THE LIBERTY S

WORLD WAR II

MW01000312

THE LIBERTY SHIPS OF WORLD WAR II

A Record of the 2,710 Vessels and
Their Builders, Operators and Namesakes,
with a History of the *Jeremiah O'Brien*

Greg H. Williams

McFarland & Company, Inc., Publishers
Jefferson, North Carolina

LIBRARY OF CONGRESS CATALOGUING-IN-PUBLICATION DATA

Williams, Greg H.
The Liberty Ships of World War II : a record of the 2,710
vessels and their builders, operators and namesakes, with a
history of the Jeremiah O'Brien / Greg H. Williams.
p.   cm.
Includes bibliographical references and index.

ISBN 978-0-7864-7945-0 (softcover : acid free paper) ∞
ISBN 978-1-4766-1754-1 (ebook)

1. Jeremiah O'Brien (Ship)—History.   2. New England
Shipbuilding Corporation—History.   3. Liberty ships—
United States—History.   4. Liberty ships—United States—Registers.
5. Liberty ships—United States—Design and construction.   I. Title.
2014021873

BRITISH LIBRARY CATALOGUING DATA ARE AVAILABLE

On the cover: Liberty ship S.S. *Jeremiah O'Brien*, San Francisco,
California © Carol M. Highsmith/Library of Congress

Printed in the United States of America

*McFarland & Company, Inc., Publishers
Box 611, Jefferson, North Carolina 28640
www.mcfarlandpub.com*

Table of Contents

Preface

This is the story of Liberty ships and the Emergency Shipbuilding Program during World War II and, for the first time, comprehensive information is provided about the builders, the namesakes, and the operators under one cover. Simple lists of companies' names in a book are fine as far as they go but they don't give the reader or researcher any sense of who was behind the greatest shipbuilding program in history. The general lack of this information was the primary motivation for undertaking this effort. Who built the ships; for what person or place was a 10,500-ton freighter named; and what is the story behind the steamship companies that operated the ships during the war? All of these questions are answered.

Liberty ships were built by management teams and workers from 12 corporations at 18 yards from Portland, Maine, down the Eastern Seaboard, around the Gulf Coast, and up the West Coast to Portland, Oregon. Some yards were publicly owned, others private, and some were under joint public/private ownership.

Also included in the book is the story of the South Portland Shipbuilding Company at South Portland, Maine, a rare example of incompetence and malfeasance in the Emergency Program. While these circumstances were in no way isolated to the management of South Portland Ship, and large-scale fraud was not especially common during the war, the Justice Department nevertheless found it necessary to maintain a War Frauds Division.

Several books have been written about Liberty ships and the Emergency Shipbuilding Program and all were helpful to some extent in doing the research for this book. The most notable books on this subject include the epic work by Professor Frederic C. Lane, of the Johns Hopkins University, *Ships for Victory*, published in 1951. Professor Lane was the official historian of wartime merchant shipbuilding and gives an excellent overall account of the entire shipbuilding program.

In 1948 the Society of Naval Architects and Marine Engineers published *The Shipbuilding Business in the United States of America* in two volumes, an excellent source of facts and figures from Colonial times to World War II and which set the total number of Liberty ships delivered at 2,710, a figure that unfortunately eluded many writers until fairly recently.

The L.A. Sawyer and W.H. Mitchell book *The Liberty Ships*, first published in Great Britain in 1970 and revised in 1985 after the *Jeremiah O'Brien* was removed from mothballs and restored to operating condition in San Francisco in 1980, has the complete list of ships, including one extra that was never delivered, and some good information about the shipyards.

John Gorley Bunker's classic book *Liberty Ships: The Ugly Ducklings of World War II*, published in 1972, is an excellent work about wartime operations with some useful appendices.

Bunker served as a 29-year-old wiper on the *Jonathan Grout* from December 1942 to August 1943 and in 1944 he was the purser on the *William B. Giles*.

The 1979 publication *America's Maritime Legacy: A History of the U.S. Merchant Marine and Shipbuilding Industry Since Colonial Times*, edited by Robert A. Kilmarx, gives a good overview of World War II shipbuilding.

By far the best source for World War II merchant marine losses, casualties, and many other details is Capt. Arthur Moore's book *A Careless Word... A Needless Sinking*, last revised in 1988.

The 2001 book *Liberty: The Ships That Won the War* by British author Peter Elphic gives a detailed account of the British Purchasing Commission's visit to the United States in 1940 and the evolution of the Liberty ship from the *Empire Wave*, the *Empire Liberty*, and the *Ocean*-class freighters.

On a more local note, relevant to the South Portland Shipbuilding Company, the Herbert G. Jones book, *Portland Ships Are Good Ships*, alludes to "production problems" at the yard but says no more. Jones could be excused, I suppose, since he lived in Portland and owned a bookstore at 647 Congress Street.

With 12 exceptions—*Midwest Farmer*, *Am-Mer-Mar*, *Pearl Harbor*, *U.S.O.*, *Johnny Appleseed*, *Molly Pitcher*, *American Mariner*, *Stage Door Canteen*, *Fort Orange*, *Star of Oregon*, *Houston Volunteers*, and *Paul Bunyan* — all American operated Liberty ships were named after real persons who were deceased, with one exception, the *Francis J. O'Gara*, named in the mistaken belief that O'Gara had perished in the Japanese-perpetrated *Jean Nicolet* atrocity. Unbeknownst to anyone in the States, he had been put aboard the submarine and was subsequently liberated from a prisoner of war camp in 1945.

Many of the namesake people have had numerous books written about them, some were well known in the region where the ship was built, while others are now completely lost to history. Some of these people led fantastic lives, had many adventures, and shaped or were shaped by great events. Some labored in obscurity to advance science, medicine, or technology, while others were prominent in the arts or entertainment and were well-known to previous generations. Many went from rags to riches, some in the opposite direction, but all contributed in some way to the fabric, history, and life of America. Every signer of the Declaration of Independence was a namesake except Francis Hopkinson, of New Jersey, who was inexplicably omitted. He is also credited with designing the American flag. Many ships were named after U.S. representatives or senators. In theses cases the term "congressman" is used generically to indicate service in the Continental Congress, the House, the Senate, or all three.

Unfortunately, a considerable number of the original War Shipping Administration biographical records relating to the namesakes have been lost and this creates a degree of uncertainty when records for the lesser known individuals are not available. All namesakes were well known at the time in the region of the country where the name was proposed but many have now fallen into obscurity.

In April 1942 the Truman War Investigating Committee submitted to the Department of Justice evidence of "possible criminal action and activities" of the MacEvoy Shipbuilding Corporation at Savannah, Georgia, and the San Jacinto Shipbuilding Corporation at Houston, Texas, for "rapacity, greed, fraud, and negligence" in building 115 barges and tugboats at a cost of $250 million that were supposed to have been delivered in early 1942 but would not be ready until 1944.

From June 30, 1942, to July 1, 1943, the Justice Department reported that FBI investigations had resulted in 323 convictions under the Sherman and Clayton anti-trust and anti-racketeering acts with prison sentences totaling 20 years and fines of $342,677. In 1943 there were 66 convictions for war fraud resulting in sentences of 94 years and $164,484.45 in "fines, savings, and recoveries" according to the FBI. These figures are negligible considering a multi-billion dollar war effort.

This is also the story of the *Jeremiah O'Brien*, one of the many nondescript Liberty ships built at South Portland and whose future the workers could never have imagined. No one then would ever have suspected that in 51 years Hull No. 230 would sail back into Portland Harbor as one of only two operating Liberty ships left in the world, the other being the *John W. Brown* at Baltimore.

Despite all that happened, South Portland ships were good ships, built and delivered under the most brutal winter weather conditions any yard worker ever faced. The heat and humidity of a Gulf Coast yard or the blazing summer heat of Southern California was bad but it never actually stopped work or a launching.

Thanks to the very helpful folks at the corporate archives divisions in California, Louisiana, Michigan, New York, Texas, and Washington for providing information on the steamship companies and a special thanks to Susan Abbott at the National Archives in Washington.

Liberty Ship Builders

Corporate Management Name, Address: Shipyard Name and Location (if different), and Number of Ships Delivered

Alabama Dry Dock & Shipbuilding Co., S. Water at foot of Canal St., Mobile	20
American Ship Building Co., 400 Colorado Ave., Lorain, Ohio:	
Delta Shipbuilding Co., New Orleans, Louisiana	188
Bath Iron Works, 120 Water St., Bath, Maine:	
South Portland Shipbuilding Corp., South Portland, Maine	18
Bechtel-McCone Corp., 256 Montgomery St., San Francisco, California:	
California Shipbuilding Corp., Wilmington	336
Marin Shipbuilding Div. (Marinship), Sausalito, California	15
Bethlehem Steel Co., Shipbuilding Div., Fairfield Yard, Baltimore, Maryland	384
J. A. Jones Construction Co., Inc., 209 W. 4th St., Charlotte, North Carolina:	
Brunswick, Georgia, Yard	85
Wainwright Yard, Panama City, Florida	102
Henry J. Kaiser, 644 Haddon Rd., Oakland, California:	
Kaiser Co., Vancouver, Washington	10
Oregon Shipbuilding Corp., Portland	322
Permanente Metals Yard No. 1, Richmond, California	138
Permanente Metals Yard No. 2, Richmond, California	351
Newport News Shipbuilding & Dry Dock Co., 4101 Washington Ave., Newport News, Virginia:	
North Carolina Shipbuilding Co., Wilmington	126
Rheem Manufacturing Co., Providence, Rhode Island	1
St. Johns River Shipbuilding Co., Jacksonville, Florida	82
Southeastern Shipbuilding Corp., Savannah, Georgia	88
Todd-Bath Iron Shipbuilding Corp., South Portland, Maine	14
Todd Shipbuilding & Dry Dock Co., 25 Broadway, New York:	
New England Shipbuilding Corp., South Portland, Maine	212
Todd Houston Shipbuilding Corp., Houston, Texas	208
Walsh-Kaiser Co., Providence, Rhode Island	10

PART I

The Beginning: The British Contract and Six Companies

The story of the New England Shipbuilding Corporation began many years before the *Jeremiah O'Brien* was launched on June 19, 1943, at South Portland, Maine. The chronological catalog of related or seemingly unrelated events leading up to any given conclusion could start at any point from the beginning of time but for this story a practical starting point might be when Todd Shipyards Corp., Bath Iron Works, and Six Companies, Inc., joined forces in 1940 to build 60 cargo ships for the British Admiralty and Ministry of War Transport, the Admiralty and MOWT being more or less a joint venture at that time.

Todd

In 1880, the Todd family lived in New Castle, Delaware. Dad, James, 47, and sons James H., 20, and William Henry, 15, were boilermakers. By 1890, William (1864–1932) was working at the Pusey & Jones Co. at the foot of Poplar St. in Wilmington, Delaware, building steam engines and lived in a boarding house at 211 E. 6th. In 1895 he was hired at the John N. Robins Co. in Brooklyn as a boilermaker. The company later became the Robins Dry Dock & Repair Co. and by the end of 1909 William was president of the company. He eventually obtained commercial financing and enough financial help from the workers to buy the company from the heirs of Thomas Clyde and on November 11, 1915, the business became the William H. Todd Corp. Then, with help from partners including John D. Reilly, the firm purchased the Tietjen & Lang Dry Dock Co. in New York and the Seattle Construction & Dry Dock Co. in Seattle and on June 14, 1916, the firm became the Todd Shipyards Corp.

William Todd died on May 15, 1932, and Reilly became president. By 1940 the company had extensive repair and shipbuilding experience with yards at New York, Galveston, Mobile, New Orleans, and Seattle but at that time they were engaged only in ship repair. The main office was at 1 Broadway, New York. Reilly, 50, lived at 40 Belmont Terrace in Yonkers with his wife Mary F., their daughter Mary A., 25, son John D., Jr., 22, a student, Mary's mother, Mary A. Murray, 74, and their 28-year-old Austrian servant Mary E. Minarich. Reilly was deputy commissioner of Public Safety in Yonkers and enjoyed golf, yachting, and swimming.

Bath Iron

Bath Iron, at Bath, Maine, has a history going back to 1826 and was organized as Bath Iron Works in 1884 under Civil War Medal of Honor recipient Brevet Major General Thomas W. Hyde, who later became a senator from Maine.

The yard's illustrious past includes building the world's first four-masted steel-hulled sailing vessel, the *Dirigo* in 1894; the first triple-expansion engine for the yacht *Meteor*, and several U.S. Navy firsts: the first ships to make 30 knots, the torpedo boat destroyers *Dahlgren* and *Craven* in 1899; the first Parsons steam turbine-powered ship, the cruiser *Chester* in 1907; and the first geared turbine ship, destroyer *Wadsworth* in 1914.

In 1940 the company was a 4-way yard under William S. "Pete" Newell, a graduate of MIT who started with the company as a draftsman, became superintendent in 1920, and in 1927 purchased the company from a bankruptcy court. Newell earned a stellar reputation as a businessman and builder of Navy destroyers. He was also president of the Bath Savings Institution and the Bath Water Works and was a director on several boards. He was also a close friend of Adm. Emory Scott "Jerry" Land, USN, who succeeded Joseph P. Kennedy as chairman of the Maritime Commission on February 18, 1938. In 1940 Newell lived at 1080 Washington St. in Bath with his wife Caroline, their 27-year-old son John, an engineer at the shipyard, and their 28-year-old French-Canadian servant Geraldine Robichand. Bath Iron was involved early in the Maritime Commission's C-1, C-2, C-3, and C-4 modernization program and was then building the C2-S-A1 freighters *Exceller* and *Extavia* for use by American Export Lines.

Six Companies

Six Companies was a consortium of Western construction companies incorporated on February 19, 1931, at Wilmington, Delaware. The principal office was at 200 Financial Center Building, 405 Montgomery St., San Francisco, California. William Henry Wattis was president, Charles A. Shea, secretary. The company was formed to bid on the long-awaited Hoover Dam and power plant project on the Colorado River at Black Canyon.

In 1900, William Wattis and his younger brother Warren L. Wattis founded the Utah Construction Co. In 1920, William, 60, was president of the company and the Utah-Idaho Sugar Co. and vice president of the Superior Rock Springs Coal Co. He lived at 2649 Jefferson Ave. in Ogden, Utah, with his wife Marie, 54, his mother Mary Stander, 96, and their 24-year-old servant Emma Raymond.

In the late 1920s he began recruiting fellow construction company executives to join him in bidding on the Hoover Dam project. The job was so large that even experienced dam and bridge builders like Utah Construction and Morrison-Knudsen could not submit bids on their own especially with the Bureau of Reclamation's requirement for a $2 million bond just to bid on the job and a prohibitively expensive $5 million performance bond. The major builders had no choice but to join forces, especially during the lean times of the Great Depression when commercial work was scarce. All of the executives who came together knew each other well and most had worked with one or another over the years to do large jobs of all kinds under various business names. A total of three bids were submitted and on March 11, 1931, the Bureau accepted Six Companies' bid of $48,890,995. William Wattis had become ill with cancer since his original efforts began and died on September 13, 1931, in San Francisco and Harry W. Morrison became president. The original companies and their interest in the group were:

- Harry W. Morrison and Morris H. Knudsen as Morrison-Knudsen Co., Inc., 319 Broadway, Boise, Idaho, 10 percent.
- Pacific Bridge Co., W. Gorrill Swigert, president, 333 Kearny St., San Francisco, 10 percent.
- J. F. Shea Co., Inc., Charles A. Shea, president, 211 Henry Building, Portland, Oregon, 10 percent.
- MacDonald & Kahn, Felix Kahn, president, and Graeme K. MacDonald, secretary, 405 Montgomery St., Room 200, San Francisco, 20 percent.
- Utah Construction Co., Marriner S. Eccles, president, 2404 Washington Blvd., Ogden, Utah, 20 percent.
- Warren A. Bechtel, a general contractor at 155 Sansome St., San Francisco, and businessman John A. McCone, executive vice president of the Consolidated Steel Corp. and founder of the Bechtel-McCone Co. had completed different projects under various business names. Bechtel recruited ex-photographer Henry J. Kaiser, a road, bridge, and paving contractor in Oakland. In 1930, the W. A. Bechtel Co., Stephen D. Bechtel, Sr., president, McCone, and Kaiser joined Six Companies as the Bechtel-Kaiser Co., Ltd., to own the remaining 30 percent.

Six Companies successfully completed the dam ahead of schedule under general superintendent Frank Crowe, although labor troubles ensued early on because of unsafe working conditions in the diversion tunnels. An unresponsive management that took advantage of the desperate state of Great Depression workers led to a general strike. During June and July of 1931, 14 workers died of heat stroke. Half of those were employed by Six Companies.

Six Companies was dissolved on June 6, 1941.

War Comes

Meanwhile, in 1931, while the dam was just getting started, an incident occurred that would lead the United States to war. On September 18 the Japanese army invaded the northeast Chinese territory of Manchuria after accusing China of an attack on Japanese-controlled Southern Manchurian Railways Co. track. Oddly enough, the train that would have passed over the wrecked track miraculously arrived at its next station right on time. Japan's intention was to seize the region's rich farmland and natural resources before increasingly bold Chinese incursion and immigration into the territory made that too difficult. That, in turn, was done to thwart increasing Japanese influence in the area. In 1928, Japanese agents assassinated the Chinese warlord Zhang Zuolin, who controlled most of the region. A Chinese puppet government was established under harsh Japanese martial law. This incident caused great consternation in the Hoover Administration and reinforced the belief among naval and military planners that war with Japan in the Pacific would someday be inevitable.

In 1932 the Japanese army attacked Shanghai. In January 1937, it was reported that Gen. Kazushige Ugaki, the Premier-Designate, was attacked in his home by three intruders after he had returned from the Imperial Palace owing to his efforts to form a Cabinet and seize power from the army militants who had hijacked the country. The general was unhurt and Emperor Hirohito was described as "worried and sleepless." The political situation in Japan was strange as the Japanese believed the emperor was divine, the country was invincible, and the Yamato People were the chosen race on Earth. However, the emperor, even if opposed to war, had no political powers and could not stop future events. There was some opposition to the army, including members of the press, but, as in Germany, opposition or outright resistance could be very dangerous.

In August the army embarked from Shanghai on a full-scale invasion of China committing horrendous atrocities including the aerial bombing of civilians. In 1937 the United States and Europe were mired in economic depression, the world was focused on the troubles in Spain, mutinies were occurring in the Royal Navy over proposed pay cuts, and Japan's impatient, militant Black Dragon Society saw no reason to delay Japan's ambitions of conquest throughout Asia and the Pacific. With the concurrent rise of Nazi Germany the wheels were set in motion that would lead to global conflict.

Six Companies and Todd Build C1-Bs

By 1938, after several major public projects were completed, including the San Francisco–Oakland Bay Bridge, and new firms had joined the group, Six Companies was looking for new work and saw shipbuilding under the Merchant Marine Act of June 29, 1936, as a lucrative option. Admiral Land, as chairman of the Commission, had appointed fellow naval constructor Howard L. Vickery, USN, to supervise shipbuilding under the Act.

John A. McEachern, of the General Construction Co., then a Six Companies member, contacted Roscoe J. Lamont, president and general manager at Todd's Seattle yard to discuss obtaining a Maritime Commission contract. Six Companies had the construction equipment and experience to build facilities and Todd had the shipbuilding know-how, although Todd was strictly in the repair business at the time. Henry Kaiser also contacted John D. Reilly—Reilly never did like Kaiser—but the two agreed on the course of future world events and after the meeting Reilly decided to get back into shipbuilding with or without Kaiser. Kaiser apparently was leery of Reilly as he made no immediate agreement. Todd went ahead and incorporated the Seattle-Tacoma Shipbuilding Corp. on July 7, 1939, and began refitting Todd's old World War I Tacoma shipbuilding yard on Commencement Bay. Their first bid on steam-powered C1 freighters was unsuccessful but after another bid was submitted, Kaiser called Reilly on September 15 to say Six Companies was in 50 percent on the deal and the next day Todd was awarded a contract for five 6,750-ton, 418-foot, 14-knot diesel-powered C1-B freighters. Lamont was president, McEachern vice president. Todd held half of the 15,000 capitalization shares and the remaining 7,500 were divided between the nine construction companies then comprising Six Companies. The *Cape Alava* was delivered in April 1941 followed by the *Cape Flattery*, *Cape Fairweather*, *Oregon*, and *Idaho*.

The American Mail Line–operated *Cape Alava* arrived at Seattle on June 18, 1941, from Shanghai, China. The second mate on the ship was 34-year-old Kenneth S. McPherson, of Seattle. In two years he would be captain of the ill-fated American Mail Line Liberty ship *Francis W. Pettygrove*.

The *Oregon* was operated by the Pacific-Atlantic Steamship Co. under Capt. Elton P. Gillette. On December 10, 1941, the ship collided with the battleship *New Mexico* (BB-40) at 2:14 p.m. about 20 miles south of Nantucket Shoals and sank. The *Oregon* was bound from South Africa to Boston with 14,000 bales of wool. Seventeen fatalities were reported on the *Oregon* and one fireman on the *New Mexico* was transferred to the naval hospital at Portsmouth, Virginia, on December 11.

The British Purchasing Commission

On September 1, 1939, Germany invaded Poland. England declared war on Germany on the 3rd, Winston Churchill was again appointed First Lord of the Admiralty, and the very same day the British cargo liner *Athenia* was torpedoed by *U-30* with the loss of 19 sailors and 98 passengers. On the 8th, President Roosevelt declared a "limited" national emergency. Americans believed Germany would be stopped fairly soon and the Germans believed the British would sue for peace just as fast. Within the first two weeks of war the U-boats sank 30 British merchant ships, the carrier *Courageous* on the 17th, and the *Royal Oak* on October 14 at Scapa Flow. This was a rough beginning for England and it was only the beginning.

On February 15, 1940, Hitler told his U-boat commanders to regard all British merchant ships as men-of-war. By then, the effectiveness of arch-appeaser Neville Chamberlain as prime minister was being questioned and he resigned on May 7. King George VI then asked Churchill to take over and he became prime minister on May 10, the same day Germany invaded France. France surrendered on June 22 and on the 27th President Roosevelt declared a national emergency. In July German aircraft began bombing British coastal shipping and the naval base at Portsmouth then concentrated their attacks on airfields, roads, railways, shipyards, and factories. Churchill had no intention of surrendering and one of his first major concerns was the loss of so many ships. England was on the ropes and the world watched as the Battle of Britain unfolded, wondering, and doubting, if the tough little island nation could hold on. Germany's U-boat war at sea threatened to close vital supply routes to England and by August 1940 England had lost about 385 ships.

Most of England's shipyards were busy building warships and to help alleviate the merchant shipping crisis, Churchill asked prominent people in the maritime industry to form a delegation and go to the United States and Canada to have freighters built. At the top of the list was the North Sands, Sunderland, firm of Joseph L. Thompson & Sons, Ltd. Thompson had designed the 434-foot, 7,463-ton freighter *Empire Wave*, launched on March 28, 1941, and it was agreed to bring those plans to the United States.

But during the Depression years the company, under Maj. Robert Norman Thompson, had worked hard to develop cheaply built, economical ships and they had another ship, a nice, practical, slightly larger, 441-foot tramp steamer designed for the Ministry of War Transport. Thompson workers were, in fact, building the first one, the *Empire Liberty*. The 10,000-deadweight ton, single screw, all-riveted, flush-decked, 2-masted, 5-hold, 11-knot ship had coalfired Scotch fire-tube boilers, a 2,500-hp triple-expansion engine, split-island deckhouses, and lifelines on the main deck instead of bulwarks.

On September 2, 1940, the firm's managing director, Robert Cyril Thompson, 33, the eldest son of Major Thompson, joined a group of other shipping men and met with various officials at the Admiralty at Whitehall to plan the trip to America.

On the 21st, Thompson; Harry Hunter, of the North Eastern Marine Engineering Co., William M. Brown, Geoffrey N. E. T. U. Worsley, and William A. C. Yearsley departed Liverpool on the Cunard White Star liner *Scythia* and arrived at New York on October 3. They first called on various British officials in the United States including the British ambassador to the United States, Philip Henry Kerr (The Right Honourable the Marquess of Lothian, KT CH PC) where they discussed generalities.

Thompson and Hunter then met with William Bennett, Lloyds of London principal surveyor for the United States and Canada, at his office at 17 Battery Place, New York, along with John S. Heck, principal Lloyds engine surveyor, and Richard R. Powell, representing the Admiralty in the United States. The delegation wanted 60 ships, the last ships delivered by June 1942. When a ship was done the holds would be filled with vitally needed supplies and head for home.

Their next stop was the Department of Commerce at 14th and E streets NW in Washington for a visit with Admiral Land. The admiral was born on January 9, 1879, at Cañon

City, Colorado, to Scott Ephraim Land, of Ontario, Canada, and Jane Taylor Emory. He graduated from the naval academy in 1902 and then went to sea. On April 15, 1909, he married Elizabeth Stiles in Newton, Massachusetts, and then went to the Brooklyn Navy Yard to design submarines. He and Elizabeth lived at 149 Willow St. in Kings with their 20-year-old Irish servant Margaret Cullen. In the fall of 1919 he and Elizabeth went to London where he was assistant naval attaché. In 1932 he became chief of the Bureau of Construction & Repair and in 1937 he and Elizabeth settled into retirement.

At the meeting the men were astounded to learn that there were no existing shipyards anywhere in the country that could build that many ships to their specifications within the given timeframe. The Great Depression had taken its toll on American shipbuilding and the big 50-way World War I American International Shipbuilding Corp. yard at Hog Island near Pittsburgh was long gone. The existing shipyards in the country with ways 400 feet or longer were engaged primarily in naval construction and the Maritime Commission's modernization program of fast, modern, turbine-powered cargo and passenger liners that were suitable as naval auxiliaries under the Commission's construction and operating differential subsidy programs to compete with cheap foreign labor. The yards were also being rapidly expanded to accommodate the build-up in shipping.

Undaunted, they toured the country, visited prospective shipyards—where they generally received a somewhat cool reception based on the notion that England was doomed anyway—or met with builders who seemed too eager and more interested in the money than in actually completing the contract. They even did extensive aerial surveys of potential shipyard sites. They visited the Seattle-Tacoma Shipbuilding yard and when they met Henry Kaiser on October 23 they got their first positive response. When their inquiries about the Todd operation to the Maritime Commission came back positive they went back to New York to see John D. Reilly, president of Todd Shipyards, and a member of the Lloyds American Committee. He was interested but he also knew it was too tall an order for his company alone so he contacted his friend William Newell at Bath Iron Works and a fellow member of the Lloyds Committee. Newell was enthusiastic and even hosted a clambake for a group of government and shipping men to pitch his ideas for building the ships on property at South Portland he already owned. With the enthusiastic urging of Henry Kaiser, negotiations commenced but no work could be done without federal approval and the use of war-related materials. Admiral Land felt Todd was the best choice to lead the effort and, with other Maritime Commission members and federal war production officials included in the talks, the government consented to the venture. But there were further matters to address.

Construction changes were suggested that would greatly speed up delivery, primarily the use of electric welding instead of rivets, and the use of water-tube boilers. American shipbuilders had gotten away from the Scotch marine fire-tube boiler, where hot gases in tubes heat the water around them, and were using water-tube boilers instead. In this type, water flows through tubes enclosed in a firebox. They were of sturdier, simpler construction, much less prone to failure, and were readily available from Babcock & Wilcox, Foster Wheeler, and Combustion Engineering.

Construction would go much faster with welding and it was far easier and quicker to train a welder than a good riveter, which could take up to a year. Welding for ships had developed gradually after World War I and in 1920 the all-welded coastal freighter *Fullagar* was built in England. By 1938 the technique, including the use of automatic welding machines for heavy plate, was advanced enough in the United States to use on large vessels. Rivets were still used where there were structural concerns. Germany was very advanced in electric welding having seen the technique as a way to save weight and get around the Treaty of Versailles, which

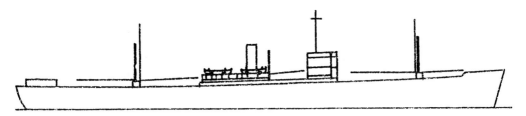

Outboard profile of the *Ocean*-class tramp steamer. The basic Thompson-designed 442-foot by 57-foot hull was used for the British-built *Empire*-class ships, the Canadian-built *Forts* and *Parks*, the American-built *Ocean*-class, and the Liberty ship, as modified.

limited Germany to six battleships of 10,000 displacement tons and six cruisers of 6,000 tons. The 609-foot, 10,000 warships *Deutchland* (1931) and the *Admiral Scheer* (1933) were the first large ships to have all-welded hulls, which reportedly saved about 500 displacement tons per ship. With a main battery of six 11-inch guns they were referred to by the British as "pocket battleships" since light and heavy cruiser main batteries were typically in the range of 6- to 8-inch guns and battleships carried 12- to 14-inch guns. The Maritime Commission's first all-welded ship was the 492-foot *Exchequer* built by Ingalls Shipbuilding at Pascagoula, Mississippi, for American Export Lines. The ship never saw service with the company as it was turned over to the Navy after completion and operated as the seaplane tender *Pocomoke* (AV-9).

Coal would remain the fuel for the ships simply because England had far more coal than oil. The after part of No. 3 hold on the *Empire*-class ships was designed as a coal bunker and, unavoidably, took up valuable cargo space. The split-island deckhouse scheme was a common practice of the day and prevalent on English tramp ships that used Asian crews with separate berthing and mess facilities.

Sir Amos L. Ayre, the Admiralty's director of merchant shipping, liked Thompson's *Empire Liberty* design but he made a few modifications to the hull design, which he believed would further speed construction and on November 16, 1940, the Admiralty informed Cyril Thompson they had decided to go with the *Empire Liberty* design instead of the *Empire Wave*. Thompson got busy making the necessary changes in designs and specifications.

The big New York naval architectural firm of Gibbs & Cox was chosen to draw up the revised plans. In 1919, astute attorney and naval architect William Francis Gibbs, of Philadelphia, became chief of construction for the International Mercantile Marine Co. and in 1922 opened a naval architectural office in New York with his brother Frederic Herbert Gibbs as Gibbs Bros., Inc. In 1929 they were joined by yacht designer Daniel H. Cox, late of Cox & Stevens, and the firm became Gibbs & Cox, Inc. In 1940 they were at 1 Broadway.

In 1940 William was 54 and lived at 170 E. 79th St. with his wife Vera. Frederic, 51, was single and lived at The New Weston Hotel, 34 E. 50th St. at Madison Ave., New York, right around the corner from St. Patrick's cathedral. Cox was 68 and lived at 264 Victoria Place, Lawrence, Hempstead, New York, with his wife Frances L., 57, son Daniel S., 33, daughter Frances B., 27, and cook Rose Morris, 64, and butler Floyd Wilson, 40. Frances B. was a postcard artist.

The matter of building ways came next. The British would have to finance the building of two new shipyards, one on the East Coast and one on the West Coast, to which they agreed. Initial documents and contracts were drawn up and Thompson left for home on the 496-foot Furness-Prince Co. motor liner *Western Prince* to submit them to the MOWT and the Admiralty for approval, but on the morning of December 14 the ship was torpedoed by *U-96* and Thompson spent nine hours in a lifeboat before being rescued. Thompson got his papers home and the Admiralty and Ministry of War Transport agreed to the changes and provisions. Harry Hunter left Liverpool on November 24 on the Holland-America cargo liner *Edam* with 27 diplomats, merchants, army, naval, and government officials and arrived at New York on December 12. On December 20, 1940, a contract was signed for two shipyards and 60 cargo ships, 30 to be built on the West Coast and 30 on the East Coast. The revised design was named the *Ocean* class, each ship having *Ocean* in its name.

Two new companies, subsidiaries of the Todd Shipyards Corp., were organized at South Portland, Maine, and Richmond, California. The Todd-Bath Iron Shipbuilding Corp. at South Portland was owned 35 percent by Todd, 35 percent by Six Companies, and 30 percent by Bath Iron Works. William Newell was president. The Todd-California Shipbuilding Corp. at Richmond was owned 35 percent by Todd and 65 percent by Six Companies with Henry Kaiser as president of the 7-way shipyard. He appointed one of his managers, Clay P. Bedford, to oversee the day-to-day operations at the yard although neither man had ever built a ship before.

Kaiser was already well known for his imagination, innovation, and efficiency and had realized early on that building anything big was simply a matter of handling large amounts of materials efficiently. One day he was visiting a road building job site and noticed how hard the workers struggled to push heavy wheelbarrows fitted with clunky, steel wheels. He ordered all the wheelbarrows fitted with pneumatic rubber tires that ran on ball bearings and after that his workers were twice as productive as any competitor.

Back East, Newell's plan for the Todd-Bath yard called for excavating three drydocks with watertight gates containing seven building berths approximately 465 feet long and one 1,000-foot fitting-out pier located in South Portland at Cushing Point just north of Spring Point. The basins would be excavated 20 feet down through soil to a rock ledge and the concrete walls separating the three basins would have tracks laid on top for cranes to run back and forth on, to deliver steel and sections of the ship for installation. The site was the old Cumberland Shipbuilding Corp. yard that Newell had secretly purchased around 1938 in anticipation of building an 80,000 ton Gibbs & Cox–designed warship for Russia and felt this scheme would be best in light of the terrain and large tidal swings on Casco Bay. The warship was never built but Newell knew the graving dock scheme would work. Kaiser reportedly was skeptical at the time but used the same idea later in the war to build Army transports at his Richmond Yard No. 3 with five 590-foot basins.

Ephraim E. Sanders of Sanders Engineering Co. at 415 Congress St., Room 205, was hired to do the job. Workers started felling trees and clearing the site on January 3, 1941, and completed the final work on October 22 while ships were being built.

The Todd-California yard was built on piles with conventional slipways. The first British keel was laid there on April 14, 1941, and the *Ocean Voyager* and *Ocean Venture* were launched the following September 27 as part of Liberty Fleet Day. At Todd-Bath the first keel was laid on May 24, 1941, and the *Ocean Liberty* and *Ocean Freedom* were launched on December 20. The first British ship to leave left in February 1942 with full holds and the last ship was delivered on November 18, 1942. Todd-Bath workers had a remarkable record considering the brutal winter weather conditions unheard of on the West Coast and complications created by initial difficulties in getting the right sized cranes.

Epilogue

Sixteen *Ocean*-class freighters were lost during the war, including nine built by Todd-Bath. One had a very short life. The *Ocean Crusader* was launched at Todd-Bath on October

18, 1942, and sunk on November 26 by *U-262*. The *Empire Liberty* survived the war and operated under the Greek flag from 1943 until being scrapped in 1960 at Osaka, Japan.

During May 1943, the Thompson yard at Sunderland was bombed and destroyed. Robert Thompson enlisted in the Royal Air Force and became an airplane mechanic stationed in Italy. After the war he returned to the shipyard. He died on March 9, 1967, leaving a son Robert Patrick Thompson, the last Thompson at Sunderland before shipbuilding there ended altogether.

John Alexander McCone (1902–1991) became involved with the building of Liberty ships at California Shipbuilding and after the war he was associated with the big multinational ITT Corp., successor to the International Telephone & Telegraph Co. In 1958 he became chairman of the Atomic Energy Commission and in 1961 he replaced Allen Dulles as director of the CIA. His later relationship with President Johnson and his opposition to American involvement in Vietnam led to his resignation in early 1965.

PART II

Building the Liberty Ships

With war on the horizon, the Merchant Marine Act of 1936 intended to rebuild a merchant marine that had languished during the Great Depression and had become all but obsolete. The original shipbuilding plan was to build 500 modern ships over 10 years that would serve as both commercial and naval auxiliary vessels and to build them here at home instead of utilizing much cheaper shipyards overseas. In 1936 there were only ten shipyards with 46 ways 400 feet or longer in the country. The Construction Differential Subsidy Program was designed so that each steamship company wishing to participate could submit plans for the ships they needed that would serve their particular routes and customers. The Maritime Commission and the Navy reviewed the plans, made whatever changes they felt necessary to fulfill the ship's dual role, and then took bids from shipyards. The low bidder got the job and the completed ship was sold to the company for the cost an overseas shipyard would have charged to build the same vessel, generally around one-half the domestic amount.

It was felt early-on that this program would be sufficient to meet the country's needs if war came but the extreme effectiveness of Hitler's U-boats after 1939 changed that notion very quickly and the realization that the United States would in all likelihood be fighting a two-ocean made the emergency shipbuilding program a necessity. Admiral Land had hoped to avoid having to build any emergency ships at all but he realized it would have to happen since the time to build a modern, geared turbine-powered ship piece-by-piece on the ways was far too long to keep up with the war losses England was already experiencing.

On January 3, 1941, President Roosevelt announced the emergency shipbuilding program would begin with 200 ships and Admiral Land was given the job of deciding exactly what they would look like. After considering several design options he decided on January 8 to build a class of freighter very similar in size and tonnage to the *Ocean*-class ships but with further modifications from the original *Empire Liberty*. The new ship would have five holds, three masts, a single midship house, oil-fired water-tube boilers, a triple expansion reciprocating steam engine, bulwarks on the main deck instead of lifelines, and accommodations for a combined merchant and Navy Armed Guard crew of 54. Being an emergency vessel, about 35 standard Maritime Commission features and amenities found in the modern "C" ships were eliminated. Some involved crew comfort and safety such as smaller cabins that were not fully-insulated, the use of combustible plywood interior bulkheads, and no mechanical ventilation system in the crew's quarters or engine room.

The choices for engines at the time included triple expansion, geared steam turbine, gas turbine, diesel, diesel-electric, and turbo-electric. Some good-sized cargo liners built during

14

the Depression years were diesel because a diesel engine used considerably less fuel than a steam plant. But a marine diesel was much heavier than a steam engine and by 1941 all diesel production was being controlled by the Navy anyway.

A turbine engine operated efficiently only at high speeds and needed gears to reduce its rpms to ship propeller shaft speeds, but they required extremely precise machining to 3/10,000th of an inch and were very time-consuming to produce. All theses engines from the very few major producers like Westinghouse and General Electric were going to naval construction and the modern merchant ships. While a geared turbine plant would take up more room than a triple expansion engine, it was estimated that a gas turbine engine would free up room for an extra 1,000 tons of cargo but in the end the "obsolete" triple expansion was chosen for availability, ease of construction, operation, and maintenance.

The basic shape of the Thompson hull was designed for simple construction, not speed, so the reciprocating engine was perfectly suited for the job and the idea of sacrificing speed for cargo space made sense considering the sheer number of freighters that would be coming off the ways. Hundreds of plodding ships at sea at all times simply overwhelmed the Axis and every civilian who worked at a defense-related job or produced the goods that filled their holds contributed substantially to the ultimate victory.

Gibbs & Cox was chosen to draw up the further revised plans mainly because the firm already had drawings for the *Ocean*-class hull in hand and they had the manpower to quickly complete the revisions for the new ship. When President Roosevelt was shown illustrations of the new "Liberty" ship he called it "a dreadful looking object."

In February 1941 the Maritime Commission published the "Specifications for the Construction of a Single Screw Cargo Vessel Design EC2-S-C1" and distributed copies to the contracting shipyards. The foreword stated:

> These specifications and plans depict a ship for special emergency production and operation. They are entirely separate and apart from the Maritime Commission's merchant marine program and are not intended to take any part in the U.S. Merchant Marine under normal peace time conditions.
>
> All requirements for compliance with Bureau of Marine Inspection and Navigation are based on the minimum emergency requirements of that body for this particular emergency and shall be submitted to the Maritime Commission before incorporation in plans or in ships. Where these plans and specification differ from the requirements of any governmental regulatory body, the provisions of the plans and specifications shall apply, excepting as specifically directed otherwise by the Commission.
>
> Special certificates will be issued by the Bureau of Marine Inspection and Navigation covering ships built under these emergency conditions.

The Commission insisted on normal durability standards, adherence to all the American Bureau of Shipping rules for building steel vessels, and first-class workmanship. They were often referred to as "five year ships" or "one voyage ships"—unglamorous compared to prewar ships and slow by modern standards—but nevertheless durable, efficient, utilitarian vessels that served their purpose and then some, as future events would prove.

Mass Production

Admiral Vickery was placed in charge of getting the ships built. He wanted every yard to build the same exact ship and to use the prefabrication methods for mass production that was done at Hog Island during World War I where sections of the ship were fabricated at inland plants, brought to the shipyard on rail cars, and assembled on the ways. A ship was launched there every 5½ days then brought to one of the 28 outfitting docks for completion. But the steel industry, faced with its own overwhelming production requirements, opposed the idea as there was "an extremely tight bottleneck in machine tools" so Admiral Vickery abandoned the idea. Each yard would have to have an on-site fabricating plant and get the machining tools, cranes, and steel as quickly as they became available.

Still, no yards existed that could prefabricate and assemble several identical ships at the same time. A shipyard like that would require large areas for plate shops, steel storage, building sites—indoor and outdoor—for the prefabricated units and storage sites for the completed units and all the myriad equipment and fittings shipped by subcontractors that had to be on hand for immediate installation on the ways or at the outfitting dock—anchors, furniture, lifeboats, rafts, booms, masts, winches, electrical equipment, settling tanks, engine parts, generators, pumps, etc.

To begin the emergency shipbuilding program, the Maritime Commission decided to build nine new yards with a total of 65 ways at public expense at South Portland, Baltimore, Mobile, New Orleans, Houston, Los Angeles, Richmond, Wilmington, North Carolina, and Portland, Oregon. The joint Todd-Kaiser-Six Companies operation was affected by the new shipyards in Oregon, California, and Texas and on January 16, 1941, three new companies were incorporated:

The Oregon Shipbuilding Corp. was organized under Henry Kaiser at Portland. The yard was built on the east bank of the Willamette River near its confluence with the Columbia River. The Maritime Commission paid $70,000 for the land, $23,474,000 for facilities, and the National Housing Agency spent $26 million to build the town of Vanport City with 9,914 homes to house 40,000 people. The McLoughlin Heights housing project was built to accommodate workers at another Kaiser yard across the Columbia River in Vancouver, Washington, where naval construction was going on. Vanport was destroyed by a flood on May 30, 1948, killing 15 residents.

The California Shipbuilding Corp. was set up at Wilmington under Todd-Six Companies as a joint public/private venture with the Maritime Commission leasing the land and spending $26,688,818 on facilities. The large Channel Heights housing project was built on 165 acres near San Pedro.

The Houston Shipbuilding Corp. on Irish Bend Island in the Houston Ship Channel was organized under Todd general manager Arthur Stout. The Maritime Commission spent $279,780 on land and $14,479,387 on facilities.

The financing of the emergency shipbuilding program presented the Maritime Commission with a unique set of problems. The old cost-plus shipbuilding contract from World War I that bred inefficiency and higher costs had been scrapped. A new system developed jointly by the Maritime Commission and the shipbuilding industry specifically for the mass-production of Liberty ships was the Man-Hours contract. The yards were constructed without profit to the builder and ships were built on a performance standard established by the Maritime Commission. The original plan set a base fee per ship of $110,000, a minimum fee of $60,000 payable in two installments, half on launching and half on delivery, and a maximum fee of $140,000. As Admiral Land stated in 1945:

> The key idea to the plan was that the contractor would have to produce ships before he would get anything beyond costs. We worked out the location of the yards, the arrangement with the contractors to build the facilities and the ships and a contracting plan for the building of the yards and facilities at cost with no profit to the contractor, and the building of the ships on the basis of an estimated cost with a base fee plus or minus bonuses and penalties dependent on meeting, exceeding, or falling short of required bogeys in completion dates, man hours and costs.

The admiral used a golf term to explain what was considered "par" in fulfilling the contracts. The Maritime Commission knew that private capital would not invest $20 million in a shipyard used to build one type of ship that would be obsolete and useless after the war, along with the idle shipyard, so the emphasis for any profit was output in ships rather than capital investment. As workers became much more efficient and innovative, the base fee became $35,000 per ship with a minimum of $20,000 and the maximum of $60,000.

Liberty ships would prove to be the largest class of ship ever built and the prefabrication methods perfected by Henry Kaiser and his workers in his West Coast yards set ship-building records that still stand. From the original order of 200 in 1941, a total of 3,140 were contracted for; 429 contracts were cancelled in 1945, and one ship, the *Louis C. Tiffany*, burned up at Bethlehem's Fairfield yard and was declared a total loss. That left a grand total of 2,710 delivered to the Maritime Commission. Some were bareboat chartered to the Navy and modified and others shipped off under Lend-Lease to foreign operators. These ships would not only win the war of supply but these "ugly ducklings" would be seen in virtually every deepwater port on earth into the mid–1970s, a fantastic notion probably not contemplated by many at the time.

Naming the Ships

It was decided early on that Liberty ships would be named after prominent persons "not now living" because Admiral Land did not want to have to deal with pushy bigshots or politicians demanding that a ship be named for them or a family member. Commission member John M. Carmody was appointed chairman of the naming committee in Washington. Names could be submitted for consideration by individuals, local committees, professional associations, historical societies, counties, school children or 4-H Clubs who won the major "drives" that were organized nationwide to sell war bonds or collect scrap metal. The winning county, kid, club, or school was given the right to nominate a name for a ship and since it was traditional for a female to sponsor ships, a girl was chosen and she and her escorts got an all expenses paid trip to the shipyard and back for the christening ceremony.

United Features Syndicate columnist Drew Pearson's "The Washington Merry-Go-Round" column of February 10, 1943, had an item about a New Mexico boy named Connie Mack who won a scrap drive. When the War Production Board's Conservation Division sent him an invitation to officiate in the christening of a Liberty ship they mistook him for a girl. He replied:

> I gathered scrap to whip the Jap,
> And make a better world.
> And in my scrap to whip the Jap,
> They thought I was a girl.
> But when our scrap does reach the Jap,
> We'll have them on the run.
> So thank you, Mr. Roosevelt,
> I had a lot of fun.

Sometimes a name suggestion became controversial. An editorial in the December 15, 1942, edition of the Uniontown, Pennsylvania, *Evening Standard* stated:

> No S.S. Harry Bridges
> The serious suggestion that a Liberty ship be named for Harry Bridges, leader in a C.I.O. group which, until Russia was attacked, was delaying American war production, is shocking. Not only

should the idea be repudiated, but the person who sponsored it in the Maritime Commission should be relieved from any type of duty which requires sound judgment.

There was no SS *Harry Bridges*. Admiral Land was noted for his disdain for organized labor and those ships that were named for labor leaders probably irritated him. The majority of names tended to be those of people who were significant to the region where the ship was built but for states where there were no shipyards the Commission distributed names chosen there throughout all the shipyards.

The shipyards in the South, most notably North Carolina Ship, named vessels after prominent Confederate States figures, generals, and notable Southern figures. Todd Houston pretty much stuck to Texas history and Confederate generals. All the Union generals and abolitionists were honored on the West Coast and northern shipyards far, far from Dixie.

In early 1944 *Collier's* listed 105 prominent Americans who had died the previous year— all worthy namesake candidates—politicians, financiers, writers, entertainers, diplomats, the works, including John Pierpont Morgan—but only 12 actually had their name painted on a hull.

Officials in Lumberton, North Carolina, tried unsuccessfully to have a ship named after Angus Wilton McLean, an ex-governor of the state, but by November 1944 all the ships then building had assigned names and Robert W. Horton, Maritime Commission PR director, informed the group in January 1945 that the last batch of names would be those of merchant seamen "who have lost their lives in active war service."

Many names chosen were of local significance only. The 4-H Club in Duval County, Florida, for example, won a scrap drive and submitted the name of William L. Watson. Watson was the U.S. Department of Agriculture agent for Duval County and did extensive work with 4-H but apart from a few people in Florida state government and another handful of people in Washington he was virtually unknown to the rest of the nation, yet here was his name painted on a 10,500-ton ship sailing all over the world. The preponderance of agricultural figures who were namesakes reflects the agricultural nature of the country at the time.

The Sponsor

After a name was approved it was assigned to a hull and then a sponsor had to be found. By World War II the tradition of having women sponsor ships had been firmly established. As in naval construction, a relative of the namesake was the first choice but when none was available sponsors were chosen by various means. At Oregon Shipbuilding Corp. any employee could fill out a paper slip which was put into a large wooden box set up and turned by a crank. A name was picked out and the person whose name was chosen got to nominate a sponsor. Being a sponsor was quite an honor as most launchings were somewhat formal affairs with maids of honor for the sponsor and the lucky lady was presented with the broken champagne bottle she used to smash against the bow of the ship, which was tightly wrapped in wicker so glass wouldn't fly all over, and usually a silver goblet, pitcher, serving tray, photo album, or other mementoes of some sort. The actual package varied with each yard. Sometimes a sponsor failed to show up or was significantly delayed and in that case a female shipyard worker or the daughter of a company officer or employee who happened to be handy was hastily chosen to carry out the duty.

At California Shipbuilding a worker won a lottery to name a sponsor. He turned his ticket over to the Infantile Paralysis Foundation and the Foundation gave the honor to 10-year-old Lorene Mitchell, the daughter of Sally Mitchell, a Los Angeles laundry worker and single mother. The two lived at 712 E. 32nd St. After the shipyard workers heard her story they raised $6,000 for a trust fund for her and in October 1942 she was given the honor of sponsoring the *Horace Mann*. Company officials threw in a $500 war bond for her in addition to the usual commemorative items.

The Sailors

Section 216 of the Merchant Marine Act of 1936 provided for a U.S. Maritime Service to train merchant seamen. It was established in 1938 within the Maritime Commission and training stations were set up on Hoffman Island in New York and on Government Island off Alameda, California. In 1939 an officer candidate school opened at Fort Trumbull in New London, Connecticut, and in 1940 on Gallops Island in Boston Harbor. In 1941 the West Coast training station for unlicensed seamen was moved from Alameda to Port Hueneme, California.

In February 1942 the Coast Guard took over all training. The West Coast station was moved to Avalon on Catalina Island and stations were established at St. Petersburg, Florida, and Sheepshead Bay in Brooklyn. Courses included general instruction in all shipboard duties and emergencies, gunnery on the 20-mm Oerlikon, signaling, and cargo handling. Sheepshead students could practice on a dry-land Liberty ship mockup named the SS *Sheepshead Bay*.

In 1943 male applicants between 16 and 50 could apply for training. Those under 18 required a Work Permit from a High School or Board of Education, up to 21 required parental consent, and married men needed their wife's consent. Those between 18 and 26 who could not have been inducted into the Armed Forces, were 4-F, 1-C, 1-A-L, or were honorably discharged. Approximately 15.1 percent of the eligible population nationwide was 4-F. South Carolina ranked first with 22.1 percent and Idaho least at 8.7 percent. The physically unfit had to have a letter from the Draft Board.

After six weeks, students chose Deck or Engine, 8 more weeks, or Steward training, 2 to 10 more weeks, or take exams for Radio, 22 weeks, Hospital-Purser, 22 weeks, Carpenter, 8 weeks, or they could apply for officer training in the Cadet Corps. Basic Cadet Schools were opened at Pass Christian, Mississippi, and San Mateo, California. After 90 days the students went aboard ship for a minimum of six months, usually one or two voyages. In September 1943 the Merchant Marine Academy at Kings Point, New York, opened as the only Advanced Cadet School and after that students from the Basic Schools were sent there for nine months to complete their studies after their initial sea time. In addition to the federal schools there were five state-run maritime academies, in the Bronx, San Francisco, Philadelphia, Hyannis in Massachusetts, and Castine, Maine.

Technically, it was still possible under federal law for a 12-year-old boy to go to sea, with his consent, as an apprentice indentured to the master until he turned 18. The manpower needs of the war inspired some to take advantage of this provision. In 1940, 12-year-old George Mark Waggoner was sent to the Oregon State Training School in Woodburn as a ward of the state. On February 9, 1942, he was offered a "choice" between prison or sea service. He "chose" the sea and in April he was taken to Portland to get mariners documents then shipped out as a messboy on the *Edgar Allan Poe*. By the time he was 18 he had been on three ships that had been attacked.

When the War Manpower Commission was established on April 18, 1942, it sought to utilize "manpower confined in prisons and reformatories not convicted of crimes of violence." It was still illegal to put minors in a dangerous work situation and to make matters worse, the parents whom most of these kids were fleeing got two thirds of his pay until he turned 18. According to George, most of the 15 and 16-year-olds like him were "throwaways" from bad family situations.

After six months, the master could appoint an apprentice an Ordinary Seaman. After 14 months at sea, a sailor could apply for the Maritime Service Officers Candidate School for a Third Mate's or Third Assistant Engineer's license and in another six months sit for Second Mate or Second Assistant Engineer then up to Master or Chief Engineer with six months in between each step.

Some new positions were even created. Prior to the war, Pursers were found only on passenger vessels. They were licensed by the Bureau of Marine Inspection & Navigation as Chief, Senior Assistant, and Junior Assistant Pursers. They kept company records, payroll, handled foreign currency exchange, cash accounts, and took charge of passengers' valuables. On cargo ships the master was usually able to handle the normal paperwork involved in a typical voyage and if he needed extra help he could call on Sparks, the radio operator, who would pitch in using his or her typewriter. But with the New Deal and then World War II, federal bureaucracies blossomed like the desert after a rain and there was no way a ship captain could handle the amount of paperwork required for a voyage under the War Shipping Administration. Over 100 forms were issued to ships operating under General Agency Agreements, hence the need for Pursers on freighters. Pursers also handled the slop chest in addition to their clerical duties. They could also attend a school for medical training and were then rated as Purser–Pharmacist's Mates. Since Pursers were a novelty on freighters and most men who were hired had never been a purser, or even been to sea before, the job title varied considerably. Novices were referred to as the ship's clerk, typist, or the junior assistant purser. On large liners, with an office staff of six or eight people, the junior assistant purser worked up the cargo manifest, so this title naturally transferred to freighters.

The subject of allowing women to serve on merchant vessels inevitably came up and in July 1943 a congressional proposal was made to allow women to serve as cooks. Many women had served aboard ships in peacetime as wireless operators, cooks, stewardesses, hairdressers, clerks, etc., and a few even held master's licenses. Joseph Curran, head of the National Maritime Union, President Roosevelt, Admiral Land, and Edward Macauley, deputy administrator of the War Shipping Administration, met to discuss the matter. Curran expressed the opinion that women should be allowed to serve as cooks and President Roosevelt concurred but Land and Macauley were opposed. Curran pointed out that Russian women were serving in all military capacities and Scandinavian ships carried women crewmembers. Roosevelt apparently chose to drop the matter altogether since the idea died.

By 1945 it was estimated that 200,000 trained seamen were in the merchant marine. All were members of a maritime union. Conflicts between the merchant and Armed Guard crews occasionally arose over perceived pay differences when some of the Armed Guard sailors got the notion that the merchant crew was underworked and overpaid. After all, they got lots of overtime pay, belonged to big, powerful unions, got $100 bonuses for being in a war zone and bonuses for carrying explosives. There were also cases when the Armed Guard stood at battle stations for 48 hours in freezing weather to keep the guns in working order under threat of imminent attack. On the other hand, a merchant seaman's pay stopped if the ship he was on sank or if he was in a lifeboat or even taken prisoner.

Merchant seaman who were sick or injured were entitled to treatment at one of the nine U.S. Public Health Service Marine Hospitals or five Relief Stations if they had "60 days of continuous service" prior to seeking medical care. This rule, from Section 595 of the Public Health Service regulations, caused considerable headaches for sailors and providers. Those injured as a result of enemy action were treated by Army or Navy personnel near the scene. There were no post-war benefits for merchant seamen and many lived with debilitating injuries and problems that went uncared for unless he could pay for them himself. Many Armed Forces veterans who were injured in the line of duty were unsuccessful in filing claims for post-war care.

Merchant sailors were allowed one day of shore leave for each week at sea, up to 30 days, and any sailor who was eligible for military service and overstayed his leave could find himself in the Army. This was especially important since on March 7, 1943, the War Manpower Commission allowed the drafting of men between 38 and 45 years of age by abolishing the 4-H classification.

Most merchant sailors, like their military counterparts, had more or less uneventful service time. Many Liberty ships left a West Coast port fully loaded and spent months shuttling around isolated, makeshift ports discharging their various cargoes as needed while under control of Navy port directors, usually an ensign or lieutenant, junior grade, who was trying his best to keep things moving in the right direction and keep the brass happy. There were few, if any, amenities at those ports and, just like Mr. Roberts on the USS *Reluctant* in the movie, they went back and forth between Tedium and Boredom with an occasional side trip to Monotony.

It would appear from the records that more than a few merchant seamen who sailed out of East Coast ports had no desire to make any voyages in the Pacific. They high-tailed it back home, visited the folks for a few days, then signed on another ship at New York before the draft board came calling.

While critics of the merchant marine like to cite the disciplinary problems aboard ships all one has to do is read the records of World War II naval vessels to see one deck or summary court martial after another, usually for being absent over leave but occasionally for much worse offenses. In the aggregate, the number of "performers" on merchant ships was no greater on average than those in the Navy. In most instances it was a case of a youngster who had never been away from home off on a big adventure, sometimes a really big adventure, like when an older group of merchant sailors rented a hotel suite in Rio de Janeiro and hosted a party for the youngsters and the Armed Guard kids.

The Armed Guard

In the days of sail most merchant vessels carried some form of arms like sabers, muskets, or cannon as protection against pirates. These weapons were used by the crew. But as technology increased, ships and armaments became more complicated and by the turn of the century it was no longer possible for a merchant crew to run the ship and operate and maintain the available guns by themselves. But when the United States entered World War I, furious debates took place in Congress over whether or not merchant ships should be armed at all. Sanity prevailed and the Navy Armed Guard was created. By World War II it was a foregone conclusion that guns would be put aboard Maritime Commission ships for defensive purposes and that the Navy Armed Guard would be re-activated. Each Liberty ship had a Navy Armed Guard contingent whose number varied from 12 to 28 including an officer-in-charge who, like everyone else aboard, was subordinate to the master of the vessel. The ratings in the Armed Guard aboard Liberty ships varied but were normally gunner's mates, radiomen, signalmen, seamen, and sometimes pharmacist's mates and boatswain's mates. They served on all Maritime Commissioned-owned vessels operated by private shipping companies and the U.S. Army.

The armament on the early Liberty ships was light, often surplus 37-mm or .30 caliber weapons left over from the Great War. In the early days of the war, sailors were ordered to the duty, the North Atlantic being an especially dangerous place, but as time went on the armament improved, and anti-submarine warfare improved immensely in the Atlantic.

Japanese submarine attacks against merchant ships in the Pacific and Indian Oceans, for whatever reason, were a tiny fraction of what the Germans did in the Atlantic and Mediterranean. In May 1943, the Japanese announced they had sunk 50,000 tons of Allied shipping. Admiral Halsey, barely containing himself, said Japanese attacks were "inconsequential" and a "flat lie." By then, duty in the Armed Guard had become a highly desired billet. Almost all the sailors were naval reservists and the detachment was commanded by a naval reserve ensign or lieutenant, junior grade. The living conditions on a Liberty ship were usually far superior to those of other small naval units like patrol craft. The Armed Guard sailors had their own dining room with sit-down meals chosen from a menu and served by civilian waiters. Still, a war was on and the Armed Guard had a very high percentage of casualties, as did the merchant marine in general.

The principal supplier of guns for merchant ships was the Northern Ordnance Co., a subsidiary of the Northern Pump Co. The Northern Fire Apparatus Co. was founded in 1907 at Minneapolis to build fire pumps and was purchased in 1929 by John Blackstock Hawley, Jr., a civil engineer from Texas. He changed the name to Northern Pump and started building guns for the Navy in 1932. In September 1940, the company moved to a large plant at Fridley, Minnesota, and in January 1941 they began producing the iconic 5"/38 cal. deck gun for the Navy's Bureau of Ordnance. They delivered their 1,000th mount on December 4, 1941. The company developed a simplified version of the 5"/38 for merchant ships, the Mark 37, for quicker production, and also furnished the 3"/50 and 20-mm guns for merchant ships. According to the Bureau, over 3,600 5"/38s were put aboard 6,229 merchant vessels.

On June 26, 1943, the Armed Forces newspaper *Stars and Stripes* reported that Admiral Vickery had announced that Liberty ships would be carrying helicopters for defense against submarines. Experiments were to begin in July and the plan was to add a 40 × 50-foot flight deck to each ship. It obviously never happened, couldn't have happened in any case, and one wonders why such an idea was stated at all. The admiral said it had already been done on tankers.

The Todd-Kaiser Liberty Ship Operation

While initially successful, the relationship between Todd executives and Henry Kaiser soon began to sour. Back in 1939 Kaiser had obtained an option to buy a large limestone deposit on Permanente Creek four miles west of Cupertino, California, to make cement in anticipation of Six Companies building Shasta Dam. Pacific Constructors, Inc., got the job instead so Kaiser formed the Permanente Cement Co., built a plant, and got a contract to supply the 1.1 million tons of cement used to build the dam. The cement was shipped by railroad and mixed with aggregate and water at the site. In February 1941 he got a $3,500,000 loan from the Reconstruction Finance Corp. to set up a magnesium production plant next to the cement plant and formed the Permanente Metals Corp. Todd reluctantly went along with the plan in the national interest and agreed, again with considerable reservations, to use future fixed-fee profits from the Todd-California shipyard to pay back the loan. This was the beginning of troubles for Todd and others were on the horizon.

Once the emergency shipbuilding program got underway, the Maritime Commission realized that the three new yards would not be able to deliver the ever-growing number of ships required for the anticipated two-ocean war so in March 1941 they negotiated for the expansion of the existing yards and the construction of two new shipyards at South Portland and Richmond.

In Maine, Newell got an aerial photograph of the land to the west of the Todd-Bath yard and began plotting the layout for the new yard based on the piece-by-piece construction methods used for the British ships but using conventional sloping ways instead of basins. An immediate problem was the lack of available space and this one issue would prove to be the cause of major headaches for a lot of people, including the neighbors. Newell had about 35 acres of industrial land to work with that was hemmed in by residential neighborhoods and summer cottages. By contrast, the Bethlehem-Fairfield yard in Baltimore was over 700 acres and the fabricating shop was two miles from the ways. Ten-ton sections were built indoors then combined outside into 25-ton sections. Ten locomotives, 200 flatcars, 50 railroad cranes, and 82 cranes of various types and capacities moved parts around and put everything together.

The South Portland Shipbuilding Corp. was incorporated on April 4, 1941, at the offices of attorneys Charles M., Josiah H., and Wadleigh M. Drummond, in business as Drummond & Drummond, 120 Exchange St. in Portland, with a capital stock value of $250,000 divided into 2,500 shares with a par value of $100 each. Charles Drummond, stenographer Ethel G. Doughty, and Josiah Drummond owned one share each and they were the board of directors—Charles president, Ethel treasurer, and Josiah as clerk. The company was owned 50/50 by Todd and Bath Iron, but Todd, unfortunately, as events would prove, had no part in its management. William Newell was paid $10,000 a year to run the operation and Thatcher B. Pinkham, 43, a production supervisor at Bath, became general manager. In California, the Richmond Shipbuilding Corp. was set up under Henry Kaiser.

On April 28, 1941, the Maritime Commission signed a straight cost-plus contract with South Portland Ship for a new 4-way yard to be built on the Fore River to the west of the Todd-Bath basin yard.

With the concurrence of the Commission, architect Alonzo Jesse Harriman, 151 Dennison St., Auburn, Maine, was hired for all "architectural, engineering, and supervisory service." Harriman had worked with Newell at Bath Iron back in the 1920s when Newell was the engine supervisor and Harriman was a machinist. Ellis C. Snodgrass, 67 Colonial Rd., Portland, was general contractor. William Newell and Thomas R. Allen, the 60-year-old general manager at Bath Iron, advised Harriman as to the general layout of the yard but neither Newell nor Allen had any experience with mass production facilities. Allen and Robert D. Crean, a 27-year-old plant supervisor with Bath Iron, were sent to oversee the construction although neither one had any construction experience and, after a short period of time at the beginning, did not spend any time at the site until October 1. Additionally, South Portland had no purchasing department and left all that to Harriman, a job not normally performed by architects. The shops were built of wood since it was immediately available and steel wasn't, but there was no fabrication plant at the yard. All fabrication was to be done at the Todd-Bath east yard or by the Bath Iron Works Harding plant 35 miles away.

Regarding this, Prof. Frederick C. Lane stated: "It should be recalled that all these arrangements were worked out before the declaration of war, and before the possibilities and principles of multiple production had been demonstrated." Except the "principles of multiple production" had been demonstrated years before at Hog Island. The on-site prefabrication methods used for World War II shipbuilding had yet to be perfected by the Kaiser operation.

When the Maritime Commission decided to add two additional ways at South Portland along with a fabrication plant and steel storage area the space situation became very acute. As a site to store steel, Newell proposed leasing Thompson's Point on the north side of the Fore

River (just west of the present I-295 bridge) and seven road miles from the shipyard. The area contained "abandoned railroad engine and car repair shops" and was owned by the Portland Terminal Co., a subsidiary of the Maine Central Railroad. William Newell was a director of Maine Central. The Maritime Commission rejected the idea and acquired land next to the shipyard through eminent domain for the purpose. The problem of transporting steel to the yard by railroad or truck was discussed. Newell had approached the Maine Central back in 1940 about running a 3-mile spur to Cushing Point. He was told it would cost anywhere from $350,000 to $400,000 plus operation and maintenance would be done by the shipyard. Arrangements were then made for trucking.

The First Liberty Ships and Liberty Fleet Day

Since the beginning of war in Europe in 1939, and almost certain war with Japan in the very near future, it was felt that a show of strength and determination should take place as the launching of the first emergency Liberty ships was approaching and more fast, modern Maritime Commission merchant vessels were coming off the ways. Builders around the country were consulted and Saturday, September 27, 1941, was chosen for the mass launching of 14 ships. The first Liberty ship keel laid down was the *Patrick Henry* on April 30, 1941, and that ship became the star of the show at Bethlehem Steel's Fairfield yard at Baltimore. President Roosevelt recorded a speech before he left for Hyde Park that emphasized the need for more ships. He said, in part:

> The ship workers of America are doing a great job. They have made a commendable record for efficiency and speed. With every new ship they are striking a telling blow at the menace to our nation and the liberty of free people throughout the world. They struck fourteen such blows today. They have caught the true spirit with which all this nation must be imbued if Hitler and other aggressors of his ilk are to be prevented from crushing us.

The Maritime Commission scheduled coordinated launchings based on Eastern Standard Time. A recording of the president's speech was played at each yard. The ships launched were:

Surprise, 8,591-ton Maritime Commission C-2 motor freighter built by the Sun Shipbuilding & Dry Dock Co., Chester, Pennsylvania, for United States Lines, 1 Broadway, New York. Launched at 6 a.m.

Operated in the Atlantic and Mediterranean under charter to the Ministry of War Transport until April 1943. Scrapped in 1970.

James McKay, 6,762-ton Maritime Commission C-1 freighter built by the Bethlehem–Sparrows Point Shipyard, Baltimore, for Lykes Bros. Steamship Co., 925 Whitney Bank Building, 624 Common St., New Orleans. Launched at 10 a.m.

Capt. Herman N. Olsen's ship rendezvoused with Convoy HX 217 on December 3, 1942, but was reported as a straggler and making fastest speed toward Belfast. The ship was expected in Belfast on the 12th but after being overdue for 30 days was presumed lost with all aboard. The ship and crew disappeared and were never seen or heard from again. Later reported sunk by *U-600* on December 8, six days out from Halifax, Newfoundland, at 57°50'N/23°10'W. Capt. Olsen, a 51-year-old Norwegian, lived at 476 W. Austin St., Paris, Texas, with his Texan wife Lelia M.

Ocean Voyager, 7,174-ton British Ministry of War Transport freighter built by the Todd-California Shipbuilding Corp., Richmond, California. Launched at 12 noon.

Operated by H. Hogarth & Sons (Hogarth Shipping Co., Ltd.), 120 St. Vincent St., Glasgow. Bombed by aircraft and sunk on March 19, 1943, in Tripoli Harbor with the loss of five crew.

Patrick Henry, 7,191-ton Maritime Commission Liberty ship built by the Bethlehem-Fairfield Shipyard, Baltimore. Launched at 12:30 p.m. Operated by American Export Lines, 25 Broadway, New York, under charter to the British Ministry of War Transport.

Departed Trinidad on May 26, 1942, for Baltimore and rescued three Royal Navy airmen 15 miles out and arrived at Baltimore on June 3. Pilot Arthur M. Breton, 20, of Wakefield, Yorkshire; and observers Harry Ashford, 20, of Birmingham; and Patrick D. P. Fagan, 26, of Port Talbot, Glenmorgan, South Wales, were turned over to the British consul for repatriation. Made one voyage in the Pacific and was scrapped in 1958.

Alcoa Polaris, 6,679-ton Maritime Commission C-1 freighter built by the Consolidated Steel Corp., Los Angeles, California, for the Alcoa Steamship Co., 17 Battery Place, New York. Launched at 1:15 p.m.

Departed Trinidad on May 20, 1942, for Cape Town. On June 1 they were diverted to assist the Liberty ship *George Clymer*, whose propeller shaft had broken en route to Cape Town from Portland, Oregon, on her maiden voyage. Operated by Alcoa until 1963 then returned to the Maritime Administration and subsequently scrapped. The *Clymer* was adrift for seven days and sank a month later.

Frederick Funston, 11,971-ton Maritime Commission troopship built by the Seattle-Tacoma Shipbuilding Corp., Tacoma, Washington, for the War Department. Launched at 1:30 p.m.

Transferred to the Navy on April 8, 1943, and operated as the APA-89. Participated at Salerno, Saipan, Leyte, and Iwo Jima. Returned to the Army on April 1, 1946, operated by the Navy's MSTS in 1950, and scrapped in 1969.

African Planet, 6,507-ton Maritime Commission C-3 passenger/cargo ship built by the Ingalls Shipbuilding Corp., Pascagoula, Mississippi, for American South African Line, 26 Beaver St., New York. Launched at 2:30 p.m.

The ship was transferred to the Navy and converted to the transport *George Clymer* (AP-57).

Louise Lykes, 6,511-ton Maritime Commission C-2 freighter built by the Federal Shipbuilding & Dry Dock Co., Kearney, New Jersey, for Lykes Bros. Steamship Co., 925 Whitney Bank Building, 624 Common St., New Orleans. Launched at 2:30 p.m.

Operated in the Indian and Atlantic Oceans. Sunk on January 9, 1943, in the North Atlantic by *U-384* with the loss of all 80 persons aboard.

Adabelle Lykes, 5,093-ton Maritime Commission freighter built by the Pusey & Jones Corp., Wilmington, Delaware, for Lykes Bros. Steamship Co., 925 Whitney Bank Building, 624 Common St., New Orleans. Launched at 3 p.m.

Operated in the Atlantic and Pacific and removed from service in 1961.

Steel Artisan, 5,686-ton Maritime Commission C-3 freighter built by the Western Pipe & Steel Co., San Francisco, California, for the Isthmian Steamship Co., 25 Broadway, New York. Launched at 3 p.m.

Transferred to the Navy and completed as the escort carrier *Barnes* (CVE-7) then transferred to Great Britain under Lend-Lease and operated by the Royal Navy as HMS *Attacker*. Returned to the U.S. in 1946 and scrapped.

Sinclair Superflame, 7,874-ton Maritime Commission tanker built by the Bethlehem Steel Co., Fore River Yard, Quincy, Massachusetts, for the Sinclair Refining Co., 630 5th Ave., New York. Launched at 4:45 p.m.

Departed Philadelphia on February 3, 1942, for Cristobal, Panama, and observed a torpedo track at 33°15'N/78°52'W on the 5th. Operated mostly in the Pacific and scrapped in 1966.

John C. Fremont, 7,176-ton Maritime Commission Liberty ship built by the California Shipbuilding Corp., Los Angeles. Launched at 5:30 p.m.

Operated in the Atlantic, Mediterranean, and Pacific by American President Lines, 311 California St., San Francisco, California. Hit a mine in Manila Bay, Philippines, on March 31, 1945. Subsequently sold for scrap.

Star of Oregon, 7,176-ton Maritime Commission Liberty ship built by the Oregon Shipbuilding Corp., Portland, Oregon. Launched at 6:30 p.m.

Operated by States Steamship Co., 1010 Washington St., Tacoma, Washington. Capt. Ellis P. Thomas's ship was torpedoed and shelled off Trinidad by *U-162* on August 30, 1942, at 11°48'N/59°45'W. One sailor, oiler James V. Carbone, 28, of Portland, Oregon, was lost and 54 survivors were landed at Trinidad.

Ocean Venture, 7,174-ton British Ministry of War Transport freighter built by the Todd-California Shipbuilding Corp., Richmond, California. Launched at 8:30 p.m.

Operated by the Larrinaga Steamship Co., Ltd., 30 James St., Liverpool. Sunk on February 8, 1942, by *U-108* in the North Atlantic at 37°05'N/74°15'W. Thirteen survivors and one deceased crewman were picked up by USS *Roe* (DD-418) on the 10th and brought to Norfolk.

A sequel to Liberty Fleet Day occurred on National Maritime Day, May 22, 1942, when 21 ships were launched. On May 20, 1933, Congress declared May 22 National Maritime Day to commemorate May 22, 1819, when the *Savannah* left Savannah, Georgia, on its historic 25-day journey to Liverpool, England, the first steamship to cross the Atlantic, although mostly under sail. The date is commemorated every year by Presidential proclamation. The launchings were little comfort on that day in 1942, however, as merchant ship and crew losses continued to mount. On the 29th the Navy Department announced that 233 ships had been sunk in Atlantic, Gulf, and Caribbean waters—one out of every two that were then coming off the ways. The first and last ships launched were at the Seattle-Tacoma Shipbuilding Corp. The Navy auxiliary aircraft carrier *Barnes* (ACV-20) went into the water at 12:01 a.m. and the escort carrier *Altamaha* (CVE-18) at 11:38 p.m. That day, Oregon Ship in Portland, Oregon, broke a world record by launching six Liberty ships in one day.

The Todd-Kaiser-Six Companies Split

The war offered Henry Kaiser unprecedented opportunity to expand his holdings and branch out into new ventures. He apparently felt hamstrung by Todd's presence in his affairs and at the end of October 1941 Six Companies made the Todd-California Shipbuilding Corp. a subsidiary of the Permanente Metals Corp. and ceased to use the Todd name. Todd's interest in the company was only 35 percent so it wasn't difficult for Kaiser to exert influence over these matters.

On December 7 the long-expected attack by Japan occurred at Pearl Harbor. During the last week of December, Admiral Land announced that the 10 private shipyards with 40 ways capable of building a 400-foot plus ship that existed in 1937 had been increased to 40 yards with 275 ways, around 1,000 ships were under construction or had been contracted for, and all the yards had on-site schools for training new workers. Around 175 ships had been requisitioned and transferred to the Navy and War Departments and most of the 198 World War I Shipping Board ships laid up in reserve fleets had been reconditioned and returned to service through sale or charter.

On January 17, 1942, a contract was signed with South Portland for the construction of 16 Liberty ships on a cost-plus-fixed-fee basis. The fixed-fee was $110,000 per ship with bonuses for good performance and penalties for poor performance. The upper fee-plus-bonus limit for each ship was $140,000 with a minimum fee of $60,000 per ship in the event of penalties.

At the same time Todd-Bath and Permanente Metals each received contracts for the construction of 68 Liberty ships, 33 of those to be built at the Todd-Bath east area yard. At this same time Newell again went ahead and leased Thompson's Point and put John W. Osborn in charge there.

On February 10, 1942, John Reilly reported to the Todd board of directors that Kaiser wanted to use the profits from the West Coast shipbuilding business to invest in synthetic rubber. When the war began, two commodities became immediately critical: rubber and 100-octane gasoline for aircraft. The Japanese occupied the best sources of natural rubber in Ceylon and Malaya so it was vital that a synthetic substitute be found as quickly as possible.

Todd acknowledged it was a vital necessity, but they were in the ship business while Kaiser was an industrialist who saw ships as just another large thing to build and when he again wanted to invest in non-ship related activities it was too much for Todd and on February 14 the partnership with Kaiser was formally dissolved. After the appropriate financial and legal adjustments were made, Kaiser took sole control of Oregon Ship, Richmond Ship, and Permanente Metals. The old Todd-California yard became Permanente Metals Yard No. 1 and Richmond Shipbuilding's new yard became Permanente Metals Yard No. 2. Kaiser relinquished his interest in Todd's Seattle-Tacoma operations, the Todd-Bath Iron yard, and South Portland Ship. Those two yards were then owned 50/50 by Bath Iron and Todd. The Houston Shipbuilding Corp. became Todd Houston Shipbuilding under Todd's sole control and Bechtel-McCone took control of California Shipbuilding.

The Higgins Contract and a Few Diversions

In March 1942, the Maritime Commission awarded a contract for a 28-way shipyard and 234 Liberty ships to boat builder Andrew Jackson Higgins, president of Higgins Industries at New Orleans. At the same time a contract for a 6-way yard and 34 ships was awarded to the W. A. Bechtel Co. at Sausalito, California, but in July the Higgins contract was cancelled. The decision was extremely controversial and a highly-publicized Congressional investigation ensued. The official explanation from Washington was a "lack of steel" but an independent investigation by labor organizations concluded that "East Coast industrialists" were afraid of post-war competition from Higgins if he was allowed to expand into large shipbuilding and they twisted Admiral Land's arm.

The "steel" argument seemed plausible at the time since it was early in the war and enormous demands were being put on the industry. As time went on, however, it turned out that labor was directly involved and the steel issue would eventually catch up with Henry Kaiser.

According to Gar A. Roush, editor of *Mineral Industry* magazine in Pennsylvania, the numerous coal strikes during 1942 drastically reduced the supply of coke for blast furnaces and annealing ovens and a shortage of scrap iron in the latter half of 1942 contributed somewhat. The main reason for the coal strikes that occurred was wages failing to keep up with inflation.

Mobilizing for total war required wage and price controls but in June 1942 the War Labor Board granted a 15 percent wage increase to match the inflation that had occurred since January 1941. On October 3, 1942, President Roosevelt froze all wages, rents, and farm prices. Organized labor still felt squeezed by the wage controls and constantly complained that inflation was far worse than officially reported by the Labor Department and the A.F.L. and C.I.O. wanted a return to free market collective bargaining. John L. Lewis, head of the United Mine Worker's union, demanded a $2 a day increase and refused to meet with the War Labor Board or abide by their decisions. Instead, he took his case directly to Secretary of the Interior and Fuel Administrator Harold L. Ickes, without success. Four major coal strikes and a government takeover ensued but Lewis got $1.75 a day raise. On December 30, 1942, anthracite coal miners began a strike that lasted 22 days, ending only after President Roosevelt threatened government action.

The coal miner's victory emboldened other unions but on April 8, 1943, Roosevelt again froze wages, prices, and salaries to control inflation. Lewis vigorously protested, Roosevelt said on the 29th that he would use war powers to deal with strikers, and on April 30 bituminous miners struck again. On May 1 Roosevelt directed Secretary Ickes to seize all coal mines and 80,000 anthracite miners went out in eastern Pennsylvania. The next day, 30 minutes before Roosevelt was going to go on the air and blast the miners as unpatriotic, Lewis called for a "15-day truce" to work things out. On May 28, President Roosevelt appointed James F. Byrnes director of the new Office of War Mobilization and on June 1 tens of thousands of bituminous coal miners in 25 states walked off the job over conflicts between the Union and Appalachian mine operators. Roosevelt ordered them back to work by the 3rd, or else, and the next day Lewis said get back to work by the 7th, or else. The normal work week for coal miners was 42 hours but on August 16 it was upped to 48 hours. In October 1943 a bituminous coal miner made $1.16 an hour averaging $45.22 a week and on November 2 Secretary Ickes granted miners a $1.50 a day increase, up 27 percent a week from October 1942.

Further strikes and wage increases ensued and all this affected steel production. By the end of 1943 approximately 89 million short tons was produced, 3 percent over 1942, but at the same time below the 91.5 short tons that was expected.

The coal strikes notwithstanding, Henry Kaiser's speed in putting ships together, particularly after the 24-day keel laying-to-launching of the *John Fitch* in his Yard 2, prompted allegations that he was buying black market structural steel. Leon Henderson, administrator of the Office of Price Administration in Cleveland, got involved and also raised some questions. Kaiser denied there was a black market but he was enjoined from buying steel "in violation of price ceilings." Kaiser replied:

> There is no such thing as a "black market" in steel. Neither I nor anyone connected with me has ever bought steel on this so-called "black market." What is called a "black market" is nothing more than perhaps a hundred thousand dealers, customers of the steel corporations, who carry stocks of steel in their warehouses for sale at ceiling prices specified by Leon Henderson. We have not at any time paid prices in excess of those established and approved by Henderson.

While Kaiser had his own steel mill in Fontana, California, to help with his supply needs, much of the continual speed-up in his ship deliveries was due to the ideas and innovations of workers who came up with inventions, jigs, and shortcuts to save time, often thousands of man-hours per ship. This was happening everywhere and each company had a system for recognizing and awarding these hardworking, creative people. In March 1944 the Truman Committee reported that workers at the Boeing Aircraft Corp. had cut the man-hours for a B-17 Flying Fortress from 35,400 to 18,700; Consolidated Vultee was building a Liberator in 15,400 man-hours, down from 24,300; Oregon Ship was turning out a Liberty ship in 294,135 man-hours instead of the early 1,146,560; and Bath Iron Works went from building a 2,100-ton destroyer in 1,675,000 man-hours to 925,000.

Admiral Land reported that as of December 31, 1942, 746 merchant vessels had been delivered, including 542 Liberty ships, 62 tankers, 59 C-class freighters, 5 coastal freighters, 5 ore carriers, 15 special type ships, and 55 ships for Great Britain. In 1942 alone over 800 naval craft had been completed.

All this despite a "No-Strike Pledge" for the duration early on by organized labor. The National Bureau of Economic Research, Inc., reported there were 2,968 strikes of various durations in 1942 alone costing 4,182,557 idle man days and 3,736 strikes in 1943.

In the later part of 1944 new contracts for Liberty ships were halted as the yards concentrated on building Victory ships but on December 28, James F. Byrnes, War Mobilization & Reconversion director, announced he was directing the WSA to resume construction of 24 Liberty ships for delivery in the second half of 1945. Byrnes was sketchy on details but the insinuated purpose was the acute need to supply liberated countries and the advances made by German forces into Western Europe.

While Kaiser knew that shipping had to be replaced, he had felt for some time that transatlantic supply to Britain and Russia could be achieved with far better results by using large, fast aircraft instead of slow ships vulnerable to U-boat attack. He pitched his ideas to Congress and on August 7, 1942, Donald M. Nelson, chief of the War Production Board, announced the approval of Kaiser's scheme and announced that 100, 70-ton planes would be built and if successful, 400 more would follow, all similar to Glenn L. Martin's Mars flying boat. Kaiser then teamed up with Howard Hughes to design and build the wooden HK-1 (Hughes-Kaiser) flying boat dubbed the "Spruce Goose" but the easily-frustrated Kaiser soon became annoyed with delays and left the project to Hughes. Kaiser's plan never materialized and the famous HK-1 flew only once. The plane can be seen today at the Evergreen Aviation & Space Museum at 500 NE Captain Michael King Smith Way in McMinnville, Oregon. Henry Kaiser left enduring legacies, among them the Kaiser Permanente medical system.

Meanwhile, on May 15, 1942, South Portland Ship launched their first Liberty ship, the *John Davenport*. On September 30 the British-financed basin yard at South Portland was purchased by the United States and on October 19 the land was purchased from the Todd-Bath Iron Shipbuilding Corp.

War Production Spending Concerns and the Investigation at South Portland

The sudden gearing up for war after the inactivity and loss of income during the decade-long Great Depression created a certain amount of confusion and upheaval in virtually every corner of American society. On April 3, 1939, President Roosevelt signed the Administrative Reorganization Act to consolidate executive bureaus and on August 9 he established the War Resources Board composed of civilian advisors under Edward Stettinius, Jr., to collaborate with the Army & Navy Munitions Board to formulate and coordinate economic mobilization policies. The wealthy Stettinius had been president of the Diamond Match Co., and had worked with J. P. Morgan in 1915 to supply arms to Britain and France. The group was abolished on November 24 and Stettinius would go on to administer the Lend-Lease program.

On September 8, 1939, President Roosevelt declared a national emergency and established the Office for Emergency Management within the Executive Branch, which would serve as an umbrella agency for all war-related mobilization.

On January 3, 1940, he asked Congress for $1.8 billion for defense and $460 million in new taxes. On May 29 he revived the World War I Council of National Defense to stockpile, allocate, and deliver vital raw materials.

On January 7, 1941, Roosevelt established the Office of Production Management. The board was composed of a Director General, Associate Director General, divisions of Production, Purchase, and Priorities, and the Secretary of War and the Secretary of the Navy. The primary purpose was stated in Article 2(a):

> Formulate and execute in the public interest all measures needful and appropriate in order (1) to increase, accelerate, and regulate the production and supply of materials, articles and equipment and the provision of emergency plant facilities and services required for the national defense, and (2) to ensure effective coordination of those activities of the several departments, corporations, and other agencies of the Government which are directly concerned therewith.

Automotive industry executive William S. Knudsen was appointed Director General and was commissioned a lieutenant general in the Army. Donald M. Nelson, a former Sears & Roebuck purchasing manager, was Director of Purchases, and labor organizer Sidney Hillman was second in command.

As boards and conflicting personalities came and went and defense production was going into high gear, rumors of mismanagement came to the attention of Senator Harry Truman. He decided to investigate the matter personally and discovered fixed-fee contracts were being let to inefficient contractors and that a greater proportion of the spending was going to Eastern companies.

On March 1, 1941, the Senate formed the Senate Committee Investigating the War Program to look into all manner of defense spending and organization, including the ship modernization program. Truman was chairman and on August 14, 1941, House Resolution 281, authorized the Committee on Merchant Marine & Fisheries to conduct investigations, stating in part

> to conduct thorough studies and investigation of the progress of the national-defense program, insofar as it relates to matters coming within the jurisdiction of said committee, or administered by the United States Maritime Commission, or any other agency under the jurisdiction of said committee, with a view to determining whether such program is being carried forward efficiently, expeditiously, and economically.

On May 27, 1941, President Roosevelt declared an unlimited national emergency and on August 28 his Executive Order 8875 established the Supply Priorities and Allocations Board within the OPM to replace the Priorities Board, which apparently was seen as ineffective. Vice President Henry A. Wallace was chairman and the executive director was Donald M. Nelson, The Board's first meeting was on September 2, 1941.

On January 16, 1942, Executive Order 9024 established the Office for Emergency Management, superseding the Supply Priorities and Allocations Board.

January 28, 1942, Executive Order 9040 abolished the OPM and created the War Production Board in the Office for Emergency Management to "perform the functions and exercise the powers vested in the Supply Priorities and Allocations Board" of August 28, 1941. Donald Nelson was chairman and Ferdinand Eberstadt was vice chairman.

Plans for shipyard investigations were formulated and this purpose. Rep. Schuyler O. Bland (D-Virginia) chaired the Bland Committee to conduct these particular investigations.

The investigators were immediately confronted with convoluted legal and tax issues. In 1934, the Vinson-Trammell Act required contracts for naval construction to be awarded on a competitive bid basis and limited the profits of prime contractors and subcontractors to 10 percent of the contract amount and the contractor was required to pay any amount over 10 percent net profit to the government within the "income taxable year." Any amount owed and not paid voluntarily could be "recaptured" through legal action. Section 505(b) of the Merchant Marine Act of 1936 contained the same provisions for merchant vessel construction.

As war became inevitable, Knudsen and Hillman felt that the profit limitations and the recapture provision would hamper the country's preparedness efforts and they urged Congress to repeal the law. The Maritime Commission felt its program was working well with the 10 percent limitation on shipbuilders but were concerned about future subcontractors and suppliers being subjected to the recapture process and potential embarrassment from the auditing of their books. Section 402 of the Second Internal Revenue Act of 1940 exempted prime contractors and corporate subcontractors working under Maritime Commission contractors from the recapture provision. As R. Earle Anderson, former director of finance for the Maritime Commission, stated in 1948:

> The extinction of the profit-limiting provisions of the Vinson-Trammell Act for both prime and subcontractors and of the corresponding provisions of the Merchant Marine Act as related to subcontractors was probably one of the causes of the public and Congressional clamor which later led to the enactment of the renegotiation laws.

Contract manipulators and lobbyists were thick in Washington as one article in the *St. Petersburg Times* on March 14, 1942, stated: "They operate along three general lines: (1) straight commissions (2) as special company officials whose commission payments are disguised as payroll charges, and (3) as subcontract distributors."

The average cost of a Liberty ship was $1,780,000 but the same vessel built in peacetime would have cost about $500,000 according to economists. The difference was attributed to a 24-hour work schedule with overtime and increased supply costs such as shipping engines half way across the country by train to yards needing them.

On April 18, 1942, President Roosevelt's Executive Order 9139 established the War Manpower Commission within the Office of Emergency Management and appointed Paul V. McNutt chairman. The 1912 Eight-Hour law was suspended, while retaining overtime for work in excess of eight hours a day and 40 hours a week. On February 9, Roosevelt mandated a 48-hour work week in 32 war-related industries, including shipbuilding.

The labor shortage on the West Coast obligated contractors like Henry Kaiser to recruit workers from the Midwest and southeast. Ads were printed in newspapers and "Kaiser Special" trains brought workers out West. Many fled poverty, bad marriages, and unstable homes to make more money in one month than they had seen in a long time. The "Okies" who came out to California to work in agriculture went to work in defense plants or joined the service. Money was no doubt the driving factor for not only contractors but also the individual worker. Everyone wanted to win the war, but it was nice to have a little walking around money. At the Kaiser yard in Richmond in late January 1944, one couple, both 25, were convicted of "tethering" their 6-year-old daughter in their basement while they both worked the swing shift. The husband got 90 days in jail and the wife six months probation. The judge said they needed to forget their "apparent interest in money and take better care of their children."

The speed in which Liberty ships were delivered and several incidences of structural failures was formally addressed in early January 1944 when Adm. Land said that 75 to 80 percent of structural faults could be corrected but not 100 percent as they were caused by "locked up stresses" inherent in all-welded hulls. On March 27, 1944, the Truman War Investigating Committee composed of Senators Truman, Monrad C. Wallgren, Charles W. Kilgore, Samuel D. Jackson, and chief counsel Hugh Fulton met in Seattle with five representatives of shipping companies who had operated Liberty ships in Northern Pacific waters to address the issue of structural cracking and charges of faulty construction filed by Marcus P. Dukes and four other Oregonship inspectors. Edgar F. Kaiser represented Oregonship. It was determined that out of 234 structural failures to date, 139 were from Kaiser yards. The national average for failures was 12.21 percent per yard. Alabama Dry Dock and Delta Shipbuilding had a higher rate of failure than Kaiser. Of 116 built at Richmond No. 1, seven ships cracked; out of 258 from Yard 2, 19 had cracking problems. At Calship, 50 ships split open out of 206 studied. The Kaiser yard in Vancouver, Washington, had a 40 percent failure rate while 69 Oregonship vessels out of 306 developed cracks. The committee moved on to San Francisco on March 30.

The rapid construction of all-welded ships presented problems with metal stresses and distortion that were eventually overcome through strict attention to the sequence of welding the various parts together.

THE INVESTIGATION AT SOUTH PORTLAND

When the Committee on Merchant Marine and Fisheries investigations got underway South Portland Ship became the immediate subject of study since it had "the poorest performance record of any company engaged in the construction of Liberty ships." Investigators were at South Portland Ship from August to November 1942.

In March of 1942, prior to the arrival of the investigators, Adm. Vickery, John D. Reilly, and William H. Harrison, a member of the War Production Board, visited South Portland Ship and concluded that a new "deputy president" was needed. The group found Carl N. Klitgaard, a 41-year-old Danish marine superintendent with Standard Oil of New Jersey, who agreed to step in after the Maritime Commission secured his release from Standard Oil. He lived with his wife Ellen, also a Dane, and their three children at 18 Westcott Blvd. on Staten Island. Carl reported to South Portland Ship in May 1942 as an independent deputy to William Newell but with complete authority to fulfill all the contracts. Newell apparently was happy with the arrangement and Klitgaard set about getting as much prefabrication work done, given the limitations of space and crane-lifting capacity.

On Sunday, August 30, 1942, the *James G. Blaine* was scheduled to be launched but the welders took "voluntary time off" and went home, delaying the launching by a week. On Monday, Mr. Klitgaard said that further absenteeism would result in mass firings and there would be "Army uniforms" for "shipyard vacationists" and "names will be turned over to the Selective Service board by the company." Klitgaard had planned to leave the shipyard in September but Adm. Land and Rep. Bland, chairman of the Committee on Merchant Marine and Fisheries, begged him to stay on despite his grueling work schedule and constant frustration. He stayed on until December.

On November 24, 1942, Representative Bland submitted the investigator's report. Regarding Mr. Klitgaard, the report stated:

> Mr. Klitgaard's specific task was to build a shipbuilding organization, and one of his first tasks was to send the general manager, Mr. Thatcher B. Pinkham, on a visit to other shipyards. That as late as May of this year just 1 year after the original facilities and ship construction contracts had been made, a new manager should have to be brought into the yard, is the most eloquent testimony

obtainable of the failure of South Portland Ship to supply what was expected of it, to wit, an organization capable of building ships.

Mr. Klitgaard's first task in this direction was the elimination of incompetents, all of whom had come from Bath Iron Works, who had been placed in important posts in the yard by South Portland management. For example, he removed Mr. Thomas R. Allen, who had been vice president in charge of production, the gentleman who, with Mr. Newell, made a tour of the west-coast yards so that he could learn mass-construction methods and then objected to the use of automatic-welding machines. In the original master plans prepared for the construction of Liberty ships, the use of automatic welding was contemplated. By reason of the opposition of the corporation, voiced by Mr. Allen particularly, the substitution of hand welding was permitted and was utilized until it became evident that such outmoded methods could not produce the desired results. Nevertheless, it was only through the continued insistence of the Commission that the more modern and speedy automatic welding procedure was instituted in the spring of this year.

Mr. Klitgaard also removed Mr. John W. Osborn, who had been the general manager at Thompsons Point and who had formerly held other posts in the yard. It was Mr. Osborn who failed to establish a proper method of checking trucking which made it possible for the double billing by Materials Handling. Mr. Klitgaard also removed Mr. Crean, the 27-year-old ship fitter, who had been placed in the important position of hull superintendent, after serving as general manager during the early construction of facilities. Most of the people removed were relatives or favorites of officers or stockholders of Bath Iron Works.

The report described the overall effort and stated:

Members of the investigating staff were in Portland from shortly after August 1 until November 1. During that time they made a thorough examination of all phases of the activities of South Portland Ship in the performance of its facilities and ship-construction contracts. They investigated certain vendors who dealt with the shipyard. They investigated the files of the Maritime Commission at the yard, at the regional office in Philadelphia and in Washington. Extensive hearings have been held and the testimony of many witnesses taken both in Portland and in Washington.

The investigator's report was arranged under various topic headings and will explain in further detail the reasons for Mr. Klitgaard's actions:

The Maritime Commission

The Maritime Commission's Regional Director of Construction for the East Coast was John Frank McInnis, Jefferson Building, 1015 Chestnut St., Philadelphia. His office had control of all Maritime Commission shipbuilding from Maine to Georgia.

The first thing the investigators noticed was an extreme leniency and generosity on the part of the Maritime Commission toward South Portland from the beginning.

Investigators were astounded to learn the company's contract with the Maritime Commission essentially said the company did not have to fulfill the contract, as stated: "the contractor shall not be deemed to have guaranteed that this contract can be performed." Admiral Land, according to Professor Frederic C. Lane, was "an old personal friend of Mr. Newell." The investigation was no doubt painful for the admiral, who told Newell on August 26, 1942, that he had "no intention of butting in to his affairs."

The Maritime Commission was faulted for not moving sooner to fix things:

These conditions have been well known to the Maritime Commission during the whole period of the yard's history.... Aside from that [appointing the new manager] it has done nothing to improve conditions at the yard other that to plead with South Portland Ship for better performance.

The bottom line was stated in the report:

The record of South Portland Ship is the worst of any company engaged in the construction of Liberty ships. Your committee is unable to subscribe to the principle that South Portland Ship should be paid $5,000,000 for its incompetence, inefficiency, and obvious inability to perform its contract duties solely because other yards furnish examples of bad management. The specific suggestion of your committee is that the contracts with South Portland Ship should be terminated immediately.

Inadequate Management

Concerning the management of the yard, the committee stated:

The fundamental trouble with South Portland is that it lacked sufficient managerial personnel and skill to accomplish the vast task of operating a yard capable of performing its contracts. That lack still exists.

William Newell ended up in the committee's hot seat during the hearings in Washington. Here he is being questioned by Department of Justice attorney James V. Hayes trying to explain why Thomas Allen, a man with no building construction experience, was made supervisor of facilities construction:

MR. HAYES: Was Mr. Allen ever in the building construction business?
MR. NEWELL: I do not know, Mr. Hayes. I believe his father was a contractor, but I am not sure of that. I do think, however, that I recall hearing Mr. Allen say that Mr. Allen was with his father, who was a contractor in Philadelphia.
MR. HAYES: So far as you know Mr. Allen had never engaged in building construction before? He was a shipbuilder as I understand your testimony.
MR. NEWELL: Yes, but I told you his father was a contractor, and I believe as a young man he had done some work with his father.

Allen's father, Thomas R., was actually a building inspector in Philadelphia and then a residential brick and stone mason in West Deptford, New Jersey.

To ease the management shortage, South Portland promoted tradesmen to "executive and subexecutive" posts. In Newell's defense in this regard, he had only so many people to choose from initially. The most experienced foremen and supervisors from Bath Iron who could be spared went to the Todd-Bath Iron yard and the "second string" went to South Portland, but then things got out of hand. The report continued:

On the pay roll there are approximately 100 superintendents, foremen, and assistant foremen. Of these, 75 had no prior experience in the direction of men.

Given the nature of the national emergency, that was probably happening in every industry in America. Field appointments in all the military branches and merchant seamen promoted to acting capacities aboard shorthanded ships was common and the committee no doubt found the same situation in just about every shipyard and defense plant their investigators went to.

A good military example is Army Air Corps pilot John D. Landers, born August 23, 1920, in Wilson, Oklahoma. He grew up in Joshua, Texas, where his father, Obediah, was a gas company engineer and mom, Mamie, was the lunch room manager at a local public school. In 1941 he was a flying cadet and was commissioned a 1st lieutenant on December 12 with only 209 hours—20 hours in P-40s—and ended the war as a highly decorated 24-year-old ace colonel in command of the 361st Fighter Group in Europe. But by early 1944 the average time in training alone was 250 hours and the average newly-commissioned 1st lieutenant had 600 hours under his belt.

Bath Iron had no experience in building large, prefabricated, single-class, ships and they had no prefabrication experience at all. Between 1921 and 1942 Bath Iron had built only six vessels over 2,000 gross tons and none had exceeded 6,597 tons. Bath built a lot of vessels between the wars but was known best for building Navy destroyers.

The Yard Layout

After an inspection of the yard itself, the investigating committee reported:

The lay-out is bad for a yard which was intended to exploit to the full use of prefabrication and preassembly in the construction of ships. The assembly building is much too close to the head of the ways, and a portion of the distance between is taken up with a roadway for the passage of trucks and with a railroad track. The remaining space is too small to take care of the preassembled units in sufficient number.

The placing of the assembly building in a position so close to the head of the ways was described by a witness as a $5,000,000 blunder. The explanation for the blunder lies likely in the fact that Bath Iron Works and its president, Mr. Newell, have engaged principally in custom-tailor ship construction and were not acquainted with the methods of mass construction used and intended to be used in the building of Liberty ships. Thus, the only participation by South Portland Ship in the performance of the facilities contract was the furnishing of a bad lay-out and the appointment of two inexperienced men to supervise construction.

Record of Deliveries

Shortcomings in virtually every management area a shipbuilding concern could have were found but no fault is mentioned with the workers or of workmanship:

As of November 1, 1942, South Portland had delivered 8 ships. Next lowest is a yard which delivered 13 ships, and the next lowest delivered 17 ships. The 2 best yards delivered 80 and 85 ships.... A more significant comparison exists between the Todd-Bath yard ... and the Richmond No. 1 yard, located in California. Both these yards on the same day received contracts for the construction of facilities and of 30 identical merchant ships from the British. That was in December 1940. In addition, both yards, in January 1942, received contracts for the construction of 33 Liberty ships. At November 1, 1942, the Richmond No. 1 yard had delivered all of the 30 British ships and 15 Liberty ships. At the same date the Todd-Bath yard had not yet completed its British contract, 3 ships remaining to be delivered, and had delivered no Liberty ships.

Appropriations & Record Keeping

The next area of attack was faulty record keeping. The architect for the yard buildings, Alonzo Harriman, by all accounts highly competent, estimated that 2½ million board feet of lumber would be needed. But South Portland kept no records and it was found that around 1,200,000 extra board feet—75 car loads—had been delivered over the amount ordered and had not been accounted for.

Until about February 1942, no records pertaining to the rental of equipment for the use by the general contractor were kept and that was a violation of Maritime Commission rules. Due to faulty record keeping for appropriations, approximately $600,000 was unaccounted for as of March 1942. In referring to the effort expended in sorting it out the committee stated:

The appropriations made by the Maritime Commission for the construction of the facilities were divided into separate amounts for the construction of particular items, i. e., crane ways, assembly building, etc. The plan was that as each commitment was made by South Portland Ship for services or materials upon a particular structure, such commitment would be charged against the appropriation and thus a record would be available to determine the degree of exhaustion of the particular appropriation. There was, however, a progressive failure to record commitments exceeded recorded commitments by approximately $600,000. In order to bring the records up to date, it became necessary at that time to cease purchases and to instruct vendors to make no further deliveries for a period of about 2 weeks.

The important point in connection with the failure to keep adequate records is the time loss that resulted. It is impossible now to determine how many man-hours, not merely of subordinates but of men in executive posts, were wasted in their endeavors to settle the controversies that resulted from this failure.

Building Techniques

The Maritime Commission's resident Hull Inspector at South Portland, Herman Stephan, had complained from the very beginning that no prefabrication was being done but Newell called William G. Esmond, the Maritime Commission's chief of the Construction Division, Hull Section, and "had him overruled." Esmond's feeling was that the builders should use whatever methods they felt best for their situation. Stephan complained about many things at South Portland and in early 1942 he was transferred to North Carolina.

Shipbuilding deficiencies involved the failure to use prefabrication techniques and automatic welding machines primarily due to Bath Iron's management team's lack of experience with that production method. The Maritime Commission suggested that Newell and Allen visit West Coast shipyards to observe the methods used there, which they did:

> But whatever they may have learned with respect to the far speedier methods of ship construction in use there, they applied none of it to the South Portland yard, and continued to build ships piece by piece.

On his return, Allen particularly was noted to make strenuous objections to the use of automatic welding machines—the reason was not stated—and continued to use the much slower hand welding.

Thompson's Point

When the yard was expanded from four ways to six, William Newell proposed using a little peninsula on the north bank of the Fore River called Thompson's Point, an old railroad yard, as a fabrication and storage site but it was seven miles from the shipyard. The Maritime Commission refused the proposal and acquired property for that purpose adjacent to the shipyard. But in January 1942 Newell went ahead and leased Thompson's Point from its owners, the Portland Terminal Co., a subsidiary of the Maine Central Railroad Co., and put John W. Osborn in charge there. It just so happened that William Newell was a director of Maine Central and South Portland's legal counsel, Wadleigh M. Drummond, Esq., 108 Vaughn St., Portland, was a director of "one of the underlying railroad corporations involved."

The committee found that for the previous five years, the revenue from Thompson's Point never exceeded $15,000 but South Portland's lease was for $36,000 a year with a minimum of two years, plus property taxes of $5,541 a year, and any improvements made would become the property of Portland Terminal. South Portland Ship had the option of buying the property for $555,000 at any time during the lease.

The committee found the assessed value of the property was less than $120,000 and the book value of the buildings was $103,000. Improvements made to the property totaled $520,000. The committee charged that excessive rent was collected on a grossly inflated market value and one provision in the lease was particularly troubling:

> The property consists of a point of land extending into a body of water known as the Fore River, which is part of Portland Harbor. The main line of the Boston & Maine Railroad, which operates the Maine Central Railroad, crosses Fore River on a trestle located between Thompsons Point and Portland Harbor at a distance of approximately three-quarters of a mile from the former. The lease contains a covenant to the effect that the leasee will in no way, directly or indirectly, attempt to promote the use of Fore River as a navigable waterway, and that if, at any time within 20 years, the railroad is compelled to build a bridge to permit navigation there, SPS will defray the entire cost of such structure and its maintenance until January 1, 1962.

It is difficult to understand why South Portland Ship should ever have entered into such a lease. It is impossible to justify it. He [Mr. Newell] could offer no explanation for the inclusion in the lease of the strange and unusual provisions relating to the construction of the bridge. In response to questions concerning that provision, his testimony was that he didn't remember the lease contained such provision. He finally admitted that either the railroad company of which he is a director had driven a "sharp bargain" or "somebody was asleep" in his organization.

No prudent businessman, dealing with his own money, would ever have entered into such a lease. Its improvidence and imprudence can be explained only by keeping in mind that all costs incurred are reimbursable by the Maritime Commission.

The lease was immediately terminated, "primarily on the ground that the rent was excessive" and the investigating committee "called the whole transaction to the attention of the War Frauds Unit of the Department of Justice."

Transporting Material

South Portland Ship never hired its own people to transport steel from the storage area to the ways about 200 yards away. Instead, John Osborn hired the Materials Handling Corp. with three tractor-trailer rigs and also rented a flatcar from the Maine Central Railroad Co. at .50¢ a day to haul the steel from the storage area to the ways. Eventually Osborn rented two more flatcars and a small gas-powered locomotive. The three flatcars and the locomotive required 11 workers during each 24-hour period

Materials Handling charged South Portland $4.75 an hour for each rig for 24 hours. At the time of the investigation South Portland was paying Materials Handling over $1,000 a day and had already paid them $325,000. The company never had enough trucks of its own and rented additional equipment.

Materials Handling was owned primarily by Kenneth T. Burr, treasurer of the Bancroft & Martin Rolling Mill Co., 7 Main St., South Portland, his wife Edith M., and their daughter Barbara who lived at 16 Chadwick St., Portland. Other owners were employees of Bancroft & Martin. Bancroft & Martin was never engaged in the trucking business and incorporated Materials Handling in January 1941 to haul goods for Todd-Bath. Of the $3,000 startup money, $2,000 was put up by Burr and $1,000 by "an old friend of Mr. Burr," Mortier D. Harris, manager of the Harris Co., a ship chandlery, grocery, and hardware store at 188 Commercial St. in Portland, manager of the Harris Oil Co., 17 Main, South Portland, and a director of Todd-Bath and South Portland Ship. Harris lived with his wife Edna at 140 Clifford St., South Portland. Barbara Burr was a 22-year-old, $25 a week stenographer at Bancroft & Martin who made an extra $9,875 as a director of Materials Handling. Dad made $10,000. All three were being paid by Bancroft & Martin at the same time.

The investigators found that a company called the Truck Leasing Corp., established in 1940 under president Andrew J. Reilley at 353 Cumberland Ave., Portland, would rent a fuelled truck but no driver to Hunnewell Trucking, Inc., an old established furniture and piano moving firm under president John F. Robinson at 551 Commercial St., Portland, for $6.50 a day. Hunnewell rented the truck with fuel and a driver to Materials Handling for $2.75 per hour and Materials Handling would rent the truck, with fuel and driver, to South Portland Ship for $3.50 per hour. Between January 1941 and September 30, 1942, Materials Handling paid its officers $38,000, and cleared $87,394.30 according to investigators, "after writing off depreciation based on an 18-month life for equipment, a rate of depreciation wholly unjustified by any standard." The total amount paid to Materials & handling was $145,000 on a $3,000 investment.

Another supplier of equipment to Materials Handling was the William H. Gilbert

Partnership, noted by investigators to be "a by-product of the shipbuilding boom in Portland." William H. Gilbert, Jr., was treasurer of the A & N Transportation Co., Inc., 269 Ocean St., South Portland, and partnered with Mortier D. Harris, manager of Harris Oil Delivery, Inc., 188 Commercial St., and his brothers Bernard F., an employee, Elery S., treasurer, and Omah S., clerk. The Gilbert Partnership made $74,000.

From 1936 to 1940 Hunnewell's average profit was around $2,000 a year minus the officers' salaries "which never exceeded $12,000 in any one year." In 1941, the first year of doing business with Materials Handling, the company made $5,000 and the officers' salaries were $24,000. As of September 30, 1942, the company's profit was $71,000 after paying the officers $36,000.

All the firms made some money from Todd-Bath but the majority of their profits came from South Portland Ship. The Committee stated:

> The profits and salaries mentioned above exceed $300,000.... One would suppose that the owners of Materials Handling would be quite satisfied with the profits they were making, but such appears not to be the case. Examination has disclosed that they have engaged in a systematic course of double billing the yard.... We have advised the War Frauds Unit of the Department of Justice of the condition which we discovered.

After the investigation, Materials Handling issued a credit to South Portland for $6,079.50 but the Committee stated:

> We are convinced that the double billing amounted to a much larger sum.
>
> Our endeavors to get some explanation from the executives of South Portland Ship as to why the yard did not do its own trucking or why it did not seek competitive bids—no such bids were ever asked—or why favored treatment was accorded Materials Handling were totally fruitless.

Labor Relations

South Portland had approximately 13,000 employees at the time and Todd-Bath had around 25,000. Todd-Bath Iron workers belonged to the CIO while workers at South Portland were affiliated with their arch-rival, the AFL. According to Prof. Lane:

> The rank and file in the west yard were conscious of working for a management that had not succeeded in organizing for the job it was to do. They complained of poor supervision, of nepotism, and of not having enough work to keep them busy. They did not have faith in the company.

The Committee's investigators also found serious problems with labor relations, pay, and worker morale, as the report stated:

> Perhaps the worst example of the management's bungling has been its handling of labor relations. The result is that there is a complete lack of morale in the yard. The chief reason for this lack of morale is the failure of South Portland Ship to act on an agreement it made on July 2, 1942, with the metal-trades department of the American Federation of Labor covering wages and working conditions in the yard. In general, the wages agreed to by the parties were higher than the prevailing rates in the yard. Although the agreement was executed on July 2, 1942, and was stated to be retroactive to May 4, 1942, the management did not pay any part of the agreed increases until the latter part of October, when a few of the men were increased "as evidence of good faith."

South Portland's Profits

The Committee stated:

> The fees paid to South Portland Ship as of October 31, 1942, are, for all practical purposes, net earnings of South Portland Ship. Its total investment is $250,000. All costs and expenses incurred by it, including salaries of officers, even $6,575 of the $10,000 salary paid to Mr. Newell, are being reimbursed to it by the Maritime Commission. It has already received a return on its investment of

almost 200 percent. Under its contracts with the Commission it is to build 84 ships. Judging by its performance to date, its fees will not exceed $60,000 per ship, as on the ships built so far the penalties imposed for bad performance keep to fees at the minimum figure. Even at the minimum figure, however, its total fees will amount to $5,040,000, or a return of 2,000 percent on investment. This high return on investment must be considered in the light of the fact that South Portland Ship incurs no risk. Up to the present time it has financed its operations by short-term bank loans, a simple matter when one is enabled to borrow on the security of a Government contract. Incidentally, even the interest expense incurred on such loans is reimbursable.

A work stoppage occurred in October and all concerned became aware of the Congressional report published in November. On Tuesday evening, December 1, 1942, at approximately 9:30 p.m. around 80 percent of the company's welders, tackers, and drillers stopped work, some briefly while others went home two hours early. The dispute was over wage increases authorized by the War Labor Board. Employees were upset that the company planned on phasing in the raises department by department, two departments per week, and said they were three weeks overdue already. Work stopped for the rest of the night. Elinor Herrick, Todd's chief of personnel, said she was working with the A. F. of L. machinist's union president, Edward Miller, on job classifications that would determine who got raises and who didn't. Miller said the walkout was unauthorized. Work stopped again on December 3 and these delays in launching disrupted plans already made by groups of school children who won scrap drives and were scheduled to christen ships.

Rep. Bland was severely critical of the Maritime Commission and wrote to President Roosevelt: "South Portland is receiving a fee of [$5,040,000 on a $250,000 investment] for the trouble of incorporating a company, choosing a name for that company, holding an occasional directors' meeting and delegating the performance of its duties." He was especially critical of the Commission's decision to remove Stephan from the yard while retaining people who overlooked the discrepancies.

On January 4, 1943, Boston steamship agent Andrew B. Sides, who apparently had ties with Todd, was made president and Walter L. Green was brought over from Todd's Seattle-Tacoma Shipbuilding Corp. to become vice president and general manager. In 1942, Chester L. Churchill was an architect in Boston who was retained by Sides to help with the expansion work. He lived with his wife Louise at 20 Holly Rd. in Waban and was probably acquainted with Sides. In 1943 he was director of the Planning & Technical Div. at the Massachusetts Committee on Public Safety.

Sides, 58, lived at 25 Fenwick Rd. in Newton, Massachusetts, with his wife Helen F., 48, their daughter Virginia, 21, and son Andrew, 18, and the next year they moved to a home on Mitchell Rd. in South Portland.

On January 12, 1943, a hearing was held in Washington before the Maritime Commission where John Reilly, William Newell and other Bath executives proposed that Todd formally take over South Portland. The Commission agreed and financial arrangements were made regarding the new company: No fees on the first 16 ships; the Burr operation was limited to 6 per cent profit on net sales before taxes; the value of Thompson's Point would be based on the assessed value in condemnation hearings, the Commission would pay $4,151,000 for facilities; and fee schedules on the ships to be contracted for would be reduced, and the new management would "on trial" for 60 days.

As the result of these investigations and problems, the stockholders of South Portland Ship met at the offices of Drummond & Drummond on March 15 and voted to change the name of the company to the New England Shipbuilding Corporation. Todd-Bath Iron Shipbuilding and South Portland Ship merged under Todd's sole control and on April 1, 1943, the new company became the New England Shipbuilding Corporation. Andrew B. Sides was made president and Walter L. Green vice president and general manager. Bath Iron would retain just short of 50 percent ownership of the new company.

The old Todd-Bath Iron yard became known as the East Yard while South Portland was the West Yard. Walter Green's wife, Stella, sponsored the *Mary Wilkins Freeman* on November 13, 1943.

This situation was, as the Committee found, by no means confined to South Portland Ship. Problems with production and management were occurring in most every other defense industry in the country.

Todd-Bath Iron delivered 14 ships before the merger and South Portland delivered 18 ships. The first Liberty ship launched at New England Ship was the *Joseph Warren* on April 5, 1943. On April 30 it was announced that two workers in the crane department, John B. Openshaw, 30, of Portland, and Charles R. Winslow, 21, of South Windham, were charged with "depredation against federal government property" and fined $25 each for cutting and stealing rubber gasket material.

No one knew the Germans would surrender in May 1945 and that Japan would follow in August but both were clearly on the ropes. GIs had a saying, "Home alive in '45" and many women working grimy jobs in the defense industry and anxious to return home said "When it's curtains for the Axis, its curtains for me." Shipping contracts were being cancelled and during the first week of February 1945 the company made plans to start reducing the workforce. Andrew A. Pettis, president of Local 50, Industrial Union of Marine & Shipbuilding Workers (CIO) representing NESCo workers, was notified that 8,000 jobs would be lost by April 30. Ten percent of workers in the west area would be off the payroll by February 28 and 23 percent of east area workers and another 60 percent of west area jobs would be gone by April 30 with further layoffs by June 30.

A total of 236 Liberty ships were delivered by Todd-Bath Iron, South Portland Ship, and the New England Shipbuilding Corp.

Epilogue

After the war, Andrew and Helen Sides moved to Waban, Massachusetts, where Andrew stayed in the shipbuilding business but they kept a summer home in Rockland, Maine. In 1947, Andrew, Jr. was an ensign in the Navy and in 1960 he was president of Bath Iron Works.

The Todd-Bath Iron Shipbuilding Corp. was liquidated in 1951. The New England Shipbuilding Corp. became the Todd Atlantic Shipyards Corp. after the war while still owned 50 percent by Bath Iron. In 1958 Todd bought out Bath's interest in the yard for $223,000. William Newell died in February 1960 and his grand scheme in South Portland is now the Spring Point Marina. The site of the old South Portland Shipbuilding yard is now a tank farm directly across the Fore River from the Maine State Pier. In February 2011 Todd Shipyards was purchased by Vigor Industrial, of Portland, Oregon, for $130 million. Bath Iron continues today as a major shipbuilder.

In August 1943, a serious rift arose between Admiral Vickery, William Gibbs, of Gibbs & Cox, and the Navy. Back in 1941 Admirals Land and Vickery had foreseen the need for a single class of fast, mass produced turbine-powered merchant ship that could outrun U-boats during the war and have an economic peacetime use while still retaining the ability to serve as naval auxiliaries. He had approached Gibbs & Cox to complete a design for 100 ships while he worked to get turbines mass produced. But, according to Vickery, Gibbs squandered $5 million in the effort so he took the job away from them and Gibbs had disliked Vickery ever since. In the meantime, naval planners, hoping for a 7-ocean postwar Navy, had sought to commandeer these turbines for their own ships and had even brought Gibbs into the fray on their side. It turned out that Gibbs, an "astute Wall Street lawyer," got about $9 million of Navy work every year and employed 2,000 draftsmen just for Navy work alone. Gibbs knew that Maritime Commission work would largely cease when the war ended but naval construction would go on forever. Gibbs, the War Production Board, the Maritime Commission, and the Navy all fought over who would get the turbines. The Navy was not fond of Vickery either but he was backed by President Roosevelt and Admiral Land and what would be called the Victory ship was designed by the Maritime Commission's Technical Division under James L. Bates.

The ink hadn't yet dried on the Instrument of Surrender signed on board the *Missouri* before people wanted to know where $910 million spent on the emergency shipbuilding program went and how much of it fat cats like Henry Kaiser had walked away with. The war was over, millions of men had lost their jobs in the shipyards and defense plants, and thousands of ships were now sitting idle. People wanted answers from Comptroller General Lindsay C. Warren.

Approximately 5,600 ships were built under Maritime Commission contracts and approximately half a billion dollars was spent for Liberty ships. Yale lawyer, Navy veteran, and general counsel Marvin J. Coles determined the average profit on each ship was $66,631 but no two shipyards had the same costs or the same profits. The entire contract scheme was based on performance—the fastest producers earned the most money. Henry Kaiser came out on top with an average profit of $86,000 on 489 ships at an average cost of $1,700,000 in 42 days average delivery time. The two ships completed at his Vancouver yard cost $2,100,000 each with a profit of $110,000 each. At the other end, the St. Johns River yard built 82 ships at an average time of 82 days each with an average profit of only $23,000. These figures were before taxes, however, which took $72 out of every $100 of profit.

Vice Admiral Vickery died on March 21, 1946, at 53.

PART III

Liberty Ship Construction by Shipyard

All Liberty ships were launched with their Maritime Commission assigned name when they were around 75 to 85 percent complete. Ships that were transferred to foreign governments under Lend-Lease, either outright or under bareboat charter agreements, were renamed by the nation involved and operated by the government or by private shipping firms.

After launching it was off to the outfitting or "wet dock" where the remaining detail work was completed and the ship cleaned up, painted, and stocked with supplies for the voyage by the operating general agent and the War Shipping Administration. A master was assigned to the ship by the company and he began bringing crew members aboard. They came through the company's office, a union hiring hall, or a local War Shipping Administration office.

When approaching completion, surveyors and various inspectors went aboard to calculate the ship's tonnages and record various construction details for federal documentation purposes. Hull and Boiler Certificates and a Builder's Certificate signed by the "master carpenter" were sent to Washington and the ship was issued an Official Number to be "carved on the main beam" and at some point shortly before delivery a radio license and call sign were issued by the Federal Communications Commission.

If a ship was requisitioned by the Navy, War Department, or allocated to a foreign government under Lend-Lease before being surveyed, no Official Number or call sign was issued. It was probably an awkward situation for shipyard officials when the sponsor or a family member asked about "their" ship after the christening with the champagne, the matrons of honor, the speeches, the photo album and the other commemorative items, only to find out the ship, as launched, no longer exists. "She's in the Navy now" they were probably told, or "she's flying the Russian flag somewhere."

In other cases, a ship was taken after it was delivered to the Maritime Commission but before delivery to a general agent for operation. In this case the ship had and Official Number and perhaps a call sign but never sailed under its original name during the war. On the other hand, some ships made one or more voyages under their original name before being requisitioned. In both of these cases the original name, official number, and call sign are recorded here.

The basic dry cargo Liberty freighter had the Maritime Commission designation of EC2-S-C1 (E=Emergency, C2=a cargo ship with a waterline length between 400 and 450 feet, S=Steam, and C1=design designation). Others were modified for specific cargoes and had their own configurations and designations: Tankers, Z-ET1-S-C3; Colliers, EC2-S-AW1; Boxed Aircraft Transports, Z-EC2-S-C5; and Tank Transports, Z-EC2-S-C2. All ships are EC2-S-C1 except where noted.

The "Sam" ships were built for the British Ministry of War Transport under Lend-Lease and operated by private shipping firms under the Red Duster. "SAM" stands for "Superstructure Aft of Midship" since the typical British tramp freighter had a split island scheme.

The operator shown is the one listed by the Bureau at the time of publication or, in cases where the Navy took control of the ship after one or more voyages and no agent is listed in the *Record*, the agent comes from the Shipping Articles for Voyage No. 1. Agents normally ran a ship for the duration of the war but changes sometimes occurred. In the ship entries that follow, the month and year shown represents the general outfitting and delivery date as recorded in the American Bureau of Shipping's *Record*. This is followed by the Official Number and call sign.

The operator is followed by a brief biographical note about the person or a description of the geographical namesake in the case of foreign-operated ships.

Troop Ship Conversions

Ships taken by the Army or Navy were operated to carry primarily cargo or troops, designated AK for cargo or AP for troops. The second deck, known as the 'tween deck, under the main deck and above the much deeper lower holds, was converted into living and berthing spaces for the much larger Navy crews and troops. Typically, the No. 1 hold had berths for 348 troops in the 'tween deck and 436 troops in the lower hold with an inclined, staircase type ladder between the two decks, which all the below decks spaces had.

The troops ate their meals in the No. 2 hold 'tween deck, which also accommodated refrigerated and dry stores and had an electrical shop aft. An inclined ladder went up to a "booby" hatch on the main deck. The No. 3 hold 'tween deck had the galley for the troops, troop messing, a bake shop, and dry stores with a ladder to the main deck. The No. 4 hold 'tween deck had 84 crew berths and potable water tanks. The No. 5 hold 'tween deck had a 14-bed sickbay on the starboard side and troop berthing for 63 officers on the port side, a troop officer's pantry and messing, medical stores, a surgery suite, pharmacy, medical records office, an isolation ward, and two cells for "mental" cases. All the personnel spaces had showers, toilets, and wash basins. LCMs (Landing Craft, Medium) were carried on top of No. 2 hold and LCVPs (Landing Craft, Vehicle, Personnel) were carried on top of No. 4 hold. All of these functions and spaces were on the main deck on a Liberty merchant vessel, nothing in the cargo spaces.

Crew Information

Much information available today about the crews, passengers, and survivors is due to the fact that during the war the nation's immigration laws were strictly enforced under the Immigration Acts of February 5, 1917, and May 26, 1924. On arrival in foreign ports, the master was required to submit a list of every alien crew member employed on board the vessel to the American Consulate and to submit a crew list and obtain clearance from the consul before departing for the United States. He could be fined $10 "for each change in crew" not reported. On arrival in the United States at a port of entry the master was required to present a detailed list of all aliens that were aboard, or had been aboard, during the voyage and a $10 fine could be imposed for each incomplete report. On arrival, Immigration, Customs, and Public Health officials boarded every vessel coming in from foreign ports and paperwork detailing every person aboard was filled out by the Immigration Inspector along with naturalization documentation for foreign-born citizens. The $2 head tax normally imposed on alien passengers was waived for merchant seamen and Navy Armed Guard sailors but not for civilian passengers. Alien seamen could not go ashore over 29 days, could be restricted to the ship while in port by the Inspector if they had ever been deported, or were turned over to their consul for repatriation. On June 15, 1943, President Roosevelt signed Executive Order 9352 granting alien seamen entry into the United States without visas. This order superseded Executive Order 8429 of June 5, 1940, which required alien sailors to have proper documents. Forms supplied by the State Department contained a "List of Races or Peoples" used to identify ethnicity at the time: Albanian, Armenian, Bohemian, Bosnian, Bulgarian, Chinese, Croatian, Cuban, Dalmatian, Dutch, East Indian, English, Estonian, Filipino, Finnish, Flemish, French, German, Greek, Hebrew, Hercegovinian, Irish, Italian, Japanese, Korean, Latvian, Lithuanian, Magyar, Manx, Montenegrin, Moravian, Negro, Pacific Islander, Polish, Portuguese, Rumanian, Russian, Ruthenian (Russniak), Scandinavian (Norwegians, Danes and Swedes), Scotch, Serbian, Slovak, Slovenian, Spanish, Spanish American, Syrian, Turkish, Welsh, West Indian (except Cuba).

The General Agency Agreement specified the crewing of the vessels. Article 3A subdivision (d) stated:

> The General Agent shall procure the Master of the vessels operated hereunder, subject to the approval of the United States. The Master shall be an agent and employee of the United States, and shall have and exercise full control, responsibility and authority with respect to the navigation and management of the vessel. The General Agent shall procure and make available to the Master for engagement by him the officers and men required by him to fill the complement of the vessel. Such officers and men shall be procured by the General Agent through the usual channels and in accordance with the customary practices of commercial operators and upon the terms and conditions prevailing in the particular service or services in which the vessels are to be operated from time to time. The officers and members of the crew shall be subject only to the orders of the Master. All such persons shall be paid in the customary manner with funds provided by the United States hereunder.

Before the voyage started, the sailors signed the customary Shipping Articles, an agreement between the master and the sailor, in the presence of the Shipping Commissioner at the port of departure. Below is a typical front sheet of wartime Shipping Articles made out on signing a crew for the *Nathaniel Wyeth*. The underlined portions were filled in by the Purser:

IT IS AGREED between the Master and seamen, or mariners, of the <u>S. S. Nathaniel Wyeth of Portland, Oregon</u> *of which* <u>William Shutz</u> *is at present Master, or whoever shall go for Master, now bound from the Port of* <u>Portland, Oregon</u> *, to* <u>a point in the Pacific Ocean to the westward of Portland, Oregon, and thence to such ports and places in any part of the world as the Master may direct or as may be ordered or directed by the United States Government or any Department, Commission or Agency thereof</u> *, and back to a final port of discharge* on the Pacific Coast (inserted) *in the United States, for a term not exceeding* <u>NINE (9)</u> *calendar months.*

GOING ON SHORE IN FOREIGN PORTS IS PROHIBITED
EXCEPT BY PERMISSION OF THE MASTER

NO DANGEROUS WEAPONS OR GROG ALLOWED,
AND NONE TO BE BROUGHT ON BOARD BY THE CREW

A voyage could be stated as any number of months, but typically 6, 9, or 12. As operator only, the agent could not be held liable for damages resulting from the negligence of the master or another crewmember in the case of a sailor's injury [337 U.S. 810].

Ship Losses

When a ship was lost to enemy action, the event was almost always witnessed by sailors on other ships, but a total of 31 ships, including six Liberty ships, simply disappeared and the ship and those aboard were never seen or heard from again. They never reached port, no one knew what happened, and there was no information to give to the families. The ships could have foundered—lost to the ordinary perils of the sea—or were attacked, usually by submarines. In that case there were no witnesses other than the submarine's commander. Most of the attacked ships had become separated from their convoys—known as stragglers. A distress call from the ship might have been heard by someone but when rescue vessels or aircraft reached the reported location, nothing of the ship or crew was ever found. The ship was declared overdue and the sailors were declared missing and presumed lost. War Risk and life insurance policy claims were paid and all were left to ponder the mystery. It was only years after the war ended, when Axis records were examined and pieces of the puzzle were put together by historians, that some light was shed on the events.

The ships in this section are grouped together under each builder according to their month and year of build but not necessarily in their order of delivery. The number shown for each entry has no relation to the Maritime Commission contract number or builder's hull number; it merely serves as a numerical accounting of the number of ships built by each yard. The last Liberty ship delivered was the *Albert M. Boe*, on October 30, 1945, from New England Ship.

Alabama Dry Dock & Shipbuilding Co.
Mobile, Alabama

In 1916, David R. Dunlap, Jr., was president and general manager of Alabama Iron Works at Mobile. In December he consolidated four companies and incorporated Addsco. When war came, Dunlap lived with his wife Talulah at 25 Fearn Way in Mobile. The Maritime Commission spent $19,303,079 on facilities at the 12-way yard, 306-acre yard. The first keel was laid on July 28, 1941.

From September 17 to 20, 1942, approximately 12,000 Industrial Union of Marine and Shipbuilding Workers (CIO) stopped work. Dunlap maintained a segregated workforce but in May 1943 President Roosevelt was expected to sign an executive order establishing the Fair Employment Practices Commission to deal mainly with discrimination in railroad unions. Twelve black welders were put on all-white crews but on the 24th a riot broke out on the night shift. The black workers attempted to leave the yard but were attacked and 11 were reported seriously injured. Local law enforcement and the National Guard were called in and Governor Chauncey Sparks in Montgomery ordered all beer and liquor stores in Mobile and Baldwin County closed. Executive Order 9346 was signed on May 27. The yard built 20 Liberty ships, all delivered by January 1943. The average building time for the ships was 137.5 days. The yard started building T2 tankers under the same ownership but with new management.

1. J. L. M. CURRY, 5–42, 241520, KERQ (1825–1903) Jabez Lamar Monroe Curry was a Georgia educator, Confederate officer, and author. Operated by Lykes. On March 1, 1943, the ship left Murmansk, Russia, in Convoy JW 51A but broke apart in heavy seas on the 7th. The ship was abandoned, survivors were picked up, and the ship sunk by gunfire the next day by HMS *St. Elstan* (FY.240).

2. JOHN MARSHALL, 5–42, 241738, KEVH (1755–1835) John James Marshall was the 4th chief justice of the Supreme Court. Operated by Waterman.

3. HENRY CLAY, 6–42, 241847, KEUU (1777–1852) Henry Clay, Sr., was a Kentucky congressman and Secretary of State. Operated by Lykes.

4. ALEXANDER H. STEPHENS, 7–42, 241863, KFYV (1812–1883) Alexander Hamilton Stephens was a Georgia congressman and vice president of the Confederate States of America. Operated by Mississippi Shipping.

5. ARTHUR MIDDLETON, 7–42, 241864, KEYW (1742–1787) Declaration of Independence signer from South Carolina. Operated by Lykes. Capt. John V. Smith's ship, loaded with munitions, was torpedoed on January 1, 1943, by *U-73* off Oran, Algeria. Of the 61 people aboard only three Armed Guard sailors survived.

6. THOMAS HEYWARD, 7–42, 241868, KFQY (1746–1809) Thomas Heyward, Jr., was a Declaration of Independence signer from South Carolina. Operated by Waterman.

7. JUDAH P. BENJAMIN, 8–42, 242047, KGET (1811–1884) Judah Philip Benjamin was a Louisiana senator, head of the Confederate War Department and a financial genius. Operated by American South African.

8. JEFFERSON DAVIS, 8–42, 242068, KFHO (1808–1889) Jefferson Finis Davis was president of the Confederate States of America. Operated by International Freighting.

9. THOMAS LYNCH, 8–42, 242150, KFVT (1749–1779) Thomas Lynch, Jr., was a Declaration of Independence signer from South Carolina. Operated by J. H. Winchester.

10. JOEL CHANDLER HARRIS, 9–42, 242183, KGID (1848–1908) Atlanta newspaperman and author. Operated by J. H. Winchester.

11. NATHANIEL BACON, 10–42, 242280, KHKK (1647–1676) resident of colonial Jamestown who led a popular, armed rebellion against Gov. William Berkeley in 1676. Operated by International Freighting. On November 24, 1942, Capt. David M. Dantaler's brand-new ship collided at New York with Capt. Aabroslus Vandenkerckhove's Belgian Overseas Transports, S.A., tanker *Esso Belgium*, of Liverpool. The tanker went on its way while the *Bacon* was beached. It was refloated and repaired and in March 1943 got underway and arrived back at New York on May 27 from Oran, Algiers. On December 19, 1945, Capt. Harvey A. Huff's ship hit a mine in Italian waters. There were no casualties but the ship was beached and declared a total constructive loss. The bow section was salvaged and joined with the after portion of the *Bert Williams* at Genoa, Italy, to create a new ship named the *Boccadasse*.

12. ISRAEL PUTNAM, 10–42, 242316, KHKH (1718–1790) Israel "Old Put" Putnam was a dynamic—some said reckless—Army general who served at Bunker Hill. Operated by North Atlantic & Gulf.

13. JOSEPH WHEELER, 11–42, 242404, KHMR (1836–1906) Confederate cavalry general, Alabama congressman, and major general in the Spanish-American War. Served as a general for and against the United States. Operated by South Atlantic. Patrick Morrissey, 60, was chief mate on the Black Diamond Liberty ship *Henry B. Brown* when they arrived at New York on July 12, 1943, from Bizerte, Tunisia. In August he came aboard the *Wheeler* at New York as master and arrived back there from Liverpool on October 15. On the 31st they arrived at the Army Depot at Mobile, Alabama, arriving on the 31st. On December 2, the ship was bombed by German aircraft at Bari, Italy, and completely burned with the loss of 26 merchant crew, including Capt. Morrissey, and 15 Armed Guard sailors.

14. JAMES HOBAN, 11–42, 242490, KHLR (1762–1831) Irish architect who designed the White House. Operated by Waterman.

15. CLARK MILLS, 12–42, 242544, KHLT (1810–1883) noted sculptor in bronze of famous Americans. Operated by Waterman. Capt. Charles B. Raeburn's ship was hit by a

German aerial torpedo on March 9, 1944, off Bizerte, Tunsia. There were no reported casualties.

16. BENJAMIN H. LATROBE, 12–42, 242563, KHLU (1764–1820) Benjamin Henry Boneval Latrobe was a British architect who designed the U.S. Capitol. Operated by American Export Lines until July 29, 1945, when the ship was turned over to a French crew at Baltimore. Christian Valensei, president of the French Supply Council and head of the French Shipping Mission in the United States had petitioned for the use of Liberty ships "to transport vast amounts of materials required to rehabilitate the nation's economy."

17. SIMON WILLARD, 12–42, 242651, KHLW (1605–1676) fur trader who, with Peter Bulkeley, cofounded Concord, Massachusetts. Operated by Waterman.

18. COLIN P. KELLY, JR., 1–43, 242695, KKGI (1915–1941) Colin Purdie Kelly, Jr., was an Army B-17 pilot from Madison, Florida, who bombed the Japanese heavy cruiser *Asigara* on December 10, 1941, in the Philippine Islands. While returning to Clark Field his plane was attacked by Zero fighters and disabled. Kelly stayed at the controls while his crew bailed out but before he could get out the plane exploded. Operated by Waterman. In January 1943 the ship left Mobile under Capt. Frank L. Murdock, 28. Oscar G. Jones, 31, was chief mate. They departed Bombay, India, on April 6 and arrived at New York on August 4. Jones In 1945 Jones was captain when the ship hit a mine on April 6th off Belgium and became a total constructive loss. No reported casualties.

19. WILLIAM C. GORGAS, 1–43, 242781, KKFA (1854–1920) William Crawford Gorgas was a physician and Surgeon General who eradicated yellow fever in the Panama Canal Zone. Operated by Waterman. Capt. James C. Ellis, Jr.'ship was torpedoed on March 11, 1943, by *U-444* and *U-757* in the North Atlantic. Capt. Ellis, 33 merchant crew, and 21 Armed Guard sailors were lost.

20. LAWTON B. EVANS, 1–43, 242787, KIGW (1862–1934) Lawton Bryan Evans was an educator and author of American and Georgia history books from Lumpkin, Georgia. Operated by Waterman.

Bethlehem Steel Co., Shipbuilding Division
Fairfield Yard, Baltimore, Maryland

The Bethlehem Steel Co. signed a contract for a 13-way yard on February 4, 1941, to be built in the Fairfield area of Baltimore. The Maritime Commission spent $1,798,561 on land and $33,233,156 for facilities on the 741–acre yard, which eventually had 16 ways. The Commission-owned yard delivered or partially built 384 Liberty ships under legendary vice president and general manager Jack Macy Willis (1885–1961). Willis got into shipbuilding at age 13 as a rivet boy with Union Iron Works in San Francisco and worked his way up to supervisory positions in Navy yards. In 1914 he left Norfolk for Baltimore to work at the reorganized Skinner yard and when the company was taken over by Bethlehem Steel in 1921 he became general manager. In 1940 he lived at 5 W. Ruxton Rd. in Ruxton, Maryland, with his wife Lenore, 46, and daughters Elsie, 18, Nancy, 16, and Frances, 14.

The yard built the *Patrick Henry*, the first Liberty ship keel laid down on April 30, 1941, and the *John W. Brown*, one of only two surviving operational Liberty ships left in the world. The *Brown* is open for visitors at Baltimore and cruises the East Coast. One almost complete ship, the *Louis C. Tiffany*, caught fire in the yard and was declared a total loss. The average building time for the ships was 53.8 days.

On October 6, 1961, Willis and his chauffeur, Milton Lewis, 62, died when their car ran into a tractor-trailer rig on the Chesapeake Bay Bridge at around 6:20 a.m., just before dawn. The truck had stopped because of a flat tire. The two were on a fishing trip to the Eastern Shore.

1. PATRICK HENRY, 12–41, 241252, KIVU (1736–1799) governor of Virginia and Revolutionary War patriot. Operated by Lykes. Departed Loch Ewe, Scotland, on September 2, 1942, in the 39-ship, heavily escorted Convoy PQ 18 to Murmansk, Russia. The convoy was attacked repeatedly and only 20 ships reached port.

2. CHARLES CARROLL, 1–42, 241299, KKZK (1737–1832) Charles Carroll of Carrollton was a Declaration of Independence signer from Maryland and the last living signer. Operated by American Export Lines.

3. FRANCIS SCOTT KEY, 1–42, 241317, KTBH (1779–1843) lawyer who witnessed the bombardment of Fort McHenry in Baltimore Harbor in September 1814 and wrote the lyrics to what would become the National Anthem. Operated by Lykes. The *Key*, the *John Randolph*, *Richard Henry Lee*, and *Zebulon B. Vance* were the first Liberty ships to make the infamous and deadly Arctic PQ convoy trips to Murmansk and Archangel, Russia, known as the "Murmansk Run" from September 1941 to September 1942. The *Key* sailed in Convoy PQ 15 in April 1942 on a nine-day run to Murmansk.

4. ROGER B. TANEY, 2–42, 241315, KTXS (1777–1864) Roger Brooke Taney was an Attorney General, Secretary of the Treasury, and 5th chief justice of the Supreme Court. Operated by Waterman. Capt. Thomas J. Potter's ship was torpedoed on February 7, 1943, by *U-160* in the South Atlantic with the loss of all the engineers on watch: 3rd assistant engineer Alfred T. Schulte, oiler Hugh E. Williams, and fireman/watertender Arthur L. Hand.

5. RICHARD HENRY LEE, 2–42, 241369, KAXU (1732–1794) Declaration of Independence signer from Virginia. Operated by Calmar.

6. JOHN RANDOLPH, 2–42, 241394, KBMZ (1773–1833) Virginia congressman. Operated by Union Sulphur. Capt. Paul C. Mugge's ship hit a mine on July 5, 1942, off the northwest coast of Ireland and sank with the loss of five merchant crew.

7. AMERICAN MARINER, 2–42, U.S. Maritime Service Training Ship. Z3-EC2-S-C1 operated by the Coast Guard at Pier 73 at the foot of E. 25th St. across East River Drive. Apprentice seamen from the Sheepshead Bay Maritime Training Center took three week cruises on Long Island Sound. The ship had a master, 24 officers, and 133 enlisted men who acted as crew and instructors.

8. CHRISTOPHER NEWPORT, 3–42, 241439, KBXH (1565–1617) master of the *Susan Constant* and commodore to the *Constant*, *Discovery* and *Godspeed*, the first Virginia Co. vessels to land settlers in Virginia in 1607 and establish Jamestown. Operated by Calmar. Capt. Charles E. Nash's ship left Reykjavik, Iceland, on June 28, 1942, in Convoy PQ 17 for Archangel and Murmansk, Russia, via the Denmark Strait. The ship was sunk on July 6, 1942, by a German torpedo bomber in the Barents Sea. Andrew J. Platt, second engineer; Leroy F. Deutsch, oiler; and Mose G. Parker, fireman/watertender, the three engineers on watch were lost.

9. CARTER BRAXTON, 3–42, 241422, KBTH (1736–1797) Declaration of Independence signer from Virginia. Operated by Union Sulphur.

10. SAMUEL CHASE, 4–42, 241445, KBYU (1741–1811) Declaration of Independence signer from Maryland and Supreme Court justice. Operated by American-Hawaiian. Capt. William K. Martin, 64, left Baltimore in April 1942 for Reykjavik, Iceland, and left from there on June 28 in Convoy PQ 17 for Russia, via the Denmark Strait. The ship was damaged by near bomb misses and had to stop, but chief engineer Albert W. Seel and his black gang got

the ship going and they reached Morotovak, Russia, as one of only 11 ships out of the 33-ship convoy to arrive at their destination. The crew of 33 merchant seamen and 12 Navy gunners under Lt. John Sexton reached New York on October 20.

11. GEORGE WYTHE, 5–42, 241595, KESU (1726–1806) Declaration of Independence signer from Virginia and the first American professor of law. Operated by AGWI Lines.

12. BENJAMIN HARRISON, 3–42, 241405, KBQL (1726–1791) Declaration of Independence signer from Virginia. Operated by Calmar. Capt. Einar J. Christensen's ship left Reykjavik, Iceland, on June 28, 1942, in Convoy PQ 17 for Archangel and Murmansk, Russia, via the Denmark Strait. They were one of only 11 ships out of the 33-ship convoy to reach their destination and arrived at New York on October 20 from Loch Ewe, Scotland. They departed New York on or about December 9, 1942, and on March 16, 1943, the ship was torpedoed by *U-172*, east of the Azores. Two crewmen, chief mate Oswald A. Sorensen, and chief engineer Charles T. Lofgren, and one Armed Guard sailor, possibly S1c Paul Ray Thompson, USNR, of Greensboro, North Carolina, were reported missing and lost.

13. JOHN WITHERSPOON, 4–42, 241487, KEIB (1723–1794) John Knox Witherspoon was a Declaration of Independence signer from New Jersey. Operated by Seas Shipping. John S. Clark was chief mate on the Seas Shipping (Robin Line) freighter *Robin Adair* when they arrived at New York on March 16, 1942, from Port of Spain, Trinidad. He then took command of the *Witherspoon* and left Reykjavik, Iceland, on June 28, 1942, in Convoy PQ 17 for Archangel and Murmansk, Russia, via the Denmark Strait. The ship was torpedoed on July 6 by *U-255* off Novaya Zemlya in the Arctic Ocean. Able seaman Otis F. Tydings was lost.

14. RICHARD BLAND, 4–42, 241495, KENZ (1710–1776) Virginia delegate to the Constitutional Convention. Operated by American South African. Capt. Lawrence Dodd left Philadelphia on May 1 for Halifax, Nova Scotia, and left there on the 14th in a 42-ship convoy for Great Britain. On the 24th the *Bland* and eight other ships detached from the convoy and arrived at Iceland a few days later. On June 27 they joined Convoy PQ 17 but the *Bland* ran aground in heavy fog. Temporary repairs were made at Reykjavik over several weeks and they sailed to Loch Ewe, Scotland. They arrived at Murmansk on December 27 and on March 1, 1943, they left in Convoy JW 51A. On the 10th the ship was torpedoed by *U-255* off Iceland in heavy seas with the loss of 19 merchant crew, including Capt. Dodd and 15 Armed Guard sailors.

15. FRANCIS L. LEE, 4–42, 241544, KESO (1734–1797) Francis Lightfoot Lee was a Declaration of Independence signer from Virginia. Operated by Seas Shipping.

16. ROBERT TREAT PAINE, 5–42, 241589, KETK (1731–1814) Declaration of Independence signer from Massachusetts. Operated by AGWI Lines and converted to an Army troopship.

17. THOMAS NELSON, 5–42, 241597, KEWP (1738–1789) Thomas Nelson, Jr., was a Declaration of Independence signer from Virginia. Operated by Calmar. Capt. Axel M. Michelson's ship was hit by a kamikaze on November 12, 1944, at Dulag, Leyte, Philippines, with the loss of three Armed Guard sailors and 164 soldiers. The ship returned to San Francisco.

18. THOMAS STONE, 5–42, 241654, KEWS (1743–1787) Declaration of Independence signer from Maryland. Operated by American West African.

19. GEORGE CALVERT, 4–42, 241545, KEST (1579–1632) George Calvert, First Baron Baltimore, was the founder and first governor of the Province of Maryland. Operated by A. H. Bull. Capt. Severin Broadwick was master of the A. H. Bull–operated Hog Island freighter *Mary*, torpedoed on March 3, 1942, by *U-129* off Dutch Guiana. He was taken to the large repatriation center for merchant seamen at Port of Spain, Trinidad, and arrived at

New York on the 31st aboard Capt. Frank K. Crosby's Eastern Steamship Lines passenger ship *Yarmouth*. He took command of the *Calvert* and on May 20, 1942, the ship was sunk by *U-753* in the Gulf of Mexico with the loss of three Armed Guard sailors. Capt. Broadwick lived at 3117 Chesterfield Ave. in Baltimore.

20. ST. OLAF, 5–42, 241653, KFAU (995 AD-1030 AD) Olaf II Haraldsson was King of Norway and canonized as Norway's patron saint. Operated by Union Sulphur and converted by the War Department to the Army hospital ship *St. Olaf*.

21. ESEK HOPKINS, 5–42, 241698, KEUC (1718–1802) Commander-in-Chief of the Continental Navy during the Revolutionary War. Operated by Moore-McCormack. Departed Loch Ewe, Scotland, on September 2, 1942, in the 39-ship, heavily escorted PQ 18 convoy to Murmansk, Russia. The convoy was attacked repeatedly leaving only 20 ships to reach port.

22. THOMAS MCKEAN, 5–42, 241699, KEWO (1734–1817) Declaration of Independence signer from Delaware. Operated by Calmar. Capt. Mellin E. Respess, 40, arrived at La Guardia airport in New York aboard Pan Am's *Dixie Clipper* on April 17, 1942, from Bermuda and headed home to 3804 West N. Ave. in Baltimore then took command of the *McKean*. The ship was torpedoed on June 29, 1942, by *U-505* northeast of Puerto Rico with the loss of one merchant sailor, wiper Russell C. Funk, and four Armed Guard sailors. Capt. Respass was a passenger on the freighter *Onondaga* when the ship was torpedoed by *U-129* on July 23, 1942. He was lost along with 18 of the crew.

23. PETER MINUIT, 5–42, 241652, KFNJ (1580–1638) Pieter/Pierre Minuit or Peter Minnewit was director of the Dutch West India Co. who traded goods of value to Indians in exchange for Manhattes Island. Operated by Grace Line.

24. ALEXANDER MACOMB, 6–42, 241720, KEYE (1782–1841) noted War of 1812 Army commander and Commanding General of the Army from 1828–1841. Operated by A. H. Bull. Capt. Carl M. Froisland's ship was torpedoed on July 3, 1942, by *U-215* off Cape Cod with the loss of four merchant crew and six Armed Guard sailors.

25. ELEAZAR WHEELOCK, 6–42, 241774, KFDN (1711–1779) Congregationalist minister and founder and first president of Dartmouth College. Operated by Calmar.

26. HENRY ST. G. TUCKER, 6–42, 241775, KFGP (1780–1848) Henry St. George Tucker was a Virginia congressman. Operated by American South African.

27. RICHARD BASSETT, 6–42, 241806, KFOG (1745–1815) governor of Delaware. Operated by A. H. Bull.

28. WILLIAM JOHNSON, 6–42, 241807, KFUN (1771–1834) Supreme Court justice. Operated by A. H. Bull.

29. THOMAS RUFFIN, 6–42, 241809, KGJA (1787–1870) chief justice of the North Carolina supreme court. Operated by A. H. Bull. Capt. Severin Broadwick's ship was torpedoed on March 9, 1943, by *U-510* north of French Guiana. Second engineer Peder S. Govertson, oiler Julio Rozenfeld, and fireman/watertender Howard L. Hewitt died in the engine room. Convoy escort USS *Courage* (PG-70) rescued 42 survivors. Chief engineer Samuel E. Gardner, Jr., and two Armed Guard sailors died from wounds aboard the *Courage*.

30. OLIVER ELLSWORTH, 6–42, 241820, KFMR (1745–1807) Continental Congressman, Kentucky senator, chief justice of the Supreme Court. Operated by AGWI Lines. Capt. Otto E. Buford departed Loch Ewe, Scotland, on September 2, 1942, in Convoy PQ 18. The ship was torpedoed on September 13 by *U-408* south of Spitzbergen. There were no reported casualties.

31. WILLIAM PACA, 6–42, 241830, KFUZ (1740–1799) Declaration of Independence signer from Maryland. Operated by Calmar.

32. BENJAMIN RUSH, 6–42, 241874, KETT (1745–1813) Declaration of Independence signer from Pennsylvania. Founder of Dickinson College at Carlisle. Operated by United Fruit.

33. JAMES GUNN, 6–42, 241875, KFGW (1867–1927) engineer and cofounder of the Harvard Business School. Operated by Seas Shipping.

34. JOHN HENRY, 6–42, 241876, KFID (1750–1798) Maryland congressman and governor. Operated by Eastern Steamship.

35. THEODORE FOSTER, 6–42, 241877, KFPV (1752–1828) Rhode Island senator. Operated by Shepard.

36. WILLIAM MACLAY, 7–42, 241878, KFVA (1737–1804) Pennsylvania senator. Operated by A. H. Bull.

37. WILLIAM PATTERSON, 7–42, 241879, KFVC (1752–1835) Baltimore City shipping magnate and director of the Baltimore & Ohio Railroad. Operated by A. H. Bull.

38. SAMUEL JOHNSTON, 7–42, 241908, KFOV (1733–1816) North Carolina governor and congressman. Operated by Eastern.

39. JOSEPH STANTON, 7–42, 241940, KFJX (1739–1807) Joseph Stanton, Jr., was a Rhode Island congressman. Operated by AGWI Lines.

40. LUTHER MARTIN, 7–42, 241941, KGBH (1748–1826) proponent of the Bill of Rights in the Constitution. Operated by AGWI Lines.

41. WILLIAM WIRT, 7–42, 241942, KGBF (1772–1834) U.S. Attorney General. Operated by International Freighting. Capt. Cameron D. Simmons, 50, left Baltimore in July 1942 carrying flammable liquids. On January 7, 1943, the ship came under air attack off Algeria while in convoy. The ship was damaged but Armed Guard Lt. (jg) Robert H. McIlwaine, USNR, watched his gun crew shoot down four German planes and two more "probable' hits. The ship arrived at New York on April 3 from Liverpool, England.

42. JOHN H. B. LATROBE, 7–42, 241954, KGBL (1803–1891) John Hazelhurst Boneval Latrobe was a West Point graduate, promoter of the Baltimore & Ohio railroad, cofounder of the Maryland Historical Society in 1844, and stove inventor who joined the effort to colonize Liberia with freed slaves. Operated by Calmar.

43. REVERDY JOHNSON, 7–42, 241955, KGBM (1796–1876) Maryland senator and noted attorney in the Dred Scott case and Fitz John Porter court martial. Operated by American Export Lines.

44. JOHN WALKER, 7–42, 241986, KFJH (1835–1907) chief of the Bureau of Navigation, commander of the White Squadron, and president of the Isthmian Canal Commission. Operated by United Fruit.

45. JOHN P. POE, 7–42, 241987, KHSY (1836–1909) John Prentiss Poe, Sr., was a Maryland attorney general and dean of the University of Maryland law school. Operated by A. H. Bull.

46. RICHARD H. ALVEY, 7–42, 241988, KGIM (1826–1906) Richard Henry Alvey was chief justice of the Maryland supreme court. Operated by A. H. Bull.

47. ANDREW HAMILTON, 8–42, 242059, KGEY (1676–1741) Scotland-born lawyer from Pennsylvania who defended John Peter Zenger in a landmark First Amendment case. Operated by International Freighting.

48. BERNARD CARTER, 8–42, 242060, KGFB (1834–1912) noted Maryland legislator and Baltimore corporate attorney. Operated by American South African.

49. JOHN CARTER ROSE, 8–42, 242061, KGFZ (1861–1927) editor of the *Baltimore Sun*, district attorney, and federal judge. Operated by American West African. Capt. Magnus Leknes' ship was torpedoed on October 8, 1942, by *U-201* east of Trinidad with the loss of

five merchant crew and three Armed Guard sailors. The survivors arrived at New York aboard the Holland-America Line steamer *Westerland* on October 26 from Pernambuco, Brazil.

50. WILLIAM TILGHMAN, 8–42, 242062, KGIZ (1756–1827) chief justice of the Pennsylvania supreme court. Operated by A. H. Bull.

51. BENJAMIN CHEW, 8–42, 242079, KGJP (1722–1810) Pennsylvania supreme court justice. Operated by Calmar.

52. JARED INGERSOLL, 8–42, 242084, KGJR (1749–1822) Connecticut congressman. Operated by American West African.

53. WILLIAM RAWLE, 8–42, 242086, KGGJ (1759–1836) founder and first president of the Historical Society of Pennsylvania. Operated by A. H. Bull.

54. HORACE BINNEY, 8–42, 242124, KGHH (1780–1875) Pennsylvania congressman. Operated by American Export Lines. Cecil Douglas Davies, Jr., 24, signed on the American Export Lines Liberty ship *Charles Carroll* as 2nd mate on October 1, 1942, at New York and arrived back there from Greenock, Scotland, on May 2, 1943. On June 4, 1943, he signed on the *John L. Motley* as chief mate at Baltimore and arrived at New York on September 19 from Oran, Algeria. The *Motley* was bombed at Bari, Italy, on the next voyage with heavy loss of life. On December 24, 1943, he was back on the *Carroll* as chief mate at Savannah, Georgia, and arrived at New York on April 24, 1944, from Hull, England. In June 1944 was master of the *Binney* and left Baltimore on the 22nd and arrived at New York on August 16, 1944, from Liverpool. After two more voyages they left New York on April 3 and on May 8, 1945, they hit a mine off Ostend, Belgium. There were no reported fatalities.

55. JOHN SERGEANT, 9–42, 242125, KGKG (1779–1852) Pennsylvania congressman. Operated by Marine Transport.

56. PIERCE BUTLER, 9–42, 242126, KFNL (1866–1939) Supreme Court justice. Operated by Calmar. Capt. George P. Moodie's ship was torpedoed on November 21, 1942, by *U-177* off South Africa. There were no reported casualties. Survivors left Durban, Natal, on December 9 on the *Empress of Scotland* and arrived at New York on the 19th. Capt. Moodie lived at 330 Fingerboard Rd. on Staten Island.

57. JONATHAN ELMER, 9–42, 242165, KHAP (1745–1817) Continental Congressman and New Jersey senator. Operated by Marine Transport. The ship reached New York on June 28, 1945, from France carrying 390 troops who had gone through 70-mile-an hour winds and 40-degree rolls.

58. TRISTRAM DALTON, 9–42, 242166, KHAU (1738–1817) the first senator from Massachusetts. Operated by A. H. Bull.

59. WILLIAM FEW, 9–42, 242210, KHHJ (1748–1828) Georgia senator and Constitutional delegate. Operated by Merchants & Miners.

60. WILLIAM GRAYSON, 9–42, 242211, KHGD (1736–1790) Virginia congressman. Operated by Black Diamond.

61. JOHN MITCHELL, 9–42, 242207, KHJZ (1870–1919) president of the United Mine Workers Union. Operated by Black Diamond.

62. JOHN W. BROWN, 9–42, 242209, KHJL (1867–1941) born in Canada, came to America in 1887, and settled in Greenfield, Mass. Became a carpenter in Maine and in 1900, at age 33, married a 16-year-old Massachusetts girl named Eva. He became a citizen on February 10, 1904. In 1910 they lived in Surry and had a daughter, Dorothy, 5, and Bertha, a newborn, and John's 5-year-old daughter-in-law Doris. In 1930 they lived at 907 High St. in Bath and Eva worked as a practical nurse. John joined the labor movement and cofounded the United Brotherhood of Carpenters and the United Mine Workers Union. In 1941 he was a 73-year-old widower living at the Hotel Sedgewick on High St. in Bath and still working as a newspaper

columnist. He died from a gunshot wound when his hunting rifle accidentally discharged. Operated by States Marine. The ex-troopship ship was used as a floating maritime school in New York City and the interior was gutted for classroom space. The ship is now operating and open for visitors and offers cruises from Baltimore.

63. BENJAMIN HAWKINS, 9–42, 242288, KHCR (1754–1816) North Carolina senator. Operated by States Marine.

64. RALPH IZARD, 9–42, 242289, KHCS (1741–1804) South Carolina senator. Operated by American-Foreign.

65. CAESAR RODNEY, 9–42, 242269, KHJW (1728–1784) Declaration of Independence signer from Delaware. Operated by International Freighting.

66. JAMES CALDWELL, 9–42, 242270, KHKJ (1734–1781) Presbyterian minister in New Jersey known as the "soldier parson" during the Revolution. His wife Hannah was killed by the British and he was shot by an American soldier. Operated by A. H. Bull.

67. NICHOLAS BIDDLE, 9–42, 242271, KHNT (1786–1844) president of the Bank of the United States. Operated by Seas Shipping.

68. CARDINAL GIBBONS, 10–42, 242324, KHMH (1834–1921) James Gibbons was the archbishop of Baltimore, promoted to cardinal in 1886. Operated by Sword Line.

69. GEORGE WEEMS, 10–42, 242325, KHKI (1784–1853) established freight and passenger steamboat service on the Rappahannock River in 1828. Operated by Moore-McCormack.

70. GRACE ABBOTT, 10–42, 242326, KHLG (1878–1939) social worker and child labor activist from Grand Island, Nebraska, who helped draft the Social Security Act and was the first female nominated for a cabinet position but she was not confirmed. Operated by Calmar.

71. THOMAS SIM LEE, 10–42, 242427, KHJU (1745–1819) governor of Maryland. Operated by AGWI Lines.

72. COTTON MATHER, 11–42, 242452, KHPW (1662–1728) Puritan pioneer and author who was involved with the treatment of smallpox in Massachusetts and in the Salem witch trials. Operated by American Export Lines.

73. WILL ROGERS, 11–42, 242520, KFDC (1879–1935) William Penn Adair Rogers was an entertainer who died on August 15, 1935, in a plane crash with pilot Wiley Post in Alaska. Operated by Merchants & Miners. Capt. Thomas M. Lewis left New York in March 1945 and on April 12 the ship was torpedoed by *U-1024* in the Irish Sea. There were no casualties and the ship arrived at New York on December 15 from Liverpool and was repaired.

74. DANIEL CHESTER FRENCH, 11–42, 242514, KHQA (1850–1931) sculptor of the Lincoln Memorial. Operated by Stockard. Hit a mine on May 6, 1944, off Bizerte, Tunisia, and sank with the loss of nine merchant crew, four Navy Armed Guard sailors, and 24 soldiers.

75. DANIEL WILLARD, 12–42, 242577, KKAZ (1861–1942) "Uncle Dan" Willard was president of the Baltimore & Ohio Railroad. Operated by Calmar. The ship was sponsored by Willard's only granddaughter, 14-year-old Mary Beale Willard.

76. THADDEUS KOSCIUSZKO, 12–42, 242599, KJJF (1746–1817) Andrzej Tadeusz Bonawentura Kościuszko was a Polish brevet brigadier general in the Continental Army during the Revolutionary War. Operated by Grace Line.

77. PEARL HARBOR, 12–42, 242617, KKGL, American naval base on Oahu, Territory of Hawaii, attacked by Japan on December 7, 1941. Operated by AGWI Lines.

78. LORD DELAWARE, 12–42, 242642, KJKC (1577–1618) Thomas West, 3rd Baron De La Warr, was the British governor of Virginia at Jamestown and namesake for all things Delaware. Operated by International Freighting.

79. JAMES WOODROW, 1–43, 242683, KJLT (1828–1907) theologian, scientist, and president of the University of North Carolina. Operated by American South African.

80. WILLARD HALL, 1–43, 242686, KKGE (1780–1875) established public education in Delaware and served in congress. Operated by Stockard.

81. WOODBRIDGE N. FERRIS, 1–43, 242687, KKFZ (1853–1928) Woodbridge Nathan Ferris was a governor of Michigan and a senator. Operated by Calmar.

82. WILLIAM MCKINLEY, 2–43, 242810, KKGA (1843–1901) 25th President of the United States. Operated by American West African.

83. THOMAS R. MARSHALL, 2–43, 242705, KKGB (1854–1925) Thomas Riley Marshall was the governor of Indiana and a vice president. Operated by American-Foreign.

84. ANDREW G. CURTIN, 2–43, 242771, KKGC (1815–1894) Andrew Gregg Curtin was the first Republican governor of Pennsylvania and a congressman. Operated by Calmar. Capt. Robert E. Redding's ship arrived at New York on November 7, 1943, from London. Departed on or about December 5 under Capt. Jacob Jacobson and was torpedoed on January 25, 1944, by *U-716* in the Barents Sea in Convoy JW 56A. Galley utilityman Joseph Simmons, 18, and messman Desso Yeoman, 21, drowned and one Navy Armed Guard sailor was lost. HMS *Inconstant* (H.49) rescued 66 survivors.

85. HORACE GRAY, 2–43, 242772, KKAE (1828–1902) Supreme Court justice. Operated by American Export Lines. Capt. Charles Fox Brown expected to depart Pier F, Jersey City, New Jersey, on December 4, 1944. His ship was torpedoed on February 14, 1945, by *U-711* off Kola Inlet, Russia. There were no reported casualties. Survivors left Southampton, England, on the United States Lines motorship *John Ericsson* and arrived at New York on April 16.

86. SAMUEL BLATCHFORD, 2–43, 242802, KKAH (1820–1893) noted admiralty lawyer and Supreme Court justice. Operated by AGWI Lines.

87. MOLLY PITCHER, 2–43, 242809, KEXY (1744–1832) believed to be Mary Ludwig, wife of 4th Pennsylvania artilleryman William Hays who became a camp follower and served at Valley Forge. At the Battle of Monmouth she provided water to swab cannon barrels and took over her husband's place when he became incapacitated. Operated by Prudential. Capt. David M. Daly's ship was torpedoed on March 17, 1943, by *U-167* off Portugal with the loss of 1st engineer William F. Sims, Jr., 2nd engineer Jack Bewley, and two Armed Guard sailors.

88. HENRY B. BROWN, 2–43, 242819, KKAO (1836–1913) Henry Billings Brown was a Supreme Court justice. Operated by Black Diamond.

89. GEORGE SHIRAS, 2–43, 242817, KKAP (1832–1924) George Shiras, Jr., was a Supreme Court justice. Operated by Prudential.

90. RUFUS W. PECKHAM, 2–43, 242822, KKAQ (1838–1909) Rufus Wheeler Peckham was a Supreme Court justice. Operated by A. H. Bull.

91. WILLIAM R. DAY, 2–43, 242823, KKAT (1849–1923) William Rufus Day was Secretary of State and a Supreme Court Justice. Operated by Marine Transport.

92. MAHLON PITNEY, 2–43, 242842, KKAV (1858–1924) New Jersey congressman and Supreme Court justice. Operated by Grace Line.

93. LOUIS D. BRANDEIS, 3–43, 242841, KKAW (1865–1941) Louis Dembitz Brandeis was a Supreme Court justice. Operated by Moore-McCormack.

94. NATHAN CLIFFORD, 3–43, 242906, KKAY (1803–1881) Maine congressman, Attorney General, Supreme Court justice. Operated by American-Foreign.

95. GEORGE SHARSWOOD, 3–43, 242901, KKMV (1810–1883) Pennsylvania supreme court chief justice. Operated by Dichmann, Wright & Pugh.

96. HENRY L. BENNING, 3–43, 242902, KKMX (1814–1875) Henry Lewis Benning was a Georgia supreme court justice and Confederate general. Namesake for Fort Benning. Operated by Cosmopolitan.

97. JAMES W. DENVER, 3–43, 242982, KKNB (1817–1892) James William Denver was the namesake for Denver, Colorado, a California congressman, and governor of Kansas. Operated by Calmar. Capt. Everett W. Staley left Boston on the Ore Steamship Co. freighter *Cubore* in September 1942 and arrived at New York on December 6 from Havana. He paid off and took command of the *Denver*. The ship was sunk on April 11, 1943, by *U-195* west of the Canary Islands with two fatalities from exposure to the elements, 2nd engineer Malcolm C. Davis and oiler Virgil J. Hurd.

98. JOHN GALLUP, 3–43, 242983, KKNH (1593–1650) early Narragansett Bay trader and pioneer. Operated by Smith & Johnson.

99. JOHNS HOPKINS, 3–43, 242984, KKMY (1795–1873) railroad investor and benefactor of his namesake hospital. Operated by North Atlantic & Gulf. Capt. Frank A. Middleton's ship hit a mine on October 2, 1944, off Marseille, France, in heavy seas. There were no reported casualties and the ship was repaired.

100. THOMAS CRESAP, 3–43, 242985, KKMZ (1702–1790) English-born Col. Cresap was a Maryland pioneer and agent to Lord Baltimore. Operated by Isthmian.

101. HENRY GILBERT COSTIN, 3–43, 242981, KKNG (1898–1918) Private Costin was a Medal of Honor recipient from Baltimore who was lost during the Meuse-Argonne campaign during World War I on October 8, 1918, while taking out machinegun positions. Operated by Cosmopolitan.

102. CLIFFORD D. MALLORY, 3–43, 242980, KKNI (1881–1941) Clifford Day Mallory was vice president of the Clyde Line and Mallory Steamship Cos., a Shipping Board Emergency Fleet Corp. officer, and founder of C. D. Mallory & Co. Operated by Marine Transport.

103. WILLIAM H. WELCH, 3–43, 243007, KKNL (1850–1934) William Henry Welch was a physician and one of the "Big Four" (the Four Horsemen) founders of Johns Hopkins Hospital. Operated by T. J. Stevenson. Stranded on February 26, 1944, near Loch Ewe, Scotland, in very heavy seas. Out of 74 on board only five merchant crewmen and seven Armed Guard sailors survived. Capt. Lee Marshall, of Philadelphia, was lost.

104. WILLIAM OSLER, 3–43, 243065, KKNN (1849–1919) Sir William, 1st Baronet, was a Canadian physician, one of the "Big Four" (the Four Horsemen) founders of Johns Hopkins Hospital, and first professor of medicine. Operated by States Marine. Capt. Frank Kraat departed Philadelphia in March 1943 and arrived at New York on November 7 from Trinidad. The ship was taken by the War Department and converted to the Army hospital ship *Wisteria*.

105. HOWARD A. KELLY, 3–43, 243058, KKNP (1858–1943) Howard Atwood Kelly was a pioneer of abdominal surgery, one of the "Big Four" (the Four Horsemen) founders of Johns Hopkins Hospital, founder of the Kensington Hospital for Women, and professor of obstetrics who established gynecology as a specialty. Operated by A. L. Burbank.

106. WILLIAM S. HALSTED, 3–43, 243103, KKNQ (1852–1922) William Stewart Halsted was a surgeon and one of the "Big Four" (the Four Horsemen) founders of Johns Hopkins Hospital. Operated by International Freighting. Converted to an animal transport ship.

107. FRANKLIN P. MALL, 4–43, 243146, KKNS (1862–1917) Franklin Paine Mall was a noted physician in various fields, anatomist, and professor at Johns Hopkins who married Mabel Glover, one of his female students, in 1894. Operated by Black Diamond.

108. JOHN HOWLAND, 4–43, 243147, KKNU (1873–1926) physician who opened the first American pediatric service at Johns Hopkins Hospital. Operated by American President Lines.

109. WILLIAM H. WILMER, 4–43, 243102, KKNV (1863–1936) William Holland Wilmer was a noted ophthalmologist and first director of the Dept. of Ophthalmology at Johns Hopkins. Operated by Dichmann, Wright & Pugh.

110. JOHN J. ABEL, 4–43, 243096, KKNW (1857–1938) John Jacob Abel was a Johns Hopkins biochemist, pharmacologist, and member of the original medical school faculty. Operated by Calmar.

111. SANTIAGO IGLESIAS, 4–43, 243101, KKNX (1872–1939) Santiago Iglesias Pantin was the resident Commissioner of Puerto Rico in the U.S. Congress from 1933 to 1939. Operated by Grace Line. Converted to an animal transport ship.

112. JOHN BANVARD, 4–43, 243094, KKOA (1815–1891) author and artist from New York noted for his panoramic views of the Mississippi Valley. Operated by Seas Shipping. Stranded on October 31, 1944, in the Azores and declared a total constructive loss.

113. EDWARD N. HURLEY, 4–43, 243195, KKOC (1864–1933) Edward Nash Hurley was chairman of the U.S. Shipping Board. Operated by Isthmian.

114. CHARLES M. SCHWAB, 4–43, 243194, KKOD (1862–1939) Charles Michael Schwab was an engineer, president of Carnegie Steel and first president of U.S. Steel. He built up Bethlehem Steel to a major company by developing the H-beam, forerunner of the I-beam, and was a director general of the U.S. Shipping Board Emergency Fleet Corp. Operated by Calmar.

115. CHARLES PIEZ, 4–43, 243193, KKOE (1866–1933) a director general of the U.S. Shipping Board Emergency Fleet Corp. Operated by Isthmian.

116. BERNARD N. BAKER, 4–43, 243192, KKOF (1854–1918) Bernard Nadal Baker was a partner in the Baltimore shipping firm of the Baker-Whitely Towing Co., and a glass manufacturer appointed by President Wilson to run the $50 million U.S. Shipping Board in December 1916. Operated by American Export Lines.

117. BUSHROD WASHINGTON, 4–43, 243222, KJRN (1762–1829) President Washington's nephew was a Supreme Court justice. Operated by American South African. Capt. Jonathan Mayhew Wainwright's ship was sunk on September 14, 1943, by German aircraft off Salerno with the loss of six merchant crew and one Armed Guard sailor. Capt. Wainwright was the son of Maj. Gen. Jonathan Mayhew "Skinny" Wainwright, IV (1883–1953) who surrendered U.S. forces in the Philippines. Capt. Wainwright took command of the American South African Liberty ship *Anna Howard Shaw* at New York in December 1943.

118. ROALD AMUNDSEN, 4–43, LKPF (1872–1928) Roald Engelbregt Gravning Amundsen was a Norwegian polar explorer who reached the South Pole in 1911. Operated under the Norwegian flag by Neptune Shipping.

119. JOHN WOOLMAN, 4–43, 243225, KJNZ (1720–1772) New Jersey merchant, preacher, and abolitionist. Operated by American West African.

120. JOSEPH P. BRADLEY, 4–43, 243226, KJWD (1813–1892) Joseph Philo Bradley was a Supreme Court justice. Operated by Grace Line.

121. LEVI WOODBURY, 4–43, 243227, KJSS (1789–1851) New Hampshire governor and senator, Secretary of the Navy and Treasury, first Supreme Court justice to attend a law school. Operated by J. H. Winchester.

122. WARD HUNT, 4–43, 243235, KJXQ (1810–1886) Supreme Court justice. Operated by A. H. Bull.

123. WINFRED L. SMITH, 4–43, 243237, KKYA (1874–1937) president of M. P. Smith & Sons, 116 Broad St., New York, a stevedore and floating derricks company founded by his father Merbourne in 1857. Operated by American Export Lines.

124. WILLIAM PEPPER, 5–43, 243307, KKYC (1843–1898) William Pepper, Jr., was

a physician, founder of the Philadelphia public library, and provost of the University of Pennsylvania. Operated by Calmar.

125. SILAS WEIR MITCHELL, 5–43, 243305, KKYF (1829–1914) pioneering neurologist and president of the Association of American Physicians. Operated by Black Diamond.

126. JOSEPH LEIDY, 5–43, 243302, KKYG (1823–1891) noted paleontologist and professor of anatomy and natural history from Philadelphia. Operated by Stockard.

127. JAMES R. RANDALL, 5–43, 243341, KKYJ (1839–1908) James Ryder Randall was a journalist and poet who wrote "Maryland, My Maryland"—the official state song. Operated by International Freighting.

128. JOHN MORGAN, 5–43, 243342, KKYI (1824–1907) John Tyler Morgan was a senator from Alabama for 30 years. Operated by Wessel, Duval. Capt. Joseph D. Lydon left Baltimore on June 1, 1943, loaded with munitions and collided with an inbound ship, the brand new 9,310-ton Texas Co. tanker *Montana* off Cape Henry, Virginia. The *Morgan* blew up with the loss of 41 merchant crew and 25 of the 28 Armed Guard sailors aboard. The *Montana* was heavily damaged.

129. WILLIAM W. GERHARD, 5–43, 243350, KKYH (1809–1872) William Wood Gerhard was a physician who advanced the study of typhus and typhoid fever. Operated by American South African. Capt. Olaf J. Anderson's ship was torpedoed on September 21, 1943, by *U-593* off Italy with loss of two Armed Guard sailors.

130. JOHN L. MOTLEY, 5–43, 243384, KKYQ (1814–1877) John Lathrop Motley was a noted historian of the Dutch people and minister to the Austrian Empire. Operated by American Export Lines. Capt. Constantine Tsimenis departed Baltimore in June 1943 and arrived at New York on September 19. They left the Army Pier at Philadelphia on or about October 23, 1943, and were bombed on December 2, 1943, by German aircraft at Bari, Italy, with the loss of Capt. Tsimenis, 39 merchant crew, and 24 Armed Guard sailors.

131. WILLIAM H. WEBB, 5–43, 243405, KOLI (1816–1899) William Henry Webb was a New York shipbuilder. He is considered to be the first professional naval architect who cofounded the Society of Naval Architects & Marine Engineers and was founder of the Webb Institute at Glen Cove, New York, a naval architecture and marine engineering school that continues today. Operated by States Marine.

132. USS LUZON (ARG-2), 5–43, NPYA, internal combustion engine repair ship commissioned on October 12, 1943.

133. STEVENSON TAYLOR, 5–43, 243432, KKYZ (1848–1926) president of the American Bureau of Shipping. Operated by Calmar.

134. CHARLES A. MCALLISTER, 5–43, 243444, KKYV (1867–1932) Charles Albert McAllister was engineer-in-chief of the Revenue Cutter Service Aviation Section and president of the American Bureau of Shipping. Operated by United States Navigation.

135. USS MINDANAO (ARG-3), 5–43, NPYG, internal combustion engine repair ship commissioned on November 6, 1943. On November 10, 1944, the ship was at Seeadler Harbor, Manus Island, when the ammunition ship *Mount Hood* (AE-11) blew up at 8:50 a.m. The ship was severely damaged, 15 sailors died in the explosion, and many more were wounded. A total of 378 people in the harbor died from concussion or falling debris and about 400 were injured. Twenty-one small vessels within 500 feet disappeared, 10 ships within half a mile were damaged, and 26 ships up to a mile and a half away were hit by fragments. Many of the ARG's crew had reported aboard only four days before. According to an Army Ordnance Office study, a total of 12 shipboard explosions occurred during the war that resulted in 1,817 fatalities and 2,777 injured.

136. FREDERICK DOUGLASS, 5–43, 243476, KKZG (c. 1818–1895) Frederick

Augustus Washington Bailey was a slave in Talbot County, Maryland, who escaped and became a celebrated speaker, author, and statesman as Frederick Douglass. Operated by Luckenbach. Capt. Adrian Richardson departed New York in June 1943 and arrived back there from Glasgow, Scotland, on August 7. The ship was sunk on the next voyage on September 18, 1943, by *U-238* in the North Atlantic. There were no reported casualties.

137. JOHN E. SCHMELTZER, 5–43, 243487, KOPU (1882–1943) John Emile Schmeltzer was a member of the U.S. Shipping Board and the Maritime Commission's Technical Division. Operated by Prudential.

138. HAYM SOLOMON, 5–43, 243643, KKZE (1740–1785) financier and broker who converted loans from France for the American Revolution into usable cash to purchase supplies. Operated by Luckenbach.

139. EDVARD GRIEG, 5–43, LKPH (1843–1907) Edvard Hagerup Grieg was a famous Norwegian composer. Operated under the Norwegian flag.

140. CONRAD WEISER, 5–43, 243475, KOPE (1696–1760) Johann Conrad Weiser, Jr., was an interpreter and liaison between the Pennsylvania colonists and Indians. Operated by Dichmann, Wright & Pugh.

141. CHRISTIAN MICHELSEN, 6–43 (1857–1925) prominent shipping man and the first Norwegian prime minister. Operated under the Norwegian flag. Sunk on September 26, 1943, by *U-410* off Bizerte, Tunisia.

142. LOUISA M. ALCOTT, 6–43, 243345, KKYM (1832–1888) Louisa May Alcott was a novelist and author of *Little Women*. Operated by Stockard.

143. THOMAS NELSON PAGE, 6–43, 243453, KKYT (1853–1922) Virginia lawyer, author, and ambassador to Italy. Operated by Grace Line.

144. JAMES MCCOSH, 6–43, 243559, KORZ (1811–1894) the 11th president of Princeton University. Operated by Isthmian.

145. JOSEPH H. NICHOLSON, 6–43, 243560, KOSK (1770–1817) Joseph Hooper Nicholson was a Maryland lawyer, judge, and congressman. Operated by Wessel, Duval.

146. WILLIAM TYLER PAGE, 6–43, 243563, KOSN (1868–1942) Capitol page, author of the *American's Creed* in 1918, and Clerk of the House of Representatives. Operated by Polarus.

147. ALBERT C. RITCHIE, 6–43, 243634, KXDH (1876–1936) Albert Cabell Ritchie was governor of Maryland. Operated by Merchants & Miners.

148. CHARLES BULFINCH, 6–43, 243635, KIAC (1763–1844) regarded as the first American-born building designer to practice architecture as a profession. Worked in Boston and Washington, D.C. Operated by Luckenbach.

149. GEORGE W. WOODWARD, 6–43, 243637, KXDG (1809–1875) George Washington Woodward was a Pennsylvania congressman. Operated by Prudential.

150. EDWARD L. GRANT, 6–43, 243682, KXDQ (1883–1918) Edward Leslie "Harvard Eddie" Grant was a Harvard law school graduate who played major league baseball. He retired from the New York Yankees in 1913 and opened a law office in Boston. In April 1917 he enlisted in the Army and was a captain in the 77th Infantry Division. On October 5, 1918, he was mortally wounded when a shell exploded near him in the Meuse-Argonne. Operated by American West African.

151. PIERRE L'ENFANT, 6–43, 243687, KHLY (1754–1825) Pierre "Peter" Charles L'Enfant was a French-born architect and civil engineer who laid out the District of Columbia. Operated by Polarus.

152. SAMUEL MCINTYRE, 6–43, 243690, KHLZ (1757–1811) noted Federal and Palladian style architect. Operated by Isthmian.

153. ROBERT J. COLLIER, 6–43, 243688, KXFT (1876–1918) Robert Joseph Collier succeeded his father, Peter F. Collier, as publisher and editor of *Collier's Weekly*. Operated by J. H. Winchester.

154. JOSHUA W. ALEXANDER, 6–43, 243686, KXFU (1852–1936) Joshua Willis Alexander was Secretary of Commerce. Operated by American Export Lines.

155. JOHN A. DONALD, 6–43, 243684, KXDV (1853–1922) president of the Donald Steamship Co. in New York who was appointed by President Wilson to run the $50 million U.S. Shipping Board Emergency Fleet Corp. in December 1916. Operated by Smith & Johnson.

156. NATHAN TOWSON, 7–43, 243720, KXGX (1784–1854) Nathaniel Towson, of Towsonton, Maryland, was a highly effective artillery officer in the War of 1812. Operated by United States Navigation.

157. WILLIAM H. JACKSON, 7–43, 243723, KXGW (1843–1942) William Henry Jackson photographed the Yellowstone area and helped create the national park. Operated by T. J. Stevenson.

158. JANET LORD ROPER, 7–43, 243719, KXNT (1871–1943) "Mother Ropeyarns" was a fisherman's widow and house mother at the large Seaman's Church Institute, the "hotel for seamen," in New York City from 1915 to 1943. She established the Missing Seamen's Bureau and helped locate many missing sailors. Operated by International Freighting.

159. ROBERT ERSKINE, 7–43, 243758, KXHA (1735–1780) Scottish hydraulic engineer, pump inventor, and militia colonel during the Revolutionary War who built defenses to keep British ships from using the Hudson River. Operated by T. J. Stevenson. Capt. Frank A. Davis' ship foundered on January 6, 1944, during heavy weather at Bizerte, Tunisia. Deck cadet Joseph L. Driscoll, 20, was lost.

160. JOHN WANAMAKER, 7–43, 243752, KXHB (1838–1922) innovative Philadelphia department store merchant considered the father of modern advertising and marketing. Also served as Postmaster General. Operated by Isthmian.

161. JOHN STEVENSON, 7–43, 243750, KXHD (1812–1886) John White Stevenson was a Kentucky congressman and governor. Operated by United States Lines.

162. ROBERT EDEN, 7–43, 243757, KXHG (1741–1784) Sir Robert Eden, 1st Baronet of Maryland, was the 23rd Proprietary Governor of Maryland. Operated by Stockard.

163. GEORGE H. PENDLETON, 7–43, 243789, KXHH (1825–1889) George Hunt "Gentleman George" Pendleton was an Ohio congressman. Operated by Calmar.

164. GEORGE W. CHILDS, 7–43, 243790, KXHJ (1829–1894) George William Childs was a bookstore clerk, sailor, and publisher/co-owner of the *Public Ledger* newspaper in Philadelphia. Operated by Dichmann, Wright & Pugh. Sometime before March 17, 1944, Capt. John Niemeyer's ship suffered extensive damage from grounding in the Clyde and became disabled. The ship was towed to Tyne by the tug *Thames* and was scuttled on June 8, 1944, as part of Gooseberry 2 by order of naval authorities at San Lorenzo Beachhead, France.

165. GEORGE M. COHAN, 7–43, 243791, KXHK (1878–1942) George Michael Cohan was an entertainer, composer, and playwright. The ship was launched on Sunday, July 4, 1943, Cohan's 64th birthday. Operated by Black Diamond.

166. JAMES A. FARRELL, 7–43, 243869, KXHN (1863–1943) James Augustine Farrell was a wire salesman with U.S. Steel & Wire, became a manager in 1899, and cofounded the Isthmian Steamship Co. in 1910. He became president of U.S. Steel, the parent company, in 1911 and died on March 28, 1943, at New York City. Operated by American South African. Capt. Michael E. Martin departed New York around April 12 and the ship was torpedoed on June 29, 1944, by *U-984* off St. Catherine's Point, England, with the loss of four Army passengers and many wounded.

167. JOSE MARTI, 7–43, 243872, KXHP (1853–1895) José Juliáin Martí Pérez was a Cuban writer and revolutionary leader. Operated by A. H. Bull.

168. CROSBY S. NOYES, 7–43, 243868, KXHS (1825–1908) Crosby Stuart Noyes was co-owner of the *Washington Evening Star* in Washington, D.C. Operated by Merchants & Miners.

169. LOUIS MARSHALL, 7–43, 243892, KXHT (1856–1929) prominent attorney and cofounder of the American Jewish Committee. Operated by Wessel, Duvall & Co.

170. TOWNSEND HARRIS, 7–43, 243894, KXHU (1804–1878) New York merchant and founder of the City College of New York who was the first U.S. consul general to Japan and in 1856 concluded the first trade agreements. Operated by Marine Transport.

171. GEORGE VICKERS, 7–43, 243889, KXHX (1801–1879) Maryland senator. Operated by T. J. Stevenson.

172. THOMAS U. WALTER, 7–43, 243921, KXXC (1804–1887) Thomas Ustick Walter was an architect who designed the U.S. Capitol's House (south) and Senate (north) wings and the dome. Became second president of the American Institute of Architects. Operated by William J. Rountree.

173. JOHN W. POWELL, 8–43, 243891, KXHY (1834–1902) John Wesley Powell was a naturalist who was seriously wounded at Shiloh. He was the first explorer through the Grand Canyon and became director of the U.S. Geological Survey. Operated by Cosmopolitan.

174. EDWIN L. DRAKE, 8–43, 243914, KXXB (1819–1880) Edwin Leslie "Colonel" Drake was a railroad conductor who got interested in oil, went to work for Seneca Oil, and reportedly was the first person to drill for oil in the United States while employed by Seneca in Pennsylvania in 1858. Operated by International Freighting.

175. JOHN T. HOLT, 8–43, 243918, KXXE (1854–1942) "one of the best known sea captains who sailed out of Baltimore at the turn of the Century" according to the Hagerstown, Maryland, *Daily Mail* of July 30, 1943. Operated by Calmar.

176. THORSTEIN VEBLEN, 8–43, 243922, KXXD (1857–1929) Torsten Bunde Veblen, of Cato, Wisconsin, was a controversial economist and sociologist. Operated by J. H. Winchester.

177. ARUNAH S. ABELL, 8–43, 243983, KXXF (1806–1888) Arunah Shepherdson Abell founded the Baltimore Sun newspaper. Operated by Blidberg Rothchild.

178. JOSHUA THOMAS, 8–43, 243991, KXXG (1776–1853) Tangier Island, Virginia, preacher known for warning the British in 1814 that attacking Baltimore would mean losing the war. Operated by American Export Lines.

179. WILLIAM S. THAYER, 8–43, 243994, KXXI (1864–1932) William Sydney Thayer was a Johns Hopkins professor and chief medical consultant for the American Expeditionary Force during World War I. Operated by A. L. Burbank. Daniel A. Sperbeck, 55, signed on the *Thomas W. Bickett* as chief mate on August 20, 1943, at New York and arrived back at there on December 7 from Bizerte, Tunisia. He then became master of the *Thayer*. The ship was torpedoed on April 30, 1944, by *U-711* in the Barents Sea with the loss of 23 merchant crew, seven Armed Guard sailors, and 23 passengers.

180. SAMWATER, 8–43, 169923, BFBP, built for the British Ministry of War Transport. Operated by Glen Line.

181. SAMHAIN, 8–43, 169630, BFPC, built for the British Ministry of War Transport. Operated by Ellerman & Bucknall.

182. JAMES M. GILLIS, 8–43, 244078, KXXU (1811–1865) Lt. James Melville Gillis, USN, was an astronomer put in charge of the first naval observatory, built at Foggy Bottom near the Lincoln Memorial in 1842. Operated by Smith & Johnson.

183. SAMBRAKE, 8–43, 169919, BFPD, built for the British Ministry of War Transport. Operated by Ellerman & Bucknall.

184. SAMOA, 8–43, 169749, BFPF, built for the British Ministry of War Transport. Operated by Alfred Holt & Co.

185. SAMITE, 8–43, 169717, BFPG, built for the British Ministry of War Transport. Operated by Alfred Holt & Co.

186. JOHN W. GARRETT, 8–43, 244079, KTWF (1820–1884) John Work Garrett was president of the Baltimore & Ohio Railroad. Operated by Stockard.

187. SAMARKAND, 9–43, 169715, BFJP, built for the British Ministry of War Transport. Operated by Alfred Holt & Co.

188. SAMOS, 9–43, 169674, MYLR, built for the British Ministry of War Transport. Operated by Elder Dempster Lines.

189. SAMARINA, 9–43, 169748, MYLN, built for the British Ministry of War Transport. Operated by Westcott & Laurence.

190. SAMARA, 9–43, 169431, MYLM, built for the British Ministry of War Transport. Operated by Ellerman & Bucknall as the *Samshire*.

191. SAMUR, 9–43, 169641, MYLL, built for the British Ministry of War Transport. Operated by Lamport & Holt.

192. SAMPA, 9–43, 169632, MYLT, built for the British Ministry of War Transport. Operated by Houlder Bros. & Co.

193. SAMAYE, 9–43, 180496, MYLP, built for the British Ministry of War Transport. Operated by Cayzer, Irvine & Co.

194. SAMORA, 9–43, 169638, MYLQ, built for the British Ministry of War Transport. Operated by Cayzer, Irvine & Co. as the *Sampenn*.

195. SAMOTHRACE, 9–43, 169687, MYLS, built for the British Ministry of War Transport. Operated by the Pacific Steam Navigation Co.

196. MARIE M. MELONEY, 9–43, 244208, KYMK (1878–1943) reporter Marie Mattingly married William B. Meloney, editor of the *New York Sun*. She became editor of *This Week Magazine*, raised money for Marie Curie, and became a social activist and household, health, and food consumer advocate. She died on June 23, 1943, at Pawling, New York. Operated by Calmar.

197. USS TUTUILA (ARG-4), 9–43, NPYN, internal combustion repair ship commissioned on April 8, 1944.

198. HEYWOOD BROUN, 9–43, 244263, KYMM (1888–1939) Heywood Campbell Broun, Jr., was a war correspondent and New York sportswriter who founded the American Newspaper Guild. Operated by Boland & Cornelius.

199. PHILIP F. THOMAS, 9–43, 244270, KYMQ (1810–1890) Philip Francis Thomas was a Maryland congressman, governor, and Secretary of the Treasury. Operated by Calmar.

200. USS OAHU (ARG-5), 9–43, NPZB, internal combustion repair ship commissioned on April 4, 1944.

201. HAWKINS FUDSKE, 9–43, 244262, KYNP (1911–1942) chief mate and acting master lost on the Panama Transport Co. tanker *Esso Bolivar*, torpedoed on March 7, 1942, by *U-126* off Cuba. He was awarded the Merchant Marine Distinguished Service medal for saving lives and launching lifeboats although severely wounded. He was a Norwegian naturalized on September 18, 1934, and lived in a large rooming house in Wilmington, Delaware, used by many single merchant seamen. Operated by Isthmian.

202. GEORGE UHLER, 9–43, 244283, KYOH (1853-c. 1935) Philadelphia marine

engineer and president of the Marine Engineer's Association who was appointed Supervising Inspector General of Steamboats in March 1903. Operated by Isthmian.

203. HENRY LOMB, 9–43, 244284, KYOM (1828–1908) Rochester, New York, cabinet maker who loaned money to optician John J. Bausch in 1854 and later became a partner in Bausch & Lomb. Operated by A. H. Bull.

204. MARGARET BRENT, 9–43, 244286, KYON (c. 1600–c. 1670) arrived at St. Mary's City, Maryland, from Gloucestershire, England, in 1638 and became the first female land owner in America. In 1647 she became the executor of Gov. Leonard Calvert's estate. Operated by Luckenbach.

205. PATRICK C. BOYLE, 9–43, 244338, KYOQ (1846–1920) Ireland-born miner and mechanical engineer who pioneered the Pennsylvania oil industry and published the Oil City Derrick magazine. Operated by Boland & Cornelius.

206. BEN F. DIXON, 9–43, 244334, KYQA (1846–1910) Benjamin Franklin Dixon was a Confederate soldier at age 15 and was wounded several times. He became a prominent North Carolina physician, minister, superintendent of the Oxford Orphan Asylum, and president of the Greensboro Female College. Operated by United Fruit.

207. FRANCIS VIGO, 9–43, 244336, KYQC (1747–1836) Giuseppe Maria Francesco Vigo was an East Coast Italian merchant who spied for America during the Revolutionary War and contributed substantial war funding. He was was instrumental in founding the Jefferson Academy in Vincennes, Indiana, now Vincennes University, and is the namesake for Vigo County, Indiana. Operated by American South African.

208. SAMARIZ, 9–43, 169653, MYLZ, launched as the *John J. McGraw*, the longtime, 30-year manager of the New York Yankees who died in 1934 after being the only man to win ten major league pennants for a single club. The ship was transferred to the British Ministry of War Transport as *Samariz* but was operated by Lamport & Holt as the *John J. McGraw*.

209. SAMWYO, 10–43, 169658, built for the British Ministry of War Transport. Operated by Cayzer, Irvine.

210. SAMKANSA, 10–43, 169656, MYLY, built for the British Ministry of War Transport. Operated by the Orient Steam Navigation Co.

211. SAMMEX, 10–43, 169657, MYMC, built for the British Ministry of War Transport. Operated by the General Steam Navigation Co.

212. SAMDAK, 10–43, 169652, MYMD, built for the British Ministry of War Transport. Operated by Moss-Hutchison.

213. HORACE BUSHNELL, 10–43, 244380, KTLP (1802–1876) editor of the *New York Journal of Commerce*, theology professor, and Congregational minister from Connecticut. Operated by R. A. Nicol. Capt. William J. Lacey's ship was torpedoed on March 20, 1945, by *U-995* off Russia with the loss of five merchant crew. Survivors left Southampton, England, on the United States Lines motorship *John Ericsson* and arrived at New York on April 16.

214. JOYCE KILMER, 10–43, 244390, KTDR (1886–1918) Alfred Joyce Kilmer was a poet who wrote "Trees" and was shot by a sniper on July 30, 1918, while serving in the Fighting 69th New York Infantry Regiment in the Marne. Operated by Dichmann, Wright & Pugh.

215. W. R. GRACE, 10–43, 244394, KTLS (1832–1904) William Russell Grace turned a ship chandlery business in Peru into a large chemical and shipping company as W. R. Grace & Co. Grace Line was a subsidiary. Operated by Grace Line.

216. SAMUTA, 10–43, 169678, MYLV, built for the British Ministry of War Transport. Operated by Andrew Weir & Co.

217. SAMNEBRA, 10–43, 169655, MYLW, built for the British Ministry of War Transport. Operated by Cayzer, Irvine.

218. SAMOTA, 10–43, 169654, MYLX, built for the British Ministry of War Transport. Operated by Elder Dempster Lines.

219. SAMWIS, 10–43, 169968, MYMW, built for the British Ministry of War Transport. Operated by T. & J. Harrison.

220. SAMNESSE, 10–43, 169690, MYMX, built for the British Ministry of War Transport. Operated by Alfred Holt & Co.

221. SAMYORK, 10–43, 169691, MYNF, built for the British Ministry of War Transport. Operated by Andrew Weir & Co.

222. VIGGO HANSTEEN, 10–43, LKPM (1900–1941) Norwegian a lawyer who got in the way of Nazi Germany and was shot on September 10, 1941. Operated under the Norwegian flag.

223. STAGE DOOR CANTEEN, 10–43, 244486, KTME, recreational center for servicemen on 44th St. in New York City that featured prominent performers. Operated by North Atlantic & Gulf.

224. USS CEBU (ARG-6), internal combustion engine repair ship commissioned on April 15, 1944.

225. LEWIS EMERY, JR., 10–43, 244482, KTMJ (1839–1924) Pennsylvania oil man, head of the Oil Producers' Association in 1872, and state senator who ran for governor. In 1917, when he was 78, he married Eleta Card, a 40-year-old Canadian gal. Operated by Merchants & Miners.

226. HAROLD L. WINSLOW, 10–43, 244523, KTMK (1893–1938) Navy boatswain's mate who made ensign, became a U.S. Shipping Board inspector, then got a master's license. He was captain of the big 17,910-ton United States Lines passenger ship *Republic* when they rescued 11 sailors from the schooner *Gander Deal* in huge seas in 1929. He died by his own hand on August 2, 1938. Operated by United States Lines.

227. U.S.O., 10–43, 244578, KURN, the United Service Organizations, Inc., was founded in February 1941 at the request of President Roosevelt to provide recreation and entertainment to servicemen overseas. Since merchant seamen were often not welcome at the USO the United Seamen's Service was created in August 1942 and over 125 centers were opened. Henry Kaiser was the first president of the U.S. S., "born to aid exhausted, wounded and battle-traumatized merchant seafarers in faraway places and unsafe harbors." The USO continues today. Operated by Blidberg Rothchild.

228. USS INDUS (AKN-1), 11–43, NWAG, anti-torpedo net cargo ship commissioned on February 15, 1944.

229. SAMOIS, 11–43, 169680, MYNA, built for the British Ministry of War Transport. Operated by Westcott & Laurence.

230. SAMSYLVAN, 11–43, 169679, MYND, built for the British Ministry of War Transport. Operated by Shaw, Savill & Albion.

231. SAMVERN, 11–43, 169841, MYNG, built for the British Ministry of War Transport. Operated by William Thomson & Son. Hit a mine on January 18, 1945, in the Schelde Estuary and sank.

232. SAMOKLA, 11–43, 169698, MYNJ, built for the British Ministry of War Transport. Operated by Cayzer, Irvine & Co.

233. SAMLOUIS, 11–43, 169685, MYNL, built for the British Ministry of War Transport. Operated by Ellerman's Wilson Line.

234. SAMSIP, 11–43, 169743, MYNN, built for the British Ministry of War Transport. Operated by New Zealand Shipping. Hit a mine on December 7, 1944, in Schelde Estuary.

235. SAMSETTE, 11–43, 169681, MYNP, built for the British Ministry of War Transport. Operated by Alfred Holt & Co.

236. SAMOINE, 11–43, 169693, MYNQ, launched as the *Edward Bruce*, the New Deal director of the Public Works of Art Project who died on January 26, 1943. The ship was transferred to the British Ministry of War Transport as *Samoine* but was operated by Thompson, Stanley & John as the *Edward Bruce*.

237. SAMFLORA, 11–43, 169677, MYNR, built for the British Ministry of War Transport. Operated by Union-Castle Mail Steamship Co.

238. SAMBUFF, 11–43, 169700, MYNS, built for the British Ministry of War Transport. Operated by the Union-Castle Mail Steamship Co.

239. CHARLES SCRIBNER, 11–43, 244589, KUER (1821–1871) book and magazine publisher. Operated by William J. Rountree.

240. JOHN LA FARGE, 11–43, 244632, KUFI (1835–1910) noted mural painter and stained glass artist. Operated by American Range-Liberty Lines.

241. SAMBURGH, 11–43, 169745, MYNT, built for the British Ministry of War Transport. Operated by Andrew Weir & Co.

242. SAMCLEVE, 11–43, 169701, MYNV, built for the British Ministry of War Transport. Operated by Alfred Holt & Co.

243. FRANCIS C. HARRINGTON, 11–43, 244684, KUFZ (1887–1940) administrator of the Work Projects Administration and director of the Panama Canal Railroad. Operated by International Freighting. Capt. James Hassell's ship was off Normandy on June 7, 1944, when they hit a mine and the engine room was flooded. Destroyer escort *Blessman* (DE-69) was in the area taking off 38 sailors and 6 officers from the mined transport *Susan B. Anthony* (AP-72) but when flames erupted from the transport's stack, Cdr. Thomas L. Gray, USNR, waved them away before the transport sank. *Blessman* then headed for the *Harrington* and came alongside just after noon. Twenty-two injured and four deceased soldiers were removed and all were taken to the *LST(H)-134*. Chief engineer Leonard W. Valentine, 46, was awarded the Merchant Marine Distinguished Service medal for supervising extremely difficult work in repairing serious damage over five days. Wiper Patrick Nolen paid off the ship on July 8 and engine cadet John P. Fazio was sent home by the War Shipping Administration. The ship left Belfast, Ireland, on August 6 and arrived at New York on the 20th.

244. SAMGARA, 11–43, 169744, MYNW, built for the British Ministry of War Transport. Operated by Alfred Holt & Co.

245. BARBARA FRIETCHIE, 11–43, 244768, KVAJ (1766–1862) erroneously credited with waving the Stars and Stripes in the face of Stonewall Jackson in Frederick, Maryland, a deed actually done by Mary S. Quantrell. Operated by Dichmann, Wright & Pugh.

246. SAMFIELD, 11–43, 169765, MYPD, built for the British Ministry of War Transport. Operated by Cayzer, Irvine.

247. LEO J. DUSTER, 11–43, 244714, KVAM (1894–1943) officer with the American Legion. Operated by Standard Fruit.

248. USS CULEBRA ISLAND (ARG-7), 11–43, NPZW, internal combustion engine repair ship commissioned on May 19, 1944.

249. USS SAGITTARIUS (AKN-2), 12–43, NWAK, anti-torpedo net cargo ship commissioned on March 18, 1944.

250. JAMES C. CAMERON, 12–43, 244712, KVAW (1800–1942) James was a 32-year-old Canadian bosun with 11 years of service when he arrived at New York on June 25, 1940, on the Socony-Vacuum tanker *Royal Arrow*. In 1942 he was third mate on the Socony tanker *Brilliant* and was one of seven crew lost when the ship was torpedoed by *U-43* on

November 18 in the North Atlantic. Posthumously awarded the Merchant Marine Distinguished Service medal. Operated by Isbrandtsen.

251. SAMBOSTON, 12–43, 169723, MYPF, built for the British Ministry of War Transport. Operated by Ellerman & Papayanni.

252. HUGH M. SMITH, 12–43, 244778, KVDS (1865–1941) Hugh McCormick Smith was an ichthyologist, director of the Bureau of Fisheries, and curator of zoology at the Smithsonian Institution. Operated by Marine Transport.

253. SAMTROY, 12–43, 169722, MYPG, built for the British Ministry of War Transport. Operated by Andrew Weir & Co.

254. A. J. CERMAK, 12–43, 244777, KVDZ (1873–1933) Anton Joseph "Pushcart Tony" Cermak was mayor of Chicago on February 15, 1933, when he was shot by an assassin aiming for President Roosevelt. The wound became infected and he died on March 6. Operated by Blidberg Rothchild.

255. SAMVARD, 12–43, 180345, MYPJ, launched on December 3 as the *Ammla* (American Merchant Marine Library Association) and sponsored by Annie Howard, 44, of Newport, Rhode Island, founder and president of the association and a native of England. Transferred to the British Ministry of War Transport as *Samvard* and operated by William Thomson & Co. in 1944 as *Ammla*.

256. LOUIS KOSSUTH, 12–43, 244861, KVEF (1802–1894) Lajos Kossuth de Udvard et Kossuthfalva was a Hungarian lawyer and president of the Kingdom of Hungary. Operated by A. H. Bull. Capt. Carl Norman's ship hit a mine on August 23, 1944, off Normandy. There were no reported fatalities. Fireman/watertender John Zudahagi and 2nd cook Charles D. Jones paid off at Cardiff, Wales. The ship arrived at New York on December 28 from Cardiff.

257. SAMPORT, 12–43, 169786, MYPK, built for the British Ministry of War Transport. Operated by Cayzer, Irvine & Co.

258. SAMYALE, 12–43, 169764, MYPL, built for the British Ministry of War Transport. Operated by Elder Dempster.

259. JOSHUA B. LIPPINCOTT, 12–43, 244860, KVEM (1813–1886) Joshua Ballinger Lippincott was a Philadelphia bookstore clerk at age 14 and at 18 took over the bankrupt firm. In 1836 he founded J. B. Lippincott & Co. to manufacture Bibles and prayer books. Operated by American Export Lines.

260. SAMBALT, 12–43, 169766, KYPM, built for the British Ministry of War Transport. Operated by Cayzer, Irvine & Co.

261. FRANK R. STOCKTON, 12–43, 244857, KVEP (1834–1902) Francis Richard Stockton was a popular Philadelphia author of children's fairy tales. Operated by Calmar.

262. BEN H. MILLER, 12–43, 169763, MYPR (1908–1942) Benjamin H. Miller was a *Baltimore Sun* and *Evening Sun* correspondent reporting for the AP. In May 1942 he was on a Production-for-Victory tour of factories around the country flying with pilot Cecil J. Lucas, 43, of Wichita. On May 18 the plane crashed outside Wichita, Kansas. Lucas, 43, businessman William Knorr, of Wichita, and Miller died. Miller lived with his wife Theodora, 37, at 1202 Eutaw Pl. in Baltimore. Operated under the British flag by Ellerman & Papayanni Line, Ltd.

263. SAMHARLE, 12–43, 169767, MYPS, built for the British Ministry of War Transport. Operated by Alfred Holt & Co.

264. SAMKEY, 12–43, 169788, MYPV, built for the British Ministry of War Transport. Operated by New Zealand Shipping.

265. BYRON DARNTON, 12–43, 244913, KVEU (1897–1942) *New York Times* war correspondent lost in an accident on October 18, 1942, off New Guinea when a bomb accidentally fell from a B-25. Operated by Boland & Cornelius.

266. SAMSACOLA, 12–43, 169789, MYPW, built for the British Ministry of War Transport. Operated by Stanley & John Thompson.

267. FREDERICK BANTING, 12–43, 169810, MYPX (1891–1941) Sir Frederick Grant Banting, KBE, MC, FRS, FRSC, was a Canadian physician who won the Nobel Prize in Medicine for discovering insulin. He died in Newfoundland. Operated under the British flag by Ellerman's City Line, Ltd.

268. MARTIN VAN BUREN, 12–43, 244916, KVPJ (1782–1862) 8th President of the United States. Operated by West India. Capt. James H. Hiss' ship was torpedoed by *U-1232* on January 14, 1945, off Nova Scotia. There were no fatalities but three Armed Guard sailors from Lt. (jg) Norman L. Stephens' crew, Jimmy Olroyd, S1c, of Decatur, Illinois; Charles Polonyi, GM3c, of Cornwall-on-Hudson, New York; and Jimmy Rose, S1c, of Detroit, Michigan, were blown off the fantail and suffered wounds.

269. SAMTWEED, 12–43, 169809, MYPY, built for the British Ministry of War Transport. Operated by Hall Line.

270. SAMFORTH, 1–44, 169800, MYQN, built for the British Ministry of War Transport. Operated by Alfred Holt & Co.

271. SAMCLYDE, 1–44, 169779, MYQP, built for the British Ministry of War Transport. Operated by Andrew Weir & Co.

272. USS TUSCANA (AKN-3), 1–44, NWAS, anti-torpedo net cargo ship commissioned on March 28, 1944.

273. SAMETTRICK, 1–44, 169783, MYQQ, built for the British Ministry of War Transport. Operated by P. & O. Steam Navigation.

274. SAMCREE, 1–44, 169780, MYQR, built for the British Ministry of War Transport. Operated by Alfred Holt & Co.

275. SAMFEUGH, 1–44, 169793, MYQS, built for the British Ministry of War Transport. Operated by Charles Hill & Sons.

276. SAMEVERON, 1–44, 169782, MYQT, built for the British Ministry of War Transport. Operated by the Orient Steam Navigation Co.

277. SAMTAY, 1–44, 169798, KYQV, built for the British Ministry of War Transport. Operated by the Blue Star Line.

278. SAMNID, 1–44, 169784, MYQW, built for the British Ministry of War Transport. Operated by the Blue Star Line.

279. SAMOUSE, 1–44, 169799, MYQX, built for the British Ministry of War Transport. Operated by Cunard White Star.

280. ELOY ALFARO, 1–44, 245015, KVOI (1842–1912) José Eloy Alfaro Delgado was the president of Ecuador killed by a mob on January 28, 1912. Operated by Smith & Johnson.

281. SAMCHESS, 1–44, 169823, MYQY, built for the British Ministry of War Transport. Operated by Cayzer, Irvine & Co.

282. BENJAMIN SCHLESINGER, 2–44, 245060, KVXY (1876–1932) managing editor of the *New York Jewish Daily Forward* and president of the International Ladies' Garment Workers' Union. Operated by Moore-McCormack.

283. VAN LEAR BLACK, 1–44, 245063, KVXZ (1875–1930) Maryland financier who ran the *Baltimore Sun* newspaper in 1915. He became an aviation enthusiast and financed Adm. Byrd's expedition to the North Pole in 1926. Four years later he mysteriously fell off the stern of his 141-foot motor yacht *Sabalo*. Operated by Merchants & Miners. Arrived at Baltimore on July 29, 1944, from Bizerte, Tunisia, then operated by the Navy as the *Crater*-class cargo ship *Allegan* (AK-225), commissioned on September 21, 1944.

284. SAMESK, 2–44, 169824, MYQZ, built for the British Ministry of War Transport. Operated by New Zealand Shipping.

285. MORRIS HILLQUIT, 2–44, 245110, KVYI (1869–1933) labor lawyer and founder of the Socialist Party of America. Operated by AGWI Lines.

286. MEYER LONDON, 2–44, 245109, KVYN (1871–1926) New York Socialist Party congressman. Operated by T. J. Stevenson. Capt. Fred Rylander's ship was torpedoed on April 16, 1944, by *U-407* off Libya. There were no reported casualties.

287. MORRIS SIGMAN, 2–44, 245111, KVQP (1880–1931) president of the International Ladies' Garment Workers' Union. Operated by American Export Lines.

288. SAMLEVEN, 2–44, 169817, MYRC, built for the British Ministry of War Transport. Operated by Port Line.

289. WILLIAM D. BYRON, 2–44, 245143, KVYP (1895–1941) William Devereux Byron, II, was a Maryland congressman who died on February 27, 1941, when Eastern Airlines Flight 11 crashed on approach to Chandler Field at Atlanta, Georgia. Nine of the 16 aboard the DC-3 died and fighter ace and Eastern's president, Eddie Rickenbacker, was seriously injured. Operated by Dichmann, Wright & Pugh.

290. SAMLYTH, 2–44, 169834, MYRD, built for the British Ministry of War Transport. Operated by Moss-Hutchison.

291. SAMSTRULE, 2–44, 169835, MYRF, built for the British Ministry of War Transport. Operated by Elders & Fyffes.

292. SAMINVER, 2–44, 169829, MYRG, built for the British Ministry of War Transport. Operated by the Blue Star Line.

293. THOMAS DONALDSON, 2–44, 245166, KVYQ (1815–1877) lawyer, engineer, legislator, and cofounder of the Maryland Historical Society in 1844. Operated by American Export Lines. Capt. Robert Headden's ship was torpedoed on March 20, 1945, by *U-968* off Kola Inlet with the loss of four merchant crew. Survivors left Southampton, England, on the United States Lines motorship *John Ericsson* and arrived at New York on April 16.

294. SAMLOSSIE, 2–44, 169836, MYRJ, built for the British Ministry of War Transport. Operated by P. Henderson & Co.

295. JOHN L. ELLIOTT, 2–44, 245165, KVYR (1868–1942) John Lovejoy Elliott was a New York City social activist, Settlement House founder, and cofounder, with Mary K. Simkhovitch, of the Association of Neighborhood Workers in December 1900. Operated by Stockard.

296. USS LEYTE (ARG-8), 2–44, NPZV, internal combustion engine repair ship commissioned on August 17, 1944.

297. SAMGAUDIE, 3–44, 169849, MYRK, built for the British Ministry of War Transport. Operated by Thos. & Jno. Brocklebank.

298. WARREN DELANO, 3–44, 245211, KVYW (1779–1865) wealthy trader who was irritated that China wouldn't buy British goods. He took part in getting opium from India and introducing it into China. By creating a massive addiction problem it was believed that Chinese money would begin to flow into British coffers. Warren's daughter Sara married Franklin Roosevelt and Warren was President Franklin Delano Roosevelt's grandfather. Operated by Marine Transport.

299. SAMAFFRIC, 3–44, 169850, MYRL, built for the British Ministry of War Transport. Operated by William Thomson & Co.

300. SAMCONON, 3–44, 169853, MYRM, built for the British Ministry of War Transport. Operated by B. & S. Shipping.

301. SAMNETHY, 3–44, 180023, MYRN, built for the British Ministry of War Transport. Operated by the E. R. Management Co.

302. STEPHEN W. GAMBRILL, 3–44, 245210, KWJA (1873–1938) Stephen Warfield Gambrill was a Maryland congressman. Operated by American Range–Liberty Lines.

303. SAMEDEN, 3–44, 169851, MYRP, built for the British Ministry of War Transport. Operated by Port Line.

304. ROBERT ELLIS LEWIS, 3–44, 245275, KWND (1914–1943) *Philadelphia Inquirer* reporter who became the public information director for the Red Cross in the Southwest Pacific. He was lost in a plane crash at Port Moresby, New Guinea, in November 1943. Operated by West India.

305. SAMCOLNE, 3–44, 169852, MYRQ, built for the British Ministry of War Transport. Operated by Anchor Line.

306. SAMLEA, 3–44, 180036, MYRR, built for the British Ministry of War Transport. Operated by Ellerman & Bucknall.

307. SAMSHEE, 3–44, 169956, MYRS, built for the British Ministry of War Transport. Operated by Hain.

308. SAMJACK, 4–44, 180554, MYPT, built for the British Ministry of War Transport. Operated by Alfred Holt & Co.

309. SAMSPELGA, 4–44, 180550, MYRX, built for the British Ministry of War Transport. Operated by J. Morrison & Son.

310. SAMDONARD, 4–44, 180490, MYRY, built for the British Ministry of War Transport. Operated by Cayzer, Irvine.

311. SAMGALLION, 4–44, 169983, MYRZ, built for the British Ministry of War Transport. Operated by E. J. Sutton & Co.

312. SAMNEAGH, 4–44, 169853, MYSE, built for the British Ministry of War Transport. Operated by P. Henderson & Co.

313. EDWARD B. HAINES, 4–44, 245356, KWJD (1849–1911) founded *The Paterson Evening News* in Paterson, New Jersey, in 1890. Operated by Cosmopolitan.

314. SAMHOPE, 4–44, 180037, MYSC, built for the British Ministry of War Transport. Operated by Sir William Reardon Smith & Sons.

315. JOHN H. MURPHY, 4–44, 245415, KWJC (1841–1922) John Henry Murphy, Sr., was the African-American publisher of the *Baltimore Afro-American*, "The Afro," newspaper. Operated by States Marine.

316. SAMSTURDY, 4–44, 169871, MYSD, built for the British Ministry of War Transport. Operated by Common Brothers.

317. LAWRENCE J. BRENGLE, 4–44, 245416, KWQD (1878–1936) a very prominent name in Frederick, Maryland, for generations. The ship was named for the Philadelphia marine underwriter and executive manager of the United States Salvage Association. Operated by Blidberg Rothchild.

318. SAMDAUNTLESS, 4–44, 169875, MYSF, built for the British Ministry of War Transport. Operated by William Thomson & Co.

319. SVERRE HELMERSEN, 4–44, LKPV (1910–1941) Norwegian merchant marine fireman shot by the Nazis as a resister. Operated under the Norwegian flag by Nortraship.

320. SAMTRUSTY, 4–44, 169915, MYSG, built for the British Ministry of War Transport. Operated by Donaldson Bros. & Black.

321. DEBORAH GANNETT, 4–44, 245470, KWWG (1760–1827) In 1782, Deborah Sampson, of Plympton, Massachusetts, enlisted in the 4th Massachusetts Light Infantry under the name of her deceased brother, Robert Shurtlieff Sampson, and on July 3 she was seriously wounded in New York. Her identity was not discovered but the next year she became ill and

her true identity became known. She was honorably discharged from the Army and in 1785 she married Benjamin Gannet. Operated by T. J. Stevenson.

322. SAMCONSTANT, 5–44, 169877, MYSJ, built for the British Ministry of War Transport. Operated by Furness, Withy & Co.

323. FRANCIS D. CULKIN, 4–44, 245509, KWWH (1874–1943) Francis Dugan Culkin was a New York congressman who died on August 4, 1943, at Oswego, New York. Operated by Wessel, Duval.

324. SAMFAITHFUL, 4–44, 180550, MYSK, built for the British Ministry of War Transport. Operated by Royal Mail Lines.

325. SAMWINGED, 4–44, 169874, MYSK, built for the British Ministry of War Transport. Operated by Sir William Reardon Smith & Sons.

326. SAMLOYAL, 5–44, 169887, MYSL, built for the British Ministry of War Transport. Operated by B. & S. Shipping Co.

327. SAMFLEET, 5–44, 180572, MYTF, built for the British Ministry of War Transport. Operated by Andrew Weir & Co.

328. SAMGLORY, 5–44, 180544, MYSM, built for the British Ministry of War Transport. Operated by Dodd, Thomson & Co.

329. JAMES KERNEY, 5–44, 245564, KWWI (1873–1934) longtime owner and editor of the *Trenton Times* in Trenton, New Jersey. Operated by A. L. Burbank.

330. SAMSOARING, 5–44, 169984, MYTL, built for the British Ministry of War Transport. Operated by P. & O. Steam Navigation.

331. SAMCREST, 5–44, 169998, MYTD, built for the British Ministry of War Transport. Operated by Ellerman & Bucknall.

332. JAMES D. TRASK, 5–44, 254672, WODG (1890–1942) Astoria, Long Island, New York, physician who was active in public health at Yale University. Operated by International Freighting.

333. SAMFREEDOM, 5–44, 180532, MYTK, built for the British Ministry of War Transport. Operated by Counties Ship Management Co.

334. SAMTRUTH, 5–44, 180553, MYTC, built for the British Ministry of War Transport. Operated by Haldin & Philipps.

335. USS MONA ISLAND (ARG-9), 5–44, NQBY, internal combustion engine repair ship commissioned on October 17, 1944.

336. SAMTORCH, 5–44, 180039, MYTJ, built for the British Ministry of War Transport. Operated by Ellerman & Papayanni.

337. SAMLISTAR, 6–44, 180534, GWDK, built for the British Ministry of War Transport. Operated by Mungo, Campbell & Co.

338. USS CHOURRE (ARV-1), 6–44, NIQF, aircraft repair ship commissioned on December 7, 1944.

339. SAMSPEED, 6–44, 180011, MYTB, built for the British Ministry of War Transport. Operated by Lyle Shipping.

340. SAMLUZON, 6–44, 180035, MYSZ, built for the British Ministry of War Transport. Operated by Morel, Ltd.

341. SAMNEGROS, 6–44, 180025, MYSY, built for the British Ministry of War Transport. Operated by George Nisbet & Co.

342. SAMINDORO, 6–44, 180492, MYTG, built for the British Ministry of War Transport. Operated by Headlam & Son.

343. CHUNG TUNG, 6–44, operated under the Chinese flag by the Republic of China.

344. SAMTANA, 6–44, 180038, GWFP, built for the British Ministry of War Transport. Operated by Lyle Shipping.

345. SAMSKERN, 6–44, 169993, GWKD, built for the British Ministry of War Transport. Operated by Evan Thomas Radcliffe & Co.

346. SAMSYLARNA, 6–44, GWKS, built for the British Ministry of War Transport. Operated by Sir R. Ropner & Co. Hit by an aerial torpedo on August 4, 1944, and beached.

347. SAMLAMU, 6–44, 180533, WQNY, built for the British Ministry of War Transport. Operated by Sir William Reardon & Sons.

348. SAMUEL F. B. MORSE, 6–44, 245810, WPQZ (1791–1872) Samuel Finley Breese Morse was a noted portrait painter interested in electricity. He and Leonard D. Gale built on the work of Joseph Henry, of Princeton, to invent the single-wire telegraph and devised the Morse code. Operated by Marine Transport.

349. DEXTER W. FELLOWS, 6–44, 245913, WPSC (1871–1937) Dexter William Fellows, of Fitchburg, Massachusetts, was the "King of Press Agents" as pitchman for Ringling Brothers, Barnum & Bailey Circus "The Greatest Show on Earth!" for 40 years. Operated by A. L. Burbank.

350. ASSISTANCE (BAR-17), 6–44, operated by the Royal Navy under Lend-Lease as HMS *Assistance* (F.173).

351. OAKLEY WOOD, 6–44, 245941, WPSM (1872–1935) Barber Steamship Lines executive and president of the U.S. Ship Operators Association. Operated by American West African.

352. WILLIAM S. BAER, 7–44, 245915, WQUY (1872–1931) William Stevenson Baer was an orthopedic surgeon at Johns Hopkins who discovered a cure for chronic osteomyelitis using maggots. Operated by Marine Transport.

353. SIDNEY WRIGHT, 7–44, 245943, WPXP (1790–1822) shipbuilder Noah Brown's foreman who built the pontoons used to float the 492-ton brigs *Lawrence* and *Niagara* over a sandbar in Lake Erie in 1813. Operated by Dichmann, Wright & Pugh.

354. WILLIAM HODSON, 7–44, 245944, WOEK (1891–1943) Minnesota children's activist and New York Commissioner of Welfare. Operated by R. A. Nicol.

355. GEORGE R. HOLMES, 7–44, 246062, WNXP (1895–1939) International News Service Washington Bureau Chief for 20 years. Operated by Sprague.

356. MARY PICKERSGILL, 7–44, 246065, WRES (1776–1857) widowed Philadelphia flagmaker Rebecca Young and her daughter Mary moved to Baltimore. In 1795 Mary married John Pickersgill and when he died in 1805 she took up flagmaking. In 1813 she was hired to make a 30 × 42 foot garrison flag the British would have no trouble seeing in their impending attack. The flag Francis Scott Key saw still flying at Fort McHenry in September 1814 "by the dawn's early light" inspired his poem. Operated by Parry.

357. JOSEPH B. EASTMAN, 7–44, 246063, WREW (1883–1944) Joseph Bartlett "Joe" Eastman was a member of the Interstate Commerce Commission and director of the Office of Defense Transportation who died on March 15, 1944, in Washington. Operated by Polarus.

358. WALTER KIDDE, 7–44, 246067, WREY (1877–1943) founded Walter Kidde & Co., a construction company in New Jersey in 1890. He helped build shipyards then worked for the New Jersey State Highway Commission designing roads. In 1918 he purchased the rights to a shipboard fire suppression system, greatly improved it, and went into the fire extinguisher business. Operated by American Range–Liberty Lines.

359. DILIGENCE (BAR-18), 7–44, operated by the Royal Navy under Lend-Lease as HMS *Diligence* (F.174).

360. FREDERIC A. KUMMER, 7–44, 246159, WRFO (1873–1943) Frederic Arnold

Kummer was a New York civil engineer who dealt with a wide variety of construction problems and was an artist, author, celebrated screen writer, and playwright. He died on November 22, 1943. Operated by Blidberg Rothchild.

361. EDWARD A. SAVOY, 7–44, 246156, WRFQ (1855–1943) Edward Augustine Savoy was an African-American who worked at the State Dept. for 64 years as chief messenger to 22 secretaries of state and keeper of the secretary's door. He was widowed by 1930 and lived with his daughter Edith Morgan, a teacher, and her husband Robert W. Morgan, a retail merchant at 503 24th St. NE. He was retired by 1940 at age 85 and died on August 23, 1943, in Washington. Operated by Merchants & Miners.

362. VINCENT HARRINGTON, 7–44, 246161, WRFR (1903–1943) Vincent Francis Harrington was a congressman from Iowa who resigned to serve in the Army Air Corps and died of a heart attack in England on November 29, 1943. Operated by Dichmann, Wright & Pugh.

363. USS APPANOOSE (AK-226), 7–44, NXUE, *Crater*-class cargo ship commissioned on September 26, 1944.

364. S. WILEY WAKEMAN, 7–44, 246245, WSKP (1876–1940) Samuel Wiley Wakeman was a vice president and director of Bethlehem Steel who died on May 10, 1940. Operated by T. J. Stevenson.

365. USS XANTHUS (AR-19), 8–44, repair ship commissioned on May 9, 1945.

366. FREDERICK W. WOOD, 8–44, 246242, WSVV (1857–1943) Frederick William Wood was a mining engineer with the Pennsylvania Steel Co. who discovered ore deposits in Cuba in 1882 and was then asked to find a spot where the imported ore could be mixed with American coal. By 1890 he had designed a steel mill at Sparrows Point, Maryland, which became the Maryland Steel Co., a subsidiary of Pennsylvania Steel, with Wood as president. In 1891 they started building ships and in 1916 the company was sold to Charles M. Schwab, of Bethlehem Steel. Wood resigned in 1918 and became vice president of the American International Shipbuilding Corp. and oversaw the building and operation of the Hog Island yard. Operated by Cosmopolitan.

367. USS WEBSTER (ARV-2), 8–44, NIQI, aircraft repair ship commissioned on March 17, 1945.

368. S. M. SHOEMAKER, 8–44, 246333, KRTD (1861–1933) Samuel Moor Shoemaker was a Maryland agriculturist and dairy expert on the family's Burnside Farm Road in central Baltimore County. Operated by Marine Transport.

369. USS PALAWAN (ARG-10), 8–44, NPXQ, internal combustion engine repair ship commissioned on May 3, 1945.

370. ALEXANDER V. FRASER, 8–44, 246328, KRVW (1804–1868) appointed the first commander of the Treasury Department's Revenue Marine Bureau on April 12, 1843. Operated by Pope & Talbot.

371. FREDERICK H. BAETJER, 8–44, 246331, KSBA (1874–1933) Frederick Henry Baetjer was a Johns Hopkins physician and early user of X-ray technology. Operated by Dichmann, Wright & Pugh.

372. JESSE COTTRELL, 9–44, 246424, KSBF (1878–1944) Jesse Samuel Cottrell was city editor of the *Chattanooga News*, a Tennessee politician, and a reporter representing the *Atlanta Georgian & American* newspaper in Washington during the World War. In June 1918 became a captain with the General Staff of the Army's Military Intelligence Division in Philadelphia and was minister to Bolivia. He died on November 24, 1944. Operated by Pope & Talbot.

373. WILLIAM LIBBEY, 9–44, 246427, KSCT (1855–1927) William Libbey, Jr., was

a professor of geology at Princeton, mountain climber, president of the National Rifle Association, and a member of the 1912 Summer Olympic rifle team at Stockholm. Operated by American-Foreign.

374. BENJAMIN PEIXOTTO, 9–44, 246422, KSDQ (1834–1890) Benjamin Franklin Peixotto was an attorney in San Francisco who was president of B'nai Brith during the Civil War. In 1870 he was appointed by President Grant as consul general at Bucharest, Rumania, to help recognize Jewish civil rights as a condition of recognizing Romania's sovereignty in 1878. Operated by Merchants & Miners.

375. USS LAERTES (AR-20), 9–44, repair ship commissioned on March 26, 1945.

376. GEORGE M. VERITY, 9–44, 246507, KTHG (1865–1943) George Matthew Verity started out as a wholesale grocer in Ohio but by 1889 he was vice president and manager of the American Steel Roofing Co. in Cincinnati. With a $500 loan and innovative industry and labor practices he built a steel mill at Middletown, Ohio, on the Great Miami River. The American Rolling Mill Co. was the first steel company with a safety program and eight-hour days for all employees. He retired in 1930. Operated by United States Lines.

377. CHARLES C. GLOVER, 10–44, 246502, KSZF (1846–1936) Charles Carroll Glover was president of Riggs Bank in the District of Columbia. As a civic projects leader he helped found the National Zoo, the National Cathedral, Embassy Row, the Washington Stock Exchange, and donated the land where the Lincoln and Jefferson Memorials were built. He was famously arrested by Speaker James "Champ" Clark for assaulting Thetus Sims (D-Tenn.) in 1913 over an accusation. He is the namesake for the bridge on Massachusetts Ave. NW over Rock Creek in Georgetown. Operated by Dichmann, Wright & Pugh. Stranded on a reef 20 miles off St. Nazaire, France, in October 1945 in heavy seas.

378. JOHN HANSON, 10–44, 246574, KSZI (1721–1783) Maryland resident who was president of the Continental Congress. He is considered by some historians to be the first president of the United States. Operated by A. L. Burbank.

379. CHARLES A. MCCUE, 10–44, 246573, KSZN (1879–1942) horticulturist and Forest Service agriculture specialist who served with the Association of Land-Grant Colleges and Universities. Named the Cape May potato in New Jersey. Operated by Pope & Talbot.

380. MILAN R. STEFANIK, 10–44, 246631, KSZO (1880–1919) Milan Rastislav Štefánik was a Czechoslovakian astronomer, diplomat, World War I French Army pilot and general, freedom fighter, and national hero in creating the Czechoslovak Republic. He died in a plane crash on May 4, 1919, en route home from Italy. Operated by Merchants & Miners.

381. USS KERMIT ROOSEVELT (ARG-16), 10–44, internal combustion engine repair ship commissioned on May 31, 1945. The son of Theodore R., who founded the Roosevelt Steamship Co. and United States Lines. He committed suicide on June 4, 1943.

382. USS DIONYSUS (AR-21), 10–44, repair ship commissioned on April 28, 1945.

383. USS HOOPER ISLAND (ARG-17), 10–44, NKFP, internal combustion engine repair ship commissioned on July 13, 1945.

384. USS SAMAR (ARG-11), 10–44, NICA, internal combustion engine repair ship commissioned on June 5, 1945.

California Shipbuilding Corp.
Terminal Island, Wilmington, California

The 151-acre Calship yard was established on January 16, 1941, under joint ownership of Todd Shipbuilding Corp. and Henry Kaiser. The Maritime Commission leased the land and spent $26,688,818 for facilities. The first keel was laid on May 24, 1941. In February 1942 the yard came under control of Bechtel-McCone with John A. McCone as president and Stephen D. Bechtel as chairman of the board. The 14-way yard delivered 306 Liberty cargo ships and 30 Liberty tankers for a total of 336. The average building time for the ships was 60.7 days.

1. JOHN C. FREMONT, 3–42, 211222, KHIX (1813–1890) John Charles Frémont was a Western explorer, Army officer, and California senator. Operated by American President Lines. Capt. Ludwig J. Yttergaard's ship hit a mine on March 31, 1945, at Manila, Philippines. No fatalities were reported.

2. THOMAS PAINE, 3–42, 241331, KAJK (1737–1809) author of *Common Sense.* Operated by Lykes.

3. BENJAMIN FRANKLIN, 3–42, 241309, KBOF (1706–1790) oldest signer of the Declaration of Independence. Operated by Isthmian.

4. JOHN PAUL JONES, 3–42, 241476, KEHN (1747–1792) John Paul was born in Scotland, came to America, and became a naval commander as John Paul Jones. Operated by Pacific-Atlantic.

5. PAUL REVERE, 4–42, 241509, KEPN (1734–1818) Boston silversmith, dentist, Tea Party organizer, patriot "alarm and muster" member, gunpowder maker, and the first metalworker to form copper into sheets. Operated by American-Hawaiian.

6. DANIEL BOONE, 4–42, 241519, KERI (1734–1820) Kentucky pioneer, frontiersman, and early American folk hero. Operated by American-Hawaiian. Capt. Larz Neilson arrived at San Francisco on November 10, 1943, from Fremantle, Australia. The ship was then operated by the Navy as the *Crater*-class cargo ship *Ara* (AK-136), commissioned on January 4, 1944.

7. ROBERT MORRIS, 4–42, 241560, KETI (1734–1806) Declaration of Independence signer from Pennsylvania. Operated by Luckenbach.

8. SAMUEL ADAMS, 4–42, 241551, KETL (1722–1803) Declaration of Independence signer from Massachusetts. Operated by Luckenbach.

9. ALBERT GALLATIN, 4–42, 241518, KERH (1761–1849) Abraham Alfonse Albert Gallatin was a linguist, Pennsylvania congressman, long-serving Secretary of the Treasury, and in 1831 founded New York University. Operated by American-Hawaiian. Capt. Cyrus Lee Brown's ship arrived at San Francisco from Sydney, Australia, on November 11, 1942. They departed Mobile, Alabama, in July 1943 and on August 28 the ship was hit by three torpedoes fired from *U-107* but none exploded. They arrived at New York on October 26, 1943, from New Castle, England. Sunk on January 2, 1944, by *I-26* in the Arabian Sea. No casualties were reported.

10. NATHAN HALE, 5–42, 241560, KEZI (1755–1776) Revolutionary War American spy. Operated by Coastwise (Pacific Far East) Line.

11. OLIVER HAZARD PERRY, 5–42, 241549, KETH (1785–1819) noted War of 1812 naval officer. Operated by Luckenbach.

12. ELBRIDGE GERRY, 5–42, 241553, KEUM (1744–1814) Elbridge Thomas Gerry was a Declaration of Independence signer from Massachusetts and vice president. Operated by Seas Shipping.

13. ZEBULON PIKE, 5–42, 241668, KEXE (1779–1813) Zebulon Montgomery Pike was an explorer and namesake for Pikes Peak, Colorado. He was lost during the War of 1812 at the Battle of York. Operated by American-Hawaiian.

14. BENJAMIN GOODHUE, 5–42, 241616, KEZC (1748–1814) Massachusetts senator. Operated by American-Hawaiian and converted to an Army troopship.

15. RUFUS KING, 5–42, 241607, KEVG (1755–1827) Massachusetts and New York congressman and minister to Great Britain. Operated by Coastwise (Pacific Far East) Line. Stranded on July 7, 1942, off Brisbane, Australia.

16. ABIEL FOSTER, 5–42, 241606, KETM (1735–1806) New Hampshire congressman. Operated by Matson.

17. CALEB STRONG, 5–42, 241748, KFAX (1745–1819) Massachusetts governor and senator. Operated by American-Hawaiian.

18. PAINE WINGATE, 5–42, 241751, KPNG (1739–1838) New Hampshire congressman. Operated by Luckenbach.

19. WILLIAM FLOYD, 5–42, 241701, KEWX (1734–1821) Declaration of Independence signer from New York. Operated by Luckenbach.

20. ABRAHAM CLARK, 6–42, 241615, KEXI (1725–1794) Declaration of Independence signer from New Jersey. Operated by Grace Line.

21. HENRY KNOX, 6–42, 241617, KEUV (1750–1806) Continental Army officer and the first Secretary of War. Operated by Matson. Capt. Eugene M. Olsen's ship was torpedoed by *I-37* on June 19 in the Indian Ocean with the loss of 13 merchant crew and 13 Armed Guard sailors.

22. JOHN LANGDON, 6–42, 241618, KFIF (1741–1819) New Hampshire congressman. Operated by Moore-McCormack.

23. JAMES MONROE, 6–42, 241749, KFHB (1758–1831) 5th President of the United States. Operated by Matson.

24. JOHN HATHORN, 6–42, 241795, KFIC (1749–1825) Revolutionary War colonel. Someone got the idea of putting a huge chain across the Hudson River to block British ships. Hathorn helped decide the location for the Great Chain and in 1778 wrote the final report that recommended going from West Point across to Constitution Island. He also served as a New York congressman. Operated by Hammond.

25. EDWIN MARKHAM, 6–42, 241793, KFWZ (1852–1940) Charles Edwin Anson Markham was an Oregon native and poet laureate of Oregon. Operated by Matson.

26. GEORGE MATTHEWS, 6–42, 241794, KFFU (1847–1942) worked in an Elmira, New York, flour mill and then became a milling magnate in Buffalo. He donated $1 million to the YMCA to aid black men and boys in the Buffalo area. Operated by Grace Line.

27. F. A. C. MUHLENBERG, 6–42, 241834, KFFI (1750–1801) Frederick Augustus Conrad Muhlenberg was a Pennsylvania congressman. Operated by Luckenbach and converted to an Army troopship. Capt. Kristian K. Kristiansen's ship was bombed by German aircraft at Naples, Italy, on January 25, 1944, with the loss of six merchant crew and one Armed Guard sailor. The ship was repaired.

28. JOHN B. ASHE, 6–42, 241837, KFHU (1748–1802) John Baptista Ashe served at Valley Forge and the Battle of Eutaw Springs. He was a North Carolina congressman when he was elected governor but he died before taking office. Operated by American-Hawaiian.

29. JOHN PAGE, 6–42, 241836, KFIX (1743–1808) Virginia congressman and governor. Operated by Matson.

30. JAMES SCHUREMAN, 6–42, 241835, KFHF (1756–1824) New Jersey congressman. Operated by Luckenbach.

31. ISAAC COLES, 6–42, 241900, KFGV (1747–1813) Virginia congressman. Operated by American President Lines.

32. EGBERT BENSON, 6–42, 241899, KFDJ (1746–1833) New York congressman. Operated by Luckenbach.

33. PETER SILVESTER, 6–42, 241902, KFNK (1734–1808) New York congressman. Operated by Coastwise (Pacific Far East) Line. Converted to an animal transport ship. Sunk

on February 6, 1945, by *U-862* in the Indian Ocean with the loss of able seaman Jack Funk, seven Armed Guard sailors, and 24 soldiers.

34. STEPHEN JOHNSON FIELD, 6–42, 241903, KFZP (1816–1899) Supreme Court justice. Operated by American-Hawaiian. Capt. Pierce Powers' ship was bombed by Japanese aircraft on January 23, 1943, at Milne Bay, New Guinea. No fatalities were reported.

35. JOSEPH MCKENNA, 6–42, 241929, KFYZ (1843–1926) California congressman, Attorney General, and Supreme Court justice. Operated by Grace Line.

36. WILLIAM M. STEWART, 7–42, 241933, KFZG (1827–1909) William Morris Stewart was a 49er, lawyer, controversial Nevada senator, and cofounder of Chevy Chase, Maryland. Operated by Matson.

37. WILLIS VAN DEVANTER, 7–42, 241934, KFZK (1859–1941) Supreme Court justice who resigned on May 18, 1937, in the wake of President Roosevelt's attack on the Court after his National Industrial Recovery Act (NRA) was declared unconstitutional. Operated by Moore-McCormack.

38. FRANCIS PARKMAN, 7–42, 241974, KGAI (1823–1893) Francis Parkman, Jr., was a noted North America and Oregon Trail historian. Operated by Pope & Talbot.

39. GEORGE THACHER, 7–42, 241975, KFGD (1754–1824) George Thatcher represented Massachusetts in the Continental Congress. Operated by Moore-McCormack. Capt. Henry O. Billings sailed with Moore-McCormack and was chief mate on the company's steamer *Argentina* when the ship arrived at New York on June 2, 1941, from Rio de Janeiro. He sat for his master's license then took command of the *Thacher*. The ship was sunk on November 1, 1942, by *U-126* off Africa with the loss of five merchant crew, including Capt. Billings, five Armed Guard sailors, and eight soldiers.

40. JOHN STEELE, 7–42, 241976, KFIF (1764–1815) North Carolina congressman and Comptroller of the Treasury. Operated by American-Hawaiian.

41. JUAN CABRILLO, 7–42, 241977, KGAM (1499–1543) João Rodrígues Cabrillo was a Portuguese explorer representing Spain who was the first European to visit the coast of California. Operated by American-Hawaiian.

42. JOHN FISKE, 7–42, 242037, KGCB (1842–1901) celebrated and popular American historian from Boston. Operated by American President Lines.

43. JUNIPERO SERRA, 7–42, 242039, KGII (1713–1784) Miguel Josep Serra was a Spanish Franciscan friar who founded a series of 21 missions in Alta California. Operated by Sudden & Christenson.

44. JOHN A. SUTTER, 7–42, 242036, KCFG (1803–1880) Swiss-born Johann August Sutter was a California pioneer who built Sutter's Fort and the sawmill where carpenter James Marshall discovered gold in 1848. Operated by Sudden & Christenson.

45. RICHARD HENRY DANA, 8–42, 242040, KGFH (1815–1882) noted sailor and lawyer who wrote *Two Years Before the Mast*. Operated by American Mail Line. The ship left New York in early January 1943 under Capt. Edward Raymond Kidd. In mid-year the ship was in the Persian Gulf when a mutiny occurred. Capt. Kidd called on Armed Guard detachment commander Lt. William Hadruck Burras for assistance to suppress the mutiny and provide security. Nine mutineers were subsequently turned over to the Army at Khorramshahr, Iran, and the ship proceeded to Australia. Four crewmen had enough of the voyage and paid off in Fremantle, including the chief mate. One deserted there, one was hospitalized at Durban, South Africa, two at Bahia, Brazil, and one deserted at Bahia. Replacements were hired and the ship arrived at New York on September 3, 1943, from Port of Spain, Trinidad.

46. JAMES FORD RHODES, 8–42, 242083, KGJL (1848–1927) Cleveland steel magnate and historian. Operated by Oliver J. Olson.

47. GEORGE BANCROFT, 8–42, 242086, KGTV (1800–1891) historian, Secretary of the Navy, and founder of the naval academy at Annapolis. Operated by Hammond.

48. WILLIAM H. PRESCOTT, 8–42, 242085, KGIY (1796–1859) William Hickling Prescott was a Spanish historian, advocate for the blind, and regarded as the first American scientific historian. Operated by American President Lines.

49. HINTON R. HELPER, 8–42, 242136, KGFS (1829–1909) Hinton Rowan Helper was a North Carolina anti-slavery author. In 1857 he wrote The Impending Crisis of the South. Operated by Matson.

50. WILLIAM F. CODY, 8–42, 242139, KGFK (1846–1917) William Frederick "Buffalo Bill" Cody was a frontiersman and Wild West showman. Operated by American President Lines.

51. ROBERT F. STOCKTON, 8–42, 242137, KGIT (1795–1866) Robert Field Stockton was an innovative naval constructor who captured California from Mexico and became a New Jersey senator. Operated by Matson.

52. STARR KING, 8–42, 242138, KGFU (1824–1864) Thomas Starr King was a minister in San Francisco and is credited with keeping California in the Union during the Civil War. Operated by McCormick. Sunk on February 10, 1943, by *I-10* off Sydney, Australia. There were no reported casualties.

53. LELAND STANFORD, 8–42, 242174, KGGA (1824–1893) Amasa Leland Stanford was a lawyer, 49er, merchant, and one of the "Big Four" who founded the Central Pacific Railroad. He became the governor of California, a senator, president of the Southern Pacific Railroad, and in 1891 founded the Leland Stanford, Jr., University in Palo Alto. Operated by United States Lines.

54. FRANCIS DRAKE, 8–42, 242173, KGGB (1545–1596) English sailor who made the second circumnavigation of the world. Namesake for Drake's Bay in Marin County, California, where it it believed he visited. Operated by Isthmian.

55. PETER H. BURNETT, 8–42, 242175, KGGC (1807–1895) Peter Hardeman Burnett was an Oregon pioneer and the first governor of the state of California. Operated by American President Lines. Capt. Charles A. Darling's ship was torpedoed by *I-9* on January 22, 1943, off Australia, with the loss of one Armed Guard sailor. The ship was repaired.

56. EWING YOUNG, 8–42, 242200, KHHI (1799–1841) Oregon pioneer and wealthy merchant who inspired the formation of the Oregon Territory. Operated by Pacific-Atlantic.

57. PETER CARTWRIGHT, 9–42, 242201, KHHV (1785–1872) Methodist preacher, abolitionist, and Illinois politician who was defeated by Abraham Lincoln in an 1846 congressional election. Operated by American President Lines.

58. BRIGHAM YOUNG, 9–42, 242199, KHHD (1801–1877) second president of the Church of Jesus Christ of Latter Day Saints. A dispute with Joseph Smith's ex-associate Sidney Rigdon led him to take his followers into the desert where they founded Salt Lake City. First governor of the Utah Territory. Operated by Matson for one voyage in the Pacific under Capt. Arvid Gosta (Gustav) Torleif Cahling then by the Navy as the *Crater*-class cargo ship *Murzim* (AK-95), NGJS, commissioned on May 14, 1943.

59. HORACE MANN, 9–42, 242234, KHHR (1796–1859) noted reformer of public education and Massachusetts congressman. Operated by Isthmian.

60. JANE ADDAMS, 9–42, 242235, KHGO (1860–1935) Chicago social reformer who cofounded the Hull House with Ellen G. Starr, the first Settlement House in the United States. Her life partner was Mary R. Smith. Operated by American President Lines and converted to an Army troopship.

61. CLARA BARTON, 9–42, 242233, KHGT (1821–1912) Clarissa "Clara" Harlowe

Barton was known as the "Angel of the Battlefield" during the Civil War and in 1878 founded the American Red Cross. She consorted with John J. Elwell. Operated by Coastwise (Pacific Far East) Line.

62. WENDELL PHILLIPS, 9–42, 242281, KHHE (1811–1884) noted Boston lawyer and abolitionist. Operated by Weyerhaeuser.

63. WILLIAM ELLERY CHANNING, 9–42, 242282, KHIC (1780–1842) prominent Unitarian theologian. Operated by American-Hawaiian.

64. FELIPE DE NEVE, 9–42, 242279, KHIP (1724–1784) Spanish governor of Las Californias. Operated by AGWI Lines.

65. HENRY WARD BEECHER, 9–42, 242306, KHIE (1813–1887) prominent Congregationalist preacher and social reformer who became mired in scandal. Operated by Union Sulphur. In December 1945 the ship was 340 miles northwest of Bermuda heading home with 541 soldiers from Marseille, France, when the propeller fell off.

66. HORACE GREELEY, 9–42, 242307, KHGH (1811–1872) abolitionist publisher of the *New York Tribune* and founder of the Liberal Republican Party. Operated by Oliver J. Olson.

67. JAMES GORDON BENNETT, 9–42, 242308, KHGK (1795–1872) founder of the New York Herald. Operated by Matson.

68. SAMUEL GOMPERS, 9–42, 242309, KHIN (1850–1924) English cigar maker and longtime president of the American Federation of Labor. Operated by Weyerhaeuser. Capt. John J. Lapoint's ship was torpedoed on January 29, 1943, by *I-10* in the South Pacific with the loss of three merchant crew and one Armed Guard sailor. Capt. Lapoint commanded one of the lifeboats, picked up survivors, and kept his crew of 49 survivors alive for 33 days until they were rescued. He boarded Capt. Harold R. Gillespie's liner *Matsonia* on February 6 at Noumea, New Caledonia, and arrived at San Diego, California, on February 25. He was awarded the Merchant Marine Distinguished Service medal.

69. JOSEPH PULITZER, 10–42, 242372, KHLV (1847–1911) Pulitzer József, of Hungary, owned the *St. Louis Post Dispatch* and the *New York World* and was a New York congressman. Operated by American President Lines.

70. MALCOLM M. STEWART, 10–42, 242373, KHIN (1877–1937) chairman of the Middle West Foreign Trade Committee at Cincinnati and a major booster of the merchant marine. Operated by Moore-McCormack.

71. GEORGE A. CUSTER, 10–42, 242370, KHIX (1839–1876) George Armstrong Custer was commander of the 7th Cavalry at Little Bighorn, Montana, in June 1876. Operated by American South African.

72. GEORGE G. MEADE, 10–42, 242371, KHMY (1815–1872) George Gordon Meade was a civil engineer who designed lighthouses. He was an engineer in the Army when he defeated Lee at Gettysburg. Operated by Weyerhaeuser.

73. BOOKER T. WASHINGTON, 10–42, 242392, KHLF (1856–1915) Booker Taliaferro Washington was an African-American political leader and head of the Tuskegee Institute. Operated by Luckenbach. The master, Capt. Hugh N. Mulzac, was the first African-American shipmaster in American history.

74. FITZ-JOHN PORTER, 10–42, 242393, KHNA (1822–1901) Fitz John Porter was a noted Civil War Army general. Operated by McCormick. Capt. Herbert E. Gregg's ship was torpedoed on March 1, 1943, by *U-518* one day out from Bahia, Brazil, with the loss of one Armed Guard sailor. Engine cadet Frederick R. Zito was awarded the Merchant Marine Distinguished Service medal for rescuing a fireman/watertender trapped in the lifeboat falls while abandoning ship.

75. JAMES B. MCPHERSON, 10–42, 242432, KHNO (1828–1864) James Birdseye McPherson was an Army engineer who commanded the Right Wing of Sherman's Army during the Atlanta campaign. He was shot and killed on July 22 while trying to escape Confederate skirmishers under Lt. Gen. John Bell Hood, his longtime friend and classmate. Operated by American-Hawaiian.

76. SAMUEL HEINTZELMAN, 10–42, 242399, KHQO (1805–1880) Samuel Peter Heintzelman was a distinguished Army officer of many campaigns. Operated by Coastwise (Pacific Far East) Line. Capt. Johann W. G. Wilkie's ship left Fremantle, Australia, on July 1, 1943, for Calcutta but never arrived. The ship, 42 crew, and 19 Armed Guard sailors disappeared and were never seen or heard from again. Post-war research determined the ship was torpedoed in the Indian Ocean, possibly by *U-511*.

77. JOHN SEDGWICK, 10–42, 242433, KHRO (1813–1864) Union general lost at the Spotsylvania Courthouse on May 9, 1864, the highest ranking Union casualty of the war. The ship was known as "the 7 ship": 7 letters in Calship; the yard's 77th ship, launched at 7 p.m. on October 7 on way No. 7 and pushed by 7 tugs in 7 minutes to Outfitting Dock No. 7. Operated by Pope & Talbot.

78. WILLIAM LLOYD GARRISON, 10–42, 242435, KHHU (1805–1879) noted abolitionist. Operated by Shepard.

79. SMITH THOMPSON, 10–42, 242434, KHQP (1768–1843) Secretary of the Navy and a Supreme Court justice. Moore-McCormack.

80. JOSEPH STORY, 11–42, 242460, KHQX (1779–1845) Massachusetts congressman and Supreme Court justice. Operated by American-Hawaiian.

81. GABRIEL DUVAL, 11–42, 242457, KHRE (1752–1844) Maryland congressman and Supreme Court justice. Sometimes seen as Duvall or DuVal. Operated by Lykes.

82. HENRY BALDWIN, 11–42, 242459, KHRG (1780–1844) Pennsylvania congressman and Supreme Court justice. Operated by United States Lines.

83. BROCKHOLST LIVINGSTON, 11–42, 242456, KHRJ (1757–1823) Henry Brockholst Livingston was a Supreme Court justice. Operated by A. H. Bull.

84. THOMAS JOHNSON, 11–42, 242496, KHRL (1732–1819) Continental congressman, first governor of Maryland, and Supreme Court justice. Operated by Union Sulphur.

85. PHILIP P. BARBOUR, 11–42, 242492, KHRM (1783–1841) Philip Pendleton Barbour was a Virginia congressman and Supreme Court justice. Operated by Grace Line.

86. PETER V. DANIEL, 11–42, 242491, KHRR (1784–1860) Peter Vivian Daniel was a Supreme Court justice. Operated by Isthmian.

87. SAMUEL NELSON, 11–42, 242494, KHRN (1792–1873) Supreme Court justice. Operated by Lykes.

88. ROBERT C. GRIER, 11–42, 242518, KHRT (1794–1870) Robert Cooper Grier was a Supreme Court justice. Operated by Isthmian.

89. BENJAMIN R. CURTIS, 11–42, 242513, KHRY (1809–1874) Benjamin Robbins Curtis was a Supreme Court justice. Operated by United States Lines.

90. MARION MCKINLEY BOVARD, 11–42, 242517, KKBW (1847–1891) first president of the University of Southern California. Operated by American-Hawaiian.

91. STEPHEN M. WHITE, 11–42, 242551, KKBZ (1853–1901) Stephen Mallory White was a California native, lawyer, district attorney, and senator who developed a deepwater harbor at San Pedro, forerunner of the present Port of Los Angeles–Long Beach. Operated by United States Lines.

92. WILLIAM EATON, 12–42, 242554, KKCB (1764–1811) minister to Tunis during the Barbary Wars. Operated by Isthmian.

93. LINCOLN STEFFENS, 12–42, 242548, KKCD (1866–1936) San Francisco native Lincoln Joseph Steffens was a reporter with the *New York Evening Post*, a muckraker, and fierce critic of corruption in municipal government. Operated by Parry.

94. HUBERT HOWE BANCROFT, 11–42, 242572, KKCE (1832–19187) James and George Derby were publishers and booksellers in Buffalo, New York. In 1852 they decided to open a branch in San Francisco, the new boom town, so they sent two clerks, George Kenny and Hubert Bancroft overland to get started while they put $5,000 worth of stock on a ship going around the Horn. But before the merchandise got to San Francisco George Derby died and the venture was called off. Kenny and Bancroft purchased the merchandise and opened their own stationary and bookstore. Bancroft later became an eminent historian of California and namesake for the library at UC Berkeley. Operated by Isthmian.

95. JAMES W. MARSHALL, 12–42, 242573, KISZ (1810–1885) James Wilson Marshall, of New Jersey, was a farmer in Missouri, a soldier in the Mexican War, and a carpenter at Sutter's Fort in California. On January 24, 1848, he discovered something shiny in a stream that changed the course of American history. Operated by Pope & Talbot. Capt. Ragnar W. Roggenbihl's ship was bombed by German aircraft off Salerno, Italy, on September 13, 1943, with the loss of 13 merchant crew, 17 Armed Guard sailors, and a number of Army troops. The ship was scuttled on June 8, 1944, at Normandy as Gooseberry 2.

96. GEORGE CHAFFEY, 12–42, 242571, KKCG (1848–1932) Canadian-born engineer who electrified Los Angeles, developed irrigation systems, and founded Ontario, California. Operated by J. H. Winchester.

97. FRANK JOSEPH IRWIN, 12–42, 242601, KHAV (1893–1942) national commander of the Disabled American Veterans of the World War. Operated by Hammond.

98. HELEN HUNT JACKSON, 12–42, 242602, KITV (1830–1885) Helen Fiske was a prominent poet, author, and Native American activist who married Army captain Edward B. Hunt in 1852. He died in 1863 in an accident and in 1875 she married wealthy banker and railroad man William S. Jackson. Operated by Parry.

99. ABEL STEARNS, 12–42, 242600, KITM (1798–1871) Southern California pioneer, merchant, stagecoach operator, and cattle rancher in Pueblo de Los Angeles. Operated by A. H. Bull.

100. BENJAMIN IDE WHEELER, 12–42, 242626, KIRV (1854–1927) professor at Cornell who became president of the University of California. Operated by American-Hawaiian. Capt. Daniel J. Coughlin's ship was bombed by Japanese aircraft on October 26, 1944, at Leyte, Philippines, with the loss of able seaman Charles H. Malpass and one Armed Guard sailor.

101. AMOS G. THROOP, 12–42, 242628, KTRZ (1811–1894) Amos Gager Throop founded Throop University, now the California Institute of Technology. Operated by United States Lines.

102. WILLIAM MULHOLLAND, 12–42, 242627, KISO (1855–1935) merchant seaman, well digger, foreman with the Los Angeles City Water Co., and superintendent of the City of Los Angeles Water Dept. Operated by American West African.

103. GASPAR DE PORTOLA, 12–42, 242655, KITS (1716–1784) Don Gaspar de Portolà de Rovira was a Spanish explorer, founder of San Diego and Monterey, and governor of Baja and Alta California. Operated by Lykes. Capt. Robert E. Johnson's ship was fatally damaged on a reef in the Caribbean Sea on June 7, 1943. The ship was used at the Coast Guard Fire Fighting School at Fort McHenry, Baltimore, for experiments in the indirect extinguishment methods of fuel oil fires.

104. LUIS ARGUELLO, 12–42, 242656, KKCO (1784–1830) Luis Antonio Argüello

was the first native born governor of Alta California under Mexican rule. Operated by United States Lines.

105. SEBASTIAN VIZCAINO, 12–42, 242659, KISV (1548–1624) Spanish explorer of the West Coast who named San Diego, Catalina Island, and Santa Barbara. Operated by American West African. In 1944, Don Hewitt was the Merchant Marine war correspondent for Stars and Stripes newspaper. The April 13, 1944, edition featured a story about Capt. John C. Giriat's crew on the *Vizcaino*. There were 42 merchant seaman from 16 to 55 years old and 27 Armed Guard sailors under Ens. Cassel R. Rhulman, Jr., USNR, when they arrived at New York on April 1, 1944, from London. Hewitt started out by saying, "They were fighting this war long before the Allies' power to strike back approached anything like it is today. They rode out the enemy's punches long before the rest of our forces were called into full scale operations." On May 14, 1933, Capt. Giriat, of New Rochelle, New York, signed on the Pacific-Atlantic Steamship Co. freighter *San Marcos* as a workaway at Portland, Oregon, and decided to stay at sea. In April 1933 he was ordinary seaman on the States Steamship Lines passenger vessel *General Lee* from Portland, Oregon, to Yokohama, to San Francisco. He came ashore when he made third mate and went to work for Sears Roebuck & Co. where he organized the marine division. In October 1942 he was 2nd mate on the J. H. Winchester Liberty ship *Daniel Carroll*. One of the galley utility boys, Joseph A. "Joe" Berthelot, 16, of Wayne, Michigan, had five voyages into war zones under his belt since signing on the motortanker *Jamestown* in September 1943 at New York. Fireman/watertender, Cicero James "Jimmy" Ray, 29, was an African-American boxer who was on his way to some big cards when he was drafted. He went to the Sheepshead Bay Maritime School, signed on then decided to quit the ring. Royce Alfred Tewksbury, 40, from Portsmouth, New Hampshire, quit a good job ashore to sign up as a wiper for his first trip. His son was a Navy pilot. One of the ABs from Boston, Gustave Walter "Gus" "Guadalcanal Gus" Portrait, 36, had enlisted in the Army on March 10, 1942 as a private. He said he had been on Guadalcanal and "had six Japs to his credit" but had come down with malaria and was honorably discharged on July 27, 1943. He went to work in a defense plant but got restless and decided to put his prewar experience sailing yachts to good use and signed on the *Vizcaino* on December 9, 1943, at Boston. English-born able seaman Dennis "Danny" Dobbins, 29, had been torpedoed twice and shipwrecked on a sailing vessel. He had signed on at St. John's, Newfoundland, on January 26. Wiper William J. "Bill" Harvey, 20, said he was at Hickam Field when Pearl Harbor was attacked and helped with the salvage work. He was declared Class IV-F by the draft board and went to work in a shipyard building Liberty ships and decided to see what sailing on one was like. Fireman/watertender Francis K. "Frank" Sweeney, 23, of Providence, Rhode Island, got the idea to join the merchant marine and had been torpedoed off North Africa. The saloon messman, Maxwell S. "Max" Wadlington, 28, of Evanston, Illinois, had been a machinist at the Norfolk Navy Yard and was making his first trip at sea. Ordinary Seaman William J. "Bill" Rowe, 20, was building Liberty ships at Portland, Maine, when he got the urge to ship out. John Francis "Johnny" Westcott, 25, of Newfoundland, was a galley utilityman who had been torpedoed in 1941 and was in the convoy that landed the first Allied expeditionary force in Britain. He had signed on with Dobbins. Ordinary seaman Theodore "Ted" Gioshes, 20, had an essential job in a defense plant but "was getting sick of hanging around at home" and was on the first ship to get through the German blockade at Malta. Chief Steward Antonio "Tony" Cunha, 55, had been at sea since 1915 and said he was torpedoed once in the Great War and once in the second. Third engineer Charles F. "Charlie" Metz, 49, of Waltham, Massachusetts, had a wife and kids and a good job ashore but he wanted to see his son in England—a gunner with the Eighth Air Force. Metz said, "He couldn't get home to see us, so I did the next best thing. I came over to see him." Chief mate Quinley E.

"Quin" Stewart, 52, had 30 years at sea. Don Hewitt (1922–2009) would go on to create the CBS news magazine program 60 Minutes.

106. KING S. WOOLSEY, 12–42, 242685, KKEC (1832–1879) King Sam Woolsey was an Arizona pioneer, Indian fighter, and legislator. Operated by A. H. Bull.

107. ARCHBISHOP LAMY, 12–42, 242680, KKEP (1814–1888) Jean-Baptiste Lamy was the archbishop of Santa Fe, New Mexico. Operated by Pope & Talbot.

108. JOHN BIDWELL, 12–42, 242684, KIPZ (1819–1900) California pioneer and independence fighter. Operated by Grace Line.

109. LOUIS MCLANE, 12–42, 242720, KKGO (1786–1857) Delaware congressman and Secretary of the Treasury and State. Operated by American-Hawaiian.

110. HUGH S. LEGARE, 1–43, 242715, KKGW (1797–1843) Hugh Swinton Legaré was a South Carolina congressman, U.S. Attorney General, and Secretary of State. Operated by Lykes.

111. JAMES BUCHANAN, 1–43, 242716, KKHC (1791–1868) James Buchanan, Jr., was the 15th President of the United States. Operated by Matson.

112. JOHN M. CLAYTON, 1–43, 242731, KKHJ (1796–1856) John Middleton Clayton was a Delaware senator and Secretary of State. Operated by American-Hawaiian. Capt. Nels E. Nelson's ship was bombed by Japanese aircraft on January 1, 1945, at Mindoro Island, Philippines, with the loss of two merchant crew and four Armed Guard sailors. The crew and Armed Guard were sent ashore and Capt. Charles S. Robbins, master of the damaged Liberty ship *Juan de Fuca*, came aboard and signed on a new crew at Tacloban, Leyte, Philippines, between January and May that included his former deck and engine officers and chief steward, George W. Laporte, from the *Juan de Fuca*. On May 4 he signed on radio operator Dillion G. Sherritze and on the 5th signed on six able seamen, three Filipino ordinaries, and rounded out the steward and engine departments. The new crew included 14 Filipinos nationals and two Norwegian nationals. Able seaman Kristen M. Eltweldt, 40, and oiler Hans Svendsen, 37, had been captured by the Japanese on December 8, 1941, and imprisoned until recently liberated. Capt. Robbins headed for Pearl Harbor and arrived there on June 3. The immigration inspector, Arthur Corcoran, removed the Filipinos and sent them home on the *Sacagawea*. A War Shipping Administration official went aboard the *Clayton* on the 14th to inspect the ship, which prompted him to remove the crew and put the ship in dry dock. After further inspection it was taken over by the Navy and on June 2, 1945, became the *Harcourt* (IX-225) and hauled supplies to Eniwetok and occupied Japan. In the meantime, Capt. Nelson, 43, took command of the American-Hawaiian Liberty ship *Lyman Beecher* at Los Angeles and arrived at New York from Cadiz, Spain, on July 20, 1945.

113. WILLIAM L. MARCY, 1–43, 242736, KKHR (1786–1857) William Learned Marcy was a New York senator, governor, and Secretary of War and State. Operated by American-Hawaiian. Capt. Graham Griffiths' ship was sunk by a German torpedo off Juno Beach, Normandy, on August 7, 1944. A British soldier aboard was lost in the attack.

114. LEWIS CASS, 1–43, 242732, KKHU (1782–1866) Michigan senator, governor, and Secretary of State. Operated by Waterman. Stranded on the Mexican coast on January 25, 1943, and broke in two.

115. JEREMIAH S. BLACK, 1–43, 242749, KEXR (1810–1883) Jeremiah Sullivan Black was chief justice of the Pennsylvania supreme court, Attorney General and Secretary of State. Operated by Isthmian.

116. ELIHU B. WASHBURNE, 1–43, 242746, KEYB (1816–1887) Elihu Benjamin Washburne was an Illinois congressman and Secretary of State. Operated by Matson. Capt. George Lambert Mollison was master of the Matson ship *Mapele* and arrived at Seattle on

January 13, 1942, then took command of the *Washburne*. The ship was torpedoed on July 3, 1943, by *U-513* off Brazil. No casualties were reported.

117. HARRISON GRAY OTIS, 1–43, 242748, KFBG (1765–1848) Massachusetts congressman and mayor of Boston. Operated by American-Hawaiian. Captain Roy Moyes' ship hit a mine on August 4, 1943, at Gibraltar Harbor with the loss of second engineer Carl H. Regan and fireman/watertender John M. Lawson.

118. JOSEPH H. HOLLISTER, 1–43, 242760, KFKX (1820–1873) pioneered the sheep and wool industry in California. Operated by United States Lines.

119. PHOEBE A. HEARST, 1–43, 242761, KKIT (1842–1919) Phoebe Elizabeth Apperson, of Missouri, married George Hearst in 1862 and the two moved to San Francisco where their son, William Randolph, was born on April 29, 1863. He got into the newspaper business. Operated by American President Lines. Capt. Stephanos Bacoyanis' ship was torpedoed on April 30, 1943, by *I-19* in the South Pacific. There were no reported casualties.

120. ZANE GREY, 1–43, 242763, KKIR (1872–1939) Pearl Zane Grey was a baseball player, dentist, and adventure writer. Operated by Isthmian.

121. PIO PICO, 1–43, 242831, KHZI (1801–1894) Pio de Jesús Pico was the last Mexican governor of Alta California. Operated by Marine Transport.

122. JOHN DRAKE SLOAT, 1–43, 242829, KHZJ (1781–1867) commander of the Pacific Squadron who formally claimed Alta California for the United States on July 7, 1846. Operated by American-Hawaiian.

123. CARLOS CARRILLO, 1–43, 242826, KHZF (1783–1852) Carlos Antonio Carrillo was a governor of Alta California. Operated by American President Lines and converted to an Army troopship.

124. GEORGE E. HALE, 2–43, 242852, KKJF (1868–1938) George Ellery Hale was a solar astronomer who invented the spectrohelioscope and discovered solar vortices and that sunspots were magnetic. Operated by Waterman.

125. WILLIAM S. YOUNG, 2–43, 242854, KHZL (1790–1827) William Singleton Young was a Kentucky congressman who died in office. Operated by A. H. Bull.

126. JEAN JAURES, 2–43 (1859–1914) Auguste Marie Joseph Jean Léon Jaurès was a French Socialist Party leader who was assassinated by French nationalist Raoul Villain in a Paris cafe. Operated under the French flag.

127. VOIKOV, 2–43 (1888–1927) Pyotr Lazarevich Voykov was a Russian revolutionist who disposed of the bodies of Tsar Nicholas II and his family and who was assassinated on June 7, 1927. Operated under the Russian flag.

128. JAMES ROBERTSON, 2–43, 242884, KKJI (1742–1814) explorer and cofounder of Nashville, Tennessee. Operated by American President Lines. Capt. Harold F. DeLasaux's ship was torpedoed on July 7, 1943, by *U-105* off Brazil with the loss of one Armed Guard sailor.

129. WILLIAM J. WORTH, 2–43, 242887, KKJJ (1794–1849) William Jenkins Worth was a general noted for his service in the War of 1812 and the Seminole and Mexican Wars. Namesake for Fort Worth and Lake Worth, Texas. Operated by American-Hawaiian.

130. HOWARD STANSBURY, 2–43, 242903, KKJQ (1806–1863) Army topographical engineer who surveyed and explored the Great Salt Lake region in Utah. Operated by De La Rama.

131. ROBERT STUART, 2–43, 242908, KKJR (1785–1848) explorer and partner of John Jacob Astor in the Pacific Northwest fur trade. Fort Astoria was built in 1811 but after Indians burned their ship *Tonquin* off Vancouver Island, Stuart and six others left Fort Astoria in 1812, discovered the fabled South Pass in the Rocky Mountains along the way, and arrived at St. Louis the next year. Operated by American South African.

132. WILLIAM DUNBAR, 2–43, 242910, KKQS (1749–1810) English-born Philadelphia merchant. He and John Ross planted indigo and cotton in Mississippi. He invented a screw press to form cotton into square bales, thought cottonseed might make a useful oil, and then, as a scientist and noted meteorologist, was appointed by President Jefferson to lead a scientific expedition to the newly-acquired Louisiana Purchase. Operated by South Atlantic.

133. GEORGE C. YOUNT, 2–43, 242930, KKQV (1794–1865) George Calvert Yount was a farmer, soldier, and trapper who arrived in California in 1831. He received two land grants from the Mexican government and became the first European settler in the Napa Valley. Namesake for Yountville, California. Operated in the Pacific by American President Lines under Capt. Harold Lucas then by the Navy as the *Crater*-class cargo ship *Ascella* (AK-137), NHDB, commissioned on January 7, 1944.

134. SOLOMON JUNEAU, 2–43, 242933, KKQY (1793–1856) also known as Laurent-Salomon Juneau, a French-Canadian fur trader who cofounded Milwaukee, Wisconsin. Operated by Weyerhaeuser. Capt. Walter F. Graham's ship was torpedoed by a German midget submarine on April 9, 1945, off Boulogne, France, with the loss of two Armed Guard sailors. The ship was repaired and repatriated soldiers back to New York in August.

135. EDMUND FANNING, 2–43, 242929, KKQX (1769–1841) explorer and namesake of Fanning Atoll in the Central Pacific, now known as Tabuaeran. Operated by Isthmian.

136. PHINEAS BANNING, 2–43, 242990, KKSJ (1831–1885) noted for developing a port at Wilmington, California. Operated by Waterman.

137. EDMUND RANDOLPH, 2–43, 242987, KKSL (1753–1813) governor of Virginia, Secretary of State, and first the U.S. Attorney General. Operated by AGWI Lines.

138. EDWARD LIVINGSTON, 3–43, 242988, KKSM (1764–1836) New York and Louisiana congressman, Secretary of State, and minister to France. Operated by American West African.

139. JOSIAH ROYCE, 3–43, 243014, KKSO (1855–1916) noted realist philosopher and historian born in Grass Valley, California. Operated by Isbrandtsen.

140. DANIEL DRAKE, 3–43, 243013, KKSP (1785–1852) founder of the Ohio Medical College. Operated by United States Lines.

141. BENJAMIN LUNDY, 3–43, 243012, KKSQ (1789–1839) noted abolitionist. Operated by American-Hawaiian.

142. THEODORE DWIGHT WELD, 3–43, 243033, KKSS (1803–1895) noted abolitionist. Operated by Seas Shipping. In September 1941, Michael Formanack, 59, signed on as chief mate on the Shepard Steamship freighter *Sea Thrush* at New York. They arrived at New York from Durban, South Africa, on January 3, 1942. He had made the previous voyage and intended to stay aboard but took command of the *Weld*. On September 20, 1943, the ship was sunk by *U-238* off Iceland with the loss of 20 merchant crew, 13 Armed Guard sailors, and Capt. Formanack.

143. THEODORE PARKER, 3–43, 243032, KKSV (1810–1860) prominent Boston preacher, abolitionist, and social activist. Operated by AGWI Lines. Capt. Robert Vagner's ship hit a mine off England on November 16, 1944. There were no casualties and the ship was repaired.

144. JAMES G. BIRNEY, 3–43, 243030, KKSW (1792–1857) James Gillespie Birney was a lawyer, abolitionist, and Kentucky legislator. Operated by American West African.

145. LYDIA M. CHILD, 3–43, 243076, KKSZ (1802–1880) Lydia Maria Francis was a novelist, teacher, abolitionist, and poet who wrote *Over the River and Through the Wood*. She married David Lee Child in 1828. Operated by McCormick. Capt. Carl M. Enstrom's ship was torpedoed on April 27, 1943, by *I-178* off Australia. No casualties were reported.

146. RACHEL JACKSON, 3–43, 243078, KKTA (1767–1828) Rachel Donelson Robards, of Virginia, married Andrew Jackson in 1791 and again in 1794. Operated by Black Diamond.

147. MARIA MITCHELL, 3–43, 243077, KKTB (1818–1889) first American female professional astronomer who discovered "Miss Mitchell's Comet" in 1847. Operated by A. L. Burbank.

148. MARGARET FULLER, 3–43, 243088, KKTC (1810–1850) Sarah Margaret Fuller was the first full-time female journalist to review books and was Horace Greely's first female correspondent. In 1846 he sent her to Italy where she met Giovanni Ossili. In 1848 they had a son, Angelino, and in 1850 the family boarded the freighter *Elizabeth* for America. On July 19 all three perished when the ship went aground off Fire Island in heavy seas. Operated by AGWI Lines.

149. WILLIAM B. ALLISON, 3–43, 243089, KKTD (1829–1908) William Boyd Allison was an Iowa congressman. Operated by Waterman. Capt. Robert H. Sonneman's ship was hit by a Japanese aerial torpedo on May 24, 1945, with the loss of six merchant crew. The ship was taken over by the Navy and named *Inca* (IX-229) but on July 14 became *Gamage* (IX-227).

150. USS MINTAKA (AK-94), 3–43, NKGP, *Crater*-class cargo ship commissioned on May 10, 1943.

151. ALICE F. PALMER, 3–43, 243112, KKTF (1855–1902) Alice Elvira Freeman was a professor of history and president of Wellesley College when she married George Herbert Palmer. Operated by American President Lines. Capt. George Pederson's ship was torpedoed on July 10, 1943, by *U-177* in the Indian Ocean. There were no reported casualties. Capt. Pederson, 44, was from Silverdale, Washington. He and other survivors arrived at New York on October 17, 1943, on the Seas Shipping Co. steamer *Robin Tuxford*.

152. JAMES M. GOODHUE, 3–43, 243116, KKTI (1810–1852) James Madison Goodhue founded the *Minnesota Pioneer* in 1849, the state's first daily newspaper, today the *St. Paul Pioneer Press*. Namesake for Goodhue, Minnesota. The comic strip *Peanuts* got its start in the paper in 1947 as *Li'l Folks* by Charles Schultz. Operated by American West African.

153. HENRY H. SIBLEY, 3–43, 243115, KKTK (1811–1891) Henry Hastings Sibley was the first governor of Minnesota and a congressman from Wisconsin. Operated by American-Foreign.

154. HENRY M. RICE, 3–43, 243160, KKTL (1816–1894) Henry Mower Rice was a fur trader turned Minnesota senator. Operated by Alcoa.

155. JOHN S. PILLSBURY, 4–43, 243163, KKTN (1827–1901) John Sargent Pillsbury was a flour magnate and governor of Minnesota. Operated by Grace Line.

156. KNUTE NELSON, 4–43, 243164, KKTS (1843–1923) On February 2, 1843, a young lady, Ingebørg Haldorsdatter Kvilekval, had an out-of-wedlock son in Voss, Norway, that she named Knud Evanger. In 1849 they came to New York and when they landed she proclaimed herself a widow and he was Knud Helgeson Kvilekval. They made their way to Chicago to live with her brother Jon and in 1850 mom married Nils Olson Grotland. Nils called his new stepson Knud Nelson. The family moved to Wisconsin, Knud was wounded in the Civil War then became a lawyer, a Wisconsin politician, and Minnesota congressman, and governor as Knute Nelson. Operated by Seas Shipping.

157. JAMES B. WEAVER, 4–43, 243177, KKTU (1833–1912) James Baird Weaver was an Iowa congressman. Operated by International Freighting. Capt. Jim Sweeney, of Drexel, Pennsylvania, had a son in the Army "on the northern front" and the *Weaver* was the first American freighter to reach Antwerp, Belgium, on December 1, 1944. The front was only 60 miles

away. The first ship in was the British freighter *Fort Cataraqui*. The *Weaver* carried cranes, machinery, supplies, and 100 Army stevedores under Lt. Payne W. Labre, of Escanaba, Michigan, to get the port up and running again. Around 18,000 Belgians, unemployed since 1940, were also brought in to unload ships, store, and distribute goods.

158. SIMON NEWCOMB, 4–43, 243178, KKTX (1835–1909) Canadian-born astronomer, mathematician, economist, timekeeping scientist, and author who retired as a rear admiral with the Naval Observatory's Nautical Almanac department. Operated by Pope & Talbot.

159. AMY LOWELL, 4–43, 243175, KKUA (1874–1925) Amy Lawrence Lowell was a Massachusetts poet who won a 1926 Pulitzer Prize and reportedly consorted with Mercedes de Acosta. Operated by Seas Shipping.

160. WILLIAM G. FARGO, 4–43, 243191, KKUB (1818–1881) William George Fargo and Henry Wells founded the American Express company and in 1864 Wells Fargo & Co. in California. Operated by General Steamship.

161. WILLIAM JAMES, 4–43, 243190, KHPY (1842–1910) physician who was the first professor of psychology in America, at Harvard. Operated by American-Hawaiian.

162. JACQUES CARTIER, 4–43, 243187, KOAF (1491–1557) French explorer of North America and the first European to map the Gulf of Saint Lawrence. Operated by AGWI Lines.

163. STANFORD WHITE, 4–43, 243234, KOAH (1853–1906) noted architect of majestic homes and designer of the Pennsylvania Station. He was murdered on June 25, 1906, in a love triangle. Operated by United States Lines. Capt. Bernard B. Backston departed Los Angeles and arrived at New Orleans, possibly operated coastwise, then departed New Orleans in early September for England. Departed Liverpool on October 18 and arrived at New York on November 3. The ship was then taken by the War Department and converted to the Army hospital ship *Blanche F. Sigman*. 1st Lt. Blanche Faye Sigman, 36, was an Army nurse from Byesville, Ohio, who served in North Africa, survived a bombing at sea on the way to Italy, and was lost when a bomb hit the medical tent she was working in at Anzio on February 7, 1944. As her namesake ship passed the Anzio beachhead in October 1944, with hundreds of wounded aboard, the flag was lowered in her honor.

164. BENJAMIN N. CARDOZO, 4–43, 243220, KOAK (1870–1938) Benjamin Nathan Cardozo was a Constitutionalist Supreme Court justice who died on December 1, 1938, and was promptly replaced by New Dealer Felix Frankfurter. Operated by the Navy as the *Crater*-class cargo ship *Serpens* (AK-97), NJGY, commissioned on May 28, 1943.

165. WILLIAM CARSON, 4–43, 243236, KOAN (1825–1912) 49er from Canada who failed at mining but by 1853 had become a successful Humboldt Bay lumberman with partner John Dolbeer. Carson's spectacular mansion is a famous landmark in Eureka, California. Operated by Grace Line.

166. CHARLES H. WINDHAM, 4–43, 243241, KOAR (1871–1932) father and mayor of Long Beach, California, who spearheaded the building of the breakwater that created the harbor. Operated by American West African.

167. JUAN FLACO BROWN, 4–43, 243243, KOBB (1820–1859) In September 1846, Capt. Archibald Gillespie's troops were besieged by Mexican forces at Fort Hill, Los Angeles. Reinforcements were urgently needed. Robert Stockton was at Monterey so very early on the 23rd, John "Juan Flaco" Brown left Fort Hill but when he got to Monterey he learned Stockton was in San Francisco. He continued on, arrived the evening of the 26th, and reinforcements were sent. He was then known as the Paul Revere of California. Operated by De La Rama.

168. THADDEUS S. C. LOWE, 4–43, 243247, KOBC (1832–1913) Thaddeus Sobieski Constantine Lowe took photos from balloons during the Civil War, pioneering aerial

reconnaissance. In 1893 he and David J. McPherson built an incline scenic railway at Rubio Canyon on Echo Mountain north of Los Angeles and the Mount Lowe Railway ran until 1938. Operated by American-Hawaiian.

169. MIGUEL HIDALGO, 4–43, 243290, KOBL (1753–1811) Don Miguel Gregorio Antonio Ignacio Hidalgo-Costilla y Gallaga Mandarte Villaseñor was a priest and leader in the Mexican War of Independence. The *Hidalgo* was the first American ship christened with Mexican champagne, a rare cordon bleu from the Santo Tomas winery. Operated by American President Lines.

170. JOSIAH D. WHITNEY, 4–43, 243289, KOBI (1819–1896) Josiah Dwight Whitney was a Harvard geology professor and chief of the California Geological Survey. Operated by Matson Navigation for one voyage in the Pacific under Capt. Arvid Gosta (Gustav) Torleif Cahling then by the Navy as the *Livingston* (AP-163) commissioned on November 10, 1943.

171. WILLIAM M. GWIN, 4–43, 243292, KOBL (1805–1885) William McKendree Gwin was a physician and Mississippi congressman turned 49er who struck it rich and became a California legislator and senator. Operated by American President Lines for one voyage under Capt. Carl H. Hermance then by the Navy as the *Lesuth* (AK-125), NHCF, commissioned on November 1, 1943.

172. MARK KEPPEL, 4–43, 243303, KOBO (1867–1928) prominent Los Angeles County schools superintendent. Operated by Hammond.

173. WILEY POST, 4–43, 243306, KOBS (1890–1935) Wiley Hardeman Post was an aviation pioneer who discovered of the jet stream and was the first to fly solo around the world. He died in a crash with passenger Will Rogers in Alaska. Operated by Moore-McCormack.

174. GEORGE GERSHWIN, 5–43, 243300, KOBU (1898–1937) Broadway musical composer. Operated by American-Hawaiian.

175. GENERAL VALLEJO, 5–43, 243325, KKMU (1807–1890) Mariano Guadalupe Vallejo was a legislator, rancher, and military commander in Alta California. Namesake for Vallejo, California. Operated by Waterman for one voyage in the Pacific under Capt. Andrew J. Shrader then by the Navy as *Megrez* (AK-126), NHDX, commissioned on October 26, 1943.

176. ANDREW ROWAN, 5–43, 243324, KKGH (1857–1943) Andrew Summers Rowan was an Army officer during the Spanish-American War. It was vital that a message regarding reinforcements get to Cuban rebel leader Gen. Calixto Garcia. Rowan got through and his feat was immortalized as the "Message to Garcia." He died at San Francisco on January 11, 1943. Operated by Waterman for one voyage in the Pacific under Capt. John G. Jenson, arriving at San Diego on October 6, 1943. Operated by the Navy as the *Crater*-class cargo ship *Rutilicus* (AK-113), NTTZ, commissioned on October 30, 1943.

177. THOMAS HILL, 5–43, 243326, KOIW (1829–1908) popular painter of Western landscapes. Operated by AGWI Lines.

178. BENJAMIN D. WILSON, 5–43, 243359, KOJI (1811–1878) Benjamin Davis Wilson was a California pioneer and politician and the first non–Hispanic owner of Rancho San Pascual in Southern California. Operated by American West African.

179. EDWARD W. SCRIPPS, 5–43, 243360, KOJO (1854–1926) Edward Willis Scripps was a newspaper publisher, founder of the United Press Association, later the United Press International news service, and funded the Scripps Institution of Oceanography at La Jolla, California. Operated by Alcoa.

180. SUCHAN, 5–43, the Suchansky Rudnik geographical area was a vital coal source for the Russian Pacific fleet. Shortened to Suchan in 1932, and shortly thereafter changed to Gamarnik, after revolutionary commissar Yan Gamarnik, then back to Suchan in 1937. In 1972 the name became Partizansk. Operated under the Russian flag.

181. IGNACE PADEREWSKI, 5–43, 243374, KOKD (1860–1941) Ignacy Jan Paderewski was the Republic of Poland's second prime minister. Operated by T. J. Stevenson.

182. CHARLES LUMMIS, 5–43, 243369, KOKE (1859–1928) Charles Fletcher Lummis was a journalist, American Indian historian, and author. Operated by States Marine and converted to an Army troopship.

183. JEDEDIAH S. SMITH, 5–43, 243375, KOKF (1799–1831) Jedediah Strong Smith was a very early California and Oregon explorer, mountain man, author, cartographer, and pathfinder. Operated by R. A. Nicol.

184. JOSIAH NELSON CUSHING, 5–43, 243421, KOMI (1840–1905) Cushing was famous for his missionary work in Burma. The ship was sponsored by patriotic singer Kate Smith, known for her rendition of Irving Berlin's "God Bless America." Operated by American-Hawaiian.

185. JOHN BURROUGHS, 5–43–243420, KOMH (1837–1921) writer and naturalist prominent in the early conservation movement. Operated by Matson.

186. CHARLES CROCKER, 5–43, 243410, KOMF (1822–1888) one of the "Big Four" who founded the Central Pacific Railway and president of the Southern Pacific Railroad. Operated by American West African.

187. JOHN S. CASEMENT, 5–43, 243467, KOOQ (1829–1909) John Stephen "Jack" Casement was a noted Union general and railroad contractor. Operated by Luckenbach.

188. P. T. BARNUM, 5–43, 243470, KOOW (1810–1891) Phineas Taylor Barnum was a showman, hoaxster, promoter, and partner in the Barnum & Bailey circus. Operated by United States Lines.

189. THOMAS OLIVER LARKIN, 5–43, 243471, KOOX (1802–1858) the only American consul to the California Republic. Operated by the Navy as the *Bootes* (AK-99), NJTP, commissioned on July 5, 1943.

190. JOHN ALDEN, 6–43, 243493, KOQE (1599–1687) shipwright and cooper who was celebrated as the first person on the *Mayflower* to step ashore on Plymouth Rock. Signer of the Mayflower Compact and cofounder of Plymouth Colony. Operated by Sudden & Christenson.

191. JUAN BAUTISTA DE ANZA, 5–43, 243495, KOQN (1736–1788) Juan Bautista de Anza Bezerra Nieto was a Spanish explorer and governor of New Mexico. Operated by the Navy as the *Crater*-class cargo ship *Lynx* (AK-100), NAXK, commissioned on July 26, 1943.

192. LYMAN STEWART, 5–43, 243496, KOQO (1840–1923) cofounder of Union Oil of California. Operated by Coastwise.

193. CHARLES D. POSTON, 6–43, 243514, KOQU (1825–1902) Charles Debrille Poston, of Kentucky, was an Arizona pioneer known as the Father of Arizona, and the first Arizona Territory delegate to Congress. Operated by United States Lines.

194. CLARENCE DARROW, 6–43, 243515, KOQY (1857–1938) Clarence Steward Darrow was a famous lawyer and vigorous supporter of President Roosevelt but condemned the National Industrial Recovery Act of May 27, 1933 (NRA) as "ghastly." Operated by Matson.

195. JOSIAH EARL, 6–43, 243522, KORJ (1814–1892) pioneered refrigeration for the California fruit industry. Operated by Hammond.

196. FRANKLIN K. LANE, 6–43, 243586, KOWI (1864–1921) Franklin Knight Lane was Secretary of the Interior. Operated by W. R. Chamberlin.

197. JACOB S. MANSFIELD, 6–43, 243588, KOWK (1835–1894) Nevada newsman and Tucson merchant who donated land for the University of Arizona in 1886 and served as a regent. Operated by American President Lines.

198. JAMES H. MCCLINTOCK, 6–43, 243590, KOWP (1864–1934) James Henry

McClintock was an Arizona newspaperman and commander of the Rough Riders B Troop who was wounded on June 24, 1898, during the Spanish-American War. Operated by American President Lines for one voyage in the Pacific under Capt. James E. Barnhart. Arrived at San Francisco from Espiritu Santo on October 12, 1943, then operated by the Navy as the *Kenmore* (AP-162) commissioned on November 14, 1943.

199. DAVID E. HUGHES, 6–43, 243654, KXEZ (1831–1900) David Edward Hughes was a music professor who invented the teleprinter, spark-gap transmitter, and crystal radio set. Operated by States Marine.

200. BILLY MITCHELL, 6–43, 243648, KXED (1879–1936) Gen. William Mitchell commanded American air units in France during the Great War, became deputy director of the Army Air Service, and formed the belief that aircraft and aircraft carriers made battleships obsolete. His outspoken views got him busted to colonel and he was court-martialed for insubordination. In the end he was proved right and the "father of the Army Air Corps" is the only namesake for a military aircraft, the Mitchell B-25 bomber. Calship workers named the ship in his honor. Operated by Luckenbach.

201. JAMES SHIELDS, 6–43, 243659, KXFF (c. 1806–1879) Army general in the Mexican War, governor of the Oregon Territory, and a senator from Illinois, Minnesota, and Missouri. Operated by Matson.

202. EUGENE B. DASKAM, 6–43, 243683, KXFY (1841–1920) Eugene Benjamin Daskam was a federal monetary official. Operated by the Navy as the *Crater*-class cargo ship *Triangulum* (AK-102), NTWF, commissioned on July 30, 1943.

203. ANDREW T. HUNTINGTON, 6–43, 243679, KXGE (1842–1915) Andrew Tyler Huntington was the Treasury Department's chief of the Division of Loans & Currency for 25 years. Operated by American President Lines.

204. D. W. HARRINGTON, 6–43, 243680, KXGD (1837–1919) Delavan W. Harrington was a Treasury Department official. Operated by the Navy as the *Crater*-class cargo ship *Sculptor* (AK-103), NTTT, commissioned on August 10, 1943.

205. WILFRED GRENFELL, 6–43, 243710, KXMO (1865–1940) Sir William Thomason Grenfell was a British physician, missionary, and associate of Dwight L. Moody. In 1912 he founded the International Grenfell Association to aid fishermen in Newfoundland, Labrador, and lived in Vermont. Operated by Grace Line.

206. WILLIAM F. MACLENNAN, 6–43, 243711, KXMK (1840–1909) Treasury Department chief of the Division of Bookeeping & Warrants. Operated by Waterman.

207. FLORENCE CRITTENTON, 6–43, 243707, KXMT (1878–1882) Charles Nelson Crittenton (1833–1909) was a salesman who married Josephine Slosson in 1859. In 1861 he started selling patent medicines at 115 Fulton St. in New York and became very successful. The couple lived at 2019 Fifth Ave. Their first child, Charles, Jr., died of scarlet fever. Daughter Adeline was born in 1864 and in 1877 Florence arrived but when she was four she also died of scarlet fever. Her death devastated Crittenton and he retired from business and became a preacher and social activist. On April 19, 1883, he established the Florence Night Mission at 29 Bleeker St. in her honor to aid prostitutes and unwed mothers. By the 1950s the Florence Crittenton Homes Assoc., Inc., had 53 maternity homes in 28 states. The National Florence Crittenton Mission received a federal charter in 1898 and continues today. Operated by Waterman.

208. JOSEPH PRIESTLEY, 6–43, 243729, KXMU (1733–1804) electrical theorist who discovered oxygen and invented soda water. Operated by Coastwise (Pacific Far East) Line.

209. STEPHEN T. MATHER, 6–43, 243730, KXMV (1867–1930) Stephen Tyng Mather was a borax merchant who became the first director of the National Park Service. Operated by Luckenbach.

210. FRANK SPRINGER, 6–43, 243727, KXMW (1848–1927) president of Lucien B. Maxwell's Maxwell Land Grant Company and cofounder of the huge CS Cattle Co. with his brother Charles in New Mexico. Operated by American-Hawaiian.

211. FINLEY PETER DUNNE, 6–43, 243747, KXMX (1867–1936) popular writer for the Chicago Post. Operated by Seas Shipping.

212. MARINA RASKOVA, 7–43, 243754, KXNC (1912–1943) first female Soviet Air Force navigator and instructor. During World War II she commanded the all-female 125th Guards Bomber Aviation Regiment, one of three all-female Russian combat aviation regiments. She died in a forced landing accident on January 4, 1943. Operated by Norton Lilly.

213. CHARLES A. WARFIELD, 7–43, 243744, KXNF (1751–1813) Maryland physician and member of the Sons of Liberty who led a party of rebels to burn the brig *Peggy Stewart* at Annapolis on October 19, 1774. Owners James Dick and Anthony Stewart were smuggling tea from London on the account of Thomas C. Williams. Operated by Alcoa.

214. STEPHEN VINCENT BENET, 7–43, 243784, KXNG (1898–1943) Pennsylvania novelist and poet who wrote *John Brown's Body*. He died on March 13, 1943, in New York City. Operated by James Griffiths & Sons.

215. STEPHEN H. LONG, 7–43, 243783, KXNH (1784–1864) Stephen Harriman Long was an Army engineer, explorer, influential designer of steam locomotives, and a railroad pioneer. Operated by Luckenbach.

216. ANSON P. K. SAFFORD, 7–43, 243773, KXNJ (1830–1891) Anson Pacely Killen Safford was the third and 5'-6" "Little Governor" of the Arizona Territory. He was an education advocate, banker, and cofounder of Tarpon Springs, Florida. Operated by United States Lines.

217. WILLIAM R. NELSON, 7–43, 243845, KXNK (1841–1915) William Rockhill Nelson was a lawyer, Kansas City real estate developer, and founder and editor of the *Kansas City Star*. Operated by the Navy as the *Crater*-class cargo ship *Naos* (AK-105), NKSU, commissioned on July 16, 1943.

218. SAMHOLT, 7–43, 169673, MSLM, built for the British Ministry of War Transport. Operated by Cunard White Star.

219. SAMSON, 7–43, 169667, MSLN, built for the British Ministry of War Transport. Operated by Cunard White Star.

220. BILLY SUNDAY, 7–43, 243849, KXNO (1862–1935) William Ashley Sunday was a baseball player turned evangelist. Operated by Luckenbach.

221. SAMARITAN, 7–43, 167642, MSLP, built for the British Ministry of War Transport. Operated by Cunard White Star Line.

222. ZONA GALE, 7–43, 243859, KXNU (1874–1938) first female writer to win the Pulitzer Prize for drama and a founding member of the Lucy Stone League. In 1928 she married William L. Breese. Operated by American-Hawaiian and converted to an animal transport ship.

223. BRAND WHITLOCK, 7–43, 243887, KXNV (1869–1934) Joseph Brand Whitlock was a journalist, lawyer, mayor of Toledo, Ohio, and ambassador to Belgium. Operated by United States Lines.

224. VERNON L. KELLOGG, 7–43, 243895, KXNW (1867–1937) Vernon Lyman Kellogg was an entomology professor at Stanford, evolutionary biologist, director of the American Commission for Relief in Belgium, and an ex-pacifist. Operated by Grace Line.

225. HOWARD T. RICKETTS, 7–43, 243890, KXNX (1871–1910) Howard Taylor Ricketts was a pathologist who studied Rocky Mountain spotted fever and typhus, from which he died. Namesake for the Rickettsia bacteria. Operated by Luckenbach.

226. INA COOLBRITH, 7–43, 243910, KXWW (1841–1928) Don Carlos Smith and

Agnes Coolbrith Smith's daughter Josephine Anna Smith was born in Nauvoo, Illinois. Don was the brother of Mormon founder Joseph Smith. When Don died Agnes married Joseph Smith, Jr., but he was murdered in June 1844 and Agnes moved to St. Louis where she married William Pickett. In 1851 they went to Los Angeles where Agnes and "Josephina" used Coolbrith as their last name. After a disastrous marriage at 17 to Robert B. Carsley she became a teacher, published poetry, and became a San Francisco librarian and writer as Ina Coolbrith. Operated by Luckenbach.

227. ROBERT G. INGERSOLL, 7–43, 243913, KXNY (1833–1899) Robert Green Ingersoll was a political leader and famous orator known as the "Great Agnostic." Operated by Waterman.

228. SAMSURF, 8–43, 169639, BKXT, built for the British Ministry of War Transport. Operated by Cunard White Star.

229. ARTHUR P. DAVIS, 8–43, 244005, KXOF (1861–1933) Arthur Powell Davis was a civil engineer, hydrographer of the Panama Canal route, chief engineer of the Bureau of Reclamation in 1908, and in 1914 the director. He was the first engineer to suggest using dams to produce electrical power, primarily as a way to offset the cost of the dam by selling electricity. Operated by American West African.

230. SAMBLADE, 8–43, 169670, BKXV, built for the British Ministry of War Transport. Operated by Port Line.

231. WYATT EARP, 8–43, 244068, KXOI (1848–1929) Wyatt Berry Stapp Earp was a gambler and Kansas and Arizona law enforcement officer. Operated by the Navy as the *Crater*-class cargo ship *Caelum* (AK-106), NHLT, commissioned on October 22, 1943.

232. SAMBO, 8–43, built for the British Ministry of War Transport. Operated by Cunard White Star. Torpedoed on November 10, 1943, by *I-27* in the Gulf of Aden.

233. SAMSTEEL, 8–43, 169643, BKXX, built for the British Ministry of War Transport. Operated by Union-Castle Mail Steamship Co.

234. SAMPAN, 8–43, 169802, BKXY, built for the British Ministry of War Transport. Operated by Union-Castle Mail Steamship Co.

235. EDWIN ABBEY, 8–43, 244059, KXZT (1852–1911) Edwin Austin Abbey was a famous Philadelphia illustrator, artist, and muralist. Operated by Shepard.

236. SAMAROVSK, 8–43, 169827, BKXZ, launched as the *Henry M. Robinson*. Henry Mauris Robinson (1868–1936) was a U.S. Shipping Board commissioner and chairman of the Bituminous Coal Commission. The ship was transferred to the British Ministry of War Transport as *Samarovsk* but was operated by Lamport & Holt as the *Henry M. Robinson*. The *Robinson* was the first ship paid for by Calship workers with war bond purchases.

237. GEORGE KENNY, 8–43, 244061, KXZV (1823–1902) George Lee Kenny was employed as a clerk by publishers and booksellers James and George Derby in Buffalo, New York. in 1852 they decided to open a branch in San Francisco so they sent George and Hubert Howe Bancroft overland to get started and put $5,000 worth of stock on a ship going around the Horn. Before the merchandise got there George Derby died and the venture was called off. Kenny and Bancroft then opened their own stationary and bookstore. Operated by American West African.

238. DAVID R. FRANCIS, 8–43, 244098, KYAD (1850–1927) David Rowland Francis was mayor of St. Louis, governor of Missouri, Secretary of the Interior, and ambassador to Russia during World War I. Operated by Luckenbach.

239. THOMAS G. MASARYK, 8–43, 244103, KYAE (1850–1937) Tomáš Garrigue Masaryk was founder and first president of the Czecho-Slovak Republic. Operated by Seas Shipping. Capt. Robert H. Sloan's ship was torpedoed on April 16, 1944, by *U-407* about

seven miles off Dema, Libya. The ship was beached and the cargo salvaged. There were no reported casualties.

240. GUTZON BORGLUM, 8–43, 244101, KYAG (1871–1941) Gutzon de la Mothe Borglum was the sculptor of Stone Mountain, Georgia, and Mount Rushmore in South Dakota. Operated by Isthmian.

241. JOSEPH REYNOLDS, 8–43, 244135, KYAH (1785–1864) General in the War of 1812, judge, and New York congressman. Operated by Hammond.

242. SAMPEP, 8–43, 169795, BFNV, built for the British Ministry of War Transport. Operated by Houlder Bros. & Co.

243. DON MARQUIS, 9–43, 244175, KYKZ (1878–1937) popular comic writer. Operated by Oliver J. Olson. On September 27, 1944, Capt. Peter J. C. Johnson's ship collided with the 10,195-ton War Emergency Tankers, Inc, tanker *Missionary Ridge* south of Manus Island with the loss of three soldiers. The damaged ship was taken by the Navy and on May 31, 1945, became the *Don Marquis* (IX-215).

244. JOSEPH FRANCIS, 9–43, 244181, KYLA (1801–1893) inventor of the unsinkable lifeboat. Operated by Mississippi Shipping.

245. WILLIAM KELLY, 9–43, 244138, KYIF (1811–1888) college-educated metallurgist and partner in a Pittsburgh dry goods store. After a destructive fire, Kelly moved to Kentucky to get into the iron and steel business and in 1846 he bought an iron manufacturer in Eddyville. He began experimenting and soon developed the much-improved steel-making process Henry Bessemer would later patent. Operated by the Navy as the *Crater*-class cargo ship *Rotanin* (AK-108), NTTW, commissioned on November 23, 1943.

246. FRANK WIGGINS, 9–43, 244177, KYAN (1849–1924) Los Angeles agricultural and industrial booster, secretary of the Chamber of Commerce, and trade school founder. Operated by Isthmian.

247. SAMBUR, 9–43, 169946, BFNT, built for the British Ministry of War Transport. Operated by Ellerman's Wilson Line. In 1944 the name was changed to *Samwharfe*.

248. ALBERT P. RYDER, 9–43, 244206, KVLG (1847–1917) Albert Pinkham Ryder was an eccentric but very popular seascape artist. Operated by South Atlantic.

249. SAMARINDA, 9–43, 169672, BFNZ, built for the British Ministry of War Transport. Operated by T. & J. Harrison.

250. ALBINO PEREZ, 9–43, 244282, KYLI (unk.-1837) unpopular governor of New Mexico who was killed by rebels. Operated by American President Lines.

251. SAMTREDY, 9–43, 169668, BFNY, built for the British Ministry of War Transport. Operated by Prince Line.

252. SAMCALIA, 9–43, 169669, MYLK, built for the British Ministry of War Transport. Operated by Furness, Withy & Co.

253. SAMIDA, 9–43, 169721, MYLJ, built for the British Ministry of War Transport. Operated by P. & O. Steam Navigation. Torpedoed on April 9, 1945, in the English Channel by a German midget submarine.

254. SAMNEVA, 9–43, 169844, MYLF, built for the British Ministry of War Transport. Operated by Alfred Holt & Co.

255. SAMMONT, 9–43, 169846, MYLB, built for the British Ministry of War Transport. Operated by William Thomson & Co.

256. JOHN GOODE, 9–43, 244180, KYLL (1829–1909) John Goode, Jr., was a United States and Confederate States congressman from Virginia. Z-ET1-S-C3 operated by the Los Angeles Tanker Operators.

257. HENRY C. WALLACE, 9–43, 244178, KYLM (1866–1924) Henry Cartwell

"Harry" Wallace, of Ohio, published *Wallaces' Farmer* and was Secretary of Agriculture. Z-ET1-S-C3 operated by the Los Angeles Tanker Operators.

258. ALBERT J. BERRES, 9–43, 244319, KTNZ (1873–1940) Albert Julius Berres, Sr., was a prominent metal and printing trades union official and entertainment executive. Z-ET1-S-C3 operated by Union Oil Co, of California.

259. PAUL CHANDLER, 10–43, 244364, KTTB (1889–1943) Dr. Paul Gladstone Chandler was a school teacher in Kentucky, a professor at Kent State, and president of Clarion College. Operated by Stockard.

260. RICHARD J. CLEVELAND, 10–43, 244324, KTOB (1773–1860) Richard Jeffry Cleveland was a shrewd-trading shipmaster and popular author. Z-ET1-S-C3 operated by Pacific Tankers.

261. JOSIAH G. HOLLAND, 10–43, 244322, KTOG (1819–1881) Josiah Gilbert Holland was a novelist whose pen name was Timothy Titcomb and who cofounded *Scribner's Monthly*, in which his novels were serialized. Z-ET1-S-C3 operated by Pacific Tankers.

262. OSCAR F. BARRETT, 10–43, 244363, KTOJ (1860–1935) Oscar Fitzallen Barrett was a prominent boatbuilder, coal merchant, and tug and barge operator on the Ohio, Mississippi, and Missouri Rivers. Z-ET1-S-C3 operated by Pacific Tankers.

263. JAMES COOK, 10–43, 244359, KTOL (1728–1779) Royal Navy officer who commanded three major explorations in the Pacific Ocean. Z-ET1-S-C3 operated by Pacific Tankers.

264. CHRISTOPHER L. SHOLES, 10–43, 244462, KTOM (1819–1890) Christopher Latham Sholes was a newspaperman and inventor of the first practical typewriter featuring the "qwerty" keyboard in use today. Z-ET1-S-C3 operated by Pacific Tankers.

265. ORSON D. MUNN, 10–43, 244469, KTON (1824–1907) Orson Desaix Munn was editor and publisher of *Scientific American* magazine. Z-ET1-S-C3 operated by Union Oil of California.

266. ALAN SEEGER, 10–43, 244457, KTOU (1888–1916) American poet who was lost at Belloy-en-Santerre during the Battle of the Somme on July 4, 1916, while serving with the French Foreign Legion. Z-ET1-S-C3 operated by the Los Angeles Tanker Operators.

267. HORACE SEE, 10–43, 244514, KTRA (1835–1909) chief engineer at Wm. Cramp & Son who was instrumental in bringing triple and quadruple expansion engines to the United States and for making significant improvements in their operation. Z-ET1-S-C3 operated by Pacific Tankers.

268. CARLETON ELLIS, 10–43, 244511, KTRL (1876–1941) noted chemist who held 753 patents and invented margarine, polyester, paint remover, and gasoline additives. Z-ET1-S-C3 operated by Pacific Tankers.

269. CHARLOTTE P. GILMAN, 10–43, 244512, KTRS (1860–1935) little Charlotte Perkins lost herself in reading during a difficult childhood. In 1884 she married Charles Stetson, had a daughter, and left the marriage four years later. In 1900 she married her first cousin, Houghton Gilman, a Wall Street attorney, and went on to become a prominent feminist, social activist, and writer. Z-ET1-S-C3 operated by the Los Angeles Tanker Operators.

270. MORTON PRINCE, 10–43, 244541, KTRX (1854–1929) Morton Henry Prince was a physician, neurologist, and pioneer of psychology. Z-ET1-S-C3 operated by Pacific Tankers.

271. HARVEY W. WILEY, 10–43, 244539, KUJV (1844–1930) Harvey Washington Wiley was a chemist who advocated for the Pure Food & Drug Act of 1906 and was first commissioner of the Food & Drug Administration. Z-ET1-S-C3 operated by Pacific Tankers.

272. JOHN H. MARION, 11–43, 244540, KUJW (1835–1891) John Huguenot Marion

was a Louisiana printer who became a miner in Arizona then in 1867 was co-owner of the *Prescott Miner* newspaper and editor of the *Arizona Courier*. Z-ET1-S-C3 operated by Pacific Tankers.

273. JOHN P. ALTGELD, 11–43, 244594, KUKN (1847–1902) John Peter Altgeld was governor of Illinois. Z-ET1-S-C3 operated by Pacific Tankers.

274. BEYLGOROD, 11–43, Beylgorod-Dnestrovski is a port city in southwest Ukraine. Z-ET1-S-C3 operated under the Russian flag.

275. MAIKOP, 11–43, capital of the Republic of Adygeya, Russia. Z-ET1-S-C3 operated under the Russian flag.

276. SCHUYLER COLFAX, 11–43, 244655, KULH (1823–1885) Schuyler Colfax, Jr., was an Indiana congressman and vice president. Z-ET1-S-C3 operated by the Los Angeles Tanker Operators.

277. SIDNEY HOWARD, 11–43, 244656, KULI (1891–1939) Sidney Coe Howard wrote the screenplay for *Gone with the Wind*. Z-ET1-S-C3 operated by the Navy as the *Armadillo* (IX-111) commissioned on November 18, 1943.

278. DAVID RITTENHOUSE, 11–43, 244650, KULL (1732–1796) first director of the U.S. Mint. Z-ET1-S-C3 operated by the Navy as the *Beagle* (IX-112) commissioned on November 20, 1943.

279. WILLIAM H. CARRUTH, 11–43, 244682, KULS (1859–1924) William Herbert Carruth was a noted professor of comparative literature at Stanford University. Z-ET1-S-C3 operated by the Navy as the *Camel* (IX-113) commissioned on November 22, 1943.

280. NATHANIEL B. PALMER, 11–43, 244679, KULU (1799–1877) Nathaniel Brown Palmer was a seal hunter, Antarctic explorer, clipper ship designer, and sea captain who discovered Palmer Island. Namesake for Palmer Archipelago. Z-ET1-S-C3 operated by the Navy as the *Caribou* (IX-114) commissioned on November 25, 1943.

281. WILLIAM WINTER, 11–43, 244683, KUMA (1836–1917) dramatic critic and author. Z-ET1-S-C3 operated by the Navy as the *Elk* (IX-115) commissioned on November 26, 1943.

282. CYRUS K. HOLLIDAY, 11–43, 244731, KUMP (1826–1900) Cyrus Kurtz Holliday was a cofounder of Topeka, Kansas, and first president of the Atchison, Topeka & Santa Fe Railway. Z-ET1-S-C3 operated by the Navy as the *Gazelle* (IX-116) commissioned on November 29, 1943.

283. RALPH A. CRAM, 12–43, 244757, KUYZ (1863–1942) Ralph Adam Cram was a noted Gothic style architect. Operated by Smith & Johnson.

284. JOHN A. ROEBLING, 12–43, 244751, KVCP (1806–1869) Johann August Röbling was an engineer and wire rope manufacturer who designed a bridge in Brooklyn that used a lot of wire rope. Operated by Mississippi Shipping.

285. ORLAND LOOMIS, 12–43, 244756, KVCY (1893–1942) Otland Steen "Spike" Loomis was a lawyer and Wisconsin politician who was elected governor in 1942 but died on December 7, 1942, from a heart attack before taking office. Operated by American West African.

286. SYLVESTER PATTIE, 12–43, 244832, KVGW (1782–1828) fur trapper in New Mexico whose party reached California on March 12, 1828. They were arrested by Mexican authorities ten days later as Spanish spies and imprisoned at San Diego. Pattie died on April 24 becoming the first American buried in California soil. Operated by Pacific-Atlantic.

287. LEOPOLD DAMROSCH, 12–43, 244829, KVGZ (1832–1885) Prussian physician and noted New York orchestra conductor. Operated by Isthmian.

288. JOHN DAVEY, 12–43, 244842, KUWU (1846–1923) English-born agriculturist

who came to the United States in the 1870s and started a landscaping and greenhouse business in Ohio. He branched out into tree care in 1880 as the Davey Tree Expert Co. at Warren, Ohio, and is considered the father of tree surgery, greatly contributing to agriculture. Operated by American-Hawaiian.

289. MEYER LISSNER, 12–43, 244880, KUWZ (1871–1930) lawyer who organized the Los Angeles City Club in 1907, founded the Good Government Fund in 1911, edited the *California Outlook*, was a member of the U.S. Shipping Board, and founded the State Industrial Accident Commission. Operated by Waterman.

290. EDWARD PAINE, 12–43, 244827, KVGU (1745–1841) Ohio pioneer, trader, and founder of Painesville, Ohio. Operated by United States Lines.

291. FRANKLIN H. KING, 12–43, 244875, KUXA (1848–1911) Franklin Hiram King was an agricultural soil scientist and inventtor of the grain storage silo. Operated by AGWI Lines.

292. BEN B. LINDSEY, 12–43, 244873, KVHA (1869–1943) Benjamin Barr Lindsey was a judge in Colorado who became a noted marriage, family, and juvenile delinquency expert. Regarded as the father of the juvenile court who also served as a Los Angeles Superior Court judge. He died on March 26, 1943, at Los Angeles. Operated by Interocean.

293. HENRY MILLER, 12–43, 244841, KUWT (1858–1896) waterboy for telegraph linemen and a lineman who became the first president of the National Brotherhood of Electrical Workers in 1890. On July 10, 1896, Miller was working on a power pole in Washington, D.C., when he suffered a severe electric shock and fell from the pole. Operated by Moore-McCormack. Capt. Charles W. Spears's ship was torpedoed by *U-870* on January 3, 1945, off Gibraltar. Chief Mate Nikolais Grinins, 36 Lee Ave., Yonkers, New York, was on the monkey bridge when the torpedo hit. He fell to the deck and was showered with burning oil, catching his clothes on fire. The crew got the fires out and then got off the ship in two lifeboats. A skeleton crew went back aboard later and got the ship going. There were no reported casualties and the ship made port on April 23.

294. PHILIP C. SHERA, 12–43, 244917, KVHF (1905–1942) Philip Carter Shera was a 3rd assistant engineer lost on the *Java Arrow*, torpedoed on May 5, 1942, by *U-333* off Vero Beach, Florida. Shera was awarded the Merchant Marine Distinguished Service medal posthumously for remaining alone in the engine room to answer bells before a second torpedo hit. Shera's son, Philip C., Jr., was an engineer in 1945. Operated by American-Hawaiian.

295. JOHN W. SEARLES, 12–43, 244843, KUWW (1828–1897) John Wemple Searles discovered borax in the Mohave Desert in 1862 and started the San Bernardino Borax Mining Co. in 1873. Namesake for Searles Lake and Valley. Operated by General Steamship.

296. JAMES W. JOHNSON, 12–43, 244915, KVHJ (1871–1938) James Weldon Johnson was an African-American lawyer, writer, and leader in the National Association for the Advancement of Colored People. Operated by Coastwise (Pacific Far East) Line.

297. CARL R. GRAY, 12–43, 244729, KUYN (1867–1939) Carl Raymond Gray was president of the Great Northern and Union Pacific Railroads. Z-ET1-S-C3 operated by the Navy as the *Gemsbok* (IX-117) commissioned on December 3, 1943.

298. SANFORD B. DOLE, 12–43, 244765, KUYT (1844–1926) Sanford Ballard Dole was a lawyer, president of the Republic of Hawaii, and governor of the Territory of Hawaii in 1910. Z-ET1-S-C3 operated by the Navy as the *Giraffe* (IX-118) commissioned on December 12, 1943.

299. SHERWOOD ANDERSON, 12–43, 244918, KVHB (1876–1941) noted author, copywriter, and Ohio businessman. Operated by Moore-McCormack Lines.

300. NICHOLAS LONGWORTH, 12–43, 244764, KUYW (1783–1863) pioneered

grape cultivation and winemaking in America. Z-ET1-S-C3 operated by the Navy as the *Ibex* (IX-119) commissioned on December 13, 1943.

301. CHARLES T. YERKES, 12–43, 244761, KUYX (1837–1905) Charles Tyson Yerkes was a controversial developer who controlled much of the "L" transportation system in Chicago and funded the Yerkes Observatory. Z-ET1-S-C3 operated by the Navy as the *Jaguar* (IX-120) commissioned on December 15, 1943.

302. JOHN H. QUICK, 12–43, 244929, KVHK (1861–1925) John Herbert Quick was a lawyer and noted Iowa novelist known as Herbert Quick. Operated by AGWI Lines.

303. CHARLES FORT, 12–43, 244925, KVHN (1874–1932) Charles Hoy Fort was a popular science writer and investigator of "anomalous phenomena." Operated by Seas Shipping.

304. JOHN DREW, 12–43, 244928, KVHO (1853–1927) John Drew, Jr., was a noted stage actor, the "leading matinee idol of his day," and the uncle of John, Ethel, and Lionel Barrymore. He died in San Francisco on July 9, 1927. Operated by Sudden & Christenson.

305. WILLIAM WOLFSKILL, 12–43, 244950, KVHS (1798–1866) Southern California citrus pioneer who developed the Valencia orange. Operated by Union Sulphur.

306. HART CRANE, 1–44, 244945, KVHT (1899–1932) Harold Hart Crane was a poet from Ohio. Operated by Alcoa.

307. JACK SINGER, 1–44, 244916, KVQS (1914–1942) sports reporter with the *Journal-American* who was in Florida covering the New York Giants in the spring of 1942 when he was hired by the International News Service as a war correspondent. He was on the carrier *Wasp* (CV-7) on September 15, 1942, off Guadalcanal when the ship was torpedoed by *I-19* and he was mortally wounded. He lived with his wife, Etta, 24, at 2325 Morris Ave. in the Bronx. Operated by American West African. Capt. Julius M. Jacobsen's ship was damaged by a Japanese aerial torpedo on August 10, 1945, at Naha, Okinawa. There were no reported casualties. The ship was further damaged by Typhoon Louise on October 9, 1945, and declared a total constructive loss.

308. CHARLES PADDOCK, 1–44, 244980, KVQV (1900–1943) Charles William Paddock was a World War I Marine veteran, Olympic sprinter, and newspaperman. In 1943 Capt. Paddock was in the Marine Corps as an aide to Maj. Gen. William Peterkin Upshur when both died in a plane crash near Sitka, Alaska, on July 21 during an inspection tour. A pair of Paddock's track shoes was carried aboard the ship in a glass case. Operated by Seas Shipping.

309. EDWARD J. O'BRIEN, 1–44, 244981, KVQZ (1890–1941) Edward Joseph Harrington O'Brien was a noted poet, editor, and author of *The Best American Short Stories*. Operated by General Steamship.

310. HENRY L. GANTT, 1–44, 244983, KVRB (1861–1919) Henry Laurence Gantt was an engineer and pioneer of efficient industrial project management. Operated by American-Hawaiian.

311. WILLIAM GLACKENS, 1–44, 245012, KVRG (1870–1938) William James Glackens was a realist artist and cofounder the Ashcan School of American art. Operated by Isthmian.

312. AUGUSTIN STAHL, 1–44, 245003, KVRM (1842–1917) Puerto Rican physician and scientist who advocated for independence. Operated by Polarus.

313. JULIAN W. MACK, 1–44, 245008, KVRN (1866–1943) Julian William Mack was a federal judge, social activist, and cofounder of the American Jewish Committee. He died on September 5, 1943. Operated by American President Lines.

314. CLARENCE H. MATSON, 1–44, 245037, KVRP (1872–1943) Clarence Henry

Matson was manager of the Department of Foreign Commerce and Shipping with the Los Angeles Chamber of Commerce and co-developer of the Los Angeles–Long Beach Harbor. He died in Los Angeles on October 17, 1943. Operated by Matson.

315. JAMES A. WILDER, 1–44, 245038, KVRR (1868–1934) James Austin Wilder was a travel author who organized the Sea Scouts in Hawaii and became Chief Sea Scout of the Boy Scouts of America. Operated by Pope & Talbot.

316. CAROLE LOMBARD, 1–44, 245036, KVRT (1908–1942) Jane Alice Peters was an actress who was lost when TWA Flight 3 hit a mountain just west of Las Vegas, Nevada. She was returning to California from a War Bond tour in her home state of Indiana. Operated by Black Diamond.

317. ALLEN C. BALCH, 2–44, 254049, KVWZ (1864–1943) Allen Christopher Balch was a Cornell-trained electrical and mechanical engineer who partnered with William G. Kerckhoff to found the Pacific Light & Power Co. in California in 1902 and retired as president of San Joaquin Light & Power. Operated by American President Lines.

318. RAYMOND T. BAKER, 2–44, 245055, KVXM (1877–1935) Raymond Thomas Baker was a mining financier, ambassador to Russia, and director of the U.S. Mint. Operated by Coastwise Line.

319. A. B. HAMMOND, 2–44, 245047, KVWY (1848–1934) Andrew Benoni Hammond was a Pacific Northwest railroad, lumber, and shipping magnate. Operated by Hammond.

320. ELINOR WYLIE, 2–44, 245113, KWCC (1885–1928) Elinor Morton Hoyt married Philip Hichborn in 1906, divorced, and took up with married lawyer Horace Wylie. They ran off to England and she became a famous poet and novelist. Operated by McCormick. Capt. Gustav Winsens left Los Angeles in February 1944 and arrived at New York on July 10 from Port Said, Egypt. Capt. David A. Jones took over and expected to leave the Bayonne Navy Depot on April 19. The ship hit a mine on October 6, 1944, off France. There were no reported casualties. The ship was taken over by the Navy and became the USS *Triana* (IX-223).

321. JOHN DOCKWEILER, 2–44, 245115, KWCF (1895–1943) John Francis Dockweiler was a lawyer and California congressman who died on January 31, 1943. Operated by Interocean.

322. HENRY E. HUNTINGTON, 2–44, 245114, KWCD (1850–1927) Henry Edwards Huntington was Collis Huntington's nephew who owned the Pacific Electric Railway in Los Angeles. Operated by United States Lines.

323. RUSSELL H. CHITTENDEN, 3–44, 245209, KWKR (1856–1943) Russell Henry Chittenden was a noted Yale biochemistry professor who pioneered digestive and nutritional subjects. Operated by McCormick. Stranded on Vassel Island off New Guinea on March 13, 1945.

324. DAVID A. CURRY, 2–44, 245155, KWFP (1860–1917) Indiana natives David Alexander Curry and his wife Jennie were furniture dealers in Palo Alto, California, when they opened Camp Curry in Yosemite Valley in 1899. The camp offered affordable lodging in a dozen tents with a common dining area and entertainment. The Currys lived with Jennie's parents, Robert and Margery Foster at 837 Cowper St. with their son David F., 11, and daughters Mary, 5, and Margery 4. They opened a new and used furniture store at 336 University Ave. David died at Camp Curry on April 30, 1917. Operated by South Atlantic.

325. J. FRANK COOPER, 3–44, 245208, KWKV (1885–1943) James Frank Cooper was a Goodyear Tire & Rubber Co. balloon and blimp designer who invented the rubber life raft. Operated by De La Rama.

326. SHERMAN O. HOUGHTON, 2–44, 245158, KWGI (1828–1914) Sherman Otis

Houghton was a Mexican War veteran and 49er who struck it rich, became a lawyer, and a California congressman. Operated by Pope & Talbot.

327. OSCAR UNDERWOOD, 2–44, 245157, KWGL (1862–1929) Oscar Wilder Underwood was an Alabama congressman. Operated by Seas Shipping.

328. HORATIO ALLEN, 2–44, 245206, KWKN (1802–1889) New York civil engineer who was chief engineer of the Delaware & Hudson Canal Co. When the company wanted to start a rail line in 1828, Allen was sent to England to buy a locomotive and he purchased a brand-new one built in Stourbridge by Foster, Rastrick & Co. The next year it became the first steam locomotive in America, the *Stourbridge Lion*, and ran at Honesdale, Pennsylvania. Operated by Burns.

329. ROBERT L. HAGUE, 3–44, 245285, KWKX (1880–1939) Robert Lyons Hague was marine superintendent, vice president, and director of Standard Oil of New Jersey. During World War I he was in charge of the U.S. Shipping Board's Steel Construction division in San Francisco. Operated by Alaska Steamship.

330. I. N. VAN NUYS, 3–44, 245280, KWKY (1836–1912) Isaac Newton Van Nuys was a merchant and real estate developer who founded Van Nuys, California. Operated by Burns.

331. JOE FELLOWS, 3–44, 245345, KXLZ (1865–1942) In 1907, Joseph Fellows opened the Joe Fellows Yacht & Launch Co. at Wilmington, California, and in 1917 he partnered with Victor Stewart to become the legendary Fellows & Stewart, Inc. Operated by Pope & Talbot.

332. C. K. MCCLATCHY, 4–44, 245342, KWSG (1858–1936) Charles Kenny McClatchy was the editor of the *Sacramento Bee* and founder of McClatchy Newspapers. Operated by Matson.

333. IDA M. TARBELL, 3–44, 245279, KWLL (1857–1944) Ida Minerva Tarbell, of Pennsylvania, was a teacher who pioneered investigative journalism, wrote popular biographies, lectured, and became a muckraker who thouroughly disliked John D. Rockefeller and Standard Oil in general for destroying her father's independent oil business. She died on January 6, 1944, at Bridgeport, Connecticut. Operated by American Mail Line.

334. PETER LASSEN, 4–44, 245513, WDDR (1800–1859) Danish-born explorer who walked the Oregon Trail to the California Trail then blazed the Lassen Cutoff. He was shot under mysterious circumstances in Virginia on April 26, 1859, while prospecting with two others. Namesake for Lassen County, California. Operated by W. R. Chamberlin.

335. FREDERICK C. HICKS, 3–44, 245343, KWCG (1872–1925) born Frederick Hicks Cocks. Hicks became a New York congressman, banker, and Alien Property Custodian. Operated by Union Sulphur.

336. MARTIN JOHNSON, 5–44, 245512, WCZO (1884–1937) Martin Elmer Johnson was a noted wildlife photographer and travel writer with wife Osa Helen Johnson. Martin and Osa were aboard a Western Air Express plane that crashed near Newhall, California. Osa survived. Operated by Shepard.

Delta Shipbuilding Co., Inc.
740 S. Claiborne Ave., New Orleans, Louisiana

The 8-way, 150-acre jointly-owned yard under Chief Engineer Marion Heath was established in 1941 as a subsidiary of the American Ship Building Co. of Lorain, Ohio. The Maritime Commission leased the land and spent $13,072,523 for facilities. The first keel was laid on

October 1, 1941. The yard built 132 Liberty dry cargo ships, 32 Liberty tankers, and 24 Liberty colliers for a total of 188. The average building time for the ships was 82.8 days.

1. WILLIAM C.C. CLAIBORNE, 5–42, 241641, KFWQ (c. 1773–1817) William Charles Cole Claiborne was a Tennessee congressman, governor of the Mississippi Territory, and first governor of the state of Louisiana. Operated by Mississippi Shipping.

2. T. J. JACKSON, 6–42, 241821, KFRX (1824–1863) Thomas Jonathan "Stonewall" Jackson was a Confederate general. Operated by Mississippi Shipping.

3. THOMAS B. ROBERTSON, 7–42, 241822, KFQT (1779–1828) Thomas Bolling Robertson was a Louisiana congressman, governor, and federal judge. Operated by Mississippi Shipping.

4. ABRAHAM BALDWIN, 7–42, 241952, KEXH (1754–1807) Georgia representative in the Continental Congress and founder and president of the University of Georgia, the first state-chartered institution of higher learning in the United States. Operated by Mississippi Shipping.

5. THEODORIC BLAND, 7–42, 241956, KFPT (1741–1790) Theodorick Bland, Jr., was a physician who served in the Revolutionary War and represented Virginia at the Continental Congress and in the first Congress. Operated by United Fruit. In July 1945 Capt. Peder Pederson's ship was under charter by the Army when he left Baltimore. The same month, a Tunisian Axis prisoner of war, Alfredo Raffaele Pumilia, 24, escaped and attempted to surrender to the Army but wouldn't take him. That November the *Bland* was at Casablanca when Alfredo saw a chance of getting to his uncle, Pietro Buttacavoli, in Brooklyn. He disguised himself as part of an 8-man Army detail that was assigned to the ship, slipped away, and found a nice hiding place. He was discovered in short order but no authority would admit him at any port the ship touched, including Antwerp, Belgium. He was still aboard when the *Bland* reached Baltimore on January 1, 1946, and then New York on the 18th. He was interviewed there and told a reporter, sadly, "The people and country here are very free." He was turned over to the Department of Justice and deported on December 11.

6. BENJAMIN CONTEE, 8–42, 241953, KEZA (1755–1815) Episcopal priest and Maryland delegate to the Confederation Congress. Operated by Mississippi Shipping. Capt. Even Evenson's ship was hit by an aerial torpedo on August 16, 1943, off Bone, Algeria, with 1,800 Italian prisoners of war aboard, of whom 264 were lost. The ship made Bone on the 18th. Messman Clyde M. Walker, 28, was hospitalized at Bone, on October 27. Capt. William H. F. Muir came aboard on January 4, 1944, at Gibraltar and took the ship to New York, arriving on January 24. The ship was scuttled off Normandy as part of Gooseberry 1. Capt. Evenson was awarded the Merchant Marine Distinguished Service medal.

7. GEORGE GALE, 8–42, 242100, KFFR (1756–1815) Continental Army veteran and Maryland congressman. Operated by Mississippi Shipping.

8. WILLIAM B. GILES, 8–42, 242187, KFUJ (1762–1830) William Branch Giles was a Virginia congressman and governor. Operated by Mississippi Shipping.

9. JONATHAN GROUT, 9–42, 242184, KFJQ (1737–1807) represented Massachusetts in the first Congress and built the first semaphore telegraph in the United States. Visual signals were transmitted from tower to tower across a distance. Grout's telegraphic system went from Martha's Vineyard to Boston. Operated by Mississippi Shipping.

10. DANIEL HUGER, 9–42, 242181, KFBS (1779–1854) South Carolina senator. Operated by Mississippi Shipping. Capt. James B. Adams' ship was hit by a bomb at Bone, Algeria, on May 9, 1943, with the loss of third mate Bernard Goulden and one Armed Guard sailor. The ship was repaired. Capt. Adams, chief mate Foster DeWight Carpenter, purser

Alexander Waigandt, second cook Paul I. Valentine, deck cadet Elmer C. Donnelly, and engine cadet Phil Cox Vannais were awarded the Merchant Marine Distinguished Service medal for heroic attempts to control fires and save the ship.

11. GEORGE LEONARD, 9–42, 242241, KFFT (1729–1819) lawyer, judge, Massachusetts congressman, of the famous Massachusetts Leonards. Operated by United Fruit.

12. ANDREW MOORE, 10–42, 242296, KEYN (1752–1821) Continental Army captain at Saratoga and Virginia congressman. Operated by North Atlantic & Gulf.

13. JOSIAH PARKER, 10–42, 242368, KFKD (1751–1810) Virginia congressman. Operated by Mississippi Shipping (Delta Line).

14. THOMAS SCOTT, 10–42, 242416, KFRM (1739–1796) Pennsylvania congressman who is said to have proposed siting the capital on the banks of the Potomac River. Operated by Waterman. Capt. Jack A. Teston's ship was torpedoed on February 17, 1945, by *U-968* off Kola Inlet, Russia. No casualties were reported. Survivors left Southampton, England, on the United States Lines motorship *John Ericsson* and arrived at New York on April 16.

15. JOSHUA SENEY, 10–42, 242415, KFKB (1756–1798) Maryland congressman. Operated by Black Diamond.

16. THOMAS SINNICKSON, 11–42, 242447, KFRN (1744–1817) New Jersey congressman. Operated by Stockard. Capt. Joseph Linder's ship was torpedoed on July 7, 1943, by *U-185* off Brazil with the loss of one Armed Guard sailor.

17. JONATHAN STURGES, 11–42, 242453, KFJS (1740–1819) Connecticut congressman. Operated by Mississippi Shipping. Capt. Thorbjorn Leerburg's ship was torpedoed on February 23, 1943, by *U-707* in the North Atlantic with the loss of 29 merchant crew and 22 Armed Guard sailors.

18. JONATHAN TRUMBULL, 11–43, 242547, KFJV (1710–1785) governor of Connecticut Colony and the State of Connecticut governor. Namesake for Trumbull, Connecticut. Operated by United Fruit.

19. JOHN VINING, 11–42, 242591, KHQH (1758–1802) Delaware congressman. Operated by Standard Fruit.

20. ALEXANDER WHITE, 12–42, 242650, KIBN (1738–1804) Virginia congressman. Operated by American South African.

21. HENRY WYNKOOP, 12–42, 242603, KIBT (1737–1816) Pennsylvania congressman. Operated by United Fruit. Capt. Glen P. Feltus, 52, left New York on February 28, 1943, for Loch Ewe, Scotland, in Convoy HX 228. Very early on the morning of March 11 the Italian sub *Torelli* torpedoed the British steamer *Orari* and just about the same time, around 1 a.m., the *Wynkoop* struck a submerged object and rolled violently. Loud noises were heard and everyone assumed they had been torpedoed. Capt. Feltus ordered the ship hove to and lifeboats lowered but in the excitement No. 3 boat was let go too fast and capsized apparently with 2nd cook John Wood Fox, 29, of West Virginia, messman John A. Brudnok, 18, and radio operator William R. Fletcher, Jr., in it and they were lost in the sea. According to Navy gunner William B. Tinneny, of Philadelphia, a sub surfaced in front of the *Wynkoop* and began shelling the ship ahead of them. Ens. John Theodore McNaughton's Armed Guard crew got the ship's 4-inch stern gun going. At this time oil was observed spread all over the sea. More lifeboats were launched and rafts let go with 26 merchant crew and seven Armed Guard sailors in them. Two Armed Guard sailors who got off, Thomas J. Phillips, SM3c, and Eugene P. Walsh, S1c, were apparently picked up by rescue vessels. Chief cook Henry Homer Howerton, 48, bosun John William Mugford, 52, three gunners, one able seaman, and one ordinary seaman were brought aboard when the motor-lifeboat they were in came alongside after daylight but it was too rough to recover the lifeboat. Two lifeboats were missing, one with five Navymen and the

other with 26 merchant seamen were not accounted for bur apparently rejoined the ship later. Capt. Feltus was rerouted to Belfast, Northern Ireland, and arrived there on the 15th. On March 19 radio operator Burwell G. Atwood, 32, signed on. The next day Capt. Feltus left the ship and chief mate Jessie Howard Sheffield took over as master. On April 5, at Oban, Ireland, British subject John J. Hern, 60, signed as chief mate. The ship then went to Mullwall Docks in London and on June 9 two more British subjects signed on: 2nd cook & baker James H. McKenzie, 56, and Walter A. J. Overton, 31, galley utility. The ship arrived at Pier 9, North River, New York, on July 9 from London. Capt. Sheffield stayed on and expected to sail on July 23rd. In the meantime, Capt. Feltus, of 4111 Ithaca St., Long Island, New York, arrived at New York on April 3, 1943, on the *Queen Elizabeth* from Gourock, Scotland. John Brudnok had signed on for his first voyage at New York on October 22, 1942, on the *Benjamin Hawkins*, the ship's maiden voyage, as a messman and arrived back at New York on January 10, 1943, from Safi, French Morocco. He paid off and signed on the *Wynkoop*. It was assumed the object the she ship struck was a submarine from the wolf pack that attacked the convoy.

22. SAMUEL JORDAN KIRKWOOD, 12–42, 242634, KKEN (1813–1894) Iowa governor and Secretary of the Interior. Operated by A. H. Bull. Capt. Samuel Olsen's ship was torpedoed on May 6, 1943, by *U-195* off Ascension Island. There were no reported casualties. The survivors left Durban on May 7 aboard the Seas Shipping Co. (Robin Line) steamer *Robin Tuxford* and arrived at New York on June 11. Capt. Olsen was awarded the Merchant Marine Distinguished Service medal.

23. ABRAHAM LINCOLN, 12–42, 24265, KKEO (1809–1865) 16th President of the United States. Operated by United Fruit.

24. PAT HARRISON, 1–43, 242721, KKES (1881–1941) Byron Patton "Pat" Harrison was a Mississippi senator known as the "Gadfly of the Senate" for his schmoozing abilities. Operated by Standard Fruit. Capt. Karl H. Kellar, 56, left New Orleans in January 1943, arrived at New York from Nuevitas, Cuba, on March 5, and expected to sail from Hoboken, New Jeresy, on or about March 14 for Boston. On May 8 the ship hit a mine in Gibraltar Harbor. Oiler Lawrence M. Keddie and fireman/watertender Anthony Kunitsky, 18, were lost. Chief engineer Michael Stevens was awarded the Merchant Marine Distinguished Service medal for rescuing a seriously injured fireman/watertender from the engine room.

25. LEONIDAS POLK, 1–43, 242794, KKHW (1806–1864) Episcopal bishop of Louisiana and a Confederate general who was lost near Marietta, Georgia, on June 14, 1864, from artillery fire from a 5th Indiana battery. Operated by Mississippi Shipping.

26. CHARLES BRANTLEY AYCOCK, 9–42, 242297, KHIH (1859–1912) governor of North Carolina. Operated by Mississippi Shipping.

27. WILLIAM BLOUNT, 9–42, 242274, KHIF (1749–1800) delegate to the Constitutional Convention and governor of the Tennessee Territory. Operated by Parry.

28. WADE HAMPTON, 12–42, 242552, KIDH (1818–1902) South Carolina governor and senator. Operated by Mississippi Shipping. Capt. John L. Reynolds' ship was hit by two torpedoes on February 28, 1943, from *U-405* in the North Atlantic with the loss of four merchant crew and five Armed Guard sailors. The ship did not sink but everyone abandoned ship except the captain, chief engineer Worsham Chandler, bosun John Sandova, and able seaman Rexford Dickey. Sandova and Dickey later decided to go over the side and got on a raft in freezing water. The captain and chief were picked up the next morning by a boat crew from HMS *Vervain* (K.190). Sandova and Dickey weren't picked up until March 3 by HMS *Beverley* (H.64) but by then Sandova had died of exposure.

29. RICHMOND MUMFORD PEARSON, 11–42, 242493, KIDI (1805–1878) chief justice of the North Carolina Supreme Court. Operated by Mississippi Shipping.

30. DAVID G. FARRAGUT, 1–43, 242714, KKGM (1801–1870) David Glasgow Farragut, of Norfolk, Virginia, was a Union naval officer famous for stating "Damn the torpedoes, full speed ahead!" at Mobile Bay on August 5, 1864. Operated by United Fruit.

31. MAYO BROTHERS, 12–42, 242674, KKEW, William James Mayo (1861–1939) and Charles Horace Mayo (1865–1939) were physicians who assisted their father in his Rochester, Minnesota, practice and were founding members of the Mayo Clinic. Operated by Waterman.

32. WILLIAM HARPER, 2–43, 242946, KIDM (1790–1847) William Joseph Harper was a prominent South Carolina lawyer, chancellor in the Missouri Territory, and senator from South Carolina. Operated by Waterman.

33. PIERRE SOULE, 2–43, 242895, KIDS (1801–1870) French refugee, Louisiana senator, and minister to Spain who wrote the Ostend Manifesto advocating the annexation of Cuba, an issue in the 1860 presidential election. Operated by Moore-McCormack. Capt. Patrick Driscoll's ship was torpedoed by *U-380* on August 23, 1943, off Palermo, Sicily. There were no reported casualties.

34. WALTER Q. GRESHAM, 2–43, 242834, KIFK (1832–1895) Walter Quintin Gresham was Postmaster General and Secretary of State. Operated by Standard Fruit. Capt. Byron Miller's ship was torpedoed on March 18, 1943, by *U-221* 600 miles west of Ireland with the loss of 22 merchant crew and five Armed Guard sailors.

35. BLACK HAWK, 2–43, 242835, KKEM (1767–1838) Sauk Indian chief. Operated by United Fruit.

36. ROBERT M. LA FOLLETTE, 2–43, 242795, KKEJ (1855–1925) Robert Marion "Fighting Bob" La Follette was a Wisconsin governor and senator who sponsored the La Follette Seaman's Act of 1915, to improve wages and working conditions for seafarers. Imprisonment for desertion was abolished but the Act also applied to foreign seamen in U.S. ports, which lead to desertions by alien seamen. Operated by Mississippi Shipping.

37. RICHARD OLNEY, 2–43, 242856, KKLP (1835–1917) Attorney General and Secretary of State. Operated by Marine Transport. Capt. Erich Richter's ship hit a mine on September 22, 1943, off Bizerte, Tunisia, with the loss of oiler Alvin J. Luke and fireman/ watertender Baylus F. Malcolm.

38. ROBERT BACON, 3–43, 242951, KK— (1860–1918) financier and Assistant Secretary of State. Operated by R. A. Nicol. Capt. Clyde H. Henderson's ship was torpedoed on July 14, 1943, by *U-178* about 50 miles off Mozambique with the loss of three merchant crew and two Armed Guard sailors.

39. PHILANDER C. KNOX, 3–43, 243016, KKLR (1853–1921) Philander Chase Knox was a banker, Attorney General, Pennsylvania senator, and Secretary of State. Operated by Wessel, Duval.

40. LUCIUS Q. C. LAMAR, 3–43, 243081, KKLY (1825–1893) Lucius Quintus Cincinnatus Lamar was a Georgia congressman, Secretary of the Interior, and Supreme Court justice. Operated by Waterman.

41. JAMES MCHENRY, 3–43, 243054, KKLZ (1753–1816) Army surgeon, Maryland congressman, Secretary of War, founder of the Navy Department, and namesake for Fort McHenry in Baltimore. Operated by Cosmopolitan.

42. SAMUEL DEXTER, 3–43, 243200, KKMB (1761–1816) Massachusetts congressman and Secretary of War and Treasury. Operated by Waterman. Stranded on January 24, 1944, at Barra Island, Scotland.

43. ROGER GRISWOLD, 3–43, 243044, KKMD (1762–1812) Connecticut congressman and governor. Operated by Waterman.

44. TIMOTHY BLOODWORTH, 4–43, 243144, KIBU (1736–1814) senator from North Carolina. Operated by Lykes.

45. ELIAS BOUDINOT, 3–43, 243126, KIBY (1740–1821) president of the Continental Congress, Congressman from New Jersey, and director of the Mint. Operated by Wessel, Duval.

46. AEDANUS BURKE, 4–43, 243198, KICW (1743–1802) South Carolina congressman. Operated by Mississippi Shipping.

47. THOMAS FITZSIMONS, 4–43, 243273, KIDA (1741–1811) Pennsylvania congressman. Operated by Standard Fruit.

48. HENRY GROVES CONNOR, 4–43, 243372, KIDK (1852–1924) federal district court judge in North Carolina. Operated by Standard Fruit.

49. WILLIAM M. EVARTS, 5–43, 243377, KLZO (1818–1901) William Maxwell Evarts was a New York senator, Secretary of State, and Attorney General. Operated by Waterman and converted to an Army troopship.

50. F. T. FRELINGHUYSEN, 5–43, 243393, KMHC (1817–1885) Frederick Theodore Frelinghuysen was a New Jersey senator and Secretary of State. Operated by Waterman.

51. TARLETON BROWN, 4–43, 243285, KMHD (1757–1846) South Carolina soldier who went from private to captain during the Revolutionary War and fought in many engagements. Operated by Mississippi Shipping.

52. JAMES E. HOWARD, 5–43, 243362, KMHE (1815–1876) James Edmonds Howard founded the Howard Ship Yards & Dock Co. in 1834 at Jeffersonville, Indiana, to build steamboats, tugs, and barges. In 1836 he moved the yard to Madison, Indiana, and in 1844 moved back to Jeffersonville. In 1846 he moved to Shippingsport, Kentucky, then to Louisville, and in 1849 back to Jeffersonville where his brother Daniel joined him. The company was James Howard & Co. when his brother John and his son Edmonds joined in 1865. James drowned in 1876. He built 1,123 boats. In 1925 the government took control of the firm and in 1942 it became the Jeffersonville Boat & Machine Co. Operated by Waterman.

53. HENRY S. FOOTE, 5–43, 243373, KMHH (1804–1880) Henry Stuart Foote was a Mississippi senator and governor. Operated by Lykes.

54. CHARLES HENDERSON, 5–43, 243302, KNCD (1848–1915) clergyman and noted sociologist. Operated by Mississippi Shipping. On the night of January 21, 1944, the ship collided with the 1,242-ton coastwise motor tanker *Plattsburgh Socony* about five miles off the Delaware Capes. The tanker's cargo ignited and ordinary seaman Harvey Raach, of Milwaukee, was lost and several others suffered burns. The ship returned for repairs and on February 2 Capt. Charles E. Hill, 32, came aboard as skipper and a new Armed Guard crew came aboard on the 27th. Capt. Herbert J. Louis, 42, left Charleston, South Carolina, in September 1944 as skipper of the Marine Transport Lines Liberty ship *Jonathan Elmer* and arrived at New York on December 21 from Oran, Algeria. On or about December 23 the *Henderson* left New York under Capt. Nathan Smukler, 53, and arrived back there on February 19, 1945, where all but seven of the crew paid off. Capt. Louis then took command of the *Henderson*. Herman Hanes signed on for the voyage but was was hospitalized on the 23rd with varicose veins. The left New York, arrived at Lynn Haven on the 27th, and left Norfolk on March 9 with a cargo of explosives. They joined Convoy UGS 80 and arrived at Bari, Italy, on April 5 and began discharging their cargo. Four days later the ship exploded while unloading 500 pound bombs. Army investigators concluded the bombs were being dragged to the hatch opening then lifted without safety nets and one or more fell and detonated. The entire merchant crew of 41, except the chief engineer, were aboard at the time and were lost. All 13 Armed Guard sailors perished. The only survivor from the ship was the chief engineer who was ashore

at the time. According to the Army, the explosion killed 542 people and injured around 1,800. Buildings within half a mile were leveled and other vessels in the vicinity were seriously damaged.

55. ROBERT LOWRY, 5–43, 243452, KNCH (1830–1910) Confederate general and governor of Mississippi. Operated by Standard Fruit. The launching was celebrated by Adm. Vickery as the 1,000th Liberty ship.

56. GEORGE POINDEXTER, 5–43, 243486, KNCP (1779–1853) Mississippi governor and congressman. Operated by Mississippi Shipping.

57. JOHN A. QUITMAN, 6–43, 243565, KOTQ (1798–1858) John Anthony Quitman was a Mississippi governor and congressman. Operated by Waterman.

58. JOHN SHARP WILLIAMS, 6–43, 243624, KXCO (1854–1932) Mississippi congressman. Operated by Parry.

59. JULIEN POYDRAS, 5–43, 243468, KOOR (1746–1824) French-born Julien de Lallande Poydras was a delegate to Congress from the Territory of New Orleans. Operated by Waterman.

60. JOSEPH N. NICOLETTE, 6–43, 243566, KOTB (1786–1843) Jean-Nicholas Nicholette was a French geographer and mathematician who mapped the Mississippi and Missouri River areas of Minnesota and the Dakotas. Operated by Waterman.

61. RICHARD M. JOHNSON, 6–43, 243598, KOXK (1780–1850) Richard Mentor Johnson was a Kentucky congressman and controversial 9th vice president. Operated by Mississippi Shipping.

62. EDWARD SPARROW, 6–43, 243619, KXCC (1810–1882) wealthy Louisiana senator in the Provisional Confederate and first and second Confederate Congresses. Operated by Calmar.

63. JOHN MCDONOGH, 7–43, 243694, KXGL (1779–1850) prominent Baltimore shipping man who settled in New Orleans. Operated by Waterman.

64. GEORGE W. KENDALL, 9–43, 243898, KXKD (1809–1867) George Wilkins Kendall was the cofounder with Francis Lumsden of *The Picayune* newspaper in New Orleans in 1837. In 1841 he was a correspondent with the Texas Santa Fe Expedition and was captured by Mexican troops, marched 2,000 miles, and imprisoned in Mexico City where he got smallpox. He was released the next year and was a correspondent during the Mexican War. Z-ET1-S-C3 operated by American Republics.

65. MARY ASHLEY TOWNSEND, 9–43, 243968, KXKE (c. 1832–1901) Mary Ashley Van Voorhis, of Lyons, New York, married Gideon Townsend. She then became a celebrated poet and writer. Z-ET1-S-C3 operated by International Freighting.

66. JOHN STAGG, 9–43, 243900, KXKJ (1864–1915) John Weldon Stagg was pastor of the First Presbyterian Church in Birmingham and president of the Alabama Presbyterian College for Men. Z-ET1-S-C3 operated by Bernuth, Lembcke.

67. TOBIAS F. STANSBURY, 9–43, 243923, KXKO (1757–1849) Tobias Emerson Stansbury served in the Revolutionary War and commanded the Baltimore Brigade in the War of 1812. Z-ET1-S-C3 operated by Barber Asphalt.

68. LAFCADIO HEARN, 9–43, 243966, KXKV (1850–1904) Patrick Lafcadio "Koizum Yakumo" Hearn wrote books about Japan and New Orleans. Z-ET1-S-C3 operated by Tankers Co., Inc.

69. ANDREW MARSCHALK, 10–43, 244037, KXKI (1767–1838) printer, Army officer, and publisher of the *Mississippi Gazette*. Z-ET1-S-C3 operated by American Republics.

70. JACOB THOMPSON, 10–43, 244041, KXKL (1810–1885) Mississippi congressman and Secretary of the Interior. Z-ET1-S-C3 operated by Republic Oil Refining.

The *William E. Pendleton* heading out with full holds and aircraft on top of the hatches. Photo courtesy of Bill Hultgren.

71. DAVID HOLMES, 10–43, 244097, KXKW (1770–1832) Virginia congressman, Mississippi senator and governor. Z-ET1-S-C3 operated by Bernuth, Lembcke.

72. WILLIAM E. PENDLETON, 10–43, 244194, KYIR (1824–1901) ship captain and prominent bar pilot at New Orleans. Z-ET1-S-C3 operated by Barber Asphalt.

73. IRWIN RUSSELL, 10–43, 244330, KYJD (1853–1879) young lawyer and noted Mississippi dialect poet. Z-ET1-S-C3 operated by American Republics.

74. REGINALD A. FESSENDEN, 10–43, 244192, KYJF (1866–1932) Reginald Aubrey Fessenden was a Canadian-born pioneer of radio technology credited with the first transmission of voice and music. Z-ET1-S-C3 operated by International Freighting.

75. JOSEPH GOLDBERGER, 10–43, 244331, KTNC (1874–1929) physician, researcher of pellagra, and student of the links between poverty and disease. Z-ET1-S-C3 operated by Spencer Kellogg.

76. HENRY L. ELLSWORTH, 11–43, 244222, KYJE (1791–1858) Henry Leavitt Ellsworth was the first Commissioner of Patents. Z-ET1-S-C3 operated by Republic Oil Refining.

77. WILLIAM CROMPTON, 11–43, 244373, KTMZ (1806–1891) English-born cotton weaver who came to Taunton, Massachusetts, in 1836 and the next year got a patent for a unique loom that made high quality cotton goods. Z-ET1-S-C3 operated by Republic Oil Refining.

78. ANDREW A. HUMPHREYS, 11–43, 244370, KTNB (1810–1883) Andrew Atkinson Humphreys was a Civil War general and Army Chief Engineer. Z-ET1-S-C3 operated by International Freighting.

79. OSCAR S. STRAUS, 11–43, 244449, KTND (1850–1926) Oscar Solomon Straus was Secretary of Commerce and Labor. Z-ET1-S-C3 operated by Spencer Kellogg.

80. ALBERT G. BROWN, 11–43, 244531, KUPR (1813–1880) Albert Gallatin Brown was a Mississippi governor and congressman. Z-ET1-S-C3 operated by American Trading & Production.

81. ELIZA JANE NICHOLSON, 11–43, 244533, KUPS (1843–1896) Eliza Jane

Poitevent, of Gainesville, Mississippi, began writing in New Orleans after the Civil War under the name Pearl Rivers. In May 1872 she married Alva Holbrook, a 60+-year-old gentleman who was co-owner of the *Daily Picayune* newspaper but the marriage was a shambles. When he died in 1876, $80,000 in debt, she ran the newspaper, becoming the first female professional journalist in the South and the first American female newspaper publisher, editor, and writer. She had been in love with George Nicholson, the paper's married business manager. The two married in June 1878 and the paper thrived. Z-ET1-S-C3 operated by Republic Oil Refining.

82. THOMAS F. CUNNINGHAM, 12–43, 244536, KTNF (1864–1937) president of the New Orleans Board of Trade and president of the Delta Line in the 1930s. Z-ET1-S-C3 operated by Spencer Kellogg.

83. CHARLES A. WICKLIFFE, 12–43, 244634, KUUE (1788–1869) Charles Anderson Cunningham was a Kentucky congressman, governor, and Postmaster General. Z-ET1-S-C3 operated by Barber Asphalt.

84. JEAN-BAPTISTE LE MOYNE, 12–43, 244689, KUUF (1680–1767) Sieur de Bienville was an explorer, governor of Louisiana, and founder of Mobile, Biloxi, and New Orleans. Z-ET1-S-C3 operated by Spencer Kellogg.

85. HORACE H. HARVEY, 12–43, 244674, KUYH (1860–1938) Capt. Horace Hale Harvey was a Gulf Coast mariner who developed the Louisiana Intracoastal Waterway. Z-ET1-S-C3 operated by Bernuth, Lembcke.

86. PAUL TULANE, 12–43, 244681, KUYJ (1801–1887) New Orleans dry goods merchant who donated a large sum of money to the University of Louisiana, afterward renamed The Tulane University of Louisiana. Z-ET1-S-C3 operated by the Navy as the *Kangaroo* (IX-121) commissioned on December 20, 1943.

87. WILLIAM B. BANKHEAD, 12–43, 244758, KVDA (1874–1940) William Brockman Bankhead was an Alabama congressman and Speaker of the House. Z-ET1-S-C3 operated by the Navy as the *Leopard* (IX-122) commissioned on December 26, 1943.

88. LEIF ERICSON, 12–43, 244754, KUWE (c. 970-c. 1020) Leiv Eriksson was a Norwegian explorer. Z-ET1-S-C3 operated by the Navy as *Porcupine* (IX-126) commissioned on December 30, 1943.

89. JUDAH TOURO, 12–43, 244844, KVKQ (1775–1854) New Orleans merchant and philanthropist seriously wounded in 1815 at New Orleans. Z-ET1-S-C3 operated by the Navy as the *Mink* (IX-123) commissioned on January 9, 1943.

90. MASON L. WEEMS, 1–44, 244804, KVLQ (1759–1825) Mason Locke Weems—"Parson Weems"—wrote apocryphal stories about George Washington. Z-ET1-S-C3 operated by the Navy as the *Moose* (IX-124) commissioned on January 28, 1944.

91. OPIE READ, 1–44, 244846, KVKS (1852–1939) Opie Percival Read was a writer and founder of the *Arkansas Traveler*. Z-ET1-S-C3 operated by the Navy as the *Panda* (IX-125) commissioned on January 6, 1944.

92. J. C. W. BECKHAM, 1–44, 244966, KUWH, 1869–1940) John Crepps Wickliffe Beckham was a Kentucky senator and governor. Z-ET1-S-C3 operated by Navy as the *Raccoon* (IX-127) commissioned on February 1, 1944.

93. EUGENE W. HILGARD, 1–44, 244892, KUWM (1833–1916) Eugene Woldemar Hilgard was a German-born geologist in Mississippi, a chemist at the Smithsonian, a professor at the University of Michigan and UC Berkeley, and director of the California State Agricultural Experiment Station. Z-ET1-S-C3 operated by the Navy as the *Whippet* (IX-129) commissioned on January 14, 1944.

94. USS ACUBENS (AKS-5), 2–44, NBNZ, general stores issue ship commissioned on July 15, 1944.

95. NORMAN O. PEDRICK, 2–44, 244967, KUWK (1875–1942) Norman Owens Pedrick was president of the Gulf Shipping Conference and president of the Mississippi Shipping Co. Z-ET1-S-C3 operated by the Navy as *Stag* (IX-128), commissioned on February 16, 1944, then converted to the water distilling ship AW-1.

96. LEON GODCHAUX, 2–44, 244990, KUWN (1824–1899) pioneer in the sugar refining industry and "Sugar King of the South." Z-ET1-S-C3 operated by the Navy as *Wildcat* (IX-130) commissioned on February 17, 1944, then converted to the water distilling ship AW-2.

97. WARREN STONE, 2–44, 245081, KWES (1808–1872) physician who cofounded the Louisiana Medical College. Operated by the Navy as the *Crater*-class cargo ship *Arkab* (AK-130), NHEB, commissioned on May 15, 1944.

98. JAMES B. ASWELL, 3–44, 245148, KVPV (1869–1931) James Benjamin Aswell was an educator and Louisiana congressman. Operated by Marine Transport.

99. LINN BOYD, 3–44, 245080, KWEU (1800–1859) Kentucky congressman. Operated by American Export Lines.

100. RUFUS E. FOSTER, 3–44, 245188, KWAN (1871–1942) Rufus Edward Foster was a federal judge and dean of the Tulane law school. Operated by Mississippi Shipping.

101. R. S. WILSON, 3–44, 245149, KWAO (1875–1937) Robert Samuel Wilson was a director of the Mississippi State University extension service. Operated by American Export Lines.

102. USS SEGINUS (AK-133), 4–44, NBCT, *Crater*-class cargo ship commissioned on June 14, 1944.

103. GEORGE A. MARR, 3–44, 245273, KWJQ (1866–1943) Great Lakes shipping promoter and secretary of the Lake Carriers Association. Operated by Overlakes.

104. USS SYRMA (AK-134), 3–44, NHEJ, *Crater*-class cargo ship commissioned on March 21, 1944.

105. JOHN M. PARKER, 4–44, 245334, KWJV (1863–1939) John Milliken Parker was the 37th governor of Louisiana. Operated by T. J. Stevenson.

106. CECIL N. BEAN, 4–44, 245333, KWJW (1870–1940) Cecil Noyes Bean was a prominent marine engineer who joined the Bureau of Marine Inspection & Navigation in September 1917. Operated by American Range-Liberty Lines.

107. USS BURIAS (AG-69), 4–44, NQST, miscellaneous auxiliary ship commissioned on April 24, 1944.

108. USS KOCHAB (AKS-6), 4–44, general stores issue ship commissioned on May 2, 1944.

109. USS BASILAN (AG-68), 4–44, NQQY, miscellaneous auxiliary ship commissioned on October 10, 1944.

110. ANDREW STEVENSON, 5–44, 245456, KXAV (1784–1857) Virginia congressman. Operated by Eastern Gas & Fuel.

111. CHARLES W. WOOSTER, 5–44, 245526, WESG (1780–1848) Charles Whiting Wooster was master of the ship *Fair American* at 21 and captain of the privateer *Saratoga* in the War of 1812. His 22 prizes made him wealthy and his celebrated battle with the British vessel *Rachel* on December 11, 1812, off Venezuela made him famous. He served with the Chilean navy and was a New York harbor pilot. Operated by Standard Fruit and converted to an animal transport ship.

112. EDWIN A. STEVENS, 6–44, 245527, 6–44, WFUW (1795–1868) Edwin Augustus Stevens invented a plow, innovated the forced draft system for closed firerooms in steamships, and endowed the Stevens Institute of Technology. Operated by American Export Lines.

113. W. C. LATTA, 5–44, 245531, WFZH (1850–1935) William Carroll Latta was a prominent Purdue University horticulturist noted for corn and oat experiments in Indiana. Operated by International Freighting.

114. WILLIAM WHEELWRIGHT, 6–44, 245612, WLIM (1798–1873) founder of the Pacific Steam Navigation Co. who provided waterborne and rail service to South American ports. Operated by International Freighting.

115. FRANK ADAIR MONROE, 7–44, 245607, WKZK (1844–1927) chief justice of the Louisiana Supreme Court. Operated by American South African.

116. ALEXANDER W. DONIPHAN, 7–44, 245718, WOGT (1808–1887) Alexander William Doniphan wrote New Mexico's Bill of Rights and prevented the summary execution of Mormon founder Joseph Smith. Operated by Parry.

117. AMASA DELANO, 7–44, 245719, WPGV (1763–1823) sea captain, author, kin to Franklin Delano Roosevelt. Operated by A. L. Burbank.

118. CYRUS ADLER, 7–44, 245852, WQBJ (1863–1940) professor of Semitic languages at Johns Hopkins. Operated by West India.

119. GEORGE W. ALTHER, 7–44, 245854, WQBO (1918–1943) second mate on the *Timothy Pickering*, bombed by German aircraft off Avola, Sicily, on July 14, 1943. Alther was awarded the Merchant Marine Distinguished Service medal posthumously for saving the life of an Armed Guard sailor who was trapped below decks by flames. Operated by Mississippi Shipping.

120. BRIG. GEN. CLINTON W. RUSSELL, 7–44 (1891–1943) flight technology pioneer in the Army Air Corps who died on March 23, 1943, at Fort Jay, New York. Aircraft repair ship operated by the U.S. Army.

121. WALKER D. HINES, 7–44, 245863, WQCI (1870–1934) Walker Downer Hines was a railroad executive and second director of the Federal Railroad Administration. Operated by American-Foreign.

122. COLLIN MCKINNEY, 8–44, 246035, WQBZ (1766–1861) Texas Revolutionary and co-author of the *Texas Declaration of Independence*. Namesake for McKinney, Texas. Operated by American Export Lines.

123. ALCEE FORTIER, 8–44, 246000, WRLL (1856–1914) author, historian, noted Tulane professor, and recorder and preservationist of French culture in Louisiana. Operated by A. H. Bull and converted to an animal transport ship.

124. MILTON B. MEDARY, 8–44, 246180, WRME (1874–1929) Milton Bennett Medary, Jr., was a noted Philadelphia architect who served on federal commissions. Operated by Standard Fruit.

125. FERDINAND R. HASSLER, 8–44, 246036, WRMK (1770–1843) Ferdinand Rudolph Hassler was a surveyor who was director of the U.S. Coast Survey and the Bureau of Weights & Measures. Operated by A. H. Bull.

126. O. L. BODENHAMER, 8–44, 246302, WRMX (1891–1933) Ossee Lee Bodenhamer was a World War I veteran who was elected national commander of the American Legion in 1929. Operated by Norton Lilly.

127. FREDERICK VON STEUBEN, 8–44, 246170, WROC (1730–1794) Friedrich Wilhelm Ludolf Gerhard Augustin von Steuben was a Prussian army officer and baron who served in the Continental Army and helped establish West Point. Operated by Seas Shipping.

128. FLOYD W. SPENCER, 9–44, 246094, WRPP (1890–1940) Floyd William Spencer was a beloved Louisiana agricultural youth leader and administrator at Baton Rouge. Over $3 million in war bonds were sold by the 4-H Clubs of Louisiana to fund a ship the clubs named. Operated by Stockard.

129. MILTON H. SMITH, 9–44, 246301, WSOX (1836–1921) Milton Hannibal Smith was president of the Louisville & Nashville Railroad. Operated by Mississippi Shipping.

130. E. G. HALL, 9–44, 246218, WSOZ (1866–1938) possibly Canadian-born Edmund G. Hall, president of the Minnesota State Federation of Labor. Hall came to America in 1880 and in 1930 lived in Minneapolis with his Norwegian wife Martha, 63, and daughter Irene, 28. Operated by Alcoa.

131. ROBERT F. BROUSSARD, 9–44, 246426, WSPG (1864–1918) Robert Foligny Broussard was a Louisiana congressman. Operated by Norton Lilly.

132. ANCIL F. HAINES, 10–44, 246421, WSPM (1872–1937) 11-year-old runaway farm boy who became a Pacific Northwest ferry service operator, shipping executive, then president of the Pacific Steamship Co. He was working for Dollar Steamship and American Mail Line when he died in Seattle. Operated by Wessel, Duval.

133. GEORGE POMUTZ, 10–44, 246298, WSPS (1818–1882) Gheorghe Pomuţ was a Romanian-born soldier who came to New York in 1850, became a Union general and was the American consul in Saint Petersburg, Russia, during negotiations for the purchase of Alaska. Operated by Mississippi Shipping.

134. AM-MER-MAR, 10–44, 246599, KSQX, named for the **Am**erican **Mer**chant **Mar**ine. Operated by Mississippi Shipping.

135. ISAAC DELGADO, 10–44, 246423, KSRS (1839–1912) prominent New Orleans sugar merchant, philanthropist, and founder of the New Orleans Museum of Art. Operated by Prudential.

136. SIEUR DE LA SALLE, 10–44, 246497, KSQZ (1643–1687) "Sir de La Salle" was René-Robert Cavelier, also Robert de La Salle, a French explorer of the Great Lakes and Mississippi Valley regions. Operated by A. L. Burbank.

137. CHRISTIAN BERGH, 10–44, 246601, KSRU (1763–1843) prominent New York shipbuilder on the East River. Henry Bergh's father. Operated by Standard Fruit.

138. ALRED J. EVANS, 10–44, 246494, KSSI (1874–1944) sea captain and chief surveyor for the Board of Underwriters of New York. Operated by United States Lines.

139. KATHERINE B. SHERWOOD, 10–44, 246675, KTBR (1841–1914) Kate Margaret Brownlee was a prominent journalist and poet who married probate judge Isaac Sherwood in Toledo, Ohio. Operated by Prudential.

140. J. RUFINO BARRIOS, 11–44, 246674, KTBU (1835–1885) Justo Rufino Barrios was president of Guatemala. Operated by Parry.

141. THOMAS P. LEATHERS, 10–44, 246612, KTBX (1817–1896) flamboyant captain of the stern-wheeler *Natchez* who famously raced Capt. John W. Cannon's *Robert E. Lee* on the Mississippi River in June 1870. Operated by Boland & Cornelius.

142. ALES HRDLICKA, 11–44, 246728, KTBZ (1869–1943) born in Humpolec, Bohemia, and travelled the world looking for the origin of the human race. He was the first president of the American Association of Physical Anthropologists and retired from the Smithsonian Institution in 1942 and died on September 5, 1943, in Washington. Operated by Alcoa.

143. BENJAMIN SILLIMAN, 10–44, 246670, KTEA (1779–1864) early science professor, mineralogist, and first chemist to distill petroleum. Namesake for Sillimanite. Operated by West India.

144. KING HATHAWAY, 11–44, 246835, KTIZ (1878–1944) Horace King Hathaway was an industrial engineering management consultant and professor at Stanford University. Operated by Standard Fruit.

145. USS CYBELE (AKS-10), 11–44, general stores issues ship commissioned April 16, 1945.

146. USS HECUBA (AKS-12), 11–44, NCWY, general stores issues ship commissioned on April 21, 1945.

147. JOSEPH WEYDEMEYER, 11–44, 246943, KYTY (1818–1866) Joseph Arnold Weydemeyer was a Prussian army officer, Marxist labor leader, newspaperman, and Union general. The International Fur & Leather Workers' Union in New York sold $2 million in War Bonds to pay for the ship. Operated by Standard Fruit.

148. USS GRATIA (AKS-11), 11–44, NCWW, general stores issues ship commissioned on May 5, 1945.

149. USS HESPERIA (AKS-13), 12–44, NCXA, general stores issues ship commissioned on April 1, 1945.

150. HELENA MODJESKA, 12–44, 246904, ANCO (1840–1909) Helena Modrzejewska was a noted Shakespearean actress of obscure Polish extraction. Operated by Black Diamond.

151. MARTIN BEHRMAN, 12–44, 247007, ANDW (1864–1926) longest serving mayor of New Orleans. Operated by Isbrandtsen.

152. WILLIAM H. KENDRICK, 12–44, 246944, ANCT (1882–1937) William H. "Teepi" Kendrick was "West Virginia's beloved 4-H Leader" and State Club Agent for West Virginia. Operated by J. H. Winchester.

153. ANDREAS HONCHARENKO, 12–44, 247042, ANGC (1830–1916) first known Ukrainian immigrant to the United States and publisher of the *Alaska Herald*. Operated by De La Rama.

154. JAMES EAGAN LAYNE, 12–44, 247006, ANCZ (1903–1943) 2nd assistant engineer lost on the Standard Oil tanker *Esso Baton Rouge*, torpedoed by *U-202* on February 23, 1943, south of the Azores. Layne lived with his wife Marjorie, 37, daughter Beverly, 12, and son Jimmie, 5, at 1633 Jeanette St., Baton Rouge, Louisiana. Operated by United States Navigation. Capt. William A. Sleek was master of the *Webster Victory* when they arrived at New York on December 4, 1945, from Marseilles, France, and then took command of the *Layne*. The ship was torpedoed on March 21, 1945, by *U-1195* off Plymouth, England. There were no reported casualties.

155. BENJAMIN A. FISHER, 12–44, 247043, ANDG (1900–1942) chief engineer from Tampa, Florida, lost on the *Alcoa Guide*, sunk by *U-123* on April 16, 1942, about 300 miles off Cape Hatteras. Operated by Alcoa.

156. NACHMAN SYRKIN, 1–45, 247101, ANHM (1868–1924) Russian-born founder of the American Jewish Congress and advocate for a Jewish homeland in Palestine. Operated by Norton Lilly.

157. CARL ZACHARY WEBB, 1–45, 247132, ANDH (1922–1942) wiper lost on the Standard Oil tanker *Allan Jackson*, torpedoed on January 18, 1942, by *U-66* off North Carolina. Carl lived with his dad Robert O., 55, mom Florence Z., 58, sisters Dorothy, 22, and June, 15, Fay, 24, and her husband Henry A. Kuhlman, 27, at 1726 Pruyn St., Baton Rouge, Louisiana. Operated by Standard Fruit.

158. WILLIAM W. MCKEE, 1–45, 247224, ANHC (1916–1942) ordinary seaman lost on the Waterman freighter *Bienville*, bombed by Japanese aircraft and shelled by a cruiser in the Bay of Bengal. When he was ashore, William lived with his older brother George and his wife Aline, 31, and their daughter Estelle, 5, and son Berringer, 4, on Henley Rd. in Mobile County, Alabama. Operated by Cosmopolitan.

159. HYDRA, 1–45, Greek island occupied by Germany from 1941 to 1943 causing widespread starvation. Operated under the Greek flag.

160. DAREL M. RITTER, 2–45, 247317, ANOP (1922–1943) fireman/watertender

lost on the *Henry Knox*, torpedoed by *I-37* on June 19, 1943, in the Indian Ocean. Operated by Boland & Cornelius.

161.　FRANK E. SPENCER, 1–45, 247214, ANJN (1900–1942) messman lost on the Cuba Distilling Co. Hog Island tanker *Carrabulle*, torpedoed by *U-106* on May 26, 1942, in the Gulf of Mexico. Frank shipped out in 1940, signed on the *Carrabulle*, and arrived at New Orleans on May 20, 1942, from the Dominican Republic. Operated by South Atlantic.

162.　ROY K. JOHNSON, 2–45, 247320, ANOQ (1918–1942) oiler lost on the American-Hawaiian freighter *Alaskan*, torpedoed by *U-172* on November 28, 1942, off Brazil. Operated by Calmar.

163.　DONALD S. WRIGHT, 3–45, 247421, ANQI (1924–1943) deck cadet lost on the *Cornelia P. Spencer*, torpedoed on September 21, 1943, by *U-188* off Somalia. Operated by A. L. Burbank.

164.　JAGGER SEAM, 3–45, 247161, ANKE, EC2-S-AW1 possibly not operated.

165.　LA SALLE SEAM, 3–45, 247274, ANLW, EC2-S-AW1 possibly not operated.

166.　SEWANEE SEAM, 4–45, 247414, ANQL, EC2-S-AW1 possibly not operated.

167.　LINTON SEAM, 4–45, 247412, ANQK, EC2-S-AW1 operated by Sprague.

168.　LAURENCE J. GALLAGHER, 5–45, 247511, ANSS (1894–1943) master of the *Melville E. Stone*, lost on November 24, 1943, when the ship was torpedoed by *U-516* in the South Atlantic. EC2-S-AW1 operated by Norton Lilly.

169.　MERRIMAC SEAM, 5–45, 247566, ANST, EC2-S-AW1 operated by Wellhart.

170.　REDSTONE SEAM, 5–45, 247645, ANWJ, EC2-S-AW1 operated by United States Lines.

171.　BON AIR SEAM, 5–45, 247706, ANWW, EC2-S-AW1 operated by Sprague.

172.　JEWELL SEAM, 5–45, 247768, ANWX, EC2-S-AW1 operated by Eastern Gas & Fuel.

173.　GLAMORGAN SEAM, 6–45, 247867, ANZL, EC2-S-AW1 operated by Sprague.

174.　HERRIN SEAM, 6–45, 247868, ANZO, EC2-S-AW1 operated by M. & J. Tracy post-war.

175.　POCAHONTAS SEAM, 6–45, 247869, ANZN, EC2-S-AW1 operated by American Steamship.

176.　SEWELL SEAM, 6–45, 247870, ANZM, EC2-S-AW1 operated by Eastern Gas & Fuel.

177.　POWELLTON SEAM, 7–45, 247951, AOAD, EC2-S-AW1 operated by A. H. Bull.

178.　BECKLEY SEAM, 7–45, 247987, AOAO, EC2-S-AW1 operated by Norton Lilly.

179.　EAGLE SEAM, 7–45, 247991, AOAP, EC2-S-AW1 operated by Marine Transport.

180.　BANNER SEAM, 7–45, 248164, AOFB, EC2-S-AW1 operated by M. & J. Tracy post-war.

181.　CHILTON SEAM, 8–45, 248165, AOFC, EC2-S-AW1 operated by A. H. Bull post-war.

182.　IMBODEN SEAM, 8–45, 248271, AODG, EC2-S-AW1 operated by Eastern Gas & Fuel.

183.　STREATOR SEAM, 8–45, 248276, AOGP, EC2-S-AW1 operated by Eastern Gas & Fuel.

184.　FREEPORT SEAM, 9–45, 248564, AOGE, EC2-S-AW1 operated by A. H. Bull post-war.

185.　MINGO SEAM, 9–45, 248384, AOGF, EC2-S-AW1 operated by American-Hawaiian.

186. PITTSBURGH SEAM, 9–45, 248386, AOGG, EC2-S-AW1 operated by Eastern Gas & Fuel.

187. JELLICOE SEAM, 10–45, 248567, AOJX, EC2-S-AW1 operated by American Export Lines.

188. RODA SEAM, 10–45, 248703, AOGC, EC2-S-AW1 operated by T. J. Stevenson.

J. A. Jones Construction Co.
209 W. 4th St., Charlotte, North Carolina

James Addison Jones was born on August 20, 1868, in Charlotte, North Carolina, and at age 17 went to work in a brickyard and in 1890 he lived at 507 W. 7th Street. By 1895 he was in business for himself as a brickmason and married Minnie, his office stenographer. Their son Raymond was born when they lived at 1203 S. Caldwell St. By 1902 Jones was a general contractor and in 1910 he had an office in room 404 in the Realty Building in downtown Charlotte and the family lived at 1011 S. Tryon. By 1915 the company had moved to larger offices in 800–801 Realty Building. The company survived the Great Depression through good management policies and became one of the largest contracting firms in the nation.

In 1940 at age 70 he lived in Charlotte at 600 East Blvd. with his wife Maud, 50, daughters Dorothy May Pierce, 30; Helen Estelle, 25, a stenographer at the company; Emma Renn, 23 (named after second wife Emma); and sons Robert Joseph, 21, a civil engineer at the company; Charles Borne, 18; and Mattie Alexander, 31, the family cook.

Like Six Companies, Inc., the firm had no shipbuilding experience and when Admiral Land called Jones at home to ask if he would build a 6-way shipyard and ships for the Maritime Commission at Panama City, Florida, Jones said, "We don't know anything about ships" and went back to bed. Land had heard about the company's excellent work in building camps for the Army. A week later, Jones' son, Edwin L. Jones, who managed the business, learned of the phone call and got back to the admiral. The company's general abilities and excellent management proved adequate for the task.

At Panama City, the Commission spent $19,600 on land and $12,475,814 on facilities. The 6-way yard was under executive vice president Raymond A. Jones, who lived with his wife Lucille at 355 Bunkers Cove Rd. The first keel was laid on July 9, 1942. They built 66 Liberty cargo ships, 8 Liberty Army tank transports, and 28 Liberty crated aircraft transports for a total of 102. The average building time for the ships was 83.3 days.

In January 1942 it was decided to build a shipyard at Brunswick, Georgia, and the old boatbuilding firm, the Brunswick Marine Construction Corp., was awarded a contract to build a 6-way yard under president and general manager Adolph N. Shelander. The company was at the foot of Dartmouth St. and Shelander lived with his wife Selma at 826 Union (telephone 173). He was also treasurer of Royal, Fendig & Shelander, a general insurance and real estate company at 1517 Newcastle. When Admiral Vickers found the construction schedule lagging they agreed to turn over the contract to J. A. Jones and the appropriate financial adjustments were made.

At Brunswick, the Commission spent $384,565 on land and $12,926,601 on facilities. The 6-way yard, under vice president and general manager Emil J. Kratt, built 85 Liberty ships and 14 Maritime Commission C1-M-AV1 coastal freighters for a total of 99 ships. Kratt lived with his wife Lucy at 1212 Palmetto Ave. The first keel was laid on July 6, 1942, and the average building time for the ships was 79.7 days.

Wainwright Yard, Panama City, Florida

    1. E. KIRBY SMITH, 3–43, 242926, KIFA (1824–1893) Edmund Kirby Smith was a Confederate general and college professor. Operated by Marine Transport.

    2. NEWTON D. BAKER, 3–43, 243064, KIFC (1871–1937) Newton Diehl Baker was mayor of Cleveland, Ohio, and Secretary of War. Operated by Luckenbach.

    3. JOHN BASCOM, 4–43, 243059, KLEG (1827–1911) Alaska educator and president of the University of Wisconsin. Operated by Moore-McCormack. Capt. Otto Heitmann left New Orleans in May 1943 and arrived at New York on August 8 from Glasgow, Scotland. They left New York on Voyage No. 2 and arrived back at New York on October 15 where 27 sailors paid off and 29 signed on. Capt. Heitmann expected to leave the Army Base on December 1. On December 3, 1943, the ship was sunk during an air raid at Bari, Italy, with the loss of four merchant crew and 10 Armed Guard sailors including their commander, Ens. Kay Kopl Vesole, of Iowa, who was awarded the Navy Cross for aiding survivors with total disregard for his own safety and became the namesake for the USS *Vesole* (DD-878). Captain Heitmann, second mate William R. Rudolph and third mate Allen G. Collins were awarded the Merchant Marine Distinguished Service medal, Collins posthumously, for heroic efforts in rendering aid to the injured. Rudolph summoned help from British and Norwegian vessels with a flashlight.

    4. WILLIAM J. BRYAN, 5–43, 243071, KLEI (1860–1925) William Jennings Bryan was a Nebraska congressman, Secretary of State, and orator who popularized the "stump speech" type of campaign tour. Operated by Standard Fruit.

    5. JOSEPH M. MEDILL, 5–43, 243561, KLHP (1823–1899) lawyer, founder of the *Chicago Tribune*, and mayor. Operated by Moore-McCormack.

    6. ELIHU ROOT, 6–43, 243558, KLXY (1845–1937) Secretary of War and State. Operated by AGWI Lines.

    7. JOHN HAY, 6–43, 243519, KLZN (1838–1905) John Milton Hay was President Lincoln's private secretary and Secretary of State. Operated by A. H. Bull.

    8. DWIGHT L. MOODY, 6–43, 243527, KORS (1837–1899) Dwight Lyman Moody was a preacher and president of the Chicago YMCA who refused to join the Union Army. Operated by Lykes.

    9. PETER ZENGER, 7–43, 243524, KORL (1697–1746) John Peter Zenger was a New York journalist whose trial for seditious libel established truth as an absolute defense against libel. Operated by A. H. Bull.

    10. ROBERT LANSING, 8–43, 243781, KXLT (1864–1928) Secretary of State. Operated by Moore-McCormack.

    11. VICTOR HERBERT, 9–43, 243785, KXLI (1859–1924) Victor August Herbert was a composer and founder of the American Society of Composers, Authors, & Publishers. Operated by Marine Transport.

    12. JULIUS ROSENWALD, 9–43, 243912, KXWZ (1862–1932) co-owner of Sears, Roebuck & Co. who funded education for Southern black children and founded the Chicago Museum of Science & Industry. Operated by Blidberg Rothchild.

    13. USS LUNA (AKS-7), 10–43, NAZB, general stores issues ship commissioned on February 7, 1944.

    14. DUNCAN U. FLETCHER, 8–43, 243777, KXLM (1859–1936) Duncan Upshaw Fletcher was a Florida senator. Operated by Lykes.

    15. DOLLY MADISON, 10–43, 243776, KXLP (1768–1849) Dolley Madison was James Madison's wife. Operated by Merchants & Miners.

16. MARY BALL, 11–43, 244166, KYHQ (1708–1789) Mary Ball married Augustine Washington on March 6, 1731, in Virginia and the next year they had a son they named George. Z-EC2-S-C2 operated by United Fruit.

17. JOHN BARTON PAYNE, 11–43, 244179, KYLV (1855–1935) Secretary of the Interior. Z-EC2-S-C2 operated by Isthmian.

18. FREDERIC C. HOWE, 12–43, 244291, KYPR (1867–1940) Frederic Clemson Howe was the Immigration Commissioner for the Port of New York. Z-EC2-S-C2 operated by United Fruit.

19. WILLIAM B. WILSON, 12–43, 244704, KVBR (1862–1934) Scotch-born William Bauchop Wilson was the first Secretary of Labor, appointed by President Wilson in 1913. Z-EC2-S-C2 operated by Eastern Steamship.

20. SARAH J. HALE, 12–43, 244741, KVCF (1788–1879) Sarah Josepha Buell was a schoolteacher who married attorney David Hale in 1811 and they had five children. When he died in 1823 she decided to wear black mourning clothes for the rest of her life and she turned to writing poetry, including "Mary Had a Little Lamb," wrote novels, and became the editor of *Ladies' Magazine*. Z-EC2-S-C2 operated by International Freighting.

21. NATHAN B. FORREST, 12–43, 244772, KVKB (1821–1877) Nathan Bedford Forrest was a wealthy planter and partner in Forrest & Maples, slave dealers, who ran a "Negro Mart" in Memphis. He enlisted in the Confederate army as a private and retired as a cavalry general. Z-EC2-S-C2 operated by American Export Lines.

22. EDGAR E. CLARK, 1–44, 244902, KUVQ (1856–1930) Edgar Erastus Clark was chairman of the Interstate Commerce Commission. Z-EC2-S-C2 operated by Stockard.

23. STEPHEN R. MALLORY, 1–44, 244907, KVMH (1813–1873) Stephen Russell Mallory was a Florida senator and chairman of the Confederacy's Committee on Naval Affairs. Z-EC2-S-C2 operated by Isbrandtsen.

24. WALTER L. FLEMING, 1–44, 244908, KUVZ (1874–1932) Walter Lynwood Fleming was a noted Civil War historian. Operated by Waterman.

25. SALVADOR BRAU, 1–44, 244948, KUWA (1842–1912) Salvador Brau Asencio was a noted Puerto Rican journalist and historian. Operated by William J. Rountree.

26. HAROLD T. ANDREWS, 2–44, 244944, KVQJ (1926–1944) ordinary seaman on the *West Nohno* who saved the life of an engineer trapped in the forepeak tank on September 15, 1942, at Suez, Egypt. Andrews was awarded the Merchant Marine Distinguished Service medal posthumously. Operated by Boland & Conelius.

27. RUSSELL SAGE, 2–44, 244992, KVQK (1816–1906) financier, railroad executive, New York congressman. His widow established Russell Sage College. Operated by Marine Transport.

28. WILLIAM W. LORING, 3–44, 244995, KVVE (1818–1886) William Wing Loring was a United States and a Confederate general. Operated by T. J. Stevenson.

29. MINNIE M. FISKE, 3–44, 245030, KVWR (1865–1932) Marie Augustus Davey, of New Orleans, was a leading Broadway actress who married Harrison Fiske in 1890 and was known as Minnie Maddern Fiske but billed herself as "Mrs. Fiske." Operated by American South African.

30. JOHN W. GRIFFITHS, 3–44, 245085, KWBN (1809–1882) John Willis Griffiths was a naval architect who designed a fast, sleek-hulled ship with a unique, concave bow shape. The *Rainbow* was built in 1845 and radically altered the "clipper ship" design and notion of speed versus cargo space. China traders Howland & Aspinwall owned the ship that Capt. John Land ran from New York to Canton, China, and back in 180 days. Operated by Blidberg Rothchild.

31. AUGUSTUS SAINT-GAUDENS, 3–44, 245120, KWBO (1848–1807) Irish-born sculptor of Civil War figures and other notable Americans. Operated by Black Diamond.

32. JOHN M. BROOKE, 3–44, 245181, KWBP (1826–1906) John Mercer Brooke was one of the first Naval Academy graduates, Confederate naval officer, and chief of the Bureau of Hydrography who was instrumental in realizing the transatlantic cable. Operated by North Atlantic & Gulf.

33. MAJ. GEN. HERBERT A. DARGUE, 4–44 (1886–1941) pioneer Army aviator who earned the Distinguished Flying Cross. Aircraft repair ship operated by the U.S. Army.

34. ALANSON B. HOUGHTON, 4–44, 245387, KWJZ (1863–1941) Alanson Bigelow Houghton was a Massachusetts congressman. Operated by American South African.

35. SAMUEL G. FRENCH, 4–44, 245438, KWKB (1818–1910) Samuel Gibbs French was a Confederate general. Operated by Oliver J. Olson.

36. MAJ. GEN. WALTER R. WEAVER, 4–44 (1885–1944) Army aviator who pioneered aircraft maintenance procedures. Aircraft repair ship operated by the U.S. Army.

37. JOSEPHINE SHAW LOWELL, 4–44, 245436, KWVZ (1843–1905) Josephine "Effie" Shaw married Massachusetts businessman Charles R. Lowell in 1863. He was drafted the next year into the 2d Massachusetts Horse Cavalry and Josephine went with him to Virginia where she cared for wounded on the battlefield although she was pregnant. Charles was mortally wounded and one month later she delivered their daughter Carlotta. She moved to Staten Island, went into business, became a social reformer, and was the first female commissioner of the New York State Board of Charities then founded the New York Consumers' League. Operated by Luckenbach.

38. RICHARD V. OULAHAN, 5–44, 245437, KWWA (1867–1931) Washington correspondent for the *New York Times*. Operated by Black Diamond.

39. JAMES H. KIMBALL, 5–44, 245462, KXAY (1874–1943) Dr. James Henry Kimball was Chief Meteorologist in the New York Weather Bureau. The office provided Atlantic weather data for steamships and aircraft. He died on December 21, 1943, in New York. Operated by American Export Lines.

40. STEPHEN FURDEK, 5–44, 245491, KXBZ (1855–1915) noted Slovakian priest in Cleveland. Operated by Merchants & Miners.

41. JEAN RIBAUT, 5–44, 245577, WJVC (1520–1565) Jean Ribault was a French naval officer who explored Florida and established a colony for French Protestants. Operated by A. H. Bull.

42. LE BARON RUSSELL BRIGGS, 5–44, 245580, WKMN (1855–1934) LeBaron Russell Briggs, Jr., was a Harvard dean and president of Radcliffe College. Operated by R. A. Nicol.

43. HOWARD GRAY, 6–44, 245697, WPCH (1878–1944) federal Public Works Administration official active in Alabama 4-H. Operated by Black Diamond.

44. H. H. RAYMOND, 6–44, 245724, WPIQ (1864–1935) Harry H. Raymond was president and general manager of the Clyde and Mallory Steamship Cos. He was appointed by the Shipping Board as the first Federal Controller of Shipping in January 1918. Operated by AGWI Lines.

45. T. A. JOHNSTON, 12–44, 246994, WQEA (1848–1934) In 1881 Thomas A. Johnston was the second president of the Kemper Family School in Boonville, Missouri. Operated by J. H. Winchester.

46. M. MICHAEL EDELSTEIN, 6–44, 245899, WQEV (1888–1941) Morris Michael Edelstein was a New York congressman. Operated by Smith & Johnson.

47. NICK STONER, 6–44, 245900, WQZQ (1762–1850) Nicholas Stoner was a

soldier, explorer, pioneer, and legendary figure in the Adirondacks mountain region. Operated by North Atlantic & Gulf.

48. WILLIAM D. BLOXHAM, 6–44, 245901, WQZR (1835–1911) William Dunningham Bloxham was the governor of Florida. Operated by William J. Rountree.

49. WILLIAM E. DODD, 7–44, 245926, WREQ (1869–1940) William Edward Dodd was a historian and ambassador to Germany during the rise of Hitler. Operated by Marine Transport.

50. J. H. DRUMMOND, 7–44, 246026, WRPZ (1827–1902) Josiah Hayden Drummond was the attorney general of Maine. Operated by American Export Lines.

51. WILLIAM L. WATSON, 7–44, 246030, WRQA (1879–1935) first Duval County, Florida, Agricultural Agent who was very active in the Florida 4-H program. Operated by Black Diamond.

52. JOHN R. MCQUIGG, 7–44, 246027, WRQB (1866–1928) Gen. John Rea McQuigg was an Army engineer in World War I, a lawyer, and national commander of the American Legion. Operated by American South African.

53. PEDRO MENENDEZ, 8–44, 246127, WSSM (1519–1574) Pedro Menéndez de Avilés was a Spanish admiral who founded St. Augustine, La Florida, and was governor of Spanish Florida. Operated by Moore-McCormack.

54. CARL E. LADD, 8–44, 246092, WSIT (1888–1943) Carl Edwin Ladd was dean of the New York State Colleges of Agriculture, Cornell University, and director of Extension Services and Home Ecomics who died unexpectedly on July 23, 1943. Operated by States Marine.

55. GEORGE ADE, 8–44, 246171, WSSN (1866–1944) noted playwright. Operated by American West African.

56. EDWARD K. COLLINS, 8–44, 246421, WSUZ (1802–1878) Edward Knight Collins founded the United States Mail Steamship Co. in 1847, known as the Collins Line. Operated by Smith & Johnson.

57. C. FRANCIS JENKINS, 9–44, 246256, WSYJ (1867–1934) Charles Francis Jenkins was a pioneer in the motion picture industry and the inventor of mechanical television. Philo Farnsworth's all-electronic version of TV eventually prevailed in the marketplace. Operated by AGWI Lines.

58. RAYMOND V. INGERSOLL, 9–44, 246387, KSSK (1875–1940) Raymond Vail Ingersoll was president of the Brooklyn Borough in New York and promoter of civic improvements and in public housing. Operated by Polarus.

59. BENJAMIN F. COSTON, 9–44, 246378, KSSN (1820–1848) Benjamin Franklin Coston was a naval scientist, pyrotechnic engineer, and inventor of the marine flare. Operated by Union Sulphur.

60. WILLIAM P. DUVAL, 9–44, 246390, KSSQ (1784–1854) William Pope Duval was a Kentucky congressman and governor of Florida. Operated by Blidberg Rothchild.

61. STEPAS DARIUS, 10–44, 246447, KSSW (1896–1933) Lithuanian-born aviators Steponus Darašius (airline owner Stephen Darius of Chicago) and Stasys Girskis (Stanley T. Girenas of Chicago) attempted to fly their Bellanca CH-300 Pacemaker *Lituanica* nonstop from New York to Kaunas, Lithuania, but both died in a crash near Kuhdamm, Germany, on July 17, 1933. Operated by William J. Rountree.

62. ALEXANDER E. BROWN, 10–44, 246472, KSYW (1852–1911) Alexander Ephraim Brown devised a system for loading coal from rail cars onto ships and incorporated the Brown Hoisting & Conveying Machine Co. at Cleveland, a major improvement that did not break the coal. Operated by South Atlantic.

63. CHIEF OSCEOLA, 10–44, 246603, KTEE (1804–1838) William Powell and Polly Coppinger, of Creek Indian heritage, had a son named Billy Powell. Billy was raised in the Creek tribe and became a leader of the Florida Seminole Indians. He was captured on September 21, 1837, and died at Fort Marion in St. Augustine on January 30, 1838, of illness. Operated by United States Navigation.

64. RICHARD HALLIBURTON, 10–44, 246609, KTEP (1900–1939) merchant seaman, colorful adventurer and author who hired Capt. John Welch to sail his 75-foot Chinese junk *Sea Dragon* from Hong Kong to the Golden Gate International Exposition at Treasure Island in San Francisco Bay but all aboard perished in a gale. Operated by Isbrandtsen.

65. SAMUEL G. HOWE, 10–44, 246611, KTEG (1801–1876) Samuel Gridley Howe was a physician, abolitionist, philanthropist, and husband of Julia Ward Howe. Operated by Isbrandtsen.

66. GRANVILLE S. HALL, 11–44, 246656, KTEK (1844–1924) G. Stanley Hall founded the *American Journal of Psychology* and was the first president of the American Psychological Association and of Clark University. Operated by A. L. Burbank.

67. STEPHEN SMITH, 11–44, 246768, KYUH (1823–1922) surgeon, pioneer of public health, and founder of the American Public Health Association. Operated by American West African.

68. CHARLES D. WALCOTT, 11–44, 246796, KYUJ (1850–1927) Charles Dolittle Walcott was a noted paleontologist, director of the U.S. Geological Survey, and secretary of the Smithsonian Institution. Operated by American Export Lines.

69. ART YOUNG, 11–44, 246752, KYUK (1866–1943) Arthur Henry "Art" Young was a noted socialist magazine political cartoonist who most often appeared in *The Masses* magazine. He died in New York on December 29, 1943. Operated by A. L. Burbank.

70. CHARLES H. MARSHALL, 11–44, 246833, KYUO (1792–1865) The Black Ball Line of packet ships was founded in 1816 by Benjamin Marshall. Capt. Charles Henry became president in 1835. Operated by Polarus.

71. RANSOM A. MOORE, 11–44, 246852, ANAU (1861–1941) Ransom Asa Moore was the founder of the Wisconsin Agricultural Experiment Association. Operated by J. H. Winchester.

72. SOTER ORTYNSKY, 12–44, 246915, ANBO (1866–1916) Stephen Soter Ortynsky was the first bishop to represent Eastern-rite Catholics in the United States. Operated by Wessel, Duval.

73. BJARNE A. LIA, 12–44, 246934, ANBP (1907–1944) master of the tanker *Bostonian* who was lost when benzol leaked in the pump room on August 12, 1944, off Fort Pierce, Florida. Operated by Moore-McCormack.

74. WENDELL L. WILKIE, 12–44, 246935, ANBQ (1892–1944) Wendell Lewis Wilkie was an industrial leader who lost to FDR in 1940 but became a goodwill ambassador-at-large until suffering a fatal heart attack on October 8, 1944, in New York. Operated by Stockard.

75. FREDERICK E. WILLIAMSON, 1–45, 247016, ANEC (1876–1944) Frederick Ely Williamson was a prominent railroad man and in 1931 president of the New York Central Railroad. Z-EC2-S-C5 operated by International Freighting.

76. MICHAEL JAMES MONOHAN, 1–45, 247056, ANFA (1893–1942) engineer lost on the *Gulfamerica*, torpedoed and shelled by *U-123* on April 10, 1942, off Jacksonville, Florida. Z-EC2-S-C5 operated by Alcoa.

77. CHARLES A. DRAPER, 1–45, 247053, ANFB (1897–1943) radio operator lost on the *Walter Q. Gresham*, torpedoed by *U-221* off Ireland. Z-EC2-S-C5 operated by Polarus.

78. RAFAEL R. RIVERA, 1–45, 247058, ANFC (1921–1943) 3rd mate lost on the

William C. Gorgas, torpedoed by *U-757* on March 10, 1943, in the North Atlantic. Z-EC2-S-C5 operated by States Marine.

79. JAMES W. WHEELER, 2–45, 247118, ANFD (1913–1942) ordinary seaman lost on the *Carrabulle*, torpedoed on May 26, 1942, by *U-106* in the Gulf of Mexico. Z-EC2-S-C5 operated by Calmar.

80. RAYMOND VAN BROGAN, 2–45, 247120, ANFF (1915–1942) able-bodied seaman lost on the *Caddo*, torpedoed on November 23, 1942, by *U-518* in the North Atlantic. Z-EC2-S-C5 operated by A. H. Bull.

81. WILLIAM J. RIDDLE, 2–45, 247202, ANIJ (1917–1942) fireman/watertender lost on the *Carrabulle*, torpedoed by *U-106* on May 26, 1942, in the Gulf of Mexico. Z-EC2-S-C5 operated by Moore-McCormack.

82. DUDLEY H. THOMAS, 3–45, 247267, ANIK (1905–1942) chief steward lost on the *Azalea City*, torpedoed on February 20, 1942, by *U-432* off Maryland. Z-EC2-S-C5 operated by A. L. Burbank.

83. JOHN L. MCCARLEY, 2–45, 247272, ANIL (1916–1942) able-bodied seaman lost on the *Pan Kraft*, bombed by German aircraft on July 5, 1942, in the Barents Sea. Z-EC2-S-C5 operated by the U.S. Army.

84. VERNON S. HOOD, 3–45, 247352, ANPR (1917–1943) 3rd assistant engineer lost on the *John Drayton*, torpedoed and shelled on April 21, 1943, by the Italian sub *Leonardo da Vinci*. Z-EC2-S-C5 operated by Overlakes.

85. EDWIN D. HOWARD, 3–45, 247375, ANQC (1923–1943) deck cadet lost on the *John L. Motley*, destroyed during an air attack at Bari, Italy, on December 2, 1943. Z-EC2-S-C5 operated by Waterman.

86. WESLEY W. BARRETT, 3–45, 247377, ANQD (1922–1942) messman lost on the tanker *Rawleigh Warner*, torpedoed by *U-67* on June 23, 1942, off Louisiana. Z-EC2-S-C5 operated by American West African.

87. WARREN P. MARKS, 3–45, 247409, ANQH (1924–1943) engine cadet lost on the *Timothy Pickering*, bombed by German aircraft on July 14, 1943, off Sicily. Z-EC2-S-C5 operated by Shepard.

88. FRANK O. PETERSON, 4–45, 247502, ANTC (1917–1943) 2nd assistant engineer lost on the *James W. Marshall*, bombed by German aircraft on September 15, 1943, off Salerno. Z-EC2-S-C5, operator unknown.

89. BARNEY KIRSCHBAUM, 4–45, 247501, ANTD (1901–1943) master of the *Collingsworth*, lost on January 9, 1943, when the ship was torpedoed by *U-124* off Dutch Guiana. Z-EC2-S-C5 operated by the U.S. Army.

90. MARY CULLOM KIMBRO, 4–45, 247543, ANTL (1889–1942) stewardess lost on the passenger ship *City of Birmingham*, torpedoed by *U-202* on June 30, 1942, off Cape Hatteras. Mary's next of kin was Dr. Marvin McTyeire Cullom, MD, of Nashville. Z-EC2-S-C5 operated by United Fruit. On the afternoon of January 5, 1946, the ship was docked at the Prospect Terminal Corp. yard at the foot of 17th St. in Brooklyn to have the guns and mounts removed when oil leaked from the tankers *Chisolm Trail* and *Apache Trail* and a fire started on the water endangering those three ships and the *Haverford Victory*. Firefighters put out the blaze in half an hour averting a conflagration.

91. JAMES G. SQUIRES, 5–45, 247855, ANZI (1913–1943) 2nd cook & baker lost on the *Malantic*, torpedoed by *U-409* on March 9, 1943, in the North Atlantic. Squires was awarded the Merchant Marine Distinguished Service medal posthumously for holding a line from his lifeboat to the rescue ship in heavy seas while others escaped until he was too exhausted to save himself. Z-EC2-S-C5 operated by Waterman.

92. JAMES F. HARRELL, 6–45, 247854, ANZH (1903–1943) master of the *Gulfstate*, lost when the ship was torpedoed by *U-155* on April 2, 1943, off Florida. Z-EC2-S-C5 operated by United States Navigation.

93. CLAUDE KITCHIN, 6–45, 247857, ANZJ (1869–1923) North Carolina congressman. Z-EC2-S-C5 operated by United Fruit.

94. FRANCIS J. O'GARA, 6–45, 247897, ANZT (1917–1981) O'Gara, 31, of Philadelphia, made one trip as clerk on the *William H. Welch* under Capt. Lee Marshall and sometime after they arrived at New York on November 15, 1943, he accepted a position as the War Shipping Administration's representative at the Calcutta office and took passage on the ill-fated *Jean Nicolet*. The ship was torpedoed on July 2, 1944, by *I-8* in the Indian Ocean. The sub surfaced and of the 100 people on board, 70 were murdered by the Japanese crew. O'Gara was taken prisoner on board the sub and transferred to a prison camp. He was thought to have perished in the atrocity but survived and was liberated on October 28, 1945, becoming the only living namesake for a Liberty ship. He died on September 18, 1981. Z-EC2-S-C5 operated by Calmar.

95. FRANK FLOWERS, 7–45, 248132, AOEL (1875–1944) Chief Commissary Steward aboard the troopship USS *Leviathan* (SP-1326) awarded the Navy Cross for organizing a Steward Department that became a model for all ships. Z-EC2-S-C5 possibly not operated during the war.

96. EDWIN H. DUFF, 7–45, 248131, AOEM (1874–1944) Edwin Hamilton Duff was a noted admiralty lawyer and lobbyist in Washington. Z-EC2-S-C5 operated by United States Lines.

97. JOSEPH V. CONNOLLY, 8–45, 248134, AOEO (1895–1944) Joseph Vincent Connolly was a highly respected Hearst executive who was president of King Features Syndicate and the International News Service. Mrs. Connolly sponsored the ship, which *The Pelham Sun* newspaper in New York described as an aircraft carrier. Z-EC2-S-C5 operated by South Atlantic.

98. WALTER W. SCHWENK, 8–45, 248173, AOFF (1901–1945) Walter William Schwenk served in the Navy, went to work for the Maritime Commission in 1940, and became Atlantic Coast director of the War Shipping Administration on April 15, 1944. He died on March 12, 1945, following an operation. Z-EC2-S-C5 operated by the U.S. Army.

99. CHARLES H. CUGLE, 8–45, 248408, AOHV (1881–1931) Charles Hurst Cugle worked for the Steamboat Inspection Service and wrote books about maritime practices including Cugle's Practical Navigation. Z-EC2-S-C5, no wartime operator.

100. ROBERT F. BURNS, 9–45, 248387, AOHQ (1919–1942) fireman/watertender lost on the freighter *Topa Topa*, torpedoed on August 29, 1942, by *U-66* in the South Atlantic. Z-EC2-S-C5, operator unknown.

101. EDWARD W. BURTON, 9–45, 248395, AOHR (1900–1942) able-bodied seaman lost on the Sun Oil Co. motor tanker *Mercury Sun*, torpedoed on May 18 by *U-125* off Cuba. Z-EC2-S-C5 operated by Cosmopolitan.

102. ORA ELLIS, 9–45, 248492, AOJA (1885–1942) 2nd Cook & Baker lost on the *William C. McTarnahan*, torpedoed by *U-506* on May 16, 1942, in the North Atlantic. Z-EC2-S-C5 operated by Waterman.

BRUNSWICK YARD

1. JAMES M. WAYNE, 5–43, 243252, KHQB (c. 1790–1867) James Moore Wayne was a Georgia congressman and Supreme Court justice. Operated by Waterman.

2. WILLIAM B. WOODS, 6–43, 243472, KHQC (1824–1887) William Burnham Woods was a veteran of Shiloh, Vicksburg, the Atlanta Campaign, and was a Supreme Court justice. Operated by A. H. Bull. Capt. Edward A. Clark, 26, left Savannah, Georgia, in June 1943 and arrived at New York on August 8 from England. He stayed aboard the ship and on March 10, 1944, they were torpedoed by *U-952* off Sicily with the loss of one Armed Guard sailor and 51 soldiers.

3. JOSEPH R. LAMAR, 6–43, 243491, KIQB (1857–1916) Joseph Rucker Lamar was a Supreme Court justice. Operated by AGWI Lines.

4. THOMAS TODD, 6–43, 243601, KIQL (1765–1826) Supreme Court justice. Operated by Standard Fruit.

5. ROBERT TRIMBLE, 7–43, 243782, KIQS (1776–1828) Supreme Court justice. Operated by AGWI Lines.

6. JOHN CATRON, 7–43, 243916, KIQU (1786–1865) Supreme Court justice. Operated by American-Foreign.

7. JOHN MCKINLEY, 8–43, 243988, KIQY (1780–1852) Alabama congressman and Supreme Court justice. Operated by Dichmann, Wright & Pugh.

8. JOHN A. CAMPBELL, 8–43, 244042, KIRC (1811–1889) John Archibald Campbell was a Supreme Court justice. Operated by Moore-McCormack.

9. JOHN M. HARLAN, 9–43, 244134, KIRI (1833–1911) John Marshall Harlan was a Supreme Court justice. Operated by Moore-McCormack.

10. HOWELL E. JACKSON, 9–43, 244223, KIRA (1832–1895) Howell Edmunds Jackson was a Supreme Court justice. Operated by Marine Transport.

11. EDWARD D. WHITE, 9–43, 244260, KIRD (1844–1921) Edward Douglass White, Jr., was chief justice of the Supreme Court and a Louisiana senator. Operated by A. H. Bull.

12. HORACE H. LURTON, 10–43, 244264, KIRM (1844–1914) Horace Harmon Lurton was a Supreme Court justice at age 65, the oldest appointee. Operated by Cosmopolitan.

13. HENRY W. GRADY, 10–43, 244313, KYPV (1850–1889) Henry Woodfin Grady was publisher of the *Atlantic Constitution* and worked to bring the Confederate states back into the Union as spokesman for the "New South." Operated by Wilmore.

14. JAMES A. WETMORE, 11–43, 244350, KTMN (1863–1940) James Alphonso Wetmore was a lawyer and administrator of federal architectural services as Executive Supervising Architect. Operated by William J. Rountree.

15. FREDERICK BARTHOLDI, 11–43, 244490, KTMO (1834–1904) Frédéric Auguste Bartholdi was the French designer of the Statue of Liberty. Operated by West India. Stranded on December 24, 1943, on Skye.

16. JOHN B. GORDON, 11–43, 244662, KUGA (1832–1904) John Brown Gordon was a Confederate general and Georgia senator and governor. Operated by T. J. Stevenson.

17. EDWARD P. ALEXANDER, 11–43, 244709, KUGH (1835–1910) Edward Porter Alexander was an engineer, railroad official, Confederate general, inventor of railroad equipment, and author. Operated by Wilmore.

18. ROBERT BATTEY, 12–43, 244740, KVCD (1828–1895) Confederate surgeon and gynecologist who performed the first successful removal of diseased overies (oophorectomy) on August 27, 1872, known as "Battey's Operation." Operated by Cosmopolitan.

19. SAMDEE, 12–43, 169814, MYPZ, built for the British Ministry of War Transport. Operated by Thos. & Jno. Brocklebank.

20. JOE C. S. BLACKBURN, 12–43, 244822, KVFQ (1838–1918) Joseph Clay Stiles Blackburn was a Kentucky congressman. Operated by Black Diamond.

21. JOHN B. LENNON, 12–43, 244823, KVKP (1850–1923) John Brown Lennon was general secretary of the Journeyman Tailors Union of America, treasurer of the American Federation of Labor, and served on federal Labor Department boards and commissions. Operated by Smith & Johnson.

22. GEORGE G. CRAWFORD, 1–44, 244904, KVLY (1869–1936) George Gordon Crawford was one of the first two graduates of the Georgia Institute of Technology in 1890 who became president of the Tennessee Coal, Iron & Railroad Co. at Birmingham and president of the Jones & Laughlin Steel Co. in Pittsburgh. Operated by American Range–Liberty Lines.

23. DAVID B. JOHNSON, 1–44, 244901, KVMD (1856–1928) David Bancroft Johnson was superintendent of the Columbia Graded Schools in South Carolina and organized the Winthrop Training School, the first state college for women in South Carolina to train teachers. Operated by Wilmore.

24. HOWARD E. COFFIN, 1–44, 244973, KVOH (1873–1937) Howard Earle Coffin was an auto engineer and cofounder of the Hudson Motor Car Co. Operated by South Atlantic.

25. R. NEY MCNEELY, 2–44, 245010, KVOJ (1883–1915) Robert Ney McNeely was a North Carolina teacher, lawyer, and state representative who was appointed consul to Aden. He was lost when the P. & O. liner *Persia* was torpedoed off Crete by *U-38*. Operated by South Atlantic.

26. BENJAMIN H. HILL, 2–44, 245083, KVOT (1823–1882) Benjamin Harvey Hill was a United States and Confederate States congressman from Georgia. Operated by A. L. Burbank.

27. JOSEPH M. TERRELL, 2–44, 245102, KVOV (1861–1912) Joseph Meriwether Terrell was a Georgia senator and governor. Operated by R. A. Nicol.

28. ROBERT R. LIVINGSTON, 2–44, 245153, KVYX (1746–1813) Robert Robert Livingston, Jr., was a New York congressman who helped draft the Declaration of Independence and was minister to France. Operated by A. H. Bull.

29. SAMALNESS, 3–44, 180019, MXSW, built for the British Ministry of War Transport. Operated by Haldin & Philipps.

30. ISAAC SHELBY, 2–44, 245224, KWAE (1750–1826) governor of Kentucky, soldier, and namesake for numerous locations. Operated by Smith & Johnson. Capt. John H. Lanctot left Red Hook on November 22, 1944, and hit a mine on January 5, 1945, off Italy. There were no reported casualties.

31. SAMFAIRY, 3–44, 180004, MYTM, built for the British Ministry of War Transport. Operated by Haldin & Philipps.

32. SAMFOYLE, 3–44, 169864, MYTN, built for the British Ministry of War Transport. Operated by Cunard White Star.

33. SAMFINN, 4–44, 169876, MYTP, built for the British Ministry of War Transport. Operated by Donaldson Bros. & Black.

34. SAMVIGNA, 4–44, 169914, MYTQ, built for the British Ministry of War Transport. Operated by Hain Steamship.

35. SAMSELBU, 4–44, 169878, MYTR, built for the British Ministry of War Transport. Operated by Runciman Shipping. Hit a mine off Belgium on March 19, 1945.

36. SAMLEYTE, 4–44, 180546, GSXC, built for the British Ministry of War Transport. Operated by C. T. Browning & Co.

37. SAMAUSTRAL, 5–44, 169891, GSVP, built for the British Ministry of War Transport. Operated by J. & C. Harrison.

38. SAMINGOY, 5–44, 180548, GSVX, built for the British Ministry of War Transport. Operated by New Zealand Shipping.

39. SAMLORIAN, 5–44, 169929, GSWD, built for the British Ministry of War Transport. Operated by E. R. Management Co.

40. SAMOLAND, 6–44, 180491, GSWL, built for the British Ministry of War Transport. Operated by Watts, Watts & Co.

41. DONALD W. BAIN, 6–44, 245720, WPGY (1841–1892) Donald William Bain was the state treasurer of North Carolinian. Operated by Norton Lilly.

42. AUGUSTINE B. MCMANUS, 6–44, 245809, WPYY (1877–1941) Augustine Boas McManus was a naval officer and scientist with the Navy Hydrographic Bureau who testified at trials involving the *Titanic* disaster. Operated by William J. Rountree.

43. JAMES B. DUKE, 6–44, 245886, WPZA (1856–1925) James Buchanan Duke was an industrialist and patron of Duke University. Operated by Wessel, Duval.

44. W. P. FEW, 7–44, 245946, WQAE (1867–1940) William Preston Few was the first president of Duke University. Operated by Isbrandtsen.

45. ALEXANDER S. CLAY, 7–44, 246058, WQAF (1853–1910) Alexander Stephens Clay was a Georgia senator. Operated by South Atlantic.

46. F. SOUTHALL FARRAR, 7–44, 246073, WQAG (1871–1940) Fernando Southall Farrar was a Virginia agriculturist and 4-H leader. Operated by Union Sulphur.

47. JAMES W. CANNON, 7–44, 246105, WRFV (1852–1921) James William Cannon worked in the textile industry. In the mid–1890s he and his son Charles founded Cannon Mills in North Carolina and produced the first towels made in the South. When James died they owned 12 mills and employed 15,000 people. Cannon towels are still sold today. Operated by International Freighting.

48. FRANK PARK, 8–44, 246121, WRFW (1864–1925) Alabama congressman. Operated by United States Navigation.

49. EUGENE T. CHAMBERLAIN, 8–44, 246169, WRFX (1856–1920) Eugene Tyler Chamberlain was the U.S. Commissioner of Navigation. Operated by Isbrandtsen.

50. THOMAS B. KING, 8–44, 246223, WSKL (1800–1864) Thomas Butler King was a Georgia congressman. Operated by Wessel, Duval.

51. R. WALTON MOORE, 8–44, 246244, WSUU (1859–1941) Robert Walton Moore was a Virginia congressman. Operated by Parry.

52. NIELS POULSON, 8–44, 246281, WSLR (1843–1911) came to America from Denmark in 1864, worked as a brick mason, then as a draftsman in Washington, D.C. While there he got interested in architectural iron work and in 1868 he moved to New York to work for Architectural Iron Works, the largest firm of its kind in the country. Also there was an architectural draftsman named Charles M. Eger. When Poulson decided to go out on his own in 1876 to manufacture iron work Eger joined him and the two worked as Poulson & Eger. In 1897 they incorporated as the Hecla Iron Works, with Poulson as president and Eger vice president. Over the years they made many significant contributions to the manufacturing of architectural and ornamental iron work including fireproof stairs, elevator enclosures, and library shelves. They provided the Library of Congress with plans for library shelves free of charge. Operated by Dichmann, Wright & Pugh.

53. ARTHUR J. TYRER, 8–44, 246330, KSFD (1868–1936) Department of Commerce official, founding member of the Bureau of Navigation in 1903, and supervising inspector general of the Steamboat Inspection Service. Operated by Grace Line.

54. CASSIUS HUDSON, 9–44, 246381, KSMS (1873–1940) North Carolina agricultural advisor who developed 4-H Youth Development programs. Operated by Alcoa.

55. LUNSFORD RICHARDSON, 9–44, 246462, KSMT (1854–1919) Selena, North Carolina, pharmacist who founded the Vick Chemical Co. and invented many home remedies

including Vicks Croup & Pneumonia Salve, later Vicks VapoRub. Operated by William J. Rountree.

56. JOHAN PRINTZ, 9–44, 246495, KSMZ (1592–1663) Johan Björnsson Printz was governor of the Swedish colony of New Sweden, based in present-day Wilmington, Delaware, from 1623 to 1653. Operated by Parry.

57. CHARLES S. HAIGHT, 10–44, 246541, KSND (1838–1891) Charles Sherman Haight was a New Jersey congressman. Operated by Marine Transport.

58. R. J. REYNOLDS, 10–44, 246577, WSLD (1850–1918) Richard Joshua Reynolds was a tobacco magnate. Operated by Black Diamond.

59. DUNCAN L. CLINCH, 10–44, 246582, KZSU (1787–1849) Duncan Lamont Clinch was an Army officer in the Seminole Wars and a Georgia congressman. Operated by American Export Lines. Hit a mine in December 1945 off Le Havre, France. The ship was lost but there were no casualties.

60. ABIGAIL GIBBONS, 10–44, 246624, KSZY (1801–1893) Abigail Hooper was a New York abolitionist and school teacher who married abolitionist James S. Gibbons in 1833. In 1845 she and her abolitionist father, Isaac Hooper, founded the Women's Prison Association. Abby became a nurse during the Civil War and on July 14, 1863, the Hooper home was burned during the New York Draft Riots. Operated by American-Foreign.

61. CHARLES W. STILES, 10–44, 246685, KSZZ (1867–1941) Charles Wardell Stiles was a Dept. of Agriculture zoologist whose work with hookworms and groundwater contaminants greatly aided public health. Operated by Seas Shipping.

62. MURRAY M. BLUM, 11–44, 246738, KTAB (1920–1943) radio operator from Brooklyn on the *Leonidas Polk* who drowned on December 3, 1943, while attempting to save another crewmember who had fallen overboard after a collision with the small Dutch vessel *Princess Irene* nine miles west of the Mull of Galloway. Blum was awarded the Merchant Marine Distinguished Service medal posthumously. Operated by Mississippi Shipping.

63. LAURA BRIDGMAN, 11–44, 246761, KTAF (1829–1889) Laura Dewey Lynn Bridgman contracted scarlet fever when she was two and became deaf and blind and lost her sense of taste and smell. Her two older sisters died. In 1837 Laura went to the Perkins Institution for the Blind in Boston where Dr. Samuel Howe educated her using tactile methods to indentify letters and numbers. She became the first person to be educated in English using this method. Operated by Seas Shipping.

64. RICHARD RANDALL, 11–44, 246800, KYTN (1750–1801) Robert Richard Randall was a wealthy New York privateer captain and philanthropist who endowed what would become the Trustees of the Sailors' Snug Harbor in the City of New York. Operated by Isbrandtsen.

65. EDWARD R. SQUIBB, 11–44, 246834, KYTQ (1819–1900) Edward Robinson Squibb was a Navy physician who founded his own pharmaceutical company. Operated by West India.

66. JOHN H. HAMMOND, 11–44, 246849, KYTU (1855–1936) John Hays Hammond was a San Francisco-born mining engineer who became embroiled in South African politics and served as president of the American Institute of Mining Engineers. Operated by William J. Rountree.

67. ALBERT K. SMILEY, 11–44, 246912, KYTW (1828–1912) Albert Keith Smiley was co-owner with his twin Quaker brother Alfred H. of the famous 251-room resort hotel Mohonk Mountain House at New Platz, New York. Operated by International Freighting.

68. IRA NELSON MORRIS, 12–44, 246942, ANBG (1875–1939) U.S. minister to Sweden who saved the life of Ellen Neilson, a 19-year-old Brooklyn girl, in December 1921 on

the liner *United States* when they were in heavy seas and she was going overboard. Operated by Seas Shipping.

69. GEORGE W. NORRIS, 12–44, 246967, ANBH (1861–1944) George William Norris was a Nebraska senator and member of President Roosevelt's "Brain Trust" of campaign supporters. Operated by Prudential.

70. ARTHUR M. HULBERT, 12–44, 246964, ANBI (1870–1937) New Jersey State Leader of Boys' and Girls' Club Work, Rutgers College Agricultural College Station, Division of Extension in Agriculture and Home Economics. Operated by Alcoa.

71. M. E. COMERFORD, 12–44, 246985, ANBJ (1865–1939) Michael Comerford opened some of the first motion picture theaters in Pennsylvania and New York. Operated by Merchants & Miners.

72. FELIX RIESENBERG, 12–44, 247015, ANDZ (1879–1939) licensed mariner, explorer, civil engineer, U.S. Shipping Board chief officer, and marine textbook author. Operated by American West African.

73. VADSØ, 12–44, port city in Norway. Operated under the Norwegian flag by Nortraship.

74. WILLIAM F. JERMAN, 12–44, 247086, ANEU (1914–1942) master of the *Cities Service Empire*, lost when the ship was torpedoed by *U-128* on February 22, 1942, off the East Coast. Operated by Black Diamond.

75. WILLIAM COX, 1–45, 247122, ANEV (1898–1942) African-American fireman on the coastal collier *David H. Atwater*, shelled by *U-552* on April 2, 1942, off Virginia. Operated by Blidberg Rothchild.

76. GEORGE R. POOLE, 1–45, 247115, ANEW (1885–1943) 1st assistant engineer lost on the Gulf Oil tanker *Gulfstate*, torpedoed by *U-155* on April 3, 1943, off Florida. Operated by Stockard.

77. HAROLD O. WILSON, 1–45, 247147, ANHY (1906–1943) oiler lost on the *Flora MacDonald*, torpedoed on May 30, 1943, by *U-126* off Sierra Leone. Operated by United States Navigation.

78. JAMES BENNETT MOORE, 1–45, 247135, ANHZ (1899–1942) 2nd assistant engineer lost on the Calmar freighter *Massmar* when the ship wandered into an Allied minefield off Greenland. Operated by A. L. Burbank.

79. HALTON R. CAREY, 2–45, 247160, ANIA (1921–1942) ordinary seaman lost on the Atlantic Refining tanker *W. D. Anderson*, torpedoed on February 22, 1942, by *U-504* off Florida. Operated by American Liberty.

80. HAROLD DOSSETT, 2–45, 247190, ANIB (1914–1942) messman lost on the *Samuel Q. Brown*, torpedoed by *U-103* on May 23, 1942, off Cuba. Operated by Norton Lilly.

81. PATRICK S. MAHONY, 2–45, 247196, ANIC (1888–1942) master of the Standard Oil tanker *J. A. Moffett, Jr.,* lost when the ship was torpedoed by *U-571* on July 8, 1942, off Florida. Operated by Black Diamond.

82. BELGIAN EQUALITY, 2–45, operated under the Belgian flag.

83. CHARLES C. RANDLEMAN, 3–45, 247263, ANLP (1911–1942) messman lost on the *William C. McTarnahan*, torpedoed by *U-506* on May 16, 1942, in the Gulf of Mexico. Operated by American-Foreign. Stranded on August 31, 1945, on Apo Reef off Mindoro Island, Philippines.

84. ROY JAMES COLE, 3–45, 247349, ANMX (1906–1943) chief engineer lost aboard the *Expositor*, torpedoed by *U-606* on February 22, 1943, in the North Atlantic. Operated by Blidberg Rothchild.

85. PATRICK B. WHALEN, 3–45, 247348, ANMY (1884–1942) 1st assistant engineer

lost on the *Illinois*, torpedoed on June 1, 1942, by *U-172* in the Caribbean. Operated by Isbrandtsen.

Kaiser Company, Inc.
Vancouver, Washington

The land was a 245-acre dairy farm on which Dr. John McLoughlin's orginial Fort Vancouver was built in 1824. The Maritime Commission spent $50,681 on land and $26,644,740 on facilities. The 12-way yard, under executive vice president Edgar F. Kaiser, general manager Michael Miller, and general superintendent John Hallett delivered the *George Vancouver* and the *Elias Howe* out of the original 65-ship contract. The keel for the *Vancouver* was laid on April 15, 1942, and launched 165 days after surveyors first walked the property. Construction then switched to the new Landing Ship, Tank (LST) "mystery ship" and the escort "jeep" aircraft carrier. In 1943 eight more Liberty ships were launched but finished and delivered from Kaiser's Oregon Shipbuilding Corp. the Kaiser Co. launched 10 ships. The average building time for the ships was 80.4 days.

1. GEORGE VANCOUVER, 7–42, 242020, KGBT (1757–1798) Royal Navy officer who explored the northwest Pacific Coast in 1791–95 and namesake for all things Vancouver in Canada and the Pacific Northwest. Operated by American President Lines.

2. ELIAS HOWE, 7–42, 242092, KGCM (1819–1867) inventor of the sewing machine. Operated by Pacific-Atlantic. Capt. Joseph W. Dickover, 26, signed on as master on December 17, 1942, at Seattle and arrived at Bellingham, Washington, on February 2, 1943, from New Westminster, B. C. The ship was torpedoed on September 24, 1943, by *I-10* in the Gulf of Aden with the loss of second engineers Theo R. Payne and fireman/watertender Jerry E. Stott. Capt. Dickover and chief mate Harold L. Codling signed on the *Joseph LeConte* for return to United States

3. JUAN DE FUCA, 1–43, 242751, KKHM (1536–1602) Spanish alias for Greek sailor Ioánnis Fokás who explored the Pacific Northwest. Operated by Weyerhaeuser. Capt. Charles S. Robbins' ship was attacked by Japanese aircraft on December 21 and December 30, 1944, in the Philippines with the loss of two soldiers. On the 30th the ship was hit by an aerial torpedo and while Robbins was trying to find shelter the ship ran onto a reef and started breaking up. He abandoned his damaged ship and cargo only after being ordered off by military authorities. On January 31, 1945, Robbins went aboard the damaged American-Hawaiian Liberty ship *John M. Clayton* at Tacloban as master, signed on a new crew, and arrived at Pearl Harbor on June 3. Capt. Robbins was awarded the Merchant Marine Distinguished Service medal. On September 23, 1945, the *Juan de Fuca* was taken over by the Navy and became the *Araner* (IX-226).

4. FRANCISCO CORONADO, 1–43, 242786, KIGU (1510–1554) Francisco Vázquez de Coronado y Luján was a governor in Mexico who explored what is now the American Southwest and searched for the Seven Cities of Gold. Namesake for Coronado peninsula in San Diego and for many things throughout the Southwest. Operated by Pacific-Atlantic.

5. JOHN CABOT, 1–43, 242808, KIGJ (1450–1498) Zuan Chabotto was an Italian sailor bankrolled by King Henry VII to explore North America and is believed to have made landfall on Newfoundland. Operated by Weyerhaeuser.

6. MOSES CLEAVELAND, 2–43, 242862, KJDD (1754–1806) lawyer, surveyor, soldier, and founder of Cleveland, Ohio. Operated by Union Sulphur.

7. JOSEPH HENRY, 2–43, 242868, KJDF (1797–1878) electromagnetic physicist, meteorologist, and first secretary of the Smithsonian Institution. Operated by Northland.

8. LAURA KEENE, 2–43, 242905, KJCY (1826–1873) stage name of Mary Frances Moss, a British actress and New York theater owner/manager who was the star performer in *Our American Cousin* at Ford's Theater on April 14, 1865, and who identified John Wilkes Booth to the authorities. Operated by Sudden & Christenson.

9. WALTER REED, 2–43, 242934, KFKE (1851–1902) Army doctor and pioneer of epidemiology who discovered that yellow fever was transmitted by mosquitoes. Namesake for Walter Reed General Hospital. Operated by Hammond and converted to an Army troopship.

10. RUSSELL A. ALGER, 3–43, 242952, KFKG (1836–1907) Russell Alexander Alger was governor of Michigan and Secretary of War. Operated by Union Sulphur.

Marinship Corp.
Sausalito, California

In March 1942 the Maritime Commission awarded the W. A. Bechtel Co. a contract for a 6-way yard and 34 ships at Sausalito, California. The Commission spent $305,239 on land and $16,617,824 on facilities. The Commission-owned yard was operated as the Marin Shipbuilding Division of W. A. Bechtel with Kenneth K. Bechtel president and William E. Waste vice president and general manager. The yard built 15 Liberty ships. The first keel was laid on June 27, 1942, and the average building time for the ships was 112.2 days.

1. WILLIAM A. RICHARDSON, 10–42, 242461, KHLB (1795–1856) William Anthony Richardson was the second mate aboard the British whaler *Orion* when they arrived at Yerba Buena in 1822—the future San Francisco, California—and stayed on to make many contributions to the development of the area. Namesake for Richardson Bay. Operated by United States Lines.

2. WILLIAM T. COLEMAN, 11–42, 242476, KHMC (1824–1893) William Tell Coleman was a 49er from Kentucky who went into the shipping business in San Francisco, joined the Committees of Vigilance, and in 1856 moved to New York. Operated by J. H. Winchester. Capt. Samuel J. Reynard's ship left San Francisco in December 1942 with ammunition and aviation gasoline for the Mediterranean. On March 19, 1943, they were moored at Tripoli Harbor when German aircraft attacked and the ship immediately astern of them, the *Ocean Voyager*, with the same type of cargo, was hit and immediately caught fire. Radio operator James C. Huett, 19, and engine cadet Walter G. Sittmann, 23, volunteered to cut the after mooring lines, only six feet from the burning British ship, which they did and the *Coleman* was able to maneuver out of the way. Huett and Sittmann were awarded the Merchant Marine Distinguished Service medal for their efforts. The *Ocean Voyager* lost five crew and the *Coleman* arrived at New York on August 25.

3. WILLIAM KENT, 12–42, 242564, KHLO (1864–1928) California congressman who was instrumental in creating the National Park Service in 1916 and who advocated for creating the Muir Woods National Monument. (National Parks are created by Congress, National Monuments by Presidential proclamation). Operated by American President Lines.

4. JOHN MUIR, 12–42, 242613, KHLL (1838–1914) wilderness preservationist who was instrumental in creating Yellowstone and Sequoia National Parks. Founder of the Sierra Club and namesake for Muir Woods National Monument. Operated by Alaska Packers.

5. LYMAN BEECHER, 12–42, 242638, KIJS (1775–1863) Presbyterian minister, cofounder of the American Temperance Society, and father of Henry Ward Beecher and Harriet Beecher Stowe—three Liberty ships in the family. Operated by American-Hawaiian.

6. PHILIP KEARNY, 1–43, 242690, KHLK (1815–1862) Philip Kearny, Jr., was a noted Army general lost at Chantilly. Namesake for Kearny, New Jersey. Operated by American-Hawaiian.

7. THOMAS HART BENTON, 1–43, 242753, KHMG (1782–1858) Missouri senator who advocated for Westward Expansion, the movement known as Manifest Destiny. Operated by Matson.

8. FRANCIS PRESTON BLAIR, 1–43, 242827, KIKA (1791–1876) Kentucky journalist and member of President Jackson's "kitchen cabinet." Operated by Sudden & Christenson. Stranded on July 15, 1945, on an Australian reef and declared a total constructive loss. There were no reported casualties.

9. MARK HOPKINS, 2–43, 242894, KIKB (1813–1878) Mark Hopkins, Jr., was one of the "Big Four" who founded the Central Pacific Railroad. Operated by Matson.

10. ANDREW D. WHITE, 2–43, 242920, KIKC (1832–1918) Andrew Dickson White was cofounder with Ezra Cornell of Cornell University and was the first president. Also first president of the American Historical Association and an ambassador. Operated by the U.S. Army Transport Service.

11. SEBASTIAN CERMENO, 3–43, 242965, KIKI (1560–1602) Sebastião Rodrigues Soromenho was a Portuguese explorer who visited California in 1595 under the auspices of King Philip II. Operated by Oliver J. Olson. The ship was torpedoed on June 27, 1943, by *U-511* in the Indian Ocean with the loss of five merchant crew including all three watch engineers in the engine room.

12. PETER DONAHUE, 3–43, 243038, KIKJ (1822–1885) Irish-born brothers Peter and James Donahue founded Union Iron Works in San Francisco in 1849 building mining equipment then locomotives. In 1885 they delivered the *Arargo*, the first steel ship built on the West Coast. Operated by Matson.

13. SUN YAT-SEN, 4–43, 243206, KMYS (1866–1925) founder of the Republic of China. Operated by North Atlantic & Gulf.

14. HENRY DURANT, 7–43, 243770, KKMS (1802–1875) Yale graduate who was involved with several academies and in 1868 was a founder and first president of the University of California at Berkeley. Operated by Norton Lilly.

15. JACK LONDON, 8–43, 243987, KKCF (1876–1916) John Griffith Chaney was a journalist and, as an Oakland, California, resident Jack London, one of the first commercially successful writers of fiction. Operated by Pacific-Atlantic.

New England Shipbuilding Corp.
169 Front St., South Portland, Maine

Created on April 1, 1943, under Todd Shipyards management subsequent to the merger of the Todd-Bath Iron Shipbuilding Corp. and the South Portland Shipbuilding Corp. The Maritime Commission spent $1,027,763 acquiring land and $22,273,278 on facilities, including the former South Portland yard. Todd executive Andrew B. Sides was president and Walter L. Green was vice president and general manager. The company built 212 Liberty ships with an average building time of 73.8 days. In September 1944 a major hurricane hit the Atlantic Coast. Damage and deaths occurred with high winds in South Portland.

1. RICHARD HOVEY, 4–43, 243043, KHZY (1864–1900) Illinois poet who wrote "Men of Dartmouth." Operated by Coastwise Transportation. Capt. Hans Thorsen's ship arrived at New York on November 7, 1943, from Liverpool, England, and moved to Charleston, South Carolina, arriving on the 20th. Capt. Thorsen expected to sail sometime after December 3 for "World Ports." On March 29, 1944, the ship was torpedoed by *I-26* in the Arabian Sea. The three engineers on watch: 1st assistant engineer Ole J. Albertsen, 35; fireman/watertender Joaquin Guervia, 59; oiler Beaufort L. Lankford, 19; and one Armed Guard sailor were lost. Capt. Thorsen and three others were taken prisoner. Junior third engineer Arthur J. Dreschler was awarded the Merchant Marine Distinguished Service medal for fabricating a makeshift distiller that produced 60 gallons of fresh water for 38 survivors who spent 16 days in a lifeboat.

2. JOHN SULLIVAN, 4–43, 243097, KHZU (1740–1795) irascible New Hampshire delegate to the Continental Congress who became a general, federal judge, and eventually the state's first governor. Operated by Shepard.

3. JOSEPH WARREN, 4–43, 243098, KKLN (1741–1775) physician and president of the Massachusetts Provisional Congress who was at Lexington and Concord and dispatched William Dawes and Paul Revere on their fabled midnight errand. He was a Major General lost at Bunker Hill while serving as a rifleman on Breed's Hill. Operated by Wessel, Duval.

4. EMMA WILLARD, 4–43, 243092, KKLO (1787–1870) Emma Hart was an educator in Middlebury, Vermont, in 1807 when she married physician John Willard, 48, and opened a boarding school. She became an activist for womens' education and founded the Troy Female Seminary in Troy, New York. Operated by Eastern Gas & Fuel.

5. JOHN CHANDLER, 4–43, 243095, KIAA (1762–1841) Maine senator. Operated by American Export Lines.

6. CHARLES SUMNER, 4–43, 243260, KKZI (1811–1874) Massachusetts senator. Operated by Sprague.

7. WILLIAM PHIPS, 4–43, 243267, KHZN (1651–1694) governor of the Province of Massachusetts Bay. Operated by Eastern Steamship.

8. JOHN HOLMES, 4–43, 243262, KIBB (1773–1843) Massachusetts congressman, Maine senator. Operated by A. L. Burbank.

9. EMILY DICKINSON, 5–43, 243261, KIAB (1830–1886) Emily Elizabeth Dickinson was a reclusive poet from Massachusetts. Operated by Eastern Gas & Fuel.

10. ASA GRAY, 5–43, 243337, KKZJ (1810–1888) physician, botanist, and professor of natural history at Harvard. Operated by Sprague.

11. MARY LYON, 5–43, 243346, KKZM (1797–1849) Mary Mason Lyon was a teacher and founder of Mount Holyoke Female Seminary. Operated by Cosmopolitan.

12. HENRY WILSON, 5–43, 243339, KMHP (1812–1875) Jeremiah Jones Colbath legally changed his name before he became President Grant's vice president. Operated by American Export Lines.

13. THOMAS W. HYDE, 5–43, 243266, KKZT (1841–1899) Thomas Worcester Hyde was awarded the Medal of Honor for service at Antietam, became general manager of Bath Iron Works in 1888, and was a senator from Maine. Operated by Calmar.

14. EUGENE FIELD, 5–43, 243338, KIAS (1850–1895) author of children's poetry and humor. Operated by American Export Lines.

15. GEORGE F. PATTEN, 5–43, 243414, KLBL (1787–1869) prominent builder and ship operator at Bath, Maine. Operated by International Freighting.

16. CHARLES W. ELIOT, 5–43, 243441, KKZR (1834–1926) Charles William Eliot was president of Harvard from 1869 to 1909. Operated by Sprague. Capt. Walter O'Brien's

ship departed New York on or about April 12 for the Normandy Invasion and sank on June 28, 1944, after hitting two mines off Juno Beach. There were no reported fatalities.

17. HARRIET BEECHER STOWE, 6–43, 243431, KKZS (1811–1896) Harriet Elizabeth Beecher married Calvin E. Stowe in 1836, a professor at the school she was attending, and went on to write *Uncle Tom's Cabin*. Operated by Eastern Gas & Fuel.

18. WILLIAM PEPPERELL, 6–43, 243427, KOMK (1696–1759) Kittery shipping man who financed the 1746 expedition to capture the French fortress of Louisbourg on Île Royale, present day Cape Breton Island, during King George's War, a part of the French and Indian War. Operated by Calmar.

19. EUGENE HALE, 6–43, 243489, KNAZ (1836–1918) Maine congressman. Operated by American Export Lines.

20. ROBERT TREAT, 6–43, 243498, KNBV (1622–1710) governor of the Connecticut Colony. Operated by Eastern Steamship.

21. THOMAS B. REED, 6–43, 243499, KOOP (1839–1902) Thomas Brackett Reed was a Maine congressman. Operated by Calmar.

22. GEORGE CLEEVE, 6–43, 243620, KXCD (1601–1667) founder of Portland, Maine. Operated by American Export Lines. Capt. Daniel L. MacDonald's ship was torpedoed by *U-969* off Bone, Algeria, on February 22, 1944, and beached. 2nd engineer Andrew T. Brown was the only fatality and the ship was a total constructive loss.

23. JACOB H. GALLINGER, 6–43, 243621, KXCE (1837–1918) Jacob Harold Gallinger was a New Hampshire congressman. Operated by Sprague.

24. JEREMIAH O'BRIEN, 6–43, 243622, KXCH (1740–1818) leader of the first American naval victory during the Revolutionary War at Machias, District of Maine. Operated by Grace Line.

25. JOSHUA L. CHAMBERLAIN, 6–43, 243626, KXCR (1828–1914) Joshua Lawrence Chamberlain was a Civil War general, governor of Maine, and president of Bowdoin University. Operated by Eastern Gas & Fuel.

26. SILVESTER GARDINER, 6–43, 243629, KXCX (1708–1786) Maine lawyer, physician and namesake of Gardiner, Maine. Operated by American Export Lines.

27. JOHN A. POOR, 243693, 7–43, KXGN (1808–1871) John Alfred Poor developed railroads in Maine. Operated by International Freighting. Torpedoed on March 19, 1944, by *U-510* in the Arabian Sea with the loss of 25 merchant crew and nine Navy Armed Guard sailors.

28. ROBERT JORDAN, 7–43, 243696, KXGG (1611–1679) in 1648 Rev. Jordan acquired the Plymouth Company land granted to Moses Goodyear and Robert Trelawny, encompassing Cape Elizabeth and South Portland, Maine, under very dubious circumstances. Operated by American Export Lines.

29. ROBERT ROGERS, 7–43, 243697, KXGK (1731–1795) commander of Rogers' Rangers in the French and Indian War. Operated by Moore-McCormack.

30. HARRY A. GARFIELD, 7–43, 243692, KXGT (1863–1942) Harry Augustus "Hal" Garfield was President Garfield's son and president of Williams College. Operated by Eastern Gas & Fuel.

31. ARTHUR L. PERRY, 8–43, 243825, KXIL (1830–1905) Arthur Latham Perry was an economics professor and president of Williams College who strongly opposed tariffs in foreign trade. Operated by Calmar.

32. NELSON DINGLEY, 7–43, 243842, KXIN (1832–1899) Nelson Dingley, Jr., was governor of Maine and a congressman. Operated by States Marine.

33. EZRA WESTON, 8–43, 243831, KXHZ (1747–1805) famous shipowner from

Duxbury, Massachusetts. Operated by International Freighting. Capt. Earl W. Larrabee's ship was torpedoed on August 8, 1944, by *U-667* off Lands End, England. There were no reported casualties.

34. JAMES BOWDOIN, 8–43, 243836, KXIS (1726–1790) James Bowdoin II was a political figure in Massachusetts who endowed Bowdoin College in the District of Maine. Operated by Eastern Gas & Fuel.

35. JOSIAH QUINCY, 8–43, 243841, KXIE (1709–1784) spy who watched the British fleet in Boston Harbor and notified General Washington of movements and events. Operated by Black Diamond.

36. WILLIAM STURGIS, 8–43, 243942, KXIJ (1782–1863) Boston merchant and shipmaster in the China and fur trade. Operated by Calmar.

37. FERDINANDO GORGES, 8–43, 243935, KXYJ (1566–1647) Sir Gorges is considered the father of English colonization in North America and founder of the District of Maine in 1622 but never actually came to the New World. Operated by Moore-McCormack.

38. JOHN MASON, 8–43, 243939, KXYN (c. 1600–1672) Massachusetts pioneer and cofounder of Norwich, Connecticut. Operated by Sprague.

39. HENRY JOCELYN, 8–43, 243937, KXIX (1606–1683) Maine pioneer and governor. Operated by Calmar.

40. BARTHOLOMEW GOSNOLD, 9–43, 243934, KXYI (1572–1607) master of the *Godspeed* and commodore of the *Susan Constant* and *Discovery* in the Virginia Co. expedition to Jamestown, Virginia, in 1607. He explored Maine and settled in Cape Cod. Operated by Marine Transport.

41. ANNA HOWARD SHAW, 9–43, 244114, KXYP (1847–1919) teacher, first female Methodist minister, associate of Mary A. Livermore, physician, president of the National American Women Suffrage Association, head of the Women's Committee of the United States Council of National Defense during World War I, and first female to be awarded the U.S. Army's Distinguished Service Medal. Operated by American South African.

42. CYRUS H. K. CURTIS, 9–43, 244116, KYHV (1850–1933) Cyrus Hermann Kotzschmar Curtis founded of the Curtis Publishing Co. and published the *Ladies' Home Journal* and the *Saturday Evening Post*. Operated by American Export Lines.

43. HELLAS, 9–43, ancient name for Greece. Operated under the Greek flag.

44. FORT ORANGE, 9–43, PEDH, the first permanent New Netherland Dutch settlement located at Albany, New York, in 1624. Operated under the Dutch flag.

45. PARK HOLLAND, 9–43, 244268, KYIN (1752–1844) pioneer and surveyor of the District of Maine. Operated by William J. Rountree.

46. PEREGRINE WHITE, 9–43, 244269, KYNV (1620–1704) William and Susanna White's son was born on board the *Mayflower* while the vessel was at anchor at Cape Cod Hook shortly after arriving in November 1620. The first child born to Pilgrims in America. Operated by Black Diamond.

47. JOHN FAIRFIELD, 10–43, 244265, KYNQ (1797–1847) Maine Congressman and governor. Operated by American Export Lines.

48. AMERIKI, 9–43, America in Greek, Operated under the Greek flag.

49. JOHN N. ROBINS, 10–43, 244266, KYIG (1852–1923) founder of the Robins Dry Dock & Repair Co., one of three companies that merged into Todd Shipyards. Operated by American Export Lines.

50. SUMNER I. KIMBALL, 10–43, 244272, KYOB (1834–1923) Sumner Increase Kimball was the founder of the U.S. Life Saving Service. Operated by Eastern Gas & Fuel. Capt. Harry Atkins, his ship, 39 merchant seamen, and 24 Armed Guard sailors disappeared

in January 1944 and were never seen or heard from again. It was later discovered they had been torpedoed on January 16 by *U-960* east of the Strait of Belle Isle.

51. THOMAS CLYDE, 10–43, 244273, KYIM (1867–1937) president of Clyde Steamship and founder of AGWI Lines. Operated by Moore-McCormack.

52. ENOCH TRAIN, 10–43, 244261, KYNN (1801–1868) ran a packet service from Boston to Liverpool, Russia, South America, and San Francisco and in 1855 formed the Boston & European Steamship Co. Operated by Boland & Cornelius.

53. ROBERT L. VANN, 10–43, 244271, KYNZ (1880–1940) Robert Lee Vann, of North Carolina, was an African-American attorney and founder of the *Pittsburgh Courier*. In 1940 he lived with his wife Jessie, 55, and their 34-year old maid Ethel Mackert, in a $35,000 home at 7337 Monticello. Operated by United Fruit. Capt. John Godfrey's ship hit a mine on March 1, 1945, off Ostend, Belgium, and sank. There were no reported casualties.

54. OMAR E. CHAPMAN, 10–43, 244484, KTMV (1855–1912) famous Maine sea captain. Operated by Boland & Cornelius.

55. SAMTUCKY, 10–43, 169684, MYYM, built for the British Ministry of War Transport. Operated by Prince Line.

56. SAMPHILL, 11–43, 169683, MYNZ, built for the British Ministry of War Transport. Operated by Royal Mail Lines.

57. GEORGE POPHAM, 11–43, 244480, KTMX (1550–1608) colonizer of the Maine region. Operated by Luckenbach.

58. SAMRICH, 11–43, 169702, MYPB, built for the British Ministry of War Transport. Operated by Shaw, Savill & Albion.

59. SAMTRENT, 11–43, 169724, MYPC, built for the British Ministry of War Transport. Operated by the Union-Castle Mail Steamship Co.

60. SAMAKRON, 11–43, 169699, MYNX, built for the British Ministry of War Transport. Operated by Royal Mail Lines.

61. SAMLONG, 11–43, 169689, MYNY, built for the British Ministry of War Transport. Operated by Prince Line.

62. MARY WILKINS FREEMAN, 11–43, 244588, KTMU (1852–1930) Mary Eleanor Wilkins married Dr. Charles M. Freeman in 1902. Mary became a prominent Massachusetts author who worked as a secretary for Dr. Oliver Wendell Holmes. Operated by Boland & Cornelius.

63. J. WILLARD GIBBS, 11–43, 244640, KUGK (1839–1903) Josiah Willard Gibbs was a Yale mathematician and physicist who developed physical chemistry as a science, known as the "father of vector analysis." Operated by Calmar.

64. JAMES MANNING, 12–43, 244637, KUGV (1738–1791) cofounder and first president of what became Brown University. Operated by American Export Lines.

65. ROBERT R. RANDALL, 12–43, 244645, KUHH (1750–1801) Robert Richard Randall was a prosperous New York privateer captain, merchant, and philanthropist who endowed the Sailors Snug Harbor retirement home on Staten Island. Operated by Pope & Talbot.

66. MERCY WARREN, 12–43, 244643, KUHL (1728–1814) Mercy Otis married James Warren and from their Barnstable, Massachusetts, home she became active in politics and wrote as a historian, poet, and dramatist opposing British rule while her husband served in Massachusetts political offices. Operated by West India.

67. WEBB MILLER, 12–43, 244807, KVFR (1891–1940) Webster Miller, general manager of the United Press in Europe covering the war, died in a subway accident during the London blitz. Operated by American Range–Liberty Lines.

68. EUGENE E. O'DONNELL, 12–43, 244854, KVKU (1883–1933) sea captain and president of Eastern Steamship Lines. Operated by Eastern Steamship.

69. GEORGE S. WASSON, 12–43, 244859, KVFT (1855–1932) noted Maine artist, boatbuilder, and author of *Sailing Days on the Penobscot*. Operated by R. A. Nicol. Capt. William Munda's ship hit a mine on January 31, 1944, off England and sank. There were no reported casualties. The ship was scuttled off Normandy as part of Gooseberry 1. Survivors were returned to New York on the *Aquitania*, arriving at New York from Greenock, Scotland, on July 3, 1944.

70. SAMDON, 12–43, 169781, MYQC, built for the British Ministry of War Transport. Operated by Cayzer, Irvine.

71. SAMSPRING, 12–43, 169755, MYPN, built for the British Ministry of War Transport. Operated by Royal Mail Lines.

72. SAMTAMPA, 12–43, 169787, KYPP, built for the British Ministry of War Transport. Operated by the Houlder Line.

73. SAMAVON, 12–43, 169785, MYQB, built for the British Ministry of War Transport. Operated by Prince Line.

74. SAMYTHIAN, 1–44, 169801, MYQD, built for the British Ministry of War Transport. Operated by Kaye, Son & Co.

75. SUSAN COLBY, 1–44, 244993, KVPD (1817–1919) Susan F. Colby was the daughter of New Hampshire governor Anthony Colby and was the first principal of the New London Academy. In 1851 she married James B. Colgate and moved to New York. She is the namesake for Colby Junior College in New London, New Hampshire. Operated by Moore-McCormack.

76. SAMEARN, 1–44, 169816, MYQF, built for the British Ministry of War Transport. Operated by the Houlder Line.

77. SAMTEVIOT, 2–44, 169856, MYQG, built for the British Ministry of War Transport. Operated by Trinder Anderson & Co.

78. EDWARD KAVANAUGH, 1–44, 244934, KVNP (1795–1844) Maine congressman and acting governor. Operated by Parry.

79. GEORGE T. ANGELL, 1–44, 244936, KVNS (1823–1909) George Thorndike Angell was a lawyer who founded the Massachusetts Society for the Prevention of Cruelty to Animals. Operated by American Export Lines.

80. EDWARD H. CROCKETT, 1–44, 244988, KVPC (1911–1943) "Harry" Crockett was an Associated Press war correspondent from Massachusetts who was lost on the minelayer HMS *Welshman* (M.48) under Capt. William Howard Denis Friedberger, RN, when the boat was torpedoed by *U-617* off Tobruk, North Africa, on February 1, 1943. A total of 157 aboard were lost. Operated by American Export Lines. Capt. Albert Baldi, 45, arrived at New York on June 29, 1944, from Algiers and departed around July 25. The ship was torpedoed on September 29, 1944, by *U-310* in the North Atlantic. 1st engineer John D. Hicks, Jr., was lost. Survivors were sent home on the liner *Aquitania* and arrived at New York on October 9.

81. RENALD FERNALD, 2–44, 245086, KVPE (1595–1656) first surgeon in New Hampshire and cofounder of Portsmouth. He left Downs, England, with 88 others on the bark *Warwick* and arrived at Piscataqua, Strawberry Bank, now Portsmouth, on July 4, 1630. Operated by North Atlantic & Gulf.

82. SARAH ORNE JEWETT, 2–44, 245087, KWAF (1849–1909) author and first female PhD in literature from Bowdoin College. Operated by Prudential.

83. WASHINGTON ALLSTON, 2–44, 245088, KVPF (1779–1843) noted South Carolina landscape artist. Operated by Eastern Gas & Fuel.

84. FREDERICK W. TAYLOR, 2–44, 245178, KWAG (1856–1915) Frederick Winslow

Taylor was a noted tennis player and a mechanical engineer who pioneered the scientific efficiency of management in manufacturing. Operated by American Export Lines.

85. SAMTYNE, 2–44, 169847, MYQK, built for the British Ministry of War Transport. Operated by Royal Mail Lines.

86. SAMSTRAE, 2–44, 169862, MYQL, built for the British Ministry of War Transport. Operated by Headlam & Son.

87. SAMANNAN, 3–44, 169822, MYQJ, built for the British Ministry of War Transport. Operated by Blue Star Line.

88. SAMDERWENT, 3–44, 169059, MYRV, built for the British Ministry of War Transport. Operated by Cayzer, Irvine.

89. SAMWYE, 3–44, 169848, MYRT, built for the British Ministry of War Transport. Operated by Andrew Weir & Co.

90. SAMSPERRIN, 3–44, 169937, MYSS, built for the British Ministry of War Transport. Operated by Hain Steamship Co.

91. ARTHUR SEWALL, 3–44, 245239, KWJF (1835–1900) Maine railroad man, shipbuilder, and prominent shipowner. Operated by Eastern Steamship. Capt. Harold C. Jessen's ship was sunk by *U-772* on December 29, 1944, off Portland Bill, England, with the loss of junior engineer Joseph A. Gauvin, and fireman/watertender Irving G. Harrington.

92. STANTON H. KING, 3–44, 245255, KWJE (1867–1939) Stanton Henry King was a sailor, "chantey man of the U.S. Shipping Board recruiting service," and superintendent of the Sailors' Haven in Charlestown for 47 years. Operated by Boland & Cornelius.

93. SAMDARING, 3–44, 180586, MYSN, built for the British Ministry of War Transport. Operated by Prince Line.

94. PARK BENJAMIN, 3–44, 245253, KWOM (1849–1922) patent lawyer and noted science author. Operated by North Atlantic & Gulf.

95. SAMDERRY, 3–44, 180024, MYST, built for the British Ministry of War Transport. Operated by J. & C. Harrison.

96. LILLIAN NORDICA, 3–44, 245251, KWOL (1857–1914) stage name of famed opera singer Lillian Allen Norton. Operated by Black Diamond.

97. ELIJAH KELLOGG, 4–44, 245413, KWUS (1813–1901) popular author of boy's adventure books. Operated by Blidberg Rothchild.

98. CHARLES DAURAY, 4–44, 245411, KWUN (1838–1931) French-Canadian priest who rose to monsignor in the Diocese of Providence, Rhode Island. Operated by United States Navigation.

99. RAYMOND B. STEVENS, 4–44, 245418, KWUU (1874–1942) Raymond Bartlett Stevens was a New Hampshire congressman. Operated by R. A. Nicol.

100. SAMWAKE, 4–44, built for the British Ministry of War Transport. Operated by Stanley & John Thompson. Torpedoed on July 30, 1944, by a German E-boat in the English Channel.

101. BELGIAN TENACITY, 4–44, operated under the Belgian flag.

102. SAMADRE, 4–44, 169916, BTQN, built for the British Ministry of War Transport. Operated Hain.

103. SAMBANKA, 4–44, 180032, BTQV, built for the British Ministry of War Transport. Operated by H. Hogarth & Sons.

104. SAMORESBY, 4–44, 169917, BTQQ, built for the British Ministry of War Transport. Operated by B. & S. Shipping Co.

105. GEORGE ELDRIDGE, 4–44, 245414, KWUT (1812–1900) noted sea captain, hydrographer, and cartographer of the Atlantic Coast. Operated by William J. Rountree.

106. SAMADANG, 4–44, 180493, BTQR, built for the British Ministry of War Transport. Operated by Joseph Robinson & Sons.

107. SAMSUVA, 5–44, 169594, built for the British Ministry of War Transport. Operated by Sir R. Ropner & Co. Torpedoed on September 29, 1944, by *U-310* off North Cape.

108. SAMIDWAY, 5–44, 169905, BTQT, built for the British Ministry of War Transport. Operated by Alfred Holt & Co.

109. SAMSMOLA, 5–44, 180487, GWCY, built for the British Ministry of War Transport. Operated by Ellerman's Wilson Line.

110. GEORGE HAWLEY, 5–44, 245574, WJPC (1869–1934) prominent coal and shipping man in Boston. Operated by Sprague. Capt. John J. Murley, 48, was master of the Sprague Liberty ship *Calvin Coolidge* when they arrived at New York on April 4, 1944, from Naples, Italy. He then took command of the *Hawley*. The ship was torpedoed by *U-1199* on January 21, 1945, just off the Chesapeake Bay's Wolf Trap Lighthouse. Clarence E. Boneham, 2nd engineer, and fireman/watertender Claude L. Greene, Jr., were lost.

111. HADLEY F. BROWN, 5–44, 245576, WJTU (1877–1935) Hadley Fairfield Brown was a lumberjack, soldier, machinist, outdoor guide, sailor, superintendent at Hog Island, became president of the Maryland Dry Dock Co. at Fairfield in 1927. Operated by Eastern Gas & Fuel.

112. JOHN CHESTER KENDALL, 5–44, 245578, WKKY (1877–1941) founder and director of the University of New Hampshire extension service and agricultural experiment station. Operated by Blidberg Rothchild.

113. JOSEPH I. KEMP, 5–44, 245751, WLOT (1872–1943) Joseph Ingersoll Kemp was a pilot at the Boston Navy Yard and famous trial captain the Fore River Shipbuilding Co. who conducted builder's trials and delivered vessels to their owners. Operated by American Range–Liberty Lines.

114. JOSEPH SQUIRES, 5–44, 245752, WPIZ (1909–1942) able-bodied seaman lost when the Waterman freighter *Maiden Creek* foundered off Long Island on December 31, 1942, in heavy seas and covered in ice. Squires was awarded the Merchant Marine Distinguished Service medal posthumously for remaining on board to lower the lifeboats so others could survive. Operated by Dichman, Wright & Pugh.

115. MIAOULIS, 6–44 (1768–1835) Andreas "Miaoulis" Vokos was an admiral during the Greek war of Independence. Operated under the Greek flag.

116. ERNEST W. GIBSON, 6–44, 245746, WPIW (1871–1940) Ernest William Gibson was a Vermont congressman. Operated by International Freighting.

117. HARRIET TUBMAN, 6–44, 245747, WPIX (c. 1820–1913) Araminta Ross was an escaped African-American slave, Union Army nurse, spy, underground railroad worker, and housemother for indigents. Operated by Polarus.

118. JOSEPH-AUGUSTIN CHEVALIER, 6–44, 245750, WPIY (1847–1929) founder and first priest of St. Augustine's parish in Manchester, New Hampshire. Operated by Blidberg Rothchild.

119. WILLIAM LEAVITT, 6–44, 245756, WPOO (1823–1911) Maine sea captain and surveyor and agent for the American Bureau of Shipping at Portland, Maine. Operated by Boland & Cornelius.

120. THOMAS H. SUMNER, 6–44, 245925, WQAJ (1807–1876) Thomas Hubbard Sumner was a sea captain and innovator of celestial navigation methods. Operated by A. L. Burbank.

121. ARAM J. POTHIER, 6–44, 245909, WQAS (1854–1928) Aram Jules Pothier was a governor of Rhode Island. Operated by Blidberg Rothchild.

122. JOSEPH C. LINCOLN, 7–44, 245919, WQAR (1870–1944) Joseph Crosby Lincoln was a prominent maritime novelist. Operated by Mystic.

123. GEORGE L. FARLEY, 7–44, 245915, WRDF (1873–1941) George Lewis "uncle George" Farley was a Massachusetts school superintendent and State 4-H Leader from 1916 until he died. Operated by Boland & Cornelius.

124. ANDREW J. NEWBURY, 7–44, 245910, WRDC (1845–1919) commissioner of New Jersey Pilotage & Docking and president of the Marine Society of New York. Operated by Wilmore.

125. AUGUSTUS P. LORING, 7–44, 245911, WRDD (1856–1938) Augustus Peabody Loring was a noted Boston lawyer specializing in trust law and the author of *A Trustee's Handbook*. Operated by Eastern Steamship.

126. B. CHARNEY VLADECK, 7–44, 245912, WRDE (1886–1938) Baruch Charney Vladeck was a labor leader, managing editor of the *Jewish Daily Forward*, and a New York City councilor. Operated by Merchants & Miners.

127. JAMES SULLIVAN, 7–44, 246123, WRGC (1744–1808) governor of Massachusetts. Operated by West India.

128. EDWARD E. SPAFFORD, 7–44, 246157, WRII (1878–1943) Edward Elwell Spafford was a Navy veteran from New York and national commander of the American Legion. Operated by United States Navigation.

129. LOT M. MORRILL, 8–44, 246125, WRFZ (1813–1883) Lot Myrick Morrill was a governor of Maine, senator, and Secretary of the Treasury. Operated by Wessel, Duval.

130. JOSEPH N. DINAND, 8–44, 246124, WRGX (1869–1943) Joseph Nicholas Dinand was president of Holy Cross University. He died on July 29, 1943. Operated by Eastern Steamship.

131. HAROLD I. PRATT, 8–44, 246122, WRHH (1877–1939) Harold Irving Pratt was a director of Standard Oil of New Jersey, member of the Council on Foreign Affairs, and founder of the Pratt Institute. Operated by Blidberg Rothchild.

132. MARCUS H. TRACY, 8–44, 246126, WRKI (1859–1936) Marcus Hunter Tracy founded M. H. Tracy & Co. and the Tracy Steamship Co., Inc., agents and managers. Operated by Wilmore.

133. THOMAS BRADLEE, 8–44, 246186, WSMK (1885–1931) director of the Vermont Agricultural Extension Service. Operated by Wilmore.

134. WILLIAM TYLER, 8–44, 246225, WSNM (1806–1849) first Catholic bishop in Rhode Island. The Rhode Island Council of the Knights of Columbus sold $4,253,675 in War Bonds to sponsor and pay for the ship. Operated by Sprague.

135. GEORGE N. SEGER, 8–44, 246172, WSNZ (1866–1940) George Nicholas Seger was a New Jersey congressman. Operated by R. A. Nicol.

136. MICHAEL MORAN, 8–44, 246179, WSOL (1832–1906) founder of the Moran Tugboat Company. Operated by Moore-McCormack.

137. WILLIAM LYON PHELPS, 8–44, 246334, KSNJ (1865–1943) author and syndicated columnist of "A Daily Thought" who taught English at Yale for 41 years and died at New Haven on August 21, 1943. Operated by A. L. Burbank.

138. ARCHIBALD R. MANSFIELD, 9–44, 246376, KSNF (1871–1934) Archibald Reuel Mansfield was a minister and first superintendent of the Seaman's Church Institute in New York. Operated by Lykes.

139. C. H. M. JONES, 9–44, 246382, KSNK (1886–1944) London-born Charles Henry M. Jones was a shipping reporter and public relations man for Todd Shipyards Corp. at 1 Broadway, New York. Operated by American West African.

140. GALEN L. STONE, 9–44, 246383, KSNG (1862–1926) Galen Luther Stone was cofounder of Eastern Steamship Lines and president of the Atlantic Gulf & West Indies Steamship Co. Operated by Eastern Steamship.

141. ROBERT B. FORBES, 9–44, 246445, 9–44, KSNQ (1804–1889) Robert Bennet Forbes was a sea captain, innovator of ship construction techniques, and China merchant. Operated by Boland & Cornelius.

142. FRANK P. REED, 9–44, 246433, KSNR (1875–1942) Frank Pearsall Reed was a leader of the Iowa State College 4-H Boys Club for over 25 years. Operated by R. A. Nicol.

143. FERDINAND GAGNON, 9–44, 246432, KSNO (1849–1886) French-Canadian who fled English rule in Quebec in 1868 and became a journalist who worked to unite French Canadians in Canada and America. Operated by Eastern Gas & Fuel.

144. ELIJAH COBB, 9–44, 246431, KSNV (1768–1846) Massachusetts sea captain and author. Operated by Merchants & Miners.

145. ROBERT R. MCBURNEY, 9–44, 246479, KSZD (1837–1898) Robert Ross McBurney arrived from Ireland in 1854 and in 1862 became the first paid staff member of the New York City YMCA. Operated by Weyerhaeuser.

146. EDWARD L. LOGAN, 10–44, 246604, KTAM (1875–1939) Gen. Edward Lawrence Logan was president of the National Guard Association of the United States. Namesake for Logan International Airport in East Boston. Operated by Eastern Steamship.

147. JAMES T. FIELDS, 10–44, 246605, KTAL (1817–1881) James Thomas Fields was a poet and editor of the *Atlantic Monthly*. Operated by West India.

148. MICHAEL ANAGNOS, 10–44 (1837–1906) noted Greek-American educator. Operated under the Greek flag. Owned by the Greek government and operated by the United Greek Ship Owner's Corp. Collided on June 1, 1945, with the Luckenbach Liberty ship *Samuel L. Jeffery* in Panama Bay, Canal Zone.

149. LOAMMI BALDWIN, 10–44, 246607, KSOD (1744–1807) soldier who served at Lexington and Concord and became an engineer. Considered the father of American civil engineering and also creator of the Baldwin apple. Operated by A. L. Burbank & Co.

150. CHARLES TUFTS, 10–44, 246707, KTAU (1781–1876) Massachusetts brick maker who donated 100 acres on which Tufts University was built. Operated by Prudential.

151. KENYON L. BUTTERFIELD, 10–44, 246735, KTAW (1868–1936) Kenyon Leech Butterfield was an agricultural scientist who developed Cooperative Extension Services at the Land Grant Colleges and president of the Rhode Island College of Agriculture and Michigan State College. Operated by R. A. Nicol.

152. ABRAHAM ROSENBERG, 10–44, 246598, KTAX (1870–1935) cofounder of the International Ladies' Garment Workers' Union. Operated by Seas Shipping.

153. WILSON B. KEENE, 10–44, 246689, KTAY (1887–1935) Wilson Bird Keene was a prominent New Jersey shipping man and banker. Operated by Lykes.

154. USS IOLANDA (AKS-14), 10–44, NCXC, general stores issue ship commissioned on June 14, 1945.

155. BELGIAN UNITY, 11–44, operated under the Belgian flag.

156. WINTHROP L. MARVIN, 11–44, 246769, KTIN (1863–1926) Winthrop Lippitt Marvin was a member of the Massachusetts Civil Service Commission, secretary of the Merchant Marine Commission, and general manager of the American Steamship Owners Association. Operated by Isthmian.

157. MATTHEW SHEEHAN, 11–44, 246764, KYXT (1885–1944) Irish-born employee of Barber Steamship Lines of New York for 36 years. Operated by Blidberg Rothchild.

158. USS BELLE ISLE (AG-73), 11–44, miscellaneous auxiliary ship commissioned on July 13, 1945.

159. USS LIGURIA (AKS-15), 11–44, NCXG, general stores issue ship commissioned on July 12, 1945.

160. USS COASTERS HARBOR (AG-74), 11–44, miscellaneous auxiliary ship commissioned on July 29, 1945.

161. FREDERICK BOUCHARD, 11–44, 246797, ANAD (1879–1941) New York tugboat man who started the Bouchard Transportation Co. Operated by International Freighting.

162. BERT WILLIAMS, 11–44, 246831, KTIT (1875–1922) Egbert Austin "Bert" Williams was an African-American humorist and recording artist. Operated by Blidberg Rothchild. In 1948 the ship broke apart while under tow and in 1951 the stern section was joined to the bow portion of the salvaged *Nathaniel Bacon* at Genoa, Italy, to create a new ship named the *Boccadasse.*

163. EDMOND MALLET, 11–44, 246848, ANAT (1842–1907) noted Canadian writer and historian. Operated by Marine Transport.

164. USS CUTTYHUNK ISLAND (AG-75), 11–44, miscellaneous auxiliary ship commissioned on September 1, 1945.

165. CALVIN AUSTIN, 12–44, 246913, ANCP (1850–1936) a director of the Eastern Steamship Line. Operated by Eastern Steamship.

166. THOMAS F. MEAGHER, 12–44, 246917, KTIR (1823–1867) Thomas Francis Meagher was an Irish nationalist leader of the Young Irelanders during the Rebellion of 1848, an American Civil War general who organized the Irish Brigade, and the acting governor of the Montana Territory. Operated by Parry.

167. JOSEPH LEE, 12–44, 246952, ANCV (1862–1937) president of the Massachusetts Civic League that established urban playgrounds for children and president of the National Recreation Association. Operated by Smith & Johnson.

168. JOSHUA SLOCUM, 12–44, 246983, ANDM (1844–1909) first to sail alone around the world. Operated by Smith & Johnson.

169. JULIA P. SHAW, 12–44, 247008, ANDX (1864–1944) Julia Perrine was the daughter of a Dayton, Ohio, businessman. She married George Shaw and became a noted philanthropist. Operated by A. L. Burbank.

170. PAUL BUCK, 12–44, 247085, ANFZ (1901–1942) master of the *Stephen Hopkins* lost during an engagement with the German raider *Stier* and tender *Tannenfels* on September 27, 1942, in the South Atlantic. Capt. Buck was awarded the Merchant Marine Distinguished Service medal posthumously. Operated by Luckenbach.

171. USS AVERY ISLAND (AG-76), 12–44, miscellaneous auxiliary ship commissioned on July 31, 1945.

172. USS INDIAN ISLAND (AG-77), 12–44, miscellaneous auxiliary ship commissioned on July 27, 1945.

173. WILLIAM A. DOBSON, 12–44, 247047, ANGA (1853–1943) William Alexander Dobson was a noted Philadelphia naval architect who worked in a variety of positions over a distinguished career including Wm. Cramp & Sons, the Navy Bureau of Construction, and the American Bureau of Shipping. He died on June 3, 1943. Operated by Marine Transport.

174. F. SCOTT FITZGERALD, 1–45, 247153, ANFY (1896–1940) Francis Scott Key Fitzgerald was a "Lost Generation" novelist and a shirttail relative of the famous lawyer. Operated by R. A. Nichol.

175. EZRA MEECH, 1–45, 247152, ANJP (1773–1856) Vermont congressman. Operated by Dichmann, Wright & Pugh.

176. USS KENT ISLAND (AG-78), 1–45, miscellaneous auxiliary ship commissioned on August 1, 1945.

177. ALFRED E. SMITH, 1–45, 247151, ANJQ (1873–1944) Alfred Emanuel Smith was governor of New York. A section of New York sidewalk was installed in the ship during construction. Operated by Moore-McCormack.

178. LEON S. MERRILL, 2–45, 247165, ANJX (1864–1933) Leon Stephen Merrill was dean of the Maine College of Agriculture, director of the Agricultural Extension Service, and the federal Food Administrator for Maine during World War I. Operated by Black Diamond.

179. FRANCIS A. RETKA, 2–45, 247159, ANJV (1877–1938) Rev. Francis Andrew Retka was chaplain and director of the Polish Orphan Asylum at Emsworth, Pennsylvania. Operated by Boland & Cornelius.

180. JAMES A. BUTTS, 2–45, 247162, ANJW (1926–1942) 1st assistant engineer lost on Grace Line's steamer *Santa Rita*, torpedoed on July 9 by *U-172* northeast of Puerto Rico. Operated by Calmar.

181. T. S. GOLD, 2–45, 247171, ANJY (1818–1906) Theodore Sedgwick Gold founded agricultural schools and was instrumental in creating the University of Connecticut. Operated by Wessel, Duvall.

182. CLARENCE F. PECK, 2–45, 247265, ANLR (1904–1942) wiper lost on the *Carrabulle*, sunk by *U-106* on May 26, 1942, in the Gulf of Mexico. Operated by Shepard.

183. WILLIAM BEVAN, 2–45, 247281, ANLS (1895–1942) chief engineer lost on the *David H. Atwater*, shelled by *U-552* on April 2, 1942, off Virginia. Operated by Eastern Steamship.

184. CHARLES N. COLE, 3–45, 247264, ANLQ (1887–1942) 3rd assistant engineer lost aboard the *Lemuel Burrows*, torpedoed by U-404 on March 14, 1942, off Atlantic City, New Jersey. Operated by Stockard.

185. GEORGE A. LAWSON, 3–45, 247376, ANNA (1918–1942) African-American messman lost on the Southern Transportation tugboat *Menominee*, shelled by *U-754* on March 31, 1942, off Virginia. Operated by Sword Line.

186. RICHARD D. LYONS, 3–45 (1921–1942) utilityman lost on the Socony-Vacuum Oil tanker *Atlas*, torpedoed by *U-552* on April 9, 1942, off North Carolina. Greek government owned, operated by United Greek Shipowners Corp.

187. CARL OFTEDAL, 3–45 (1907–1941) physician and leader of the Norwegian Stavanger resistance group who was executed by the Nazis after the group was exposed by an infiltrator. Operated under the Norwegian flag.

188. DONALD H. HOLLAND, 3–45, 247343, ANNC (1920–1943) able-bodied seaman lost on the *John L. Motley*, destroyed during an air attack at Bari, Italy, on December 2, 1943. Operated by Luckenbach.

189. WILFRED R. BELLEVUE, 3–45, 247371, ANND (1911–1942) 1st assistant engineer from Rochester, New Hampshire, lost on the Sinclair Refining tanker *Joseph M. Cudahy*, torpedoed on May 4, 1942, off Florida by *U-507*. Operated by William J. Rountree.

190. FRED E. JOYCE, 3–45, 247406, ANNE (1890–1942) 3rd assistant engineer lost on the freighter *Sawokla*, sunk by the German commerce raider *Michel* on November 29, 1942, off Madagascar. Operated by Stockard.

191. ELIAS REISBERG, 3–45 (1887–1943) Russian Ukraine native who came to New York in 1906 and in 1909 helped organize the strike of 20,000 shirtwaist makers. In 1916 he was manager of Local 25 of the Waist & Dressmakers Union then moved to the Philadelphia office in 1921. In 1935 he was named director of the cotton garment department of the Inter-

national Ladies Garment Workers Union of the A. F. of L. Operated under the French flag by Compagne Générale Transatlantique. The *Reisberg* was the first French-operated Liberty to reach Le Havre, on May 6, with Lend-Lease wool, wood pulp, paper, and steel.

192. WILLIAM H. LANE, 4–45 (1902–1942) master of the *Hampton Roads*, lost when the ship was torpedoed by *U-106* on June 1, 1942, off Cuba. Operated under the French flag by Compagne Générale Transatlantique.

193. BELGIAN AMITY, 4–45. Operated under the Belgian flag.

194. JOSEPH CARRIGAN, 4–45, 247542, ANNB (1922–1942) wiper lost on the Socony-Vacuum tanker *Ario*, torpedoed by *U-158* on March 15, 1942, off North Carolina. Operated by United States Navigation. Capt. Karl Knudsen's ship hit a mine on August 31, 1945, north of Brunei, Borneo, and declared a total loss. There were no reported casualties.

195. ELWIN F. KNOWLES, 4–45, 247713, ANNF (1901–1943) master of the *John Harvey*, lost when the ship was bombed by German aircraft at Bari, Italy, on December 2, 1943. Operated by AGWI Lines.

196. ERNEST L. DAWSON, 4–45 (1892–1943) 1st assistant engineer lost aboard the *Expositor*, torpedoed by *U-606* on February 22, 1943, in the North Atlantic. Operated under the French flag by Compagne Générale Transatlantique.

197. LEIF M. OLSON, 4–45, 247714, ANWZ (1914–1942) 2nd mate lost on the Socony-Vacuum Oil Co. tanker *Caddo*, torpedoed by *U-518* on November 23, 1942, in the North Atlantic. Operated by Boland & Cornelius.

198. OLIVER WESTOVER, 5–45 (1902–1943) chief mate lost on the *John Drayton*, torpedoed on April 21, 1943, by the Italian sub *Leonardo da Vinci*. Operated under the French flag by Compagne Générale Transatlantique.

199. LESVOS, 5–45, island in the North Aegean Sea also known as Mytilini and Lesbos occupied by Germany and liberated on September 10, 1944. Operated under the Greek flag.

200. DODEKANISOS, 5–45, a group of islands in the Aegean Sea. Operated under the Greek flag.

201. ALLEN G. COLLINS, 6–45 (1912–1943) 3rd mate lost on the *John Bascom*, bombed at Bari, Italy, on December 2, 1943. Collins manned a gun until seriously wounded by a bomb blast. He then assisted others into the last lifeboat before himself and died several days later of wounds. He was awarded the Merchant Marine Distinguished Service medal posthumously. Operated under the French flag by Compagne Générale Transatlantique.

202. JOHN ROBERT GORDON, 6–45 (1918–1943) engine cadet lost on the *Nathaniel Greene*, torpedoed by *U-565* on February 24, 1943, off Oran, Algeria. Operated under the French flag by Compagne Générale Transatlantique. The ship rammed the Portland–South Portland bridge on the way out on June 14 causing $20,000 worth of damage.

203. HAROLD H. BROWN, 6–45 (1917–1942) ordinary seaman lost on the *David H. Atwater*, shelled by *U-552* on April 2, 1942, off Virginia. Operated under the French flag by Compagne Générale Transatlantique.

204. STANLEY R. FISHER, 6–45, 248019, AOBA (1922–1942) ordinary seaman lost on the Weyerhaeuser freighter *Potlatch*, torpedoed by *U-153* on June 27, 1942, in the South Atlantic. Operated by United States Lines.

205. ROBERT W. HART, 8–45, 248274, AOCD (1880–1942) master of the AGWI Lines freighter *San Jacinto*, lost when the ship was torpedoed and shelled by *U-201* on April 21, 1942, off North Carolina. Z-RC2-S-C5, operated by AGWI Lines.

206. J. HOWLAND GARDNER, 8–45, 248272, AOCE (1871–1943) John Howland Gardner was president of the Society of Marine Architects. Z-RC2-S-C5 operated by United States Navigation.

207. SAMUEL R. AITKEN, 8–45, 248534, AOJO (1882–1938) Northern Ireland-born vice president of Moore-McCormack in New York and served with the Shipping Board during the Great War. In 1930 Aitken lived at 100 Woodland Ave. in East Orange, New Jersey, with his wife Margaret, 49, son George, 17, his mother-in-law Jean Scott, 81, and their 20-year-old Irish servant Anna Clarke. In July 1938 son George became engaged to Olive Ann Pearsall, daughter of Charles Pearsall, retired president of the Columbian Steamship Line. George attended the Stevens Institute and was employed by United Fruit. This personal situation involving two families illustrates the often complicated, intertwined nature of the shipping business that has existed since pre–Colonial times. Z-RC2-S-C5 operated by Moore-McCormack.

208. LORENZO C. MCCARTHY, 9–45, 248532, AOJN (1881–1941) the Very Reverend became president of Providence College in 1927. Z-RC2-S-C5, possibly not operated during the war.

209. CARDINAL O'CONNELL, 9–45, 248714, AOLY (1859–1944) William Henry "Number One" O'Connell was archbishop of Boston. Z-RC2-S-C5 operated by the U.S. Army.

210. TOM TREANOR, 10–45, 248717, AOMB (1908–1944) Thomas C. Treanor was the advertising manager for the *Los Angeles Times* in 1940. He became a correspondent and was lost in Europe when a U.S. tank turned into his jeep at Ermont, France, on August 18, 1944. He left a wife Eleanor, 34, sons Thomas, Jr., 10, John, 9, and daughter Cordelia, 5, at their home at 226 S. Westmoreland in Los Angeles. Z-RC2-S-C5 operated by the U.S. Army.

211. WALTER F. PERRY, 10–45, 248852, AONT (1911–1942) able-bodied seaman lost on the *John Winthrop*, torpedoed by *U-619* on September 24, 1942, in the North Atlantic. Z-RC2-S-C5, operator unknown.

212. ALBERT M. BOE, 10–45, 248849, AONR (1916–1944) chief engineer on the Army Transport *FS-214* when the starboard engine exploded on April 13, 1944. Boe ordered everyone in the engine room topside and then took measures to save the ship from fire at his own expense. Z-RC2-S-C5 operated by the U.S. Army. The chief was posthumously awarded the Merchant Marine Distinguished Service medal. The *Boe* was the last Liberty ship delivered.

North Carolina Shipbuilding Co.
Wilmington, North Carolina

The 160-acre Maritime Commission-owned, 9-way yard was operated by the Newport News Shipbuilding & Dry Dock Co. The Commission spent $334,487 on land and $20,058,871 for facilities. The yard built 126 ships. The first keel was laid on May 22, 1941, and the average building time was 64.8 days.

1. ZEBULON B. VANCE, 2–42, 241316, KTED (1830–1894) Zebulon Baird Vance was a North Carolina senator and governor. Operated by American Export Lines. The *Vance* was one of the first Liberty ships to make the infamous and deadly Arctic "PQ" convoy trips to Murmansk and Archangel, Russia, known as the "Murmansk Run" from September 1941 to September 1942. the ship experienced a very unusual series of crew changes. In August 1942 Capt. Guy W. Hudgins left Newport News with Nicholas Harisanoff, 50, as chief mate, Oliver A. Simonson, 40, chief engineer, and Thomas J. Taylor, 35, chief steward. Ens. C. A. Griffin, USNR, was Armed Guard commander with 20 sailors. On September 26 bosun Bernard G. Zastrow, 32, paid off at Liverpool. On September 29 2nd cook & baker Christos Joanidos, 53,

paid off at Glasgow, Scotland, and on October 3 Penn Scott, 37, signed on at Liverpool as 2nd cook & baker. On October 14 galley utilityman Robert M. Gaffney, 18, paid off at Manchester, England, and Canadian citizen Armand Legendre 19, came on in his place. Third engineer William Murphy, 40, also paid off on the 14th and on October 15 British subject Charles Cowell, 32, signed on at Manchester as 3rd engineer. On October 17 British subject William J. Weston, 37, signed on as 2nd cook & baker and Irishman Edward T. Kearns, 29, signed on as galley utility. On December 3 Weston and Kearns paid off at Glasgow and Legendre paid off on December 8. On December 14 Cowell got off at Glasgow. On December 18 third cook Frank B. Kolbuch, 48, paid off at Glasgow. On December 20 able seaman Bernard G. Sayers, 35, paid off at Glasgow. On December 21 deck maintenance man Wilbur H. Tharp, 27, was declared a deserter at Glasgow. On December 23 oiler 33, John J. Weldon paid off at Glasgow. On December 29 chief cook Leroy Dunbar, 42, got off at Glasgow and the next day Penn Scott paid off. On December 30 one Scot and five British sailors were signed on. On January 28, 1943, able seaman Richard Heath, 38, was left in a hospital at Oran, Algeria. On February 18 able seaman Arthur Blomquist died on board at Gibraltar and was buried ashore in the cemetery at Saint Avold, France, as a casualty of war. The next day, February 19, messman Thomas F. Zoll died on board and was buried at Saint Avold as a casualty of war and chief engineer Simonson died in a hospital at Gibraltar and was buried at Saint Avold as a casualty of war. The ship arrived at New York from Gibraltar on March 12, 1943, and Capt. Clinton H. Keaton, 41, expected to sail from Pier D, Jersey City, New Jersey, on April 9 wih only five crew from the previous voyage. They arrived at New York on November 5 from Trinidad. The ship was converted by the War Department to the Army hospital ship *John J. Meany*. St. Louis, Missouri, native Maj. John Joseph Meany, 27, was an Army Medical Corps physician with the air corps who died at Tunisia, North Africa, on March 20, 1943. He graduated from the St. Louis University medical school in 1939 and worked at City Hospital before the war.

2. NATHANIEL GREENE, 2–42, 241419, KBSR (1742–1786) Revolutionary War general from Rhode Island. Operated by United States Lines. Capt. George A. Vickers departed Loch Ewe, Scotland, on September 2, 1942, in the 39-ship, heavily escorted PQ 18 convoy to Murmansk, Russia. The convoy was attacked repeatedly leaving 20 ships to reach port. Capt. Vickers' ship was torpedoed on February 24, 1943, by *U-565* off Oran, Algeria, with the loss of four merchant crew. The ship received the Maritime Commission Gallant Ship award for fending off attacks en route to Russia and Capt. Vickers was awarded the Merchant Marine Distinguished Service medal.

3. VIRGINIA DARE, 3–42, 241468, KRUW (1587-?) daughter of Ananais and Elizabeth Dare and granddaughter of John White, governor in 1587 of the settlement on Roanoke Island. She was the first child born at the Roanoke Island settlement. Operated by South Atlantic. Capt. Arthur L. Johnson was awarded the Merchant Marine Distinguished Service medal posthumously for navigating his ship under air attack en route to Russia in Convoy PQ 18 in September 1942 while the ship's gunners shot down seven bombers. Capt. Vernon A. Davis' ship hit a mine on March 13, 1944, off Bizerte, Tunisia, and broke in two. There were no reported casualties. The *Dare* received the Maritime Commission Gallant Ship award.

4. WILLIAM HOOPER, 3–42, 241469, KDOO (1742–1790) Declaration of Independence signer from North Carolina. Operated by American West African. Capt. Edward L. Graves' ship left Reykjavik, Iceland, on June 28, 1942, in Convoy PQ 17 for Archangel and Murmansk, Russia, via the Denmark Strait. The ship was torpedoed on July 4 by *U-334* in the Barents Sea with the loss first assistant engineer Alfred M. Erdle, oiler John McCaffery, and fireman/watertender Jones C. Hine, all on duty below.

5. DANIEL MORGAN, 3–42, 241546, KEPY (1736–1802) Revolutionary War officer

and Virginia congressman. Operated by American South African. Capt. George T. Sullivan's ship left Reykjavik, Iceland, on June 28, 1942, in Convoy PQ 17 for Archangel and Murmansk, Russia, via the Denmark Strait and was torpedoed on July 5, 1942, by *U-88* in the Barents Sea with the loss of four crew.

6. FRANCIS MARION, 4–42, 241581, KESP (1732–1795) South Carolina Continental Army officer known as the "Swamp Fox" who used guerrilla tactics. Operated by Seas Shipping.

7. JOSEPH HEWES, 5–42, 241596, KFJW (1730–1779) Declaration of Independence signer from North Carolina and director of the Continental Navy. Operated by A. H. Bull and converted to an Army troopship.

8. CHARLES C. PINCKNEY, 5–42, 241680, KFAY (1746–1825) Charles Cotesworth Pinckney was the South Carolina delegate to the Constitutional Convention and minister to France. Operated by American South African. Frank T. Woolverton, 33, signed on the 6,220-ton, 1920 American South African freighter *Henry S. Grove* on December 11, 1941, and arrived back at New York on April 23, 1942. He then took command of the *Pinckney* and left Baltimore in June 1942, departed Suez, Egypt, on September 23 and arrived at New York on December 4. The ship left around January 5, 1943, and was torpedoed on the 27th by *U-514* southwest of the Azores. Out of 42 merchant crew, 36 were lost, including Capt. Woolverton, 21 Armed Guard sailors, and two Army officers. Frank was a divorced New Yorker who lived at 1048 Sterling Place in Kings.

9. JOHN PENN, 6–42, 241645, KFIY (1741–1788) Declaration of Independence signer from North Carolina. Operated by Lykes. Capt. Albin Johnson departed Loch Ewe, Scotland, on September 2, 1942, in the 39-ship, heavily escorted PQ 18 convoy to Murmansk, Russia, and was sunk on September 13, 1942, by German aircraft in the Barents Sea with the loss of 2nd assistant engineer Guy Donaldson, Jr., oiler Francis L. Stephenson, and fireman/watertender Arthur W. Cantrell, all on watch below.

10. JOHN C. CALHOUN, 6–42, 241677, KFHV (1782–1850) John Caldwell Calhoun was a political theorist and vice president from South Carolina. Operated by Calmar. Capt. Daniel L. Madison's ship was damaged by explosion on September 7, 1944, while unloading ammunition at Finschaven, New Guinea. No fatalities reported but the ship was declared a total constructive loss.

11. JOHN CROPPER, 6–42, 241681, KFHZ (1755–1821) Revolutionary War general from Virginia. Operated by AGWI Lines.

12. WILLIAM MOULTRIE, 6–42, 241682, KEWZ (1730–1805) Revolutionary War general and governor of South Carolina. Operated by Seas Shipping. The gun crew under Lt. Jeremiah T. Mahoney, 26, of New York City, was credited with shooting down eight German aircraft and damaging 12 others in September 1942 while in Convoy PQ 18 from Loch Ewe, Scotland, to Arkhangeisk, Russia. The ship received the Maritime Commission Gallant Ship award and the master, Richard E. Hocken, was awarded the Merchant Marine Distinguished Service medal.

13. THOMAS SUMTER, 6–42, 241776, KFXS (1734–1832) soldier, South Carolina congressman and namesake for Fort Sumter. Operated by AGWI Lines and converted to an Army troopship.

14. JEREMIAH VAN RENSSELAER, 6–42, 241777, KFHQ (1738–1810) New York congressman and lieutenant governor. Operated by AGWI Lines. Capt. Lucius W. Webb left New York in July 1942 and arrived back there on December 9. Capt Webb left the Bush Terminal Army Base in Brooklyn and was torpedoed on February 2, 1943, by *U-456* in the North Atlantic with the loss of 35 merchant crew, including Capt. Webb, and 11 Armed Guard sailors.

15. ARTEMAS WARD, 6–42, 241778, KEYT (1727–1800) Massachusetts congressman. Operated by American Export Lines. Capt. Julius C. Klepper, 48, arrived at New York from Murmansk, Russia, on June 28, 1942, as master of the American Export Lines freighter *Expositor*. He then took command of the *Artemas Ward*. Departed New York on February 20, 1944, for England and collided on March 4 with Capt. Bjarne T. Halleland's 10,195-ton Tankers Co. tanker *Manassas* in the Bristol Channel. The heavily damaged ship was beached then sunk on July 16, 1944, at Normandy as part of Gooseberry 2. The tanker arrived at New York on September 30.

16. EDWARD RUTLEDGE, 7–42, 241779, KEUG (1749–1800) Declaration of Independence signer from South Carolina and the youngest signer. Operated by AGWI Lines.

17. ABEL PARKER UPSHUR, 7–42, 241780, KEXF (1790–1844) Secretary of the Navy and State who died in a shipboard accident. The USS *Princeton* was the Navy's first steam-powered, propeller-driven warship. In February 1844 Capt. Robert Stockton's ship was making trial runs that included several port visits along the way. Guests were invited aboard and the new 12-inch Peacemaker cannon would be fired for demonstration purposes. On the 28th Secretary Upshur was one of around 200 guests aboard when Navy Secretary Thomas Gilmer requested the cannon be fired. The gun had overheated from previous use earlier that day but Capt. Stockton reluctantly agreed. The cannon exploded killing six people, including Upshur, and 22 were wounded, including Capt. Stockton and Sen. Thomas Hart Benton. Operated by International Freighting.

18. WILLIAM HAWKINS, 7–42, 241781, KFWN (1863–1937) Texas supreme court justice. Operated by Barber.

19. HUGH WILLIAMSON, 7–42, 241913, KFGS (1735–1819) noted scholar who represented North Carolina at the Constitutional Convention. Operated by American South African.

20. WILLIAM GASTON, 7–42, 214914, KFUV (1788–1844) North Carolina congressman. Operated by American West African. Capt. Henry W. Chase's ship was torpedoed on July 24, 1944, by *U-861* in the South Atlantic. There were no reported casualties.

21. WILLIAM R. DAVIE, 7–42, 241915, KFVF (1756–1820) William Richardson Davie was a North Carolina governor and founder of the University of North Carolina. Operated by South Atlantic.

22. WILLIAM A. GRAHAM, 7–42, 241978, KFUI (1804–1875) William Alexander Graham was a North Carolina senator, governor, and Secretary of the Navy. Operated by J. H. Winchester.

23. ALEXANDER MARTIN, 8–42, 242009, KEYP (1740–1807) North Carolina governor and senator. Operated by American South African.

24. JAMES K. POLK, 8–42, 242067, KFGZ (1795–1865) James Knox Polk was the 11th President of the United States. Operated by American South African. Capt. Herbert V. Olsen's ship was torpedoed by *U-510* on March 9, 1943, with the loss of one Armed Guard sailor. The ship was repaired.

25. RICHARD D. SPAIGHT, 8–42, 242185, KFOI (1758–1802) Richard Dobbs Spaight was a North Carolina governor and senator. Operated by American West African. Capt. Russell H. Quynn's ship was torpedoed on March 10, 1943, by *U-182* northeast of Durban, South Africa, with the loss of messman William J. O'Brien. The survivors left Durban on May 7 aboard the Seas Shipping Co. (Robin Line) steamer *Robin Tuxford* and arrived at New York on June 11.

26. ROGER WILLIAMS, 9–42, 242103, KFOO (1603–1683) founder of the colony of Providence Plantation in Rhode Island. Operated by International Freighting.

27. JOHN DRAYTON, 9–42, 242101, KGGR (1766–1822) governor of South Carolina. Operated by A. H. Bull. Capt. Carl Norman's ship was sunk on April 21, 1943, by the Italian submarine *Leonardo da Vinci* off Durban, South Africa with the loss of 21 merchant crew and five Armed Guard sailors. The survivors left Durban on May 7 aboard the Seas Shipping Co. (Robin Line) steamer *Robin Tuxford* and arrived at New York on June 11.

28. THOMAS PINCKNEY, 9–42, 242104, KGJA (1750–1828) soldier, South Carolina congressman, minister to Great Britain. Operated by American West African.

29. SAMUEL ASHE, 9–42, 242186, KFOP (1725–1813) governor of North Carolina. Operated by American South African.

30. BENJAMIN WILLIAMS, 10–42, 242180, KEZF (1754–1814) North Carolina congressman and governor. Operated by Calmar.

31. JAMES TURNER, 10–42, 242182, KFHI (1766–1824) governor of North Carolina. Operated by International Freighting.

32. DAVID STONE, 10–42, 242346, KFBY (1770–1818) North Carolina senator and governor. Operated by American-Foreign.

33. JAMES B. RICHARDSON, 10–42, 242349, KHMK (1770–1836) James Burchill Richardson was the 41st governor of South Carolina. Operated by North Atlantic & Gulf.

34. NATHANIEL ALEXANDER, 10–42, 242350, KFLG (1756–1808) surgeon, congressman, and governor of North Carolina. Operated by Merchants & Miners.

35. PAUL HAMILTON, 10–42, 242351, KHMT (1762–1816) governor of South Carolina and Secretary of the Navy. Operated by Black Diamond. Capt. Robert G. Winans' ship left Norfolk with a cargo of high explosives and was torpedoed on April 20, 1944, by German aircraft off Algeria and exploded. All 47 merchant seamen, 17 Armed Guard sailors, and 504 Army Air Corpsmen aboard perished.

36. HENRY MIDDLETON, 11–42, 242347, KHMW (1770–1846) South Carolina governor and senator. Operated by Merchants & Miners.

37. COLLIS P. HUNTINGTON, 11–42, 242471, KHVV (1821–1900) Collis Potter Huntington was one of the "Big Four" founders of the Central Pacific Railroad, was president of Southern Pacific Railroad, and founded the Newport News Shipbuilding & Dry Dock Co. in 1889. Operated by Parry.

38. BENJAMIN SMITH, 11–42, 242341, KHMU (1756–1826) governor of North Carolina. Operated by South Atlantic. Capt. George W. Johnson's ship was torpedoed off Liberia by *U-175* on January 23, 1943. There were no reported casualties.

39. CORNELIUS HARNETT, 11–42, 242472, KHVW (1723–1781) Continental Congressman from North Carolina. Operated by Black Diamond.

40. HENRY BACON, 11–42, 242473, KHVX (1866–1924) designer of the Lincoln Memorial. Operated by South Atlantic. Capt. William P. Lawton left Philadelphia in December 1942 on Voyage No. 1 and arrived at New York on August 24, 1943, from Port of Spain, Trinidad. In June 1944 Capt. Alfred Carini, 62, took command of the South Atlantic Liberty ship *Button Gwinett* in New York and then the *Henry Bacon*. The ship was sunk by German aircraft in the Barents Sea on February 23, 1945, with 35 Norwegian refugees on board. Capt. Carini was lost with 14 merchant crew and seven Armed Guard sailors. Chief engineer Donald F. Haviland was awarded the Merchant Marine Distinguished Service medal posthumously for giving his place in a lifeboat to a young kid and then going back aboard the ship.

41. JOSEPH ALSTON, 11–42, 242474, KUWD (1779–1816) governor of South Carolina. Operated by AGWI Lines.

42. ABNER NASH, 11–42, 242469, KHVZ (1740–1786) Virginia legislator and governor of North Carolina. Operated by North Atlantic & Gulf.

43. PAUL HAMILTON HAYNE, 12–42, 242477, KHWH (1830–1886) poet and writer from South Carolina. Operated by States Marine.

44. MARSHALL ELLIOTT, 12–42, 242593, KHWJ (1844–1910) Aaaron Marshall Elliott, of North Carolina, was a Harvard-educated linguist who taught German and Romance languages at Johns Hopkins University. Operated by Merchants & Miners.

45. JAMES IREDELL, 12–42, 242590, KHWK (1751–1799) Supreme Court justice. Operated by AGWI Lines. Capt. Alfred L. Jones' ship was bombed by German aircraft off Naples, Italy, on October 23, 1943. There were no fatalities and the ship was scuttled off Normandy as part of Gooseberry 2.

46. PENELOPE BARKER, 12–42, 242594, KHWM (1728–1796) Penelope Padgett, of Edenton, North Carolina, married John Hodgson and when he died around 1847 she married wealthy planter James Craven. He died in 1755 and she inherited his estate. She married Thomas Barker and became an avid supporter of the American Revolution. She became famous for hosting the "Edenton Tea Party" on October 25, 1774, at Elizabeth King's home in Edenton where 52 women signed a statement of protest against taxation without representation and to boycott British goods. Operated by North Atlantic & Gulf. Capt. John Kounce's ship was torpedoed on January 25, 1944, by *U-278* in the Barents Sea in Convoy JW 56A with the loss of ten merchant seamen, five Armed Guard sailors, and a British physician. HMS *Inconstant* (H.49) rescued 51 survivors.

47. ALEXANDER LILLINGTON, 12–42, 242622, KHWN (c. 1725–1786) John Alexander Lillington was a delegate to the Third Provincial Congress from North Carolina and served as a colonel during the Revolutionary War who gained fame by holding British forces heading for Wilmington at Moore's Creek in 1776. Reinforcements arrived to secure the bridge and defeat the Loyalist's advance. He is the namesake for Lillington, North Carolina. Operated by South Atlantic.

48. POCAHONTAS, 12–42, 242623, KKFB (c. 1595–1617) alias of Matoaka who saved the life of John Smith, of Jamestown, Virginia, when her father, Chief Powhatan, wanted to murder him. She moved to England and lived as Rebecca Rolfe. Operated by Marine Transport.

49. RICHARD CASWELL, 12–42, 242624, KHWO (1729–1789) first governor of North Carolina. Operated by South Atlantic. Capt. Solomon A. Suggs' ship was torpedoed on July 16, 1943, by *U-513* off Brazil. Capt. Suggs was lost along with eight other merchant seamen. That October, his son, Solomon, Jr., signed on as an able seaman on the *Edward D. White* out of Brunswick, Georgia.

50. CHRISTOPHER GADSDEN, 12–42, 242665, KIGK (1724–1805) South Carolina delegate to the Continental Congress and Revolutionary War soldier who fought a duel with Robert Howe, his former Continental Army commander, on August 17, 1778. Operated by AGWI Lines.

51. JAMES J. PETTIGREW, 1–43, 242666, KIDL (1828–1863) J. Johnston Pettigrew was a lawyer, author, diplomat, and linguist. He was a Confederate soldier left for dead at the Battle of Seven Pines, taken prisoner, recovered from his wounds, and was transferred in a prisoner exchange. As a general he was again wounded at Gettysburg then fatally wounded on July 14 near Falling Waters, West Virginia, during the retreat from Gettysburg. Operated by Moore-McCormack.

52. GEORGE DAVIS, 1–43, 242728, KKHD (1830–1896) Confederate States Attorney General. Operated by J. H. Winchester. Capt. John H. Jewell left Wilmington, North Carolina, in January 1943 and arrived back at New York on May 5 from Oran, Algeria. On August 13, on Voyage No. 2, the ship came under heavy air attack in Convoy MKS 21 and Lt. (jg) Frederick

B. Ryan's gunners claimed two aircraft out of the 15 or so shot down. On August 27, about 100 miles out from New York, the *Davis* and the steamer *Erita* both collided with the 1918, 5,627-ton Pan American Petroleum & Transport Co. tanker *Pan Royal*. As the tanker was sinking, bosun Charles M. Dake, Jr., jumped into the sea and rescued two sailors from the ship. Prior to that, in April 1942, the 23-year-old ordinary seaman signed on the Lykes. freighter *Scottsburg* at Boston. On June 15 the ship was torpedoed by *U-151* and he single-handedly launched a lifeboat and rescued 12 shipmates. The ship that picked them up, possibly the Panamanian freighter *Cold Harbor*, was also torpedoed the same day at the same location by *U-502* and Dake assisted a struggling sailor into a raft. He was awarded the Merchant Marine Distinguished Service medal

53. DANIEL H. HILL, 1–43, 242727, KKGV (1821–1889) Daniel Harvey Hill was a Confederate general and president of the University of Arkansas. Operated by American Export Lines.

54. JOHN HARVEY, 1–43, 242730, KEZK (1724–1775) North Carolina assemblyman from Perquimans County who was very active in supporting the patriot cause and instrumental in leading the colony away from British rule. He died from complications from a fall off a horse. Operated by AGWI Lines. Capt. Elwin F. Knowles left Norfolk in February 1943 and returned to New York from Casablanca, Morocco, on April 14. On December 2, 1943, Knowles' ship was sunk by air attack at Bari, Italy, with a cargo of mustard gas bombs. Only two merchant crew who were ashore at the time survived out of 38 crew, 28 Armed Guard sailors, and ten soldiers aboard.

55. BETTY ZANE, 1–43, 242663, KFDD (1765–1823) In September 1782, during the American Revolution, Indian allies of the British attacked the area near present-day Wheeling, West Virginia. William and Nancy Ann Zane, their daughter Elizabeth "Betty," and sons Ebenezer, Silas, Jonathan, Isaac, and Andrew grabbed their guns and left their cabin for nearby Fort Henry. Betty was reloading rifles and just about the time her father fell wounded they began to run short of gunpowder. There was a secret supply of powder at the cabin and Elizabeth knew exactly where it was. When she left the fort the Indians left her alone but on the return trip with powder and ammunition they saw what she was up to and shot at her but she made it back unscathed and the attack was repelled. Operated by States Marine.

56. WALTER RALEIGH, 1–43, 242735, KKHS (c. 1553–1618) English explorer, sponsor of the Roanoke Colony, and namesake for Raleigh, North Carolina. Operated by American West African.

57. ROBERT HOWE, 1–43, 242734, KKHX (1732–1786) North Carolina legislator and effective Revolutionary War general embroiled in politics and personal problems who fought a duel with Christopher Gadsden, a former Continental Army subordinate, on August 17, 1778. Operated by American South African.

58. NATHANIEL MACON, 1–43, 242780, KKIK (1757–1837) North Carolina congressman. Operated by A. H. Bull.

59. LEIV ERIKSSON, 1–43, LKPD (c. 970 AD–c. 1020) Norse explorer. Operated under the Norwegian flag.

60. FRIDTJOF NANSEN, 1–43, LKPE (1861–1930) Polar explorer, marine zoologist, Norwegian independence activist. Awarded the Nobel Peace Prize for the Nansen Passport used by those displaced persons in World War I. Operated under the Norwegian flag.

61. EPHRAIM BREVARD, 2–43, 242800, KKKF (1744–1781) North Carolina educator and Continental Army surgeon who signed a document on May 20, 1775, at Charlotte referred to by North Carolinians as the Mecklenburg Declaration of Independence to declare

independence from Great Britain, which some assert to be the first such Colonial document. He was captured by the British and sent to Florida where his health failed. Operated by States Marine.

62. GEORGE E. BADGER, 2–43, 242818, KKKJ (1795–1866) North Carolina senator and Secretary of the Navy. Operated by Grace Line.

63. FLORA MACDONALD, 2–43, 242816, KKKL (1722–1790) Fionnghal Nic-Dhòmhnaill helped Bonnie Prince Charles escape from the Hanoverian militia on Benbecula Island when he fled there after the Battle of Culloden. She married British army captain Allan MacDonald in 1750 and in 1774 came to America and settled in North Carolina. Her husband was taken prisoner at Moore's Creek in 1776, released two years later. She returned to Scotland in 1779 and he in 1784. Operated by Calmar. Capt. Ernest W. Jones' ship was torpedoed on May 30, 1943, by U-126 off Sierra Leone with the loss of seven merchant seamen.

64. JAMES SPRUNT, 2–43, 242873, KKKP (1846–1924) Civil War blockade runner, North Carolina cotton exporter, vice-consul to Great Britain, consul to Germany, and noted Cape Fear historian. Operated by Black Diamond. Capt. Elie C. Carr's ship was torpedoed on March 10, 1943, by U-185 off Cuba with the loss of all 43 merchant crew and 28 Armed Guard sailors aboard.

65. MATT W. RANSOM, 2–43, 242879, KKKQ (1826–1904) Matt Whitaker Ransom was a Confederate general, North Carolina senator, and minister to Mexico. Operated by Smith & Johnson. Capt. John Metsall's ship hit a mine on April 1, 1943, off Casablanca. He ordered the ship abandoned but Metsall and six volunteers went back aboard and got underway and made port. The damaged ship was scuttled on July 16, 1944, as Gooseberry 1 at Normandy. Ordinary seaman George E. Baker was awarded the Merchant Marine Distinguished Service medal for rescuing the one-armed chief engineer who had become trapped in the life net while abandoning ship.

66. FURNIFOLD M. SIMMONS, 2–43, 242877, KKKV (1854–1940) Furnifold McLendel Simmons was a North Carolina congressman. Operated by R. A. Nicol.

67. EDWARD B. DUDLEY, 2–43, 242876, KKLC (1789–1855) Edward Bishop Dudley was a North Carolina congressman and governor. Operated by Bulk Carriers Corp. Capt. Gibson D. Hillary's ship left New York in Convoy HX 232 but fell behind and disappeared. The 42 merchant crew and 27 Armed Guard sailors aboard were never seen or heard from again. It was later determined the ship had been torpedoed on April 11, 1943, by U-615.

68. WILLIE JONES, 2–43, 242880, KKLD (1740–1801) North Carolina delegate to the Continental Congress who opposed ratification of the Constitution. Operated by A. L. Burbank.

69. JAMES MOORE, 2–43, 242878, KKLF (c. 1650–1706) British governor of the Carolinas who fought Spaniards and Indians. Operated by Dichmann, Wright & Pugh.

70. ALFRED MOORE, 3–43, 242969, KHWP (1755–1810) Supreme Court justice. Operated by Prudential.

71. WOODROW WILSON, 3–43, 242970, KKWH (1856–1924) Thomas Woodrow Wilson was the 28th President of the United States. Operated by American Export Lines.

72. WILLIAM D. PENDER, 3–43, 242967, KKXJ (1834–1863) William Dorsey Pender was a Confederate major general mortally wounded at Gettysburg on July 2, 1863. Operated by American South African.

73. WILLIAM D. MOSELEY, 3–43, 242966, KKXK (1795–1863) William Dunn Moseley was governor of Florida. Operated by Polarus.

74. DAVID L. SWAIN, 3–43, 242962, KKXL (1801–1868) David Lowry Swain was a governor of North Carolina. Operated by Moore-McCormack.

75. JONATHAN WORTH, 3–43, 243009, KKXM (1802–1869) governor of North Carolina. Operated by AGWI Lines.

76. MATTHEW T. GOLDSBORO, 3–43, 243010, KKXN (1805–1877) assistant chief engineer with the Wilmington & Weldon Railroad in North Carolina who surveyed the route and advised Arnold Borden to build a hotel at the junction of the railway at a crossroad intended as a stopping point for the train crews. Namesake for Goldsboro, North Carolina, incorporated on January 18, 1847. Operated by South Atlantic.

77. ELISHA MITCHELL, 3–43, 243026, KKXO (1793–1857) geology professor at the University of North Carolina, Chapel Hill, who measured a peak in the Appalachians in 1835 that proved to be the highest peak east of the Mississippi. Named Mount Mitchell in 1882. Operated by American Export Lines.

78. CHRISTOPHER GALE, 3–43, 243025, KKXP (c. 1670–1735) achieved wealth trading with Indians in Carolina and was the first chief justice of the General Court, the highest court in the Carolina Colony and served as attorney general during turbulent times. Operated by Luckenbach.

79. WILLIAM L. DAVIDSON, 3–43, 243028, KKXS (1746–1781) William Lee Davidson was a general in the North Carolina militia during the Revolutionary War who was wounded at Colson's Mill and lost during the battle of Cowan's Ford on February 1, 1781. Namesake for Davidson College in North Carolina. Operated by Polarus.

80. WALKER TAYLOR, 3–43, 243027, KKXW (1864–1937) Wilmington insurance man, civic leader, and founder of the Brigade Boys & Girls Club. Operated by A. H. Bull.

81. ROGER MOORE, 3–43, 243125, KNAH (1838–1900) North Carolina Confederate Army officer and noted Ku Klux Klan Division Chief at Wilmington during an 1898 race war. Operated by Merchants & Miners.

82. ROBERT ROWAN, 4–43, 243134, KNAI (c. 1738–1798) noted Carolina merchant and patriot. Namesake for Rowan County, North Carolina. Operated by Isthmian. Capt. Ivar H. Rosenquist's ship was sunk on July 12, 1943, by German aircraft at Gela, Sicily. There were no reported casualties.

83. THOMAS W. BICKETT, 4–43, 243137, KNAJ (1869–1921) T. Walter Bickett was governor of North Carolina. Operated by T. J. Stevenson & Co.

84. HORACE WILLIAMS, 4–43, 243132, KNAL (1858–1940) Henry Horace Williams was a philosophy professor at the University of North Carolina. Operated by Prudential.

85. JOSE BONIFACIO, 4–43, 243133, KNAO (1763–1838) José Bonifácio de Andrada was a statesman, naturalist, professor, chemist, and leader of the Brazilian movement for independence from the Portuguese Empire. Namesake for the mineral andradite and was instrumental in discovering lithium. Operated by States Marine.

86. THOMAS L. CLINGMAN, 4–43, 243136, KNAM (1812–1897) Thomas Lanier Clingman was a North Carolina senator. Operated by Cosmopolitan.

87. DAVID CALDWELL, 4–43, 243131, KNAT (1725–1824) preacher, educator, patriot, and founder of the Guilford Academy in Guilford County, North Carolina. Operated by Isbrandtsen.

88. WAIGSTILL AVERY, 4–43, 243138, KNAV (1741–1821) Waightstill Avery was attorney general of North Carolina for the Crown who signed the Mecklenburg Resolves, helped draft the North Carolina Constitution, and was the first attorney general of North Carolina. Operated by Polarus.

89. CORNELIA P. SPENCER, 4–43, 243130, KNAW (1825–1908) Cornelia Phillips, of New York City, married James M. Spencer in 1855 and moved to Alabama and had a daughter. When James died in 1861 she moved to Chapel Hill, North Carolina, where her brother

taught mathamatics at the University. She took up writing, became an author and newspaper columnist popular enough to influence the state legislature to close the University in 1870 and then reopen it five years later. Operated by A. L. Burbank. Capt. Elmer H. Kirwan's ship was torpedoed on September 21, 1943, by *U-188* well off Somalia with the loss of able seaman Melvin E. Franklin and deck cadet Donald S. Wright. Capt. Kirwan signed on Capt. Irving Jensen's Moore-McCormack Liberty ship *Joseph LeConte* at Alexandria, Egypt, for repatriation on October 12 and arrived at New York on November 15,

   90. WALTER HINES PAGE, 5–43, 243139, KNAX (1855–1918) founder of the *State Chronicle* newspaper in Raleigh, North Carolina, who wrote for the *Evening Post*, and was ambassador to Britain. Operated by American Export Lines.

   91. JOSEPH A. BROWN, 5–43, 243344, KOIX (1733–1785) Joseph Addison Brown was a North Carolina state legislator and farmer who introduced strawberries into Chadbourn in 1895. The annual North Carolina Strawberry Festival celebrates his work. Operated by Blidberg Rothchild.

   92. ROBERT F. HOKE, 5–43, 243348, KOIY (1837–1912) Robert Frederick Hoke was a Confederate major general from North Carolina. Operated by American Export Lines. On June 24, 1943, Frederick N. MacLean signed on the American Export Lines Liberty ship *Bernard N. Baker* at New York as chief mate and arrived back there on August 7 from Liverpool. He took command of the *Hoke* and that ship was torpedoed by *I-26* on December 28, 1943, in the Arabian Sea. There were no reported casualties but the ship was abandoned in a sinking condition and became a total constructive loss. In 1944 he was master of the American Export Lines Liberty ship *Hoke Smith*.

   93. OLE BULL, 5–43, LKPG (1810–1880) famous Norwegian musician. Operated under the Norwegian flag.

   94. JOHN OWEN, 5–43, 243343, KOJA (1787–1841) 24th governor of North Carolina. Operated by William J. Rountree.

   95. PHILIP DODDRIDGE, 5–43, 243347, KOJB (1733–1832) West Virginia congressman. Operated by Marine Transport.

   96. JOHN GRIER HIBBEN, 5–43, 243447, KOJY (1861–1933) president of Princeton University. Operated by Seas Shipping.

   97. KEMP P. BATTLE, 5–43, 243449, KOKA (1831–1919) Kemp Plummer Battle was president of the University of North Carolina. Operated by Luckenbach and converted to an Army troopship.

   98. ROBERT DALE OWEN, 5–43, 243451, KOND (1801–1877) owner of New Harmony, Indiana, and congressman who introduced the bill creating the Smithsonian Institution. Operated by Black Diamond.

   99. JOHN P. MITCHELL, 5–43, 243448, KNOF (1879–1918) John Purroy Mitchell, of the South Carolina Mitchells, was the 34-year-old "boy" mayor of New York City who joined the Army Air Service and died on July 6, 1918, in a training accident at Gerstner Field near Lake Charles, Louisiana. Operated by Seas Shipping.

   100. CHARLES D. MCIVER, 6–43, 243445, KONK (1860–1906) Charles Duncan McIver was an educator and founder and first president of the University of North Carolina at Greensboro. Operated by Marine Transport. Julius Palu, 37, was a naturalized Estonian who signed on the *McIver* as chief mate at New York on July 7, 1944, and arrived back at New York from Marseilles, France, on January 11, 1945. He assumed command and on March 23, 1945, the ship was sunk by a torpedo or mine off Belgium. There were no reported casualties and 40 survivors were sent home on Capt. Jean Bracchet's French Line steamer *Athos II* arriving at New York on April 7 from Southampton, England. Capt. Palu lived at 2913 Randall Ave. in the Bronx.

101. EDWARD RICHARDSON, 6–43, 243516, KORF (1750–1798) Mecklenburg County, North Carolina, pioneer, Revolutionary war soldier, and grandson of William Richardson Davie. Operated by United States Navigation and converted to an Army troopship.

102. HANNIS TAYLOR, 6–43, 243517, KORG (1851–1922) Alabama lawyer, jurist, and minister to Spain. Operated by Isbrandtsen.

103. JOHN M. MOREHEAD, 6–43, 243521, KORH (1796–1866) John Motley Moorehead was governor of North Carolina and namesake for Morehead City. Operated by Moore-McCormack.

104. JOHN LAWSON, 6–43, 243623, KXCN (1674–1711) pioneer of the Carolinas, surveyor, and author. Operated by South Atlantic.

105. JOSEPH LE CONTE, 6–43, 243625, KXCP (1823–1901) manufacturer of explosives for the Confederate States, physician, geologist, scientist, namesake for features in Yosemite National Park, and professor at UC Berkeley. Operated by Moore-McCormack.

106. LEE S. OVERMAN, 6–43, 243627, KXCT (1854–1930) Lee Slater Overman was a North Carolina senator. Operated by Bllidberg Rothchild. Capt. Creston C. Jenkins' ship hit a mine on November 11, 1944, off Le Havre, France. There were no reported casualties.

107. THOMAS J. JARVIS, 6–43, 243631, KXCZ (1836–1915) Thomas Jordan Jarvis was a North Carolina governor and senator who helped establish the East Carolina Teachers Training School. Operated by William J. Rountree.

108. ARTHUR DOBBS, 6–43, 243617, KXCB (1689–1765) Colonial governor of North Carolina. Operated by Calmar.

109. WILLIAM T. BARRY, 6–43, 243632, KXDF (1785–1835) William Taylor Barry was governor of Kentucky and Postmaster General. Operated by American South African.

110. HILARY A. HERBERT, 7–43, 243640, KMYQ (1834–1919) Hilary Abner Herbert was Secretary of the Navy and an Alabama congressman, Secretary of the Navy. Operated by Cosmopolitan.

111. HUTCHINSON I. CONE, 7–43, 243780, KXJD (1871–1941) Hutchinson Ingram Cone was an 1894 Naval Academy graduate, chief of the Bureau of Steam Engineering, and commander of American naval aviation forces in Europe during the Great War. He retired as a rear admiral and was the namesake for the USS *Cone* (DD-866) commissioned on August 18, 1945. Operated by Moore-McCormack.

112. LAWRENCE D. TYSON, 7–43, 243788, KXJF (1861–1929) Lawrence Davis Tyson was a Tennessee senator. Operated by Polarus.

113. DAVID F. HOUSTON, 7–43, 243775, KXJH (1866–1940) David Franklin Houston was president of the Agricultural & Mechanical College of Texas, now Texas A&M, Secretary of Agriculture and the Treasury. Operated by Wessel, Duval.

114. JOHN MERRICK, 7–43, 243778, KXVA (1859–1919) African-American slave, barber, cofounder of the North Carolina Mutual Life Insurance Co. at Durham and the Mechanics & Farmers Bank. Lincoln Hospital trustee. Operated by Calmar.

115. CHARLES A. DANA, 7–43, 243774, KXJL (1819–1897) Charles Anderson Dana was the publisher of the *New York Sun*. Operated by R. A. Nicol.

116. CLEMENT CLAY, 7–43, 243867, KXJN (1816–1866) Clement Claiborne Clay was an Alabama congressman and governor. Operated by Prudential.

117. RICHMOND P. HOBSON, 7–43, 243874, KXJP (1870–1937) Richmond Pearson Hobson was a rear admiral who was awarded the Medal of Honor for service during the Spanish-American War. Alabama congressman and namesake for the USS *Hobson* (DD-464) commissioned on January 22, 1942. Operated by Isbrandtsen.

118. THOMAS W. OWEN, 8–43, 243875, KXJO (1735–1806) Thomas William

Owen was the leader of the Bladen County, North Carolina, militia during the Revolutionary War. Served at Camden and Elizabethtown and retired as a major. Operated by American West African.

119. CHATHAM C. LYON, 8–43, 243866, KXJQ (1850–1931) Chatham Calhoun Lyon was a North Carolina Superior Court judge for Bladen County. Operated by American South African.

120. JAMES I. MCKAY, 8–43, 243870, KXJR (1793–1853) James Iver McKay was a North Carolina congressman. Operated by United States Navigation.

121. JOHN N. MAFFITT, 8–43, 243989, KXYS (1819–1886) John Newland Maffitt was the "Prince of Privateers" in the Confederate States Navy. Operated by Polarus.

122. GEORGE DURANT, 8–43, 243985, KXYT (1632–1691) English-born settler who purchased land in Virginia from Indian chiefs in 1661–62 around Albermarle Sound, annexed to the Carolina Colony in 1665. Known as the "father of North Carolina." Operated by Stockard.

123. AUGUSTUS S. MERRIMON, 8–43, 243984, KXYU (1830–1892) Augustus Summerfield Merrimon was a North Carolina senator. Operated by States Marine.

124. SAMPHIRE, 8–43, 169631, MYLM, built for the British Ministry of War Transport. Operated by P. Henderson & Co.

125. THOMAS POLLOCK, 8–43, 244014, KXYW (1654–1722) Carolina Colony pioneer, attorney, shipowner, trader, large landowner, and governor. Operated by Grace Line.

126. SAMBRIAN, 8–43, 169716, BFNS, built for the British Ministry of War Transport. Operated by Cayzer, Irvine & Co.

Oregon Shipbuilding Corp.
Foot of N. Burgard St., Portland, Oregon

The Kaiser-controlled company was organized on January 16, 1941, with Charles A. Shea as the first president. Those in the know said it would take 2½ years to build the 11-way yard and deliver 32 ships so they were probably a little surprised to see the 2-story, 130 foot by 260 foot mold loft and template storage building with roof trusses spanning 130 feet go up in eight days. The Maritime Commission spent $70,000 for land and $23,474,000 on facilities. President Jack A. McEachern built 322 Liberty ships with Henry Kaiser's son Edgar as vice president. McEachern was president of the J. A. McEachern Co., a construction firm that merged with the General Construction Co., of Spokane, Washington, in 1926. Oregon-ship was the first yard to receive the Maritime Commission's "flag of merit." The first keel was laid on May 19, 1941, and the average building time for the ships was 44.9 days.

1. STAR OF OREGON, 12–41, 241206, KFHX, named for the 1842 schooner *Star of Oregon*, the first vessel built in the Oregon Territory. Operated by States Steamship. Torpedoed on August 30, 1942, by *U-162* northeast of Tobago with the loss of one merchant seaman passenger.

2. MERIWETHER LEWIS, 1–42, 241205, KFFL (1774–1809) naturalist, explorer, and ex–Army captain of the Lewis & Clark expedition. Operated by American Mail Line. Capt. John E. Beal, 36, left New York in October 1942 and arrived back at the Java St. Pier on January 10, 1943. The ship departed with a cargo of explosives and disappeared. None of the 44 merchant crew or 28 Armed Guard sailors were ever seen or heard from again. Post-war research determined the ship had been torpedoed on March 2, 1943, by *U-634* in the North

Atlantic. One career seaman, fireman/watertender John Killoran, 51, signed articles on January 25 at New York but inexplicably failed to join the ship and was declared a deserter. On February 10 he signed on the *Bret Harte* and was still sailing when the war ended.

3. WILLIAM CLARK, 2–42, 241257, KJXR (1770–1838) of the Lewis & Clark expedition and governor of the Missouri Territory. Operated by Isthmian. Capt. Walter E. Elian's ship was torpedoed on November 4, 1942, by *U-354* in the North Atlantic with loss of 18 merchant crew, including Capt. Elian, and 13 Armed Guard sailors.

4. ROBERT GRAY, 2–42, 241271, KKKR (1755–1806) Gray was captain of the *Lady Washington* and John Kendrick skippered the *Columbia Rediviva* when the two set out from Boston in September 1787 to explore the Pacific Coast. Gray was instrumental in establishing the fur trade in North America and, after swapping vessels with Kendrick, discovered the Columbia River and became the first American shipmaster to circumnavigate the world. His ship is the namesake for the Columbia River and he is the namesake for Gray's Harbor, Washington. Operated by Waterman. Capt. Alfred Rasmussen's ship disappeared in April 1943 and the 39 merchant seamen and 23 Armed Guard sailors were never seen or heard from again. It was later determined that the ship had been torpedoed on April 23, 1943, by *U-306* south of Greenland.

5. THOMAS JEFFERSON, 2–42, 241361, KAYI (1743–1826) Declaration of Independence signer from Virginia and 3rd President of the United States. Operated by Waterman.

6. JOHN BARRY, 2–42, 241375, KAYR (1745–1803) first commodore of the Navy. Operated by Lykes. Joseph Ellerwald was chief mate on the Lykes Liberty ship *Thomas Paine* in 1942, the *Tillie Lykes* in 1943, and the *Nancy Lykes* when they arrived in San Francisco on April 16, 1944. His first command was torpedoed on August 28, 1944, by *U-859* in the Arabian Sea with the loss of chief mate Gordon W. Lyons and messman Tan See Jee.

7. JOHN HANCOCK, 2–42, 241368, KAZY (1737–1793) Declaration of Independence signer from Massachusetts. Operated by Lykes. Capt. Levi J. Plesner's ship was torpedoed on August 18, 1942, by *U-553* west of Cuba. There were no reported casualties.

8. PHILIP LIVINGSTON, 3–42, 241406, KBOZ (1716–1778) Declaration of Independence signer from New York. Operated by American-Hawaiian.

9. ALEXANDER HAMILTON, 3–42, 241415, KBSK (1755–1804) first Secretary of the Treasury. Operated by Sudden & Christianson.

10. STEPHEN A. DOUGLAS, 3–42, 241440, KBWB (1813–1861) Stephen Arnold Douglas was an Illinois congressman who lost to Abraham Lincoln in 1860 and died shortly after in Chicago from typhoid fever. Operated by Matson.

11. ROBERT FULTON, 3–42, 241453, KBUY (1765–1815) built the first practical steamboat, the *Clermont* in 1807. Went 150 miles from New York to Albany in 52 hours. Operated by Pope & Talbot.

12. THOMAS MACDONOUGH, 3–42, 241467, KDEE (1783–1825) naval commander of the Lake Champlain Squadron in 1812 who defeated the British at Plattsburg Bay. Operated by Matson.

13. JOHN JAY, 3–42, 241485, KDGG (1745–1829) first chief justice of the Supreme Court. Operated by Sudden & Christenson.

14. WILLIAM DAWES, 4–42, 241489, KDPB (1745–1799) rode with Paul Revere on their midnight ride. Operated by Weyerhaeuser. Capt. John A. Froberg's ship was torpedoed on July 22, 1942, by *I-11* off Australia with loss of four Armed Guard sailors and one soldier.

15. PHILIP SCHUYLER, 4–42, 241500, KEPA (1733–1804) Revolutionary War general and New York senator. Operated by American Mail Line.

16. GEORGE CLYMER, 4–42, 241506, KEPH (1739–1813) Declaration of Independ-

ence signer from Pennsylvania. Operated by American Mail Line. Capt. Edward Ackerman's ship was sunk on June 6, 1942, by German raiders in the South Atlantic with the loss of fireman/ watertender John R. Shatto.

17. HENRY W. LONGFELLOW, 4–42, 241507, KEPK (1807–1882) Henry Wadsworth Longfellow was a Maine educator and one of the five Fireside Poets whose work was read by families sitting around the fireplace and by children in school. Operated by Coastwise and converted to an Army troopship.

18. JAMES WILSON, 4–42, 241522, KERK (1742–1798) Declaration of Independence signer from Pennsylvania. Operated for three voyages by American President Lines under Capt. Fred P. Willarts. The ship arrived at San Francisco, on March, 1943, from Suva, Philippines, and was taken by the Navy and operated as the *Crater*-class cargo ship *Sterope* (AK-96), NKGV, commissioned on May 14, 1943.

19. JOHN HART, 4–42, 241523, KERU (1711–1779) Declaration of Independence signer from New Jersey. Operated by Pope & Talbot.

20. JOHN DICKINSON, 4–42, 241565, KESZ (1732–1808) member of the Continental Congress from Philadelphia and governor of Pennsylvania and Delaware. Operated by Pope & Talbot.

21. FISHER AMES, 4–42, 241564, KEUR (1758–1808) Massachusetts congressman. Operated by American Mail Line.

22. ROBERT G. HARPER, 4–42, 241572, KEVO (1765–1825) Robert Goodhue Harper was a South Carolina congressman. Operated by Pacific-Atlantic.

23. EDGAR ALLAN POE, 4–42, 241586, KEUF (1809–1849) Baltimore editor and writer. Operated by Weyerhaeuser. Capt. Jack Edgerton's ship was torpedoed by *I-21* on December 8, 1942, off Noumea, New Caledonia, with the loss of two engineers. Engine cadet William M. Thomas, Jr., was awarded the Merchant Marine Distinguished Service medal for rescuing a seriously injured oiler and carrying him off the ship.

24. NATHANIEL HAWTHORNE, 5–42, 241587, KEVJ (1804–1864) Massachusetts writer and author of *The Scarlet Letter*. Operated by Pacific-Atlantic. Capt. Richard C. Brennan's ship was torpedoed on November 7, 1942, by *U-508* off Isla de Margarita with the loss of 30 crew, including Capt. Brennan, seven Armed Guard sailors, and one passenger.

25. JOHN G. WHITTIER, 5–42, 241623, KEUY (1807–1892) John Greenleaf Whittier was one of the five Fireside Poets and namesake for Whittier, California. Operated by American Mail Line.

26. WILLIAM CULLEN BRYANT, 5–42, 241622, KEWU (1794–1878) editor of the *Saturday Evening Post* and one of the five Fireside Poets. Operated by James Griffiths and in 1943 by Alcoa.

27. JAMES RUSSELL LOWELL, 5–42, 241636, KFHE (1819–1891) one of the five Fireside Poets and a diplomat. Operated by McCormick. Capt. Richard N. Forman's ship was torpedoed on October 15, 1943, by *U-371* off Algeria. There were no reported casualties.

28. HENRY D. THOREAU, 5–42, 241660, KFGO (1817–1862) Henry David Thoreau was an author, poet, lakeside camper, and philosopher. Operated by Luckenbach.

29. RALPH WALDO EMERSON, 5–42, 241661, KFOB (1803–1882) lecturer, essayist, and poet. Operated by American President Lines.

30. JAMES WHITCOMB RILEY, 5–42, 241671, KFHL (1849–1916) Indiana "Hoosier Poet" and children's author. Operated by James Griffiths.

31. SAMUEL MOODY, 5–42, 241679, KFPG (1676–1747) the eccentric Parson Moody preached at the First Parish Church at York, District of Maine, in 1698. "Father Moody Sunday"

was observed at the church as part of the "Days of Our Forefathers" series of commemorations held at the church. Operated by Pacific-Atlantic.

32. JOHN SEVIER, 5–42, 241703, KFJE (1745–1815) cofounder of Tennessee, first governor, and congressman. North Carolina congressman. Operated by Grace Line. Capt. Charles F. Drury, 42, left Portland, Oregon, in May 1942 and arrived at New York on August 9 from the Canal Zone via San Antonio, Chile, and moved to the Claremont Terminal in New Jersey on the 17th. Capt. Drury expected to leave around September 11. The ship was torpedoed on April 6, 1943, by *U-185* in the Caribbean. There were no reported casualties.

33. JONATHAN EDWARDS, 5–42, 241716, KFJN (1703–1758) noted philosophical theologian. Operated by James Griffiths.

34. OLIVER WENDELL HOLMES, 5–42, 241721, KEMS, Holmes, Sr. (1809–1894) was one of the five Fireside Poets and Jr. (1841–1935) was a Supreme Court justice. Operated by States Steamship.

35. WALT WHITMAN, 5–42, 241760, KFTQ (1819–1892) Walter Whitman was a journalist, essayist, and poet. Operated by Weyerhaeuser. Capt. Oscar W. Carlson's ship was torpedoed by German aircraft off Algiers on January 20, 1943. There were no casualties and the ship was repaired.

36. MARK TWAIN, 5–42, 241759, KFWW (1835–1910) Samuel Langhorne Clemens was a Mississippi River steamboat captain, pilot, and novelist. Operated by American Mail Line.

37. WASHINGTON IRVING, 6–42, 241790, KFWJ (1783–1859) New York author, historian, and minister to Spain. Operated by Luckenbach.

38. JAMES FENIMORE COOPER, 6–42, 241813, KFWK (1789–1851) historian and author of *Last of the Mohicans*. Operated by American President Lines.

39. THOMAS BAILEY ALDRICH, 6–42, 241788, KFWM (1836–1907) editor of the *Atlantic Monthly*. Operated by Luckenbach.

40. BRET HARTE, 6–42, 241829, KFXE (1836–1902) noted author of stories about early California. Operated by Weyerhaeuser.

41. ANNE HUTCHINSON, 6–42, 241814, KEYQ (1591–1643) Anne Marbury married merchant Wiiliam Hutchinson in England, had 11 children, and sailed to Boston in 1634 on the *Griffin*. Her religious views resulted in her banishment and she, her husband, and several others moved to Providence Plantations. In 1642 they moved to New Netherland and were murdered by Siwanoy Indians in present-day Bronx, New York. Operated by Sudden & Christenson. Capt. John Stenlund's ship was torpedoed on October 26, 1942, by *U-504* off South Africa. Three merchant seamen were lost.

42. JOHN HARVARD, 6–42, 241865, KFIA (1607–1638) preacher who left his estate to the new Massachusetts Bay Colony school at Cambridge and became its namesake. Operated by American-Hawaiian.

43. ELIHU YALE, 6–42, 241894, KFDV (1649–1721) governor of the East India Co. post at Madras and financier of the Collegiate School of Connecticut, renamed Yale. Operated by McCormack. Capt. Thure Walter F. Ekstrom arrived at Norfolk, Virginia, on November 24, 1943, and expected to sail on December 24. The ship was sunk on February 15, 1944, by a German bomb off Anzio with the loss of three merchant seamen and two of Ens. Daniel Mungall, Jr.'s Armed Guard sailors.

44. CORNELIUS GILLIAM, 6–42, 241888, KFXW (1798–1848) Oregon pioneer and namesake for Gilliam County. Operated by Pacific-Atlantic.

45. GEORGE H. WILLIAMS, 6–42, 241946, KFXV (1820–1910) George Henry Williams was the chief justice of the Oregon Territory and senator, U.S. Attorney General, and mayor of Portland. Operated by American Mail Line.

46. MATTHEW P. DEADY, 7–42, 241947, KFYD (1824–1893) Matthew Paul Deady was an Oregon lawyer and federal judge. Operated by American-Hawaiian. Capt. Kenneth D. Fry became skipper on January 11, 1944, at New York and arrived back there from Alexandria, Egypt, on May 22 and went to Sullivan's Drydock. Fry expected to sail for the Pacific Coast on June 8. The ship was damaged by Japanese aircraft on November 2, 1944, at Tacloban, Leyte, Philippines, with the loss of two Armed Guard sailors and 25 soldiers. The ship was repaired.

47. JASON LEE, 7–42, 241982, KFZM (1803–1845) Oregon pioneer. Operated by Pope & Talbot.

48. MARCUS WHITMAN, 7–42, 242006, KFZR (1802–1847) Marcus and Narcissa Whitman were missionaries who brought the first large wagon train over the Oregon Trail in 1843, established a mission in Cayuse country near Walla Walla, Washington, and were murdered by Indians. Operated by Matson. Capt. Joseph Smith's ship was torpedoed by the Italian sub *Leonardo da Vinci* on November 8, 1942, off Brazil. There were no reported casualties.

49. JOHN MCLOUGHLIN, 7–42, 242021, KFZU (1784–1857) Jean-Baptiste McLoughlin was a physician and officer with the Hudson's Bay Co. engaged in fur trading. In 1829 McLoughlin established a lumber mill at the confluence of the Willamette and Clackamas Rivers that became Oregon City, the terminus of the Oregon Trail. Oregon City was the first city west of the Rocky Mountains to incorporate and was the capital of the Oregon Territory from its beginning in 1848 until 1851. Operated by Pacific-Atlantic.

50. JESSE APPLEGATE, 7–42, 242030, KGCD (1811–1888) Oregon pioneer who opened the Applegate Trail, an alternate Oregon Trail route into southern Oregon and northern California from Fort Hall, Idaho. Operated by American President Lines.

51. GEORGE ABERNETHY, 7–42, 242048, KGBZ (1807–1877) governor of the Oregon Territory. Operated by Grace Line.

52. JOSEPH LANE, 7–42, 242051, KGBY (1801–1881) general in the Mexican War, first governor of the Oregon Territory in 1848, Oregon senator, and namesake for Lane County. Operated by Matson.

53. HARVEY W. SCOTT, 7–42, 242081, KGCJ (1838–1910) Harvey Whitefield Scott was a newsman, Portland collector of customs, part owner and editor-in-chief of *The Oregonian* newspaper, Abigail Scott Duniway's brother, and namesake for Mount Scott in Happy Valley. Operated by Grace Line. Grace Line skipper Axel E. Uldall left Portland, Oregon, in July 1942 and arrived at New York on October 20 from Havana, Cuba. On Voyage No. 2 the ship was torpedoed on March 3, 1943, by *U-160* off South Africa. There were no reported casualties.

54. JAMES W. NESMITH, 7–42, 242082, KGBW (1820–1885) James Willis Nesmith was an Oregon senator. Operated by McCormick. Capt. Reginald Rossiter's ship was torpedoed on April 7, 1945, by *U-1024* off Holyhead, England, and towed to Liverpool. There were no reported casualties.

55. JOHN C. AINSWORTH, 8–42, 242102, KGJH (1870–1943) John Commingers Ainsworth was a merchant who operated a steamboat on the Ohio River. In 1849 he got gold fever and went Out West but found little success. He then moved to the Oregon Territory to run steamers on the Willamette River and in 1860 cofounded the Oregon Steam Navigation Co. He got into railroads and eventually controlled all transportation on the Willamette and Columbia Rivers. In 1879 he sold out to Henry Villard, moved back to California, and went into banking in Oak Lawn. Operated by American Mail Line and converted to an Army troopship.

56. WILLIAM P. MCARTHUR, 8–42, 242119, KGIU (1814–1850) William Pope McArthur was the first U.S. Coast & Geodetic Survey hydrologist to map the Pacific Coast. Operated by Grace Line.

57. EUGENE SKINNER, 8–42, 242133, KGIP (1809–1864) Oregon pioneer and founder of Eugene City. Operated by American Mail Line.

58. DANIEL H. LOWNSDALE, 8–42, 242158, KGJY (1803–1862) Daniel Hillman Lownsdale was a Kentucky native who cofounded Portland, Oregon, and opened the first tannery. Operated by Luckenbach.

59. ELIJAH WHITE, 8–42, 242163, KGGX (1806–1879) physician, missionary, Oregon pioneer, and federal Indian agent for the Oregon Territory. Operated by American Mail Line.

60. HARRY LANE, 8–42, 242192, KGJT (1865–1917) Oregon physician, senator, mayor of Portland, and grandson of Joseph Lane. Operated by American Mail Line.

61. GEORGE CHAMBERLAIN, 8–42, 242191, KGJS (1854–1928) Mississippi lawyer and 11th governor of Oregon. Operated by Luckenbach.

62. JONATHAN HARRINGTON, 8–42, 242208, KGGW (1745–1775) one of Capt. John Parker's 77 Minute Men lost on Lexington Green on the morning of April 19, 1775. He died while trying to reach his nearby home, and was possibly the first one shot. Eight were lost that day and ten wounded. Operated by Matson.

63. WILLIAM H. SEWARD, 8–42, 242222, KGHJ (1801–1872) William Henry Seward was a governor of New York, senator, and Secretary of State who brokered the purchase of Alaska. Operated by Oliver J. Olson.

The *William H. Seward* photographed coming in to New York Harbor on June 27, 1943, from Bone, Algeria. This ship's last voyage was in the Pacific and was laid up in the reserve fleet at Benicia, California, with an estimated $27,300 worth of damage. On April 27, 1960, the ship was sold to the Hugo Nem Corp. of New York for scrap on their bid of $96,187. Hugo Nem then sold the ship to a Japanese company and on June 5 the tug *Sudbury II* rigged a towline to the *Seward* and the *James L. Breck* and headed for Japan. U.S. Coast Guard photograph.

64. GIDEON WELLES, 9–42, 242240, KGKH (1802–1878) Secretary of the Navy. Operated by Pope & Talbot.

65. EDWIN M. STANTON, 9–42, 242239, KGKI (1814–1869) Edwin McMasters Stanton was Attorney General and Secretary of War under Lincoln. Operated by Matson.

66. CLEVELAND ABBE, 9–42, 242254, KGKJ (1838–1916) noted astronomer and meteorologist. Operated by American President Lines.

67. ANDREW CARNEGIE, 9–42, 242277, KHAO (1835–1919) Scottish immigrant and telegraph operator who invested his money in railroads, became a bond broker, and then a steel magnate and noted philanthropist. Operated by American President Lines.

68. PIERRE S. DUPONT, 9–42, 242246, KHAY (1739–1817) Pierre Samuel du Pont de Nemours was the father and partner of Eleuthère Irénée du Pont de Nemours in the manufacture of gunpowder and dynamite. Operated by Grace Line. The *Dupont's* first skipper was 80-year-old George E. Bridgett, of San Francisco. He had been retired for 15 years after 48 years at sea. They left Portland, Oregon, in September 1942 and arrived at New York on May 6, 1943, from Trinidad.

69. JAMES DUNCAN, 9–42, 242304, KHIV (1857–1928) first vice president of the American Federation of Labor. Operated by W. R. Chamberlin.

70. GEORGE H. THOMAS, 9–42, 242311, KHAX (1816–1870) George Henry Thomas was a noted Union general from Virginia. Operated by Grace Line.

71. WILLIAM S. ROSECRANS, 9–42, 242317, KHCK (1819–1898) William Starke Rosecrans was a Union general, a major California land holder, and congressman. Namesake for Fort Rosecrans National Cemetery and Rosecrans Ave. in San Diego. Operated by American President Lines. Elmer P. Barstow, 49, was chief mate on the APL Liberty ship *Ralph Waldo Emerson* when they arrived at New York on April 16, 1943, from Glasgow, Scotland. On April 23 he took command of the *Rosecrans* at New York and arrived back there on September 14 from Algeria. He expected to leave the Army base at Brooklyn around October 10. The ship was sunk on January 6, 1944, by a mine off Naples, Italy. There were no reported casualties.

72. HENRY VILLARD, 9–42, 242327, KHCB (1835–1900) Ferdinand Heinrich Gustav Hilgard was a newspaper war correspondent during the Civil War, became an investor, then president of the Northern Pacific Railway and benefactor of the University of Oregon. Operated by Coastwise (Pacific Far East) Line.

73. JOSEPH N. TEAL, 9–42, 242333, KHOP (1858–1929) Joseph Nathan Teal was born in Eugene City and became a prominent Portland lawyer and businessman. Operated by Hammond.

74. SAMUEL SEABURY, 9–42, 242352, KHBY (1729–1796) first Episcopal bishop in America, British Loyalist, and first Bishop of Connecticut. Operated by American-Hawaiian.

75. MARK HANNA, 10–42, 242366, KRGU (1837–1904) Marcus Alonzo "Mark" Hanna was an Ohio coal and iron magnate and Ohio senator. Operated by Moore-McCormack.

76. HENRY GEORGE, 9–42, 242377, KHBK (1839–1897) sailor, typesetter, San Francisco, California, newspaper editor/owner and noted economic writer. Operated by American-Hawaiian.

77. EDWARD EVERETT, 10–42, 242376, KHBD (1794–1865) Massachusetts congressman, president of Harvard, Secretary of State, and vice president. Operated by Lykes.

78. JAMES MCNEIL WHISTLER, 10–42, 242397, KHBU (1834–1903) noted painter. Operated by American President Lines.

79. SALMON P. CHASE, 10–42, 242405, KHCU (1808–1873) Salmon Portland Chase was an Ohio governor and Supreme Court justice. Operated by Pacific-Atlantic.

Attacked by German aircraft off Naples, Italy, on November 1, 1943, with the loss of Peter J. Biemel, the engine cadet.

80. STEPHEN GIRARD, 10–42, 242409, KHCX (1750–1831) Pennsylvania shipping magnate and namesake for Girard College. Operated by Isthmian.

81. HENRY DEARBORN, 10–42, 242412, KHGG (1751–1829) on Gen. Washington's staff, Maine congressman, and Secretary of War. Operated by American-Hawaiian and converted to an animal transport ship.

82. JAMES B. STEPHENS, 10–42, 242425, KHNU (1806–1889) James Bowles Stephens was an Oregon pioneer, cooper, developer of East Portland (Stephens Addition), ferry operator, and organizer of the Pacific Telegraph Co. Operated by United States Lines. Capt. John E. Green's ship was torpedoed on March 8, 1943, by *U-160* off South Africa. One Armed Guard sailor was lost. The survivors left Durban on May 7 aboard the Seas Shipping Co. (Robin Line) steamer *Robin Tuxford* and arrived at New York on June 11. Bosun Edward F. Racine was awarded the Merchant Marine Distinguished Service medal for rescuing several shipmates out from underneath an overturned lifeboat.

83. TABITHA BROWN, 10–42, 242446, KHNV (1780–1858) Tabitha Moffatt, of Massachusetts, married the Rev. Clark Brown in December 1799. He died in 1817 and she began teaching school and moved to Missouri. Her son Otis went to Oregon in 1843 and she came out in 1846 over the Oregon Trail. She was cofounder of the Tualatin Academy in 1849, now Pacific University, and was honored as the "Mother of Oregon" in 1987 by the legislature. Operated by Pacific-Atlantic.

84. ALEXANDER GRAHAM BELL, 10–42, 242455, KHSP (1847–1922) inventor of the telephone. Operated by Weyerhaeuser.

85. THOMAS A. EDISON, 10–42, 242475, KHSQ (1847–1931) Thomas Alva Edison was a prolific inventor. Operated by Grace Line. Stranded on a reef southeast of Fiji on January 2, 1943, and destroyed. There were no reported casualties.

86. SAMUEL COLT, 10–42, 242445, KHSR (1814–1862) firearms inventor and manufacturer. Operated by Union Sulphur.

87. JOHN DEERE, 10–42, 242466, KHSS (1804–1886) farm equipment innovator and manufacturer. Operated by Pacific-Atlantic.

88. CHARLES GOODYEAR, 11–42, 242487, KHST (1836–1860) innovative automobile tire manufacturer. Operated by Marine Transport.

89. ELMER A. SPERRY, 11–42, 242502, KHSW (1860–1930) Elmer Ambrose Sperry was a pioneer in electrochemistry who invented the gyroscope and the high-intensity arc lamp searchlight. Operated by Shepard.

90. JOHN P. HOLLAND, 11–42, 242503, KHSY (1840–1914) Irish-born Seán Pilib Ó hUalláchain came to America in 1873 as John P. Holland and built the U.S. Navy's first commissioned submarine in 1900. Operated by Lykes.

91. CHARLES GORDON CURTIS, 11–42, 242511, KHTE (1860–1936) Kansas congressman and vice president. Operated by Seas Shipping.

92. JAMES B. EADS, 11–42, 242516, KHBF (1820–1897) Capt. James Buchanan Eads was a wrecker on the Mississippi who invented the diving bell. Operated by Shepard.

93. S. M. BABCOCK, 11–42, 242523, KHNQ (1843–1931) Stephen Moulton Babcock created the Babcock test for determining the butterfat content in milk. Operated by A. H. Bull.

94. SAMUEL PARKER, 11–42, 242550, KIYC (1806–1886) Oregon pioneer and legislator. Operated by American Mail Line. Capt. Elmer J. Stull's ship was hit by an aerial torpedo off Sicily on July 13, 1943, while loaded with gasoline, ammunition, and general cargo. The

badly-holed and damaged ship received the first Maritime Commission Gallant Ship award upon arrival in New York. Capt. Stull, chief mate Nikolai K. Storkersen, and able seaman Fred Aubry Anderson were awarded the Merchant Marine Distinguished Service medal for extinguishing fires in a hold filled with ammunition.

95. JOSEPH GALE, 11–42, 242559, KIYF (1807–1881) Washington, D.C., resident who was a ship-wrecked sailor, mountain man, fur trapper, 49er, Oregon pioneer, ferryboat and California sawmill operator, and restless adventurer who helped build the *Star of Oregon*. Operated by Weyerhaeuser.

96. PETER SKENE OGDEN, 11–42, 242565, KIVH (1790–1854) Canadian fur trader, explorer of the American west, and namesake for Ogden, Utah. Operated by W. R. Chamberlin. Capt. William P. Mangan's ship was torpedoed on February 22, 1944, by *U-969* off Algeria. There were no reported casualties.

97. JOSEPH L. MEEK, 11–42, 242558, KIZA (1810–1875) Joseph Lafayette Meek was a pioneer fur trader who helped settle Oregon. In a very unusual twist, some of Meek's descendants worked at Oregon Shipbuilding. Steven Meek, 84, was a burner and his wife Gertrude, 62, and their grandson Steven D., 17, were welders. Joseph L. Meek was a welder and Robert E. Meek was a welder in the assembly building division. Operated by Alaska Steamship.

98. SAMUEL J. TILDEN, 11–42, 242562, KIZE (1814–1886) Samuel Jones Tilden was governor of New York. Operated by A. H. Bull. Capt. Joseph J. Blair's ship was sunk on December 2, 1943, by German aircraft at Bari, Italy, with the loss of 10 merchant crew and 17 passengers.

99. ABNER DOUBLEDAY, 11–42, 242570, KIZN (1819–1893) founder of baseball. Operated by Sword Line.

100. G. W. GOETHALS, 12–42, 242579, KHBE (1858–1928) George Washington Goethals was an Army engineer and builder of the Panama Canal. Operated by Weyerhaeuser.

101. WILLIAM T. SHERMAN, 12–42, 242581, KGFY (1820–1891) William Tecumseh Sherman was a Union general and the namesake for Sherman County, Oregon. Operated by Alaska Steamship.

102. FRANK B. KELLOGG, 12–42, 242578, KIZQ (1856–1937) Frank Billings Kellogg was a Minnesota senator and Secretary of State. Operated by Pacific-Atlantic. Louis J. "Frenchy" Guillemette, 24, was third mate on the *Julia Luckenbach* when they left New York in November 1942 and arrived back at New York from London on April 3, 1943. In May he signed on Mississippi Shipping's Hog Islander *Delrio* at New York and arrived back there on June 26 from Swansea, Wales. From February to August 1944 he was chief mate on the *Edmund F. Dickins* then skipper of the Hog Islander *Examiner*. In July 1945 at age 27 he left Seattle as captain of the *Frank B. Kellogg* and was sent to Batavia, Java, to "assist in liberating the island" but while there trouble started between the Indonesians and the Dutch. During the disturbance the crew of the *Kellogg* apparently became involved in black market activities urged on by Indonesian officials. Theses activities came to the attention of Central Intelligence Division agents in the area and regular reports were forwarded to Washington. After a month in Java the ship went to Bangkok, then Singapore, and Fremantle, Australia. When they arrived back at Seattle on May 7, 1946, the FBI was waiting with warrants for the arrest of everyone on board, Lt. Harold A. Hall's Armed Guard crew possibly excepted. Capt. Guillemette was charged with conspiracy and piracy on the high seas and his master mariner's license was revoked. He began appealing and found sympathetic allies in the State Dept. meanwhile, Frenchy and his wife Dot moved to Two Rivers, Minnesota, in 1961 and he worked as a wheelman on the Great Lakes tanker *Detroit* and became a naturalized citizen in 1963. His allies in

the State Dept. brought his case and war record to President Johnson and in March 1964 a pardon was granted, signed by Attorney General Robert Kennedy. He had no plans at that time to make use of his new unlimited license.

103. CARL SCHURZ, 12–42, 242586, KIZT (1829–1906) German-born Carl Christian Schurz was a minister to Spain, Union general, Missouri senator, and Secretary of the Interior. Operated by American Mail Line and converted to an Army troopship.

104. HENRY BARNARD, 12–42, 242610, KIZU (1811–1900) Yale graduate, advocate and reformer of public education in Connecticut and Rhode Island, and editor of the *American Journal of Education.* Operated by Sword Line.

105. JOHN S. COPLEY, 12–42, 242612, KJAG (1738–1815) John Singleton Copley was a noted portrait artist who painted average New England subjects. Operated by American Mail Line. Capt. Arthur Dowell's ship was torpedoed by *U-73* on December 16, 1943, off Oran, Algeria. There were no reported casualties and the ship was repaired.

106. CHARLES WILLSON PEALE, 12–42, 242619, KJAH (1741–1827) soldier and Revolutionary era portrait painter, especially of George Washington. Operated by Pacific-Atlantic.

107. EDWIN BOOTH, 12–42, 242631, KJAJ (1833–1893) Edwin Thomas Booth was a noted Shakespearean actor and brother of John Wilkes Booth. Operated by American Mail Line.

108. JOSEPH JEFFERSON, 12–42, 242641, KJAK (1829–1905) Joe Jefferson was a noted comedian. Operated by Weyerhaeuser.

109. RICHARD MANSFIELD, 12–42, 242658, KJAL (1854–1907) noted Shakespearean actor. Operated by Alaska Steamship.

110. JOHN BURKE, 12–42, 242664, KKDQ (1859–1937) governor of North Dakota and Secretary of the Treasury. Operated by Northland. Capt. Herbert A. Falk's ship had a full cargo of munitions when it was hit by a kamikaze on December 28, 1944, off Mindoro, Philippines. The ship disintegrated and all 40 merchant seamen and 28 Armed Guard sailors aboard were lost.

111. JIM BRIDGER, 12–42, 242673, KKDR (1804–1881) James Felix "Jim" Bridger was a Northwest frontiersman, mountain man, trapper, and multi-lingual mediator between Indians and white settlers. Operated by James Griffiths.

112. EZRA MEEKER, 12–42, 242672, KKDS (1830–1928) Ezra Manning Meeker was an Oregon pioneer and Oregon Trail preservationist. Operated by Pacific-Atlantic.

113. SACAJAWEA, 12–42, 242697, KKDV (1788–1882) Shoshone girl named Bird Woman who was kidnapped by Hidatsa Indians and sold to Toussaint Charbonneau, a member of the Lewis & Clark expedition. Operated by Alaska Transportation and converted to an Army troopship.

114. CHIEF WASHAKIE, 12–42, 242704, KKDW (c. 1804–1900) chief of the Eastern Shoshone Indians of Wyoming who aided white travelers, and Army scout betrayed by broken promises. His daughter was Jim Bridger's third wife. Operated by Northland.

115. WILLIAM E. BORAH, 1–43, 242723, KKGN (1865–1940) William Edgar Borah was an Idaho senator and leader of the "drys" during Prohibition who came to agree with President Hoover in 1932 that the law was unenforceable and should be repealed. Operated by American Mail Line.

116. M. M. GUHIN, 1–43, 242733, KKDX (1871–1941) Michael Miles Guhin fostered education in rural South Dakota. Operated by Pope & Talbot.

117. LINDLEY M. GARRISON, 1–43, 242752, KKGZ (1864–1932) Lindley Miller Garrison was Secretary of War. Operated by Alaska Transportation then converted to an Army troopship.

118. JOHN W. WEEKS, 1–43, 242750, KKHH (1860–1926) John Wingate Weeks was a Massachusetts congressman and Secretary of War. Operated by Northland then converted to an Army troopship.

119. STEPHEN B. ELKINS, 1–43, 242769, KKII (1841–1911) Stephen Benton Elkins was a New Mexico congressman, Secretary of War, West Virginia senator, and namesake for Elkins, West Virginia. Operated by James Griffiths.

120. DANIEL S. LAMONT, 1–43, 242768, KKIG (1851–1905) Daniel Scott Lamont was Secretary of War. Operated by Alaska Transportation.

121. ALEXANDER J. DALLAS, 1–43, 242767, KKIA (1759–1871) Alexander James Dallas was a Philadelphia lawyer who wrote four volumes of Supreme Court reports and was Secretary of the Treasury. Operated by Pacific-Atlantic.

122. RICHARD RUSH, 1–43, 242788, KKIQ (1780–1859) Attorney General, Secretary of State and Treasury. Operated by Seas Shipping.

123. SAMUEL D. INGHAM, 1–43, 242790, KHWT (1779–1860) Samuel Delucenna Ingham was a Pennsylvania congressman and Secretary of the Treasury. Operated by Alaska Transportation.

124. GEORGE W. CAMPBELL, 1–43, 242793, KHWZ (1769–1848) George Washington Campbell was a Tennessee senator, Secretary of the Treasury, and minister to Russia. Operated by Weyerhaeuser.

125. WILLIAM J. DUANE, 1–43, 242811, KHWU (1780–1865) William John Duane was Secretary of the Treasury. Operated by Pacific-Atlantic.

126. THOMAS EWING, 1–43, 242832, KHWW (1789–1871) Ohio senator and Secretary of the Treasury and Interior. Operated by J. H. Winchester under Capt. Ernest A. Dammann and then by the Navy as the *Crater*-class cargo ship *Giansar* (AK-111), NHLX, commissioned on October 29, 1943.

127. WALTER FORWARD, 2–43, 242833, KHWY (1786–1852) Pennsylvania congressman and Secretary of the Treasury. Operated by Pacific-Atlantic.

128. FRANKLIN MACVEAGH, 2–43, 242858, KKIL (1837–1934) Secretary of the Treasury. Operated by Alaska Steamship.

129. GEORGE M. BIBB, 2–43, 242859, KKIZ (1776–1859) George Mortimer Bibb was a Kentucky senator and Secretary of the Treasury. Operated by Isthmian.

130. ROBERT J. WALKER, 2–43, 242871, KKJC (1801–1869) Robert John Walker was Secretary of the Treasury, Mississippi senator, and governor of the Kansas Territory. Operated by McCormick. Capt. Murdoch D. MacRae was skipper of the Smith & Johnson Liberty ship *Edwin T. Meredith* when they arrived at San Francisco on May 25, 1944. He made one more voyage then joined the *Walker*. The ship was torpedoed on December 24, 1944, by *U-862* southeast of Sydney, Australia, with the loss of messman Ernest E. Ballard and utilityman Chew Toon.

131. WILLIAM M. MEREDITH, 2–43, 242897, KKJE (1799–1873) William Morris Meredith was Secretary of the Treasury. Operated by Weyerhaeuser. Captain Leonard J. Greene, of Portsmouth, New Hampshire, was master when his crew worked to salvage cargo from the *Thomas G. Masaryk*. He removed the ship's 150-pound bell and sent it home to his wife in Pepperell, New Hampshire, where it sat out on the front lawn.

132. JOHN WHITEAKER, 2–43, 242904, KKQO (1820–1902) first governor of the state of Oregon and a congressman. Operated by Isthmian under Capt. John M. Griffin then by the Navy as the *Crater*-class cargo ship *Situla* (AK-140), NHET, commissioned on January 1, 1944.

133. SAM JACKSON, 2–43, 242909, KKQQ (1860–1924) Charles S. "Sam" Jackson

came to eastern Oregon in 1880 from Virginia and by 1882 was publisher of the *East Oregonian* newspaper in Pendleton. In 1902 he moved to Portland to run the *Oregon Journal*. Operated by American Mail.

134. OWEN SUMMERS, 2–43, 242932, KKQU (1850–1911) prominent Portland merchant and father of the Oregon National Guard. Operated by Weyerhaeuser.

135. ARTHUR RIGGS, 2–43, 242937, KKQP (1871–1941) famous steamboat pilot on the Columbia, Willamette, and Snake rivers. Operated by Polarus.

136. LOT WHITCOMB, 2–43, 242940, KKOZ (1807–1857) first Willamette River steamboat operator, founder of Milwaukie, Oregon, and publisher of the first Oregon Territory newspaper. Operated by Shepard.

137. MORTON M. MCCARVER, 2–43, 242950, KKRA (1807–1875) Morton Matthew McCarver, of Kentucky, founded Tacoma, Washington, and cities in Iowa and Oregon and helped establish government in California. Operated by James Griffiths.

138. HALL J. KELLEY, 3–43, 242949, KKRB (1790–1874) Hall Jackson Kelley was an Oregon pioneer and namesake for Kelley Point at the confluence of the Columbia and Willamette Rivers. Operated by Alaska Transportation.

139. JOHN W. CULLEN, 3–43, 242989, KKRE (1838–1939) Indiana native John Winchell Cullen was an Indian war veteran, Oregon pioneer, Methodist minister, and a 2nd lieutenant in the Oregon Infantry, First Regiment in 1864–5. Operated by Alaska Steamship.

140. NATHANIEL J. WYETH, 3–43, 243005, KKRG (1802–1856) Nathaniel Jarvis Wyeth was a Boston inventor whose ideas revolutionized the ice industry and allowed ice to be shipped long distances. Apparently he was restless and became a mountain man, leading two expeditions to Oregon in the 1830s and established two trading posts, Fort Hall in Idaho and Fort William at present-day Portland, Oregon. Operated by McCormick under Capt. William Schutz and then by the Navy as the *De Grasse* (AP-164) commissioned on November 8, 1943.

141. HENDERSON LUELLING, 3–43, 243003, KKRM (1809–1878) fruit grower who brought 700 trees from Iowa to Oregon in 1848 along with eight children. Liked reproducing things. Operated by Northland. Some of the ship's deck plates separated during an Alaskan voyage and had to be rewelded.

142. DEKABRIST, 3–43, a "Decembrist" was one who participated in the failed December 14, 1825, uprising against Nicholas I. Operated under the Russian flag.

143. CUSHING EELLS, 3–43, 243021, KKRP (1810–1893) Massachusetts Congregational preacher who came to Oregon and cofounded the Tualatin Academy in 1849, now Pacific University, and founded Whitman College in Walla Walla, Washington. Operated by American Mail Line.

144. JAMES HARROD, 3–43, 243023, KKRQ (c. 1742–1792) Kentucky pioneer, British soldier, and explorer who founded Harrodstown in 1774 and became a wealthy planter. In early 1792 he and two companions went on a hunting trip but Harrod never returned and no clear explanations were forthcoming. The reason for his disappearance remains a mystery. Operated by Sudden & Christenson. Capt. Hugo B. Karsten's ship collided with the anchored Liberty ship *Raymond B. Stevens* on January 16, 1945, off Ramsgate, England, with the loss of four Armed Guard sailors. The ship was destroyed.

145. CHRISTOPHER GREENUP, 3–43, 243049, KKRR (1750–1818) Kentucky congressman and governor. Operated by Alaska Steamship and converted to an Army troopship.

146. AMOS KENDALL, 3–43, 243047, KKRT (1789–1869) lawyer, journalist, and Postmaster General. Operated by Weyerhaeuser.

147. BELVA LOCKWOOD, 3–43, 243057, KKRW (1830–1917) Belva Ann Bennett,

of New York, married Uriah McNall, a farmer, in 1848 and they had a daughter. When he died in 1853 she went to school, became an educator, a female college administrator and social activist. In 1868 she married the Rev. Ezekiel Lockwood, a dentist in Washington, D.C., and then, overcoming considerable opposition, became a lawyer. She was the first female attorney to argue a case before the Supreme Court. Operated by United States Lines.

148. KENNETH A. J. MACKENZIE, 3–43, 243060, KKRX (1859–1920) Kenneth Alexander James MacKenzie was a Canadian-born physician, cofounder and dean of the University of Oregon Medical School in Portland, and cofounder of the Oregon State Medical Society. Operated by Alaska Steamship.

149. LUCRETIA MOTT, 3–43, 243062, KKRY (1793–1880) Lucretia Coffin was a Massachusetts Quaker who attended the Nine Partners Quaker Boarding School in New York and then taught there with James Mott. She came unglued when she found out male teachers earned three times the pay of female teachers. She nevertheless married Mott in 1811 and they moved to Philadelphia where she became an abolitionist and social activist. Operated by Pacific-Atlantic.

150. PIERRE GIBAULT, 3–43, 243100, KKRZ (1737–1804) Canadian Jesuit missionary who was expelled from the Northwest Territory in 1793 by the British. He served in Virginia and supported the American Revolution. Operated by Shepard.

151. BENJAMIN H. GRIERSON, 3–43, 243106, KKSB (1826–1911) Benjamin Henry Grierson was a Union general in the Civil War. Operated by Pacific-Atlantic.

152. ALEXANDER SUVOROV, 3–43 (1730–1800) famous Russian general. Operated under the Russian flag.

153. MIKHAIL KUTUZOV, 3–43 (1745–1813) Russian Empire field marshal and diplomat. Operated under the Russian flag.

154. ALBERT B. CUMMINS, 3–43, 243155, KKSE (1850–1926) Albert Baird Cummins was an Iowa governor and senator. Operated by Alaska Steamship.

155. JAMES W. GRIMES, 3–43, 243162, KKSF (1816–1872) James Wilson Grimes was an Iowa governor and senator. Operated by Union Sulphur.

156. GEORGE L. BAKER, 4–43, 243158, KOBW (1868–1941) George Luis baker was the mayor of Portland, Oregon. Operated by Weyerhaeuser.

157. CHIEF JOSEPH, 4–43, 243172, KOCB (1840–1904) "Hin-mah-too-yah-lat-kekt" was a Wallowa Nez Perce chief in northeast Oregon. Operated by Sudden & Christenson. In June 1946 the ship was attacked by 60 Chinese pirates off China's north coast. The crew held them off until a Navy destroyer arrived.

158. ALEXANDR NEVSKY, 4–43 (1220–1263) Aleksandr Yaroslavich Nevskiy was the Prince of Novgorod and Grand Prince of Vladmir who repulsed Germanic and Swedish invaders and became a saint in the Russian Orthodox Church. Operated under the Russian flag.

159. GEORGE FLAVEL, 4–43, 243176, KOCD (1823–1893) sea captain, Oregon pioneer and Columbia River bar pilot. Operated by Alaska Steamship and converted to an Army troopship.

160. JOHN H. COUCH, 4–43, 243189, KOCE (1811–1870) John Heard Cooch was a Newburyport, Massachusetts, sailor who settled in Oregon City in 1843 and eventually became a Columbia River bar pilot and cofounder of Portland. Operated by Weyerhaeuser. Capt. David N. Welch's ship was sunk on October 11, 1943, by a Japanese aerial torpedo off Koli Point, Guadalcanal with the loss of 2nd cook & baker Robert E. Copley. Survivors left Espiritu Santo, New Hebrides, on October 31 on the *Lundys Lane* and arrived at Los Angeles on November 16.

161. GEORGE H. FLANDERS, 4–43, 243186, KOCG (1821–1892) George Hall Flanders was sea captain, brother-in-law and business partner of John H. Couch in Oregon and served in marine inspection positions. Operated by W. R. Chamberlin.

162. FRANCIS W. PETTYGROVE, 4–43, 243185, KOCI (1812–1887) Francis William Pettygrove was a cofounder of Portland, Oregon, and Port Townsend, Washington. Operated by American Mail Line. Kenneth S. McPherson, 35, was chief officer on the Hammond Co. freighter *Astoria* when they arrived at Seattle on March 23, 1943, from Prince Rupert, B. C. The company's local agent was American Mail Line and they had a new ship in Portland that needed a skipper. The *Pettygrove* was sunk on August 13, 1943, by German aircraft off Almeria, Spain, with no reported casualties.

163. HENRY FAILING, 4–43, 243203, KOCL (1834–1898) prominent Portland, Oregon, merchant and banker. Operated by Alaska Steamship then converted to an Army troopship.

164. B. F. SHAW, 4–43, 243221, KOCQ (1829–1908) Benjamin Franklin Shaw was an Oregon pioneer and Army colonel who fought Indians in the Grand Ronde Valley. Operated by Northland.

165. SIMON BOLIVAR, 4–43, 243233, KOCR (1783–1830) Simón José de la Santisima Trinidad Bolivar y Palacios Ponte y Blanco was a soldier and politician in Venezuela who lead the movement for independence from Spain. Operated by R. A. Nicol.

166. EMILIAN PUGACHEV, 4–43 (c. 1740–1775) Yemelyan Ivanovich Pugachev led a Cossack rebellion against Catherine II. Operated under the Russian flag.

167. EDWARD BELLAMY, 4–43, 243242, KOCT (1850–1898) Massachusetts journalist and socialist who inspired the founding of the Nationalist Clubs. Operated by Pacific-Atlantic.

168. STEPAN RAZIN, 4–43 (1630–1671) Stenka Timofeyevich Razin was a rebellious Cossack in south Russia. Operated under the Russian flag.

169. LENINGRAD, 4–43, city of Saint Petersburg renamed Petrograd in 1914 and Leningrad in 1924, under German siege from 1941 to early 1944. Operated under the Russian flag.

170. GILBERT STUART, 4–43, 243277, KODA (1755–1828) Gilbert Charles Stuart was a noted portrait painter. Operated by American Mail Line. Capt. John B. Kiehl's ship was hit by a kamikaze on November 17, 1944, at Tacloban, Leyte, Philippines, with the loss of five merchant crew and one Armed Guard sailor. The ship was repaired.

171. SEVASTOPOL, 4–43, second largest port city in the Ukraine, occupied by German forces from 1941 to 1944. Operated under the Russian flag.

172. RICHARD HARDING DAVIS, 4–43, 243304, KODE (1864–1916) noted correspondent during the Spanish-American, Second Boer, and Great Wars. Operated by Weyerhaeuser.

173. WILLIAM H. MCGUFFEY, 5–43, 243310, KODG (1800–1873) William Holmes McGuffey was a college professor and author of the famous *McGuffey Readers*. Operated by Weyerhaeuser.

174. CUSHMAN K. DAVIS, 5–43, 243319, KOII (1838–1900) Cushman Kellogg Davis was a Minnesota governor and senator. Operated by Alaska Steamship then converted to an Army troopship.

175. PSKOV, 5–43, Russian city occupied by German forces from July 9, 1941, to July 23, 1944, suffering much destruction. Operated under the Russian flag.

176. IGNATIUS DONNELLY, 5–43, 243340, KOIK (1831–1901) Ignatius Loyola Donnelly was a Minnesota congressman. Operated by Alaska Transportation.

177. ROBERT NEWELL, 5–43, 243349, KOGG (1807–1869) Zanesville, Ohio, native Robert "Doc" Newell was a fur trapper who learned basic medical arts and in 1840 he and his brother-in-law Joseph Meek brought the first wagon train on the Oregon Trail from Fort Hall to the Columbia River. In 1841 he brought the first wagons south to the Willamette Valley. He became a legislator, newspaper man, and Indian agent. Operated by Union Sulphur.

178. STANFORD NEWEL, 5–43, 243376, KOGJ (1839–1907) Minnesota attorney who was ambassador to the Netherlands and Luxembourg. Operated by Weyerhaeuser.

179. KUBAN, 5–43, Russian Cossacks occupied the Kuban River area in the 1860s. Operated under the Russian flag.

180. WILLIAM H. GRAY, 5–43, 243426, KOGO (1810–1889) William Henry Gray was an Oregon pioneer who arrived with the Whitman party. He moved to Salem and worked at the Oregon Institute, a Methodist school founded in 1842 that later became Willamette University. In 1843 he hosted a meeting where the provisional government was formed and later wrote a history of Oregon. Operated by Pacific-Atlantic.

181. NOVOROSSISK, 5–43, main Russian port city on the Black Sea attacked by German forces in 1942 and defended by Russian sailors, which prevented German use of the port. Operated under the Russian flag.

182. THOMAS A. HENDRICKS, 5–43, 243407, KOGW (1819–1885) Thomas Andrew Hendricks was an Indiana congressman and governor. Operated by American Mail.

183. JONATHAN JENNINGS, 5–43, 243400, KOIC (1784–1834) Indiana congressman and governor. Operated by the Navy as *Talita* (AKS-8) commissioned on March 4, 1944.

184. GEORGE W. JULIAN, 5–43, 243415, KOIE (1817–1899) George Washington Julian was an Indiana congressman. Operated by Northland then converted to an Army troopship.

185. HENRY S. LANE, 5–43, 243464, KOIF (1811–1881) Henry Smith Lane was an Indiana congressman. Operated by Pacific-Atlantic.

186. JAMES OLIVER, 5–43, 243465, KOIG (1822–1908) co-owner of the South Bend Iron Works at South Bend, Indiana, in 1855. As a youngster Oliver had experience with field plowing and felt the implement could be improved and in 1857 he patented a new design. The Oliver Farm Equipment Co. was incorporated in 1929 after mergers. Operated by Alaska Transportation.

187. ERIC V. HAUSER, 5–43, 243462, KONE (1864–1929) Eric Van Alstan Hauser was a Minneapolis native who became a contractor for the Central Oregon & Pacific Railroad, a hotel owner, and a shipbuilder. Namesake for Hauser, Oregon, and endowed the library at Reed College. Operated by James Griffiths.

188. FRANCIS E. WARREN, 5–43, 243490, KOPX (1844–1929) Francis Emory Warren was a governor of the Wyoming Territory and a senator. Operated by Coastwise.

189. GEORGE DAVIDSON, 6–43, 243491, KOQA (1825–1911) noted surveyor of the Pacific Coast. Operated by Shepard.

190. R. C. BRENNAN, 5–43, 243497, KOQP (1881–1942) Richard Charles Brennan, 60, of Portland, Oregon, was master of the *Nathaniel Hawthorne*, lost when the ship was torpedoed by *U-508* off Isla de Margarita on November 7, 1942. Before the war he was the superintendent of a stevedoring company and lived at 2925 NW Raleigh St. with his wife Naomi, 38, and daughters Patricia, 18, Catherine, 9, and Margaret, 5. Operated by Weyerhaeuser.

191. KHERSON, 6–43, Russian port city on the Black Sea. Operated under the Russian flag. Stranded on July 3, 1943.

192. VITEBSK, 6–43, city in Belarus under German occupation in 1943. Operated under the Russian flag.

193. VLADIVOSTOK, 6–43, major Russian port city. Operated under the Russian flag.

194. WILSON P. HUNT, 6–43, 243602, KOXN (1783–1842) Wilson Price Hunt was employed by John Jacob Astor's Pacific Fur Co. to hire men and lead an overland expedition from St. Louis to Fort Astoria in 1811. Operated by Weyerhaeuser.

195. BEN HOLLADAY, 6–43, 243581, KOVP (1819–1887) Benjamin "Ben" Holladay was an entrepreneur and "Stagecoach King" who started the Overland Stage to California in 1849 and unscrupulously operated railroads and steamships in Oregon. Operated by Union Sulphur.

196. JOEL PALMER, 6–43, 243591, KOWS (1810–1902) established the last leg of the Oregon Trail and cofounded Dayton, Oregon. Operated by American Mail Line.

197. THOMAS NUTTALL, 6–43, 243633, KOZW (1786–1859) English botanist and zoologist who travelled with the Wilson Price Hunt expedition to Fort Astoria in 1811 and collected plant specimens. Namesake for several plants and birds and became the curator of the Harvard University botanical gardens. Operated by American-Foreign.

198. JOHN A. JOHNSON, 6–43, 243641, KOZX (1861–1909) John Albert Johnson was the first Minnesota-born governor of the state. Operated by American Mail Line. Capt. Arnold H. Beeken, of Tacoma, Washington, ordered his ship abandoned after a torpedo from *I-12* hit the ship on October 30, 1944, about 400 miles northeast of Hawaii. Survivors were machine-gunned and lifeboats rammed. The Navy Armed Guard officer was Lt. (jg) Wynn Del Yates, of Salt Lake City. Ten aboard were lost.

199. EPHRAIM W. BAUGHMAN, 6–43, 243636, KHBZ (1835–1921) Illinois native and 49er who came to Oregon in 1851, fought in the Indian war, and worked as a fireman on the steamer *Lot Whitcomb*. By 1858 he was a pilot and captain and joined the *Colonel Wright*. In 1861 he brought the *Wright* up the Snake River to Lewiston, Idaho, the first vessel to make it past The Dalles and which led to the development of Lewiston. Operated by Pacific-Atlantic.

200. EDWARD CANBY, 6–43, 243681, KXGB (1817–1873) Edward Richard Sprigg Canby was an Army general from Kentucky who was killed by Modoc Indians in Oregon. Namesake for Canby, Oregon. Operated by American-Hawaiian.

201. SOVETSKAYA GAVAN, 6–43, vital Strait of Tartary port of entry and railway terminus during the war. Operated under the Russian flag.

202. JOHN F. STEFFEN, 6–43, 243703, KXOM (1842–1900) German-born Johann Friedrich Steffen was a noted shipbuilder at Portland, Oregon. Operated by Weyerhaeuser.

203. THOMAS CONDON, 6–43, 243705, KXOO (1822–1907) noted Oregon missionary and university professor. Operated by Alaska Steamship.

204. SIMON BENSON, 6–43, 243722, KXOP (1852–1942) Oregon lumberman and hotelier. Operated by Sudden & Christenson.

205. NAKHODKA, 6–43, Russian port city in the Sea of Japan. Operated under the Russian flag.

206. NICHOLAS J. SINNOTT, 6–43, 243762, KXOV (1870–1929) Nicholas John Sinnott was an Oregon congressman and federal Court of Claims judge. Operated by James Griffiths.

207. ASKOLD, 7–43, a traditional ancient ruler of Kiev. Operated under the Russian flag.

208. FELIX HATHAWAY, 7–43, 243779, KXQC (1798–1856) Oregon pioneer and carpenter hired to build the schooner *Star of Oregon* in 1840. Operated by Coastwise (Pacific Far East) Line.

209. JAMES WITHYCOMBE, 7–43, 243771, KXQD (1854–1919) Oregon governor.

Operated by Sudden & Christenson. Capt. William C. Gortz's ship became stranded on December 9, 1943, off Cristobal, Panama.

210. BINGER HERMANN, 7–43, 243767, KXQM (1843–1926) Oregon congressman. Operated by Weyerhaeuser.

211. DONALD MACLEAY, 7–43, 243802, KXQN (1834–1897) prominent Portland banker. Operated by American Mail Line.

212. HENRY L. HOYT, 7–43, 243834, KXQQ (1823–1898) Henry LaFayette Hoyt was an Oregon pioneer, mariner, and shipwreck survivor. Operated by General Steamship.

213. EREVAN, 7–43, Yerevan, the capital city of Armenia, was one of the 15 republics of the Soviet Union. Operated under the Russian flag.

214. DELAZON SMITH, 7–43, 243853, KXQV (1816–1860) Oregon pioneer and senator. Operated by Alaska Steamship.

215. SAMUEL K. BARLOW, 7–43, 243862, KXQX (1795–1867) Samuel Kimbrough Barlow, of Kentucky, was a Willamette Valley, Oregon, pioneer who helped establish the Oregon Trail. Operated by Weyerhaeuser.

216. JOHN P. GAINES, 7–43, 243861, KXQZ (1795–1857) John Pollard Gaines was an Oregon Territory governor and Kentucky congressman. Operated by Northland. Capt. Anthony W. Nickerson's ship broke apart on November 24, 1943, in the Bering Sea with the loss of three merchant crew, one Armed Guard sailor, and seven Army passengers.

217. SAMPLER, 7–43, 169933, BKSL, built for the British Ministry of War Transport. Operated by Port Line.

218. BAKU, 7–43, capital of Azerbaijan, held by Russian forces against German invasion in 1942. Operated under the Russian flag.

219. GEORGE H. HIMES, 7–43, 243897, KXRG (1844–1940) George Henry Himes, of Pennsylvania, was an Oregon pioneer, printer, typesetter, and the first curator of the Oregon Historical Society. Operated by Shepard.

220. J. D. ROSS, 7–43, 243915, KXRH (1872–1939) James Delmage Ross was the first administrator of the Bonneville Power Project. He was the Seattle City Light Co. superintendent of the Skagit Hydroelectric Project on the Upper Skagit River and when he died unexpectedly Ruby Dam was named for him. Operated by Pacific-Atlantic.

221. JAMES K. KELLY, 7–43, 243926, KZRK (1819–1903) James Kerr Kelly, of Pennsylvania, was an Oregon senator. Operated by Alaska Steamship.

222. THOMAS W. SYMONS, 7–43, 243931, KXRM (1849–1920) Thomas William Symons was an Oregon Army officer and surveyor from Keeseville, New York, where he was a bookbinder. He designer of several major waterway projects and improvements and was known as the "father of barge canals." Operated by Weyerhaeuser.

223. STALINABAD, 7–43, Dushanbe, capital of Tajikistan, was renamed Stalinabad in 1929 and reverted in 1961. Operated under the Russian flag.

224. GEORGE L. CURRY, 8–43, 243964, KXRP (1820–1878) George Law Curry was an Oregon Territory governor and editor of the *Oregon Free Press*. Operated by R. A. Nicol.

225. WILLIAM HUME, 8–43, 243971, KXRR (1830–1902) Maine native who got into the salmon business in 1852 at Sacramento, California. In 1864 he and his brother George and Andrew S. Hapgood built the first salmon cannery on the Pacific Coast at Broderick, California, on the Sacramento River as Hapgood, Hume & Co. In 1866 they moved to Washington 50 miles inland on the Columbia River and built the first salmon cannery in the Pacific Northwest. Operated by Weyerhaeuser.

226. SAMBAY, 8–43, 169651, BKXN, built for the British Ministry of War Transport. Operated by Glen Line.

227. CLINTON KELLY, 8–43, 244019, KXRT (1808–1875) Oregon City, Oregon, pioneer. Operated by Pacific-Atlantic.

228. EDWARD D. BAKER, 8–43, 244006, KYAO (1811–1861) Edward Dickinson Baker was a British-born Republican senator from Oregon and close friend of President Lincoln. Col. Baker was lost at Ball's Bluff in Virginia on October 21, 1861, the only senator to ever die in combat. Namesake for Baker City, Oregon. Operated by Matson.

229. SAMUEL LANCASTER, 8–43, 244013, KYAQ (1864–1941) Samuel Christopher Lancaster designed the Linfield College campus and the scenic Columbia River Highway in Oregon. Operated by Alaska Steamship.

230. JOHN JACOB ASTOR, 8–43, 244044, KYAD (1763–1848) founded the American Fur Co. and Astoria, Oregon. Operated by United States Lines.

231. CHARLES M. RUSSELL, 8–43, 244038, KYAV (1864–1926) Charles Marion "Kid" Russell was a painter of Old American Western scenes. Operated by Coastwise (Pacific Far East) Line.

232. JOSEPH SIMON, 8–43, 244045, KYAW (1851–1935) Oregon senator and mayor of Portland. Operated by Weyerhaeuser.

233. R. P. WARNER, 8–43, 244081, KYBH (1871–1936) Richmond Perez Warner was a Minnesota wholesale grocer, chairman of the St. Paul Port Authority, and vice president and director of the Oregon & Washington Colonization Company, a group formed to encourage Northwest settlement. Operated by American Mail Line.

234. HENRY L. ABBOTT, 8–43, 244088, KYBI (1831–1927) Henry Larcom Abbot was an Army surveyor who laid out railroad routes in California and Oregon. Operated by Alaska Transportation. Capt. Malcolm McClaren's ship hit a mine in Manila Bay on May 2, 1945, with the loss of 1st engineer John A. Larkin and 3rd engineer Albert E. Rutledge. The ship was taken over by the Navy and on July 14 became the USS *Gamage* (IX-227). The ship was subsequently found unfit for service and on 6 August the name was tranferred to the *William B. Allison*, which had been named *Inca* (IX-229).

235. SAMBUT, 8–43, 169803, BXXP, built for the British Ministry of War Transport. Operated by P. Henderson & Co. Sunk on June 6, 1944, in the Straits of Dover by German shore batteries.

236. DAVID THOMPSON, 8–43, 244099, KYBK (1770–1857) productive and busy Pacific Northwest land surveyor. Operated by American Mail Line.

237. DUNHAM WRIGHT, 8–43, 244104, KYBL (1842–1942) John Dunham Wright was a cousin of Abraham Lincoln's who developed the Medical Springs Resort in Union County, Oregon. Operated by Weyerhaeuser.

238. B. F. IRVINE, 8–43, 244115, KYBM (1858–1940) Benjamin Franklin Irvine owned the *Corvallis Gazette-Times* in Corvallis, Oregon. Operated by James Griffiths.

239. DAVID F. BARRY, 8–43, 244130, KYBN (1854–1934) David Frances Barry was a noted photographer of Indians. Operated by Alaska Transportation.

240. THOMAS J. WALSH, 8–43, 244149, KYBP (1859–1933) Thomas James Walsh was a Montana senator and a member of President Roosevelt's "Brain Trust" of campaign supporters. Operated by Prudential. Operated by United States Lines.

241. PETER DE SMET, 8–43, 244148, KYBQ (1801–1873) Belgium-born Pieter-Jan De Smet (Pierre-Jean De Smet) was a Jesuit missionary to Native Americans in the Midwest and in 1845–46 journied to Fort Vancouver, Washinton. Namesake for De Smet, Idaho. Operated by Alaska Steamship.

242. JAMES M. CLEMENTS, 9–43, 244157, KYBR (1849–1921) James Merritt Clements was a prominent District Court judge at Helena, Montana, and United States

Attorney for Alaska. He died at Helena on Setember 1, 1921. Operated by American Mail Line.

243. EDWARD N. WESTCOTT, 9–43, 244176, KYJM (1846–1898) Edward Noyes Westcott was a New York banker who wrote the novel *David Harum*. Operated by AGWI Lines.

244. SAMTHAR, 9–43, 169761, BFNX, built for the British Ministry of War Transport. Operated by Royal Mail Lines.

245. JOSEPH W. FOLK, 9–43, 244199, KYJP (1869–1923) Joseph Wingate "Holy Joe" Folk was governor of Missouri. Operated by Grace Line.

246. JAMES L. BRECK, 9–43, 244198, KYJQ (1818–1876) James Lloyd Breck was a noted Episcopal missionary in Wisconsin and Minnesota. Operated by Isthmian.

247. SIDNEY EDGERTON, 9–43, 244204, KYJR (1818–1900) Ohio congressman and first governor of the Montana Territory. Operated by American Mail Line.

248. ROBERT S. BEAN, 9–44, 244236, KYJU (1854–1931) Robert Sharp Bean was chief custice of the Oregon Supreme Court. Operated by United States Lines.

249. NATHANIEL CROSBY, 9–43, 244225, KYJW (1812–1856) In 1846, Nathaniel Crosby, Jr., of Cape Cod, brought the supply ship *O. C. Raymond* to the Pacific Coast and in 1849 had his whole family come out West in their 270-ton brig *Grecian* captained by his older brother Clandrick. Nathaniel, his wife Mary and their children Nathaniel, Mary, and Martha stayed in Oregon and in 1851 Capt. Crosby loaded a ship with Oregon timber, put his family aboard, and set off for the Orient. The family lived in Hong Kong while Crosby made another long voyage. Capt. Croby died in Hong Kong 1856. Operated by Waterman.

250. JOHN I. NOLAN, 9–43, 244233, KYJZ (1874–1922) John Ignatious Nolan was a California congressman. Operated by Matson.

251. BEN T. OSBORNE, 9–43, 244251, KYKC (1880–1939) Benjamin Thomas Osborne was the executive secretary of the Oregon State Federation of Labor. Operated by AGWI Lines.

252. JAMES S. LAWSON, 9–43, 244285, KYKD (1828–1893) joined the U.S. Coast Survey in January 1848 and went to the Pacific Coast in May 1850 where he spent the next 40 years. Operated by Northland.

253. MIDWEST FARMER, 9–43, 244267, KYNR, honoring the producers in the nation's breadbasket. Operated by Pacific-Atlantic.

254. SAMZONA, 9–43, 169818, MYLD, built for the British Ministry of War Transport. Operated by Royal Mail Lines.

255. WILLIAM S. LADD, 9–43, 244274, KYOE (1826–1893) William Sargent Ladd was a Portland, Oregon, banking pioneer, mayor, and developer of the unique (Ladd's Addition). Operated by Weyerhaeuser. Capt. Nels F. Anderson's ship was destroyed in a kamikaze attack on December 10, 1944, off Leyte, Philippines. There were no reported fatalities.

256. FREDERICK BILLINGS, 9–43, 244292, KYPP (1823–1890) Frederick Hale Billings cofounded of the Northern Pacific Railroad and is the namesake for Billings, Montana. Operated by Alaska Transportation.

257. ANTHONY RAVALLI, 9–43, 244311, KYPJ (1812–1884) Antonio J. Ravalli, of Ferrara, Italy, was a Jesuit missionary, physician, sculptor, and collegue of Pierre-Jean De Smet who came to the Pacific Northwest in 1844 and is the namesake for Ravalli County, Montana. Operated by American Mail Line.

258. EDMUND F. DICKINS, 9–43, 244312, KYPL (1848–1923) Edmund Finley Dickins was a noted Pacific Northwest and Alaska Coast & Geodetic Survey ship captain in San Francisco. Operated by Pacific-Atlantic. Capt. John N. Ferree's ship hit a mine on May 5, 1945, at Manila, Philippines, and declared a total loss at New York. No reported casualties.

259. JOHN F. MYERS, 9–43, 244323, KYPO (1878–1941) John Francis Myers was the directtor of education at the Oregon Blind Trade School. In 1940 he lived with his wife Rosa E. 62, and their granddaughter Rosmarie Lawrence, 16, at 724 NE 81 st Ave. John died on May 31, 1941, in Portland. Operated by Alcoa.

260. DAVID B. HENDERSON, 9–43, 244320, KYPP (1840–1906) David Brenner Henderson was an Iowa congressman and Speaker of the House. Operated by Pope & Talbot.

261. JOHN M. BOZEMAN, 9–43, 244337, KYOP (1835–1867) John Merin Bozeman was a Georgia native who failed to find gold during the Pike's Peak rush and in 1864 partnered with John Jacobs to open a cutoff from the Oregon Trail to Montana. Platted Bozeman, Montana, and was murdered in 1867 under circumstances that pointed to Jacobs. Operated by United States Lines.

262. THOMAS HOWELL, 9–43, 244339, KYPQ (1842–1912) Thomas Jefferson Howell, of Missouri, was a pioneering botanist in Oregon. Operated by W. R. Chamberlin.

263. JAMES D. DOTY, 9–43, 244360, KTTG (1799–1865) James Duane Doty was a Wisconsin congressman and governor. Operated by Isbrandtsen.

264. PRINCE L. CAMPBELL, 9–43, 244372, KTTI (1861–1925) Prince Lucien Campbell was president of the University of Oregon. Operated by American West African Line.

265. SAMOURI, 9–43, 169687, MYMZ, built for the British Ministry of War Transport. Operated by Moss-Hutchison. Torpedoed on January 26, 1944, by *U-188* in the Gulf of Aden.

266. JOHN G. BRADY, 10–43, 244389, KTTM (1847–1918) John or James was an orphan found wandering the streets of New York by Theodore Roosevelt, Sr., who gave him some money and put him on an Orphan Train for Indiana. He was taken in by John Green, became a minister, and by the 1880s he was in Alaska as John Green Brady. He became governor of the District of Alaska but got involved in illicit activities and resigned. Operated by South Atlantic.

267. JEAN NICOLET, 10–43, KTTQ, 244388 (c. 1598–1642) Jean Nicollet de Belleborne was a French explorer and trader who lived with Indians and was the first European to cross Lake Michigan and explore present-day Wisconsin. Operated by Oliver J. Olson. Capt. David Martin Nilsson, 46, had 26 years at sea and was master of the brand-new Oliver Olson Liberty ship *Samuel Huntington* when they left San Francisco in May 1942 and arrived at New York from Trinidad on December 19. That ship was sunk on January 1, 1944. The *Nicolet* was torpedoed on July 2, 1944, by *I-8* in the Indian Ocean. Thirty merchant crew, 19 Armed Guard sailors, one Army medic, and 26 passengers were murdered by the submarine crew. Capt. Nilsson was taken aboard the sub and subsequently died.

268. W. B. AYER, 10–43, 244405, KTTP (1860–1935) Winslow Bartlett Ayer, of Maine, was president of the Eastern & Western Lumber Co. at Portland, Oregon, and served as the federal Food Administrator for Oregon. Operated by Matson.

269. CHARLES NORDHOFF, 10–43, 244403, KTTU (1830–1901) journalist, author who wrote well of California and died in San Francisco. Operated by Alcoa.

270. WILLIAM L. SUBLETTE, 10–43, 244407, KTZD (1798–1845) William Lewis Sublette brought the first wagon train over the Rocky Mountains, creating Sublette's Cut-Off on the Oregon Trail. Operated by Alaska Steamship.

271. WILLIAM H. ASHLEY, 10–43, 244406, KTZA (1778–1838) William Henry Ashley was a pioneer fur trader and Missouri congressman who partnered with Andrew Henry as the Rocky Mountain Fur Co. and organized an annual rendezvous for traders to swap goods. Operated by Northland.

272. W. W. MCCRACKIN, 10–43, 244429, KUBC (1842–1913) William Wallace

McCrackin was a Pennsylvania native who became a prominent Montana banker. Operated by Isthmian.

273. FRANCIS N. BLANCHET, 10–43, 244436, KUBE (1795–1883) French-Canadian priest François Norbert Blanchet established the Catholic Church in the Oregon Country. Operated by Seas Shipping.

274. CHARLES F. AMIDON, 10–43, 244461, KUBH (1856–1937) Charles Fremont Amidon was the District Court judge for North Dakota. Operated by Grace Line.

275. JOSEPH M. CAREY, 10–43, 244467, KUBI (1845–1924) Joseph Maull Carey was a Wyoming senator and governor. Operated by Waterman.

276. STEPHEN G. PORTER, 10–43, 244487, KUDH (1869–1930) Stephen Geyer Porter was a Pennsylvania congressman. Operated by Eastern Steamship.

277. WATSON C. SQUIRE, 10–43, 244488, KUDI (1838–1926) Watson Carvosso Squire was governor of the Washington Territory governor and a Washington senator. Operated by Weyerhaeuser.

278. ABBOT L. MILLS, 10–43, 244500, KUMJ (1858–1927) Abbot Low Mills, of Brooklyn, was prominent Portland, Oregon, banker, insurance man, and legislator. Operated by Coastwise (Pacific Far East) Line. Capt. David Bowman's ship hit a mine on November 10, 1945, off Yugoslavia. There were no casualties and the ship was declared a total loss.

279. ALBERT A. MICHELSON, 10–43, 244501, KUMO (1852–1931) Albert Abraham Michelson was a physicist who was awarded 1907 Nobel Prize in physics for measuring the speed of light. Operated by R. A. Nicol.

280. EDMUND G. ROSS, 10–43, 244513, KUMR (1826–1907) Edmund Gibson Ross was a Kansas senator and governor of the New Mexico Territory. Operated by Olympic.

281. PETER WHITE, 10–43, 244524, KUMZ (1830–1908) Peter Quintard White was an upper Michigan pioneer and banker on whose land Marquette, Michigan, was built. Operated by Seas Shipping.

282. J. WARREN KEIFER, 11–43, 244557, KUNB (1836–1932) Joseph Warren Keifer was an Ohio congressman. Operated by American West African.

283. WILLIAM H. DALL, 11–43, 244563, KUNI (1845–1927) William Healey Dall was a naturalist who studied the Alaska mollusk and the Alaska interior. Operated by American Mail Line.

284. JAMES H. LANE, 11–43, 244576, KUNL (1814–1866) James Henry Lane was an Indiana representative and Kansas senator. Operated by Pacific-Atlantic.

285. WILLIAM D. HOARD, 11–43, 244601, KUNM (1836–1918) William Dempster Hoard was the father of the Wisconsin dairy industry and the state's governor. Operated by Isthmian.

286. FRANCIS W. PARKER, 11–43, 244590, KUNU (1837–1902) Francis Wayland Parker was a pioneering educator in Ohio, Boston, and Chicago. Operated by Alaska Packers.

287. HORACE V. WHITE, 11–43, 244593, KUSE (1834–1916) managing editor of the *Chicago Tribune* and collegue of Henry Villard. Director of the Oregon & Transcontinental Co., the Oregon Railway & Navigation Co., and the Northern Pacific Railroad. Operated by United States Lines.

288. ELISHA P. FERRY, 11–43, 244607, KUSM (1825–1895) Elisha Peyre Ferry was the first governor of the state of Washington and namesake for Ferry County. Operated by Waterman.

289. LUCIUS FAIRCHILD, 11–43, 244609, KUSU (1831–1896) Wisconsin governor and minister to Spain. Operated by Wilmore.

290. JANE G. SWISSHELM, 11–43, 244638, KUUC (1815–1884) Jane Grey Cannon

was a teacher who married James Swisshelm in 1836 and moved Kentucky. In 1839 she moved to Philadelphia to care for her mother and two years later went back to Kentucky where she became a journalist, abolitionist, womens activist and from there she went to St. Cloud, Minnesota, in 1857. Operated by Olympic.

291. HENRY T. RAINEY, 11–43, 244661, KUUB (1860–1934) Henry Thomas Rainey was an Illinois congressman of whom President Hoover stated: "Rainey held honorary degrees from all the schools of demagoguery. He later proved to be an ardent collectivist of a muddled variety. His opposition however, had a certain element of consistency as he was not only for overthrowing the Republican party but our economic and social system in general. He stopped at no misrepresentation and no smear was too filthy for him to use." Operated by Pope & Talbot.

292. THOMAS CRAWFORD, 11–43, 244663, KUXR (1XXX-1942) able-bodied seaman lost on the *Maiden Creek*, foundered on December 31, 1942, off Block Island in heavy seas covered with ice. Crawford was awarded the Merchant Marine Distinguished Service medal posthumously for remaining aboard to launch the lifeboats so others could survive. Operated by Pacific-Atlantic.

293. GEORGE P. MCKAY, 11–43, 244694, KUXF (1838–1918) ship captain and developer of shipping on the Great Lakes who was member of several organizations and treasurer of the Lakes Carriers' Association. Operated by Alaska Steamship.

294. RICHARD J. OGLESBY, 11–43, 244697, KUXG (1824–1899) Richard James Oglesby was an Illinois governor and senator. Operated by Alaska Transportation.

295. JOHN BALL, 11–43, 244696, KUXK (1794–1884) Oregon pioneer from New Hampshire as a member of the Wyeth expedition in 1832. Taught school at Fort Vancouver and became the first farmer in Oregon to grow wheat. Moved to Grand Rapids, Michigan in 1837. Operated by Union Sulphur.

296. SEGUNDO RUIZ BELVIS, 12–43, 244716, KUXN (1829–1867) a leader of the Puerto Rican independence movement. Operated by Shepard.

297. FRANK B. LINDERMAN, 12–43, 244710, KUXP (1869–1938) Frank Bird Linderman was a Montana author, ethnographer, and Indian advocate. Operated by Weyerhaeuser.

298. JOHN B. KENDRICK, 12–43, 244733, KVBZ (1857–1933) John Benjamin Kendrick was a Wyoming governor and senator. Operated by American Mail Line.

299. SIMEON G. REED, 12–43, 244742, KVGG (1830–1895) Simeon Gannett Reed was the cofounder of the Oregon Steam Navigation Co., namesake for Reedville, Oregon, and benefactor of Reed College. Operated by Coastwise (Pacific Far East) Line.

300. JOHN STRAUB, 12–43, 244753, KVCR (1879–1934) longtime University of Oregon professor and men's dean. Operated by Alaska Steamship. Capt. Axel W. Westerholm's ship was torpedoed on April 19, 1944, by *I-180* off Sanak Island, Alaska. Survivors reported the ship split apart at the forward end of the engine room and the boilers exploded. Capt. Westerholm, 66, of Seattle, and four Navy gunners were lost.

301. LEWIS L. DYCHE, 12–43, 244755, KVCT (1752–1915) Lewis Lindsay Dyche was a noted University of Kansas zoologist. Operated by Interocean. John W. Platt was chief officer on the USAT *Sea Barb* out of Fort Mason, San Francisco. The *Dyche* left Portland, Oregon, in December 1943 and arrived at San Francisco on August 7, 1944, from Samoa. Capt Platt relieved the previous master and left San Francisco on September 6 with a cargo of munitions and was hit by a kamikaze on January 4, 1945, in Mangarin Bay, Mindoro, Philippines, and disintegrated. All 41 merchant crew and 30 Armed Guard sailors were lost.

302. WILBUR O. ATWATER, 12–43, 244774, KVHW (1844–1907) Wilbur Olin

Atwater was a noted nutritionist, innovator of agricultural testing stations, and the first professor of chemistry at Wesleyan. Operated by Northland.

303. ISAAC MCCOY, 12–43, 244779, KVIA (1784–1846) Baptist missionary to Midwest Indians. Operated by Weyerhaeuser.

304. JOHN W. DAVIS, 12–43, 244780, KVID (1799–1859) John Wesley Davis was an Indiana congressman and governor of the Oregon Territory. Operated by Alcoa.

305. ENOS A. MILLS, 12–43, 244819, KVIG (1870–1922) Enos Abijah Mills was an outdoorsman and Rocky Mountain National Park promoter. Operated by Alaska Steamship.

306. GRACE R. HEBARD, 12–43, 244820, KVIH (1861–1936) Grace Raymond Hebard was a civil engineer, the first female trustee of the Uninversity of Wyoming, the first female attorney in Wyoming, and a professor, author, historian, and suffragette. Operated by Pope & Talbot.

307. JAMES B. MILLER, 12–43, 244828, KVIJ (1883–1915) Capt. James Blaine Miller was a member of the U.S. Coast & Geodetic Survey who worked in Alaskan waters and was lost on the RMS *Lusitania*. Operated by Alaska Packers.

308. RALPH BARNES, 12–43, 244830, KVIK (1899–1940) Oregon native Ralph Waldo Barnes was a *New York Herald Tribune* war correspondent who died when the Royal Air Force bomber he was in crashed over Albania on November 17, 1940. He was the first war correspondent lost in World War II. Operated by American Mail Line.

309. GABRIEL FRANCHERE, 12–43, 244876, KVKT (1786–1863) French-Canadian member of the Astor Expedition in 1811, Oregon fur trader, and author. Operated by Isthmian.

310. WILLIAM A. HENRY, 12–43, 244896, KVLT (1850–1932) William Arnon Henry was dean of the Wisconsin College of Agriculture and the father of scientific agriculture. Operated by Matson.

311. VALERY CHKALOV, 12–43 (1904–1938) noted Russian aviator. Operated under the Russian flag.

312. NARCISSA WHITMAN, 1–44, 244923, KVMQ (1808–1847) Narcissa and Marcus Whitman were missionaries who brought the first large wagon train over the Oregon Trail in 1843. They established a mission in Cayuse country near Walla Walla, Washington, and were subsequently murdered by Indians. Operated by Oliver J. Olson.

313. ISAAC I. STEVENS, 1–44, 244937, KVNY (1818–1862) Isaac Ingalls Stevens was the controversial first governor of the Washington Territory who was lost at the Battle of Chantilly on September 1, 1862, in Virginia. Operated by Interocean.

314. WILLIAM I. CHAMBERLAIN, 1–44, 244949, KVRY (1850–1902) William Isaac Chamberlain was the Ohio secretary of agriculture, member of the Ohio Board of Agriculture, and president of Iowa State University. Operated by American West African.

315. MARY E. KINNEY, 1–44, 244957, KVRZ (1859–1938) Mary Edna Kinney was the first female Oregon state senator. Operated by Alaska Steamship. Capt. James Blaisdell was awarded the Merchant Marine Distinguished Service medal for navigating his ship during a furious air attack at Leyte while the Armed Guard shot down five planes.

316. HARRINGTON EMERSON, 1–44, 244972, KVSA (1853–1931) cable laying engineer and pioneer efficiency expert. Operated by Coastwise (Pacific Far East) Line.

317. ELWOOD MEAD, 1–44, 244982, KVSB (1858–1936) director of the Bureau of Reclamation. Operated by Interocean.

318. SAMUEL V. STEWART, 1–44, 245011, KVSE (1872–1939) Samuel Vernon Stewart was governor of Montana. Operated by American South African.

319. JOHN W. TROY, 1–44, 245027, KVVX (1868–1942) John Weir Troy was governor of the Alaska Territory. Operated by Alaska Steamship.

320. ABIGAIL S. DUNIWAY, 1–44, 245023, KVVY (1834–1915) Abigail Jane Scott's father John, an Illinois farmer, organized a wagon train in March 1852 to go to Oregon. John's wife Anne didn't want to go because of health reasons but they set out with nine children. Anne died in June near Fort Laramie, son Willie, 3, died in August, and the party arrived in the Willamette Valley in October. Abigail became a teacher and in 1853 married Illinois farmer Benjamin C. Duniway. After he became disabled she opened a boarding school, owned a dry goods store, and moved to Portland where started a suffragist newspaper. Operated by Weyerhaeuser.

321. EDWARD LANDER, 2–44, 245066, KVBY (1816–1907) first chief justice of the Territory of Washington supreme court. Operated by Alaska Packers.

322. PETER MORAN, 2–44, 245068, KVYG (1841–1914) joined brother John, a marine engineer in Seattle, in 1882 to found Moran Bros. Ship & Engine Building Co. to build sternwheelers for the Yukon Gold Rush. Operated by American Mail.

Permanente Metals Corp., Shipbuilding Division
Richmond, California

A privately-owned Kaiser operation on which the Maritime Commission spent $791,880 for land and $35,787,472 on facilities.

Yard No. 1, at 4th and Cutting Blvd., was the former Todd-California Shipbuilding Corp. managed by Kaiser's Richmond Shipbuilding Corp., a subsidiary of Permanente Metals. Yard 1 built 138 Liberty ships. The first keel was laid on May 12, 1942, and the average building time for the ships was 48.3 days.

Yard No. 2, at the foot of S. 14th, also managed by the Richmond Shipbuilding, built 351 Liberty ships. The first keel was laid on September 17, 1941, and the average building time for the ships was 41.1 days.

The severe labor shortage on the West Coast obliged Kaiser to recruit workers from Midwest and Southeastern states. He put recruiting ads in newspapers and scheduled "Kaiser Special" trains to bring workers out West. Many jumped at the chance to flee poverty, bad marriages, or difficult family situations and start over in sunny California. The influx of "Okies" from the Dust Bowl during the Great Depression, like the Joads in *The Grapes of Wrath*, created a certain amount of social upheaval but nothing like the migration of workers during the war. Native Californians, especially, were not happy with the arrival of so many new "Okies"—a term used to describe anyone new to the area—and some members of groups like the Native Sons of the Golden West made their feelings crystal clear. The Native Sons even sued in federal court to have the names of American-born citizens of Japanese ancestry removed from voter rolls. They were unsuccessful but the numerous reports coming from the Pacific about Japanese-Americans serving in Japanese military untis further inflamed passions.

Signs like "Okie Drinking Fountain" were put up over urinals in shipyards and foods like artichokes, never seen by the newcomers, were used as sources for amusement. But it wasn't all one-sided as a little ditty composed at one yard shows:

> The miners came in '49
> The whores in '51
> And when they bunked together
> They begat the Native Son

While insulting and amusing there might be a grain of truth in that as San Francisco was a pretty wild, lawless place during that time.

A Permanente Metals study determined the average age of a Richmond worker was 42. He made $61 a week, travelled 8.9 miles to work, and a personnel study revealed the typical breakdown of wages were for food, $18.30; rent $8.50; clothes $5.50; transportation $2.45; miscellaneous $13.45; war bonds $6.10; and taxes $6.70.

The launching of the *Benjamin Warner* at Yard 2 on July 1, 1944, was celebrated as the last Pacific Coast Liberty ship. The event was celebrated with speeches by Henry Kaiser and Adm. Vickery of the Maritime Commission. They cited the figure of 519 total ships produced, which included the 30 built for the British at Yard 1, site of the former Todd-California Shipbuilding Corp.

YARD NO. 1

1. EDWARD ROWLAND SILL, 8–42, 242063, KGBR (1841–1887) newspaperman, teacher, poet, and University of California English literature professor. Operated by Luckenbach.

2. JOAQUIN MILLER, 8–42, 242121, KGIP (1837–1913) pen name of Cincinnatus Hiner Miller, the colorful and factually elusive poet who travelled the West. Operated by Isthmian.

3. LEW WALLACE, 9–42, 242135, KGEV (1827–1905) Lewis Wallace was a lawyer, Union general, governor of the New Mexico Territory, and author. Operated by Isthmian and converted to an Army troopship.

4. O. HENRY, 9–42, 242161, KGIK (1862–1910) pen name of writer William Sydney Porter. Operated by Moore-McCormack.

5. F. MARION CRAWFORD, 9–42, 242190, KHGR (1854–1909) Francis Marion Crawford was a novelist and historian. Operated by Pope & Talbot.

6. JOSEPH RODMAN DRAKE, 9–42, 242221, KHHM (1795–1820) New York City poet. Operated by Sudden & Christenson.

7. WILLIAM DEAN HOWELLS, 9–42, 242272, KHHN (1837–1920) first president of the American Academy of Arts and Letters in 1904. Operated by Sudden & Christenson.

8. JOHN HOWARD PAYNE, 9–42, 242273, KHLH (1791–1852) actor and poet. Operated by American President Lines.

9. ANDREW FURUSETH, 10–42, 242278, KHJI (1845–1938) Norwegian-born seaman's union organizer and first secretary of the Pacific Coast Seaman's Union. Operated by Matson.

10. MOSES ROGERS, 10–42, 242330, KHNC (1779–1821) master of the pioneering steamboats *Clermont*, *Phoenix*, and *Savannah*, the first steamer to cross the Atlantic, although mostly under sail. The departure from Savannah, Georgia, on May 22, 1819, was declared National Maritime Day. Operated by Luckenbach.

11. WILLIAM K. VANDERBILT, 10–42, 242353, KHIQ (1849–1920) William Kissam Vanderbilt was Cornelius "The Commodore" Vanderbilt's grandson. Operated by Isthmian. Capt. William F. Goldsmith's ship was torpedoed on May 16, 1943, by *I-19* southwest of Suva, Fiji Islands, with the loss of first assistant engineer Raymond Farr.

12. JAMES J. HILL, 10–42, 242375, KHNH (1838–1916) James Jerome Hill was the Canadian-born founder of the Great Northern Railway. Operated by Sudden & Christenson.

13. JOHN RUTLEDGE, 10–42, 242403, KHPO (1739–1800) Constitutional Con-

vention delegate, governor of South Carolina, and Supreme Court justice. Operated by Luckenbach.

14. WILLIAM CUSHING, 10–42, 242410, KHPP (1732–1810) Supreme Court justice. Operated by American Mail Line.

15. JOHN BLAIR, 10–42, 242429, KHPS (1732–1800) Constitutional Convention delegate and Supreme Court justice. Operated by Calmar.

16. ROBERT H. HARRISON, 11–42, 242454, KHPT (1745–1790) Robert Hanson Harrison was Gen. Washington's aide-de-camp and a judge in Maryland. Operated by Alaska Steamship.

17. JOHN MCLEAN, 11–42, 242467, KHPV (1785–1861) Ohio congressman, Postmaster General, Supreme Court justice. Operated by Prudential.

18. NOAH H. SWAYNE, 11–42, 242504, KHTG (1804–1884) Noah Haynes Swayne was the first Republican appointed to the Supreme Court. Operated by the Navy as the *Crater*-class cargo ship *Arided* (AK-73), NXZW, commissioned on November 13, 1942.

19. SAMUEL F. MILLER, 11–42, 242519, KHTH (1816–1890) Samuel Freeman Miller was a Supreme Court justice. Operated by Waterman.

20. DAVID DAVIS, 11–42, 242536, KHTI (1815–1886) Illinois senator and Supreme Court justice. Operated by the Navy as the *Crater*-class cargo ship *Carina* (AK-74), NYJY, commissioned on December 1, 1942.

21. MORRISON R. WAITE, 11–42, 242555, KHTQ (1816–1888) Morrison Remick "Mott" Waite was a chief justice of the Supreme Court. Operated by Coastwise (Pacific Far East) Line. Capt. Frank F. Boyd's ship was hit by a kamikaze on November 17, 1944, at Dulag, Leyte, Philippines, with the loss of 21 soldiers. The ship was repaired.

22. MELVILLE W. FULLER, 11–42, 242560, KHFR (1833–1910) Melville Weston Fuller was an Illinois lawyer and chief justice of the Supreme Court. Operated by the Navy as the *Crater*-class cargo ship *Cassiopeia* (AK-75), NYLN, commissioned on December 8, 1942.

23. STANLEY MATTHEWS, 11–42, 242580, KHTT (1824–1889) Ohio senator and Supreme Court justice. Operated by W. R. Chamberlin.

24. DAVID J. BREWER, 12–42, 242608, KHTX (1837–1910) David Josiah Brewer was a Supreme Court justice. Operated by United States Lines.

25. PIERRE LACLEDE, 12–42, 242611, KISN (1724–1778) Pierre Laclède Liguest was a French fur trader who founded St. Louis, Missouri, in 1764 with Auguste Chouteau. Operated by Grace Line.

26. FREDERIC REMINGTON, 12–42, 242637, KIST (1861–1909) Frederic Sackrider Remington was a noted painter and sculptor. Operated by Grace Line.

27. WALTER COLTON, 12–42, 242645, KITW (1797–1851) U.S. Navy chaplain and cofounder of *The Californian*, the first newspaper in California. Operated by Seas Shipping.

28. J. STERLING MORTON, 12–42, 242702, KKDP (1832–1902) Julius Sterling Morton was a newsman, acting governor of Nebraska, and Secretary of Agriculture. Operated by Isthmian.

29. GEORGE H. DERN, 12–42, 242699, KKDO (1872–1936) George Henry Dern was a miner, governor of Utah, and Secretary of War. Operated by Seas Shipping.

30. KEY PITTMAN, 12–42, 242718, KKDN (1782–1940) Key Denson Pittman was a Nevada senator. Operated by Coastwise (Pacific Far East) Line for one voyage under Capt. Alff S. Hansen and arrived at San Francisco from Auckland, New Zealand, on October 2, 1943, then taken by the Navy and operated as the *Crater*-class cargo ship *Leonis* (AK-128), NHDZ, commissioned on October 25, 1943.

31. CHIEF OURAY, 1–43, 242745, KKDM (1833–1880) "Arrow" was chief of the

Uncompahgre Ute Indians in Colorado. Operated by the Navy as the *Crater*-class cargo ship *Deimos* (AK-78), NYOV, commissioned on January 23, 1943.

32. GEORGE S. BOUTWELL, 1–43, 242766, KKGX (1818–1905) George Sewall Boutwell was a Massachusetts governor and congressman and Secretary of the Treasury. Operated by Alaska Packers.

33. BENJAMIN H. BRISTOW, 1–43, 242773, KKHB (1832–1896) Benjamin Helm Bristow was Secretary of the Treasury. Operated by American West African. Capt. Francis C. Pollard's ship hit a mine on April 22, 1945, off Belgium. There were no reported casualties.

34. WILLIAM WINDOM, 1–43, 242804, KIGG (1827–1891) Minnesota congressman and Secretary of the Treasury. Operated by Alaska Packers.

35. CHARLES J. FOLGER, 1–43, 242807, KIFO (1818–1884) Charles James Folger was Secretary of the Treasury. Operated by United States Lines.

36. WILLIAM H. ASPINWALL, 2–43, 242827, KKJX (1807–1875) William Henry Aspinwall founded the Pacific Mail Steamship Co. and supervised the railroad project across the Isthmus of Panama. Operated by Isbrandtsen.

37. KRASNOGVARDEYSK, 1–43, former city of Trotsk renamed in 1929 to "Red Guard City" until 1944 when it reverted to the Imperial Palace city of Gatchina. Operated under the Russian flag.

38. JOHN G. CARLISLE, 1–43, 242860, KKOH (1835–1910) John Griffin Carlisle was a Kentucky congressman and governor. Operated by De La Rama.

39. LYMAN J. GAGE, 2–43, 242893, KKOI (1836–1927) Lyman Judson Gage was a Secretary of the Treasury. Operated by Waterman under Capt. John F. Fuellner. Arrived at San Francisco on November 13, 1943, from Brisbane, Australia, then taken by the Navy and operated as the *Crater*-class cargo ship *Cheleb* (AK-138), NHER, commissioned on January 1, 1944. William Alton Williams, of Boerne, Texas, was a fireman third class in the commissioning crew. Shortly after commissioning they were sent to a fumigating dock without shore steam or electricity. The outside temperature was 40 degrees and Williams was the only engineer aboard when the captain, Lt. Cdr. Matthias S. Clark, USNR, ordered him to get steam up. He stated: "The hand powered oil pump took more out of this 140 lb. 17 year old than he thought he had in him. I did something I know I would have been court-martialed for, if it had been known: I dumped a whole bucket of distillate on the boiler floorplates and set it afire, as the feed oil looked like blobs of tar dribbling onto the floorplates and would not light, but by the time the other engineers got aboard, I had 170 lbs. of steam up on one boiler." When the ship got into heavy weather in the Pacific several feet of vertical welds in the skin came apart requiring fulltime pumping. They also had problems with leaking deck plates.

40. GRENVILLE M. DODGE, 2–43, 242931, KKOJ (1831–1916) Grenville Mellon Dodge was president of the Union Pacific Railroad. Operated by Grace Line.

41. JULIEN DUBUQUE, 2–43, 242963, KKOL (1762–1810) founder of Dubuque, Iowa. Operated by Alaska Packers.

42. ADONIRAM JUDSON, 3–43, 243001, KKON (1788–1850) famous Burma missionary. Operated by W. R. Chamberlin. Capt. Charles A. Jarvis, 37, left San Francisco in June 1944 and was the first freighter to dock at Tacloban, Leyte, during the Philippines invasion in October. From the 26th to 29th they were under continuous air attack. They arrived back in San Francisco from Hollandia, New Guinea, on April 9, 1945. Capt. Jarvis was awarded the Merchant Marine Distinguished Service medal.

43. JOHN G. NICOLAY, 3–43, 243031, KKOQ (1832–1901) John George Nicolay was a German-born author and President Lincoln's secretary. Operated by the Navy as the *Crater*-class cargo ship *Albireo* (AK-90), NKGD, commissioned on March 29, 1943.

44. EDWARD BATES, 3–43, 243050, KKOU (1793–1869) Missouri congressman and Attorney General. Operated by Hammond. Capt. Howard D. McLeod left San Francisco in March 1943 and arrived at New York on May 24 from Guantanamo, Cuba, and departed around June 24 on Voyage No. 2. Capt. Leo H. Luksich's ship was sunk on February 1, 1944, by a German aerial torpedo off Algeria. Oiler George C. Engle was lost.

45. JOSIAH B. GRINNELL, 3–43, 243070, KKOW (1821–1891) Josiah Bushnell Grinnell was an Iowa congressman, minister, railroad man, founder of Grinnell, Iowa, and benefactor of Grinnell College. On June 14, 1866, Grinnell was repeatedly hit on the head and face with a cane by Kentucky representative Lovell H. Rousseau, who was censured. Operated by A. H. Bull.

46. HENRY H. RICHARDSON, 3–43, 243114, KIAV (1838–1886) Henry Hobson Richardson developed the Richardsonian Romanesque architectural style in the Midwest and East. Operated by Moore-McCormack.

47. NATHANIEL CURRIER, 3–43, 243111, KIBC (1813–1888) of Currier & Ives lithographers. Operated by R. A. Nicol.

48. JAMES IVES, 3–43, 243161, KIBG (1824–1895) James Merritt Ives, of Courier & Ives lithographers. Operated by Isthmian.

49. THOMAS CORWIN, 4–43, 243179, KKWI (1794–1865) Ohio senator and minister to Mexico. Operated by the War Department.

50. JAMES GUTHRIE, 4–43, 243188, KKWK (1792–1869) Kentucky congressman, founder of the University of Louisville, and Secretary of the Treasury. Operated by AGWI Lines. Capt. Charles Jensen left San Francisco in April 1943, went to Australia and India and arrived at New York on October 4 from the Canal Zone. The ship sailed on October 31 but had an accident and returned to Pier 36 the same day. Capt. Grady L. Robertosn left San Francisco in September 1943 as master of the *Antoine Saugrain* and arrived back there on November 25. He was captain of the *Guthrie* when the ship hit a mine on April 17, 1944, off the Isle of Capri. There were no reported casualties.

51. HOWELL COBB, 4–43, 243205, KKWN (1815–1868) Thomas Howell Cobb was a Georgia congressman, governor, and Speaker of the House. Operated by the War Department.

52. HUGH MCCULLOCH, 4–43, 243271, KKWO (1808–1895) Secretary of the Treasury. Operated by Pope & Talbot.

53. MATTHEW LYON, 4–43, 243284, KKWR (1750–1822) Vermont and Kentucky congressman. Operated by Dichmann, Wright & Pugh. Capt. Jean D. Bandel's ship was torpedoed by *I-11* on August 11, 1943, in the South Pacific. There were no reported casualties. The ship was taken by the Navy and became USS *Zebra* (IX-107).

54. GEORGE D. PRENTICE, 4–43, 243270, KKWX (1802–1870) George Dennison Prentice was editor of the *Louisville Journal*. Operated by Coastwise (Pacific Far East) Line.

55. WILLIAM A. JONES, 5–43, 243322, KKWY (1817–1900) William Alfred Jones was an author and librarian at Columbia College. Operated by Norton Lilly.

56. HOMER LEA, 4–43, 243321, KKWZ (1876–1912) author and military imposter who inserted himself into Chinese revolutionary affairs. Operated by Alaska Packers.

57. ANSON BURLINGAME, 5–43, 243367, KKXA (1820–1870) Massachusetts congressman and ambassador to China. Operated by Seas Shipping.

58. LOUIS HENNEPIN, 5–43, 243395, KKXD (1626–c. 1705) Antoine Hennepin was a priest who accompanied La Salle in exploring North America. Namesake for Hennepin County, Minnesota, and other sites in Michigan and Illinois. Operated by United States Lines.

59. JOSIAH SNELLING, 5–43, 243422, KKXE (1782–1828) War of 1812 Army commander who oversaw construction of and commanded Fort Saint Anthony on a bluff over-

looking the confluence of the Mississippi and Minnesota Rivers, later renamed Fort Snelling. Operated by Sudden & Christenson. On May 28, 1945, the ship was hit by a kamikaze off Okinawa. The plane and an unexploded 500-pound bomb attached to it became embedded in a hold full of lumber and cement. The ship reached San Francisco in July and anchored way out in the Bay where a volunteer group of Seabees and a Navy bomb disposal unit extricated the plane and bomb.

60. GEORGE WASHINGTON CARVER, 5–43, 243477, KKXG (1864–1943) African-American botanist who died on January 5, 1943, at Tuskegee, Alabama. Operated by the American South African Line and converted by the Army to the hospital ship *Dogwood*.

61. JAMES A. BAYARD, 5–43, 243492, KOGB (1767–1815) James Asheton Bayard was a Delaware congressman. Operated by United States Lines.

62. ODESSA, 5–43, major port city in the Ukraine under siege and Nazi occupation until April 1944. Operated under the Russian flag.

63. MICHAEL PUPIN, 5–43, 242597, KOXJ (1858–1935) Mihajlo Idvorski Pupin was a Serbian physicist who increased the range of long-distance telephone calling. Operated by Isthmian.

64. CYRUS HAMLIN, 6–43, 243618, KOZA (1811–1900) noted Maine and Vermont educator. Operated by the Navy as the *Crater*-class cargo ship *Lyra* (AK-101), NBMK, commissioned on July 22, 1943.

65. HENRY BERGH, 6–43, 243639, KOXO (1811–1888) founded the Society for the Prevention of Cruelty to Animals. Operated by Norton Lilly. Capt. Joseph C. Chambers, 42, arrived at Honolulu on July 29 from Pacific ports. Operated by the Army Transport Service and converted to a troopship. Stranded on May 31, 1944, on the Farallon Islands 30 miles off San Francisco with over 1,000 passengers aboard.

66. JOHN CARROLL, 6–43, 243667, KOXS (1735–1815) first Roman Catholic bishop and archbishop in the United States, at Baltimore, and founder of Georgetown University. Operated by American-Hawaiian.

67. JONATHAN P. DOLLIVER, 6–43, 243695, KOXQ (1858–1910) Jonathan Prentiss Dolliver was an Iowa congressman. Operated by United States Lines.

68. JAMES HARLAN, 6–43, 243708, KOVL (1820–1899) Iowa senator and Secretary of the Interior. Operated by Seas Shipping.

69. ROBERT LUCAS, 6–43, 243721, KOVK (1781–1853) governor of Ohio and Iowa. Operated by Moore-McCormack.

70. EDWIN T. MEREDITH, 6–43, 243746, KOVI (1876–1928) Edwin Thomas Meredith was an Iowa agricultural journalist and Secretary of Agriculture who founded *Better Homes & Gardens* magazine. Operated by Smith & Johnson. On November 12, 1943, American-Hawaiian's C-1 troopship *Cape San Juan* under Capt. Walter M. Strong had 1,429 souls aboard when they were torpedoed by *I-21* off Fiji. Capt. Murdock D. McRae's Liberty ship assisted destroyer *McCalla* (DD-488) in rescuing survivors. All but 70 were saved and brought to New Caledonia. Pan-American Airways Capt. William W. Moss, flying a Martin PBM Mariner, saved 48. The transport sank the next day.

71. MARIA SANFORD, 7–43, 243792, KXRU (1836–1920) Maria Louise Sanford was a school superintendent in Pennsylvania and, as professor of history st Swarthmore, was one of the first female professors in the United States. She also taught English, rhetoric, and elocution at the University of Minnesota for 29 years. She apparently never married and in 1920, at 83, lived with her 63-year-old neice Mary Kirtland at 1050 13th Ave. SE in Minneapolis. She was still teaching at the university and Maria was a self-employed dressmaker. Operated by American President Lines.

72. USS HYPERION (AK-107), 7–43, NTCO, *Crater*-class cargo ship commissioned on August 25, 1943.

73. LEONIDAS MERRITT, 7–43, 243857, KXRZ (1844–1926) prospector who developed iron ore production in the Mesabi Range in Minnesota as head of the Merritt brothers known as the "Seven Iron Men." Operated by United States Lines. Capt. Douglas A. Wiltshire's ship was hit by a kamikaze on November 12, 1944, at Leyte, Philippines, with the loss of able seaman, Earve P. Higgins, 26, and one Armed Guard sailor. The ship was repaired.

74. FLOYD B. OLSON, 7–43, 243832, KSXB (1891–1936) Floyd Bjørnstjerne Olson was governor of Minnesota. Operated by Oliver J. Olson.

75. FRANCIS G. NEWLANDS, 7–43, 243888, KXSD (1846–1917) Francis Griffith Newlands was a Nevada congressman, cofounder of Chevy Chase, Maryland, and was instrumental in acquiring the Territory of Hawaii. Operated by Waterman.

76. AMBROSE BIERCE, 7–43, 243908, KXSF (1842–1914) Ambrose Gwinnett Bierce was a San Francisco newspaper columnist and author. Operated by American Mail Line.

77. JAMES FERGUS, 7–43, 243938, KXSG (1813–1902) Montana pioneer, rancher, merchant, and politician. Operated by Moore-McCormack.

78. WILLIAM N. BYERS, 7–43, 243972, KXSI (1831–1903) William Newton Byers founded Denver, Colorado, edited the Rocky Mountain News, and is the namesake for byerite, a type of bituminous coal. Operated by Isthmian.

79. JOSHUA HENDY, 7–43, 243990, KXSJ (1822–1891) Sunnyvale, California, ship engine builder. Operated by Coastwise and converted to an animal transport ship.

80. MARCUS DALY, 8–43, 244025, KXSM (1841–1900) Butte, Montana, "Copper King" who founded the Anaconda Mining Co. Operated by Sudden & Christenson. Capt. Alvin W. Opheim's ship was at Tacloban, Leyte, Philippines, in October 1944, during the invasion of the Philippines. The ship performed shore bombardment to defend the Leyte docks and defended itself against "vigorous attacks." Able seaman Alvin R. Crawford and ordinary seaman Richard G. Matthiesen volunteered to help the Armed Guard work the forward gun. On Wednesday, November 29, the ship got underway in convoy from Humboldt Bay, New Guinea, for Leyte. At 8:40 a.m. on Tuesday, December 5, the convoy came under air attack and Crawford and Matthiesen again manned the forward gun. The *Antoine Saugrain* was torpedoed and one damaged bomber crashed into the bow of the *Daly*. Crawford was mortally wounded and Matthiesen was severely burned and escaped the gun platform but went back through flames to rescue two Armed Guard sailors. The attacks continued throughout the day while Capt. Opheim maneuvered his ship. Matthiesen died the next morning. The ship received the Merchant Marine Gallant Ship award and Capt. Opheim, Crawford, and Matthiesen were awarded the Merchant Marine Distinguished Service medal.

81. JOHN CONSTANTINE, 8–43, 244043, KXSN (1849–1930) piloted the *Ancon* on August 15, 1914, the first ship through the Panama Canal. Operated by Isthmian.

82. SAMANA, 8–43, 169640, BKXS, built for the British Ministry of War Transport. Operated by Lamport & Holt.

83. MYRON T. HERRICK, 8–43, 244080, KYBT (1854–1929) Myron Timothy Herrick was governor of Ohio and ambassador to France. Operated by American President Lines.

84. RING LARDNER, 8–43, 244107, KYBU (1885–1933) Ringgold Wilmer Lardner was a sports writer and author. Operated by Prudential.

85. HORACE WELLS, 8–43, 244132, KYBX (1815–1848) dentist who pioneered the use of nitrous oxide for anesthesia, the effort proving disastrous for him. Operated by Isthmian.

86. WINFIELD S. STRATTON, 8–43, 244151, KYCB (1848–1902) Winfield Scott

Stratton was a very generous miner who found a huge gold deposit near Victor, Colorado, named the Independence Lode. Namesake for several Colorado Springs features. Operated by Coastwise (Pacific Far East) Line.

    87. JAMES LICK, 8–43, 244190, KYCC (1796–1876) piano maker, California land speculator, hotelier, Lick Observatory benefactor, and namesake for Lickdale, Pennsylvania. Operated by Matson.

    88. FLOYD BENNETT, 8–43, 244189, KYCD (1890–1928) Navy pilot and Arctic explorer with Adm. Richard E. Byrd. Operated by American President Lines.

    89. DAVID BELASCO, 9–43, 244211, KYCF (1853–1931) son of 49ers from England who became a noted stage actor and entertainer. Operated by Smith & Johnson.

    90. JOHN S. BASSETT, 9–43, 244224, KYCG (1867–1928) John Spencer Bassett was a history professor and author of an inflammatory article on southern race relations known as the "Bassett Affair." Operated by American President Lines.

    91. SAMPFORD, 9–43, 169797, BFNW, built for the British Ministry of War Transport. Operated by Andrew Weir & Co.

    92. VACHEL LINDSAY, 9–43, 244310, KYCM (1879–1931) Nicholas Vachel Lindsay was an Illinois poet whose work was meant to be sung. Operated by Eastern Steamship.

    93. MICHAEL CASEY, 9–43, 244309, KYKG (1857–1937) "Bloody Mike" Casey was the first business agent for the new Teamster's Union, Local 85, organized in August 1900 in San Francisco and its longtime president. Operated by American President Lines.

    94. CHUNG CHENG, 9–43 (1897–1975) Chiang Chung-cheng was the birth name of Chiang Kai-shek. Operated under the Chinese flag.

    95. HENRY WELLS, 9–43, 244358, KYKJ (1805–1878) Erie Canal freight agent who founded American Express with William Fargo and in 1864 Wells Fargo & Co. in California. Operated by Grace Line.

    96. JAMES J. O'KELLY, 9–43, 244387, KYOZ (1845–1916) James Hoseph O'Kelly was an Irish nationalist, member of the House of Commons, drama critic and art editor for the *New York Herald*, and a correspondent in Cuba during a revolt. He was captured by Spanish troops, fought Indians, and returned to Ireland. Operated by American-Hawaiian.

    97. REINHOLD RICHTER, 9–43, 244397, KYPS (1857–1898) captain in the 1st California Volunteer Infantry who was lost at Malate, Philippines, during the Spanish-American War. Operated by Seas Shipping.

    98. WILLIAM SHARON, 10–43, 244439, KYPA (1821–1885) controversial Nevada senator. Operated by United Fruit. Capt. Edward MacAughey, 39, left San Francisco, California, under Army orders and returned to San Francisco from Espiritu Santo on December 19. A year later, on December 28, 1944, his ship was hit by a kamikaze in the Philippines with the loss of six merchant crew, including Capt. MacAughey, four Armed Guard sailors, and the Army security officer. The ship was repaired.

    99. SAMARK, 10–43, 169688, MYNB, built for the British Ministry of War Transport. Operated by Ellerman's Wilson Line.

    100. SIMON BAMBERGER, 10–43, 244171, KKTZ (1846–1926) governor of Utah. Operated by American-Hawaiian.

    101. CYRUS T. BRADY, 10–43, 244489, KTUA (1861–1920) Cyrus Townsend Brady was a Naval Academy graduate, Episcopal clergyman, and author of *Indian Fights and Fighters*. Operated by American President Lines.

    102. SAMUEL BRANNON, 10–43, 244506, KTUD (1819–1889) California pioneer Sam Brannan published the *California Star*, and in 1849 started the Gold Rush by loudly announcing the find James Marshall and John Sutter tried to keep quiet. Operated by Moore-McCormack.

103. CHIEF CHARLOT, 10–43, 244532, KTUG (1830–1910) Charlo—"claw of the little grizzly"—was chief of the Bitterroot Salish in Montana. Operated by United Fruit.

104. CASPER S. YOST, 10–43, 244554, KTUJ (1863–1941) Casper Salathiel Yost was the longtime editor of the *St. Louis Globe-Democrat* and founder of the American Society of Newspaper Editors. Operated by American South African.

105. WILLIAM J. PALMER, 10–43, 244580, KTUK (1836–1909) William Jackson Palmer was cofounder of the Denver & Rio Grande Railroad and founder of Colorado Springs, Colorado. Operated by South Atlantic and converted to an animal transport ship.

106. PETER COOPER HEWITT, 10–43, 244596, KTUM (1861–1921) inventor of the mercury vapor lamp. Operated by Matson.

107. ETHAN A. HITCHCOCK, 10–43, 244608, KTUN (1798–1870) Ethan Allen Hitchcock was an Army general, grandson of Ethan Allen, and West Point commandant of cadets with multiple interests and accomplishments. Operated by Isthmian.

108. MARY BICKERDYKE, 11–43, 244633, KUNY (1817–1901) Mary Ann Ball was a house servant when she married Robert Bickerdyke in 1847. They had two kids and when he died in 1859 she took up nursing, developed a very strong personality, and became chief of nursing in Gen. Grant's command during the Civil War. Known by grateful soldiers as "Mother Bickerdyke." Operated by Seas Shipping.

109. WILLIAM W. CAMPBELL, 11–43, 244648, KUOK (1862–1938) William Wallace Campbell was a noted astronomer and president of the University of California. Operated by American President Lines.

110. MICHAEL C. KERR, 11–43, 244653, KUOO (1827–1876) Michael Crawford Kerr was an Indiana congressman. Operated by Sudden & Christenson.

111. HARRY LEON WILSON, 11–43, 244732, KUOP (1867–1939) popular novelist. Operated by Coastwise.

112. JOHN W. MELDRUM, 11–43, 244737, KUOQ (1843–1936) John William "Jack" Meldrum was a Wyoming judge, politician, and in 1884 became the first resident U.S. Commissioner of Yellowstone National Park. Operated by Sudden & Christenson.

113. CLYDE L. SEAVEY, 11–43, 244749, KVAX (1874–1943) Clyde Leroy Seavey was a member of the Federal Power Commission, the California Railroad Commission, and first city manager of Sacramento. He died on August 4, 1943. Operated by Isthmian.

114. WILLIAM A. COULTER, 11–43, 244775, KVAY (1849–1936) William Alexander Coulter was a noted San Francisco artist. Operated by Hammond.

115. LOUIS PASTEUR, 12–43, 244792, KVAZ (1822–1895) microbiologist noted for treating raw milk. The ship was christened with a bottle of pasteurized milk along with the champagne. Operated by AGWI Lines.

116. WILLIAM C. RALSTON, 12–43, 244868, KVBA (1826–1875) William Chapman "Bill" Ralston founded the Bank of California, financed 49ers, and in 1875 swam out into San Francisco Bay and drowned after his bank failed. Operated by Alaska Packers.

117. LAWRENCE GIANELLA, 12–43, 244845, KVBE (1921–1941) radio operator lost on the Lykes. freighter *Prusa*, torpedoed by *I-172* on December 19, 1941, south of Hawaii. Operated by Matson.

118. GEORGE H. POWELL, 12–43, 244858, KVIL (1872–1922) G. Harold Powell was the general manager of the California Fruit Growers' Exchange. Operated by McCormick.

119. JOSE J. ACOSTA, 12–43, 244906, KVIP (1539–1600) José Julian Acosta was a Jesuit missionary in Peru and noted historian of colonial Spain. Operated by American President Lines.

120. HEBER M. CREEL, 12–43, 244927, KVIS (1855–1932) Heber Mansfield Creel

was an Army officer, author of a Cheyenne language dictionary, and in March 1913 was appointed supervisor of Indian schools. Operated by Olympic.

121. MILLEN GRIFFITH, 12–43, 244947, KVIV (1828–1896) San Francisco tugboat operator and pioneer of the salmon canning industry in Alaska. Operated by Burns.

122. OTIS SKINNER, 1–44, 244958, KVIW (1858–1942) popular stage actor. Operated by American-Hawaiian.

123. JOHN SHERMAN, 1–44, 244975, KVSG (1823–1900) Ohio congressman. Operated by Alcoa.

124. HENRY R. SCHOOLCRAFT, 1–44, 244989, KVSN (1793–1864) Henry Rowe Schoolcraft discovered lead deposits in Missouri and led an expedition that determined Lake Itasca in central Minnesota was the primary source for the Mississippi River. Operated by Seas Shipping.

125. JOSEPH E. WING, 2–44, 245039, KVSP (1861–1915) Joseph Elwyn Wing pioneered the growing of alfalfa east of the Mississippi. Operated by Alcoa.

126. HARRIET MONROE, 2–44, 245051, KVSQ (1860–1936) literary critic, poet, and founder and longtime editor of *Poetry: A Magazine of Verse*. Operated by Mississippi Shipping.

127. FRANK J. CUHEL, 3–44, 245079, KVSR (1904–1943) Frank Josef Cuhel was a Mutual Broadcasting System war correspondent lost when the Boeing 314 *Yankee Clipper* he was in exploded at Lisbon, Portugal, on February 22, 1943. On July 10, 1939, the *Yankee Clipper* became the first aircraft to carry passengers over the Atlantic Ocean when it landed in London. Operated by Black Diamond.

128. DAULTON MANN, 3–44, 245099, KVST (1893–1941) noted shipping man and vice president of Grace Line. Operated by Grace Line.

129. ALEXANDER MAJORS, 3–44, 245119, KVSV (1814–1900) joined military suppliers Waddell & Russell as a partner in 1855, renamed Russell, Majors & Waddell. In early 1860, Majors and Benjamin Ficklin began the Central Overland California & Pikes Peak Express Co.—the "Pony Express" mail service. Operated by Isthmian. Capt. John M. Griffin's ship was hit by a kamikaze on November 12, 1944, at Leyte, Philippines, with the loss of chief cook Salvador Reyes and utility-man Salvador Padrique. The ship was repaired.

130. JAN PIETERSZOON COEN, 3–44, 245151, KWGF (1587–1629) chief founder of the Dutch East India Company. Operated by Sudden & Christenson. Princess Juliana of the Netherlands was sponsor but when she swung the bottle of Champaign she missed. Morris Nash, a public relations man on the platform also missed, then a shipyard guard, Charles Runyon, managed to break the bottle before the ship got away.

131. AUGUSTIN DALY, 4–44, 245223, KWNQ (1838–1899) John Augustin Daly was a theatrical manager and noted playwright. Operated by Alaska Steamship.

132. JAMES H. BREASTED, 4–44, 245207, KWNY (1865–1935) James Henry Breasted was a noted archeologist and historian at the University of Chicago. Operated by American President Lines. The ship departed San Francisco in March 1944 and arrived back there on June 16 from Guadalcanal. Capt. Bernard Kummel's ship was bombed by Japanese aircraft off Mindoro Island, Philippines, while at anchor on December 26, 1944. There were no reported fatalities.

133. WALTER WYMAN, 4–44, 245218, KWXO (1848–1911) the third Surgeon General. Operated by Hammond.

134. JOHN ROACH, 4–44, 245325, KWQC (1813–1887) built marine engines during the Civil War in New York and founded John Roach & Sons, iron shipbuilding pioneers at Chester, Pennsylvania. Operated by Pope & Talbot.

135. HENRY ADAMS, 4–44, 245353, KWQE (1838–1918) American historian, novelist, and great grandson of John Adams. Operated by Pacific-Atlantic.

136. SUKHONA, 4–44, major Russian river. Operated under the Russian flag.

137. JOHN ISAACSON, 4–44, 245453, KXAT (1875–1939) founder of Isaacson Iron Works and wartime operator of Jorgensen Steel, a Navy supplier near Tukwila, Washington. Operated by Sudden & Christenson.

138. SILVESTRE ESCALANTE, 4–44, 245490, KXAU (c. 1750–1799) Silvestre Vélez de Escalante was a Spanish priest and member of the Dominguez-Escalante Expedition that created the Old Spanish Trail from Santa Fe, New Mexico, to Los Angeles. Operated by Sudden & Christenson.

YARD NO. 2

1. JAMES OTIS, 3–42, 241367, KAZK (1725–1783) James Otis, Jr., was a Massachusetts Bay Colony lawyer and revolutionary leader. Operated by Pacific-Atlantic. Capt. Walter Vendshur's ship went aground near Devon, England, on February 6, 1945, and became a total loss.

2. JOHN ADAMS, 3–42, 241442, KBUT (1735–1826) Declaration of Independence signer and 2nd President of the United States. Operated by Sudden & Christenson. Capt. Conrad Peterson's ship was torpedoed on January 29, 1943, by *I-21* off New Caledonia. Five Armed Guard sailors were lost. When flaming gasoline ran into the midship house from the after deck, second engineer Cleon A. Craig heard three messmen yelling for help. He determined they were trapped in their room—the inboard room, portside aft—by a sprung door. He found a fire axe and chopped the door free then led the burned messmen to safety. Craig was awarded the Merchant Marine Distinguished Service medal.

3. KIT CARSON, 3–42, 241460, KDIL (1809–1868) Christopher Houston "Kit" Carson was a trapper mountain man, soldier, and California trail guide. Operated by Weyerhaeuser.

4. ZACHARY TAYLOR, 4–42, 241490, KEIA (1784–1850) 12th President of the United States. Operated by Pacific-Atlantic.

5. ANTHONY WAYNE, 4–42, 241578, KESF (1745–1796) "Mad Anthony" Wayne commanded Pennsylvania units during the Revolutionary War. Operated by Matson.

6. TIMOTHY PICKERING, 4–42, 241604, KEWT (1745–1829) Secretary of War and State and a Massachusetts congressman. Operated by American President Lines. Capt. Gustav E. Swanson was the *Pickering*'s skipper when they arrived at New York in November 1942. The ship was bombed on July 14, 1943, by German aircraft off Avola, Sicily, with the loss of 22 merchant crew, eight Armed Guard sailors, and 100 soldiers. Second mate George W. Alther, Jr., was awarded the Merchant Marine Distinguished Service medal posthumously.

7. STEPHEN HOPKINS, 5–42, 241648, KEWH (1707–1785) Declaration of Independence signer from Rhode Island. Operated by Luckenbach. In the summer of 1941 Paul Buck was a 37-year-old chief mate on the freighter *Harry Luckenbach* when the ship arrived at San Francisco on August 26, 1941, from Manila. He had made the previous voyages and intended to make the next one. On September 27, 1942, as master of his own ship, he chose to battle the German raider *Stier* and tender *Tannenfels* in the South Atlantic. The *Hopkins* and *Stier* sank and Capt. Buck was lost along with 31 other merchantmen and nine Armed Guard sailors. The ship received the Maritime Commission Gallant Ship award. Chief mate Richard Moczkowski, second mate Joseph E. Layman, second engineer George S. Cronk, chief

steward Ford Stilson, and engine cadet Edwin J. O'Hara were awarded the Merchant Marine Distinguished Service medal, Moczkowski, Layman, and O'Hara's posthumously.

8. SAMUEL HUNTINGTON, 5–42, 241649, KEWA (1731–1796) Declaration of Independence signer from Connecticut. Operated by Oliver J. Olson. Capt. Richard Stenman's ship was sunk on January 29, 1944, by air attack off Anzio with the loss of five merchant crew.

9. WILLIAM ELLERY, 5–42, 241722, KEWW (1727–1820) Declaration of Independence signer from Rhode Island. Operated by Pope & Talbot.

10. IRVIN MACDOWELL, 6–42, 241804, KFWV (1818–1885) supply officer, political appointee, and reluctant Army of Northern Virginia commander who was defeated at the First Battle of Bull Run. Operated by Pope & Talbot.

11. LEWIS MORRIS, 6–42, 241805, KFKV (1726–1798) Declaration of Independence signer from New York. Operated by American President Lines.

12. GEORGE B. MCCLELLAN, 6–42, 241895, KFWS (1826–1885) George Brinton McClellan was a Major General who organized the Army of the Potomac. Operated by Moore-McCormack.

13. JOHN WISE, 6–42, 241901, KFJL (1652–1725) Massachusetts political leader. Operated by Grace Line.

14. JOSEPH HOOKER, 7–42, 241971, KFWP (1814–1879) Union general. Operated by Moore-McCormack.

15. GEORGE ROSS, 7–42, 242019, KFGB (1730–1779) Declaration of Independence signer from Pennsylvania. Operated by American President Lines.

16. JAMES SMITH, 7–42, 242005, KFHH (1719–1806) Declaration of Independence signer from Pennsylvania. Operated by Matson. Capt. William H. Aguilar's ship was torpedoed by U-510 on March 9, 1943, with the loss of six merchant crew and five Armed Guard sailors. The ship was repaired.

17. GEORGE TAYLOR, 7–42, 242035, KFGC (1716–1781) Declaration of Independence signer from Pennsylvania. Operated by Matson.

18. WILLIAM WHIPPLE, 8–42, 242064, KFVI (1730–1785) Declaration of Independence signer from New Hampshire. Operated by Isthmian.

19. OLIVER WOLCOTT, 8–42, 242162, KFMT (1726–1797) Declaration of Independence signer from Connecticut. Operated by American President Lines.

20. FRANCIS LEWIS, 8–42, 242118, KFFO (1713–1802) Declaration of Independence signer from New York. Operated by Sudden & Christenson.

21. JOHN MORTON, 8–42, 242093, KFIJ (1724–1777) Declaration of Independence signer from Pennsylvania. Operated by Luckenbach.

22. GEORGE READ, 8–42, 242184, KFFZ (1733–1798) Declaration of Independence signer from Delaware. Operated by Isthmian.

23. ROGER SHERMAN, 8–42, 242149, KFON (1721–1793) Declaration of Independence signer from Connecticut. Operated by Pope & Talbot.

24. MATTHEW THORNTON, 8–42, 242193, KFLE (1714–1803) Declaration of Independence signer from New Hampshire. Operated by Hammond.

25. RICHARD STOCKTON, 8–42, 242214, KFOL (1730–1781) Declaration of Independence signer from New Jersey. Operated by Isthmian.

26. WILLIAM WILLIAMS, 9–42, 242223, KFVK (1731–1811) Declaration of Independence signer from Connecticut. Operated by Isthmian then by the Navy as the *Crater*-class cargo ship *Venus* (AK-135), commissioned on November 10, 1943.

27. ELI WHITNEY, 9–42, 242247, KFDS (1765–1825) perfected a machine to quickly separate cotton fibers from seed, known as the cotton gin. Operated by Grace Line.

28. AMBROSE E. BURNSIDE, 9–42, 242303, KGJC (1824–1881) Ambrose Everett Burnside was a Union general and Rhode Island senator and governor. Operated by Coastwise (Pacific Far East) Line.

29. PETER J. MCGUIRE, 9–42, 242299, KHJQ (1851–1906) founder of Labor Day, May Day, and cofounder of the Brotherhood of Carpenters & Joiners union. Operated by American President Lines.

30. PHILIP H. SHERIDAN, 9–42, 242318, KGIS (1831–1888) Philip Henry Sheridan was a Union Army general. Operated by Shepard.

31. DAVID BUSHNELL, 9–42, 242334, KHKD (1742–1824) Army captain at Yorktown, physician, and inventor of the time bomb and the first submarine, the *Turtle*. He also proved gunpowder would explode under water. Operated by Luckenbach.

32. JOHN FITCH, 9–42, 242245, KHJS (1743–1798) steamboat inventor. Operated by Weyerhaeuser.

33. JAMES RUMSEY, 9–42, 242348, KHLA (1743–1792) created a steam-powered water turbine to jet propel a boat and invented the water-tube boiler. Operated by American Mail Line.

34. JOHN STEVENS, 10–42, 242365, KHLP (1749–1838) soldier, New Jersey delegate to the Continental Convention who built the *Phoenix*, the first ocean-going steamboat, and established patent law. Operated by Waterman.

35. SAMUEL F. B. MORSE, 10–42, 242385, KHNM (1791–1872) Samuel Finley Breese Morse improved the single-wire telegraph system and co-invented the Morse code. Operated by Moore-McCormack and converted by the War Department to the Army hospital ship *Jarrett M. Huddleston*. Col. Huddleston, 50, was a VI Corps surgeon lost at Anzio on February 9, 1944. His son, Jarrett "Jerry" Jr., 25, was a lieutenant lost at the Battle of Ardennes on January 13, 1945. Mom, Helen, was back in Washington, D.C., and had another son, Jack W. in the Army. She was a buyer at a department store and Jack survived the war.

36. CYRUS H. MCCORMICK, 10–42, 242384, KHRX (1809–1884) Cyrus Hall McCormick perfected a machine to harvest grain. Operated by American President Lines. Capt. Heinrich H. Kronke's ship left New York in late January 1945 and arrived back at New York on March 19. On April 18 the ship was torpedoed by *U-1107* off Brest, France, with the loss of four merchant crew and two Armed Guard sailors.

37. JAMES B. FRANCIS, 10–42, 242413, KHUF (1815–1892) James Bicheno Francis was a waterworks engineer and invented the fire sprinkler system and the Francis turbine. Operated by Grace Line and converted to an Army troopship.

38. RICHARD JORDAN GATLING, 10–42, 242420, KHUI (1818–1903) invented a machinegun. Operated by Luckenbach.

39. JOHN JAMES AUDUBON, 10–42, 242414, KHUJ, bird watcher and artist. Operated by the Navy as the *Crater*-class cargo ship *Crater* (AK-70), NXTX, commissioned on October 31, 1942.

40. JOHN F. APPLEBY, 10–42, 242444, KHUN (1840–1917) John Francis Appleby invented a knotting device to bind bales of hay and grains. Operated by Moore-McCormack.

41. CHARLES M. HALL, 10–42, 242443, KHUP (1863–1914) Charles Martin Hall invented an inexpensive way to manufacture aluminum. His company became the Aluminum Company of America (Alcoa). Operated by Isthmian.

42. GEORGE WESTINGHOUSE, 10–42, 242458, KHUQ (1846–1914) steam engine, railroad machinery, and air brake inventor, who advocated the use of alternating current. Operated by Seas Shipping.

43. JOHN BARTRAM, 10–42, 242465, KHUR (1699–1777) famous early botanist, horticulturist, and explorer from Pennsylvania. Operated by A. H. Bull.

44. G. H. CORLISS, 11–42, 242488, KHUT (1817–1888) George Henry Corliss was a steam engine manufacturer. Operated by the Navy as the *Crater*-class cargo ship *Adhara* (AK-71), NXUS, commissioned on November 16, 1942.

45. RICHARD MARCH HOE, 11–42, 242526, KHUV (1812–1886) invented the revolutionary rotary printing press. Operated by the Army as a troopship then by the Navy as the *Prince Georges* (AP-165) commissioned on November 10, 1943.

46. ELIHU THOMSON, 11–42, 242515, KHUW (1853–1937) electrical engineer and entrepreneur. Operated by De La Rama. Hit a mine on September 25, 1944, in the South Pacific.

47. GEORGE B. SELDEN, 11–42, 242533, KHUY (1846–1922) George Baldwin Selden was a lawyer who built a small version of George Brayton's internal combustion engine and received a patent for the first practical "road engine." Operated by Matson.

48. ROBERT E. PEARY, 11–42, 242535, KFGE (1856–1920) Rear Admiral Robert Edwin Peary was a noted arctic explorer. Operated by Weyerhaeuser.

49. NATHANIEL BOWDITCH, 11–42, 242549, KHVB (1773–1838) author of the *Practical Navigator* for sailors. Operated by Coastwise (Pacific Far East) Line.

50. CHARLES M. CONRAD, 11–42, 242561, KKBD (1804–1878) Charles Magill Conrad was a Louisiana congressman and Secretary of War. Operated by Seas Shipping.

51. JOHN B. FLOYD, 11–42, 242534, KKBF (1806–1863) John Buchanan Floyd was governor of Virginia and Secretary of War. Operated by De La Rama and converted to an Army troopship.

52. JOSEPH HOLT, 11–42, 242587, KKBE (1807–1894) Postmaster General and Secretary of War. Operated by Prudential.

53. JOHN M. SCHOFIELD, 11–42, 242592, KKBN (1831–1906) John McAllister Schofield was a Union general, Secretary of War, and Commanding General of the Army. Operated by Sudden & Christenson.

54. JOHN A. RAWLINS, 12–42, 242598, KKBY (1831–1869) John Aaron Rawlins was a Union general and Secretary of War. Operated by Matson. Capt. Emil Brubik's ship was hit by an aerial torpedo off Okinawa on July 27, 1945, and caught fire. On September 16 heavy seas rendered the ship a total loss. There were no reported casualties.

55. GEORGE W. MCCRARY, 12–42, 242609, KKBH (1835–1890) George Washington McCrary was an Iowa congressman and Secretary of War. Operated by Alaska Packers.

56. ALEXANDER RAMSEY, 12–42, 242629, KKBK (1815–1903) Pennsylvania congressman, Minnesota governor, mayor of St. Paul, Secretary of War, and namesake for counties in Minnesota and North Dakota and towns in Minnesota and Illinois. Operated by United States Lines.

57. USS ALUDRA (AK-72), 12–42, NXWU, *Crater*-class cargo ship commissioned on December 26, 1942. Torpedoed by *RO-103* on June 26, 1943, in the Solomon Islands.

58. WILLIAM C. ENDICOTT, 12–42, 242646, KKBP (1826–1900) William Crowninshield Endicott was Secretary of War. Operated by Oliver J. Olson.

59. REDFIELD PROCTOR, 12–42, 242657, KKBU (1831–1908) Vermont governor and senator and Secretary of War. Operated by the Navy as the *Crater*-class cargo ship *Celeno* (AK-76), NYJY, commissioned on January 2, 1943.

60. DAVID GAILLARD, 12–42, 242682, KITA (1859–1913) Maj. David du Bose Gaillard was an Army engineer on the Panama Canal project who supervised the route through the Culebra Mountains from Gatun Lake to the Atlantic, one of the most difficult portions

of the Canal to build and originally named the Culebra Cut. Gaillard died on December 5, 1913, and missed the Grand Opening the next year. In 1915 the route was renamed the Gaillard Cut in his honor but in 2000 the Panamanians revoked his name and went back to Culebra. Operated by Sudden & Christenson.

    61. HENRY J. RAYMOND, 12–42, 242700, KITD (1820–1869) Henry Jarvis Raymond founded the *New York Times* and served as a New York congressman. Operated by American President Lines.

    62. WILLIAM G. MCADOO, 12–42, 242706, KKGS (1853–1930) William Gibbs McAdoo was a congressman from New Jersey and California and Secretary of the Treasury. Operated by American President Lines under Capt. Joseph D. Ryan then by the Navy as the *Crater*-class cargo ship *Grumium* (AK-112), NTVK, commissioned on October 20, 1943.

The brand-new USS *Aludra* (AK-72) heading out of San Francisco in December 1942 under Lt. Cdr. Dale E. Collins, USNR. On June 22, 1943, the ship departed Noumea, New Caledonia, for Espiritu Santo but early the next morning the Japanese submarine *RO-103* fired a torpedo that hit the port side and five hours later the ship sank with three fatalities: Namie Clyde Hoagland, F1c, USNR, and Charles Maurice Durham, S2c, USNR were reported missing. Hoagland's wife, Gay, lived at 5704 3rd Ave. N., in Birmingham, Alabama, and Durham's mother, Iva Durham, lived in Southside, Tennessee. Stanley Hugh Eichner, SM3c, USN, and Boatswain Warrant Officer Harold Lyndell Brown, USN, died of wounds and were buried at sea the next day. Brown's wife Fay, lived in Redmond, Washington, and Stan lived with his dad, John H. Eichner, in Pendleton, Oregon. National Archives photograph 19-N-40005.

63. LESLIE M. SHAW, 12–42, 242719, KKCW (1848–1932) Leslie Mortier "L.M." Shaw was governor of Iowa and Secretary of the Treasury. Operated by Luckenbach.

64. USS CETUS (AK-77), NYMF, *Crater*-class cargo ship commissioned on January 17, 1943.

65. FREDERICK JACKSON TURNER, 1–43, 242747, KKCX (1861–1932) noted University of Wisconsin and Harvard historian specializing in the American frontier. Operated by Isthmian.

66. JOSEPH G. CANNON, 1–43, 242759, KKCY (1836–1926) Joseph Gurney Cannon was an Illinois congressman. Operated by Weyerhaeuser.

67. GEORGE ROGERS CLARK, 1–43, 242758, KKGT (1752–1818) Indiana and Illinois frontiersman. Operated by De La Rama.

68. LOUIS JOLIET, 1–43, 242789, KKGS (1645–1700) Louis Jolliet was a Canadian explorer of North America and the Mississippi River and is the namesake for several towns. Operated by Seas Shipping.

69. SAMUEL DE CHAMPLAIN, 1–43, 242863, KKGP (c. 1575–1635) Samuel Champlain is the "Father of New France," a French explorer of the Great Lakes region, and founder and governor of Quebec City. Operated by United States Lines.

70. JOHN A. LOGAN, 1–43, 242828, KKHE (1826–1886) John Alexander Logan was a Union general, Illinois congressman and commander-in-chief of the Grand Army of the Republic who issued General Order No. 11 of May 5, 1868, that created Decoration Day to honor all lost in the Civil War, later Memorial Day. Operated by United States Lines then by the Navy as the *Crater*-class cargo ship *Alnitah* (AK-127), NHCI, commissioned on November 27, 1943.

71. PERE MARQUETTE, 1–43, 242830, KKHL (1637–1675) Jesuit priest, Father "Pere" Jacques Marquette, was a missionary explorer who founded Sault Sainte Marie and St. Ignace, Michigan, and explored the upper Mississippi River. Operated by Isthmian.

72. JOHN M. PALMER, 1–43, 242861, KIVZ (1817–1900) John McAuley Palmer was a Union general and Illinois governor and senator. Operated by the Navy as the *Crater*-class cargo ship *Draco* (AK-79), NYQQ, commissioned on February 16, 1943.

73. RICHARD YATES, 1–43, 242863, KIWB (1815–1873) Illinois governor and senator. Operated by W. R. Chamberlin.

74. NANCY HANKS, 2–43, 242874, KIIT (1784–1818) Nancy Hanks married Thomas Lincoln in 1806 and they had a son they named Abraham. Operated by Oliver J. Olson.

75. EDWARD P. COSTIGAN, 2–43, 242882, KIIX (1874–1939) Edward Prentiss Costigan was a Colorado senator. Operated by American President Lines.

76. TUNGUS, 2–43, Tunguska region in eastern Siberia bordering Manchuria. Operated under the Russian flag.

77. BENJAMIN BONNEVILLE, 2–43, 242900, KKPB (1796–1878) Paris-born Benjamin Louis Eulalie de Bonneville was an Army officer, fur trapper, and Rocky Mountain and Oregon territory explorer. Operated by Coastwise Line.

78. RICHARD HENDERSON, 2–43, 242907, KKPH (1735–1785) founder of Nashville, Tennessee. Operated by United States Lines. Capt. Lawrence J. Silk's ship was torpedoed on August 26, 1943, by *U-410* off Bone, Algeria. There were no reported casualties.

79. KOLKHOZNIK, 2–43, a member of a kolkhoz, a collective farm. Operated under the Russian flag.

80. JUSTIN S. MORRILL, 2–43, 242947, KKUD (1810–1898) Justin Smith Morrill was a Vermont congressman who was influential in public higher education. Operated by United States Lines.

81. THOMAS KEARNS, 2–43, 242948, KKUE (1862–1918) Utah senator. Operated by Isthmian.

82. VITUS BERING, 2–43, 242991, KKUH (1680–1741) Vitus Jonassen Bering was a Danish explorer and namesake for the Bering Sea. Operated by General Steamship.

83. DAN BEARD, 2–43, 243069, KKUK (1850–1941) engineer and artist Daniel Carter "Uncle Dan" Beard founded the Sons of Daniel Boone in 1905, renamed the Boy Pioneers of America, and founded Boy Scout Troop 1. Operated by Stockard. Capt. Wilhelm Hope's ship left New York in early January 1944 and arrived back at New York from Leith, Scotland, on March 15. Captain William R. Wilson's ship left New York around April 14 for the UK. Torpedoed by *U-1202* on December 10, 1944, off Stumble Head, North Wales, with the loss of 17 merchant crew and 12 Armed Guard sailors.

84. JANE A. DELANO, 3–43, 243093, KKUN (1862–1919) Jane Arminda Delano was an innovator of nursing methods and recruited 18,732 nurses into the American Red Cross Nursing Service during the Great War for which she was awarded the Distinguished Service Medal posthumously. Operated by General Steamship.

85. JOHN R. PARK, 3–43, 243004, KKUS (1833–1900) John Rocky Park was a physician, an educator in the Utah Territory, and president of the University of Deseret. Operated by Luckenbach. Capt. Otto L. Bartfeld's ship was torpedoed by *U-399* on March 21, 1945, off Lizard Head, England. There were no reported casualties.

86. JAMES B. HICKOK, 3–43, 243029, KKUT (1837–1876) James Butler Hickok was a fugitive from Kansas, a Civil War veteran, and self-promoter who called himself "Wild Bill" to impress audiences. Operated by Polarus.

87. HIRAM S. MAXIM, 3–43, 243022, KKUU (1840–1916) Hiram Stevens Maxim was a prolific American inventor noted for his Maxim gun, the first self-powered machine gun. Operated by Coast-wise.

88. WILLIAM B. OGDEN, 3–43, 243052, KKUV (1805–1877) William Butler Ogden was the first mayor of Chicago and the first president of the Union Pacific Railroad. Operated by Isthmian.

89. DAVID DUDLEY FIELD, 3–43, 243183, KKUW (1805–1894) lawyer and promoter of universal legal standards. Operated by Isthmian. Capt. Albion M. Burbank's ship was the first merchant vessel to arrive in the Philippines in support of the Leyte invasion, carrying troops, anti-aircraft guns, and mortar shells.

90. CHARLES P. STEINMETZ, 3–43, 243068, KKUX (1865–1923) Charles Proteus Steinmetz was the primary developer of alternating current. Operated by the War Department.

91. DAVID STARR JORDAN, 4–43, 243184, KKUY (1851–1931) first president of Leland Stanford, Jr., University. Operated by General Steamship.

92. JACQUES LARAMIE, 4–43, 243110, KKUZ (1784-c. 1821) Jacques La Ramée was a French-Canadian fur trader, Wyoming pioneer, and namesake of Laramie. Operated by Pope & Talbot.

93. LUCY STONE, 4–43, 243124, KKVA (1818–1893) women's activist and first female in Massachusetts to earn a college degree. Married abolitionist Henry Blackwell in 1854 after much discussion. Operated by Mississippi Shipping.

94. FRANCES E. WILLARD, 4–43, 243157, KKVB (1839–1898) Frances Elizabeth Caroline Willard was an educator, second president of the Women's Christian Temperance Union, and suffragist. Operated by T. J. Stevenson.

95. BETSY ROSS, 4–43, 243156, KKVE (1752–1836) after Elizabeth "Betsy" Griscom married Philadelphia upholsterer John Ross she opened her own flag-making business. She is

credited through legend as having sewed the first official American flag. Operated by the Navy as the *Crater*-class cargo ship *Cor Coroli* (AK-91), NKGG, commissioned on April 16, 1943.

96. ABIGAIL ADAMS, 4–43, 243154, KKVJ (1744–1818) in 1764, Abigail Smith's father, the Rev. Warren Smith, married her to her third cousin, country lawyer John Adams. He became the 2nd President of the United States and they had a son they named John Quincy Adams. Operated by De La Rama.

97. ELIZABETH BLACKWELL, 4–43, 243199, KKVL (1821–1910) came to America in 1832 with her family from England in 1832 and became the first degreed female medical doctor in the United States and the first female physician on the United Kingdom Medical Register. Operated by Coastwise (Pa-cific Far East) Line.

98. S. HALL YOUNG, 4–43, 243232, KKVP (1847–1927) Samuel Hall Young was a missionary who founded the first Protestant church in Alaska. Operated by American-Hawaiian.

99. J. H. KINKAID, 4–43, 243224, KKVQ (1826–1904) John Henry Kinkaid was a Nevada governor and first governor of the Alaska Territory. Operated by Coastwise (Pacific Far East) Line under Capt. Francis M. Leavy and arrived at San Francisco on September 4, 1943, from Espiritu Santo and converted to an Army troopship.

100. VALERY CHKALOV, 4–43 (1904–1938) noted Russian aviator. Operated under the Russian flag. Broke in half on December 12, 1943, in the North Pacific. The whole crew, including four women: a doctor, two stewardesses, and a bookkeeper, was saved.

101. SHELDON JACKSON, 4–43, 243265, KKVT (1834–1909) Western missionary and Alaska educator. Operated by American President Lines.

102. LUTHER BURBANK, 4–43, 243280, KHVC (1849–1926) agricultural genetic engineer. Operated by the Navy as the *Crater*-class cargo ship *Eridanus* (AK-92), NJTD, commissioned on May 8, 1943.

103. GEORGE M. PULLMAN, 4–43, 283, KHVE (1831–1897) George Mortimer Pullman manufactured railroad sleeping cars and employed the porters who staffed them on the trains. Operated by American President Lines.

104. WILBUR WRIGHT, 4–43, 243298, KHVF (1867–1912) bicycle mechanic with Orville, the Wright Brothers, aviation pioneers. Operated by Matson.

105. WILLIAM THORNTON, 4–43, 243323, KHVG (1759–1828) physician, architect who designed the U.S. Capitol, and superintendent of the Patent Office. Operated by American President Lines.

106. GLENN CURTISS, 5–43, 243320, KHVJ (1878–1930) Glenn Hammond Curtiss founded the Curtiss Aviation Co. Operated by United States Lines.

107. GEORGE EASTMAN, 5–43, 243371, KHVK (1854–1932) photography pioneer and founder of the Eastman Kodak Co. in 1880. Operated by Pacific-Atlantic.

108. CYRUS W. FIELD, 5–43, 243370, KHVL (1819–1892) Cyrus West Field cofounded the Atlantic Telegraph Co. and laid the first cable across the Atlantic Ocean in 1858 from St. John's, Newfoundland, to Ireland. Operated by Oliver J. Olson and converted to an animal transport ship.

109. ISAAC BABBITT, 5–43, 243378, KHVM (1799–1862) Taunton, Massachusetts, goldsmith who invented the tin-based alloy named Babbitt used extensively in engine bearings. Operated by the Navy as the *Crater*-class cargo ship *Etamin* (AK-93), NJTE, commissioned on May 25, 1943.

110. OREL, 5–43, or Oryol, ancient Russian fort city occupied by German forces from 1941 to 1943. Operated under the Russian flag.

111. BENJAMIN HOLT, 5–43, 243469, KHVS (1849–1920) Benjamin Leroy Holt

invented the first practical farm tractor and machine that ran over soft earth. The machine used treads instead of wheels and when a reporter described the Holt Co. contraption as looking like a "caterpillar" the name stuck and in 1910 the company became Caterpillar. Operated by Pope & Talbot.

112. ELISHA GRAVES OTIS, 5–43, 243461, KHVT (1811–1861) prolific inventor, including railroad safety brakes and elevators. Founder of the Otis Elevator Co. Operated by Matson.

113. OLIVER EVANS, 5–43, 243424, KODM (1755–1819) steam engine builder. Operated by W. R. Chamberlin.

114. JAMES J. CORBETT, 5–43, 243478, KOPH (1866–1933) James John "Gentleman Jim" Corbett was a boxer in San Francisco who greatly refined the sport. Operated by Shepard.

115. KNUTE ROCKNE, 5–43, 243479, KOPJ (1888–1931) Knute Kenneth Rockne was a celebrated football coach at Notre Dame. Operated by Grace Line.

116. WALTER CAMP, 5–43, 243500, KOQT (1859–1925) Walter Chauncey Camp was a Tennessee senator, Secretary of the Treasury, and minister to Russia. Operated by American President Lines. Capt. Henry A. Schutz's ship was torpedoed on January 25, 1944, by *U-532* in the Indian Ocean. There were no reported casualties.

117. HOBART BAKER, 5–43, 243530, KORP (1892–1918) Hobart Amory Hare "Hobey" Baker was a football player and the first American star ice hockey player. During the Great War he commanded the 141st Aero Squadron in France and died in a plane crash on December 18, 1918. Operated by General Steamship. Capt. J. A. Stevens' ship was sunk on December 28, 1944, by Japanese aircraft off Mindoro, Philippines. Chief engineer Otto C. Levang was the only fatality.

118. CHRISTY MATHEWSON, 5–43, 243526, KORR (1880–1925) Christopher "Christy" Mathewson was a baseball pitcher and one of the first inductees to the Baseball Hall of Fame. Operated by Sudden & Christenson.

119. GEORGE GIPP, 5–43, 243564, KOTU (1895–1920) "The Gipper" was a famous Notre Dame football player. Operated by Norton Lilly.

120. EDWARD A. MACDOWELL, 5–43, 243584, KOVW (1860–1908) Edward Alexander MacDowell was a famous composer and pianist. Operated by A. L. Burbank.

121. MATTHEW B. BRADY, 5–43, 243596, KOXG (1822–1896) Irish-born Mathew B. Brady was a portrait photographer at 859 Broadway in New York who organized a group of photographers to go with him into the field during the Civil War and he published his and their pictures under his name. Operated by Smith & Johnson.

122. JOSEPH SMITH, 6–43, 243593, KOWU (1805–1844) founder of the Mormons. Operated by Alaska Packers. Capt. William Salgren's ship foundered in the North Atlantic on November 11, 1944, in heavy seas. There were no casualties reported.

123. TECUMSEH, 6–43, 243630, KOZI (1768–1813) Shawnee Indian leader. Operated by Moore-McCormack.

124. GERONIMO, 6–43, 243638, KOZF (1829–1909) Apache Indian leader. Operated by Pacific-Atlantic.

125. JOHN L. SULLIVAN, 6–43, 243642, KOZQ (1858–1918) John Lawrence Sullivan was the world heavyweight prizefighter who was defeated by Gentleman Jim Corbett. Operated by Oliver J. Olson.

126. IRVING M. SCOTT, 6–43, 243666, KXDX (1837–1903) Irving Murray Scott was the general manager of Union Iron Works, a major San Francisco shipbuilder. Operated by Pope & Talbot.

127. JOSEPH S. EMERY, 6–43, 243668, KXEA (1820–1909) Joseph Stickney Emery was a stonecutter and cemetery manager who supervised the dredging of the Oakland Estuary in California, making Oakland a deepwater port. Founder of Emeryville, California. Operated by Seas Shipping.

128. GEORGE BERKELEY, 6–43, 243677, KXDZ (1685–1753) Anglo-Irish philosopher, brief resident of Rhode Island, and namesake for Berkeley, California. Operated by Dichmann, Wright & Pugh.

129. ADOLPH SUTRO, 6–43, 243691, KXEB (1830–1898) Prussian-born Adolph Heinrich Joseph Sutro was an engineer who came to the United States as a 49er and developed the Sutro Tunnel for mining the Comstock Lode. Mayor of San Francisco. Operated by Moore-McCormack.

130. JOHN W. MACKAY, 6–43, 243701, KXSO (1831–1902) John William MacKay was a 49er and one of the four "Bonanza King" silver miners of the Comstock Lode, cofounder of the Bank of Nevada, and telegraph cable owner. Operated by Grace Line.

131. JAMES W. NYE, 6–43, 243709, KXST (1815–1876) James Warren Nye was a Nevada Territory governor and senator, namesake for Nye County. Operated by the Navy as the *Crater*-class cargo ship *Ganymede* (AK-104), NTNH, commissioned on July 31, 1943.

132. WILLIAM W. MAYO, 6–43, 243731, KXSS (1819–1911) English-born William Worrall Mayo came to America in 1844 and was a physician at Rochester, Minnesota. He and his wife Louise had two sons who became famous doctors. Operated by Pope & Talbot.

133. JOHN LIND, 6–43, 243728, KXSV (1853–1930) Minnesota congressman and governor. Operated by American Mail Line.

134. OLE E. ROLVAAG, 6–43, 243738, KXSY (1876–1931) Ole Edvart Rølvaag was a novelist and head of the Norwegian Dept. at St. Olaf College in Northfield, Minnesota. Operated by Pope & Talbot.

135. JOHN T. MCMILLAN, 6–43, 243751, KXSZ (1833–1894) believed to be the early settler of Sumner County, Kansas, who operated the first sawmill in 1871 and the first gristmill to serve farmers in that area. Operated by Matson.

136. FREMONT OLDER, 6–43, 243769, KXTB (1856–1935) longtime San Francisco newspaperman who exposed corruption at city hall. Operated by American President Lines.

137. CONRAD KOHRS, 6–43, 243768, KXTH (1835–1920) Carsten Conrad Kohrs was the "Cattle King" of Montana. Operated by South Atlantic.

138. STEPHEN CRANE, 7–43, 243793, KXTI (1871–1900) New Jersey author who wrote the Red Badge of Courage. Operated by Isthmian. Capt. W. E. Green's ship departed San Francisco in July 1943 for Pacific ports. On February 1, 1944, the ship was at anchor at New Guinea when a plane was observed coming in low toward the ship. It kept coming and on approach a bomb dropped and exploded in the water. One Army officer was mortally wounded by shrapnel and 24 were wounded. Ens. Fred S. Price's Armed Guard crew shot down the plane, which they identified as an Army P-38. It was surmised that a Japanese pilot must have somehow been flying a captured plane. Capt. Green departed Brisbane, Australia, with Army medic Sgt. Clyde E. Camp aboard, and arrived at San Francisco on March 22.

139. WILLIAM BEAUMONT, 7–43, 243805, KXTK (1785–1853) noted Army surgeon and anatomist of the digestive system. Operated by American West African Line.

140. JOHN H. ROSSETER, 7–43, 243837, KXTL (1869–1936) San Francisco shipping company executive, flour miller, and director of the U.S. Shipping Board's Bureau of Operations. Operated by De La Rama.

141. HENRY DODGE, 7–43, 243833, KXTM (1782–1867) Wisconsin governor and senator. Operated by Waterman.

142. JOHN S. SARGENT, 7–43, 243839, KXTN (1856–1925) John Singer Sargent was a noted portrait painter. Operated by Mississippi Shipping.

143. CHARLES ROBINSON, 7–43, 243827, KXTP (1818–1894) Charles Lawrence Robinson was a California pioneer and legislator and first governor of Kansas. Operated by Pope & Talbot.

144. INCREASE A. LAPHAM, 7–43, 243856, KXTS (1811–1875) Increase Allen Lapham was a Wisconsin scientist and father of the U.S. Weather Service. Operated by Alaska Packers. Capt. William C. Severson made one voyage and arrived at San Francisco on September 27, 1943, from Noumea, New Caledonia. The ship was then operated by the Navy as the *Crater*-class cargo ship *Alkes* (AK-110), NKTA, commissioned on October 29, 1943.

145. CLARENCE KING, 7–43, 243860, KXTU (1842–1901) western explorer and first director of the U.S. Geological Survey. Operated by Mississippi Shipping.

146. WILLIAM PROUSE, 7–43, 243876, KXTV (1827–1894) William Cook Prows was a Mormon who discovered gold in the autumn of 1848 at Caffon (Gold Creek) in the vicinity of the future Comstock Lode of silver ore in Nevada. Operated by South Atlantic.

147. M. H. DE YOUNG, 7–43, 243893, KXUA (1849–1925) Michael Henry de Young founded the *San Francisco Chronicle*. Operated by De La Rama. Capt. William Munda's ship was torpedoed on August 14, 1943, by *I-19* in the South Pacific with the loss of 1st assistant engineer Walter F. Craft, oiler William D. Hoy, fireman/watertender William R. Lewis, and a Navy officer passenger. The ship was towed to Tongabatu Island and repaired. On October 4 the ship was taken by the Navy and named *Antelope* (IX-109).

148. SAMBRIDGE, 7–43, built for the British Ministry of War Transport. Operated by Thos. & Jno. Brocklebank. Torpedoed on November 18, 1943, by *I-27* in the Arabian Sea.

149. JOHN ROSS, 7–43, 243917, KXUD (1726–1800) Scots-born Philadelphia merchant engaged in shipping. He was a staunch Patriot who was muster-master of the Pennsylvania Navy in 1775 and resigned to procure supplies from France on his own account, which he overdrew, and later partnered with William Dunbar as a planter. Dunbar bought out Ross' heirs after he died. Operated by Seas Shipping.

150. JOSEPH A. HOLMES, 7–43, 243919, KXUH (1859–1915) Dr. Joseph Austin Holmes was a geology professor at the University of North Carolina, State Geologist, and the "father" and first director of the Bureau of Mines. He discovered that bituminous coal dust was explosive—like grain dust in a silo—and advocated for mine safety. Operated by Union Sulphur.

151. LUTHER S. KELLY, 7–43, 243967, KXUM (1849–1928) Luther Sage "Yellowstone" Kelly was a noted adventurer, soldier, Indian scout, trapper, hunter, and Western and Alaskan explorer. Operated by W. R. Chamberlin.

152. CHARLES N. MCGROARTY, 7–43, 243963, KXUN (1851–1930) Charles Neil McGroarty was chief of the Treasury Department's Loans and Currency division who supervised the sale of war bonds during the Spanish-American and World Wars. Operated by Sudden & Christenson.

153. THOMAS M. COOLEY, 7–43, 243970, KXUP (1824–1898) Thomas McIntyre Cooley was dean of the University of Michigan law school, chief justice of the Michigan supreme court, and namesake for the law school at Lansing. Operated by Pope & Talbot.

154. JOHN EVANS, 7–43, 243965, KXUQ (1814–1897) physician, railroad man, second governor of the Colorado Territory, namesake for Evanston, Illinois, and founder of Northwestern University and the University of Denver. Operated by General Steamship. Capt. George Brimble left San Francisco in October 1944 and on the morning of December 5 they were in the Molucca Strait when a Japanese plane dived on them and began firing, hitting the bridge. The plane was hit by the ship's gunners and crashed into the main mast showering the

The post-war *John Evans* after several voyages in the Pacific. The ship was mothballed in the Hudson River. On January 16, 1947, the ship was chartered by A. L. Burbank until August 28, 1949, then laid up again at Beaumont, Texas. On April 2, 1951, the ship was chartered by the Mississippi Shipping Co. then laid up in the James River on August 6, 1952. Brief service with the Military Sea Transport Service resulted in ice damage that was repaired and on November 16, 1953, Dichman, Wright & Pugh chartered the ship for one voyage then it was back to the James River in December. The ship was auctioned off for scrap and on March 14, 1961, the Northern Metals Co., of Philadelphia took possession on their winning bid of $52,532. Photograph courtesy of Bill Hultgren.

monkey bridge and funnel with debris. The plane landed in the water to starboard and its bomb exploded. The only casualty was second radio operator William J. Mauney, 19, making his first trip, who left the ship due to injuries. The ship arrived at San Francisco on January 29, 1945, from Hollandia, New Guinea.

155. SAMOVAR, 7–43, 169978, BKXQ, built for the British Ministry of War Transport. Operated by Thos. & Jno. Brocklebank.

156. WILLIAM H. ALLEN, 8–43, 244007, KYCP (1858–1936) noted and prolific architect in New Haven, Connecticut, with Richard Williams, designers of hundreds of homes and buildings throughout the nation, many on the National Register of Historic Places. Operated by Isthmian.

157. MELVILLE E. STONE, 8–43, 244026, KYCT (1848–1929) Melville Elijah Stone was the founder of the *Chicago Daily News* and general manager of the Associated Press. Operated by Norton Lilly. Capt. Lawrence J. Gallagher's ship was torpedoed on November 24, 1943, by *U-516* off Cristobal, Canal Zone, with the loss of 12 merchant crew, including Capt. Gallagher, three Armed Guard sailors, and one passenger.

158. HENRY V. ALVARADO, 8–43, 244039, KYCU (1857–1932) Henry Victor Alvarado was a judge and founder of Richmond, California. Operated by United Fruit.

159. SAMBRE, 8–43, 169638, BKXR, built for the British Ministry of War Transport. Operated by Cunard White Star.

160. H. G. BLASDELL, 8–43, 244062, KYCW (1825–1900) Henry Goode Blasdell was the first governor of Nevada. Operated by American President Lines. Roman John Wank sailed with American President Lines and in 1941 was chief mate on the company's big 16,111-ton passenger ship *President Johnson.* When they arrived at Honolulu from Hong Kong on May 27 he was 38 and had been to sea for 20 years. In July 1942 he was master of the APL Liberty ship *George Vancouver* when they left Portland, Oregon, and arrived at New York from Oran, Algeria, on June 27, 1943, a long voyage. He then took command of the *Blasdell.* The ship was en route from Southampton, England, to Utah Beach on June 29, 1944, with 436 soldiers on board when they were torpedoed by *U-984* and 76 soldiers were lost with many others injured.

161. THOMAS C. POWER, 8–43, 244082, KYCX (1839–1923) Thomas Charles Power was an engineer, surveyor, steamship company president, prominent merchant in Helena, Montana, one of the first two senators from Montana, and the namesake for Power, Montana. Operated by Mississippi Shipping.

162. WILLIAM MATSON, 8–43, 244083, KYCZ (1849–1917) founder of the Matson Navigation Co. Operated by Matson.

163. BRANDER MATTHEWS, 8–43, 244096, KYDD (1852–1929) James Brander Matthews was a writer and controversial professor of literature at Columbia. He was the first fulltime professor of dramatic literature and was instrumental in establishing theater as an area of study. Operated by Pope & Talbot.

164. WILLIAM KEITH, 8–43, 244108, KYDF (1838–1911) noted California landscape artist. Operated by Matson.

165. JOSEPH K. TOOLE, 8–43, 244105, KYDJ (1851–1929) Joseph Kemp Toole, of Missouri, was a lawyer and the first governor of Montana. Operated by AGWI Lines.

166. JEREMIAH M. DAILY, 8–43, 244117, KYDK (1869–1924) San Francisco Chamber of Commerce official and maritime industry booster. Operated by American South African. Capt. Harry Manwaring's ship was hit by a kamikaze on November 12, 1944, in San Pedro Bay, Leyte, Philippines, with the loss of four merchant crew, including Capt. Manwaring, two Armed Guard sailors, and 100 soldiers. The ship was repaired.

167. MARY PATTEN, 8–43, 244136, KYDM (1837–1861) Mary Ann Brown married shipmaster Joshua Patten and it was their custom for her to accompany him on his voyages. In June 1856, when Mary was 20, they left New York for San Francisco on the Foster & Nickerson clipper ship *Neptune's Car.* The first mate proved incompetent so Capt. Patten assumed his watches. While in the Straits of Lemaire, Capt. Patten became ill and the second mate assumed command but Mary was the better navigator and she took the ship around Cape Horn in heavy weather. With the crew's support and the obnoxious first mate in irons, they arrived at San Francisco on November 15, 1856, after 136 days. Mary is the namesake for the hospital at the Merchant Marine Academy at Kings Point. Operated by the Navy as the *Crater*-class cargo ship *Azimech* (AK-124), NHDV, commissioned on October 29, 1943.

168. HIRAM BINGHAM, 8–43, 244147, KYDO (1789–1869) noted Hawaiian missionary. Operated by Grace Line.

169. WILLIAM D. BURNHAM, 8–43, 244150, KYDU (1847–1919) Capt. William Dixon Burnham was organizer and general manager of the American-Hawaiian Steamship Co. Operated by American-Hawaiian. Capt. Emil Rosol's ship was torpedoed by *U-978* on November 23, 1944, off Cherbourg, France, with loss of ten merchant crew and eight Armed Guard sailors.

170. ANTOINE SAUGRAIN, 8–43, 244174, KYDV (1763–1820) French-born physician Dr. Antoine François Saugrain outfitted Lewis & Clark with medical supplies and was

the first physician west of the Mississippi to offer the Jenner cowpox vaccine against smallpox. Operated by AGWI Lines. Capt. Grady L. Robertson left San Francisco in September 1943 and arrived back there on November 25. Capt. Anthony Van Cromphaut's ship arrived at San Francisco on March 25, 1944, from Milne Bay, New Guinea. His ship was torpedoed on December 5, 1944, by Japanese aircraft while en route from Humboldt Bay, New Guinea, to Leyte, Philippines, in convoy. There were no reported casualties.

171. STEPHEN W. KEARNY, 8–43, 244182, KYDX (1794–1848) Stephen Walls Kearny was a noted Mexican War, frontier, and California Army colonel. Operated by De La Rama.

172. JAMES ROWAN, 8–43, 244191, KYDY, the first American sea captain to sail through The Straits on May 24, 1799, into San Franciso Bay as master of the ship *Eliza*. Operated by the Navy as the *Crater*-class cargo ship *Allioth* (AK-109), NTNM, commissioned on October 25, 1943.

173. RICHARD MOCZKOWSKI, 8–43, 244193, KYEC (1905–1942) chief mate lost on the *Stephen Hopkins*, sunk in an engagement with the German raider *Stier* and the tender *Tannenfels* on September 27, 1942, in the South Atlantic. Operated by General Steamship.

174. JOHN COLTER, 9–43, 244213, KYKK (1775–1813) explorer and member of the Lewis & Clark expedition. Operated by Norton Lilly.

175. MARY M. DODGE, 9–43, 244214, KYKM (1831–1905) Mary Elizabeth Mapes married attorney William Dodge in 1851 and became a widow seven years later. She began writing and became one of the earliest journalists in America then succeeded as a noted author of children's books and edited a magazine. Operated by South Atlantic.

176. EMILE BERLINER, 9–43, 244231, KYKN (1851–1929) inventor of a carbon microphone, gramophone, and co-inventor of the helicopter. Operated by United Fruit.

177. CHARLES G. COUTANT, 9–43, 244252, KYKP (1840–1913) Charles Griffin Coutant was the Wyoming state librarian and archivist at Cheyenne and the first official historian of the state. Operated by Polarus.

178. JOHN W. HOYT, 9–43, 244280, KYKQ (1831–1912) Dr. John Wesley Hoyt was a lawyer, physician, manager of the Wisconsin State Agricultural Society, and third governor of the Wyoming Territory. Operated by Luckenbach.

179. WAYNE MACVEAGH, 9–43, 244281, KYKT (1833–1917) Isaac Wayne MacVeagh was a Civil War soldier and 36th U.S. Attorney General. Operated by United Fruit.

180. SAMWASH, 9–43, 169770, MYLC, built for the British Ministry of War Transport. Operated by Andrew Weir & Co.

181. CHUNG SHAN, 9–43, variation of Zhongshan, any number of geographical features and a pseudonym for Sun Yat-sen. Operated under the Chinese flag.

182. JEREMIAH M. RUSK, 9–43, 244368, KYKW (1830–1893) Jeremiah McLain Rusk was a Wisconsin congressman and governor, Secretary of Agriculture. Operated by American President Lines.

183. BENJAMIN H. BREWSTER, 9–43, 244307, KYKX (1816–1888) Benjamin Harris Brewster was a U.S. Attorney General. Operated by Union Sulphur.

184. CHARLES E. SMITH, 9–43, 244318, KYNL (1842–1908) Charles Emory Smith was minister to Russia during a famine in 1890–92 and distributed $750,000 worth of aid from five ships. He also served as Postmaster General and developed the Rural Free Delivery mail service, RFD. Operated by Matson.

185. SAMORE, 9–43, 169838, MYLG, built for the British Ministry of War Transport. Operated by Ellerman's Wilson Line as the *Samdel*.

186. LOUIS A. SENGTELLER, 9–43, 244351, KYOT (1845–1889) Louis Alexander

Sengteller was a U.S. Coast & Geodetic Survey assistant who commanded the schooner *Yukon* in Pacific Coast surveys. Operated by Alaska Packers.

187. DONALD M. DICKINSON, 9–43, 244349, KTUP (1846–1917) Donald McDonald Dickinson was a lawyer, a Michigan Democratic party leader, and Postmaster General. Operated by Matson.

188. AUGUSTUS THOMAS, 9–43, 244371, KTQU (1857–1934) editor of the *Kansas City Mirror* turned playwright. He wrote the play *The Copperhead* in 1918, bringing fame to Lionel Barrymore. Operated by Coastwise. Capt. Alfred A. Pedersen's ship was hit by a Japanese bomber while at anchor in San Pedro Bay, Philippines, on October 24, 1944, and damaged beyond further use. There were no reported fatalities. Capt. Pedersen's next command was the Coastwise Liberty ship *Winfield S. Stratton*, departing from Los Angeles in January 1945.

189. GEORGE STERLING, 9–43, 244379, KTUV (1869–1926) noted California playwright and poet. Operated by Waterman.

190. WILLIAM H. MOODY, 9–43, 244393, KTVB (1853–1917) William Henry Moody was a Massachusetts congressman, Secretary of the Navy, Attorney General, and Supreme Court justice. Operated by Norton Lilly.

191. HENRY C. PAYNE, 9–43, 244396, KTVC (1843–1904) Henry Clay Payne was Postmaster General who died in office. Operated by American-Hawaiian.

192. GEORGE VON L. MEYER, 10–43, 244404, KTVD (1858–1918) George von Lengerke Meyer was Postmaster General and Secretary of the Navy. Operated by Seas Shipping.

193. JAMES D. PHELAN, 10–43, 244438, KTVG (1861–1930) James Duval Phelan was mayor of San Francisco, first president of the League of California Cities, and a California senator. Operated by American President Lines.

194. OTTO MEARS, 10–43, 244427, KTVI (1840–1931) celebrated Southwest Colorado pioneer and builder of toll roads and railroads. Operated by Matson.

195. FRANK NORRIS, 10–43, 244437, KTVM (1870–1902) Benjamin Franklin "Frank" Norris, Jr., was a writer and war correspondent noted for writing *The Octopus: A California Story*. Operated by Burns.

196. FRANCIS M. SMITH, 10–43, 244447, KTVN (1846–1931) Francis Marion Smith, of Wisconsin, came West to mine and discovered ulexite near Marietta, Nevada, and, with his brother Julius, created a borax empire. He was known as "Borax Smith" and the "Borax King" of miners in Nevada and California. They originated hauling huge loads of borax across 160 miles of desert in 30-ton loads using three huge wagons and 24 mules. Smith was also instrumental in developing the San Francisco Bay Area. Operated by Mississippi Shipping.

197. FRANK A. MUNSEY, 10–43, 244474, KTVS (1854–1925) Frank Andrew Munsey was a New York author and newspaper and magazine publisher who used high-speed presses and cheap paper to mass produce ten cent "pulp" magazines. Namesake for Munsey Park in New York. Operated by James Griffiths.

198. FREDERIC A. EILERS, 10–43, 244479, KVTV (1839–1917) German-born Frederic Anton Eilers came to America in 1859, became a miner and metallurgist, and founded the Colorado Smelting Company. He then consolidated other firms into the large American Smelting & Refining Co. Operated by United States Lines.

199. WILLIAM S. CLARK, 10–43, 244491, KTVX (1826–1886) William Smith Clark was a chemist, botanist, zoologist, commander of the 21st Massachusetts Infantry, an agricultural education innovator, and president of the Massachusetts Agricultural College. He went to Japan in 1876 and established the Sapporo Agricultural College on Hokkaido. Operated by American President Lines.

200. SAMUEL W. WILLISTON, 10–43, 244495, KTVY (1851–1918) Samuel Wendell Williston was a noted paleontologist and Yale professor who theorized about the origins of flight in birds and also studied flies. Operated by AGWI Lines.

201. EDGAR W. NYE, 10–43, 244503, KTVZ (1850–1896) Edgar Wilson "Bill" Nye was a lawyer, writer, humorist, postmaster at Laramie, Wyoming, and founder and editor of the *Laramie Boomerang*. Operated by General Steamship.

202. FRANK C. EMERSON, 10–43, 244504, KTWE (1882–1931) Frank Collins Emerson was the State Engineer of Wyoming and the 15th governor. Operated by Smith & Johnson.

203. JOHN W. FOSTER, 10–43, 244534, KTWF (1836–1917) John Watson Foster, of Indiana, was a Union colonel, editor of the *Evansville Daily Journal*, minister to Mexico, and Secretary of State. Operated by Interocean.

204. NORMAN HAPGOOD, 10–43, 244535, KTWG (1868–1937) lawyer, writer, editor of *Collier's Weekly*, and ambassador to Denmark. Operated by Sudden & Christenson.

205. BERNARDO O'HIGGINS, 10–43, 244552, KTWI (1778–1842) Bernardo O'Higgins Riquelme was instrumental in freeing Chile from Spanish rule. Operated by American President Lines.

206. NORMAN E. MACK, 10–43, 244560, KTWO (1858–1932) Norman Edward Mack published the *Buffalo Daily Times* and was chairman of the Democratic National Committee. Operated by Isthmian.

207. HENRY H. BLOOD, 10–43, 244555, KTWQ (1872–1944) Henry Hooper Blood was governor of Utah. Operated by A. L. Burbank.

208. JOHN SWETT, 10–43, 244582, KTWV (1830–1913) considered the father of California public schools. Operated by Burns. On February 23, 1945, the ship was anchored at Mindoro, Philippines, when an Army watercraft came alongside to pick up passengers going ashore. Third mate Robert A. Constantine got in and the boat proceeded to another Liberty ship, lying in ballast, to embark other passengers. Unexpectedly, the ship's engine began turning over forcing the boat toward the thrashing propeller as the ship gained headway. As passengers scrambled to get off the swamping boat, Constantine made heroic efforts that saved several lives. He was awarded the Merchant Marine Distinguished Service medal.

209. VERNON L. PARRINGTON, 10–43, 244500, KUOS (1871–1929) Vernon Louis Parrington was a pioneering University of Oklahoma football coach, a University of Washington history professor, and an author. Operated by American South African.

210. GEORGE K. FITCH, 10–43, 244591, KUOU (1826–1906) George Kenyon Fitch was co-owner of the *San Francisco Call* and *Bulletin*, served as California State Printer, and was a noted civic reformer. Operated by American-Hawaiian.

211. FRANCIS A. WARDWELL, 10–43, 244618, KUOV (1844–1928) Francis Page, of Penobscot, Maine, was adopted by Lorenzo and Marjorie Wardwell. Lorenzo was editor of the *Pembina Pioneer Express* in Pembina, North Dakota. Francis Asbury Wardwell was the first public school teacher in North Dakota and a newspaper publisher and editor. Operated by American President Lines.

212. KATE DOUGLAS WIGGIN, 10–43, 244623, KUOX (1856–1923) Kate Douglas Smith's mother moved from Philadelphia to California where Kate got involved with early education and became a teacher who established the first free kindergarten in San Francisco. In 1881 she married San Francisco lawyer Samuel B. Wiggin and was then obliged to quit her job. She took up writing as a young adult author and wrote *Rebecca of Sunnybrook Farm*. Operated by Interocean.

213. DAVID HEWES, 11–43, 244630, KUOY (1821–1915) founder of the Steam Paddy

Co. in San Francisco, sold steam shovels, and built the first steam locomotive on the Pacific Coast. He provided two gold spikes used in the ceremony connecting the Central Pacific and Union Pacific railroads at Promontory Summit, Utah Territory. Operated by American South African.

214. FERDINAND A. SILCOX, 11–43, 244631, KUTY (1882–1939) Ferdinand Augustus Silcox was a U.S. Forest Service chief who oversaw the Civilian Conservation Corps (CCC) and Works Progress Administration (WPA) projects in the national forests. Operated by Pope & Talbot.

215. JAMES KING, 11–43, 244652, KUUR (1822–1856) James King, born in the District of Columbia, was the son of William King, of Ireland. James called himself "James King of William" to distinguish himself and in 1843 married Charlotte Libbey. In 1848 he set out for California, made some money, and in 1851 sent for his wife and children. James went into banking, founded the *San Francisco Bulletin*. And on May 14, 1856, was murdered by rival newsman James P. Casey. The crime resulted in the second San Francisco Vigilence Committee being convened. King was an early member of the California Journalism Hall of Fame. Operated by Mississippi Shipping.

216. SARA TEASDALE, 11–43, 244654, KUUW (1884–1933) Sara Trevor Teasdale, of St. Louis, was a noted lyrical poet in poor health who married Ernst Filsinger in 1914. They divorced in 1929 and she died by her own hand on January 29, 1933, in New York. Operated by American President Lines.

217. R. F. PECKHAM, 11–43, 244688, KUXQ (1838–1909) Robert Francis Peckham was a noted California judge. Operated by United States Lines.

218. PETER TRIMBLE ROWE, 11–43, 244687, KUXS (1856–1942) first bishop of the Episcopal Diocese of Alaska. Operated by J. H. Winchester.

219. KEITH VAWTER, 11–43, 244702, KUXW (1872–1937) Des Moines, Iowa, bookseller who engaged lecturers for the Des Moines Lyceum and in 1899 founded the Standard Lecture Bureau. In 1901 he purchased a one-third interest in the Redpath Lyceum Bureau with Roy J. Ellison and they established the Standard Redpath Chautauqua and originated the idea of traveling lectures and performances held in tents and known as Circuit Chautauquas. Operated by Interocean.

220. JAMES G. MAGUIRE, 11–43, 244695, KUZB (1853–1920) James George Maguire was a California congressman. Operated by Burns.

221. ROBERT LOUIS STEVENSON, 11–43, 244715, KUZE (1850–1894) author of *Treasure Island* and *The Strange Case of Dr. Jekyll and Mr. Hyde*. Operated by American South African.

222. FRANCISCO M. QUINONES, 11–43, 244711, KUZK (1830–1908) Francisco Mariano Quiñones was an abolitionist who advocated for Puerto Rican independence. Operated by South Atlantic.

223. FERDINAND WESTDAHL, 11–43, 244736, KUZO (1843–1919) longtime Coast & Geodetic Survey hydrographic engineer on the Pacific Coast. Operated by W. R. Chamberlin.

224. WILLIAM F. EMPEY, 11–43, 244743, KUZP (1853–1904) William Fletcher Empey was the son of Australians Charles and Mary Empey who came to the United States in 1866 from New South Wales. Dad and son worked at the *Bulletin* newspaper in 1870. William became a citizen on November 2, 1876, and became the prominent shipping news publisher of *The Guide*. Operated by American-Hawaiian.

225. JOHN L. STODDARD, 11–43, 244752, KUZX (1850–1931) John Lawson Stoddard was a popular song and travel writer who produced travelogues. Operated by Burns.

226. FRANK H. DODD, 11–43, 244762, KUZY (1844–1916) publisher Frank Howard Dodd partnered with Edward S. Mead and formed Dodd, Mead & Co., book publishers. Dodd was president of the American Publishers Association. Operated by Matson.

227. MARY WALKER, 11–43, 244763, KVAB (1832–1919) Mary Edwards Walker was a physician who married Albert Miller. She was a civilian Army surgeon with the 52nd Ohio during the Civil War and became a prisoner of war, subsequently becoming the only female Medal of Honor recipient. She was also a social activist who wore men's clothing. Operated by Weyerhaeuser.

228. J. MAURICE THOMPSON, 11–43, 244770, KVAG (1844–1901) James Maurice Thompson was a lawyer and novelist. Operated by American President Lines.

229. WALTER WILLIAMS, 11–43, 244773, KVAH (1864–1935) professor at the University of Missouri who founded the first school of journalism. Operated by Black Diamond.

230. MARY A. LIVERMORE, 11–43, 244793, KVDX (1820–1905) Mary Ashton Rice was a teacher and abolitionist who married Daniel P. Livermore in 1845. She was a journalist and suffragist and became interested in public health. Operated by Isthmian. Capt. James A. Stewart's ship was hit by a kamikaze on May 27, 1945, at Okinawa with the loss of seven merchant crew, including Capt. Stewart, and four Armed Guard sailors. The ship was repaired.

231. SEAMAN A. KNAPP, 11–43, 244806, KVDQ (1833–1911) Seaman Asabel Knapp was a physician from Vinton, Iowa, and an agricultural pioneer who was instrumental in forming agricultural experimental stations throughout the country, served as second president of the Iowa Agricultural College, and founded Vinton, Louisiana. Operated by American South African.

232. JAMES ROLPH, 12–43, 244821, KVDO (1869–1934) James "Sunny Jim" Rolph was president of the Rolph Navigation & Coal Co., mayor of San Francisco, and governor of California. Operated by AGWI Lines.

233. ANTONIN DVORAK, 12–43, 244826, KVIY (1841–1904) Antonin Leopold Dvořák was a noted Czech symphony composer. Operated by Seas Shipping.

234. ALBERT A. ROBINSON, 12–43, 244840, KVIZ (1844–1918) Albert Alonzo Robinson was a civil engineer who supervised about 5,000 miles of track-building for the Atchison, Topeka & Santa Fe Railway, became vice president and general manager of the company, and later was president of the Mexican Central Railway. Operated by Norton Lilly.

235. RICHARD B. MOORE, 12–43, 244847, KVJA (1871–1931) Richard Bishop Moore was a chemistry professor and Dean of Science at Perdue who proposed the use of helium for airships and supervised experiments during the Great War. Operated by De La Rama.

236. ALEXANDER WILSON, 12–43, 244853, KVJF (1766–1813) Scots-born poet and unwelcome labor activist who fled to America in 1794, became a teacher and then a noted ornithologist, bird illustrator, and namesake for several species. Operated by United States Lines.

237. JOSE C. BARBOSA, 12–43, 244879, KVJG (1857–1921) José Celso Barbosa was the first Puerto Rican to become a physician in the United States, a political leader at home, and an advocate for Puerto Rican statehood. Operated by Pope & Talbot.

238. ALEXANDER MITCHELL, 12–43, 244885, KVJI (1817–1887) Scotsman who came to the United States in 1839 and went into banking at Milwaukee, Wisconsin. He founded the Marine Bank there, became president of the Chicago, Milwaukee & St. Paul Railway, and then a Wisconsin congressman. Operated by J. H. Winchester.

239. J. C. OSGOOD, 12–43, 244886, KVJO (1851–1926) John Cleveland Osgood was a clerk for a commission house in New York. He moved to Iowa and worked as a cashier for a

bank then a fuel company. In 1882 he was sent to Colorado to look for coal for a railroad. Five years later he set out on his own and organized the Colorado Fuel & Iron Co. He founded Redstone, Colorado, as a company town, and, after a series of strikes, built a hospital and school for workers. Operated by Matson.

240. FRANK H. EVERS, 12–43, 244903, KVIL (1867–1943) Frank Henry Evers was the English-born principal surveyor for the American Bureau of Shipping at the San Francisco office at 725 Castro St. He lived with his wife Anne Mary at 24 17th Ave. and died from a heart attack on October 11, 1943. Operated by American President Lines.

241. JAMES OLIVER CURWOOD, 12–43, 244905, KVJQ (1878–1927) Michigan writer known for his action-adventure stories. Operated by United States Lines.

242. EDWARD G. ACHESON, 12–43, 244914, KVJT (1856–1931) Edward Goodrich Acheson was a chemist who worked for Thomas Edison. He left Edison's lab in 1884 and invented the Acheson Process to make silicon carbide, which he called carborundum. Operated by Union Sulphur.

243. FRANCIS WILSON, 12–43, 244921, KVJU (1854–1935) probably the popular actor, comedian, and playwright who was the first Actors' Equity Association president and founder of the Francis Wilson Playhouse in Clearwater, Florida. Operated by American South African.

244. CLAUS SPRECKELS, 12–43, 244926, KVKA (1828–1908) German-born Adolph Claus J. Spreckels came to New York in April 1872, lived at 4 Bleeker St. in New York, and sold liquor. On October 20, 1892, he became a citizen, and went on to become a sugar magnate in Hawaii and California. Operated by Lykes.

245. DAVID LUBIN, 12–43, 244933, KVLX (1849–1919) Polish-born California agriculture pioneer who founded the International Institute of Agriculture in Rome in 1908. Operated by Wilmore.

246. FRANK J. SPRAGUE, 12–43, 244943, KVNH (1857–1934) Frank Julian Sprague was a naval officer who worked on shipboard electrical problems and invented and pioneered the use of electric motors for traction in trolley cars and elevators. Operated by American President Lines.

247. JEAN P. CHOUTEAU, 12–43, 244955, KVNL (1758–1849) French-born Jean Pierre Chouteau was a St. Louis, Missouri, pioneer fur trader and merchant. In 1804 he became the U.S. Agent for Indian Affairs west of the Mississippi. Operated by Grace Line.

248. JULIA L. DUMONT, 12–43, 244956, KVNM (1794–1857) Julia Louisa Corey married John Dumont in August 1812 in New York and they moved to Ohio then Indiana where she became a teacher and "the earliest female writer in the West." Operated by De La Rama.

249. ROBERT G. COUSINS, 12–43, 244970, KVNN (1859–1933) Robert Gordon Cousins was a long-time Iowa congressman. Operated by Hammond.

250. GEORGE B. PORTER, 12–43, 244969, KVSW (1791–1834) George Bryan Porter was an Army officer in the War of 1812, a lawyer, state representative in Pennsylvania, and governor of the Michigan Territory where he died of cholera. Operated by Pope & Talbot.

251. WILLIAM FORD NICHOLS, 1–44, 244994, KVSY (1849–1924) noted Episcopal bishop in California. Operated by United States Lines.

252. LILLIAN WALD, 1–44, 244991, KVSZ (1867–1940) Lillian D. Wald was born in Cincinnati, Ohio, and became a New York public health nurse and child welfare and social activist who founded the Visiting Nurse Service and the Henry Street Settlement House at 265 Henry St. In 1919 she went to the International Red Cross conference in France as a representative of the Dept. of Labor. Operated by Weyerhaeuser.

253. GEORGE LUKS, 1–44, 245006, KVTA (1867–1933) George Benjamin Luks was a Pennsylvania realist artist and illustrator of the urban Ashcan School of art. Operated by American President Lines.

254. WILLIAM VAUGHN MOODY, 1–44, 245017, KVTC (1869–1910) dramatist and author of *The Great Divide*. Operated by Alcoa.

255. OLIVER KELLEY, 1–44, 245018, KVTD (1826–1913) Oliver Hudson Kelley, of Boston, was a Minnesota frontier farmer who founded the Order of Patrons of Husbandry and was one of seven cofounders of the National Grange. Operated by Pope & Talbot.

256. ABRAM S. HEWITT, 1–44, 245014, KVTE (1822–1903) Abram Stevens Hewitt was a New York congressman and is considered the father of the New York City subway system. Operated by Black Diamond.

257. WILLIAM PEFFER, 1–44, 245041, KVTG (1831–1912) William Alfred Peffer was a Kansas senator. Operated by A. L. Burbank.

258. ADA REHAN, 1–44, 245048, KVTH (1859–1916) stage name of wildly acclaimed, Irish-born Shakespearean actress Delia Crehan. Operated by Pope & Talbot. Capt. Harold B. Ellis left San Francisco on August 16, 1945, for Chile via New Orleans for a load of nitrate. They went to Egypt, where the nitrate was discharged, then to Tripoli. At Tripoli Capt. Ellis was hospitalized and the ship continued on to Knorramshar, Iran, where Capt. Frank H. Haas came aboard as master. While there, he became ill and while he was off the ship Theresa Niedermulbicher, 41, of Poland, Anna V. Sedrakian, 36, of Iran, Mrs. Zinat Vashvarveh, 28, and her son Rutsam, 7, of Iran, a baboon named Chippy, and a "large assortment of luggage" somehow got aboard the ship. Capt. Haas arrived aboard only two hours before the ship was scheduled to sail for Ceylon but for some reason the stowaways weren't kicked off the ship and Capt Haas was unsuccessful at landing them in other ports. At some point, Chippy bit Capt. Haas on the hand and was summarily shot. At Shanghai, chief mate Lampton H. Elam became ill and after that nine crew members paid off or deserted the ship. Native seamen were hired on and when the ship arrived at New York they were landed at Ellis Island along with the stowaways. The ship arrived at Pier H in Jersey City on July 5, 1946, and a Coast Guard investigation was promptly convened.

259. URIAH M. ROSE, 1–44, 245057, KVTK (1834–1913) Uriah Milton Rose was a noted Arkansas lawyer and president of the American Bar Association. Operated by American President Lines.

260. JOHN W. BURGESS, 1–44, 245061, KVTL (1844–1931) John William Burgess was an influential professor of political science at Columbia University. Operated by South Atlantic.

261. MOSES G. FARMER, 1–44, 245067, KVTM (1820–1893) Moses Gerrish Farmer, of New Hampshire, was a pioneer telegraph operator, electrical engineer, and light bulb inventor who contributed to many forms of electrical gadgets and systems. Operated by Alaska Steamship.

262. ALFRED C. TRUE, 1–44, 245076, KVTP (1853–1929) Dr. Alfred Charles True was a director of the Dept. of Agriculture Office of Experiment Stations in 1915 that investigated irrigation, drainage, nutrition, and agricultural education. Operated by Interocean.

263. WILLIAM B. LEEDS, 1–44, 245089, KVTQ (1861–1908) William Bateman Leeds, of Richmond, Indiana, was a nursery worker who went to work for the Pennsylvania Railroad in 1883 and on August 16th of that year he married Jeanette I. Gaar, 21. Jeanette's father, John M. Gaar, 60, was the treasurer of Gaar, Scott & Co., manufacturers of threshing machines and steam engines. John, his wife Julia, and the family lived at 29 N. 11th St. and the newlyweds lived at 224 N. 11th. When her father died in 1890 Jeanette inherited a con-

siderable portion of his estate. By then William was the superintendent of the Richmond Div. of the Pittsburgh, Cincinnati, Chicago & St. Louis Railway Co. William formed a partnership with Daniel G. Reid, the Teller at the Second National Bank, and the two bought an interest in tin-plating business in Richmond and renamed it the Elliott & Reid Co., with Reid as president. In 1894 William quit the railroad, grew the business, and soon became known as the "Tin-Plate King" as president of the American Tin Plate Co. In late September 1900 he reportedly paid Jeanette $1 million for a divorce and on August 3, 1900, he wed the previously married Nonnie May Stewart Worthington, 23. The next year his business was purchased by U.S. Steel for about $40 million and Leeds went back to the railroad business but not as a depot agent. Operated by American-Hawaiian.

264. FRANCISCO MORAZAN, 1–44, 245100, KVTR (1792–1842) military man from Honduras who was the first Central American president and politician who tried to unite Central America. Operated by Isthmian.

265. WILLIAM D. BOYCE, 1–44, 245117, KVTS (1858–1929) William Dickson "W.D." Boyce was a Chicago publisher, journalist, and explorer who founded the Boy Scouts of America. Operated by Pacific-Atlantic.

266. W. B. RODGERS, 1–44, 245116, KVTU (1845–1914) Capt. William Berlean Rodgers, of Pittsburgh, founded the Rodgers Sand Co., ran boats, and was instrumental in improving waterways and waterborne commerce on the Ohio and Allegheny Rives. He advocated strongly for the Isthmian Canal and entertained prominent guests on his yacht *Troubador.* Son William, Jr. was secretary of the company. Operated by United States Lines.

267. CARL B. EIELSON, 1–44, 245122, KWCZ (1897–1929) Carl Benjamin "Ben" Eielson, of North Dakota, was an Army Air Service pilot, barnstormer, lawyer, schoolteacher in Alaska, and pioneer mail carrier. In 1928, with explorer Hubert Wilkins aboard as a passengerr, he was the first pilot to fly over the Arctic Ocean. He went on to found Alaska Airways and was lost in a crash with mechanic Earl Borland on November 9, 1929, while attempting to rescue passengers from the Swenson Fur Trading Co.'s 298-ton motor freighter *Nanuk,* trapped in ice in Siberia. He is the namesake for Eielson Air Force Base outside of Fairbanks, Alaska. Operated by Matson.

268. ALICE H. RICE, 2–44, 245147, KWDB (1870–1942) Alice Caldwell Hegan was a popular novelist who married Cale Young Rice. Operated by Coastwise (Pacific Far East) Line.

269. ELWOOD HAYNES, 2–44, 245150, KWDD (1857–1925) invented stainless steel and the first motorized vehicle. Operated by American-Hawaiian.

270. NATHAN S. DAVIS, 2–44, 245152, KWDE (1817–1904) Nathan Smith Davis was a physician and member of the New York Medical Society who founded the American Medical Association in 1847. Operated by United States Lines.

271. MORGAN ROBERTSON, 2–44, 245156, KWDL (1861–1915) Morgan Andrew Robertson was a licensed deck officer, jeweler, and author who wrote a book in 1898 about a ship named *Titan,* which was an eerie premonition of the *Titanic* disaster. Operated by General Steamship.

272. JOHN HOPE, 2–44, 245160, KWDN (1868–1936) African-American professor of classics at Atlanta Baptist College and president of Atlanta University. Operated by Alaska Steamship.

273. DANIEL G. REID, 2–44, 245164, KWDS (1858–1925) Daniel Gray Reid was cofounder and president, with William B. Leeds, of the American Tin Plate Co. He was a director of U.S. Steel after their company was bought out, and a railroad executive who endowed Reid Hospital in Richmond, Indiana. Operated by McCormick.

274. CORNELIUS VANDERBILT, 2–44, 245171, KWDV (1794–1877) shipping and railroad magnate. Operated by Alaska Steamship.

275. JAMES DEVEREUX, 2–44, 245179, KWDW (1766–1846) Boston sea captain considered to be the first American to trade with Japan as master of the ship *Franklin*. Operated by Pacific-Atlantic.

276. JOHN H. THOMAS, 2–44, 245180, KWDY (1869–1943) senior vice president of the International Mercantile Marine who was the Director of Shipping in New York Harbor during World War I for the Shipping Control Committee. Operated by United States Lines.

277. PERCY E. FOXWORTH, 2–44, 245187, KWDZ (1906–1943) in 1943, Percy Eldridge "Sam" Foxworth was chief of the Federal Bureau of Investigation's Special Intelligence Service. During the North Africa campaign, the Army captured Charles Bedaux, a French-born American millionaire who was known to have Nazi associates. Gen. Dwight D. Eisenhower contacted the FBI who detailed Foxworth and fellow agent Harold D. Haberfield to go to North Africa and interview Bedaux. The two agents boarded a C-54 military aircraft with 33 others but on January 15 the plane crashed near Paramaribo, Surinam. Bedaux later took his own life. Operated by Alcoa.

278. CARL G. BARTH, 2–44, 245204, KWEB (1860–1939) Norwegian-born Carl Georg Lange Barth was a mathematician and mechanical engineer. In 1899, Bethlehem Steel's efficiency expert, Frederick W. Taylor, hired Barth and the two collaborated on developing the speed-and-feed calculating slide rule, for which they received a patent in 1904. Operated by Olympic.

279. EDWIN C. MUSICK, 2–44, 245205, KWEC (1894–1938) Edwin Charles Musick was the chief pilot for Pan American World Airways who died with five others, including Cecil G. Sellers, on January 11, 1938, when the *Samoan Clipper* exploded while preparing for an emergency landing at Pago Pago. Operated by Grace Line.

280. SARA BACHE, 2–44, 245212, KEWJ (1744–1808) Sarah "Sally" Franklin was born to Benjamin Franklin and Deborah Read. In 1767 she married Richard Bache. Her mother

Gun captain Bill Tubbs (far right) standing in front of his 5″/38 cal. stern gun on the *Hans Heg* with part of his crew. 5″/38 means the bore of the gun is 5 inches and the barrel length is 38 times the diameter of the bore, or 160 inches. Photograph courtesy of Jim Harris, *Hans Heg* Armed Guard.

died in 1774 when her father was in France and when returned the next year, Sarah took up the role of hostess at the family home, working hard during the American Revolution to support the cause. Operated by Oliver J. Olson.

281. HANS HEG, 2–44, 245216, KWLX (1829–1863) Norwegian-born Hans Christian Heg was a 49er, Wisconsin politician, abolitionist, and colonel of the 15th Wisconsin "Scandinavian" regiment who was lost at Chickamauga on September 19, 1863. Operated by James Griffiths.

282. FRANZ SIGEL, 2–44, 245215, KWMA (1824–1902) German-born soldier, Union general, New York politician, newspaperman, and namesake for Sigel, Pennsylvania, and Sigel Township, Minnesota. Operated by Interocean.

283. ARTHUR A. PENN, 2–44, 245232, KWME (1875–1941) London-born Arthur Ambrose Penn was a musical composer employed by prominent sheet music publisher Marcus Witmark, in business as M. Witmark & Sons, 144 W. 37th St., New York. He is best known for his 1919 song "Smilin' Through." In 1940 Art lived with his wife Eleanor, 64, at 58 Berkeley Ave. in New London, Connecticut. Operated by Alaska Steamship.

284. ALLEN JOHNSON, 2–44, 245232, KWMH (1870–1931) noted professor of history at Yale and a prolific author. Operated by Alaska Packers.

285. GEORGE A. POPE, 2–44, 245233, KWMJ (1864–1942) son of Andrew Jackson Pope, California Gold Rush lumberman and cofounder of Pope & Talbot. Operated by Pope & Talbot.

286. JOSEPH J. KINYOUN, 2–44, 245267, KWMN (1860–1919) Joseph James Kinyoun was a physician who founded the U.S. Hygenic Laboratory, later the National Institutes of Health. Operated by Weyerhaeuser.

287. JUAN PABLO DUARTE, 2–44, 245282, KWMQ (1813–1876) Juan Pablo Duarte y Diez was the founder of the Dominican Republic. Operated by Sudden & Christenson.

288. JOHN F. SHAFROTH, 3–44, 245281, KWMS (1854–1922) John Franklin Shafroth was a Colorado congressman and governor. Operated by Alaska Packers.

289. CLEVELAND FORBES, 3–44, 245277, KWMW (c. 1810–1857) master of the Pacific Mail Steamship Co.

John O. Pettersen, the 66-year-old Norwegian chief mate on the *Hans Heg* under Capt. Arne Monson. A typical old-salt merchantman, Pettersen had 36 years at sea when he signed on the brand-new Liberty ship at San Francisco in February 1944. Photograph courtesy of Jim Harris, *Hans Heg* Armed Guard.

steamship *California*, the first steamer to sail in the Pacific Ocean and the first steamer to reach San Francisco, on February 28, 1849. Operated by Interocean.

290. SIDNEY H. SHORT, 3–44, 245291, KWMX (1858–1902) Sidney Howe Short, of Cleveland, Ohio, was an electrical engineer and inventor of many electrical products for communication systems and railway transportation. He owned the Short Electric Railway Company and he and his wife Mary Frank had a residence a 4 Whitehall Ct. in Middlesex, England, where he died on October 21, 1902. Operated by Coastwise (Pacific Far East) Line.

291. E. A. BRYAN, 3–44, 245304, KWPB (1855–1941) Enoch Albert Bryan was the president of Vincennes University in Indiana and of Washington State College. Operated by Oliver J. Olson. Capt. John L. M. Henrikson's ship burned on July 17, 1944, at the Port Chicago Naval Magazine in California with the loss of all aboard. Capt. Henrikson was away at the time. Army investigators concluded that 3.75 million pounds of high explosives detonated killing 325 people, injuring 392, and causing massive property damage within a 1,000 foot radius. In January 1945 Capt. Henrikson was skipper of the Olson Liberty ship *Nancy Hanks*.

292. HENRY M. STEPHENS, 3–44, 245326, KWNV (1857–1919) Henry Morse Stephens was a professor of history and founder of the University of California Extension Service. Operated by Alaska Transportation.

293. WILLET M. HAYS, 3–44, 245328, KWPA (1859–1928) Willet Martin Hays was a plant breeder in Iowa and North Dakota and Assistant Secretary of Agriculture. Operated by Hammond.

294. EDWARD E. HALE, 3–44, 245340, KWNT (1822–1909) Edward Everett Hale was an ancestor of Nathan Hale and an author, historian, and Unitarian minister. In 1903 he became Chaplain of the Senate. Operated by General Steamship.

295. CHARLES JOHN SEGHERS, 3–44, 245352, KWNR (1839–1886) Belgian Jesuit and bishop of Victoria Island who established the Alaska mission and was appointed Archbishop of Portland, Oregon. Operated by Weyerhaeuser.

296. WILLIAM J. GRAY, 3–44, 245349, KWQS (1850–1933) William James Gray was a native of New York and Pacific Coast towboat pioneer. In 1907 he was superintendent of the Shipowners' & Merchants' Tugboat Co., Pier 15, San Francisco, when he was sent to Camden, New Jersey, to supervise the construction of two new, big, steel steam tugs, *Hercules* and *Goliah*, the company was having built at the John H. Dialogue yard. Capt. Daniel C. Thomsen, skipper of the company's tug *Sea Rover*, captained the *Hercules* and towed the *Goliah* around the Horn. In 1930 Gray lived with his wife Selina Jane, 63, and Chinese cook Jack Lew, 57, in a $210/mo. flat in the Stanford Court Apartments at 901 California St., San Francisco. He dabbled in real estate and died there on August 28, 1933, from heart disease at 83 years, 4 months, and 28 days. The *Hercules* can be seen today at the San Francisco Maritime Historical Park's Hyde St. Pier. Operated by Interocean.

297. AMERIGO VESPUCCI, 3–44, 245351, KWXM (1454–1512) Italian explorer, navigator, map maker, and describer of the New World. Namesake for America. Operated by W. R. Chamberlin.

298. GEORGE MIDDLEMAS, 3–44, 245372, KXMI (1829–1903) Nova Scotia native who ran mail steamers on Puget Sound and San Francisco Bay and operated the first West Coast marine railway at Oakland, California. Operated by Oliver J. Olson.

299. ROBERT D. CAREY, 3–44, 245392, KXMG (1878–1937) Robert Davis Carey was a Wyoming senator and governor. Operated by Shepard.

300. H. WEIR COOK, 3–44, 245400, KYPC (1892–1943) Harvey Weir Cook was an ace fighter pilot in Capt. Eddie Rickenbacker's squadron in World War I and an early air mail delivery pilot. Operated by Burns.

301. LOUIS WEULE, 3–44, 245417, KXMF (1841–1927) Louis, with sons Ernest L. and Arthur F. H., were famous chronometer, nautical instrument, and watchmakers in San Francisco as the Louis Weule Co. at 106 Steuart St., close to the waterfront. Louis was a native of Hanover, Germany, who came to America in 1865 and in 1920 lived at 337 Capp St. with his wife Minna, 66. Louis died from pneumonia on November 17, 1927, two days shy of his 86th birthday. Operated by Sudden & Christenson.

302. JOSE M. MORELOS, 3–44, 245423, KXMA (1765–1815) José María Teclo Morelos y Pavón was a priest in the Mexican War of Independence who was captured and shot. Operated by Pope & Talbot.

303. BENJAMIN WATERHOUSE, 3–44, 245446, KWQT (1754–1842) physician and Harvard professor who successfully tested Jenner's smallpox vaccine theory on his own family. Operated by Coastwise.

304. WILLIAM SCHIRMER, 3–44, 245452, KWQU (1858–1939) New Jersey native, Pacific Coast sea captain, and founder of the Schirmer Stevedoring Co. and the Transoceanic Co. at San Francisco. In 1930 he lived with his wife Louise, 62, at 7949 Geary Blvd. Their son George B., 33, worked at the stevedoring company and lived next door with his wife Patricia. Operated by General Steamship.

305. J. S. HUTCHINSON, 3–44, 245464, KWQV (1826–1919) James Sloan Hutchinson was a 49er from Philadelphia who made some money in the California gold fields, went into banking, and founded the San Francisco Society for the Prevention of Cruelty to Animals. Operated by Interocean.

306. EDWARD S. HOUGH, 4–44, 245471, KWKW (1863–1924) Edward Stamford Samuel Hough was an English-born mechanical engineer who came to the United States in 1889 and settled in Alameda, California. He designed the 4,000-ton Hough Type wooden freighter built on the West Coast during World War I and was a consulting engineer for naval shipbuilding. The *North Bend* was the first Emergency Fleet Corp. ship built, launched by Kruse & Banks at North Bend, Oregon, on December 1, 1917. In 1920 Hough lived with his English wife Adelaide, 50, at 3018 E. 15th St. Operated by Alaska Steamship.

307. E. A. BURNETT, 4–44, 245481, KWQX (1865–1941) Edgar Albert Burnett was a historian and chancellor at the University of Nebraska. In 1940 he lived with his wife Nellie, 78, and servant Francis B. Neylon, 48, at 3256 Holdrege St. in Lincoln. He died on June 18, 1941. Operated by Alaska Packers.

308. WALLACE R. FARRINGTON, 4–44, 245492, KWRN (1871–1933) Wallace Rider Farrington was governor of the Territory of Hawaii and namesake for the Farrington Highway. Operated by Burns.

309. LOUIS SLOSS, 4–44, 245510, KWXJ (1823–1902) sealing fisheries pioneer, president of the Alaska Commercial Co., cofounded with Lewis Gerstle, and treasurer of the University of California. Operated by Alaska Packers.

310. TOUSSAINT LOUVERTURE, 4–44, 245514, KWXK (1743–1803) François-Dominique Toussaint L'Ouverture was a Haitian revolutionary. Operated by De La Rama.

311. LOUIS SULLIVAN, 4–44, 245511, KWXL (1856–1924) Louis Henry Sullivan was an architect considered to be the innovator of skyscrapers and "father of modernism." Operated by American Mail Line.

312. LUCIEN LABAUDT, 4–44, 245519, KWXT (1880–1943) French-born Lucien Adolphe Labaudt came to America in 1906 and San Francisco in 1910 as a pioneer of modern art. He was commissioned by *Life Magazine* to paint scenes in India during the war and died in a plane crash on December 12. Operated by Pacific-Atlantic.

313. JAMES A. DRAIN, 4–44, 245529, KWXV (1870–1943) James Andrew Drain was

a Spanish-American and World War I veteran and national commander of the American Legion who died on May 30, 1943. Operated by Interocean.

314. STALINGRAD, 4–44, city of Volograd, Russia, renamed in 1925 after Joseph Stalin and reverted in 1961 by Khrushchev. Operated under the Russian flag.

315. KAMENETS-PODOLSK, 4–44, Kamianets-Podilsky is a western Ukraine city occupied by German forces from July 1941 to March 1944. Operated under the Russian flag.

316. BENJAMIN CARPENTER, 4–44, 245571, KXAA (1725–1804) believed to be a colonial leader in Vermont during the American Revolution and lieutenant governor. Operated by Sudden & Christenson.

317. CHARLOTTE CUSHMAN, 4–44, 245573, KXAC (1816–1876) Charlotte Saunders Cushman was an opera singer and noted stage actress who played Romeo in *Romeo and Juliet*, and was a consort of fellow actor Matilda Hays. Operated by Northland.

318. HENRY MEIGGS, 4–44, 245609, KXAE (1811–1877) New York lumberman who moved his business to San Francisco in 1849 and built Meiggs Wharf then sheds, streets, and schooners. He overextended himself financially and in 1854 fled to Chile to escape fraud charges and built railroads there and in Peru where he died. Operated by Coastwise (Pacific Far East) Line.

319. MARISCAL SUCRE, 4–44, 245610, KXAI (1795–1830) "Marshal Sucre" was Antonio José de Sucre y Alcalá, a Venezuelan soldier who fought to liberate South America from Spain. Operated by James Griffiths.

320. GEORGE CLEMENT PERKINS, 4–44, 245641, WMZG (1839–1923) native of Maine who went to sea at 12 and in 1855 arrived in San Francisco. He quit the sea and eventually went into banking, milling, mining, back into the steamship business, and was the governor of California and a long-serving senator. Operated by Weyerhaeuser.

321. GILBERT M. HITCHCOCK, 4–44, 245630, WMZJ (1859–1934) Gilbert Monell Hitchcock was a Nebraska congressman and publisher of the *Omaha World Herald*. Operated by Alaska Transportation.

322. HENRY WHITE, 4–44, 245631, WMZK (1850–1927) ambassador to France who was one of the signers of the Treaty of Versailles. Operated by De La Rama.

323. INGUL, 5–44, major commercial river in the Ukraine. Operated under the Russian flag.

324. ALEXANDER WOOLLCOTT, 5–44, 245679, WMZO (1887–1943) Alexander Humphreys Woolcott was a New York reporter, critic, commentator for the *New Yorker* magazine, and a radio personality who had a stroke while on the air on January 23, 1943. Operated by Alaska Steamship.

325. E. A. CHRISTENSON, 5–44, 245680, WMZR (1874–1922) Edwin Axel Christenson and Charles E. Sudden founded the Sudden & Christenson Steamship Line in San Francisco. Operated by Sudden & Christenson.

326. RODINA, 5–44, Rodina-Mat "Mother Russia." Operated under the Russian flag.

327. BRIANSK, 5–44, the city of Bryansk, Russia, fiercely resisted German occupation. Operated under the Russian flag.

328. JOE HARRIS, 5–44, 245703, KMZW (1876–1933) Joseph William "Call Me Joe" Harris was a famous San Francisco and Berkeley clothier who catered to yachtsmen and merchant seamen. Operated by Pacific-Atlantic.

329. MELLO FRANCO, 5–44, 245714, WMZY (1870–1943) Afrânio de Mello Franco represented Brazil in the League of Nations and was a judge at The Hague. He died at Rio de Janeiro on January 1, 1943. Operated by Interocean.

330. WILLIAM ALLEN WHITE, 5–44, 245733, WMZZ (1868–1944) editor of the

Kansas Emporia Gazette and a leader of the Progressive Movement who died at Emporia, Kansas, on January 29, 1944. Operated by Pope & Talbot.

331. STEPHEN HOPKINS, 5–44, 245755, WNDD (1707–1785) Declaration of Independence signer from Rhode Island. Operated by Luckenbach.

332. CECIL G. SELLERS, 5–44, 245765, WNEF (1893–1938) Army Air Service pilot who earned the Distinguished Service Cross during World War I for carrying out a hazardous bombing mission. In 1930 he was a pilot and airport manager and lived with his wife Jeanne and two daughters in Butler, Pennsylvania. In 1938 he was a Pan American pilot who died with five other crew, including Edwin C. Musick, on January 11 when their *Samoan Clipper* exploded while preparing for an emergency landing at Pago Pago. Operated by Alaska Steamship.

333. NORMAN J. COLMAN, 5–44, 245766, WNEN (1827–1911) Norman Jay Colman was an Indiana lawyer and the first Secretary of Agriculture. Operated by American Mail Line.

334. WILLIAM SPROULE, 5–44, 245789, WNNY (1858–1935) president of Wells Fargo Express and the Southern Pacific Railroad. Operated by De La Rama.

335. GEORGE CRILE, 5–44, 245807, WNQE (1864–1943) George Washington Crile was an innovative surgeon who developed the nerve-block system of regional anesthesia, performed the first direct blood transfusion, designed the Crile "mosquito" forcep, and in 1921 cofounded the Cleveland Clinic. The clinic burned in 1939 and he died on January 7, 1943, in Cleveland, Ohio. Operated by General Steamship.

336. RALPH T. O'NEIL, 5–44, 245825, WNXX (1888–1940) Ralph Thomas O'Neil was a national commander of the American Legion. Operated by Hammond.

337. GEORGE B. MCFARLAND, 5–44, 245824, WPAK (1866–1942) George Bradley McFarland was the son of a Pennsylvania preacher who became a physician in Skaneateles, New York, and in 1915 contracted to lecture at the Royal Medical College in Bankok, Thailand, "on behalf of His Siamese Majesty's Government" and was accompanied by his wife Mary. Operated by Interocean.

338. WILLIAM H. CLAGETT, 5–44, 245865, WPAH (1838–1901) William Horace Clagett was a Montana congressman. Operated by Alaska Steamship.

339. JOSE PEDRO VARELA, 5–44, 245856, WOPU (1845–1879) Uruguayan educator, sociologist, and politician. Operated by Pacific-Atlantic.

340. SAMUEL L. COBB, 6–44, 245880, WOQO (1899–1942) master of the freighter *Alcoa Guide*, lost when the ship was torpedoed by *U-123* on April 16, 1942, off Cape Hatteras. Capt. Cobb was seriously wounded but made every effort to ram the submarine and then made his way to his cabin through flames to retrieve the secret code books and confidential papers and throw them overboard. He was awarded the Merchant Marine Distinguished Service medal posthumously. Operated by Olympic.

341. EDWARD P. RIPLEY, 6–44, 245895, WOQM (1845–1920) Edward Payson Ripley was the 14th president of the Atchison, Topeka & Santa Fe Railway. Namesake for towns in California and Oklahoma. Operated by W. R. Chamberlin.

342. CHARLES J. COLDEN, 6–44, 245898, WOOX (1870–1938) California congressman. Operated by Shepard.

343. HENRY T. SCOTT, 6–44, 245929, WQVV (1846–1927) Henry Tiffany Scott, of Baltimore, started as a timekeeper at the Union Iron Works in San Francisco with brother Irving M. Scott and in 1885 was president of a major shipbuilding company. He became president of Pacific Telephone & Telegraph, later board chairman, and was t primary organizer of the 1915 Panama-Pacific International Exposition in San Francisco. Operated by Oliver J. Olson.

344. OVID BUTLER, 6–44, 245942, WQZA (1801–1881) lawyer, newsman, and founder of Butler University in Indiana. Operated by Alaska Packers.

345. GENERAL VATUTIN, 6–44 (1901–1944) Nikolai Fyodorovich Vatutin was a heroic Soviet commander who was shot by Ukrainian insurgents on February 28, 1944, and died of wounds. Operated under the Russian flag.

346. TERRY E. STEPHENSON, 6–44, 245970, WRAB (1880–1943) Terry Elmo Stephenson was a reporter for the *Los Angeles Times* and *Santa Ana Register* and a noted Orange County historian. Donations were used to build the ship. Operated by Interocean.

347. THOMAS F. HUNT, 6–44, 246001, WRAV (1862–1927) Thomas Forsyth Hunt was a professor of agriculture at Cornell who was noted for his work involving forage and fiber animal feeds and plant diseases. Operated by Union Sulphur.

348. GENERAL PANFILOV, 6–44 (1893–1941) Gen. Ivan Vasilyevich Panfilov commanded the 316th Rifle Division defending Moscow in 1941 where he was mortally wounded on November 18. Operated under the Russian flag.

349. JUSTO AROSEMENA, 7–44, 246074, WRAT (1817–1896) Justo Arosemena Quesada was elected the first president of the state of Panama in 1855. Operated by Coast-wise.

350. SAMUEL GOMPERS, 7–44, 246097, WQZV (1850–1924) president of the American Federation of Labor. Operated by Simpson Spence & Young.

351. BENJAMIN WARNER, 7–44, 246117, WRBW (1858–1935) Polish shoemaker Benjamin Wonsol was the father of the founders of the Warner Bros. film studio. Operated by Burns.

Rheem Manufacturing Co.

Chesley Ave. at Southern Pacific RR tracks, Richmond, California

In February 1942 the Maritime Commission decided to build an emergency shipyard at Providence, Rhode Island, in order to take advantage of available labor, materials, and distribution systems. The only other yard in New England was at South Portland, Maine. They found what they thought was a nice spot at Fields Point on the Providence River and when Adm. Vickery went looking for someone to run it, executives at Bethlehem Steel recommended the Rheem Manufacturing Co., headquartered at Richmond, California. Bethlehem was also a major shareholder of Rheem stock during the war.

Richard S. and Donald L. Rheem had incorporated Rheem Manufacturing on January 22, 1931, at Richmond to build water heaters, boilers, shipping containers, and pneumatic tanks. They agreed to build Liberty ships but expressed their preference for a West Coast location. Adm. Vickery said the West Coast was pretty much at capacity and asked them if they wouldn't consider going to Providence, Rhode Island. Rheem was already a large company and had an office in New York but shipbuilding was something else entirely.

They reluctantly agreed and on March 24, 1942, signed a $6,050,000 contract to build a 6-way yard and 32 ships at Fields Point. Construction began on March 28 but on the last day of that year the plate shop burned down and on December 2 gale force winds, torrential rain, lightning, and high water struck Providence forcing the evacuation of the shipyard. The construction site proved to be a difficult one and instead of the estimated $6 million to build the yard, Rheem had already spent $27 million by February 1943.

When these expenses came to light, the Merchant Marine & Fisheries Committee sharply critized the Maritime Commission stating, in part: "The Maritime Commission did not properly safeguard government expenditures through adequate supervision and control of an inexperienced contractor's activities and expenditures" and criticized the Commission for failing to fully test and examine the site, which required "extensive filling and piling."

Rheem was also plagued by absenteeism in the workforce. In November and December 1942 and January 1943 it was estimated that 400,000 man hours were lost, the same amount of time the Maritime Commission said a Liberty ship could be built "when a yard is running right."

On February 5, 1943, it was decided to terminate Rheem's contract and turn the job over to a new company. The Walsh Construction Co. at Davenport, Rhode Island, was suggested. The company's president, Thomas J. Walsh, had previously worked with Henry J. Kaiser on construction jobs and Kaiser was already builing ships. A partnership was then formed as Walsh-Kaiser.

Rheem was able to deliver one ship, on February 13, before the yard was formally taken over by the Walsh-Kaiser Co. on Sunday, February 28, 1943. Walsh-Kaiser was given an additional $9,200,000 to complete the job. The Maritime Commission spent $297,310 on jointly-owned land and $25,787,067 on facilities.

Rheem went on to build land mines for the Army and 152-mm brass shell casings, a very odd size, for the guns on the French battleship *Richelieu*. Instead of changing the guns on the ship to match American ordnance it was decided to have custom-made shells built in the United States. Capt. Marcel Deramond's brand-new 35,000-ton ship fled Brest in 1940 for Dakar and in January 1943 made a run for the United States and reached New York on February 11. Most of the crew was pro–American, though many were anti–American.

1. WILLIAM CODDINGTON, 2–43, 242677, KIRN (1601–1678) founder of Newport, Rhode Island. The ship was at anchor after the 12-hour trial run when a brutal storm came up. Temperatures reached 10-below and the anchors dragged, but held just short of a reef. It was estimated the ship cost $12,800,000 to produce. Operated by American Export Lines.

St. Johns River Shipbuilding Co.
115 Florida Ave., Jacksonville, Florida

The company began in March 1942 under president James C. Merrill, vice-presidents Kenneth A. Merrill and Benjamin F. Crowley, and treasurer Earl D. Page. James Merrill was president of the Merrill-Stevens Dry Dock & Repair Co. in Jacksonville and Kenneth was vice president. The Commission spent $1,375,010 on land and $16,145,471 on facilities. On March 4, 1942, a contract was signed for 30 Liberty ships to be delivered between December 15, 1942, and December 31, 1943, and on April 23, 1943, another contract was executed for 52 ships to be completed between February 10, 1944, and December 29, 1944. In Commission-owned yards, the company paid the employees and was reimbursed on a weekly basis. The 6-way yard built 82 Liberty ships with the last one being delivered on February 24, 1945. The first keel was laid down on August 15, 1942, and the average building time for the ships was 77.6 days.

1. PONCE DE LEON, 4–43, 243228, KHQF (1460–1521) Juan Ponce de León was a Spanish explorer who landed in Florida and was the first governor of Puerto Rico. Operated by Grace Line.
2. JOHN GORRIE, 4–43, 243272, KITY (1803–1855) physician who developed modern refrigeration. Operated by South Atlantic.

3. FRANCIS ASBURY, 5–43, 243361, KIUO (1745–1816) noted Methodist preacher and one of the first Methodist Episcopal bishops in the United States. Operated by A. H. Bull. The ship left Jacksonville in June 1943 under Capt. Myers W. Jay and arrived at New York on August 8. Capt. Jean V. Patrick departed New York in November 1943 and hit a mine off Ostend, Belgium, on December 3, 1944, and sank with the loss of 10 merchant crew and 7 Armed Guard sailors. Second engineer Francis E. Rack and third engineer Frederick O. Williams were awarded the Merchant Marine Distinguished Service medal for rescuing the chief engineer, Robert F. Justice, from his damaged quarters. The chief subsequently died.

4. JOHN J. CRITTENDEN, 6–43, 243466, KIUV (1787–1863) John Jordan Crittenden was a Kentucky senator, governor, and Attorney General. Operated by A. H. Bull and converted to an animal transport ship.

5. SIDNEY LANIER, 7–43, 243599, KIVG (1842–1881) Sidney Clopton Lanier was a poet and musician from Georgia who served as a Confederate pilot on British blockade runners. Operated by Seas Shipping.

6. ROBERT Y. HAYNE, 7–43, 243689, KIVW (1791–1839) Robert Young Hayne was a South Carolina senator, governor, and mayor of Charleston. Operated by AGWI Lines.

7. RICHARD MONTGOMERY, 7–43, 243756, KOAA (1738–1775) Irish-born British soldier who fought in the French and Indian War, returned to England, and in 1773 came back to America, married Janet Livingston, and began farming. He was elected to the New York Provisional Congress and in June 1775 received a commission as a brigadier general in the Continental Army. He was mortally wounded on December 31, 1775, while attacking Quebec. Operated by AGWI Lines. Capt. Frederick William Henry Willecke left Jacksonville in August 1943 on Voyage No. 1 and arrived at New York on October 15, 1943, from Middlesbrough, England. Departed New York on Voyage No. 2 and arrived back at New York on April 4, 1944, from Oran, Algeria. On April 20 the ship arrived at Philadelphia to load a cargo of ordnance at Hog Island. Capt. Willecke expected to sail before the end of the month from Pier 96 with 6,862 tons of Army bombs, signal cartridges, fuses, and small arms ammunition. The trip in Convoy HX 301 was uneventful and on arrival in England the ship was directed to an anchorage in the Thames Estuary to await formation of a convoy for Cherbourg, France. The ship was assigned to an unsuitable anchorage off the north edge of the Sheerness Middle Sand by British authorities and on August 20, 1944, went aground at low tide. When the ebb tide caused the hull to crack and buckle, Capt. Willecke ordered everyone off and all were taken ashore and quartered at Southend-on-Sea. British authorities hired shipbrokers Watson & Gill, of Rochester, to oversee the salvage operation. Subcontractors were hired and unloading commenced at 10 a.m. on the 23rd using the ship's own gear powered by compressed air from a salvage vessel moored alongside. The next day at 3 p.m. the hull cracked open between No. 2 and 3 holds and all three forward holds flooded. On September 8 the ship's back broke rendering salvage of the vessel itself impossible. Unloading of No. 4 and 5 holds was completed on September 25 and the wreck was abandoned to the elements. It is still visible today at Nore Sands in the Medway Channel. Capt. Willecke, 54, left Southampton on the motorship *John Ericsson* on November 30 and arrived at New York on December 12. He was born on January 19, 1890, in Bremen, Germany, became a citizen, and lived at 60 Beach St., Stapleton, Staten Island, New York, with his wife Dora and newborn son. He was employed by the New York & Porto Rico Steamship Co. before the war.

8. JOHN PHILIP SOUSA, 8–43, 243871, KOAB (1854–1932) musician and composer known best for his military marches. Operated by Wessel, Duval.

9. HENRY WATTERSON, 8–43, 243986, KIWC (1840–1921) founder of the *Louisville Courier Journal* and a Kentucky congressman. Operated by American Export Lines.

10. GEORGE DEWEY, 8–43, 244100, KIWD (1837–1917) Admiral of the Navy of Spanish-American War fame. Operated by American Export Lines.

11. WILLIAM BYRD, 9–43, 183, KXMB (1674–1744) Colonel William Byrd II was a Colonial Virginia official, planter, and founder of Richmond. Operated by United Fruit.

12. RUFUS C. DAWES, 9–43, 244237, KXMC (1867–1940) Rufus Cutler Dawes was an oil man and banker who headed the 1933 Chicago World's Fair and the Museum of Science & Industry. Operated by Luckenbach.

13. THOMAS SULLY, 9–43, 244293, KXME (1783–1872) noted English-born portrait painter. Operated by Calmar.

14. DWIGHT W. MORROW, 10–43, 244328, KTNV (1873–1931) Dwight Whitney Morrow was a lawyer, a partner in J. P. Morgan & Co., and head of the Morrow Board that recommended the creation of an Army Air Corps. He was also ambassador to Mexico, a New Jersey senator, and had a daughter named Anne who married aviator Charles Lindberg. Operated by Sprague.

15. JOHN S. MOSBY, 10–43, 244466, KTNX (1833–1916) Col. John Singleton "the Gray Ghost" Mosby was commander of the Confederate 43rd Battalion, 1st Virginia Cavalry, known as Mosby's Raiders. Operated by Isthmian.

16. GRANT WOOD, 10–43, 244448, KTNY (1891–1942) Grant DeVolson Wood was a painter of the rural Midwest, best known for his American Gothic style. Operated by American Export Lines.

17. EDWARD M. HOUSE, 11–43, 244588, KUJL (1858–1938) Edward Mandell House was a Texas cotton grower, banker, and one of President Wilson's closest advisors. Operated by A. L. Burbank.

18. HARVEY CUSHING, 11–43, 244592, KUJO (1869–1939) Harvey Williams Cushing was a neurosurgeon at Johns Hopkins Hospital who is considered the father of modern neurosurgery and also described Cushing Syndrome involving too much cortisol in the system. Operated by Marine Transport.

19. WILLIAM G. SUMNER, 11–43, 244647, KUJT (1840–1910) William Graham Sumner was a scholar at Yale and the nation's first professor of sociology. Operated by the Navy as the *Crater*-class cargo ship *Alkaid* (AK-114), NTNQ, commissioned on March 27, 1944.

20. PETER STUYVESANT, 11–43, 244686, KUYK (c. 1612–1672) Pieter Stuyvesant was director-general of New Netherland, forerunner of New York. Operated by the Navy as the *Crater*-class cargo ship *Crux* (AK-115), NKTJ, commissioned on March 17, 1944.

21. JAMES SCREVEN, 12–43, 244713, KVBW (1744–1778) Revolutionary War colonel wounded on November 22, 1778, on Spencer Hill near Midway Church in Florida. He died on the 24th. Operated by the Navy as the *Crater*-class cargo ship *Shaula* (AK-118), NTUC, commissioned on May 5, 1944.

22. ARTHUR M. HUDDELL, 12–43, 244760, KVDD (1869–1931) Arthur McIntire Huddell was a Boston labor official who was president of the International Union of Steam and Operating Engineers when he was shot by an unknown assassin on May 22, 1931, at Washington, D.C., and died on June 1. Operated by A. H. Bull. Reported to be a museum ship in Greece.

23. NAPOLEON B. BROWARD, 12–43, 244804, KVGR (1857–1910) Napoleon Bonaparte Broward was the 19th governor of Florida and the namesake for Broward County. Operated by the Navy as the *Crater*-class cargo ship *Matar* (AK-119), NTNW, commissioned on May 17, 1944.

24. OWEN WISTER, 12–43, 244824, KVGS (1860–1938) author regarded as the father of Western fiction. Operated by William J. Rountree.

25. ELIZABETH C. BELLAMY, 12–43, 244874, KVLJ (1837–1900) Elizabeth Croom married Dr. Charles Bellamy, her first cousin, but within a year her husband died and then, after two of her children died, she took up writing about the South. Operated by the Navy as the miscellaneous auxiliary ship *Baham* (AG-71), NHDP, commissioned on August 18, 1944.

26. JOHN WHITE, 1–44, 244887, KVLO (c. 1540–1593) artist, cartographer, and in 1587 became governor of the second English settlement on Roanoke Island. Father of Elizabeth Dare who gave birth to Virginia Dare, the first child born at the settlement. Virginia's father was Ananias Dare. Operated by the Navy as the *Crater*-class cargo ship *Menkar* (AK-123), NHBZ, commissioned on January 17, 1944.

27. ROYAL S. COPELAND, 1–44, 244924, KVMS (1868–1938) Royal Samuel Copeland was a physician, New York senator, and co-author of the Merchant Marine Act of 1936. Operated by Parry.

28. JOHN EINIG, 1–44, 245007, KVQL (1854–1912) engineer and officer of the Marine Engineers Association noted for building a famous 32-inch steam whistle in Jacksonville, Florida, and also the first horseless carriage made there. Operated by United States Navigation.

29. EDWIN G. WEED, 2–44, 245005, KVQO (1837–1924) Edwin Gardner Weed was the revered Episcopal bishop in Florida. Operated by South Atlantic.

30. ANDREW TURNBULL, 2–44, 245129, KVQQ (1718–1792) Scots physician who founded the colony of New Smyrna, Florida, now New Smyrna Beach. Operated by Wessel, Duval.

31. HENRY S. SANFORD, 3–44, 245084, KWBZ (1823–1891) Henry Shelton Sanford manufactured brass tacks, served as ambassador to Belgium during the Civil War, and founded Sanford, Florida. Operated by Overlakes.

32. JAMES L. ACKERSON, 3–44, 245124, KWCA (1881–1931) James Lee Ackerson was a naval constructor and general manager and vice president of the U.S. Shipping Board Emergency Fleet Corp. from 1918 to 1920. Operated by Wessel, Duval.

33. EDWARD W. BOK, 3–44, 245272, KWKD (1863–1930) Edward William Bok was the editor of the *Ladies Home Journal* for 30 years. Operated by Luckenbach.

34. THOMAS A. MCGINLEY, 3–44, 245368, KWKF (1881–1940) Thomas Atterbury McGinley invented an improved type of high-speed screw jacks and lifting machinery as president of the Duff-Norton Manufacturing Co., 2709 Preble Ave., N. S., Pittsburgh. Operated by the Navy as the *Crater*-class cargo ship *Melucta* (AK-131), NHCO, commissioned on July 22, 1944.

35. FREDERICK TRESCA, 4–44, 245344, KWKK (1803–1886) French-born Florida lighthouse keeper, sea captain, pioneer shipping man, and Union blockade runner. Operated by the Navy as the *Crater*-class cargo ship *Propus* (AK-132), NHEH, commissioned on June 22, 1944.

36. EDWARD A. FILENE, 4–44, 245412, KWUO (1860–1937) Edward Albert Filene, of Boston, founded the Filene department store chain and was instrumental in creating credit unions. Operated by American West African.

37. RICHARD K. CALL, 4–44, 245463, KXBB (1791–1862) Richard Keith Call was a congressional delegate and governor of the Florida Territory. Operated by United States Navigation.

38. AUGUST BELMONT, 4–44, 245507, KWWQ (1813–1890) German-born August Schönberg was a house servant for the Rothchilds, studied diligently, and got promoted to a clerk's position in 1832. In 1837 he was sent to Cuba via New York and arrived at New York just in time for the Panic of 1837. He remained in New York and through his innovative financial

genius saved the Rothchild's American interests. He then decided to stay in America and change his name. In German, "schönberg" is "beautiful mountain" and he chose the French equivalent, "belmont," for his new name. He went on to become consul general to Austria and minister to the Netherlands. Operated by South Atlantic.

39. ARTHUR R. LEWIS, 5–44, 245559, KWWS (1878–1933) Arthur Raymond Lewis founded the Seas Shipping Co. in 1920 for coastwise service to supplement Farrell's Isthmian Steamship Co. and was part owner of American South African. Operated by Seas Shipping.

40. GEORGE E. MERRICK, 5–44, 245608, KWZZ (1886–1942) George Edgar Merrick planned and developed Coral Gables, Florida, and founded the University of Miami. Operated by United States Lines.

41. JAMES K. PAULDING, 5–44, 245674, WOON (1788–1860) James Kirke Paulding was a writer, publisher, and Secretary of the Navy who opposed building steam-powered warships. Operated by United States Navigation.

42. THOMAS J. LYONS, 6–44, 245677, WMYI (1894–1943) Thomas Joseph Lyons, of Brooklyn, was a delegate of the Granite Cutters' National Union who was elected president of the New York State Federation of Labor in 1939. Operated by Smith & Johnson.

43. RAYMOND CLAPPER, 6–44, 245728, WOEW (1892–1944) Raymond Lewis Clapper was a war correspondent with Scripps-Howard who was a passenger in a Navy plane lost on February 4 in a mid-air collision during the Marshall Islands invasion. Operated by T. J. Stevenson.

44. HUGH J. KILPATRICK, 6–44, 245780, WQFD (1836–1881) Hugh Judson Kilpatrick was a controversial Union cavalry general and minister to Chile. Operated by States Marine.

45. NOAH BROWN, 6–44, 245799, WQFK (1770–1850) pioneer New York shipbuilder who constructed the brigs and sloops used on Lake Erie in the War of 1812. Operated by Seas Shipping.

46. HENDRIK WILLEM VAN LOON, 6–44, 245916, WQFP (1882–1944) noted Dutch-born historian, patriot, and journalist. Operated by United States Lines.

47. STEPHEN BEASLEY, 7–44, 245986, WQGA (1742–1814) Revolutionary War Pennsylvania Navy captain who took command of the armed boat *Viper* on April 1, 1777. Operated by T. J. Stevenson.

48. JASPER F. CROPSEY, 7–44, 246006, WRQZ (1823–1900) Jasper Francis Cropsey was a noted New York architect and painter of the Hudson River School. Operated by United States Navigation.

49. WILLIAM CRANE GRAY, 7–44, 246015, WRRI (1835–1919) first bishop of the Episcopal Church's Missionary Jurisdiction of Southern Florida. Operated by International Freighting.

50. ETHELBERT NEVIN, 7–44, 246138, WRRJ (1862–1901) Ethelbert Woodbridge Nevin was a noted Pennsylvania piano player and composer. Operated by Moore-McCormack.

51. W. S. JENNINGS, 8–44, 246144, WRRK (1863–1920) William Sherman Jennings was governor of Florida. Operated by Stockard.

52. FILIPP MAZZEI, 8–44, 246158, WRRO (1730–1816) Filippo Mazzei was an Italian physician, a friend of Benjamin Franklin, and neighbor of Thomas Jefferson who was invited to help with the cultivation of grapes and olives and during the Revolution he purchased weapons for the United States. Operated by Sprague.

53. HENRY HADLEY, 8–44, 246202, WSPW (1871–1937) Henry Kimball Hadley was a famous symphony composer. Operated by T. J. Stevenson.

54. ALFRED I. DUPONT, 8–44, 246297, WSPY (1864–1935) Alfred Irénée du Pont

was an E. I. du Pont board member, vice president, and philanthropist. Operated by International Freighting.

55. IRVIN S. COBB, 8–44, 246300, WSQQ (1876–1944) Irvin Shrewsbury Cobb, of Kentucky, was a journalist in New York and ardent supporter of President Roosevelt until the infamous "court packing" scandal. He later wrote to Herbert Hoover, "[W]e are grateful because during your occupancy of the White House you never got the idea of burning down the temple of our fathers in order to destroy a few cockroaches in the basement." Operated by Seas Shipping.

56. NEGLEY D. COCHRAN, 9–44, 246385, KSSX (1863–1941) Negley Dakin Cochran was a First Amendment rights activist and editor and president of the *Toledo News-Bee* in Ohio. Operated by Smith & Johnson.

57. ANNA DICKINSON, 9–44, 246375, KSSZ (1842–1932) Anna Elizabeth Dickinson was a Philadelphia teacher, political activist, abolitionist, lecturer, mountain climber, the first woman to address Congress, playwright, and actress. Operated by Wessel, Duval.

58. JOHN RINGLING, 9–44, 246443, KSTC (1866–1936) John Nicholas Ringling was the most prominent of the five sons who started a circus and animal show in 1870 that would merge with Barnum & Bailey. Operated by Luckenbach.

59. MICHAEL DE KOVATS, 9–44, 246478, KSTJ (1724–1779) Michael Kovats de Fabriczy was a Hungarian cavalry officer in the Continental Army who was lost on May 11, 1779, while countering the British siege of Charleston. Cofounder with Casimir Pulaski of the Army's cavalry corps. Operated by Polarus.

60. JOHN H. MCINTOSH, 9–44, 246474, KSZB (1773–1836) John Houston McIntosh was a general and president of the Republic of Florida during the Patriot War of 1811. Namesake for McIntosh, Florida. Operated by Stockard.

61. JERRY S. FOLEY, 10–44, 246606, KTEW (1876–1941) Jeremiah "Jerry" Sylvester Foley was a prominent Jacksonville, Florida, businessman, president of the Brooks-Scanlon wholesale lumber company, and vice president of the Foley Lumber Company. Lester Foley was president and Jerry's wife, Marie Scanlon Foley, was secretary of Foley Lumber. Foley also had interests in banks and railroads. In 1940 the Foleys lived at 2004 Herchell with nine houseguests. Operated by American South African.

62. ROBERT MILLS, 10–44, 246610, KTEY (1781–1855) architect of the Washington Monument. Operated by Alcoa.

63. MORRIS C. FEINSTONE, 10–44, 246659, KTFE (1878–1943) Polish-born woodcarver and master designer who was executive secretary of the United Hebrew Trades, a labor union organization in New York at 175 E. Broadway. Morris lived with his wife Florence in the Hotel Park Central at 870 7th Ave. The group sold $3,212,895 worth of war bonds to pay for the ship when only $2 million was needed. Operated by Black Diamond.

64. DAVID L. YULEE, 10–44, 246671, KTFF (1810–1886) born David Levy on June 12, 1810, in the Virgin Islands. Became an attorney, a Florida Territory delegate to Congress, and the first Jewish U.S. senator. He changed his name to David Levy Yulee in 1846, adding his father's religious surname. He served as a Confederate congressman and founded the Florida Railroad Co., becoming the father of Florida railroads. Namesake for town of Yulee and Levy County in Florida. Operated by R. A. Nicol.

65. GEORGE E. WALDO, 10–44, 246754, KTFM (1851–1942) George Ernest Waldo was a New York congressman. Operated by Shepard.

66. HARALD TORSVIK, 11–44, LKPY (1904–1941) Norwegian lawyer who aided refugees fleeing to England and was arrested by the Nazis and executed. Operated under the Norwegian flag by the Norwegian Shipping & Trade Mission.

67. FREDERIC W. GALBRAITH, 11–44, 246774, KYQQ (1874–1921) Frederic William Galbraith, Jr., was a World War I veteran and second national commander of the American Legion who built up the organization to national status. He died in a car crash on June 9, 1921, in Indianapolis. Operated by South Atlantic.

68. C. W. POST, 11–44, 246811, KYUR (1854–1914) Charles William "C.W." Post was a nervous breakfast cereal manufacturer at Battle Creek, Michigan. Operated by United States Navigation.

69. JUNIUS SMITH, 11–44, 246867, KYUT (1780–1853) London merchant who left for America in 1832 on a sailing ship for the normal 40-day passage but when they arrived at New York 54 days later he became upset and got the idea for a steam packet passenger service. He then founded the British & American Steam Navigation Co. and is regarded as the father of Atlantic passenger liners. Operated by Cosmopolitan.

70. ISAAC M. SINGER, 11–44, 246895, KYUU (1811–1875) Isaac Merritt Singer was an actor who patented a rock drill for miners, then a wood block cutting machine, then the first practical sewing machine for home use. Patent infringement, license, personal and domestic promblems (18 children) consumed his time but by 1887 he was on his own as the Singer Sewing Machine Co. Operated by Moore-McCormack.

71. TELFAIR STOCKTON, 11–44, 246916, ANBR (1860–1932) noted entreprenuer and developer of Jacksonville, Florida. Operated by R. A. Nicol.

72. LOUIS BAMBERGER, 12–44, 246933, ANBS (1855–1944) founded a major department store in Newark, New Jersey, and was a major philanthropist and community supporter. Operated by Weyerhaeuser.

73. ISAAC MAYER WISE, 12–44, 246951, ANBT (1819–1900) came to New York from Austria in 1846, went to Albany as a rabbi, and began instituting reforms, such as family pews in the synagogue. Operated by North Atlantic & Gulf.

74. HENRY B. PLANT, 12–44, 246950, KYUP (1819–1899) Henry Bradley Plant, of Branford, Connecticut, started the Savannah, Florida & Western Railway in 1879 and added steamboats, hotels, and transportation projects in Georgia and Florida that was named The Plant System. Operated by A. L. Burbank. Capt. Charles J. Ward's ship was sunk on February 6, 1945, by *U-245* off Ramsgate, England, with the loss of nine merchant crew and 7 Armed Guard sailors.

75. WALTER M. CHRISTIANSEN, 12–44, 246986, ANDI (1896–1942) chief engineer lost on the *W. L. Steed*, torpedoed off the Delaware River by *U-103* on February 2, 1942. Operated by American Liberty.

76. GROVER C. HUTCHERSON, 12–44, 247005, ANDN (1919–1943) messman lost on the *Timothy Pickering*, bombed by German aircraft on July 14, 1943, off Avola, Sicily. Operated by Overlakes.

77. FRED C. STEBBINS, 1–45, 247059, ANFE (1921–1942) wiper lost on the *Jonathan Sturges*, torpedoed by *U-707* on February 23, 1943, in the North Atlantic. Operated by Union Sulphur.

78. HAROLD A. JORDAN, 1–45, 247117, ANFG (1911–1942) chief mate lost on the Parry Navigation freighter *Balladier*, torpedoed by *U-705* on August 15, 1942, in the North Atlantic. Operated by Parry.

79. JOHN MILLER, 1–45, 247154, ANFH (1901–1943) ordinary seaman lost on the Moore-McCormack freighter *Deer Lodge*, torpedoed by *U-516* on February 17, 1943, in the South Atlantic. Operated by Isbrandtsen.

80. NIKI, 1–45, "Victory" in Greek. Operated under the Greek flag.

81. FRED HERRLING, 2–45, 247215, ANIN (1889–1942) utilityman lost on the

Alaskan, torpedoed by *U-172* on November 28, 1942, in the South Atlantic. Operated by Sword Line.

82. SPETSAE, 2–45, Spetsai or Spetses, a small, pine-covered island in the Gulf of Argosaronic, Greece, that was prominent in Greece's war of independence from the Turks. Operated under the Greek flag.

South Portland Shipbuilding Corp.
169 Front St., South Portland, Maine

Ceased operation on April 1, 1943, with the forced merger of the Todd-Bath Iron Shipbuilding Corp. and South Portland Ship into the New England Shipbuilding Corp.

In January 1943 the first of 238 Redbank Village homes for workers and their families opened with a total of 500 bedrooms. A large community building had offices, shops, a clinic, kitchen, grammar school, and recreation spaces. Nextdoor was the Westbrook Street Trailer Park and the Mitchell Road Trailer Park with 300 units on 38 acres. In March 1943 the South Portland Housing Authority opened Cushing Village to house single shipyard workers in 60 buildings with 883 dormitory rooms. Each building had a large bathroom, laundry, and sitting area. The company built 18 Liberty ships. The first keel was laid down on September 24, 1941, and the average building time for the ships was 77.2 days.

1. JOHN DAVENPORT, 6–42, 241904, KFXH (1597–1669) missionary and cofounder of New Haven, Connecticut. Operated by Eastern Steamship.

2. JOHN WINTHROP, 7–42, 242038, KFJK (1587–1649) first governor of the Massachusetts Bay Colony. Operated by United Fruit. Capt. Charles M. Robertson's ship with 39 merchant crew and 15 Armed Guard sailors aboard left South Portland in July 1942 for England and were never seen or heard from again. It was later determined they were torpedoed and shelled on September 24, 1942, by *U-619* in the North Atlantic.

3. THOMAS HOOKER, 7–42, 242094, KFRD (1586–1647) founder of the Puritan Colony of Connecticut. Operated by American West African. Capt. Louis Shurtleff Hathaway's ship foundered in heavy weather on March 6, 1943, in the North Atlantic en route to New York. There were no reported casualties and the entire crew was taken to St. John's, Newfoundland.

4. ETHAN ALLEN, 8–42, 242145, KFEV (1737–1789) Vermont commander of the Green Mountain Boys. Operated by United States Lines.

5. JAMES G. BLAINE, 9–42, 242242, KHGY (1830–1893) James Gillespie Blaine was a Maine congressman and Secretary of State. Operated by Eastern Steamship.

6. HERMAN MELVILLE, 10–42, 242369, KHON (1819–1891) New York author of *Moby-Dick*. Operated by Eastern Steamship.

7. JOSIAH BARTLETT, 10–42, 242357, KFKC (1729–1795) Declaration of Independence signer from New Hampshire. Operated by Eastern Steamship.

8. WILLIAM KING, 10–42, 242448, KFUY (1768–1852) first governor of Maine who was instrumental in separating the District of Maine from Massachusetts. Operated by Marine Transport. Capt. Owen Harvey Reed's ship was torpedoed on June 6, 1943, by *U-198* off South Africa with loss of six merchant crew. Capt. Reed was taken prisoner and died on September 8, 1944, on Japanese ship.

9. JOHN CARVER, 11–42, 242512, KFHW (1576–1621) first governor of the Plymouth colony. Operated by United States Lines.

10. WILLIAM BRADFORD, 12–42, 242553, KFUM (1589–1657) signer of the Mayflower Compact and governor of the Plymouth colony. Operated by American South African.

11. JULIA WARD HOWE, 12–42, 242633, KHZX (1819–1910) Julia Ward married physician Samuel G. Howe in 1843 and had six kids. She took to writing poetry and was best known for the Battle Hymn of the Republic. Operated by American West African. Capt. Andrew A. Hammond's ship was torpedoed on January 27, 1943, by *U-442* south of the Azores. Capt. Hammond, chief engineer Thomas L. Haley, one Armed Guard sailor, and the Army security officer were lost.

12. WILLIAM BREWSTER, 12–42, 242635, KHMX (1567–1644) passenger on the *Mayflower* and religious leader of the Plymouth colony. Operated by Luckenbach and Alcoa.

13. ANNE BRADSTREET, 1–43, 242694, KHZW (1612–1672) English-born Anne Dudley married Simon Bradstreet in 1628 and the couple and her parents came to the Massachusetts Bay Colony in 1630. In 1650 she became the first female poet to be published in the colonies. Operated by AGWI Lines.

14. LOU GEHRIG, 1–43, 242821, KKFM (1903–1941) Henry Louis "Lou" Gehrig was a New York Yankees first baseman and member of the New York City parole board whose baseball career was cut short by illness. Operated by Eastern Steamship.

15. DANIEL WEBSTER, 1–43, 242815, KFBW (1782–1852) New Hampshire and Massachusetts congressman and Secretary of State. Operated by Coastwise Transportation. Capt. Benjamin Dutton's ship departed Portland, Maine, in February 1943, arrived at New York on April 24, and departed again around May 15. The ship was fatally damaged on January 10, 1944, by a German aerial torpedo off Algeria. There were no casualties reported.

16. WILLIAM PIERCE FRYE, 2–43, 242888, KHZQ (1831–1911) Maine congressman. Operated by Eastern Gas & Fuel. Capt. Meinhard Scherf's ship was torpedoed on March 29, 1943, by *U-610* in the North Atlantic with the loss of 35 merchant crew and 22 Armed Guard sailors.

17. JOHN TRUMBULL, 3–43, 242892, KIAR (1756–1843) Revolutionary War artist whose work was used on currency. Operated by Sprague.

18. HANNIBAL HAMLIN, 3–43, 242890, KHZT (1809–1891) Maine senator and governor and Lincoln's controversial vice president. Operated by Eastern Gas & Fuel.

Southeastern Shipbuilding Corp.
Savannah, Georgia

In 1940 Frank Cohen was a prominent New York City anti–Hitler Zionist and life insurance salesman who lived with his wife Ethel, their 13-year-old son Amos, and their 25-year-old West Indian servant, Jean Froset, at 88 Central Park West. That year he opened the Empire Ordnance Corp. at Philadelphia to supply armaments of all sorts to Great Britain to aid in their fight against Nazi Germany. After the United States entered the war he secured contracts to build guns for Army tanks and airplanes.

In March 1941 he leased land from the Savannah Port Authority to build a 3-way shipyard on speculation and incorporated Savannah Shipyards, Inc., in anticipatoin of wartime contracts. On November 25 he signed a contract with the Maritime Commission to build Liberty ships for $1,700,000 each. The terms stated that he had 30 days to recruit an adequate staff and show $750,000 of working capital and complete the facilities within 60 days, but on December 30 the Commission abruptly seized the property on the grounds that the facilities were inadequate and couldn't possibly be improved and completed by the deadline. On January 20, 1942, operation of the yard was taken over by George A. Rentschler, president of the General Machine Co., a Liberty ship engine builder at Hamilton, Ohio; William H. Smith, a former Todd executive, and Capt. Torkild Rieber, chairman of the Texas Oil Co. who formed Southeastern Ship. The Commission spent $1,392,698 on land and $11,166,929 on facilities to complete a 6-way yard.

Cohen initially accepted a settlement of $1,076,000 from the Maritime Commission but the Department of Justice asserted its jurisdiction in the matter and Cohen subsequently sued for $2,187,000. In July 1942 the case went to court. Cohen won, the Commission appealed, and Cohen was awarded substantially more than the original settlement offer. The Commissioned-owned yard built 88 Liberty ships. The first keel was laid down on May 22, 1942, and the average building time for the ships was 85.6 days.

1. JAMES OGLETHORPE, 2–43, 242853, KHZA (1696–1785) founder of the Georgia Colony. Operated by South Atlantic. Capt. Albert W. Long's ship was torpedoed on March 16, 1943, by *U-758* and *U-91* the next day in the North Atlantic. Capt. Long, 30 merchant seamen, 11 Armed Guard sailors, and two passengers were lost.

2. GEORGE HANDLEY, 3–43, 243002, KHZC (1752–1793) governor of Georgia. Operated by Marine Transport.

3. JAMES JACKSON, 3–43, 243037, KHZE (1757–1806) Georgia congressman. Operated by South Atlantic.

4. GEORGE WALTON, 3–43, 243051, KMHR (1741–1804) Declaration of Independence signer from Georgia. Operated by Merchants & Miners.

5. LYMAN HALL, 4–43, 243099, KMHS (1724–1790) Declaration of Independence signer from Georgia. Operated by South Atlantic.

6. JOHN MILLEDGE, 4–43, 243169, KMHV (1757–1818) Georgia congressman and governor. Operated by South Atlantic.

7. ROBERT TOOMBS, 4–43, 243229, KMHX (1810–1885) Georgia congressman and the Confederate States of America's Secretary of State. Operated by South Atlantic.

8. ROBERT M. T. HUNTER, 5–43, 243296, KMHY (1809–1887) Robert Mercer Taliaferro Hunter was an early graduate of the University of Virginia, became a congressman from that state and the Confederate States of America's Secretary of War. Operated by South Atlantic.

9. CRAWFORD W. LONG, 5–43, 243294, KMHZ (1815–1878) Crawford Williamson Long was a Georgia surgeon who first used diethyl ether as an inhaled general anesthetic. Operated by International Freighting.

10. BUTTON GWINNETT, 5–43, 243442, KETW (1735–1777) Declaration of Independence signer from Georgia. Operated by South Atlantic.

11. JOHN C. BRECKENRIDGE, 5–43, 243446, KONH (1821–1875) John Cabell Breckenridge was the Confederate Secretary of War. Operated by J. H. Winchester.

12. FELIX GRUNDY, 6–43, 243656, KXDT (1775–1840) Tennessee congressman and U.S. Attorney General. Operated by South Atlantic.

13. LANGDON CHEVES, 6–43, 243660, KXFO (1776–1857) South Carolina congressman. Operated by AGWI Lines.

14. NICHOLAS HERKIMER, 7–43, 243760, KXJY (1728–1777) Revolutionary War militia general who was wounded at Oriskany and died on August 16. Operated by AGWI Lines.

15. CASIMIR PULASKI, 7–43, 243826, KXJZ (1745–1779) Kazimierz Michal Waclaw Wiktor Pulaski was a noted Polish military commander who was recruited by Benjamin

Franklin to join the American Revolution. He saved George Washington's life and cofounded the Army's cavalry corps with Michael Kovats de Fabriczy. Operated by United Fruit.

16. HAMLIN GARLAND, 7–43, 243899. KXKA (1860–1940) Hannibal Hamlin Garland wrote novels about Midwest farmers. Operated by North Atlantic & Gulf.

17. ANDREW PICKENS, 8–43, 244004, KXKB (1739–1817) South Carolina congressman. Operated by South Atlantic.

18. WILLIAM L. YANCEY, 8–43, 244050, KXKC (1814–1863) William Lowndes Yancey was an Alabama congressman. Operated by J. H. Winchester.

19. GEORGE WHITEFIELD, 8–43, 244077, KYHE (1714–1770) English-born preacher and cofounder of Methodism who came to Savannah, Georgia in 1738. Operated by A. H. Bull.

20. JOSEPH E. BROWN, 8–43, 244158, KYHG (1821–1894) Joseph Emerson "Joe" Brown was a Georgia senator and governor. Operated by Cosmopolitan.

21. DUDLEY M. HUGHES, 9–43, 244212, KYHI (1848–1927) Dudley Mays Hughes was a Georgia congressman. Operated by Grace Line.

22. JEROME K. JONES, 9–43, 244253, KYIP (1860–1940) Jerome Kinsey Jones was an organized labor leader in Georgia and editor of the *Journal of Labor* from 1898 until he died, president of the Georgia Federation of Labor for two terms, and president of the Southern Labor Congress from 1912 to 1919. In 1920 he lived at 217 Oak St. in Atlanta with his wife Josephine, 44, and sons Charles, 20, and Jerome, 20. In 1925 he joined other Southern labor leaders in opposing an amendment creating federal child labor laws as a matter of states' rights and economics. In February 1931 his son Charles died while in police custody and the next month his wife died. In 1940 he lived in a rooming house at 853 Park St. W. and was still working 60 hours a week when he died on September 24, 1940. Operated by South Atlantic.

23. HOKE SMITH, 9–43, 244321, KYIQ (1855–1931) Michael Hoke Smith, known as M. Hoke Smith, was a trial attorney, publisher of the *Atlanta Journal*, Georgia governor and senator, and Secretary of the Interior. Operated by American Export Lines.

24. WILLIAM BLACK YATES, 10–43, 244392, KTWY (1809–1882) chaplain who served sailors in Charleston, South Carolina. Operated by T. J. Stevenson.

25. JAMES H. COUPER, 10–43, 244386, KTWZ (1794–1866) James Hamilton Couper was a Yale graduate and noted Georgia planter who advanced the use of scientific methods in farming. Operated by International Freighting.

26. JOSEPH HABERSHAM, 10–43, 244481, KTXV (1751–1815) Continental Army veteran, Georgia congressman, and Postmaster General. Operated by Isthmian.

27. JOSEPH H. MARTIN, 10–43, 244556, KTXW (1825–1883) believed to be the influential pastor of the Second Presbyterian Church at Knoxville, Tennessee. When war came he stayed with his church and in 1863 was taken prisoner by Gen. Ambrose Burnside's Federals and the church closed. He tended the sick and wounded, went to Virginia in 1867, and in 1873 became pastor of the First Presbyterian Church at Atlanta until he retired in 1882. Operated by Wessel, Duval.

28. ROBERT FECHNER, 11–43, 244597, KUHW (1876–1939) national labor union leader and director of the Civilian Conservation Corps. Operated by South Atlantic.

29. CHARLES C. JONES, 11–43, 244629, KUHX (1831–1893) Charles Colcock Jones, Jr., Presbyterian minister, lawyer, mayor of Savannah, Georgia, and historian. Operated by J. H. Winchester.

30. FLORENCE MARTUS, 11–43, 244660, KUIC (1868–1943) younger sister and housekeeper of Elba Island, Georgia, lighthouse keeper George W. Martus who used to wave at passing ships. Operated by Polarus.

31. CHARLES H. HERTY, 12–43, 244730, KUIG (1867–1938) Charles Holmes Herty was a chemist specializing in turpentine and pulp products made from pine trees. Organized the first college varsity football team at the University of Georgia. Operated by United States Navigation.

32. JOHN E. WARD, 12–43, 244771, KUIJ (1814–1902) John Elliott Ward was mayor of Savannah, Georgia, and minister to China. Operated by South Atlantic.

33. EDWIN L. GODKIN, 12–43, 244818, KUIQ (1831–1902) Irish-born Edwin Lawrence Godkin founded *The Nation* magazine and edited the *New York Evening Post*. Operated by Luckenbach.

34. A. FRANK LEVER, 12–43, 244839, KVFV (1875–1940) Asbury Francis Lever was a South Carolina congressman and founder of the 4-H Club. Supporters bought $2 million in War Bonds to pay for the ship. Operated by States Marine.

35. THOMAS WOLFE, 12–43, 244940, KVFY (1900–1938) Thomas Clayton Wolfe was a popular novelist. Operated by South Atlantic.

36. SAMVANNAH, 12–43, 169813, MYRB, built for the British Ministry of War Transport. Operated by Anchor Line.

37. BEN ROBERTSON, 1–44, 245004, KVPL (1903–1943) Benjamin Franklin "Ben" Robertson, Jr., was the foreign correspondent for the *New York Herald Tribune* who died in the crash of the Boeing 314 *Yankee Clipper* at Lisbon, Portugal, on February 22, 1943. Operated by A. H. Bull.

38. SAMUEL T. DARLING, 1–44, 245062, KVPN (1872–1925) Samuel Taylor Darling was a medical expert on tropical diseases. Operated by Grace Line.

39. ISAAC S. HOPKINS, 1–44, 245123, KVPQ (1841–1914) Isaac Stiles Hopkins was a clergyman and the first president of Georgia Tech. Operated by Isbrandtsen.

40. SAMHORN, 2–44, 169833, MYSP, built for the British Ministry of War Transport. Operated by Donaldson Bros. & Black.

41. A. MITCHELL PALMER, 2–44, 245154, KVPU (1872–1936) Alexander Mitchell Palmer was a Pennsylvania congressman and Attorney General. Operated by Isbrandtsen.

42. SAMDART, 3–44, 169950, MYSV, built for the British Ministry of War Transport. Operated by Mungo, Campbell & Co.

43. JOHN E. SWEET, 3–44, 245217, KWAI (1832–1916) John Edison Sweet made the first micrometer, designed and patented an upright steam engine, made a governor for high-speed steam engines, and cofounded the American Society of Mechanical Engineers. Operated by Black Diamond.

44. CLARK HOWELL, 3–44, 245271, KWAJ (1863–1936) editor of the *Atlantic Constitution* and Georgia politician. Operated by Parry.

45. EARL LAYMAN, 4–44, 245323, KWAK (1912–1942) Joseph Earl Layman was the 2nd Mate lost on the *Stephen Hopkins*, sunk on September 27, 1942, in a battle with the German raider *Stiers* and tender *Tannenfels*. Operated by Polarus.

46. JOHN A. TREUTLEN, 4–44, 245324, KWQB (1734–1782) John Adam Treutlen was the first post–British era governor of Georgia who was murdered on March 1, 1782, during ongoing political conflicts in the colony. Operated by South Atlantic. Capt. Gustav Andersen's ship was torpedoed by *U-984* on June 29, 1944, off St. Catherine's Point, England. There were no reported fatalities.

47. BEN A. RUFFIN, 4–44, 245321, KWPY (1879–1939) Benjamin Allen Ruffin was the president of the first Lions Clubs International post in Virginia. Operated by Marine Transport.

48. WILLIAM D. HOXIE, 5–44, 245394, KWQG (1866–1925) William Dixie Hoxie,

of Westerly, Rhode Island, was a marine engineer who patented a design for a water-tube boiler in 1920 and assigned it to Babcock & Wilcox for manufacture. Operated by Stockard.

49. SAMCEBU, 5–44, 169890, GWPP, built for the British Ministry of War Transport. Operated by the Bolton Steam Shipping Co.

50. HARRY L. GLUCKSMAN, 5–44, 245528, WFZB (1889–1938) attorney who combined the Young Men's and Young Women's Hebrew Associations into the Jewish Welfare Board in 1917 and served as executive director. Later renamed the Jewish Community Center. Operated by Merchants & Miners.

51. JULIETTE LOW, 5–44, 245530, WFZE (1860–1927) Julliette Magill Kinzie Gordon married William M. Low in 1886. They had no children and divorced in 1901. In 1912 she organized the first troop of American Girl Guides, later named the Girl Scouts. Low's niece, Daisy Gordon, the first Girl Guide, christened her aunt's ship as the married Daisy Lawrence. Operated by South Atlantic.

52. THEMISTOCLES, 6–44 (525 BC-460 BC) Greek politician and general. Operated under the Greek flag.

53. JACOB SLOAT FASSETT, 6–44, 245748, WOEQ (1853–1924) New York congressman. Operated by Stockard.

54. RICHARD UPJOHN, 6–44, 245858, WQUN (1802–1878) noted architect of Gothic Revival churches. Operated by T. J. Stevenson.

55. WILLIAM G. LEE, 7–44, 245864, WQAX (1859–1929) William Granville Lee was a railroad worker who became president of the Brotherhood of Railroad Trainmen. Operated by South Atlantic.

56. RUBEN DARIO, 7–44, 245859, WQAY (1867–1916) Félix Rubén Garcia Sarmiento Dario was a Nicaraguan poet. Operated by International Freighting. Capt. Ernst F. Carlsson's ship was torpedoed by *U-825* on January 27, 1945. There were no reported casualties and the ship was repaired.

57. BENJAMIN BROWN FRENCH, 7–44, 246091, WQAZ (1800–1870) Lincoln Administration official and identifier of John Wilkes Booth. Operated by Luckenbach.

58. STEPHEN LEACOCK, 7–44, 246098, WQBD (1869–1944) Stephen Butler Leacock was a Canadian writer and humorist. Operated by South Atlantic.

59. ALEXANDER R. SHEPERD, 8–44, 246275, WRKS (1835–1902) Alexander Robey "Boss Sheperd" was a controversial official, innovator, and governor of the District of Columbia. Operated by A. L. Burbank.

60. CHARLES A. KEFFER, 8–44, 246093, WRLA (1861–1935) Charles Albert Keffer was a noted Iowa horticulturist who worked in various states and organizations. Operated by South Atlantic.

61. RISDEN TYLER BENNETT, 8–44, 246096, WRLG (1840–1913) North Carolina congressman. Operated by American West African Line.

62. JAMES SWAN, 8–44, 246279, WRKX (1754–1830) Scottish patriot who participated in the Boston Tea Party, served at Bunker Hill, became successful in business, entered Massachusetts politics but became indebted and died in Paris after release from debtor's prison. Operated by South Atlantic.

63. MARTHA BERRY, 8–44, 246280, WRKZ (1865–1942) Martha McChesney Berry founded the Boys Industrial School in 1902, the Martha Berry School for Girls in 1909, and Berry Junior College in Rome, Georgia, in 1926. She died on February 27, 1942, in Atlanta. Operated by the Black Diamond.

64. FRANK P. WALSH, 9–44, 246277, KSOQ (1864–1939) Francis Patrick Walsh was a lawyer appointed by President Wilson to the Commission on Industrial Relations and

co-chairman of the National War Labor Board during the World War. Operated by R. A. Nicol.

65. FLOYD GIBBONS, 9–44, 246473, WSOT (1887–1939) Floyd Phillips Gibbons was a war correspondent for the *Chicago Tribune* during World War I who pioneered the use of radio for voice newscasts. He was on the British steamer *Laconia* when it was torpedoed and lost an eye while participating in the battle at Belleau Wood, for which he was decorated. He died at home in Pennsylvania. Operated by South Atlantic.

66. JONAS LIE, 9–44, 246476, WSOW (1880–1940) popular Norwegian-born painter of coastal and marine seascapes and New York City scenes. Operated by AGWI Lines. Capt. Carl L. Von Schoen, 63, left Savannah, Georgia, in September 1944 and arrived at New York on November 22 from Liverpool where 25 sailors paid off and Ricardo M. Garcia, 41, signed on along with 23 others. Capt. Von Schoen expected to sail on December 8 from the Federal Anchorage. The ship was torpedoed on January 9, 1945, by *U-1055* in the Bristol Channel with the loss of oiler Wallace D. Colson and fireman/watertender Ricardo Garcia.

67. JOHN P. HARRIS, 10–44, 246475, KSOP (1873–1926) John Paul Harris was an entertainment promoter with the Harris Comedy & Specialty Co., the company that showed the first motion picture in Pittsburgh in 1897 and in June 1905 opened the Nickelodian, the first dedicated motion picture theater in the world. Operated by Black Diamond.

68. RICHARD COULTER, 10–44, 246576, KSOJ (1827–1908) Pennsylvania banker and Union general. Operated by Overlakes.

69. ADDIE BAGLEY DANIELS, 10–44, 246571, KSOT (1869–1943) Addie Bagley Worth married Josephus Daniels, Secretary of the Navy. Operated by States Marine.

70. WILLIAM H. EDWARDS, 10–44, 246634, KSOY (1822–1909) William Henry Edwards was a noted entomologist and resident of West Virginia. Operated by A. H. Bull.

71. JOSEPH MURGAS, 10–44, 246629, KTBD (1864–1929) Jozef Murgaš was a Slovak priest whose inventions contributed to wireless communication. Operated by J. H. Winchester.

72. MILTON J. FOREMAN, 11–44, 246632, KTBE (1863–1935) Milton Joseph Foreman was an Army veteran and national commander of the American Legion. Operated by International Freighting.

73. JOSEPH S. MCDONAGH, 11–44, 246733, KTBF (1879–1944) Joseph Sylvester McDonagh was an electrician at the Brooklyn Navy Yard and secretary-treasurer of the American Federation of Labor Metal Trades Department. Operated by Overlakes.

74. JOSIAH TATTNALL, 11–44, 246734, KTBK (1794–1871) son of the Georgia senator and governor who served as a commodore in the Navy during the War of 1812 and in the Confederate States Navy. Operated by Wessell, Duval.

75. MOINA MICHAEL, 11–44, 246737, KTBN (1869–1944) Moina Belle Michael was a professor at the University of Georgia who worked with the YWCA during World War I. She adopted the red poppy from John McCrae's poem "In Flanders Fields" to honor veterans of the Great War and sold them to raise funds for diabled veterans. Operated by Stockard.

76. ROBERT PARROT, 11–44, 246869, KTTU (1804–1877) Robert Parker Parrott was an artillery officer and foundry operator who developed the Parrott Rifle. Operated by Dichmann, Wright & Pugh.

77. JOSIAH COHEN, 12–44, 246896, KTTW (1840–1930) noted Pittsburgh lawyer, judge, and legal ethicist. Operated by Overlakes.

78. RUDOLPH KAUFFMANN, 12–44, 246870, KTTY (1853–1927) managing editor of the *Washington Evening Star*. Operated by T. J. Stevenson.

79. JAMES H. PRICE, 12–44, 246970, ANBK (1878–1943) James Hubert Price was

Virginia's New Deal governor who died on November 22, 1943. Operated by Dichmann, Wright & Pugh.

80. WILLIAM L. MCLEAN, 12–44, 247009, ANBL (1852–1931) William Lippard McLean published the *Philadelphia Evening Bulletin*. The *Cummings' Evening Telegraphic Bulletin* was started in 1847 by Alexander Cummings and was the first newspaper to publish reports received by telegraph, specifically about the Mexican War. In 1859 it was purchased by Gibson Peacock and by McLean in 1895 after Peacock died and became the *Philadelphia Evening Bulletin*. The paper was run by his family until the last McLean died on August 27, 2011. Operated by William J. Rountree.

81. EDWARD J. BERWIND, 1–45, 247014, ANBM (1848–1936) Edward Julius Berwind was a Naval Academy graduate who partnered with Allison White to enter the coal industry as Berwind, White & Co. Operated by Wilmore.

82. WILLIAM W. SEATON, 1–45, 247061, ANBN (1785–1866) William Winston Seaton was co-owner with brother-in-law Joseph Gales, Jr., of the *National Intelligencer* newspaper at Washington, D.C. The two were official Congressional House reporters and published the *Annals of Congress*, the *Register of Debates*, and the *American State Papers*. Seaton was also mayor of Washington, D.C. Operated by T. J. Stevenson.

83. MACK BRUTON BRYAN, 1–45, 247060, ANEX (1907–1940) 3rd assistant engineer lost on the *City of Rayville* after hitting a German mine off Australia on November 9, 1940. Operated by Merchants & Miners.

84. WILLIAM TERRY HOWELL, 1–45, 247174, ANEY (1917–1942) wiper lost on the *Carrabulle*, torpedoed by *U-106* on May 26, 1942, in the Gulf of Mexico. Operated by International Freighting.

85. WILLIAM LEROY GABLE, 1–45, 247173, ANEZ (1892–1942) chief engineer lost on the *Carrabulle*, sunk by *U-106* on May 26, 1942, in the Gulf of Mexico. Operated by Union Sulphur.

86. HARRY KIRBY, 2–45, 247191, ANIE (1902–1942) 1st assistant engineer lost on the *Lebore*, torpedoed on June 14, 1942, by *U-172* off Panama. Operated by Blidberg Rothchild.

87. ARLIE CLARK, 2–45, 247261, ANIF (1893–1942) chief engineer lost on the *Hampton Roads*, torpedoed by *U-106* on June 1, 1942, off Cuba. Operated by

88. THOMAS W. MURRAY, 2–45, 247279, ANIO (1903–1943) bosun lost on the tanker *William C. McTarnahan*, torpedoed by *U-506* on May 16, 1942, in the Gulf of Mexico. Operated by Cosmopolitan.

Todd-Bath Iron Shipbuilding Corp.
120 Exchange St., South Portland, Maine

Ceased operation on April 1, 1943, with the forced merger of Todd-Bath Iron and South Portland Ship into the New England Shipbuilding Corp. William S. Newell's company built 14 Liberty ships. The first keel was laid down on September 9, 1942, and the average building time for the ships was 70.4 days.

1. WILLIAM P. FESSENDEN, 12–42, 242595, KKCI (1806–1869) William Pitt Fessenden was a Maine congressman and Secretary of the Treasury. Operated by American Export Lines.

2. WINSLOW HOMER, 12–42, 242596, KKCJ (1836–1910) popular illustrator, landscape and marine artist, and printmaker. Operated by AGWI Lines.

3. JOHN MURRAY FORBES, 1–43, 242632, KKCL (1771–1831) lawyer, diplomat, and pioneer China-trader with Augustine Heard. Operated by Black Diamond.

4. AUGUSTINE HEARD, 1–43, 242630, KISX (1785–1868) prominent sea captain in the China trade with John Murray Forbes. Operated by Coastwise Transportation.

5. EDWARD PREBLE, 2–43, 242696, KKFN (1761–1807) noted naval officer in the war with Tripoli and Algiers from 1801 to 1805. Operated by Eastern Steamship then taken by the Navy and operated as *Volans* (AKS-9), commissioned on March 31, 1944.

6. CALVIN COOLIDGE, 2–43, 242814, KKFS (1872–1933) John Calvin Coolidge, Jr., was the 30th President of the United States. Operated by Sprague.

7. JOHN A. DIX, 2–43, 242820, KKFV (1798–1879) John Adams Dix was a New York senator, governor, Secretary of the Treasury, and minister to France. Operated by Shepard.

8. WALTER E. RANGER, 2–43, 242886, KKFO (1855–1941) Walter Eugene Ranger was the Rhode Island commissioner of education. Operated by Eastern Steamship.

9. NOAH WEBSTER, 2–43, 242885, KKFP (1758–1843) dictionary publisher. Operated by Sprague.

10. ELIPHALET NOTT, 2–43, 242883, KKLG (1773–1866) steam engine scientist, coal stove inventor, and president of Union College at Schenectady, New York. Operated by Eastern Steamship.

11. ISAAC SHARPLESS, 3–43, 242891, KKLI (1848–1920) longtime Haverford College professor and president in Haverford, Pennsylvania. Operated by Eastern Gas & Fuel.

12. TIMOTHY DWIGHT, 3–43, 242896, KKLK (1752–1817) president of Yale University. Operated by Coastwise Transportation.

13. EZRA CORNELL, 3–43, 243041, KKLL (1807–1874) telegraph pioneer and founder of Western Union. Operated by R. A. Nicol.

14. FRANCIS AMASA WALKER, 4–43, 243042, KKLN (1840–1897) noted economist and president of the American Statistical Association and the Massachusetts Institute of Technology. Operated by Eastern Steamship.

Todd Houston Shipbuilding Corp.
Irish Bend Island, Houston, Texas

The 200-acre Houston Shipbuilding Corp. yard was established on January 6, 1941, as a joint Todd-Kaiser venture but Todd took sole control after the February 14, 1942, split with Kaiser. The Maritime Commission spent $279,780 on land and $14,479,387 on facilities. The 9-way, Commission-owned yard built 208 Liberty ships under general manager Arthur Stout. The first keel was laid down on July 18, 1941, and the average building time for the ships was 68.4 days.

1. SAM HOUSTON, 5–42, 241678, KEVY (1793–1863), Samuel Houston was the governor of Tennessee, president of the Republic of Texas, and a Texas senator. Operated by Waterman. Capt. Robert Perry's ship was torpedoed on June 28, 1942, by *U-203* near the Virgin Islands with the loss of eight merchant crewmen.

2. DAVY CROCKETT, 6–42, 241773, KEUD (1786–1836) David Crockett was a frontiersman, Mississippi congressman, and Alamo defender. Operated by Lykes.

3. MATTHEW MAURY, 6–42, 866, KFLB (1806–1873) Matthew Fontaine Maury was the first superintendent of the Naval Observatory and established a system of timekeeping that evolved through technology to make the Observatory the official time source for the

United States. He was also a world renowned oceanographer and a Confederate naval officer. Operated by Lykes. Capt. Gosta M. C. Carlsen's ship was torpedoed by *U-371* on July 10, 1943, off Algeria. There were no casualties.

4. WINFIELD SCOTT, 6–42, 241869, KFVL (1786–1866) commissioned a captain in the Army's Light Artillery in 1808 and over his 53-year career was known as "Old Fuss and Feathers" and "The Grand Old Man of the Army" serving through all the major and minor foreign and domestic conflicts. He left many namesakes around the country. Operated by A. H. Bull.

5. MICHAEL J. STONE, 6–42, 241867, KFYQ (1747–1812) Michael Jenifer Stone was a Maryland congressman. Operated by Lykes. Capt. Guy E. Parker's ship was torpedoed by *U-300* on February 17, 1945, off Gibraltar. There were no reported casualties.

6. BENJAMIN BOURN, 7–42, 241926, KEYX (1755–1808) Revolutionary War veteran and Congressman from Rhode Island. Operated by Mississippi Shipping.

7. DAVID S. TERRY, 7–42, 241928, KETY (1823–1889) David Smith Terry was an irascible and controversial California politician who left for Texas after being acquitted of murder in a duel and formed Terry's Texas Rangers during the Civil War. He was killed by a bodyguard after assaulting a Supreme Court justice. Operated by United Fruit.

8. DANIEL CARROLL, 8–42, 241927, KFBP (1730–1796) delegate to the Constitutional Convention from Maryland. Operated by J. H. Winchester. Capt. Kenneth W. Pratt's ship was torpedoed by *U-371* on February 28, 1943, off Algeria. There were no reported casualties.

9. MIRABEAU B. LAMAR, 8–42, 242930, KGAT (1798–1859) Mirabeau Buonaparte Lamar was president of Texas. Operated by Waterman.

10. STEPHEN F. AUSTIN, 8–42, 241931, KHYS (1793–1836) Stephen Fuller Austin is considered the father of Texas. Operated by Lykes. Capt. Ernest Ban's ship was torpedoed on April 20, 1944, off Algeria by German aircraft. There were no casualties reported and the ship was repaired.

11. WILLIAM B. TRAVIS, 8–42, 241932, KGBA (1809–1836) William Barret Travis was a Texas Army officer lost at the Alamo. Operated by Lykes. Capt. Karl Sandberg's ship hit a mine off Bizerte, Tunisia, on September 12, 1943, with the loss of one soldier. The ship was repaired.

12. DANIEL HEISTER, 8–42, 242066, KFBQ (1747–1804) Pennsylvania and Maryland congressman. Operated by United Fruit.

13. NICHOLAS GILMAN, 8–42, 242069, KFLX (1755–1814) New Hampshire congressman. Operated by American South African.

14. SAMUEL GRIFFIN, 8–42, 242070, KFOT (1746–1810) Virginia congressman. Operated by Seas Shipping. Capt. Francis DeSales' ship was bombed by German aircraft on May 19, 1943, at Oran, Algeria. There were no reported fatalities.

15. THEODORE SEDGWICK, 8–42, 242071, KFQA (1746–1813) Massachusetts senator. Operated by Parry.

16. THOMAS HARTLEY, 8–42, 242072, KFQW (1748–1800) Pennsylvania congressman. Operated by Merchants & Miners. Capt. James G. Hunley, 47, left Baltimore on December 30, 1943, and arrived at New York on May 8, 1944, from Murmansk, Russia, with seven Russian citizen passengers and five Russian naval aviators.

17. BENJAMIN HUNTINGTON, 9–42, 242255, KEZD (1736–1800) Connecticut congressman. Operated by Lykes.

18. JEREMIAH WADSWORTH, 10–42, 242256, KFHS (1743–1804) sea captain who supplied goods to the Continental Army and became a Connecticut congressman. Operated by Marine Transport. Capt. Arnt Magnusdal's ship was torpedoed on November 27, 1942, by

U-178 off South Africa. There were no reported casualties. Chief mate Van Rutherford McCarthy was awarded the Merchant Marine Distinguished Service medal.

19. JOHN LAURANCE, 10–42, 242257, KFIH (1750–1810) New York congressman. Operated by Lykes.

20. SAMUEL LIVERMORE, 10–42, 242258, KFPF (1732–1803) New Hampshire congressman. Operated by Stockard.

21. THOMAS T. TUCKER, 10–42, 242259, KFRT (1745–1828) Thomas Tudor Tucker was a physician, South Carolina congressman, and in 1801 was appointed Treasurer of the United States. Operated by Merchants & Miners.

22. HOUSTON VOLUNTEERS, 10–42, 242394, KHJK. The heavy cruiser *Houston* (CA-30) was sunk by Japanese ships in the Battle of the Java Sea in the early hours of February 27, 1942. It was known the ship had been lost but no details were known until November. In May 1942 a call went out for volunteers to replace the crew of the lost ship and 1,650 were accepted for naval service. The number of volunteers accepted was then set at 1,000. Operated by Lykes.

23. A. P. HILL, 10–42, 242391, KHJV (1825–1865) Ambrose Powell Hill was a Confederate general lost on April 2, 1865, at Petersburg, Virginia. Operated by Marine Transport.

24. JAMES BOWIE, 10–42, 242395, KHKW (1796–1836) knife inventor and defender of the Alamo. Operated by United Fruit.

25. JAMES LONGSTREET, 10–42, 242396, KHKT (1821–1904) Confederate general. Operated by International Freighting. Capt. Thomas J. Nelson's ship stranded on October 26, 1943, on the Jersey shore in a gale and was declared a total constructive loss.

26. LAMBERT CADWALADER, 11–42, 242398, KHKY (1743–1823) Philadelphia merchant, Revolutionary War soldier, and New Jersey congressman. Operated by Merchants & Miners.

27. THOMAS J. RUSK, 11–42, 242400, KHIY (1803–1857) Thomas Jefferson Rusk was the first Republic of Texas secretary of war and a Texas senator who died by his own hand on July 29, 1857, due to illness and the death of his wife. Operated by United Fruit.

28. JOSEPH E. JOHNSTON, 11–42, 242541, KHQJ (1807–1891) Joseph Eggleston Johnston was a Confederate general and Virginia congressman. Operated by United Fruit. The ship's skipper was Paul Jones, 35, of Mobile, Alabama, who was a direct descendant of naval hero John Paul Jones.

29. J. E. B. STUART, 12–42, 242539, KHQN (1833–1864) James Ewell Brown "Jeb" Stuart was a Confederate general lost at the Battle of Yellow Tavern on May 11, 1864, in Virginia. Operated by Merchants & Miners.

30. JOHN B. HOOD, 12–42, 242540, KIDU (1831–1879) John Bell Hood was a Confederate general. Operated by United Fruit.

31. BIG FOOT WALLACE, 12–42, 242537, KKDK (1817–1899) William Alexander "Bigfoot" Wallace was a fabled Texas Ranger. Operated by Standard Fruit.

32. JAMES MADISON, 12–42, 242538, KHMF (1750–1836) 4th President of the United States. Operated by Lykes.

33. AMELIA EARHART, 12–42, 242542, KKDG (1897–1937) Amelia Mary Earhart was the first female aviator to fly solo across the Atlantic, for which she received the Distinguished Flying Cross. She was lost in the Pacific Ocean while flying around the world. Operated by Merchants & Miners.

34. CHAMP CLARK, 1–43, 242713, KKDF (1850–1921) James Beauchamp "Champ" Clark was a Missouri congressman and speaker of the House in 1913 when he arrested George C. Glover for assaulting Thestus Simms. Operated by United Fruit.

35. JOSEPH T. ROBINSON, 1–43, 242717, KKDD (1872–1937) Joseph Taylor Robinson was an Arkansas congressman and governor. Operated by Lykes.

36. STEPHEN C. FOSTER, 1–43, 242722, KHKP (1826–1864) Stephen Collins Foster was a songwriter considered to be the father of American music having written the classics "Oh Susanna," "Camptown Races," etc. Operated by Standard Fruit.

37. WILLIAM L. SMITH, 1–43, 242725, KHKZ (1758–1812) William Laughton Smith was a South Carolina congressman. Operated by United Fruit.

38. WILLIAM EUSTIS, 1–43, 242724, KEYL (1753–1825) surgeon, Massachusetts congressman and governor and Secretary of War. Operated by United Fruit. Capt. Cecil Desmond's ship was torpedoed on March 17, 1943, by *U-435* and *U-91* in the North Atlantic. There were no reported casualties.

39. JOHN ARMSTRONG, 2–43, 242839, KKME (1758–1843) New York senator and Secretary of War. Operated by Grace Line. Grace Line skipper Capt. George E. Strom, 40, left the Army base at Norfolk, Virginia, around March 3, 1944, and arrived at Naples, Italy on the 29th. On April 21 the ship was off Anzio when they hit a mine and S1c Michael Peter Favale, USNR, from Lt. Kenneth H. Atmstrong's 28-man Armed Guard crew was mortally wounded. They put in at Naples where African-American messman William H. Robinson, 34, was declared missing from the ship on July 7 and did not sail with them. They arrived at New York on August 8 from Oran, Algeria, and the ship was repaired. Mike Favale, 20, lived with his brother Joseph, 35, his wife Josephine, 34, their son Joseph, 11, and Joseph's other brothers Arnelis, 28, Albert, 21, John 17, and sister Mary, 23, at 207 Meriline Ave. in Waterbury, Connecticut. Joseph was a laborer in a brass factory, Arnelis drove truck for a construction company, Mary was a seamstress, and Albert worked for a masonry contractor. In 1930 Petro Favale, 52, his wife Carmela, 44, both natives of Italy, lived in a home they owned with their eight kids at 8 Meriline Ave. in Waterbury. Petro worked at a masonry factory.

40. WILLIAM H. CRAWFORD, 2–43, 242843, KKMF (1772–1834) William Harris Crawford was a Georgia senator and Secretary of War and Treasury. Operated by Lykes.

41. JAMES BARBOUR, 2–43, 242837, KKMH (1785–1842) governor of Virginia, senator, and Secretary of War. Operated by Lykes.

42. JOHN H. EATON, 2–43, 242840, KKMI (1790–1856) John Henry Eaton was a Tennessee senator, governor of Florida, and Secretary of War. Operated by Parry.

43. JOEL R. POINSETT, 2–43, 242838, KKMJ (1779–1851) Joel Roberts Poinsett was a South Carolina congressman, minister to Mexico, and Secretary of War. Operated by Standard Fruit. Capt. Thomas R. Morrison arrived at New York on December 5, 1943, from Naples, Italy, to conclude Voyage No. 3. Capt. Joseph B. Lankey expected to leave Staten Island on Voyage No. 4 on December 28. The ship broke apart on March 4, 1944, in the North Atlantic. There were no casualties.

44. JOHN BELL, 3–43, 242976, KKML (1796–1869) Tennessee congressman and Secretary of War. Operated by J. H. Winchester. Capt. David D. Higbee's ship was torpedoed on August 26, 1943, by *U-410* off Algeria with the loss of oiler William J. Rasche.

45. JOHN C. SPENCER, 3–43, 242977, KKMO (1788–1855) John Canfield Spencer was Secretary of War and Treasury who strongly advocated the use of import duties to raise money for government as opposed to internal taxation. Operated by American South African.

46. JAMES M. PORTER, 3–43, 242975, KKMP (1793–1862) James Madison Porter was the first president of the Lehigh Valley Railroad, Secretary of War, and cofounder of Lafayette College. Operated by Smith & Johnson.

47. WILLIAM WILKINS, 3–43, 242978, KKMR (1779–1865) Pennsylvania senator, minister to Russia, and Secretary of War. Operated by American South African.

48. FITZHUGH LEE, 3–43, 242974, KIED (1835–1905) Confederate general and governor of Virginia. Operated by Smith & Johnson.

49. JUBAL A. EARLY, 4–43, 243141, KIES (1816–1894) Jubal Anderson Early was a Confederate general who almost reached Washington, D.C., in 1865. Operated by Lykes.

50. RICHARD S. EWELL, 4–43, 243143, KIET (1817–1872) Richard Stoddert Ewell was a Confederate major general. Operated by American South African.

51. GEORGE E. PICKETT, 4–43, 243140, KIEX (1825–1875) George Edward Pickett was a Confederate major general who commanded the First Corps, Army of Northern Virginia at Gettysburg during the disastrous Pickett-Pettigrew-Trimble "charge" on July 3, 1863. Operated by Waterman.

52. WILLIAM N. PENDLETON, 4–43, 243145, KLDG (1809–1883) William Nelson Pendleton was a Confederate general of artillery under Lee's command. Operated by Lykes.

53. MOSES AUSTIN, 4–43, 243142, KNCU (1761–1821) Texas landholder and namesake for Austin, Texas. Operated by American South African.

54. BENITO JUAREZ, 4–43, 243275, KNCW (1806–1872) Benito Pablo Juárez Garcia was a lawyer and president of Mexico. Operated by United Fruit.

55. DAVID G. BURNET, 5–43, 243276, KNEP (1788–1870) David Gouverneur Burnet was president of the Republic of Texas. Operated by Waterman.

56. JAMES S. HOGG, 5–43, 243279, KNEQ (1851–1906) James Stephen "Big Jim" Hogg was governor of Texas. Operated by Parry Navigation. Capt. Enno Hanken made one voyage then the ship was taken by the Navy and operated as the *Crater*-class cargo ship *Pavo* (AK-139), NHDH, commissioned on January 14, 1944.

57. JANE LONG, 5–43, 243419, KNHP (1798–1880) Jane Herbert Wilkinson, of Maryland, married physician James Long, of Virginia. Long became obsessed with liberating Texas from Spain and in 1819 organized his own private army to do that and they moved there. On December 21, 1821, she had a daughter they named Mary James Long and mom came to be known as the "Mother of Texas." Operated by North Atlantic & Gulf.

58. JAMES B. BONHAM, 5–43, 243417, KNWC (1807–1836) James Butler Bonham was an Alamo defender and namesake for Bonham, Texas. Operated by Lykes.

59. JAMES W. FANNIN, 5–43, 243418, KOLW (1804–1836) James Walker Fannin, Jr., died at Goliad, Texas, during the Texas Revolution. Namesake of Fannin Counties in Georgia and Texas. Operated by American South African. On July 25, 1945, Stars and Stripes reported that Capt. Dessel Oliver Scott, 35, who skippered the *Fannin* through the war without a scratch, was riding in a "command car" at Bremerhaven, Germany, with two Red Cross clubmobile hostesses, Bonnie O'Brien, of Hymore, South Dakota, and Helen Lockwood, of Cleveland, Ohio, when a cyclist cut in front of them and the driver swerved, ran over a pile of rubble, and landed in a bomb crater filled with water. All occupants had to swim 25 feet to shore. The ship arrived at New York on August 13, 1945.

60. ANSON JONES, 5–43, 243408, KOLR (1798–1858) last president of the Republic of Texas. Operated by Isthmian.

61. FREDERICK L. DAU, 5–43, 243413, KOLV (1851–1934) German-born Friedrich Leonhart Dau sailed on his family's ship *Mathilda* to the Orient in 1864 and in 1874 came to Galveston, Texas, to look after some of his father's shipping interests. In the 1880s he operated "a small fleet of ships up and down the waters around Galveston," worked as a "screwman" using screwjacks to pack bales of cotton into ships' holds, sold insurance, then Singer Sewing machines. In 1890 he married Texas-born Marie Schmidt and they had a daughter Margarite. He became a citizen on March 19, 1927, lived a quiet life, was active poltically, and was highly regarded at mathematics. Marie died on March 29, 1933, in Galveston. Operated by Calmar.

62. EDWARD BURLESON, 6–43, 243585, KOWA (1798–1851) vice president of the Republic of Texas. Operated by Lykes.

63. JAMES E. HAVILAND, 6–43, 243589, KOWM (1810–1869) James Edward Haviland was a pioneer Texas steamboat designer, builder, captain, Commissioner of Pilots for the Port of Galveston in 1866, and U.S. Steamboat Inspector. Operated by Luckenbach.

64. LORENZO DE ZAVALA, 6–43, 243594, KOWN (1788–1836) Manuel Lorenzo Justiniano de Zavala y Sáenz was finance minister of Mexico, vice president of the Republic of Texas, and signer of the Texas Declaration of Independence. Operated by United Fruit.

65. JOHN MARY ODIN, 6–43, 243592, KOWT (1801–1870) Jean-Marie Odin was the first bishop of the Diocese of Galveston, essentially the entire state of Texas. Operated by United Fruit.

66. MARY AUSTIN, 6–43, 243595, KOWZ (1868–1934) Mary Hunter, of Carlinville, Illinois, married Stafford W. Austin in California, began writing novels, poetry, plays, and became a foremost nature writer. Operated by AGWI Lines.

67. BENJAMIN R. MILAM, 6–43, 243582, KOVQ (1788–1835) Benjamin Rush Milam was a defender of the Alamo. Operated by American South African. A boiler exploded on March 8, 1945, at Locust Point, Baltimore, sinking the ship and fatally injuring pipefitter William Youngman, 49, of Baltimore. First assistant engineer John Hoffland was reported missing,

68. SIDNEY SHERMAN, 6–43, 243600, KOXL (1805–1873) manufacturer and Texas Army general who is credited with originating the "Remember the Alamo!" slogan. Operated by Luckenbach.

69. E. A. PEDEN, 6–43, 243583, KOVS (1868–1923) Edward Andrew Peden was the federal Food Administrator for Texas during World War I. Operated by United States Navigation.

70. SAM HOUSTON II, 7–43, 243759, KXKZ (1793–1863), Samuel Houston was the governor of Tennessee, Republic of Texas president, and Texas senator. Operated by Grace Line.

71. GEORGE C. CHILDRESS, 7–43, 243748, KXLB (1804–1841) George Campbell Childress authored the Texas Declaration of Independence and is the namesake for Childress, Texas. Operated by Grace Line.

72. J. PINCKNEY HENDERSON, 7–43, 243753, KXLC (1808–1858) James Pinckney Henderson was the first governor of the state of Texas. Operated by United Fruit. Capt. Clarence H. Lundy's ship was in Convoy HX 252 on August 19, 1943, when they collided with Capt. Niclas J. Joensen's Panamanian-flagged Panama Transport Co. tanker *J. H. Senior* resulting in an enormous conflagration from which there were only four survivors. On the *Henderson*, Capt. Lundy, 38 merchant crew, and 25 Armed Guard sailors were lost. Bosun Pat Sullivan was the only survivor. There were three survivors from the tanker: GM3c Walter A. Gawlick, 22, messman Eskild Lundsgaard, and oiler Sture E. Wihlborg. The ship had 14 Armed Guard sailors. Only five of the tanker's 42 crew were American citizens. Both vessels were total losses. A lawsuit under the Death on the High Seas Act of 1920 was filed by the families from both vessels, including the Armed Guard's, and in March 1950 a settlement was reached whereby the accident was declared no-fault and the United States and Panama Transport would each put up $350,000 and the total divided among the families based on the loss of income the decedent provided. No one challenged the claims of the Armed Guard families even though the court cast serious doubt on their standing to do so. The survivors also received settlements.

73. GEORGE P. GARRISON, 7–43, 243749, KXLD (1853–1910) George Pierce

Garrison was a noted university educator in Georgia and Texas and cofounded the Texas State Historical Association. Operated by Lykes.

74. ORAN M. ROBERTS, 8–43, 243755, KXLG (1815–1898) Oran Milo Roberts was a governor of Texas. Operated by United Fruit.

75. ROBERT T. HILL, 8–43, 243941, KXLH (1858–1941) Robert Thomas Hill is considered the father of Texas geology. Operated by Parry.

76. FREDERICK H. NEWELL, 8–43, 243936, KXYY (1862–1932) Frederick Haynes Newell was chief engineer then first director of the Reclamation Service. Operated by Luckenbach.

77. JOHN H. REAGAN, 8–43, 243940, KXZC (1818–1905) John Henninger Reagan was a Texas judge, senator, Confederate Secretary of the Treasury, Postmaster General, and namesake for Reagan County, Texas. Operated by Parry.

78. R. M. WILLIAMSON, 8–43, 244027, KXZE (1804–1859) Robert McAlpin "Three Legged Willie" Willamson was a crippled lawyer who advocated for Texas independence and served as senator after statehood. Operated by Standard Fruit.

79. JESSE BILLINGSLEY, 8–43, 244024, KXZG (1810–1880) Tennessee native who moved to Texas in 1834, fought in the Texas Revolution and was wounded at San Jacinto, then became a legislator and Indian fighter. Operated by William J. Rountree.

80. EDWIN W. MOORE, 8–43, 244021, KXZH (1810–1865) Edwin Ward Moore was commander of the Republic of Texas Navy and namesake for Moore County. Operated by Waterman.

81. GEORGE BELLOWS, 9–43, 244023, KXZJ (1822–1925) George Wesley Bellows was a noted artist of urban scenes. Operated by R. A. Nicol.

82. DAVID WILMOT, 9–43, 244200, KXZK (1814–1868) Pennsylvania congressman. Operated by United States Navigation.

83. SAMUEL H. WALKER, 9–43, 244203, KYJH (1817–1847) Samuel Hamilton Walker was an officer in the Armies of the Republic of Texas and the United States, co-invented the Walker Colt revolver, and was lost on October 9, 1847, during the Battle of Huamantla during the Mexican-American War. Operated by A. H. Bull and converted to an animal transport ship.

84. ERASTUS SMITH, 9–43, 244201, KYJI (1787–1837) Erastus "Deaf" (pronounced "deef") Smith fought in the Texas Revolution and is the namesake for Deaf Smith County, Texas. Operated by United Fruit.

85. JOSE NAVARRO, 10–43, 244202, KYJK (1795–1871) José Antonio Navarro was an advocate for Texas independence and a Republic of Texas congressman. Operated by Grace Line as an animal transport ship. Capt. Ernest MacClelland's ship was torpedoed on December 26, 1943, by *U-178* off Cochin, India. There were no casualties reported.

86. JOSHUA A. LEACH, 10–43, 244361, KTNG (1843–1919) Irish-born Joshua Alexander Leach was the main organizer of the Brotherhood of Locomotive Firemen on the Erie Railroad at Port Jervis, New York, in 1873. Operated by A. H. Bull.

87. HARVEY C. MILLER, 10–43, 244357, KTNH (1862–1936) Harvey Clayton Miller founded the Southern Steamship Co. in 1910, the first steamboat service between Philadelphia and Texas. Operated by J. H. Winchester.

88. GEORGE W. LIVELY, 10–43, 244356, KTNI (1791–18??) New Orleans shipowner whose vessel *George W. Lively* brought the first settlers, seeds, provisions, farm implements, and 18 settlers to Galveston Bay in the fall of 1821 after Stephen Austin received permission from the Mexican government to settle 300 families in Texas. The *Lively* is regarded as the "the *Mayflower* of Texas" and as the vessel passed Bolivar Point, Jane Long,

"the Mother of Texas" waved a greeting from the little fort she shared with her husband Dr. James Long, who was away at the time. George Lively was appointed treasurer of Harris County and was regarded as the second, though short-lived, mayor of Houston, serving briefly in 1839, apparently preferring to spend most of his time in New Orleans. Operated by Standard Fruit.

89. THOMAS W. GREGORY, 10–43, 244365, KTNJ (1861–1933) Thomas Watt Gregory was a Texas lawyer and U.S. Attorney General. Operated by American Range–Liberty Lines.

90. WILL R. WOOD, 10–43, 244366, KTNN (1861–1933) William Robert Wood was an Indiana congressman. Operated by American Export Lines.

91. WILLIAM M. RAYBURN, 10–43, 244564, KTNR (1840–1916) William Marion Rayburn was the father of House Speaker Sam Rayburn. Operated by West India.

92. L. H. MCNELLY, 10–43, 244558, KTNT (1844–1877) Leander Harvey McNelly, an ex–Texas Ranger, formed McNelly's Rangers to bring Nueces Strip cattle rustlers to justice. Operated by Parry.

93. LUCIEN B. MAXWELL, 10–43, 244559, KTNU (1818–1875) Lucien Bonaparte Maxwell was a Western pioneer, explorer, and inherited, through marriage in 1841, the 1,714,765-acre Carlos Beaubien and Guadalupe Miranda land grant in New Mexico and Colorado. Operated by States Marine.

94. ALBERT S. BURLESON, 11–43, 244551, KUIU (1863–1937) Albert Sidney Burleson was a Texas congressman and Postmaster General. Operated by American Range–Liberty Lines.

95. JOSEPH H. KIBBEY, 11–43, 244676, KUIY (1853–1924) Joseph Henry Kibbey was a Supreme Court justice and governor of Arizona. Operated by American Export Lines then by the Navy as the *Crater*-class cargo ship *Phobos* (AK-129), NHCM, commissioned on June 12, 1944.

96. OSCAR CHAPPELL, 11–43, 244680, KUIZ (1912–1942) able seaman lost on the Socony-Vacuum tanker *Dixie Arrow*, torpedoed by *U-71* on March 26, 1942, off North Carolina. Chappell was at the helm when the ship was hit by three torpedoes, injuring him and igniting the cargo of crude oil. When he observed seven crewmen trapped on the foredeck by flames he turned the ship so as to allow them to escape but in doing so the flames were directed toward the wheelhouse. He was posthumously awarded the Merchant Marine Distinguished Service medal. Operated by United Fruit.

97. J. S. CULLINAN, 11–43, 244677, KUJD (1860–1937) Joseph Stephen "Buckskin Joe" Cullinan was a prominent oil industry executive and founder of Texaco. Operated by the Navy as the *Crater*-class cargo ship *Alderamin* (AK-116), NHMA, commissioned on April 5, 1944.

98. HUGH YOUNG, 11–43, 243675, KUJE (1808–1888) Hugh Franklin Young, of Mississippi, joined the Texas militia, became a Confederate purchasing agent, and went into business in San Antonio. Operated by the Navy as the *Crater*-class cargo ship *Zaurak* (AK-117), NTCF, commissioned on March 17, 1944.

99. MATTHEW J. O'BRIEN, 11–43, 244678, KUJG (1837–1898) Matthew John O'Brien was third engineer on the 500-ton Confederate commerce raider *Sumter*, second engineeer on the notorious 900-ton, 230-foot *Alabama* and was last to leave the sinking ship off Cherbourge, France, after the duel with the *Kearsarge*. He was rescued by John Lancaster's British yacht *Deerhound* under Capt. Evan P. Jones. In October 1864 he was appointed chief engineer on the *Shenandoah*. After the war he was supervising inspector of steamboats at New Orleans. Operated by Lykes.

100. HENRY AUSTIN, 12–43, 244673, KUYB (1782–1852) lawyer cousin of Stephen F. Austin who settled on the Brazos River. Operated by Standard Fruit.

101. CHARLES MORGAN, 12–43, 244787, KVGF (1795–1878) founder of Morgan's Steamship Co., the first steamship service to Texas. Namesake for Morgan City, Louisiana. Operated by United Fruit. Sunk on June 10, 1944, by German aircraft off Utah Beach, Normandy. One able seaman, Paul O. Hilden, of Massachusetts, and seven soldiers were lost. Hilden was buried at Colleville-sur-Mer in France.

102. JOHN W. GATES, 12–43, 244791, KVGJ (1855–1911) John Warne "Bet-a-Million" Gates demonstrated the value of barbed wire to Texas cattlemen then set up the Southern Wire Co. at St. Louis. Operated by A. H. Bull.

103. ANTHONY F. LUCAS, 12–43, 244785, KVGL (1855–1921) Antun Lučić was a salt, sulfur, and petroleum explorer from Croatia who partnered with Pattillo Higgins as Anthony Francis Lucas to develop the Spindletop well at Beaumont, Texas, fueling the oil industry in America. Operated by the Navy as the miscellaneous auxiliary ship *Zaniah* (AG-70), NQSQ, commissioned on December 22, 1943.

104. WILLIAM BECKNELL, 12–43, 244797, KVGM (1787–1856) soldier and explorer who first travelled the fabled Santa Fe Trail. Operated by the Navy as the *Crater*-class cargo ship *Sabik* (AK-121), NHBW, on April 19, 1944.

105. HARRY PERCY, 12–43, 244790, KVGO (1901–1942) United Press war correspondent who died of malaria at Cairo, Egypt. Operated by States Marine.

106. REBECCA BOONE, 12–43, 244939, KVNA (1739–1813) Rebecca Ann Bryan, of Virginia, moved with her grandparents to North Carolina where their neighbors, the Boones, had a son named Daniel and they married in 1756. Operated by North Atlantic & Gulf.

107. CHARLES GOODNIGHT, 1–44, 244932, KVND (1836–1929) prominent Texas cattle rancher. Operated by Grace Line.

108. ANDREW BRISCOE, 1–44, 244931, KVNO (1810–1849) signer of the Texas Declaration of Independence. Operated by Moore-McCormack.

109. WILLIAM M. EASTLAND, 1–44, 244941, KVNX (1806–1843) William Mosby Eastland was a Texas Volunteer and Ranger during the Texas War who was taken prisoner in Mexico and shot on March 25, 1843. Namesake for Eastland, Texas. Operated by West India.

110. JOHN G. TOD, 1–44, 245026, KVPX (1808–1877) John Grant Tod was a naval officer, acting secretary of the Texas Navy, and developer of railways. Operated by McCormick.

111. CHARLES J. FINGER, 1–44, 245024, KVPZ (1869–1941) Charles Joseph Finger was a popular young adult author. Operated by Overlakes.

112. MORRIS SHEPPARD, 2–44, 245031, KVQF (1875–1941) John Morris Sheppard was a senator from Texas who authored the disastrous 18th Amendment—Prohibition—and chaired a committee to investigate corruption in New Deal relief fund expenditures. Operated by American-Foreign.

113. KATHERINE L. BATES, 2–44, 245028, KVQH (1859–1929) Katherine Lee Bates was a teacher and poet known for writing "America the Beautiful" and who lived with Katharine Coman. Operated by Moore-McCormack.

114. JACOB PERKINS, 2–44, 245052, KVQI (1766–1849) prolific inventor and pioneer of printing and steam-power technology. Operated by Isthmian.

115. JOSE G. BENITEZ, 2–44, 245101, KVTW (1851–1880) Jose Gautier Benitez was a Puerto Rican poet. Operated by the William J. Rountree.

116. ISAAC VAN ZANDT, 3–44, 245248, KVUE (1813–1847) Republic of Texas chargé de affaires to the United States. Operated by Olympic.

117. ROBERT HENRI, 3–44, 245254, KWAS (1865–1929) artist who specialized in the Ashcan movement of realism. Operated by States Marine.

118. KEITH PALMER, 3–44, 245250, KWAU (1906–1943) Royden Keith Palmer was a war correspondent for the *Melbourne Herald* and *Newsweek* magazine who was in a press tent on Bougainville Island. At 2:30 on the morning of November 7, 1943, Japanese bombers came over and he was mortally wounded by shrapnel. Operated by Merchants & Miners.

119. ANNA H. BRANCH, 3–44, 245238, KVUC (1875–1937) Anna Hempstead Branch was a famous poet and founder of the Poet's Guild. Operated by Interocean.

120. GEORGE STEERS, 3–44, 245246, KWAV (1820–1856) shipbuilder who designed the famous racing yacht *America*. He died in a horse and buggy accident. Operated by Wilmore.

121. JOHN GIBBON, 3–44, 245249, KWAY (1827–1896) Union general in the Civil War and Indian wars. Operated by Overlakes.

122. THOMAS SAY, 3–44, 245256, KWBJ (1787–1834) founder of the Academy of Natural Sciences at Philadelphia and cofounder of the Entomological Society of America. Operated by United States Navigation.

123. DANIEL E. GARRETT, 4–44, 245371, KWTE (1869–1932) Daniel Edward Garrett was a Texas congressman. Operated by the War Department as the aircraft repair ship *Maj. Gen. Robert Olds* (1896–1943) an early air power theorist and advocate who was awarded the Distinguished Flying Cross.

124. CHRISTOPHER S. FLANAGAN, 4–44, 245370, KWTD (1876–1943) Christopher Stephen Flanagan, of Quebec, Canada, was a stevedoring contractor and steamship agent who developed shipping in the Sabine, Texas, region. He died on February 16, 1943, at his home at 1347 Procter St. in Port Arthur of heart disease. Operated by Black Diamond.

125. JOHN IRELAND, 4–44, 245390, KWUC (1838–1918) first archbishop of Saint Paul, Minnesota, who was outspoken on public and civic issues. Operated by Stockard.

126. HENRY M. ROBERT, 4–44, 245389, KWUD (1837–1923) Henry Martyn Robert was an Army colonel who wrote the *Pocket Manual of Rules of Order for Deliberative Assemblies*, now *Robert's Rules of Order*, loosely based on Congressional House rules. Operated by Dichmann, Wright & Pugh.

127. SUL ROSS, 4–44, 245393, KWTU (1938–1898) Lawrence Sullivan "Sul" Ross was a Confederate general and president of the Agricultural & Mechanical College of Texas, now Texas A&M. Operated under the Russian flag.

128. JULIUS OLSEN, 4–44, 245391, KWTZ (1873–1942) long-time Hardin-Simmons University physics professor and dean at Abilene, Texas. Operated by A. H. Bull.

129. BRIG. GEN. ASA N. DUNCAN, 5–44 (1892–1942) first commander of the 8th Air Force lost when the B-17 he was in crashed in the Bay of Biscay on November 17, 1942. Operated by the U.S. Army as an aircraft repair ship.

130. FELIPI DE BASTROP, 4–44, 245562, KWWP (1759–1827) Philip Hendrik Nering Bögel, of Paramaribo, Surinam, moved to the Netherlands with his parents in 1764. In 1782 he was a tax collector when he married and had kids but in 1793 he was accused of embezzlement and fled to Louisiana where he was known as Baron de Bastrop. In 1806 he moved to San Antonio, Texas, and became Felipe Enrique Neri, Baron de Bastrop, just an ordinary pioneer settler and namesake for Bastrop, Texas. Operated by Alcoa.

131. HENRY D. LINDSLEY, 5–44, 245563, WHKH (1872–1938) Henry Dickinson Lindsley was an insurance man, mayor of Dallas, Texas, and director of the War Risk Insurance Branch of the American Expeditionary Force during the Great War. He cofounded the American Legion with Theodore Roosevelt, Jr., and was the first national commander. Operated by Marine Transport.

132. O. B. MARTIN, 5–44, 245565, WHQI (1870–1935) Oscar Baker Martin was the South Carolina superintendent of education and agriculture club pioneer who came up with Head, Heart, Hands, and Health, 4-H, and was director of the Texas A&M extension service. Operated by American-Foreign.

133. MINOR C. KEITH, 5–44, 245698, WMYB (1848–1929) Minor Cooper Keith was a Central American railroad operator, banana grower, and founder of the Tropical Trading & Fruit Co., one half of the future United Fruit Co. Operated by United Fruit.

134. NICHOLAS D. LABADIE, 5–44, 245699, WMYC (1802–1867) Nicholas Descomps Labadie was a Canadian ex-priest and physician who served at San Jacinto during the Texas War. Operated by Mississippi Shipping.

135. ARTHUR ST. CLAIR, 5–44, 245693, WMYE (1737–1818) soldier, president of the Continental Congress, and governor of the Northwest Territory who named Cincinnati. Operated by American South African.

136. RUFUS CHOATE, 5–44, 245729, WMYO (1799–1859) Massachusetts senator. Operated by Overlakes.

137. ELEAZAR LORD, 6–44, 245722, WPIG (1788–1871) first president of the New York & Erie Railroad in 1833 who established guaranteed rail service to southern New York after the Erie Canal was built upstate. Operated by Standard Fruit.

138. GUS W. DARNELL, 5–44, 245723, WPIP (1898–1942) master of the *Tillie Lykes*, lost when his ship was torpedoed on June 18, 1942, by *U-502* off Punta Herrero, Mexico. Capt. Darnell was awarded the Merchant Marine Distinguished Service medal. Operated by J. H. Winchester. Capt. C. R. Parsons' ship was sunk on November 23, 1944, by a Japanese aerial torpedo while at anchor off Samar, Philippines. Eleven were injured but there were no fatalities.

139. JUAN N. SEGUIN, 6–44, 245855, WQDM (1806–1890) Juan Nepomuceno Sequín was a captain in the Texas Army at San Jacinto, a senator, mayor of San Antonio, and namesake for Seguin, Texas. Operated by Wilmore.

140. BERTRAM G. GOODHUE, 6–44, 245850, WQDO (1869–1924) Bertram Grosvenor Goodhue was a noted architect of churches who designed the chapel at West Point. Operated by Black Diamond.

141. OLIVER LOVING, 6–44, 245857, WQDP (1812–1867) Texas cattle rancher and partner with Charles Goodnight who pioneered the driving of cattle to Midwestern markets. Operated by Alcoa.

142. ANDREW W. PRESTON, 6–44, 245848, WQDQ (1846–1924) Andrew Woodbury Preston cofounded the Boston Fruit Co. to import bananas then cofounded and was president of the United Fruit Co. Operated by United Fruit.

143. BRIG. GEN. ALFRED J. LYON, 6–44 (1892–1942) Army Air Corps pioneer who served as an observer in London during 1941 and died at Walter Reed General Hospital. Operated by the U.S. Army as an aircraft repair ship in the 6th Aircraft Repair Unit Floating.

144. JOHN B. HAMILTON, 6–44, 245918, WRBR (1847–1898) John Brown Hamilton, of Illinois, was a Marine Hospital Service physician, third Surgeon General, and pioneer of public health. Operated by American South African.

145. NATHANIEL SILSBEE, 6–44, 246009, WRRX (1773–1850) master of the ship *Benjamin* at age 19 and later a Massachusetts congressman. Operated by Wessel, Duval.

146. ROBERT WATCHORN, 7–44, 246010, WRRY (1858–1944) coal miner, first secretary of United Mine Workers, Commissioner of Immigration, and president of Watchorn Oil & Gas. Operated by Black Diamond.

147. TOMAS GUARDIA, 7–44, 246012, WRSG (1832–1882) Gen. Tomás Miguel Guardia Gutiérrez was a president of Costa Rica. Operated by Blidberg Rothchild.

148. LAURA DRAKE GILL, 7–44, 246007, WRSP (1860–1926) mathematician and lawyer who served as a Red Cross nurse in Cuba in 1898 and in 1901 became the third dean of Barnard College right after the women's school became formally affiliated with the men's Columbia University. Operated by T. J. Stevenson.

149. ANGUS MCDONALD, 7–44, 246003, WRSR (1878–1941) president of the Southern Pacific Railroad. Operated by American West African.

150. WYNN SEALE, 7–44, 246032, WSCS (1887–1934) Edward Wynn Seale was a Texas educator and president of the Texas College of Arts & Industries at Kingsville. Operated by J. H. Winchester.

151. T. E. MITCHELL, 7–44, 246185, WSDY (1874–1944) Thomas Edward Mitchell was a mining engineer, consultant, and superintendent of the Anaconda Copper Mining Co. Operated by Prudential.

152. CARLOS J. FINLAY, 8–44, 246167, WSEA (1833–1915) Carlos Juan Finlay was a Cuban physician who discovered the etiology of yellow fever. Operated by Overlakes.

153. KYLE V. JOHNSON, 8–44, 246177, WSGL (1904–1944) Kyle Vaughn Johnson was a lawyer in Arizona when he signed on the Waterman Steamship Agency freighter *Lafaytte* on April 29, 1942, at New York as an ordinary seaman under Capt. Andrew Ginder. In September the ship joined Convoy PQ 18 at Loch Ewe, Scotland, and came under furious air attack. Johnson joined Lt. (jg) George B. Lenning's Armed Guard gunners and manned a 20-mm gun. He was credited with shooting down three German planes and was awarded the Merchant Marine Distinguished Service medal when they arrived back at New York on January 20, 1943. In March 1944 he was an able seaman on the Waterman freighter *Maiden Creek II* and was lost when the ship was torpedoed by *U-371* on March 17 off Algeria. Operated by Waterman. Capt. Carl W. Moline's ship was hit by a kamikaze on January 12, 1945, off Luzon, Philippines, with the loss of chief steward Francis H. Miller and 128 soldiers. The ship was repaired.

154. JACOB A. WESTERVELT, 8–44, 246176, WSQS (1800–1879) Jacob Aaron Westervelt was a noted shipbuilder and mayor of New York City. Operated by A. H. Bull.

155. ROBERT S. LOVETT, 8–44, 246183, WSRI (1860–1932) Robert Scott Lovett was a Texas attorney and railroad officer. Operated by American Range–Liberty Lines.

156. IDA STRAUS, 8–44, 246175, WSRJ (1849–1912) Rosalie Ida Blun married Macy's Department Store cofounder Isidor Straus. Both were major supporters of the Knickerbocker Hospital in Manhattan and both were lost on the *Titanic*. Operated by Mississippi Shipping.

157. THOMAS BULFINCH, 8–44, 246187, WSSD (1796–1867) Boston banker and author of *Bulfinch's Mythology*. Operated by North Atlantic & Gulf.

158. LORADO TAFT, 8–44, 246221, WSSE (1860–1936) Lorado Zadoc Taft was a noted Illinois sculptor, writer, and educator. Operated by American South African.

159. HOWARD L. GIBSON, 8–44, 246220, WSSF (1901–1939) Kansas and Wyoming farm agent active in 4-H activities. Operated by United States Navigation. Capt. John G. M. Grant's ship collided on October 14, 1944, with the Panama Transport Co. tanker *George W. McKnight*, loaded with 1,500,000 gallons of 100 octane gasoline, northwest of Madeira with the loss of two Armed Guard sailors. Panama Transport was a foreign-flag subsidiary of Standard Oil of New Jersey. Navy escort crews under Lt. Cdr. Lawrence C. Arvin rescued 121 people out of the 128 aboard both vessels in the conflagration. The *Gibson* was declared a total constructive loss.

160. THOMAS EAKINS, 9–44, 246448, KSTK (1844–1916) Thomas Cowperhwait Eakins was a realist painter, photographer, sculptor, and fine arts educator. Operated by American Export Lines.

161. ROBERT E. CLARKSON, 9–44, 246446, KSTO (1892–1941) noted Phillips County, Montana, agricultural agent and economist who served on the Montana Relief Commission from 1934 to 1937. Operated by United States Lines.

162. IRVING BABBITT, 9–44, 246442, KSTS (1865–1933) educator, literary critic, and founder of the New Humanism movement. Operated by American South African Line.

163. MICHAEL J. OWENS, 9–44, 246444, KSUF (1859–1923) Michael Joseph Owens invented an automatic glass bottle-making machine and founded the Owens-Illinois Glass Co. Operated by American Export Lines.

164. EDWARD G. JANEWAY, 9–44, 246430, KSUG (1841–1911) Edward Garnaliel Janeway was a noted medical instructor, New York City health commissioner, and cofounder with William H. Welch, of the Department of Pathology at the Bellevue Medical College. Operated by Smith & Johnson.

165. HERBERT D. CROLY, 9–44, 246584, KTFN (1869–1930) Herbert David Croly was editor of the *New Republic* magazine. Operated by International Freighting.

166. FREDERIC E. IVES, 10–44, 246583, KTFP (1856–1937) Frederic Eugene Ives was a pioneer of color photography. Operated by Overlakes.

167. WALTER WELLMAN, 10–44, 246588, KTFQ (1858–1934) newsman, arctic explorer, and airship pilot. Operated by J. H. Winchester.

168. RICHARD J. HOPKINS, 10–44, 246587, KTFR (1873–1943) Richard Joseph Hopkins was the highly regarded lieutenant governor of Kansas, state attorney general, federal judge, and U.S. senator. Operated by Moore-McCormack.

169. J. D. YEAGER, 10–44, 246585, KTFW (1869–1935) Joseph Dilley Yeager was a director of the Nevada State Farm Bureau. Operated by North Atlantic & Gulf.

170. JOHNNY APPLESEED, 10–44, 246586, KTFX (1775–1847) John Chapman went around the Midwest planting apple trees. Operated by North Atlantic & Gulf.

171. PAUL BUNYAN, 10–44, 246709, KTHA, mythical Northeastern timber faller whose companion was Babe the Blue Ox. Operated by Dichmann, Wright & Pugh.

172. ANSON MILLS, 10–44, 246706, KTKH (1834–1924) surveyor who plotted and named El Paso, Texas. Operated by Polarus.

173. ROBERT NEIGHBORS, 10–44, 246710, KTKI (1815–1859) Robert Simpson Neighbors was a Texas Army captain, legislator, and early Indian agent and Indian advocate who was assassinated by anti–Indian settler Edward Cornett at Fort Belknap on September 14, 1859. Operated by Norton Lilly.

174. FRANCIS B. OGDEN, 11–44, 246731, KTKJ (1783–1857) Francis Barber Ogden, of New Jersey, served in the War of 1812 and was a consul in England. He had an interest in steam engines and was a friend of John Ericsson, a Swedish citizen, and in 1835 patented his friend's inventions in the United States, namely "an engine for producing motive power, whereby a greater quantity of power is obtained by a given quantity of fuel than heretofore"—the use expanding steam in engines. Ogden died in Bristol, England. Operated by Sprague.

175. EDWIN S. NETTLETON, 11–44, 246708, KTKK (1831–1901) civil engineer engaged in bringing water to the Carlsbad Irrigation District who also served as the Colorado State Engineer. Operated by William J. Rountree.

176. PONTUS H. ROSS, 11–44, 246766, KTKM (1879–1937) Pontus Henry Ross was the director of the University of Arizona Agricultural Extension Service. Operated by Moore-McCormack.

177. CLARENCE ROBERTS, 11–44, 246876, KYUW (1890–1942) Oklahoma author of *The Business of Farming*. Operated by Norton Lilly.

178. OTIS E. HALL, 11–44, 246879, KYVB (1878–1936) Otis Earle Hall was a noted extension agent and 4-H leader at Manhattan, Riley County, Kansas. Operated by American Range–Liberty Lines.

179. CHARLES L. MCNARY, 11–44, 246875, KYVC (1874–1944) Charles Linza McNary was an Oregon senator. Operated by Weyerhaeuser.

180. NAVARCHOS KOUNDOURIOTIS, 11–44 (1855–1935) "Admiral Koundouri-otis" was Paul Koundouriotis, a celebrated Greek naval commander. Operated under the Greek flag.

181. ELEFTHERIA, 11–44, "Eleftheria I thanatos"—freedom or death—is the motto adopted during Greece's war of independence from the Ottoman Empire in the 1820s. Oper-ated under the Greek flag.

182. PAUL DAVID JONES, 12–44, 246880, ANBU (1921–1944) oiler lost during a rescue attempt after benzol leaked into the pump room on the tanker *Bostonian* on August 12, 1944, off Fort Pierce, Florida. Jones was awarded the Merchant Marine Distinguished Service medal. Operated by Black Diamond.

183. WILL B. OTWELL, 12–44, 246882, ANBV (1863–1941) William B. Otwell was a nurseryman and president of the National Farm Institute in Illinois who organized youth farming events to improve farm practices. Operated by Norton Lilly.

184. JACOB CHANDLER HARPER, 12–43, 247027, ANBW (1858–1939) prominent attorney for the Scripps-McRae newspaper empire and cofounder of the Claremont Graduate School in Claremont, California. Operated by United States Navigation.

185. HAROLD D. WHITEHEAD, 12–44, 247026, ANOX (1897–1942) fireman/watertender lost on the *Sam Houston*, torpedoed on June 28, 1942, by *U-203* in the Caribbean. Operated by Alcoa.

186. CLYDE AUSTIN DUNNING, 12–44, 247025, ANFI (1921–1942) oiler lost on the *Sam Houston*, torpedoed by on June 28, 1942, by *U-203* in the South Atlantic. Operated by Norton Lilly.

187. JAMES KYRON WALKER, 12–44, 247028, ANFJ (18–19) African-American 2nd cook & baker lost on the Gulf Oil tanker *Gulfamerica*, torpedoed on April 10, 1942, by *U-123* off Jacksonville, Florida. Operated by Alcoa.

188. WALTER FREDERICK KRAFT, 12–44, 247046, ANFK (1906–1943) 1st assis-tant engineer lost on the *M. H. De Young*, torpedoed on August 13, 1943, by *I-19* in the South Pacific.

189. WILLIAM R. LEWIS, 12–44, 247049, ANFL (1923–1943) fireman/watertender lost on the *M. H. De Young*, torpedoed on August 14, 1943, by *I-19* in the South Pacific. Oper-ated by Black Diamond.

190. WILLIAM ASA CARTER, 1–45, 247045, ANFM (1922–1943) fireman/water-tender lost on the *Samuel Gompers*, torpedoed on January 30, 1943, by *I-10* in the South Pacific. Operated by Moore-McCormack.

191. JAMES ROY WELLS, 1–45, 247044, ANFN (1891–1942) fireman/watertender lost on the *Steel Navigator*, torpedoed on October 19, 1942, by *U-610* in the North Atlantic. Operated by American-Foreign.

192. WILLIAM K. KAMAKA, 1–45, 247048, ANFO (1914–1943) ordinary seaman lost on the *James Smith*, torpedoed on March 9, 1943, by *U-510* in the South Atlantic. Operated by South Atlantic.

193. DANIEL L. JOHNSTON, 1–45, 247189, ANIP (1907–1942) 2nd assistant engi-neer lost on the Socony-Vacuum Oil Co. tanker *Caddo*, torpedoed on November 23, 1942, by *U-518* in the North Atlantic. Operated by Wessel, Duval.

194. LLOYD S. CARLSON, 1–45, 247195, ANIQ (1922–1942) oiler lost on the Hammond Lumber ship *Arcata*, shelled on July 14, 1942, by *I-7* in the Gulf of Alaska. Operated by American Liberty.

195. RUSSELL R. JONES, 1–45, 247197, ANIR (1912–1942) 3rd mate lost on July 5, 1942, when the Calmar freighter *Massmar* hit a mine off Iceland. Operated by Overlakes.

196. JOHN MARTIN MILLER, 1–45, 247192, ANIS (1910–1942) ordinary seaman lost on the Weyerhaeuser freighter *Potlatch*, torpedoed on June 27, 1942, by *U-153* east of the Virgin Islands. Operated by Weyerhaeuser.

197. WALLACE M. TYLER, 2–45, 247200, ANIT (1902–1943) chief engineer lost on the *Montanan*, torpedoed on June 3, 1943, by *I-27* off the east coast of Oman. Operated by Smith & Johnson.

198. WILLIAM W. JOHNSON, 2–45, 247203, ANKF (1903–1942) 2nd assistant engineer lost on the Texas Co. tanker *Australia*, torpedoed on March 16, 1942, by *U-332* off Cape Hatteras. Operated by William J. Rountree.

199. BERNARD L. RODMAN, 2–45, 247327, ANLE (1896–1942) able-bodied seaman lost on the Hammond Lumber freighter *Arcata*, torpedoed on July 14, 1942, by *I-7* in the Gulf of Alaska. Operated by Oceanic.

200. LEONARDO L. ROMERO, 2–45, 247331, ANLF (1909–1942) utilityman lost on the *Stephens Hopkins*, sunk on September 27, 1942, in an engagement with the German raider *Stier* and tender *Tannenfels* in the South Atlantic. Operated by Polarus.

201. WILLARD R. JOHNSON, 2–45, 247333, ANLH (1914–1943) utilityman lost when the Socony-Vacuum Oil tanker *Yankee Arrow* hit a mine on August 3, 1943, in the Mediterranean. Operated by Lykes.

202. SAMUEL L. JEFFERY, 2–45, 247332, ANNI (1920–1942) fireman/watertender lost on the Socony-Vacuum Oil tanker *Ario*, torpedoed and shelled on March 15, 1942, by *U-158* off North Carolina. Operated by Luckenbach. Capt. Alfred B. Owen, 65, left Galveston, Texas, in February 1945 and arrived at New York on April 30 from Antwerp, Belgium, with 40 crew aboard. No one signed off, a quite unusual situation, and one sailor, Lawrence O. Corprow, 23, signed on. Capt. Owen left Davisville, Rhode Island, around May 22 and on June 1 his ship collided with the *Michael Anagnos* in Panama Bay, Canal Zone. The *Anagnos* was an American-built Liberty ship operating under the Greek flag. Four merchant crew and the ship were lost.

203. CLIFFORD E. ASHBY, 2–45, 247329, ANNJ (1919–1943) fireman/watertender lost on the *Malay*, shelled and torpedoed on January 19, 1942, by *U-123* off North Carolina. Operated by A. H. Bull.

204. LEKTOR GARBO, 2–45 (1891–1941) "teacher Garbo" was Ingvar Garbo, executed by the Nazis in November 1941 for resistence activities. Operated under the Norwegian flag by Nortraship.

205. FRANCIS E. SILTZ, 3–45, 247330, ANNL (1919–1942) radio operator lost on the Standard Oil tanker *W. L. Steed*, torpedoed on February 2, 1942, by *U-103* off the Delaware River. Operated by Wessel, Duval.

206. CHARLES H. LANHAM, 3–45, 247328, ANNM (1900–1942) able-bodied seaman lost on the Pennsylvania Shipping Co. tanker *Naeco*, torpedoed by *U-124* off North Carolina on March 23, 1942. Operated by American Liberty.

207. PSARA, 3–45, a Greek island in the Aegean Sea. Operated under the Greek flag.

208. EDWARD N. HINTON, 3–45, 247374, ANNO (1910–1942) able-bodied seaman lost on the Cuba Distilling Co. tanker *Carrabulle*, torpedoed on May 26, 1942, by *U-106* in the Caribbean. Operated under the French flag by Compagne Générale Transatlantique. The

ship reached Marseilles in May 1945 with 8,500 tons of cargo including 2,500 tons of evaporated milk and was the frist French-operated Liberty ship to reach southern France.

Walsh-Kaiser Co., Inc., Shipbuilding Division
1 Walsh Ave., Providence, Rhode Island

John Walsh and Mary Burns moved from Ireland to Davenport, Iowa, in 1848 and their son, Patrick Thomas Walsh, was born in March 1855 in Davenport. Patrick got involved in construction and eventually became a major railroad builder as the Walsh Construction Company. In 1942 the company was at 114½ W. 3rd St. in Davenport under president Thomas J. Walsh, general manager John S. McDonald, and executive assistant John J. Walsh. The company teamed up with Henry Kaiser to complete the Rheem Manufacturing contract as the shipbuilding division of Walsh Construction with John McDonald as general manager. The formal takeover was on Sunday, February 28, 1943. The public/private, 6-way built 10 Liberty ships before switching to other construction. The first keel was laid down on June 27, 1942, and the average building time for the ships was 208.7 days.

1. JOHN CLARKE, 4–43, 242986, KIRR (1609–1676) Dr. Clarke was a cofounder of Portsmouth and Newport, Rhode Island. The ship was launched by Rheem Manufacturing but delivered by Walsh-Kaiser. Launching was scheduled for Saturday, February 20, but was delayed by severe, subzero weather until noon on Thursday, the 25th. Operated Sprague.
2. SAMUEL GORTON, 5–43, 243236, KIRS (1593–1677) early resident of Rhode Island and Providence Plantations. Operated by American Export Lines.
3. LYMAN ABBOTT, 5–43, 243364, KOIT (1835–1922) a prominent Congregationalist theologian. Operated by the International Freighting and converted to an Army troopship. Capt. Carl P. R. Dahlstrom's ship was damaged in the German air raid at Bari, Italy, on December 2, 1943, with the loss of 2nd mate Frank J. Otremba, Jr., and bos'n Stanley Adamovicz. Capt. Dahlstrom was awarded the Merchant Marine Distinguished Service medal and the ship was repaired.
4. JAMES DE WOLF, 6–43, 243394, KOKZ (1764–1837) a privateer captain and Maine senator. Operated by American South African Line.
5. MOSES BROWN, 6–43, 243469, KOOT (1738–1836) cofounder of Brown University. Operated by American South African Line.
6. MELVILLE JACOBY, 3–44, 245141, KWAM (1915–1942), Time-Life war correspondent who died on April 29, 1942, in an airfield accident near Darwin, Australia. Operated by Wilmore.
7. FRANK GILBRETH, 4–44, 245184, KWIZ (1868–1924) Frank Bunker Gilbreth, Sr., was a construction engineer and founder of the International Congress of Management. Operated by American Export Lines.
8. CORNELIUS FORD, 5–44, 245278, KWOZ (1867–1935) New Jersey labor leader and head of the Government Printing Office from 1913 to 1921. Operated by Union Sulphur.
9. JESSE H. METCALF, 5–44, 245358, KWST (1860–1942) Jesse Houghton Metcalf was a Rhode Island senator. Operated by Eastern Steamship.
10. NELSON W. ALDRICH, 6–44, 245581, WKNG (1841–1915) Nelson Wilmarth Aldrich was a Rhode Island senator. Operated by T. J. Stevenson.

PART IV

Liberty Ship Operation and the General Agents

In order to qualify as a general agent, a company had to have total assets of at least $150,000 with at least $100,000 of that in liquid assets or "working capital." Maritime Commission vessels were operated under a General Agency Agreement that required the company to "man, equip, victual, supply and operate the vessels" and to "exercise reasonable care and diligence to maintain the vessels in a thoroughly efficient state of repair, covering hull, machinery, boilers, tackle, apparel, furniture, equipment, and spare parts" and to "effect maintenance and voyage repairs and replacements."

Initially, operators purchased War Risk Insurance from commercial underwriters but in the early months of the war the insurers experienced huge losses and it became necessary in late 1942 for the War Shipping Administration to set up an insurance division for "large value hulls" and cargoes.

Initially the operators were paid any where from 15 cents per ton to 50 cents per ton based on the number of ships the company ran, 50 cents being the rate for up to 50,000 tons and 15 cents for 250,000 tons and over. In December 1943 the rates were changed to $65 per day per ship plus $15 per day to cover business expenses and accounting, etc., with recapture provisions for "excess" profits to limit what was perceived as war profiteering. These rates were based on the average daily operating costs of the larger shipping companies. There were also provisions for reimbursing the operators for additional expenses incurred overseas. As of January 1, 1944, 90 percent of all profits over $15 per day per ship were subject to recapture in order to prevent low-overhead operators from making excess profits.

Agwilines, Inc.
Pier 13, East River, New York

Sailmaker Charles Mallory (1796–1882) hung out his own shingle in 1810 in Mystic, Connecticut, and by 1848 was fully-invested in the shipping business as an owner-operator. His son, Charles Henry Mallory (1818–1890), moved to New York in 1865 and founded C. H. Mallory & Co., ship agents and freight forwarding at Pier 20, East River, and in 1886 founded the New York & Texas Steamship Co. at Pier 20. Charles' son, Henry R. Mallory, assumed command in 1894 and in 1906 sold the company to New York "ice king" and banker

Charles W. Morse (1856–1933). On January 1, 1907, Morse folded the Eastern, Metropolitan, Clyde, Mallory, New York & Cuba Mail (Ward Line), and New York & Porto Rico steamship companies into the Consolidated Steamship Co. but in October 1907 a financial panic threw Morse's holdings into chaos and by February 1908 he was in receivership. Mallory then came back into the picture and reorganized the Clyde Line's 24 ships, the Mallory Line's 14 ships, the Porto Rico Line's 12 ships, and Ward Line's 20 ships into the Atlantic, Gulf & West Indies Steamship Lines, named by the company as AGWILINES, Inc., and variously written as Agwilines and AGWI Lines. At its height in 1911, the company covered 21,906 miles to Mexico, Cuba, San Domingo, and Puerto Rico, and chartered tramps for service anywhere in the world.

Henry Mallory retired in 1915 and was succeeded by Clifford Day Mallory (1881–1941). Upon the latter's death the company was incorporated into the Marine Transport Lines. In 1943, Lewis D. Parmalee was executive vice president. He was on the board of the American Merchant Marine Institute.

Dudley Winthrop Saltonstall was the AGWI Lines auditor from 1909 until his death on November 25, 1944, at East Orange, New Jersey, and Leonard F. Leininger was the Caribbean passenger traffic manager from 1919 to 1949. In 1940 the company had 55 ships at Pier 34, North River.

A. H. Bull Steamship Co.
115 Broad St., New York, and Pier 5, Pratt St., Baltimore

Archibald Hilton Bull (1847–1920) was born in New York and went into the shipping business, and in 1873 began running British-flagged sailing vessels as a scheduled "packet" service between New York and Puerto Rico. In 1885 he incorporated the New York & Porto Rico Steamship Co. When the United States secured Puerto Rico from Spain after the "Splendid Little War" in 1898, Bull was obliged to re-flag his vessels but an internal dispute between various company managers and the shareholders ended in 1900 with the sale of the vessels to the Berwind-White Coal Mining Co., 1 Broadway, New York.

In 1902 Bull organized the Bull Line and in 1907 Berwind-White sold his old ships to Charles W. Morse. In 1914 Bull purchased the Insular Line, which became the Bull Insular Line. In 1940 Ernest M. Bull was president and Myron Bull was the attorney.

Ernest, 65, lived at 33 Prospect Ave., Montclair, New Jersey, with his wife Edith, 61, daughters Carolyn, 32, Edith, 25, Arlyn, 24, and their Austrian cook, Margaret Messeker, 49, and Scotch maid, Elizabeth Stewart, 34. Ernest died on October 6, 1943.

Myron, 36, lived at 17 E. 89th St., New York, with his wife Frances, 33, son E. Myron, 5, daughter Frances, 2, Finnish maid Amilia Lepin, 39, and English nursemaid Eleanor Holland, 45.

The firm operated as A. H. Bull & Co., Inc., A. H. Bull Steamship Co., Bull Insular Line, Inc., and Bull Steamship Line, Inc.

A. L. Burbank & Co., Ltd.
17 Battery Place, New York

Ship broker Abram Lincoln Burbank (1885–1962) worked for A. H. Bull & Co. in 1917 and incorporated his own firm on October 16, 1928. He lived with his wife Grace, 43, daughter

Ellen, 19, and their Irish servant, Catherine Rooney, 34, at 229 Upper Mountain Ave, Montclair, New Jersey.

Alaska Packers Association, Inc.
111 California St., San Francisco, California

In 1889, several shipping companies operating sailing vessels out of San Francisco and Puget Sound to the salmon canneries in Alaska combined forces and formed the Alaska Packers Association. Henry F. Fortmann was president at the 306 Market St. headquarters. The company ran square-riggers with the prefix *"Star of"* in their names. In 1901 the company bought the *Euterpe*, overhauled her, and changed the name to *Star of India*. She still sails with a volunteer crew and is open for visitors at San Diego, California. At the same time they chartered the sailing ship *Balclutha* and when the ship went aground in 1904 the company purchased it for $500, salvaged it, and changed the name to *Star of Alaska*. The *Balclutha* can be seen today with other museum ships at the San Francisco Maritime National Historical Park at the Hyde St. Pier in San Francisco.

Austin Kent Tichenor was company president during the war. He was 79 in 1941 and lived in Alameda, California, at 1717 Dayton Ave. with his wife Tillie, 71.

Alaska Steamship Co., Inc.
Pier 2, Seattle, Washington, 903 Pacific Ave., Tacoma

In 1880, New Hampshire native Daniel B. Jackson was a 46-year-old agent for a sawmill at Port Gamble, Washington, and lived there with his wife Mary, 46, and nine kids ranging in age from 2 to 27. Son Henry, 27, was a merchant and son Leslie, 21, was a telegraph operator. Daniel decided to go into shipping and by 1884 was president of the Washington Steamboat & Transportation Company. George S. Jacobs was secretary, Walter P. Sanderson, treasurer, and Capt. Samuel Jackson was master of the company's steamer *Eliza Anderson*. Their dock was at Yesler's Wharf. In 1889, the company's name was changed to the Puget Sound & Alaska Steamship Co. and was known as the Alaska Line. The same year Daniel went to Kingston, New York, and bought the five-year-old jinxed ferryboat *City of Kingston*. He completely refurbished it, adding masts and spars for sails, and brought it around the Horn. In 1898 the company became the Alaska Steamship Co. with Charles E. Peabody as general manager. Peabody was also vice president of the Washington & Alaska Steamship Co.

On April 3, 1899, the *City of Kingston* sank in a collision with the steamer *Glenogle* off Brown Point. The company prospered through wars and mergers and in 1941 Earl Tappan Stanard was president in the New York office and Leslie W. Baker was general manager in Seattle. Offices were at Piers 1 and 2 at the foot of Yesler Way. Ftank G. Ploof was general agent in Tacoma.

Alaska Transportation Co.
Pier 58, Seattle, Washington

Incorporated in New Jersey on April 5, 1898, by Seattle attorney Andrew F. Burleigh as president and George W. Dickinson as general manager. Both were ex-officers of the Northern

Pacific Railroad. Horatio S. Byrne was secretary at the 63 Wall St. office in New York. They had a capitalization of $2,250,000, sold shares at $10 each, and had six directors in New York. The company was set up to transport miners from Puget Sound ports to Dawson City "the heart of the gold regions" via the Yukon River using nine steamboats specially built by the Moran Brothers Co. at Seattle. They expected 200,000 people would "rush to the mining regions of Alaska during the coming season."

Burleigh, 45, lived in Republic, Washington, with his 22-year-old wife Marie. Capt. James Griffiths, who would form his own company, was associated with the company in the 1920s. In 1936 Ralph T. Jones was traffic manager at Pier 7. They also had an office at 29 Broadway in New York. In 1940 John A. Talbot was president and Winston J. Jones was general manager until he joined the Navy in 1941. He was replaced by Sven J. Swanson, who was chief mate on the company's steamer *Tongass* in 1940 and *Tyee* in 1941.

Winston Jones, 37, his wife Mary, 37, and their 2-year-old son Winston, Jr., lived at Jones' 70-year-old widowed father's home at 3638 N. 36th St. in Tacoma.

Alcoa Steamship Co., Inc.
17 Battery Place, New York

In 1886, a chemist in Oberlin, Ohio, named Charles Martin Hall (1863–1914) discovered an efficient way to make aluminum. He patented his process but had trouble finding investors so he went to Pennsylvania to meet with Alfred E. Hunt, a partner of George H. Clapp as Hunt & Clapp, inspecting and metallurgical engineers and chemists who operated the Pittsburgh Testing Laboratory at 95 Fifth Ave, Room 59. Hunt and Clapp were interested and on October 1, 1888, they incorporated the Pittsburgh Reduction Co. at 95 Fifth Ave. with Hunt as president, Hall vice president, and Clapp as secretary. The company expanded and moved to 502 Murtland Building but patent and antitrust problems arose and then Hunt died on April 27, 1899, from illness contracted during Army service in the Spanish-American War. Pittsburgh banker Richard B. Mellon, of T. Mellon & Sons, then became president, Arthur V. Davis secretary, and Robert E. Withers, treasurer. Clapp went back to the testing lab. In 1907 the name was changed to the Aluminum Company of America and Hall was vice president until he died.

Around World War I the company started transporting bauxite from South America in their own ships under foreign flag. In 1941 Arthur Davis was chairman of the board and Roy A. Hunt was president.

American Export Lines, Inc.
25 Broadway, New York

Began in 1919 as the Export Steamship Corp., 67 Exchange Place, Suite 421, New York, to provide freight and passenger service to Mediterranean and Near East ports with surplus Hog Islanders purchased and operated by the company. Charles C. Torpy was president. He was a 41-year-old widower who lived in a hotel or rooming house at 46 W. 34th St. His father owned the Phoenix Mill Co. in Marietta, Ohio, where Charles had been vice president. The line flourished and in 1931–32 they took delivery of the *Excalibur*, *Excambian*, *Exeter*, and *Exochorda*, the original "Four Aces." Unfortunately, financial difficulties ensued and in 1938 twenty Hog Islanders and the Four Aces were sold and purchased, principally by Lehman Bros.

and the company was renamed American Export Lines. Financial prosperity ensued and in 1939 the firm pioneered air passenger service with flying boats from New York to Marseilles via the Azores. In 1943, John F. Gehan was vice president and general manager.

American-Foreign Steamship Corp.
80 Broad St., New York

On April 19, 1932, attorney Ira L. Rosenson, 258 Broadway, Brooklyn; Sophia Pruss, 362 Hewes St., Brooklyn; and Elias Katz, 34 Siegel St., Brooklyn incorporated the company. Of the 500 shares, par value $100, Rosenson held 498 and Pruss and Katz one each. Rosenson's office was at 258 Broadway. He was 46 and lived in a $165 a month rented house at at 295 St. John's Place, Kings, Brooklyn, with his wife Yvette, 36, son Dan, 5, and German maid Mary Gouse.

In October 1933 they purchased the 5,570-ton Shipping Board steamer *Eastern Glen* from the American South African Line and renamed it *American Oriole*. The ship was built in 1920 by Kabushiki Kaisha Uchida Zosengo at Yokohama, Japan. The company next purchased the Hog Islanders *Liberty Glo* and *Wildwood* from the South Atlantic Steamship Co. and in 1938 owned the Hog Islander *American Robin*, the ex-*Magmeric*, also purchased from South Atlantic.

In June 1940 the *American Oriole* was sold to the British, renamed *Barberrys*, and operated by the Runciman Shipping Co., Ltd., 52 Leadenhall St., London, under the Barberrys Steamship Co., Ltd., name. The ship arrived at New York from London on November 3, 1942, under Capt. George Halket Squires, 50, and on the 26th the ship was torpedoed by *U-663* northeast of St. John's, Newfoundland.

On February 26, 1984, the company's 661-foot tanker *American Eagle* was en route from Savannah, Georgia, to Orange, Texas. The chief mate, boatswain, and the pumpman were on the foredeck ventilating the forward cargo tanks. Around 10:45 a.m. an explosion occurred and they were lost. The next day the ship sank and two more perished and two were reported missing.

American-Hawaiian Steamship Co.
215 Market St., San Francisco and 90 Broad St., New York

William Dixon Burnham, of Connecticut, went to sea at 14 and was a shipmaster at 21. On September 19, 1868, he married Matilda Elizabeth Bunting, of Liverpool, England, in Liverpool. She was the daughter of Cunard Line Capt. Henry Bunting. Burnmam sailed with Flint & Co. and was noted for his early arrivals and in 1892 he was named company superintendent.

On March 7, 1899, he incorporated his own company, the American-Hawaiian Steam Navigation Co., in Flemington, New Jersey. Edwin K. Large, Jr., was the registered agent and Burnham was general manager. On May 18, 1899, the name was changed to American-Hawaiian Steamship Co.

Edwin R. Dimond was in the San Francisco office of Williams, Dimond & Co., shipping and commission agents, at 202 Market St. The New York office was at 106 Wall St. The company provided regular coast-to-coast freight service via the Panama Canal when it was opened and was known as the Panama Canal Line. Their berth was at Pier 10. Burnham retired in 1913. In 1940 John E. Cushing was president.

American Liberty Steamship Corp.
11 Broadway, New York

Established in 1943 at 11 Broadway, New York, possibly as a subsidiary of George R. Dilkes & Co., an old Philadelphia forwarding agent and coastwise shipping company. Augustus M. Dilkes was a company executive and J. Whitfield Cohen was vice president and traffic manager. The company had long provided service to Gulf ports. When the company attempted to contract for operation of War Shipping Administration ships they were found deficient for the task, possibly because they operated coastwise and didn't have the resources for foreign voyages. The WSA suggested they enter into a joint venture with American Range Lines, another Philadelphia firm. American Range had been in business since 1936 and operated the *Colabee*, *Plow City*, and *Suwied* on foreign service On August 16, 1943, an agreement was reached between the two companies and the name was changed to American Range–Liberty Lines, Inc. According to the bylaws, the joint ownership was to be held equally between the American Liberty Steamship Corp. and Lucille H. Rogers. In 1944 the company's offices moved to 75 West St.

After the war the company became embroiled in political and legal issues involving steamship service to Galveston, Texas.

American Mail Line, Ltd.
740 Stuart Bldg., Seattle, Washington

In 1912, Colorado Springs native and ex–dock worker, Hubbard Foster Alexander was 33 and lived with his wife Ruth at 502 N. Yakima Ave. in Tacoma, Washington. He was president of the Alaska Coast Co., the Alaska Pacific Steamship Co., and the Pacific Alaska Navigation Co. and ran the steamers *Admiral Dewey*, *Admiral Farragut*, and *Admiral Schley* between Alaska, Puget Sound, and Oakland, California. In 1916 he combined the companies into the Pacific Steamship Co. at 1111 Pacific Ave. and it was known as the Admiral Line. By 1920 he had the largest fleet sailing the Pacific Ocean and in 1922 he moved his headquarters to the 5th Floor of the L. C. Smith Building in Seattle. The Tacoma office stayed open but he and Ruth moved to 1065 E. Prospect St. in Seattle.

In 1924, a majority interest in the Admiral Line was purchased by Robert M. Dollar, president of the Robert Dollar Co. in the Robert Dollar Building, 311 California St. in San Francisco. Robert was managing director of the Dollar Steamship Line and Robert Stanley Dollar and John Harold Dollar were vice presidents. Robert set up the Admiral Oriental Line on the 4th Floor of the L. C. Smith Building in Seattle and R. Stanley moved to Seattle to be president of the new company. Hubbard remained president of Pacific Steamship.

In 1925, all the offices were moved to 1519 Railroad Ave. S., the Admiral Oriental Line was the agent for the American Oriental Mail Line, the Dollar Steamship Line, and the Blue Star Line, and J. Harold Dollar became president. Service was from Seattle to the Far East.

In 1927, Dollar renamed the Admiral Oriental Line the American Mail Line at the 1519 Railroad Ave. S. address. They were the agent for the Dollar Steamship and Blue Star Lines. Ancil F. Haines, Pacific Steamship's longtime vice president under Hubbard Alexander, became vice president of American Mail Line.

In 1930, Hubbard retired from Pacific Steamship and went into the petroleum business, becoming president of the Olympic Corp. and the Calmexico Petroleum Corp.

In 1941, Lawrence C. Calvert was president and Albert R. Lintner, vice president and general manager of American Mail. In 1942, Hubbard lived in Queens, New York, with his wife Mary E. Sandham and worked for the Transatlantic Navigation Co. He died in 1952.

American President Lines, Ltd.
311 California St., San Francisco, California

Robert McVey Dollar (1844–1932) was born in Falkirk, Scotland, and went to work in logging camps in Canada. From there he went to Michigan and worked in the lumber business and then moved out to California. By 1888 he owned a sawmill at Usal and that year had the 218-ton steam schooner *Newsboy* built to bring wood and passengers from Eureka to San Francisco, the first schooner in the West Coast lumber trade built with an engine.

Like Charles McCormick, Andrew Hammond, and other big West Coast lumbermen, Robert Dollar's shipping interests expanded until the Great Depression. In 1935 Dollar Steamship operations had 22 passenger and cargo ships but by 1938 the financial climate had soured and the Maritime Commission took custody of half his ships. The name given to the new line was American President Lines since all Dollar Steamship's passenger ships were named after American presidents. Other Maritime Commission-owned ships were added later to the fleet. In 1940 Donald S. Burrows was office manager.

American Range–Liberty Lines, Inc.
75 West St., New York, New York

A joint venture between American Range Lines, Inc., and the American Liberty Steamship Corp., formed only for the duration of any WSA General Agency agreements after which each company would go its own way. The GAA was signed on September 8, 1943. In time disputes arose between the two parties and, with the consent of the WSA, the joint venture was terminated on December 1, 1944.

American Range Lines, Inc.
860 Drexel Bldg., Philadelphia, Pennsylvania

Georgia native John Cypert Rogers served in the Navy in 1918, married Lucille H. Yox in 1925, and in 1930 was a 31-year-old ship broker living at 36 Sussex Rd. in Lower Merion, Pennsylvania, with Lucille, 29, daughter Joan, 3½, and two servants, Henrich and Frieda Neihouse. In 1936 he and Jacob W. Alwine went into the ship operating business with four chartered vessels as American Range Lines. Rogers died on April 6, 1940, and Alwine took over but by mid–1942 the company's operations had ceased due to war conditions. Alwine then attempted to acquire War Shipping Administration ships for operation but was found deficient for the task. All the stock in American Range was then owned by Lucille Rogers, who had since moved to Wynnewood, Pennsylvania. The WSA suggested the company join forces with the American Liberty Steamship Corp. and on August 16, 1943, an agreement was reached between the two companies. The name was changed to American Range–Liberty Lines, Inc. According to the bylaws, the joint ownership was between the American Liberty Steamship Corp. and Lucille Rogers.

In 1940, Pennsylvania-native Jacob Alwine was 36 and lived with his wife Eleanor, 33, and daughter Margery, 8, at 153 Park Place in Camden, New Jersey.

American Republics Corp.
513 Petroleum Bldg., Houston, Texas

In 1870, John Frank Cullinan, a 36-year-old native of Ireland, was a tavern keeper in McClure, Pennsylvania. His wife Mary, 35, kept house and minded their children, Patrick, 14, Elizabeth, 11, Joseph, 10, Anna, 8, Michael, 5, and Mary, 3. By 1880 the family was living in Shamburg, in the Oil Creek Valley in Venango County, where Col. Edwin Drake drilled a well in 1859 and hit oil at 70 feet. This site was the first commercial oil well in the world and created a sensation equal to the discovery of gold in California. Dad and Joseph were both laborers there and Catherine, 8, Jennie, 6, and little John F., Jr., 2, had joined the family. Joseph worked his way up in the business, worked for Standard Oil, and by 1895 he and his partner, Charles S. Todd, had their own company, the Petroleum Iron Works Co., at the corner of 2nd & Jefferson in Washington, Pennsylvania, where they manufactured steam boilers to automatically separate out the gas, and oil, water, and grain storage tanks. Joseph lived at 55 College St. in Washington. By the late 1990s Charles had moved to Philadelphia and Joseph's brother John worked as a laborer in the company.

In 1897 Joseph visited Corsicana, Texas, and decided Texas held good prospects for the future of petroleum and in 1898 he moved to Waco where he formed J. S. Cullinan Pipe Line at 129 W. Collin St., as buyers and shippers of crude oil. He lived in a boarding house at 120 N. 15th. Brother Michael was in the same office representing Petroleum Iron Works.

In 1901 Joseph and Michael moved to Corsicana and opened J. S. Cullinan & Co. at 111 W. 6th Ave. to refine and pump petroleum products. Joseph established the Texas Fuel Co., the forerunner of the Texas Oil Co., known as Texaco. Michael represented Petroleum Iron Works and also was a natural gas distributor at 110 W. 6th. Joseph was also vice president of the Corsicana Commercial Club and J. Frank Cullinan worked as a gauger at the refinery. By 1905 Joseph had a wife named Lucy and he was back in Washington, Pennsylvania, at 1006 Jefferson Ave. In 1911 he was president of the Texas Co. in Houston and vice president of the Great Southern Life Insurance Co. He and Lucey lived at 1603 Rusk Ave. with their two sons Craig and William, who were both in school.

By 1916 Joseph had so many irons in the fire that in May of that year he incorporated the American Republics Corp. as a holding company for the numerous Cullinan enterprises. He was president, J. L. Autry was vice president, J. L. Clancy secretary, and H. A. Bishop treasurer. In 1917 Joseph was president of the Fidelity Trust Co., Harvey Cullinan was president of the Eureka Paving Co., and little brother J. Frank Cullinan was president of the Producers Oil Co.

In 1920 Joseph was 60 and Lucey, 57. They lived in Houston at the family home, Shady Side, with sons John H., 26, and daughters Nina, 23, Margaret, 21, and Mary, 18. Son Craig F., 25, lived in the home with his wife Edith, 24, and there was a butler, maid, and cook. Craig was president of the American Petroleum Co. and he and Edith moved to 1102 Eagle Ave. Son John died on May 5, 1920. In addition to all his other endeavors, Joseph was president of the Texas Chamber of Commerce.

After the Great War, like so many industrialists of the day, Joseph took advantage of the surplus of Shipping Board steamers and opened an office in New York at 25 W. 43rd. to charter and operate ships under the American Republics name. H. C. Carty was vice president and Hy D. Lindsey was treasurer.

On January 1, 1927, Petroleum Iron purchased the Pennsylvania Tank Car Co. to build railroad tank cars and the Cullinans were back in Washington at 55 College St. In 1929 the company had an office in Houston with Craig as president and Frank as vice president at 1613 Petroleum Building. Harvey J. Cullinan was vice president and sales manager of the Petroleum Iron Works of Texas, Joseph had an office on the 20th floor of the Petroleum Building, and Craig was vice president of American Republics and the Fidelity Trust Co.

Craig F. Cullinan was president in 1940. The company operated three Liberty tankers during the war. In December 1950 American Republics was controlled by the Barber Oil Corp., of Houston. Famous oilman Torkild Rieber, of Texaco, was president.

American South African Line, Inc.
26 Beaver St., New York

In 1903, James Augustine Farrell, Sr. (1863–1943), became general manager of the U.S. Steel Products Export Co. and in 1910 was president of U.S. Steel.

After World War I, the U.S. Shipping Board began regular service from East Coast ports to South and East Africa with the *Eastern Glade*, *Eastern Glen*, *West Cawthon*, *West Isleta*, and *Western Knight*.

On December 31, 1925, James Farrell and Arthur R. Lewis, president of the American Cuban Steamship Line, Inc., at 39 Cortlandt St. in New York, and Arthur W. Morrison, John M. Franklin, Luke D. Stapleton, Jr., William F. Curran, and James S. Regan, at 25 Broadway, incorporated American South African with Farrell and Lewis holding 800 of the 1,000 shares owned by the directors. The company was at 25 Broadway, New York.

In 1930, Farrell was 67 and lived with his wife Catherine, 59, son James A., Jr., 29, and five servants at 944 Fifth Ave. in New York. Lewis was 50 and lived with his wife Grace, 25, sons Arthur, Jr., 21, William, 16, Barbara, 7, Marilyn, 6, niece Adele Ehrling, 20, a cook and a chamber maid at 117 Harmon Ave., North Pelham, New York.

In 1948, the company name was changed to Farrell Lines in honor of James Farrell.

American Trading & Production Corp.
American Building, 229 E. Baltimore St., Baltimore, Maryland

Established in 1931 as a subsidiary of the American Oil Co., an oil refining operation at Clarkson St. at the Baltimore & Ohio railroad tracks. Louis Blaustein was chairman of the board and president of American Oil and became president of American Trading. Jacob Blaustein was first vice president and general manager of American Oil and was vice president of American Trading. Jacob Rothchild was secretary-treasurer. They owned and operated the 8,862-ton tanker *American Trader*, built in 1923 at Chester, Pennsylvania.

Blaustein, 64, was a native of Germany who came to America in 1890. His wife, Henrietta, 61, also came from Germany in 1890 and they married in 1910. They lived at 2570 Eutaw Place in Baltimore with their 28-year-old German servant Anna Anton, a recent arrival.

They apparently operated only one Liberty ship, the *Albert G. Brown*.

American West African Line
17 Battery Place, New York

In 1880, Herbert Barber left England and brought his family to New York. He was 35, wife Sarah was 30, daughter Alice, 7, Constance, 5, Mabel, 3, and Sarah just arrived. He went into business in New York City at 85 Broadway and the family settled in Englewood, New Jersey. Daughter Annie was born in 1882, followed by sons St. George, Robert, Philip, Arthur, and daughters, Beatrice, Edith, and Elizabeth.

Younger brother James Barber arrived from England with his wife Katherine in 1886 when he was 44, and Katherine was 31. Son Edward J., 9, came over the next year and daughters Mary, Gertrude, Ada, Louise, and Florence were born in New Jersey. The family lived at 17 Lafayette Place in New York.

When James arrived they opened a steamship agency at 35 Broadway as Barber & Co. and eventually represented several lines. In 1900 both families were close neighbors in Englewood and in 1902 they incorporated the Barber Steamship Co., which became Barber Steamship Lines, Inc., in 1917 with James chairman of the board of Barber & Co. and Edward J. Barber vice president of Barber & Co. and president of Barber Steamship. Oakley Wood was vice president of Barber Steamship Lines.

American West African was established by the U.S. Shipping Board to serve West African ports. In June 1928, the ten ships and floating equipment were put up for sale at auction and five bids were received: Kermit Roosevelt, of the Roosevelt Steamship Co., $1,881,201; the A. E. Clegg Ship Owning Corp., $1,798,838; W. F. Kenney, of New York, $1,270,000.66; James A. Farrell, Jr., $1,314,000, and Oakley Wood, who submitted the winning bid of $2,263,508.80. American West African operated from Pier 36, Atlantic Basin, New York, and New Orleans. They also obtained a contract to transport mail. Most of the company's ships had names beginning with "*West.*" The business grew to a chartering and operating business serving ports worldwide and when war came again Edward J. Barber was president and Charles Barthold was vice president.

Barber Asphalt Corp.
30 Rockefeller Plaza, New York

Amzi Lorenzo Barber was born on June 22, 1843, in Vermont and became a college professor. In 1872 he decided to switch careers and got into real estate development in Washington, D.C., and that led to the problem of finishing streets to keep them clean and passable. Asphalt had been shown through studies to be an ideal material so in 1878 Barber set up A. L. Barber & Co. in Washington to acquire the material. In 1883 he incorporated the A. L. Barber Asphalt Paving Co., Inc., and moved his business to New York City where there was more opportunity.

On February 1, 1888, after years of negotiations, he obtained a 42-year lease (to 1930) on 114 acres of the world's largest known deposit of natural asphalt at Pitch Lake in Trinidad. He bought his raw material from the Trinidad Asphalt Co. and manufactured it into a suitable road paving material.

As the use of the material became more and more popular, opportunists sought to consolidate Barber's operation into a trust, which Barber opposed, but he was out-voted by the board. Gen. Francis Greene then became president. A year later the combination was taken over by John M. Mack, of Pennsylvania, who formed the National Asphalt Company of America. Barber then sold his interest and retired on January 3, 1901. National Asphalt went bankrupt and reorganized in 1903 as the General Asphalt Co., composed solely of the A. L. Barber Paving Co. In 1904 Barber returned to the business and after some trouble in Venezuela the company was reorganized as the A. L. Barber Asphalt Co.

After Barber's death in 1909 the company was run by his son-in-law, Samuel Todd Davis, husband of his daughter Lorena. In 1920 the Barber Asphalt Co. built an asphalt refinery in Perth Amboy, New Jersey.

In 1929 Harry H. Barber, a mechanical engineer, was president of the Barber-Greene Co., manufacturers of material handling machinery at 631 West Park Ave. in Aurora, Illinois. William B. Greene was vice president, treasurer, and sales manager. Barber lived with wife Blanche at 735 N. Lake and Greene lived with his wife Jane at 1300 Garfield Ave. In 1938 Barber patented an asphalt paving machine.

In 1940 the company's president was Ernest James Auten (E. James Auten), 56, at Barber, New Jersey. Auten was divorced and lived in a rented home on Shawsbury Drive in Rumson, New Jersey, with his son L. Richard, 26, a publisher, Ralph Smith, 26, their cook, and Bessie Smith, 21, their waitress. A company subsidiary, Bonafide-Genasco, Inc., manufactured roofing materials and general petroleum products at Perth Amboy under president Frank Seamans.

In October 1941 Torkild Rieber resigned from the Texas Co. (Texaco) and was elected director. In 1942 they owned the brand-new 10,169-ton tanker *Caribbean* and two barges, the *Barber* and the *Barco*. On March 25, 1942, the manufacturing of asphalt and roofing materials was suspended due to problems getting supplies through the war zones and in September all building materials came under government control. The company then took to operating ships.

In 1946 Rieber was president and the company got into Gilsonite mining with Standard Oil of California with mixed results.

Bernuth, Lembcke Co., Inc.
420 Lexington Ave., New York

Carlos Eduardo Lembcke was born in Hamburg, Germany, on January 18, 1870, arrived in New York on October 12, 1889, and opened an exporting business as C. Lembeke & Co. at 78 Wall St. Carlos became a citizen on September 20, 1899, and lived at 14 Pierrpont St. in Brooklyn.

Oscar Max von Bernuth was born in Hamburg, Germany, on July 23, 1873, and came to the United States in 1875, where his naturalized father resided, and became a clerk at various importing firms. In 1898 Oscar went to work for Carlos Lembcke and on December 20, 1907, he incorporated the Bernuth Corp. at Suffolk, New York. On November 21, 1908, he married Adeline Ellen McGillicuddy.

In 1910 Carlos' office was at 80 Wall St., Room 918 and Carlos' brother, George Albert Lembcke, was secretary of the company. George was born in Hamburg, Germany, on September 18, 1874, came to the United States in September 1894, and worked in sales. George lived at 121 W. 71st St. Carlos had space at 140 Maiden Lane where George worked and George became a citizen in 1901.

Carlos married Louise Biernatzki and they had four kids, all born in Brooklyn between 1901 and 1909. In 1911 Carlos decided to retire and move to Europe for the sake of his childrens' education and in October 1913 the family moved to Genoa, Italy, but came back to the United States when the World War started. Carlos and Louise intended to live in Switzerland when the war ended.

On July 16, 1913, George and Oscar went into business together as Lembcke, von Bernuth Co. at 80 Wall St., Room 918. Importing creosote was their main endeavor and they incorporated on August 11. Oscar was president and lived at 301 W. 108th St. George was secretary and lived at 131 Riverside Drive. On December 27, 1918, the company was Bernuth, Lembcke Co., Inc., at 171 Madison Ave.

In 1938 they had the 7,972-ton tanker *O. M. Bernuth* built. In 1940 Oscar, 66, and Adeline, 56, lived with their son Charles in his rented home at 180 Cedarhurst Ave. in Cedarhurst, New York. Charles worked at the company.

In 1942 the company owned the 4,943-ton tanker *Torres*, built in 1917. The company continues today as the Bernuth Corp. in Huntington, New York.

Black Diamond Steamship Co., Inc.
39 Broadway, New York

John Eufernio Dockendorff was born in Lima, Peru, on March 20, 1866, came to the United States in 1875, went into banking and became very successful. He married his Canadian-born wife Florence in 1900 and in 1910 lived with Florence and his stepdaughter Peisis Stallings, 15, stepsons John Stallings, 5, Cornell Stallings, 3, and three servants in Mamaronek, New York. In October 1906 their son Noyes Carroll was born and in 1917 the family lived at 205 W. 57th St., New York.

In 1920, John, fellow banker Lewis Iselin, and shipping office manager Victor J. Sudman set up an export business at 20 Broadway in New York as J. E. Dockendorff & Co. with John as president, Iselin vice president, and Sudman secretary-treasurer. Iselin was 40 and lived with his wife Marie, 36, sons Columbas, 15, Lewis, Jr., 6, daughter Marie, 12, and six servants at 16 W. 52nd St. in Manhattan. Sudman was 31, born in New York to German immigrants, and lived in a rented flat with his wife Hilda, 30, and brand-new baby George, at 273 E. 176th St. in the Bronx.

When post-war Shipping Board contracts became available Sudman, Dockendorff, Albert Chester Valentine, Michael Joseph Hanlon, and John J. Morton formed American Diamond Lines in Sudman's office at 39 Broadway and operated the Shipping Board's Hog Islanders *City of Alton, Coahoma County, Tomalva, Sac City, Saco, Sacandaga*, and *West Arrow*, built in Seattle in 1918, and *Ala*, built at Harriman, Pennsylvania, in 1921. All were operated to European ports on Shipping Board accounts.

In 1931, when the ships became available for sale, Sudman incorporated Black Diamond Lines, Inc., at 4808 Bergenline Ave., Union City, New Jersey. Sudman was president at his office at 39 Broadway and owned a 54 percent interest in the company. The Sudmans had left the Bronx long behind by then and lived at 439 Highbrook Ave. in Pelham Manor, New Rochelle, New York. Dockendorff was vice president and Valentine secretary-treasurer. The company purchased all the ships for $16.80 a ton and renamed them: *City of Alton* to *Black Gull, Coahoma County* to *Black Tern, Tomalva* to *Black Eagle, Sac City* to *Black Falcon, Saco* to *Black Hawk, Sacandaga* to *Black Heron, West Arrow* to *Black Osprey*, and *Ala* to *Black Condor*. The ships were operated by and registered to American Diamond. In 1932, according to Sudman, the company "changed their sterns and increased the speed from 10 knots to 14 knots, and they became the fastest American freighters in the overseas trade." They spent about $250,000 each on the Hog Islanders and $50,000 on the other two. They subsequently purchased the Shipping Board's *West Eldara* and *Wytheville*. American Diamond's ships were chartered to the Isthmian Steamship Co., which also sailed from New York to Antwerp and Rotterdam.

On November 4, 1939, the last of the Neutrality Acts was passed. All trans–Atlantic trade was halted and ships could no longer go to Holland or Belgium. The company then chartered foreign flag vessels for their own operation. At this time, and prior to the Spring of 1940, few ships were bought or sold on the world market but by mid–1940 the British began looking abroad for ships to replace mounting losses.

In July 1940 President Roosevelt gave a speech in which he stated that "corporations would be subject to excess profit taxes." In a later court action not related to taxes, Sudman stated, "That worried me because there were so few stockholders and if the captial had to pay excess profit taxes, and then we had to pay personal taxes again, we probably would not have had very much left. So I suggested to our attorneys, our corporate attorneys at that time, that we change the form." On September 27, 1940, Black Diamond liquidated the New Jersey corporation and created a partnership in Delaware as the Black Diamond Steamship Co., Inc., saving the company about $1 million in corporate taxes. Isthmian agreed to rewrite the charter agreement and work with the new partnership.

Just after the reorganization, the company was approached by John Gammie, an assistant general manager with Cunard White Star Line, who wanted to buy the company's ships. The ships were under charter to Isthmian at $7 a ton a month, a net proft of $4.50 a ton a month, or $250,000 a month total, a very lucrative business at that time with 64,000 tons in the fleet. Sudman initially refused to sell, believing the ships were worth about $200 a ton based on their earning capacity, but Gammie, William Boyd, and Edgar Philip Rees, the general manager at Furness Withy & Co., all British purchasing agents, kept pressing. Sudman later related a conversation with Gammie and his partners:

> You must be pretty hard up for ships. He said, "Frankly, we are." Well, if you make us an offer of $50 a ton I will discuss it again with my partners but some of the partners are objecting to selling the ships. And he said, "Well, see what you can do and let me know whether I can go ahead and go to work on them." I came back and discussed it with the partners, and the gist of the discussion was that the war had gone on now for a year. The general opinion was that the war might go on two or three or four or five years. The ships were getting older. They were 20 to 22 years of age then. Perhaps it might be wise to sell them and invest the money in new tonnage after the war was over. So as with all transactions, I tried to get my partners to agree, although I controlled the partnership, and they did agree.

On October 23, 1940, the partners agreed to the sale. The company's book value on the ships was $6 a ton. A sales agreement was signed on November 15 but permission to transfer title to a foreign flag was needed from the Maritime Commission. The Commission agreed on December 5 to transfer only the *Condor*, *Osprey*, *Heron*, and *Tern* to Cunard White Star but in early January the other four were sold to Cairn Line of Steamships, Ltd, for a grand total of $1,670,000.

Shortly after this sale, Francois Mark DeBannissis "Count" Rafailovich, supposedly a highly credentialed engineer, naval architect, and ship broker of titled royalty sued the company to recover what he believed were $83,000 in commissions due to him on the sale of the ships. The claim was dismissed after numerous appeals and he was viewed by some involved in the case as an impostor. Black Diamond operated into the 1950s.

The manner in which Black Diamond was formed was a common occurrence after the Great War. In response to war in Europe, Congress created the U.S. Shipping Board in 1917 to control American shipbuilding, shipping routes, and the activities of the companies themselves. Immediate conflicts within the Board surfaced, most notably between William Denman, who favored building cheap, wooden ships, and Gen. George Goethals, who opposed the idea. The conflict resulted in both men resigning. None of the ships built at the famous Hog Island yard took any part in the war, all being delivered too late, and by the end of the war the government had all these ships, wooden ships, plus quite a few German vessels that had been seized, including some large liners. Europe was in shambles and providing waterborne commerce to the region and to the ports previously served by European shippers was seen as a very lucrative proposition. The Board retained post-war controls, created steamship lines and routes, and leased surplus vessels to operators for specific routes to carry specific cargoes, and also began selling off some ships. Lines and ships were sold at auction, which created considerable competition from existing operators, ship brokers, and exporters. All the normal politics, scandals, accusations, business failures, lawsuits, and fines ensued.

Blidberg Rothchild Co., Inc.
80 Broad St., New York

Tryggve Sagen, 27, was a Norwegian ship owner when he arrived at New York on March 31, 1919, on the *Frederik VIII* from Christiania, Norway. Allan Blidberg was born in Sweden in 1896 and was a chief clerk when he arrived at New York from Gothenburg on April 3, 1919, on the *Stockholm*.

The two went into business as Blidberg-Sagen Co., Inc., at 52 Broadway, to serve Scandinavian and Baltic ports as operators and agents. Sagen was president, Blidberg vice president and general manager, and Sylvester E. Rothchild was secretary. Sagen was a ship broker and lived in a boarding house on Broadway in Manhattan. Rothchild was the former Vice Consul at Gothenburg, Sweden. In 1921, Sagen was a member of a Norwegian commission seeking $15.6 million from the U.S. government for 16 Norwegian vessels seized by the government during the war. By World War II the company was Blidberg Rothchild. They apparently operated into the 1970s.

Boland & Cornelius
1016 Marine Trust Building, 239 Main St., Buffalo, New York

In 1895, the Boland brothers, John J., 20, and Joseph A., 24, went into the Great Lakes steamship business as J. J. Boland. John was the steamship agent and Joseph was the broker and insurance man. Their office was at 202 Main St. in Buffalo and the two lived at 453 Elk. In 1901, Joseph decided to go into real estate. John then lived at 794 S. Park Ave. and Joseph had moved to 104 Niagara. The next year John hired 20-year-old Adam Edward Cornelius as a clerk and moved the office to 25–26 Exchange Building. Adam had been a clerk at the American Agricultural Chemical Co. and lived at home at 90 Dodge. He later came up with the idea of using self-unloading ships to save money, an idea that transformed the industry. In 1904 they became partners and in 1907 founded the American Steamship Company. In 1941 John J., Jr., ran Boland & Cornelius as an operating agency. American Steamship is still in business under GAXT Corp. ownership.

Bulk Carriers Corp.
80 Broad St., New York

Bulk Carriers Corp. was established as a subsidiary of the T. J. Stevenson Co. in the Stevens office. The company's only wartime Liberty ship was the *Edward B. Dudley*, lost in April 1943.

Burns Steamship Co.
727 W. 7th, Los Angeles, California

In 1937, Ohio native and West Coast lumber wholesaler Leroy G. Burns bought the 2,865-ton steamer *Caddopeak* from the Charles Nelson Co. of San Francisco, renamed it the *Lurline Burns*, and homeported it at San Francisco. In 1940 he was 45 and lived at 215 Roxbury in Beverly Hills with his wife, Lurline M., 48, son James A., 10, brother-in-law Charles O. Middleton, Jr., 44, a retail lumber salesman, and Benny Yelew, their 26-year-old Filipino houseboy. During the war he had an office at 727 W. 7th in Los Angeles and one in San Francisco at 311 California St., managed by Capt. Johannes Ramselius. In June 1943 the *Lurline Burns* was requisitioned by the Navy and operated as the *Besboro* (AG-66). Burns then operated War Shipping Administration ships.

Calmar Steamship Corp.
25 Broadway, New York

Calmar was a coastwise line established in 1927 by the Bethlehem Steel Co. to carry their products to the West Coast. Passengers and cargo were carried east-bound back to Atlantic ports. Henry W. Warley, 59, was president in 1943. He lived at 1035 5th Ave. in Manhattan with his wife Mary, 58. The ships were managed by Moore-McCormack.

Coastwise (Pacific Far East) Line, Inc.
1788 Front Ave., Portland, Oregon, BEacon 7301

Hector M. Hunt was a steamship agent at 623 Board of Trade Building in Portland and also treasurer and general manager of Columbia Basin Terminals. He lived with his wife Frances M. at 2401 NE 23rd. The company was incorporated in 1938 with Hunt as president, attorney James C. Dezendorf, vice president, and Frank C. McCulloch, was secretary. The wharf was at the Columbia Basin Terminal. Dezendorf was an attorney with Dey, Hampson & Nelson, 800 Pacific Bldg., and McCulloch lived at 345 Levenworth.

In 1940 Felix W. Isherwood was district manager and in San Francisco, Benjamin H. Parkinson was general manager and treasurer at 222 Sansome St. The company owned the 3,383-ton "*Coast*" freighters—*Banker, Farmer, Trader, Merchant, Miller, Shipper,* and *Trader*—homeported at Portland. Their first Liberty ship was the *Henry W. Longfellow*.

Coastwise Transportation Corp.
10 Post Office Square, Boston, Massachusetts

Incorporated in 1922 at 160 State St. in Boston as agents, operators, and owners. Harris Livermore was president, Lester H. Monks treasurer, and Charles Skentelbery marine superintendent. Monks was the resident manager at the New York office at 87 Wall St. To get started, the new company purchased seven ships from American-Hawaiian: *Bristol, Coastwise, Hampden, Middlesex, Norfolk, Suffolk,* and *Transportation*. On May 18, 1922, the *Middlesex* stranded on Trundy Ledges outside Portland Harbor and radio operator Walter McLeod got $100 from the company for standing by his radio throughout the ordeal and subsequent salvage operation.

In 1927 they had an office at 381 St John St. in Portland, Maine, and added the *Berkshire* to their fleet. In 1938 the Portland office was at 443 Congress St. and in 1943, J. J. Halloran was vice president and general manager. The company apparently no longer owned ships by 1944 but was still in business as late as 1970.

Cosmopolitan Shipping Co., Inc.
42 Broadway, New York

In 1902, August F. Mack was a freight agent for U.S. Steel and in 1913 he was president of the New York Traffic Club, a shipping organization. During the Great War he was the U.S. Shipping Board district manager in New York. He founded Cosmopolitan in 1916 at 115 Broadway. He was president and Harry Raymond, George M. Pynchon, James R. Munoz, Charles H. Crocker, and Wilfred B. Bremner were vice presidents. The directors ncorporated on July 2, 1920, at 42 Broadway and had offices in Chicago, New Orleans, Philadelphia, Baltimore, and Norfolk.

In August 1940 the company operated the 3,671-ton Norwegian freighter *Lista*. The ship left New York under tow on Wednesday August 7 with "war supplies" for Liverpool, England, when a fire started in the engine room and quickly spread throughout the ship. The company denied there was any munitions aboard and said the cargo was general merchandise, but could include airplanes. Federal and local investigators said they found no evidence of sabotage but the crew of 27 Norwegians, South Americans, and Filipinos was interrogated by the FBI.

The De La Rama Steamship Co., Inc.
De La Rama St. No. 24, Iloilo, Panay Island, Philippines, and 17 Battery Pl.,
New York

Isidro de la Rama owned a large collection of properties and sugar plantations in the Philippines when sugar was their primary export. He established the firm of Hijos de la Rama at Talisay and at the turn of the century the company owned and operated several steamships out of the port of Iloilo City, Panay Island, including the *Cabanbanan, Moleño, Taculin,* and several lighters. He had four sons who were nominally associated with the company until he died on June 10, 1897. One son, Esteban, was a general in the Philippine army in 1898 and apparently managed the de la Rama interests.

Hijos de la Rama was out of the ship owning buisiness by 1930 and the same year The De la Rama Steamship Co. was incorporated at Iloilo with Benito H. Lopez as manager and Esteban as agent. In 1934 the company owned the 560-ton steam freighter *Iloilo* and the 95-ton motor freighter *Escalante R.* In 1936 Esteban had the inter-island passenger vessel *Don Esteban* built by Krupp at Kiel, Germany, followed by the *Don Isidro.* All the company's vessels were registered in the Philippines.

In October 1938, the company obtained a $3,500,000 loan from the National Development Co. at Manila to have three passenger-freighters built in Italy. In October 1939, Capt. Natalio C. Ventosa arrived in Italy to pick up the 425-foot, 5,011-ton, 17-knot motorship *Dona Aurora,* named for the wife of Philippine president Manuel Quezon. When he arrived at Pier 2, Erie Basin, in Brooklyn on November 9 the nice looking ships received considerable attention. The *Dona Nati* was due to be delivered on Dec 5 and the *Dona Aniceta* was due on January 5, 1940. The ships were built for service from New York to the Philippines, Hong

Kong, and Shanghai. A three-month round trip to the Philippines and back cost $650. The company also chartered three Swedish-flag and three Norwegian-flag ships for trans–Pacific trade.

When war started in Europe the shipping situation in the Philippines became extremely acute. The three chartered vessels were withdrawn by their owners. Around $10 million of American money and some Philippine money was available for the purchase of ships, under strict conditions, but there were very few ships available. The company did manage to buy the 8,600-ton freighter *Wind Rush* from Shepard Steamship Co. for $737,000.

The United States purchased around 80 percent of Philippine exports, primarily sugar, and when the United States halted exports of scrap steel and aviation gas to Jalan, the Japanese blockaded Chinese ports. During one visit, the *Dona Nati* was prevented from loading $36,500 worth of rapeseed oil at Shanghai.

Capt. Ventosa's *Dona Aurora* arrived at San Francisco, California, on September 11, 1940, departed on the 14th and stopped 100 miles off the coast by a British warship. The freighter was boarded and an Italian national from the crew, an engineer, was taken off. Antonio Maria Bayot was de la Rama's representative in Los Angeles in 1941 and Luiz Francisco Meirelles, 29, a nephew of the Portuguese prime minister, ran the company's New York office. He lived at 465 Park Ave. with his wife Concepcion.

Esteban de la Rama was elected to the Philippine senate in 1941 and by May of that year the company had paid back about half a million of the loan.

Dichmann, Wright & Pugh, Inc.
803 Citizens Bank Building, 109 W. Main St., Norfolk, Virginia

In 1925, steamship agents Vilh Dichmann, Bland Saunders Wright, Frank C. Pugh, Clint B. Sellers, and Alan Smith opened an office at 111 E. Main St. in Norfolk, Virginia. Pugh had an office in Philadelphia and Sellers was in New York. In 1941 B. Saunders Wright, 51, was president and Smith secretary-treasurer. Wright lived with his wife Virginia Hughes Wright at 800 Graydon Ave., apt. 2B, in Norfolk and when he died on October 16, 1944, Alan Smith became president and John M. Levick, assistant secretary-treasurer. Virginia Wright stayed in Norfolk, went back to school, and in 1947 was a clerk at the Bay View elementary school at 1300 Bay View Blvd.

Eastern Gas & Fuel Associates
250 Stuart St., Boston

Andrew William Mellon (1835–1937) joined his father's bank in 1874, became president of the Mellon National Bank in Pittsburgh in 1902 and became a major investor in coal, coke, and iron. Mellon acquired the large Koppers coal business in West Virginia and consolidated his energy interests into the Koppers Company, a holding company for his energy investments. In 1924 the Mystic Steamship Co. was incorporated to run coastwise colliers. In 1929, Henry B. Rust was president of the Koppers Company when eight gas companies in Massachusetts were acquired and formed into a voluntary trust association known as the Eastern Gas & Fuel Associates that would be the umbrella organization for future acquisitions as a subsidiary of the Koppers Company. The trustees began acquiring various assets such as the Old Colony Gas Co., the Massachusetts Gas Co., Conneticut Coke Co., Philadelphia Coke

Co., and Philadelphia Gas Works. Eastern Gas built a ten mile long 20-inch gas line in Pennsylvania as part of a distribution system.

On January 2, 1942, Eastern Gas announced a corporate restructuring scheme whereby, among other companies, the Koppers Coal Co. became the Koppers Division and the Mystic Steamship Co. became the Mystic Steamship Division.

In 1942, apparently in an effort to avoid running afoul of antitrust laws, the Koppers Company applied to the Securities & Exchange Commission for an order "declaring that it is not a holding company" and Eastern Gas sought a declaration that it was not a subsidiary of the Koppers Company. Both petitions were denied on September 29. As so often happens in the shipping world, the actual corporate structure was somewhat murky.

Halfdan Lee, 54, of Norway, was president of Eastern Gas in 1942. He lived with his wife Nina, 51, sons John, 26, Richard, 17, daughter Alice, 23, mother-in-law Alice H. Smith, 75, and four servants at 49 Worthington Rd. in Brookline, Massachusetts. Ralph C. Goodwin was vice president of the Mystic Steamship Division.

Eastern Steamship Lines, Inc.
Piers 19 and 25, North River, New York

On October 8, 1901, bankers Galen L. Stone and "ice king" Charles W. Morse organized the Eastern Steamship Co. in Maine after buying several successful steamboat lines that had operated for many years between Boston, Maine, and Saint John, New Brunswick. Morse apparently wanted to control every steamboat line not run by a railroad and when he purchased ocean-going steamship lines he encountered financial difficulties.

On January 1, 1907, Consolidated Steamship Lines was incorporated as a holding company with controlling interest in Eastern Steamship, Metropolitan, Clyde, and Mallory steamship companies. In October 1907 a financial panic caused Morse's holdings to fail and by February 1908 they were in receivership. In 1909 Morse's Metropolitan Steamship Co. was sold to John W. McKinnon, of Chicago, with Morse as president in Maine. McKinnon was president of the Hudson Navigation Co. at Pier 32, North River.

On December 4, 1911, the Eastern Steamship Corp. was incorporated in Maine along with the assets of the Metropolitan and Maine steamship companies pursuant to a buyout authorized by Eastern Steamship Co. shareholders who were each offered a $1,000, 5 percent bond, 20 shares of new common stock, and 10 shares of new preferred stock in exchange for each 20 shares of old stock. Calvin Austin was president and general manager, Roderick A. Pepper, secretary, and Josiah W. Hayden, treasurer. Offices were at 16 State St. and 368 Atlantic Ave. at Foster's Wharf, Boston. Henry R. Mallory and Galen Stone were directors. The company had 24 steamers.

In 1914 the company became Eastern Steamship Lines at 290 & 958 Broadway, Pier 18 North River, and 4 W. 125th. Prince W. Nickerson was agent at Pier 18. The company opened an office in Boston at 332 Washington St., operating at the Union, India, and Central Wharfs.

General Steamship Corp., Ltd.
240 Battery St., San Francisco, California

Established in 1929 in San Francisco at 240 Battery Street as steamship agents and operators of chartered freight and passenger ships for worldwide service. Harry Sweet Scott, late president of the R. G. Hamilton Corp., Ltd., was president. Offices were at 240 Battery St. during the war and Scott was still president. Drew Chidester was vice president and general manager.

In 1940 Scott was 67 and lived at 618 Bolinas Rd. in Fairfax with his wife Dorothy, 44, son Harry H., 8, daughter Barbara, 9, his father and mother-in-law, a governess, a Japanese butler, a Japanese cook, a German hired man and his wife and 1-year-old son, and another single Swiss hired hand aged 51.

In 1940 Chidester lived at 2222 Hyde St. with his wife Nellie.

Grace Line., Inc.
10 Hanover Square, New York and 2 Pine St., San Francisco

In 1854, the Grace family was driven from Ireland by famine. They settled in Peru and got involved with guano harvesting, chemical manufacturing, and shipping. Eventually they incorporated in the United States and William Russell Grace, one of the sons, was president. They began their own shipping service between New York and Peru in 1882 as Grace Line with W. R. Grace & Co. as agents. In September 1947, one of the worst waterfront fires in New York history occurred when the Grace Line shed at Pier 57 caught fire and burned for a week.

Hammond Shipping Co., Ltd.
417 Montgomery St., San Francisco, California

Andrew Benoni Hammond (1848–1934) was born in New Brunswick, Canada, and at 16 went to work in the woods in Maine and Pennsylvania. In 1897 he moved to Montana and became a successful merchant and railroad builder there, in Washington, and then in California. In 1900 he purchased the John Vance redwood sawmill at Samoa, California, along with a rail line. He used steam schooners to haul lumber coastwise and tugs to tow huge log rafts. He incorporated the Hammond Lumber Co. in 1912 and by the late 1920s ran nine steamers including the 8,511-ton *Arizonan* from offices at 260 California St. in San Francisco. In 1930 he was 81 and lived with his daughters Daisy, 38, Florence, 48, and three servants at 2252 Broadway in San Francisco. He is the namesake for Hammond, Oregon.

In 1935 the Hammond Shipping Co. was organized at 310 Sansome St. under president Leonard C. Hammond and general manager and marine superintendent Ralph O. Robinson. The company was at 417 Montgomery St. during the war. In 1940 Hammond was 55 and lived at 2252 Broadway with his wife Dorothy, 53, stepson Alfred D. Bell, Jr., a salesman at Hammond Lumber, and a German butler, a servant, and a German cook. The company was bought by Georgia-Pacific in 1956.

International Freighting Corp., Inc.
17 Battery Place, New York

Established by E. I. du Pont de Nemours & Co. in 1920 as a wholly-owned subsidiary to operate ships. The office was at 120 Broadway, Room 1105. Harry J. Lesser was president, James H. Graves, vice president, and Irving L. Ernest, secretary-treasurer. They were known as I. F. C. Lines and had an office in Philadelphia.

Interocean Steamship Corp.
311 California St., Room 604, San Francisco, California

In 1919 the Dyson Shipping Co. was incorporated in New York as foreign freight for-warders. Frederick W. Gale was president, Herbert H. Van Duyne, vice president, and Edmond J. Dixon, secretary-treasurer in their office at 1542 Woolworth Building, 233 Broadway. They also had an office at 44 Beaver St., New York, 20 W. Jackson St., Chicago, and opened offices in Seattle and San Francisco. Harry Brown managed the San Francisco office at 311 California Ave. In 1929 he was a vice president when the company established Interocean Steamship in room 612. Erik Krag was manager of the General Steamship Corp. when he joined Brown as freight agent the next year. Krag became general manager and in 1933 became vice president and general manager. Elsie J. Berlund was a bookkeeper who became secretary-treasurer. Brown was president of Interocean in 1940 and president of Dyson in 1942. In 1940 Harry was 69 and lived with his wife Ida Mae, 66, Harry's son Richard G. Marshall, 22, their divorced daugh-ter Frances Rodriguez, 37, her son Michael, 4, and servant Irene McCarthy, 35, in a rented house at 716 Crescent Ave. in San Mateo. In 1942 Harry lived at 342 Polk in San Francisco and later moved to the Olympic Club.

Isbrandtsen Steamship Co., Inc.
26 Broadway, New York, and Pier 30, foot of Sedgewick, Brooklyn

Hans Julius Isbrandtsen was born in Denmark on September 7, 1891, came to America in 1915, and married his wife Gertrude, 19, a nice German girl, in 1919. He went into business with his cousin, Arnold P. Moller, and in 1930 was president of Isbrandtsen-Moller Co., Inc., at 26 Broadway. In 1939 he formed his own company to serve Far East markets while still a partner with his cousin.

In 1930, Isbrandtsen lived in a rented apartment in Brooklyn with Gertrude, 32, sons Waldermar, 12, Jakob, 8, daughter Niel, 5, and Rose M. Kilgallon, their 31-year-old Irish maid.

Isthmian Steamship Co.
71 Broadway, New York

John Pierpont Morgan and Elbert H. Gary formed the United States Steel Products Co. in 1901 by merging Carnegie Steel, Federal Steel, and National Steel. In 1903, James A. Farrell was named general manager of the U.S. Steel Products Export Co. to oversee shipping of the company's goods, mainly railroad track going to Chile. The new company found itself obliged to use foreign-flag ships for its exports but those firms were not inclined to give American shippers competitive rates, instead favoring their own countries. When Farrell became president of U.S. Steel in 1910 he purchased freighters and registered them under the British flag in two new companies: the New York & South American Line and the Maple Leaf Line. When World War I began, in 1914, the British government began requisitioning all British-flagged vessels, the Panama Canal opened, and the two companies were merged to form Isthmian Steamship Lines, in honor of the Canal, and their registry was switched to American. The office was at 11 Broadway, Room 201, with John W. Ryan as agent. By 1928 the company operated the Argonaut, Robin, and American South African ships and in 1930 owned and operated United States Steel Prod-ucts Co. ships under that name. In 1943 John McAuliffe was president of the company.

James Griffiths & Sons
655 Empire Building, Seattle, Washington

Newport, England, native Capt. James Griffiths (1861–1943) came to the United States in 1885 and opened a ship brokerage office in Seattle. He was instrumental in developing shipping with Japan's NYK Line and gradually branched out to owning and operating ships of his own. His sons, Stanley, born in England in February 1884, and Bert, born in Washington in April 1886, were the children of James' first wife Susie.

In 1936 Griffiths combined with the Olympic Steamship Co. into the Consolidated Olympic Co. to serve the Long Beach–Seattle–Tacoma route. One company travelled northbound the other southbound. The company was later the Olympic-Griffiths Line and owned the 7,216-ton freighter *Olympic Pioneer*, which hauled lumber and newsprint. Other ships were chartered.

In 1940 Griffiths was 79 and lived at 405 W. Highland Dr. with his wife Ethel, 53, three maids, his father-in-law Herbert B. Chaffee, 74, and sister-in-law Ella Scott, 54.

J. H. Winchester & Co.
19 Rector St., New York

James Henry Winchester was born at Annapolis, Nova Scotia, Canada, on June 4, 1824. He came to Eastport, Maine, in October 1831 and became a naturalized citizen on July 7, 1845. In 1850 he was a sea captain living with his wife Mary, 24, and daughters Lucy, 3, and Mary 4 mos., in Eastport. By 1860 he had quit the sea and was in the grocery and shipping business in New York at 114 South St. The family lived at 45 Elliott Place in Brooklyn. James was the majority owner of the brigantines *Nellie Celeste* and the notorious *Mary Celeste* when it was found adrift and hastily abandoned between the Azores and Portugal in December 1872, which begat a mystery that still exists. Company offices were at 356 Produce Exchange Building in New York for many years. He and Mary spent their last days in East Orange, New Jersey, and James died in 1913. The company acted as freight agents for the Shipping Board in the 1920s and became embroiled in claims resulting from the mysterious loss of goods being shipped to Bristol, England.

Winchester Noyes was president during the World War II years. He was born on March 14, 1878, in Brooklyn and entered the Navy as an ensign on April 3, 1917, and left as a lieutenant commander on December 12, 1918. He worked in naval operations in Washington. He lived with his wife Helen at 45 E. 62nd St. in New York during the war and died in April 1954. Helen died in 1957. J. Barstow Smull was vice president.

Los Angeles Tanker Operators, Inc.
541 S. Spring St., Los Angeles, California

Incorporated on July 8, 1943, at Los Angeles by Harry H. Birkholm, Morgan Adams, A. P. Scott, Eugene Overton, W. Bruce Bryant, Leander K. Vermille, and Edward D. Lyman.

Birkholm was president and lived with his wife Elsie C. at 2370 Adair in San Marino. Joseph F. Marias was executive vice president. In 1918 he ran the port of Astoria, Oregon, and in 1920 was in Portland and in 1922 was a general agent for the U.S. Shipping Board dealing with surplus and seized vessels. In 1938 he was appointed president of the newly-created

California State Board of Harbor Commissioners. In 1952 he was in San Francisco at 461 Market St. in the export business. He lived at 141 Hillside Ave., Piedmont CA.

In 1942 Bryant was the district manager for the General Steamship Corp., Ltd. He lived in South Pasadena. Morgan Adams was on the Board of Harbor Commissioners and was president of the Mortgage Guaranty Co. He lived with his wife Virginia at 3278 Wilshire Blvd.

Los Angeles Tankers also operated quite a few of the T2 *Mission*-class tankers.

Luckenbach Steamship Co., Inc.
120 Wall St., New York, and 100 Bush St., San Francisco, California

Ludwig (Lewis) Luckenbach founded a Hudson River towing company in 1850 that gradually branched out into shipping. Ludwig died in 1906 and the company was taken over by his son, Edgar F. Luckenbach. Edgar died on April 26, 1943.

Lykes Brothers Steamship Co., Inc.
925 Whitney Central Building, New Orleans, Louisiana

The Lykes family was well known in the cattle business in Texas and Cuba. They furnished beef to Confederate forces during the Civil War and in 1922 incorporated in Louisiana as steamship agents, brokers, and operators. James McKay Lykes, 41, was president. He lived at 1416 Ave. H in Galveston, Texas, with his wife Lewin, 34, daughters Frederican, 14, Gewniene, 7, sons James McKay, Jr., 13, Charles, 4, his brother-in-law Charles B. Parkhill, 21, and one servant, Andrew J. Bess, 20.

George H. Lykes was manager at the Galveston office while Reuben E. Tipton managed the New Orleans office. In 1943, Joseph T. Lykes was executive vice president. The company grew into an international shipping firm.

Marine Transport Lines, Inc.
11 Broadway, New York

In 1916, Harry H. Raymond was president of the Mallory Steamship Co. at 11 Broadway, New York. Clifford Day Mallory was secretary and Alexander R. Nicol was treasurer.

In 1919, after service as assistant director of operations with the U.S. Shipping Board Emergency Fleet Corp., Clifford founded the C. D. Mallory Corp. He was 37 and lived with his wife Rebecca, 32, daughters Margaret, 7, son Clifford, Jr., 2, and three servants on Old Church Rd. in Greenwich, Connecticut. A daughter Barbara would arrive a year later and Clifford, Jr., would be a clerk in the company office.

Clifford, Sr., died on April 7, 1941, at age 60 in Miami, Florida, as president of Mallory Transport Lines and on May 21, 1941, Marine Transport Lines was incorporated at the 11 Broadway offices. William Norman Westerlund, 48, became president. He was born in New York on April 13, 1893, and worked in the steamship business excepr for eight months during World War I when he served as a ship's writer in the Coast Guard. He lived with his wife Lyn on Hollow Tree Ridge Rd. at the town line in New Canaan, Connecticut. In 1943, Lewis D. Parmalee was executive vice president.

Matson Navigation Co.
Matson Building, 215 Market St., San Francisco, and 730 S. Broadway, Los Angeles

William Matson (1849–1917) was born in Sweden, became an orphan, went to sea at 12, and arrived in New York in 1863. Four years later he arrived at San Francisco, California, on the *Bridgewater* on a voyage around the Horn and decided to stay. Within ten years was a master mariner living at 1814½ Divisadero St. The next year moved to 443 First Ave. and then to 653 Third Ave. in 1880.

In his early days sailing the Bay he had become acquainted with the Spreckels sugar refining operation run by John D. Spreckels, president of the J. D. Spreckels & Bros. Co., the Oceanic Steamship Co., and the Western Sugar Refining Co. He frequently saw the company's tugboats at the Folsom St. Wharf and the Spreckels Line of Hawaiian Packets. Adolph B. and Claus Spreckels ran the California Sugar Refinery, the Hutchinson Sugar Plantation Co., the Western Beet Sugar Co., and the San Francisco & San Joaquin Valley Railway Co. Company offices were at 327 Market St.

He was also a guest on, and probably skippered, Claus Spreckels' yacht *Lurline*. In 1882 he was an officer with the Master Mariner's Beneficial Association at 413 Sutter and had acquired, along with other investors, a seventh-eighth interest in the Spreckels schooner *Emma Claudina* to haul general merchandise to Hilo, Hawaii, and bring back sugar for the Spreckels operation.

He married a girl named Lillie and they had a daughter they named Lurline Berenice. In time he purchased the 150-foot brigantine *Lurline* from Spreckels and a long-running cargo and passenger service was then established between San Francisco, Hawaii, and Australia.

The Matson Navigation Co. began in 1901 at 327 Market St. with Capt. Matson as president, Adolph B. Spreckels, vice president, and George A. Douglass secretary-treasurer. J. D. Spreckels & Bros. Co., general agents, was in the same office.

The Matsons lived at 1022 Guerrero St. and in 1910 he lived at 1918 Jackson with his wife Lillie, 46, daughter Lurline, 19, and three servants. He died in 1917.

In 1926 the Oceanic Steamship Co. was acquired. Oceanic began in 1878 and was known as the Spreckles Line. During the war, William P. Roth was president and Frazer A. Bailey, executive vice president. Roth lived at 1916 Jackson with his wife Lurline. The company continues today in a variety of enterprises.

McCormick Steamship Co.
461 Market St., San Francisco, California

Charles R. McCormick was born in Saginaw, Michigan, on July 6, 1870, and went into business in Menominee. He decided to move out West and arrived in San Francisco in 1904. He met up with Sidney Morse Hauptman, also from Saginaw, Michigan and they went into the wholesale lumber business as Charles R. McCormick & Co. at 303 California St. They both lived at 1606 Van Ness Ave. After the big earthquake and fire two years later they moved to Berkeley and in 1907 the business was at 25 California St. By 1910 they were back in the City where Hauptman had retired to the Hotel Victoria. Charles was 39 and living with his wife Florence, 27, and infant son Charles A. at 2310 Gough St. In 1914 the company was at 1 Drumm St. when Charles formed the Charles R. McCormick Steamship Co. and had the 951-ton wooden steamer *Wapama* built at St. Helens, Oregon, in 1915. He had a pier at the foot of Powell St. In 1939 the company had 11 ships including the 6,027-ton sister ship steamers

Charles R. McCormick and *Sidney B. Hauptman*. McCormick Steamship was an operating division of Pope & Talbot during the war. The *Wapama* has been maintained as a historical exhibit at Sausalito, California.

Merchants & Miners Transportation Co., Inc.
112 S. Gay St., Baltimore, Maryland

An old company founded in 1852 for Atlantic Coast passenger and freight coastwise service as the Merchants and Miners Coastal Shipping Line. In 1940, Arthur D. Stebbins, 71, was president and general manager. He lived with his wife Mary (M. Guinevere), 68, at 209 W. Alleghany. The company signed a General Agency Agreement on April 11, 1942, and continued in service until around 1947.

Mississippi Shipping Co., Inc.
501 Hibernia Bank Building, 812 Gravier St., New Orleans, Louisiana

On March 24, 1919, the Mississippi Shipping Company, Inc., was incorporated in the state of Louisiana, Parish of Orleans, at New Orleans to engage in all aspects the shipping business with a capital stock of $100,000 divided into 1,000 shares with a par value of $100 each.

The board of directors consisted of Matthew J. Sanders, Thomas F. Cunningham, Rudolph S. Hecht, Theodore Brent, William B. Burkenroad, George G. Westfeldt, and steamship agent William P. Ross, all of New Orleans. Sanders was president, Cunningham vice president, and Hecht secretary-treasurer. Sanders owned 200 shares, Cunningham 100, and the remainder was divided in various amounts between 25 investors.

Sanders, a 60-year-old steamship agent, was born in England and lived at 6123 Saratoga with his English wife Flora, 57, and 50-year-old widowed servant Sam Thompson.

Cunningham, 52, was single, operated a shipping warehouse, and lived in a boarding house at 125 Barrone.

Hecht, 33, was a banker who came to America in 1902 from Germany, became a citizen in 1907, and lived with his Louisiana-born wife Lynne W., 33, daughter Lynne W., 4, and three servants at 16 Audubon Place.

Brent was the federal manager of the Mississippi-Warrior Waterways at the custom house and one of President Wilson's appointees to the U.S. Shipping Board.

Norman O. Pedrick was general manager at the 402 Queen & Crescent Building office at 344 Camp St. when the company actually began business operations on May 1. The company was also the New Orleans agent for the New Orleans Brazil Line. The company chartered ships until 1930 when they purchased and operated 12 ships.

In the 1930s Cunningham was president of the Delta Line, as the company was then known, and Pedrick was secretary and general manager. In 1939 the company had 9 ships, 8 of them had names starting with "Del" as *Delalba, Delmar, Delmundo,* and so on.

On April 24, 1962, the Mississippi Shipping Co. was dissolved and the company became Delta Steamship Lines, Inc.

Moore-McCormack Lines, Inc.
5 Broadway, New York, and 5 Pine St., San Francisco

Shipping clerk Albert Voorhis Moore, Jr., 31, of Hackensack, New Jersey, and Manhattan coal dealer Emmet John McCormack, 33, went into business as shipping agents in 1913 to serve South American ports as Moore & McCormack Co., Inc., at 80 Broad St., Room 510. Moore was president, McCormack treasurer, and attorney Henry P. Molloy, was secretary. Moore moved to 517 W. 113th St. and McCormack lived at 222 78th St. in Brooklyn. Albert Moore was still president during the war years. The company went out of business in 1967.

Mystic Steamship Co.
250 Stuart St., Room 1109, Boston, Massachusetts

The company was incorporated in 1924 in Boston at 100 Arlington St. as a subsidiary of the Koppers Coal & Transportation Co. Henry S. Lyons was president, Ralph C. Goodwin, vice president, and George A. G. Wood was secretary-treasurer. The company operated from Lewis Wharf. In 1928 they owned and operated 29 vessels and in 1939 the fleet was down to four ships.

In 1940, Robert M. Folsom was president, Eugene H. Bird and Robert P. Tibalt were vice presidents, Samuel K. Phillips was secretary, and Charles A. Alden was treasurer. On December 31, 1940, all assets and property were transferred to the Trustees of the Board of the Eastern Gas & Fuel Associates and the company was then known as the Mystic Steamship Division.

On December 21, 1941, the AP reported that the 29 officers and sailors of Mystic's "grimy coastwise collier" *Edward Pierce*, at Boston under Capt. Ellenwood Folger, donated $124.61 to the Navy "to buy a bomber—a Xmas present to the U.S. Navy." It was accepted by Cdr. Robert Maborn and was believed to be the first such donation in the nation.

On January 6, 1942, the Mystic Steamship Co. was formally dissolved by shareholders, although Eastern Gas continued to use the name for ships they operated.

North Atlantic & Gulf Steamship Co., Inc.
120 Wall St., New York

On February 13, 1932, attorney George V. Reilly, William M. Stevens, and David H. Jackman, all at 150 Broadway, New York, incorporated North Atlantic & Gulf at 44 Beaver Street. Charles Walter Ulsh was president, Clifton Waller Barrett treasurer and vice president.

Ulsh was born in 1890 in Steelton, Pennsylvania. In 1918 he was sailing with the Munson Line and lived at 315 Greene Ave. in Brooklyn. In 1931 he obtained a patent for footed, pallet-like cargo platforms that could be stacked in a "nested" fashion like modern, plastic patio and lawn chairs. They were picked up by "lifting trucks" and moved around and the nested stacking of the platforms took up much less vertical space in a shed.

Munson encountered financial difficulties during the Depression and Ulsh and Barrett formed ship brokers Ulsh & Barrett at 40 Exchange Place.

Around 1940 the company purchased the 2,677-ton ex–Shipping Board steamer *Lake Furnas*, built in 1920 at Saginaw, Michigan, by the Saginaw Shipbuilding Co. and homeported at New York. In September 1929 it was named *Providence* by the Merchants & Miners Transportation Co. and homeported at Baltimore. On November 14, 1941, the ship was renamed *Norindies* and registered at New York on January 24, 1942. The ship was requisitioned by the War Shipping Administration on April 18, 1944.

In 1940, Reilly was 51 and lived at 25 5th Ave. in Manhattan with his wife Romena, 36. During the war he lived at 501 W. 110th St.

Ulsh lived at 153 Whitehall Blvd. in Garden City, Long Island, New York, with his wife Harriet, 41, son William, 16, daughter Mary, 12, and maid Anna Raymond, 30. Ulsh died in 1984.

In 1940 Barrett was 38 and lived at 103 Stratford Ave., Garden City, Long Island, New York, with his wife Cornelia, 37, sons Waller, 15, William, 7, Jon, 6, Richard and Robert, 1, and servants Rose Zadrozny, 19, and Mary Zadrozny, 22.

Northland Transportation Co.
Skinner Building and Pier 5, Seattle, Washington

In 1923, a group of merchants in Seattle became dissatisfied with the available shipping services to Alaska. Clothing manufacturer Joseph C. Black suggested starting their own steamship company and on September 22, 1923, builder Ofell Hjalmer Johnson and attorney Donald Cornue incorporated Northland Transportation with $1,128,100 in capital stock. Henry George Seaborn was president, William Semar was secretary, and Black was treasurer. Seaborn was vice president of shipbuilders Skinner & Eddy. They used Pier 5 in Seattle and the company opened an office at Ketchikan, Alaska.

They purchased the 1,255-ton motor freighter *Northland*, built in 1929 as the *W. B. Foshay* at the Lake Washington Shipbuilding Co., Houghton, Washington. Wilbur B. Foshay (1881–1957) had built a business empire from Alaska to Central America and in August 1929 opened the skyscraper Foshay Tower in Minneapolis just before the crash. In 1932 he was convicted in a stock pyramid scheme and sent upriver for 15 years so Black and Semar probably got a pretty good deal on the boat. In 1940 Northland owned six vessels, all painted white, to provide passenger and freight service to Alaskan ports.

The company was dissolved by shareholders on January 16, 1942, with Melville H. Keil as trustee and liquidation of the assets was completed by December 16, 1942. Donald Cornue joined the Navy and the company continued with Semar as general manager. They became a general agent and got their first Liberty ship, the *John Burke* the same month. His wife Elizabeth lived in their home at 3500 E. 41st.

Norton Lilly & Co.
26 Beaver St., New York

John Norton, Jr., was born in Eastport, Maine, in 1816 and in 1834 moved to New York City. He was a clerk for grocery wholesalers Oakford & Whitcomb until around 1840 when he became a partner in Russell & Norton, shipping agents and freight brokers for the Florida and West India trade at 31 Old Slip. They operated ten ships to Apalachicola, Florida, and in 1851 became the first firm to send ships to Australia.

In 1854 Norton opened his own office at 90 Wall St. and managed the freight and passenger service for the packet brig *Sea Flower* to Pensacola, Florida. 1857 he lived at 247 Clinton and in 1868 at 51 1st Place in Brooklyn. That year his son Edward N. Norton joined the firm and they were sending packets to South America. In 1878 son Augustus came into the business. Augustus died on October 17, 1889, and John died on October 30, 1890 in Brooklyn.

In 1907, steamship clerk Joseph Thomas Lilly became a partner in the firm with Edward and the company became Norton Lilly. Lilly was 35 and lived with his wife Jennie Brady, 32, at 394 8th St. in Kings, Brooklyn.

The Lillys had a summer estate at Northport, Long Island, and in 1916 Lilly bought a 300-foot Oregon fir tree from Tacoma, Washington, and had it made into a 165-foot flagpole for the estate with a 30 × 50-foot flag. Lilly died unexpectedly on November 8, 1939, at 67 at his summer estate leaving his wife and five sons and one daughter.

The company is still in business today as Norton Lilly International.

Norwegian Shipping & Trade Mission
80 Broad St., New York

According to Lloyds of London, Norway had 1,990 merchant ships in 1939 and when Germany invaded in April 1940 all but around 700 of these ships were seized, being away in foreign ports. These ships were formed into a company by the Royal Norwegian government known as Nortraship, with headquarters in London. Oivind Lorentzen was director of the Trade Mission in New York at 80 Broad St., the Armament Dept. was at 11 State St., and Ingvald Haugen was president of the Norwegian Seamen's Union.

In 1940, the major topic of discussion at the Association of Ship Brokers & Agents in New York was the possible requisitioning of vessels by the government and the second big topic was the legal ramifications of the Norwegian Trade Mission with respect to charter hire fees on Norwegian-owned ships.

The flagship of the Norwegian America Line was the luxurious 18,673-ton passenger liner *Oslofjord*, built at Bremen, Germany, in 1938 to carry 800 passengers on a New York–West Indies–Norway cruise route. On January 3, 1940, the ship was laid up at Bayonne, New Jersey, then chartered by Britain on October 28 to sail secretly to Halifax, Nova Scotia, pick up a contingent of Canadian aviators, and take them to England. The voyage over was uneventful, the pilots were landed, but on the way back to Canada on December 11, 1940, the ship hit a mine off Newcastle, England, and sank.

Norway's 25,000 merchant seamen were completely cut off from their families and country. In December 1940 the Trade Mission established the Social Welfare Committee for Norwegian Seamen in America and in 1942 purchased a 51 acre estate in Bedford, Massachusetts, for $34,000. In April 1943 they bought a 13-story building at 15 Moore St. in Manhattan from the Dime Savings Bank and spent $400,000 for conversion to a hotel. By 1943 Nortraship was the third largest shipping firm in the world and that year carried half of England's oil and gas supply and 40 percent of their food. Norway was officially neutral during the war but about 40 percent of their merchant fleet and 2,000 merchant seamen were lost through 1943.

Oliver J. Olson & Co., Inc.
1 Drumm St., San Francisco, California

Oliver John Olson was born on January 20, 1872, in San Francisco. He married Mary E. Schmetz in 1896 and went into the lumber business with Andrew F. Mahony in San Francisco. In 1910 he was president of the wholesale/retail Olson-Mahony Lumber Co. In 1923, John and Mary lived at 3476 21st St.

In 1928 Oliver went into shipping and in 1930 they lived in a $150,000 home at 540 El Camino del Mar with son Oliver, Jr., 27, George, 21, Edward, 19, daughters Virginia, 25, Mary,

23, Mary's sister Julia A. Whitney, 27, and a Chinese servant. Gee Mon Chew, 21. None of the kids worked.

By April of 1940, Mary had died and Virginia had been to college for two years, married La Forest Phillips, had three kids, La Forest, 5, Virginia, 3, and Whitney, 10 months, and all were living with Oliver. A cook, Charles Lee, 42, and nurse Mary C. Long, 24, rounded out the household. La Forest was a stock broker.

In 1940 Olson's company owned five ships. Like the Luckenbachs, Lykes, and Morans, all the ships were named after family members. Oliver died on June 26, 1940.

Olympic Steamship Co., Inc.
1519 S. Alaskan Way and Pier 6, Seattle, Washington

Incorporated on August 22, 1925, for coastwise service at 1519 Railroad Ave. S., Seattle, by attorney John Ambler, Charles A. Wallace, a clerk at the Fisher Flouring Mills Co., and William W. Shorthill, a clerk at Pacific Steamship Co., with capital stock of $100,000. Joseph L. Carman, Jr., was vice president. Carman was president of Alaska Washington Airways and Carman Manufacturing, maker of bedding and household furniture. The firm bought the 5,335-ton tanker *Dayton*, changed the name to *Olympic*, and homeported it at Los Angeles. The ship was built in 1907 in South Shields, England, as the German tanker *Harport*. The corporation dissolved on October 22, 1931, and reorganized in Nevada.

In 1936 Olympic combined with James Griffiths & Sons into the Consolidated Olympic Co. to serve the Long Beach–Seattle–Tacoma route. One company travelled northbound the other southbound. The company was later the Olympic-Griffiths Line and owned the 7,216-ton freighter *Olympic Pioneer*, which hauled lumber and newsprint. Other ships were chartered.

In 1940, Ernest Clayton Bentzen, 40, was president and general manager. He had been the district manager for the McCormick Steamship Co. in Seattle for several years. He lived with his wife Ethel Jean, 38, and daughters Estelle, 16, and Ethel Jean, 10, at 2019 E. Lynn. Olympic was strictly an operator.

Overlakes Freight Corp.
19 Rector St., New York

William M. Nicholson was born in Canada on July 2, 1864, came to America in 1882, and became a citizen three years later. He was marine engineer in Duluth, Minnesota, and in 1901 married Elizabeth Ruth Quinton. By 1920 he was a ship captain and in March 1923 incorporated the Nicholson Transit Co. at Encorse, Michigan, with a capitalization of $500,000 with plans of operating barges on the New York barge canals.

In 1929 Nicholson built Nicholson's Universal Terminal Co. Dock & Warehouse at 5451 N. Marginal Rd. in Cleveland and the Nicholson Terminal & Dock Co. at Encorse, Michigan. In 1930 Nicholson Transit operated two vessels, the 757-ton motor freighter *Liberty* and the 1,640-ton steamer *Fellowcraft*, both homeported at Detroit. He and Elizabeth lived at 165 Biddle Ave. with Nicholson's nephew, Clifford Pierce, 26, who worked at the steamship company.

In 1931 he opened the Nicholson, Erie, Dover, Ferry Line, Box 902, River Rouge, Michigan, and operated the 1,923-ton passenger vessel *Keystone*, also homeported at Detroit.

Overlakes Freight Corp. was incorporated at Wilmington, Delaware, on April 21, 1932, as a holding company for the Nicholson interests. Overlakes never owned any vessels.

In 1939 William F. Deane was president of the Aqua Terminal & Dock Corp. in Detroit. He lived with his wife Jean at 3703 Baldwin St. in Detroit. In 1941 he was president of Nicholson Terminal & Dock. Walter S. Brown was secretary-treasurer, and Nicholson was vice president and chairman of the board. Scott B. Worden was manager of the fuel department and retail and wholesale sales coal at the terminal at the foot of Great Lakes Ave. in Wyandotte.

In mid–1942 all the assets of Nicholson-Universal were purchased by Overlakes and the car carriers were converted to bulk cargo carriers. Most of the company's ships were purchased by the War Shipping Administration during the war so they were managers and operators only. Nicholson Transit owned and operated eight Great Lakes freighters during the war under marine superintendent Capt. Herbert H. Parsons. William and Ruth had no children. He died in 1954 and left a $3 million estate. Elizabeth Ruth died a year later.

Pacific-Atlantic Steamship Co.
810 Porter Building, Portland, Oregon

Established in 1929 under president Kenneth D. Dawson as a subsidiary of States Steamship Co., 810 Porter Building. In 1941 the company used the States Marine dock at Terminal 1, Pier B. Dawson, 44, was from California and lived with his wife Louise, 39, at 705 Davis #52. He was also an officer with the Port of Portland.

Pacific Tankers, Inc.
433 California St., San Francisco, California

Incorporated on May 19, 1943, with Kenneth D. Dawson as president and J. M. Warfield executive vice president. John A. McCone, president of Calship and vice president of the W. A. Bechtel Corp. in Los Angeles, was chairman of the board and owned 15 percent. Steve Bechtel was a director. Allen Cameron was general superintendent. Edmund Moran, of Moran Towing, was a stockholder. Dawson was also vice president of United States Lines and the Panama Pacific Line. He lived with his wife Louise at 2298 Pacific Ave. in San Francisco. Louise sponsored Calship's first Liberty tanker, the *John Goode*, on Tuesday afternoon, August 10, 1943.

In 1948 the company owned and operated the *McKittrick Hills* and *Montebello Hills* out of Wilmington, Delaware, and in 1949, as Western Tankers, Inc., became embroiled in an FBI investigation of the sale of ships to Aristoteles Socrates Onassis, future husband of Jackie Kennedy.

Parry Navigation Co., Inc.
39 Broadway, New York

In 1917, Alfred Walter Parry, Sr., 57, was a railroad freight agent who lived with his wife Henrietta, 48, and son Alfred, Jr., 23, in Farmingdale, New York. Junior was a ship broker with Smith & Terry, Inc., at 11 Broadway in New York City and he was the New York office manager of the Tampa Inter-Ocean Steamship Co., headquartered in New Orleans. They were also managing agents for the Shipping Board.

In 1920 the family moved to Oyster Bay and in January 1922 Junior married Esther A. Wright, 23, of Boston, who already had a son, John Brandon, 3. The marriage was formally celebrated at the New York Marine Exchange. The couple lived at 712 Fulton St. in Farmingdale.

In 1928 Junior was offered an executive vice president position with Tampa Inter-Ocean when company president and director Philip Shore decided to own and operate eight Shipping Board freighters out of New Orleans. He accepted but before making the move to New Orleans the happy couple decided to take an extended trip to the Far East and environs on the *President Polk*. After moving, they lived at 3732 Napoleon Ave. The office was at 917 Whitney Building, 228 St. Charles Street. In 1930 they moved to 2310 Dublin and in 1935 they were at 1636 Amelia.

In 1942 the Parry's moved back to Cedarhurst, Long Island, New York, and incorporated the Parry Shipping Co., Inc., at 17 Battery Place. The company operated their first Liberty ship in August 1942 as Parry Navigation while Lt. Col. Parry served with the Army Transportation Corps in the South Pacific. On March 16, 1943, Parry Navigation moved to offices on the 12th floor in the Cotton Exchange Building at 39 Broadway. In 1945 the company opened an office in San Francisco at 112 Pine St. with Charles W. Perkes as Pacific Coast manager. In 1947 the Parry Line was established and Colonel Parry was president. They later established steamship service to Galveston, Texas.

Polarus Shipping Co., Inc.
17 Battery Place, New York

Tikhon N. Agapeyeff was born in Russia on July 21, 1891, joined the Russian Imperial Navy and became a ship commander. When he got caught up in the Revolution he escaped to England and decided to continue on to the United States. He booked passage on the steamer *Saint Paul* at Liverpool and arrived at New York on July 1, 1917. His experience was found valuable and he was attached to the Naval Ordnance Depot during World War I. After the war he became a ship broker at 402 Madison Ave. as the Polarus Shipping Co. but on Ausust 1, 1921, the company dissolved and became C. M. Fetterolf & Co. at 17 Battery Place with Agapeyeff as president and Carlos M. Fetterolf vice president.

On January 10, 1923, the Polarus Shipping Co. was incorporated by Agapeyeff, attorney Marcel Levy, and exporter Charles S. Dunaif at 17 Battery Place with a capitalization of $125,000. Hendrik Robert Jolles was president and Dunaif vice president. Jolles was a banker and vice president of the City Company of New York, Inc., and lived at 1112 Park Ave. with his wife Frances.

Apapeyeff became a citizen on July 12, 1923, in New York and in 1931 became president of Polarus. Later that year he was in Halifax, Nova Scotia, with his wife Violet and daughter Barbara at the Nova Scotian Hotel when he died of a heart attack on December 4. The family lived at 630 W. 138th St. in New York. After Apapeyeff died the company was reorganized and Jolles became president. When Jolles died in April 1949 in Amsterdam at age 60 he was chairman of the board.

Pope & Talbot
461 Market St., San Francisco, California

Andrew Jackson Pope and Frederic Talbot left Machias, Maine, and arrived at San Francisco by steamer on December 1, 1849. They joined forces with Lucius D. Sanborn and

James P. Keller and began running barges on San Francisco Bay and importing lumber. Sanborn left the group and in 1851 Pope, Talbot, and Keller went up to Washington and built a sawmill and a lumber yard at Port Gamble at an area known to Indians as Teekalet. The business became the Puget Mill Company.

In 1853, Frederic's older brother Capt. William C. Talbot arrived in San Francisco with his brig *Oriental*. Frederic then decided to leave Washington and start a business in New York and William replaced him at Port Gamble. The business prospered and they operated a large fleet of lumber schooners to San Franciso's building boom. Keller died in 1862 and was replaced by the mill's superintendent, Cyrus Walker. Andrew Pope died in 1881 and his sons George A. and William H. took over. By the early 1900s the company's equipment and vessel's were showing their age and in 1908 all the schooners were sold and the company thereafter chartered the vessels it needed.

By the mid–1920s William Talbot was getting tired and in 1925 he sold all of the assets of Puget Mill to the Charles R. McCormick Lumber Co. at 215 Market St., San Francisco. Certain conditions were imposed in the sale and Puget Mill held all the mortgages. McCormick suffered serious losses during the Great Depression and in 1938 George Pope, Sr., George Pope, Jr., Frederic C. Talbot, and Talbot Walker regained most of the assets of McCormick. The business was incorporated as Pope & Talbot, Inc., at 618 NW Front Ave., Portland, Oregon, and 231 Montgomery St. in San Francisco, with Pope, Sr., as president. McCormick Steamship became an operating division of Pope & Talbot during the war.

Pope & Talbot furnished huge amounts of lumber for the war effort and lost four of its ships, including the *West Ivis* with the entire crew. The company owned 19 vessels and operated over 75 Maritime Commission ships. In 1963, the last year of shipping operations, the company owned two vessels registered at Port Gamble, Washington, and thereafter continued in the wood products business.

Prudential Steamship Corp.
17 State St., New York

Stephen Demetrios Stephanidis was born on April 23, 1891, in Constantinople, Turkey, a subject of Mehmed V, Emperor of the Ottomans. He came to America in 1904 and lived with his brother John, an attorney, at 660 Riverside Dr. in New York. He went to work as a steamship agent in the tourist trade and became a citizen on July 6, 1916.

In 1930 he lived with his wife Lillian, 37, and daughter Elizabeth "Betty," 8, in a rented flat at 169 Columbia Heights in Kings, Brooklyn, New York.

In 1933 he founded Prudential Steamship for coastwise service and in 1936 became embroiled in maritime union conflicts. In 1938 he purchased the 8,704-ton steamer *Eastern Guide* from the Pacific Coast Steamship Co. Daughter Elizabeth sponsored the Liberty ship *Sarah Orne Jewett* at New England ship in January 1944. He died in New York on March 21, 1955, at age 63.

R. A. Nicol & Co., Inc.
17 Battery Place, New York

Robert Alexander Nicol was a native of Liverpool, England, who came to America in 1906 and became a citizen in 1920. He went to work for the Oriental Navigation Co. in New

York and in 1940 he was a 60-year-old steamship agent and president of R. A. Nicol & Co. in New York. He lived with his wife Elizabeth, 51, sons Robert, 22, William, 15, and daughters Katherine, 21, and Margaret, 18, at 140 Clarewill Ave. in Montclair, New Jersey. Robert was a clerk in the office, William was a student, and no one knows what Katherine and Margaret did all day.

Republic Oil Refining Co., Inc.
Houston and Texas City, Texas

On May 13, 1926, the Republic Oil Sales Co. was incorporated at Fort Worth, Texas, by Herbert D. McCracken, vice president of the United Producers Pipeline Co. in Forth Worth; Otto C. Massey, an attorney with United Producers Pipeline, and Ovid D. Robinson, president of the Republic Oil Co. in Pittsburgh, Pennsylvania. The company had $5,000 in capital stock divided into 50 shares at $100. Robinson owned 48 shares and McCracken and Massey owned one each.

McCracken lived with his wife Eleanor at 2317 6th Ave. in Fort Worth. Massey lived with his wife Jessie D. at 1900 6th Ave. in Fort Worth, and Robinson lived at 1032 Highland (Coraopolis) in Pittsburgh.

In 1929 the Republic Oil Refining Co. was organized on the 10th floor in the Benedum-Trees Building in Pittsburgh. Robinson became president, James O. Carney, vice president and William H. Moreland, secretary-treasurer. John M Gardiner was treasurer and Daniel H. Lee assistant secretary at 2015 Clark Buillding in the Houston office. In 1930 they were at 1630 Second National Bank Building and Dana W. Hovey was manager. In 1935 he became vice president.

In October 1943 the company moved from Houston to Texas City where their plant was located. In 1947 William E. Huston was president at Texas City. Huston died on October 3, 1950, at age 64 in Pittsburgh and in 1955 John Gardiner became president. The company was dissolved on April 1, 1957.

Seas Shipping Co., Inc.
39 Cortlandt St., New York

In August 1920, Arthur R. Lewis, Sr., president of the American & Cuban Steamship Line, 39 Cortlandt St., acting as an agent for the U.S. Steel Corp., purchased the almost-new geared turbine freighters *Robin Adair* and *Robin Hood* from David E. Skinner, president of the Skinner & Eddy Corp., and their shipping company, the Robin Line. Skinner & Eddy built several 6,880-ton ships in 1919 at their Seattle yard for themselves and sold two of the last four ships they built for $144.23 a deadweight ton while Robin Line ran the remaining two.

Lewis established Seas Shipping in the Cortlandt St. office to operate the ships coastwise in conjunction with Farrell's Isthmian and American South African company ships, in which Lewis also held an interest. Eddy's Robin Line office was at 576 Sacramento St. in San Francisco and sometime prior to 1930 Lewis acquired Robin Line.

In 1930, Lewis Sr. was 50 and lived with his wife Grace, 25, sons Arthur, Jr., 21, who was in college, William S., 16, in private school, daughters Barbara, 7, Marilyn 6, and two Irish servants in a $100,000 home at 117 Harmon Ave. in North Pelham, New York. Grace was 19 when they got married.

Lewis Sr.'s relationship with James Farrell was apparently cordial but when he died in 1933, Arthur Lewis, Jr., took over the lines and all business ties with Farrell were severed. Junior took control of Seas Shipping and the Robin Line while the Farrells owned American South African and the Argonaut Line. A war between the two firms ensued over trade to South African ports and Junior apparently worked himself to death trying to outfox the Farrells and succumbed to a heart attack in March 1954. Winthrop O. Cook followed as president but in 1957 the board decided to sell all ten remaining Seas Shipping ships to Moore-McCormack.

Shepard Steamship Co., Inc.
40 Central St., Room 912, Boston, Massachusetts

In the 1920s, Horace Wentworth Shepard was president of the Shepard & Morse Lumber Co. in Boston. In 1929 Shepard Steamship was incorporated by Horace Shepard, president, Minot A. Holbrook, secretary, and Thomas H. Shepard, treasurer. The head office was in Boston with another office at 477 Congress St. in Portland, Maine. They ran the freighters *Hopatcong*, *Sage Brush*, *Sea Thrush*, and *Wind Rush*, all homeported at Portland. Horace was still president in 1940 and Morris Shepard was secretary. Horace was 45 and living with his wife Elizabeth, 45, and their son Wentworth, 17, at 115 Upland Rd., Newton, Massachusetts. He died in May 1968.

Simpson Spence & Young
78 Broad St., New York

Shipbrokers Ernest Louis Simpson, a British national, and Lewis H. Spence, an American, opened an office in New York in 1880 at 78 Broad St. as Simpson & Spence. They were joined in 1882 by Capt. William Young, who opened an office at Newcastle-upon-Tyne in England and the firm became Simpson Spence & Young.

Ernest Simpson married Charlotte Woodward Gaines and their son Ernest Aldrich Simpson (1897–1958) was an officer with the company. He married Wallis Warfield Spencer in 1928 and they divorced in 1937. Wallis Simpson married King Edward VIII, who abdicated the throne to marry her. He then became the Duke of Windsor. The firm expanded to a worldwide operation and continues today as shipbrokers headquartered in London.

Smith & Johnson
80 Broadway, New York

Sometime in the late 1920s or early 1930s, ship brokers Howell B. Smith and Algot W. Johnson opened an office at 16 William St. in Manhattan. In 1930, Smith, 30, lived at 219 Piermont Ave., South Nyack, New York, with his wife Eloise, 29, and daughters Jane, 2, and newborn Carol.

In 1940 Johnson, 39, lived with his wife Clara, 41, son Robert, 12, and daughter Lois, 11, at 173 85th St. in Kings, New York. He was a semi-professional golfer.

Smith & Johnson were wartime ship operators and brokers at 80 Broadway, New York. In 1948 the Smith-Johnson Steamship Corp. owned and operated ships from their 60 Beaver St. office.

South Atlantic Steamship Co.
7 W. 10th St., Wilmington, Delaware

In 1905, James Fairlie Cooper Myers was a merchant and director of the Germania Bank when he, Edward W. Smith, and Thomas C. Myers established the South Atlantic Steamship Line at 20 Bay St., Savannah, Georgia. Cooper was president and lived with his wife Lena at 310 Gwinnett. Son Thomas Myers, secretary-treasurer, was a bookkeeper at the Virginia-Carolina Chemical Co. and lived at home. Smith was vice president and general manager.

In 1908 the company was at 18 Bay St. and in 1912 Einar S. Trosdal was vice president and Thomas C. Myers was still secretary-treasurer. Trosdal was the Norwegian consul and lived with his wife Lucy at 113 31st St.

In 1915 Trosdal was president and the office was at 102 Bay and in 1920 moved to 24–36 Bay. From 1922 to 1928 the company apparently was inactive but two organizations, the South Atlantic Maritime Corp. and the South Atlantic Steamship Conference formed, but it appears no principal officers of South Atlantic Steamship were involved. In 1928 Trousdal was again president and James J. McQuillan, the Norwegian vice consul, was secretary-treasurer at 34 Bay St. McQuillan lived with his wife Lucile 421 St. Julian St. In 1930 Raymond D. Sullivan was vice president. He was also associated with the Dixie Stevedore Co. and lived with his wife Martha 328 45th St. In 1931 the company operated ten ships all homeported at Savannah and in 1934 the company's eleven ships were registered at 7 W. 10th St. in Wilmington, Delaware, but homeported at Savannah. Sullivan was president at Savannah. By 1939 the company was down to six ships and in 1942 owned no registered vessels.

Spencer Kellogg & Sons, Inc.
165 Broadway, New York

In 1824, Spencer Kellogg's grandfather, Supplina Kellogg, was a linseed miller making linseed oil near Amsterdam, New York. Spencer was born on June 16, 1851, at West Galway, New York. He married Jane Morris in 1875 and in 1879 moved to Buffalo and built his own linseed mill and then a second one in 1894. They had three sons, Howard, Morris, and Donald, and four daughters, Elizabeth, Gertrude, Ruth, and Doris. Spencer Kellogg & Sons incorporated in 1912 at Buffalo and by 1920 was one of the largest manufacturers of castor and other oils in the world. The company shipped products by truck, rail, and then by steamship. In 1934 they operated the 5,189-ton tank ship *Elizabeth Kellogg* as the Kellogg Steamship Corp. at 17 Battery Place, New York.

Sprague Steamship Co.
10 Post Office Square, Boston, Massachusetts

Charles H. Sprague entered the coal business around 1870 and by World War I was a major overseas supplier as C. H. Sprague & Son. Phineas W. Sprague was president in 1914 at 70 Kilby St., Room 84, in Boston. A marine department was founded in 1920 at 141 Milk St., Room 1109. The company had two wharfs in Boston, one in Providence, Rhode Island, and one at Searsport, Maine. The company continues today as Sprague Operating Resources, LLC, headquartered at Portsmouth, New Hampshire.

Standard Fruit & Steamship Co.
1400 American Bank Building, 140 Carondelet St., New Orleans, Louisiana

Joseph, John, Lucas, and Felix Vaccaro were steamship agents as Vaccaro Bros. & Company in New Orleans. Joseph was president and also president of the Crescent City Ice Manufacturing Co. and the Dixie Ice Company. In 1924 they formed the Standard Fruit & Steamship Co., known as the Vaccaro Line, to transport fruit, general cargo, and passengers between New Orleans, Spanish Honduras, Havana, Panama, and Nicaragua. In the later 1930s, W. Irving Moss was board chairman, Salvador B. D'Antoni was president, Carmelo D'Antoni, Felix, John, and Lucas J. Vaccaro, Charles Leftwich, Fred W. Salmon, and Ralph C. Lally were vice presidents. The banana division was at 204 Poydras and the company's Louisa St. wharf superintendent was Louis Provansano. The company's ships were under the Honduran flag with one lone American-flag ship, the 4,095-ton freighter *Caloria*, built in England in 1906.

States Marine Corp.
90 Broad St., New York

Established in 1930 by Henry D. Mercer. Henry was born in Lodi, New Jersey, on March 26, 1893. He went to work for the Erie Railroad, served in the Navy during World War I, became general agent for the Great Northern Railroad's New York territory and then went into shipping. He had been a vice president of the Dyson Shipping Co. In 1930 he lived with his wife Katherine, 34, and daughter Milicent, 7, at 306 Howard St. in Passaic, New Jersey. In 1941 he lived at 475 S. Parkway in Clifton, New Jersey. Cornelius S. Walsh became secretary of States Marine. The company ran chartered ships to South Africa.

States Steamship Co.
1010 Washington St., Portland, Oregon

The Columbia Pacific Shipping Co. was organized in 1920 under general manager Arthur C. Stubbe at 301 Board of Trade Building in Portland, Oregon, for service to China, Japan, and the Philippines. Stubbe was 35 and lived with his wife Amy M., 34, and daughter Amy F., 7, at 1170 Tillamook St.

In 1928, the company name was changed to States Steamship Co. with John C. Ainsworth as president and Kenneth D. Dawson vice president. Ainsworth was a prominent Portland businessman and president of the U.S. National Bank. The company had at dock on Front St. at the foot of NW 15th St. and an office at 2200 NW Front. In 1941 the dock was at Terminal 1, Pier B, and general offices were at 1010 Washington St. The company also owned the United Fruit Co. States Steamship operated only one Liberty ship, the short-lived *Star of Oregon*.

Stockard Steamship Corp.
17 Battery Place, New York

In 1936 Capt. Thor Eckert and Lester N. Stockard went into business as Eckert & Stockard, Inc., steamship agents and operators. Eckert was vice president of the Arnold Berstein Line and a director on several boards. Stockard had been a pilot in Eddie Rickenbacker's squadron during World War I and in 1939, after three years partnering with Eckert, formed Stockard Steamship. It was known as the Caribbean Line with the steamers *Caribqueen*, *Caribsea*, and *Caribstar*. The *Caribsea* was sunk on March 11, 1942, and the *Caribstar* was sunk on October 4, 1942.

Lester Stockard died in 1959 leaving his wife Mary Alice and two daughters, Susan and Lesly.

Sudden & Christenson
310 Sansome St., San Francisco, California

In 1895, Edwin Axel Christenson was a 21-year-old bookkeeper at the S. H. Harmon Lumber Co. in San Francisco. He lived at 734 Hayes St. One of his close neighbors at 716 Hayes was Capt. Robert Sudden, a master mariner who lived with his wife Catherine and their 19-year-old son Charles. In 1899 Charles moved to 746 Hayes and the same year Edwin and Charles opened a lumber, shipping, and commission business at 22 Market St. as Sudden & Christenson. Edwin was president and Charles secretary. In 1905 they moved to larger offices at 6 California St., Rooms 7 and 8 and in 1910 they moved to 110 Market St. Edwin had a wife named Eleanor and Charles had married Margerite. Charles and Margerite lived at 57 Jordan Ave. with William Rasor, Charles' brother-in-law, who was in the retail hardware business. Charles died in 1913 and in 1914 D. Walter Rasor became vice president of the lumber business at 110 Market.

In 1915, the Sudden & Christenson Steamship Line began at 110 Market with Edwin as president and Capt. Isaac N. Hibberd general manager. Hibberd was also superintendent of the Pacific Coast Steamship Co. Edwin Christenson died in a yachting accident on San Francisco Bay on May 6, 1922. Arthur B. Cahill then became president, Robert C. Sudden vice president, and Frank C. Lawler secretary-treasurer. In 1941, Cahill was president and Charles H. Chandler, Henry Hess, Frank Lawler, Louis C. Stewart were vice presidents. Offices were at 310 Sansome. The company went out of business on January 1, 1952.

Sword Line, Inc.
76 Beaver St., New York

In 1931, Capt. Charilaos "Charles" G. Poulacos and Abbott Abercrombie, 23, an assistant director with a steamship company, purchased the 3,785-ton freighter *Eastern Sword*, built in Uraga, Japan, in 1920, from the U.S. Shipping Board for $54,000. The next year they incorporated the Sword Steamship Line, Inc., at 80 Broad St., New York, for coastwise service between Atlantic and Gulf ports. Poulacos was president.

Charles was a native of Greece who came to the United States in 1915 and in 1930 was 46 and lived with his German-born wife Marie, 31, in an apartment at 159 W. 78th Ave. in New York. Marie came to America in 1923 and was a self-employed manicurist.

In 1930 Abercrombie lived on Crofon Dawn Rd. in New Castle, New York, with his father David J., 64, who was retired, mother Lucy Cate, 64, and a butler and a cook. By 1940 he was out of the shipping business and lived with wife Jean, 27, at 29 Sutton Place in New York City where he was a service man with an electrical distributing company.

By 1934 the company owned four ships. The *Eastern Sword* was sunk on May 4, 1942, by *U-162* off Venezuela.

Tankers Co., Inc.
17 Battery Place, New York

Established in 1942 and apparently operated only one Liberty tanker, the *Lafcadio Hearn*. Admiralty lawyer Roy William Chamberlain was an officer and president in 1946. He lived with his wife Esther at 3 Center Knoll in Bronxville.

In June 1947 the company's payroll manager, Frank Albert, 47, 617 W. 169th St., was accused of embezzling $57,000 to cover horse racing losses incurred in 1946.

T. J. Stevenson & Co., Inc.
80 Broad St., New York

In 1910 Henry Stevenson was a clerk in the shipping business and his son Thomas J. Stevenson started out as a clerk but by 1920 he was a steamship broker and agent. In 1930 he was 36 and lived with his wife Helen, 35, daughter Dorothy, 11, and sons Thomas, Jr., 8, and Kenneth, 4, at 8909 186th St., Queens, New York. He incorporated his own business on December 2, 1935. In 1940 the family lived at 32 Shoreview Rd., Manhasset, Long Island. Dorothy was a stenographer in dad's office when they signed a General Agency Agreement with the War Shipping Administration.

Union Oil Company of California
Union Oil Building, Los Angeles, California

In late 1890, oil men Thomas R. Bard (1841–1915), Wallace L. Hardison (1850–1909), and Lyman Stewart (1840–1923), merged their three companies at Santa Paula, California. Unocal experienced rapid growth through mergers and acquisitions and in 1939 they were operating 26 vessels out of Los Angeles and Seattle.

Union Sulphur Co., Inc.
33 Rector St., New York

In 1890, German native and mining engineer Hermann Frasch (1851–1914) invented a way to extract known sulfur deposits 1,000 feet beneath quicksand near present day Sulphur, Louisiana. Many efforts had failed and his success gained him the title of Sulphur King. He then joined forces with the American Sulphur Co. and Frasch became president of the new the Union Sulphur Company. Sulfur mining ceased in 1924 and they switched to oil production and shipping. By 1928 the company owned five freighters including the 4,421-ton *Herman Frasch*.

United Fruit Co.
1 Federal St., Boston, Massachusetts

Minor Cooper Keith (1848–1929) was the nephew of Central American railroad pioneer Henry Meiggs for whom he worked until Meiggs' death in 1877. Keith then took over the operation, got involved with fruit and banana growing, and founded the Tropical Trading &

Fruit Company. He transported bananas to the United States by ship but in 1899 encountered financial difficulties. He contacted fruit importer Andrew W. Preston (1846–1924) to discuss a merger. Preston was president of the Boston Fruit Co. and M. D. Cressy & Co. at 109 S. Market St. Myron D. Cressy was a teamster. Preston agreed and the firm became the United Fruit Co. at 60 State St., with Preston as president and Keith vice president. Attorney Bradley Palmer was a significant partner. The company used the Long Wharf. In future years, the ships of the United Fruit Steamship Corp. were known as the Great White Fleet and used Pier 3 on the North River in New York.

In 1941, Samuel Zemurray was president, H. Harris Robson, vice president, Arthur E. Nicholson secretary, and Lionel W. Udell treasurer. The passenger office was at 462 Boylston St. and there was a tanker division, the United Fruit Tanker Corp.

United States Lines Co.
1 Broadway, New York

The convoluted story of this fabled line goes back as far as 1871 when the International Navigation Co. was founded in Phildelphia, but a less complicated tale would start during the Great War when several passenger liners were among the 100 or so German ships seized by the U.S. Shipping Board as war reparations. The liners included the 10,668-ton *Friedrich der Grosse*, 18,372-ton *Kronprinzessin Cecille*, 19,360-ton *Kaiser Wilhelm II*, 21,145-ton *Amerika*, 23,788-ton *George Washington*, and the 48,943-ton *Vaterland*. All the ships' tonnages were remeasured under American rules (shown here) and the names were changed: *der Grosse* to *Huron*, *Cecille* to *Mount Vernon*, *Wilhelm II* to *Agamemnon*, *Amerika* to *America*, and *Vaterland* to *U.S.S.B. No. 1* then *Leviathan*.

Brig. Gen. John M. Franklin was president of the International Mercantile Marine Co., 11 Broadway, New York, at that time the agent for the Shipping Board's Emergency Fleet Corporation and on December 17, 1919, the company took custody of the *Leviathan* for reconditioning and operation. William Francis Gibbs was chief of construction. The IMM, known as the American Line, was formed in 1903 by financier John Pierpont Morgan to purchase the British-owned White Star Line.

When World War I began, Francis R. Mayer and his son Charles formed the France & Canada Steamship Corp. at 120 Broadway in New York and operated the largest fleet of schooners in the world. In June 1920 the Mayers formed the United States Mail Steamship Co. at 120 Broadway with the intention of running routes to Germany formerly served by North German Lloyd ships and to compete with Cunard and White Star. Francis was president and he and Charles owned almost all 200,000 shares of the company's no par value stock. The Mayers signed a five-year lease with the Shipping Board to charter the *America, George Washington, Mount Vernon, Agamemnon, Pocohontas, Susquehanna, Princess Matoika, Antigone, Madawaska, Amphion, Freedom, Huron,* and *Aeolus* for $3.30 a ton per month with an option to purchase the vessels at the end of the lease period. In an interview, Mayer said the United States could compete successfully against European shipping interests and that seamen's wages were not the issue, as seamen's wages in Europe at that time, according to him, were often higher than those of American sailors. He stated, in part:

Whether the United States is to become a force in the world's trade depends entirely upon public interest and support. The United States Mail Steamship Company has been organized with the object of placing the American flag to the forefront, and expects to compete successfully with the largest and most influential steamships lines under any flag.

The *America* left New York on June 22, 1921, for Plymouth, Cherbourg, and Bremen, but in early July the ships were abruptly seized on order of J. Barstow Smull of the Emergency Fleet Corp. for "non payment of rent." The Mayers cried foul and on July 29 Justice William F. Burr of the New York Supreme Court ordered the ships restored. But just at that point the Berwind-White Coal Co. filed a $100,000 claim against the company for coaling the ships and the Mayers declared bankruptcy. The Mayers were accused of "chicanery" and on August 28, 1921, the Shipping Board repossessed the company's German ships. Emmet J. McCormack was appointed receiver.

Kermit Roosevelt, president of the Roosevelt Steamship Co., Albert V. Moore, president of Moore & McCormack, and W. Averill Harriman, president of United American Lines then came forward and offered to operate the German ships without compensation as United States Lines.

International Mercantile Marine owned the the Red Star Line, Leyland Lines, and the White Star Line. On April 27, 1926, John H. Thomas, senior vice president of International Mercantile announced the company would sell the White Star Line to Furness, Withy & Co., Ltd., for $36,480,000. It was widely speculated the move was in preparation for the purchase of United States Lines and to use the *America*, *George Washington*, and *Leviathan* "as the basis for a great American merchant marine developed for American commerce." Later that year, J. Pierpont Morgan and Charles Steele resigned from the IMM board and the company stated it wanted to get rid of foreign flag ships, including Red Star and Leyland ships, and build an all–American fleet. IMM completed the deal and ran the ships as United States Lines but increasing debt plagued the line and in March 1929 the Shipping Board sold the line to Chicago and New York investment banker Paul W. Chapman's P. W. Chapman & Co., Inc.

In August 1929 Chapman sought a $13.5 million mail subsidy but Postmaster General Walter J. Brown denied the petition on the grounds that Chapman's financial situation did not warrant a subsidy. Chapman protested that his projected profits were predicated on a mail contract and when he failed to make payments the ships were seized and subsequently sold to a combination involving the Roosevelt Steamship Co., R. Stanley Dollar, and Kenneth D. Dawson.

In 1930 IMM took over again and ran the liners *America*, *George Washington*, *Leviathan*, *President Harding*, *President Roosevelt*, *Republic*, and freighters *American Banker*, *American Farmer*, *American Merchant*, *American Skipper*, and *American Trader* as United States Lines. In 1931 the *Republic* was returned to the Shipping Board.

In 1943, IMM formally became United States Lines with Basil Harris as president. Harris was 52 and lived with his wife Mary, 50, sons Basil, Jr., 24, Richard, 23, and a waitress and chambermaid on Dogwood Lane, in Rye, Westchester County, New York.

United States Navigation Co., Inc.
17 Battery Place, New York

Russian-born German national Edward Carl Wilhelm Oelsner (1888–1973) came to the United States in 1908 and in 1915 was a manager of the Hamburg-American Line in New York. He lived with his wife Eva, 25, and son Edward P., 3, at 1207 Carroll St., in Kings. In 1918 he was the manager of the Hamburg-American office in Chicago and lived at 1711 Jeisner Terrace with Eva and two kids.

Two years later he was a steamship broker and lived at 38 Godfrey Rd. in Montclair, New Jersey, and around that time incorporated U.S. Navigation in New York around at 17 Battery

Place to serve as general agent for Hamburg-American and North German Lloyd in the United States. Oelsner was president, Johannes W. Praesent was secretary, and Robert W. Boissevain was treasurer. The company partnered with Biehl & Co. to service Gulf ports and eventually operated chartered freight vessels to European ports from Pier 44 in Brooklyn including the *Atlantic City, Siam City, Vulcan City, Royal City,* and the British-flagged *Rioi* and *Yarborough*. In 1925, James A. Lyons, 25, joined U.S. Navigation as secretary.

In 1932 the company sued Cunard "from continuing an alleged combination and conspiracy in violation of the Sherman Anti-Trust Act' for engaging in unlawful freight rate manipulation to ports in Great Britain. At that time the company owned the old 397-ton freighter *City of Salisbury*, built in 1885 and homeported at New York.

In 1934 Oelsner and his wife bought Seacroft, the famous estate on Center Island, New York. In his day Oelsner was quite the lawn tennis player while Eva and the kids couldn't seem to stay out of traffic court for speeding and unpaid parking tickets. The family travelled extensively and on July 30, 1949, Warren Oelsner, 20, was bicycling in Hamburg with a friend, Peter Sellers, 19, of Philadelphia. They were warned by the American consul not to go toward Berlin, which they did, and were promptly taken prisoner. Army Brig. Gen. Walter Hess, Jr., affected their release on September 28 while dad waited impatiently at Helmstedt.

In 1973 Oelsner and Eva were vacationing in Torremolinos, Spain, when he died on March 7 of heart failure at age 84. Their home was then on Duck Pond Rd. in Locust Valley, New York.

Waterman Steamship Agency, Ltd.
19 Rector St., New York

In 1909 John B. Waterman was the manager of the Elder, Dempster & Co. steamship office at 56 St. Francis St. in Mobile, Alabama.

In August 1910, Horace Turner, a lumber exporter at 76 St. Francis St., Guy J. Hartwell, manager of the Mobile Auto Co., and Harry T. Hartwell, vice president and secretary-treasurer of the Mobile Towing & Wrecking Co., opened the Mobile-Atlantic Steamship Co. at 76 St. Francis St. in Horace Turner's office to operate ships on foreign voyages from the Turner-Hartwell terminal. John Waterman was hired as manager of the company.

In 1919 he went into business for himself as the Waterman Steamship Corp. in the City Bank Building at 12–14 St. Joseph St. John C. Wacker was the local manager, F. Eugene Johnson was marine superintendent, and Gordon B. Hathaway was port engineer. Waterman was 53 and lived with his wife Annie L., 39, and their 9-year-old son Carroll B. at 1045 Government Blvd., in Mobile.

John died on April 30, 1937, in Mobile at 71. Annie and Carroll lived at 2404 Springhill Ave.

In 1941, Edward A. Robinson was president of the company, Norman G. Nicholson was executive vice president, Waverly B. Garner was vice president and general counsel, H. Crawford Slaton was secretary-treasurer, and Carroll Waterman was vice president and manager of the Puerto Rican division.

Carroll became president and resigned on May 6, 1955, after the firm was sold to McLean Industries for $42 million. On Sunday, September 7, 1957, Carroll was found shot to death "in a rattlesnake-infested patch of woods about eight miles west of Mobile." He was 51 and had been reported missing since Thursday. The death was ruled a suicide due to poor health.

Wellhart Steamship Co.
31 St. James Ave., Boston, Massachusetts

Swan Hartwell was born on April 29, 1876, in Raritan, New Jersey. His father Hugh N. Hartwell was in the coal business and in 1920, Swan was president of H. N. Hartwell & Son, Inc., at 73 Water St. in Boston. In 1924, Hartwell and partners incorporated the Wellhart Steamship Co. at 10 Post Office Square, Room 860. Hartwell was president, Kingsbury Browne, vice president, and Eugene J. Wood, secretary. In 1930 they purchased the 2,846-ton freighter *Hall* from the Heald-Hall Transportation Co., 114 State St., Boston, and renamed it the *Wellhart*. The ship was built in 1893 at Wyandotte, Michigan, as the *Selwyn Eddy*.

In 1930, Hartwell lived with his wife Edna, 43, and four Irish servants at 175 Temple St. in Newton, Massachusetts. He always considered himself a coal salesman.

The company apparently operated only one Liberty ship, the *Merrimac Seam*. The ship made one wartime voyage to Port of Spain, Trinidad, under Capt. Elias Beranger and arrived at New York on August 20, 1945.

Wessel, Duval & Co., Inc.
67 Broad St., New York

Edward Augustus Holyoke Hemenway was born on April 25, 1805, in Salem, Massachusetts, graduated from Harvard, and went to work in the shipping business. He became successful in his private adventures on board Benjamin Bangs & Co. ships in the Latin American trade, invested in mining in Chile, and eventually owned a sugar plantation in Cuba and a sawmill up in the District of Maine. By 1828 he was shipping goods on his own ships as A. Hemenway & Co., primarily to Valparaiso, Chile, and became the first to offer direct sailings to the west coast of South America. In 1840 he married Mary Tileston, daughter of Thomas Tileston, a wealthy New York merchant, and they had four daughters and one son. Around 1860 he became incapacitated due to overwork. In 1865, Hector Beeche joined the firm and rose in prominence and on June 16, 1876, Hemenway, Sr., died in Cuba. Edward Augustus, Jr., the last Hemenway in the firm, had a somewhat limited role in the company and in 1885 the firm became Hemenway, Beeche & Co. In 1888, the name became Brown, Beeche & Co. and around the same time a railroad contractor named Peter "Pedro" Mathias Oehlenschlager Wessel (1851–1921) became a partner in Chile. Wessel was a Dane who moved to Valparaiso in 1866 and became a merchant and eventually a builder of railroads. In September 1877 he married Frederika M. Masten in San Francisco, California.

In the late 1880s, trouble started in Chile between the powerful president, José Balmaceda, and the congress, mainly over administrative appointments and constitutional issues. The army supported the president and the navy supported congress and the anti–Balmaceda revolutionaries. On January 6, 1891, naval officers took six warships out of Valparaiso Harbor with about 800 officers and crew, 200 deserting soldiers, 350 boatmen, and 450 revolutionary leaders and citizens on board and stood offshore. When the situation became desperate the Wessel's decided to leave. They booked passage on the steamer *Keweensaw* for San Diego, California. The ship had just been involved in a notorious incident at Valparaiso where Patrick Shields, an Irish national and fireman on the *Keweenaw*, died while in custody of the Valparaiso police. In December, at the request of District Attorney Charles A. Garter, Pedro was deposed by notary public Clement Bennett in San Francisco regarding the incident.

Wessel left California and arrived at New York on April 21, 1893, on the steamer *Alamo* and then left for Denmark where he became Consul-General to Chile. Hector Beeche's brother, Sallust, 50, a Chilean citizen, was with the company and arrived at New York on March 10, 1895, on the steamer *Finance*. Hector arrived back in New York on October 7, 1895. They opened and office at 68 Broad St. with longtime exporter and ship broker George L. Duval as manager and formed the West Coast Line of Steamers at 47 Cedar St. The company chartered ships to run between New York, Chile, Peru, and England. They used Pier 14 on the East River.

Pedro moved his family to England later that year, returned to Denmark in 1903, retired in 1920, and died on February 8, 1921, while in Cuba.

Hector Beeche, 48, arrived in New York on April 24, 1897, on the steamer *Normannia* from Cherbourg and changed the name of the company to Beeche & Co.

Duval was born on July 14, 1855, in Brooklyn. In 1872 he was an exporter and ship broker with an office at 47 Exchange Place and lived at 44 West 44th St.

In 1902, the company was Beecher, Duval & Co. and in 1906 Sallust Beeche retired and the firm became Wessel, Duval & Co., 25 Broadway, Room 1012. The West Coast Line of Steamers was in Room 1013.

On December 29, 1931, the company became Wessel, Duval & Co., Inc., and in time they were importing more than 50 percent of the nitrate used in the United States. During the war they operated 15 Liberty ships. The company continues today in energy, marketing, and agriculture from their headquarters at Cross Junction, Virginia.

West India Steamship Co.
26 Beaver St., New York

Established around 1910 by Edward R. Bacon, an attorney at 2 Wall St., Room 35, ship broker Daniel Bacon at 302 Produce Exchange Building, and Robert Bacon, whose office was at 7 W. 49th St. All were associated with the Barnes Steamship Company. In 1913, the company offered occasional freight service from New York and Norfolk to Cuba, Mexico, Colon, and the Windward Islands. Castner, Curran & Bullitt were the agents in Norfolk and Daniel Bacon became the agent in Cuba. In 1921 they offered service from Mobile, Alabama, to West Indies ports.

Weyerhaeuser Steamship Co.
24 State St., New York, and Newark, New Jersey

In 1852, Friedrich Weyerhaeuser (1834–1914) arrived in Pennsylvania from Germany and worked as a laborer building the Rock Island & Peoria Railroad. In 1856 he got a job as night watchman in a Rock Island, Illinois, sawmill. Two days later he was made a tallyman and the next year, 1857, he was made manager of the company's new yard in Coal Valley. About that time he married Sarah E. Blödel and when he got an opportunity to buy a raft of logs on good terms on his own account he went ahead. The yard he managed at Coal Valley was doing well but the company itself wasn't. He rented the sawmill from the company, made a good profit on the lumber from his logs, and then purchased the mill in partnership with his brother-in-law, Frederick C. A. Denkmann.

The partners formed two companies, Weyerhaeuser & Denkmann and the Rock Island Lumber & Manufacturing Co. at 122 Fourth Ave., in Rock Island and manufactured lumber, lath, and shingles. Weyerhaeuser was the log buyer and spent much time away purchasing timber, which was floated down the Chippewa, Black, and Mississippi Rivers to the Rock Island mill.

By 1890 Weyerhaeuser was vice president of the White River Lumber Co. at 179 E. 3rd in Saint Paul, Minnesota. John A. Humbird was president and treasurer. In 1891, Weyerhaeuser moved to 435 Summit Ave. in Saint Paul and in 1893 worked for J. C. Hill & Co.

By 1895 he had set up his own wholesale lumber business, Weyerhaeuser & Co. and moved to 266 Summit. His son, Frederick E. was with him in school.

In 1900, Weyerhaeuser and Denkmann owned the paddlewheel steamers *F. Weyerhaeuser* and *F. C. A. Denkmann*, moored at a wharf at the foot of 7th Ave. in Rock Island. Frederick was president of Weyerhaeuser & Denkmann and Denkmann was president of Rock Island Lumber and secretary-treasurer of Weyerhaeuser & Denkmann. Weyerhaeuser's oldest son John was vice president of Rock Island Lumber and lived in Lake Nebagamon, Wisconsin. Denkmann lived with his wife Rhoda Lee at 122 4th Ave. and daughter Susanne. Denkmann's son Edward P. was general superintendent of Weyerhaeuser & Denkmann. Weyerhaeuser was also very active with the Mississippi River Logging Co.

Sometime before the turn of the century, Weyerhaeuser had become interested in the forestlands of the Pacific Northwest and in 1900 he and 15 partners (Denkmann stayed in Moline) purchased 900,000 acres in Washington from the Northern Pacific Railway and essentially went into the real estate business rather than the lumber business. Their office was in Tacoma with George S. Long as general manager.

In September 1902, massive forest fires known as the Yacolt Burn consumed part of their property and in order to control their losses, the company began bringing the salvageable timber to a sawmill they purchased in Everett, Washington. The fire and subsequent salvage efforts led to the creation of modern forestry management practices.

Sarah Weyerhaeuser died in 1911, the same year the company built the Weyerhaeuser Building in Tacoma. During World War I, much wood, including spruce for airplanes, was provided from the company's holdings. After the war, demand for Pacific Northwest lumber increased dramatically in the East so the company purchased the Shipping Board freighters *Pomona* and *Hanley* and the Weyerhaeuser Steamship Co. was incorporated. In 1933 the shipping operation was moved to Newark, New Jersey, and in 1941 they owned eight ships. All were requisitioned for wartime service and the company then operated War Shipping Administration ships. Weyerhaeuser Steamship survives today as Westwood Shipping Lines.

William J. Rountree Co., Inc.
24 State St., New York

John Rountree was born in 1880, William James Rountree was born in New York on May 22, 1882, and in 1901 the two became ship brokers in New York. In 1912 William went to Singapore on business and by 1918 the firm was W. J. Rountree Co., Inc., at 23 Beaver St.

In 1925 John and William lived with Annie Jane Gould, 59, at 6 Cubberly Place in Great Kills, New York. In 1931 their office was at 15 Moore St. in Manhattan and in 1935 William was appointed agent for the Chilean–North American Line.

In 1940 William lived with his wife Lillian A., 48, at 237 Park Ave. in New York City. John was a timekeeper with a steamship company and lived with his wife Alma, 58, at 55 Parade Place in Kings, New York. Alma was a clerk with the War Dept. William Rountree died on November 24, 1949, at age 69 leaving his wife Lillian and a $356,774 estate.

Wilmore Steamship Co.
1 Broadway, New York

Around 1876, coal merchants Charles F., Edward J., and John E. Berwind, along with surveyor Allison R. White, founded Berwind, White & Co. at 216 S. 3rd St. in Philadelphia, and shipped "bituminous steam coal" from the Greenwich Wharves. Charles lived at 2010 Spruce in Philadelphia and Edward was in their New York office at 1 Broadway. In 1886 they incorporated as the Berwind-White Coal Mining Co., Inc. In 1897 the 1,141-ton schooner *Edward J. Berwind* was built at Camden, New Jersey, and homeported at Philadelphia.

In 1899, Edward was president of the Berwind-White Coal Mining Co., 305 Betz Building, in Philadelphia. In 1900, Edward was president of the Berwind-White Coal Mining Co. & Ocean Coal Co. in New York, John was vice president in New York, and Harry A. Berwind was secretary of Berwind-White in Philadelphia. In 1904 the company established a subsidiary coal land and coal purchasing and transportation company, the Wilmore Coal Co., headquartered in the same Betz Building offices. John R. Caldwell was superintendent of operations at the Windber, Pennsylvania, field office.

In 1905, Theophilus S. Shoemaker was president of the Shoemaker Coal Mining Co., 1402 Real Estate Trust Co. Building, Philadelphia, when the company opened the Wilmore No. 1 bituminous coal slope mine about one mile southwest of Bens Creek on the Pennsylvania Railroad near Wilmore Heights, Summerhill Township, Cambria County, Pennsylvania. The general manager was J. L. Shoemaker. Berwind-White purchased their coal production from their offices at nearby Windber.

On June 30, 1928, Berwind-White signed a contract with Bethlehem Steel at Quincy, Massachusetts, for two 4,411-ton colliers, the *Berwindglen* and *Berwindvale*, and in 1930 incorporated the Wilmore Steamship Co. at 1 Broadway, New York, to run the ships coastwise between Hampton Roads, Virginia, and New England ports. These were first steamships built in the United States to burn pulverized fuel and caused quite a stir in marine engineering circles.

In 1941, Edward J. Berwind was president of the Berwind-White Coal Mining Co. and president and director of the Wilmore Coal Co. and the Wilmore Steamship Co. John E. Berwind and Harry A. Berwind were vice presidents. The company operated the ships throughout the war along with War Shipping Administration ships. In 1946 the *Berwindvale* was sold to the American Gulf Steamship Corp., of Wilmington, Delaware, and the name was changed to *James Sheridan*. A brand-new 6,643-ton *Berwindvale* was built for Wilmore at New Orleans. In 1950 the old *Berwindglen* was sold to the Sheridan Towing Co., of Philadelphia, and converted to the freight barge *Mary J. Sheridan*.

The Berwind Corp. continues today in Philadelphia as an investment management company and the Wilmore Coal Co. is still in business in Windber, Pennsylvania.

W. R. Chamberlin & Co.
1 Drumm St., San Francisco, California

In 1915 William Richmond Chamberlin was 34 and president of Byxbee & Clark Co., a wholesale lumber business in San Francisco. By 1920 he was in the lumber and shipping business for himself at 593 Market St. He lived at 5740 Keith Ave. in Oakland with his wife Mabel Cora, 30, daughter Phyllis, 7, and William, Jr., a brand-new arrival. In 1928 he ran the steamers *Barbara C, Phyllis, Stanwood,* and *W. R. Chamberlin, Jr.* William R. Chamberlin was president during the war.

PART V

The Liberty Ship *Jeremiah O'Brien*

The Namesake

Morris O'Brien, was born in Dublin, Ireland, in 1715, became a tailor, and moved to Cork in 1737. He soon set off for America and in 1740 settled in Kittery, District of Maine, where he met and married Mary Cain, the widowed orphan of a sea captain. Three children, Jeremiah, Martha, and Gideon were born in Kittery. Jeremiah was born in 1744.

In 1745 Sir William Pepperell, of Kittery, proposed capturing the French fortress of Louisbourg on Île Royale, present-day Cape Breton Island, to gain control of the St. Lawrence River. Morris joined a British colonial militia under Capt. Peter Staples to participate in the expedition from May 11 to June 28.

Around 1750 the family moved to Scarborough where Morris set up shop at Dunstan Corner, the "landing road," and then began purchasing real estate. John, William, Joanna, Mary, Dennis, and Joseph were born there, where all learned to flee the regular Indian raids.

In 1764 Morris, Jeremiah, and Gideon joined an expedition to the one-year-old English lumber town at Machias where river conditions and dense pine forests made it an ideal location for a water-powered sawmill and a port with wharves. The burgeoning settlement of Boston was an ideal market just down the coast. The O'Briens were suitably impressed and decided to move there the following spring and start a lumber business of their own. They settled on the south side of the river, prospered in their business, and became prominent figures in civic affairs, especially Jeremiah.

During this time, trouble with England began escalating as restrictions on westward settlements had been prohibited in 1763 and in 1765 the Stamp Tax was levied on the colonies. By 1775, the people of Boston, especially, had become so rebellious that Parliament sent troops in under General Thomas Gage. Vice Admiral Thomas Graves, RN, controlled all shipping.

Volunteers from the other colonies and Colonial militia in support of Boston formed the New England Army and surrounded Boston to prevent supplies from reaching British troops by land. To counter this, British cruisers were intercepting merchant vessels bringing supplies to outlying towns like Machias and sending them on to Boston. To augment their fleet, British commanders were chartering local merchant vessels to bring in supplies and serve as dispatch boats and tenders to British warships.

In March 1775 the 5-ton schooner *Margueritta* was chartered at Boston and was ordered by Graves to be manned, provisioned, and armed from his flagship, Capt. John Robinson's 50-gun *Preston*. Four 3-pounders and 14 swivels were put aboard and on the 30th the schooner

286

sailed to Piscataqua with Admiral's Orders for Capt. Andrew Barkley, commander of HMS *Scarborough*. The schooner returned on April 7.

At this time there were about 100 families in Machias. On May 9, a coasting schooner from Boston arrived with news of an incident that had occurred on April 19 at a town called Lexington. A few days later, when a proclamation from the Provincial Congress of Massachusetts was received "authorizing and requiring preparations and efforts incident to a state of hostility," the town knew big trouble was afoot. A Committee of Safety was appointed and on May 27 a petition urgently requesting supplies was sent to the Provincial Congress while the town waited nervously for events to unfold.

In a letter to Capt. Barkley dated June 3, 1775, Adm. Graves stated, in part: "There is an absolute necessity for cutting off all Supplies of Provisions from the Rebels, it is the only way we can distress them at present."

Col. Jeremiah O'Brien.

Meanwhile, Gen. Gage was in need of lumber to build barracks for new troops coming in. Capt. Ichabod Jones, of Boston, owned two sloops, the 90-ton *Polly* and the 80-ton *Unity*, that were employed to bring supplies to Machias and transport their lumber to market. Jones was master of the *Unity* and Nathaniel Horton was master of the *Polly*.

Jones wanted to move his family to Machias but could not do so without permission from the British authorities. He had already sold lumber to the British so he approached General Gage with a plan to bring provisions to Machias and move his family and belongings in exchange for bringing back lumber for British use. Gage approved and told Jones to see Admiral Graves, whose permission and protection he needed for the voyage. Graves agreed and to make sure the deal went through he sent along the *Margueritta* under Master's Mate James Moore, 25, and Midshipman Richard Stillingfleet, 22, as second in command. Nathaniel Godfrey was pressed to serve on the schooner as pilot.

The little fleet arrived at Machias on Friday, June 2, and trouble started right away. Col. Benjamin Foster (1726–1818), an "old Colonial soldier" who had been at Louisbourg with Morris O'Brien, was a resident of the town. He called for a meeting to take place early on the morning of Sunday, June 11, back in the woods to decide on a course of action. All options and dangers were discussed and Foster expressed his desire to capture the British sloop. There were a few holdouts at first but all present eventually assented to the proposition. The townspeople had no real weapons, only "a few charges of powder and ball for twenty fowling pieces, thirteen pitchforks and ten or twelve narrow axes." Neighbors were alerted to the plan and the two Weston girls from Jonesboro, Hannah, 17, and Rebecca, 19, started out towards Machias with about 35 pounds of powder and ball. Jeremiah O'Brien was elected to be captain of the *Unity*.

Thomas Flinn's schooner *Falmouth Packet* arrived from Windsor the same day to load lumber and the next day it was seized by Col. Foster, John Scott Long, and Ephraim Chase to use in capturing the *Margueritta*. Morris O'Brien, now aged 65, was strongly urged to remain ashore and young Joseph, 16, was told to stay with Morris but he hid himself aboard the *Unity*. All six O'Brien boys were then aboard when the time came.

The Rev. James Lyons, chairman of the Machias Committee, submitted a report to the Massachusetts Provincial Congress, dated June 14:

Gentlemen; We, the faithful & distressed inhabitants of Machias, beg leave, once more, in the most respectful manner, to approach your presence, & spread before you a just and full representation of our very critical situation.

On the 2d instant Capt Ichabod Jones arrived in this River with two sloops, accompanied with one of the Kings Tenders: On the 3d instant, a paper was handed about for the people to sign, as a prerequisite to their obtaining any provisions, of which we were in great want. The contents of this paper, required the signers to indulge Capt Jones in carrying Lumber to Boston, & to protect him and his property, at all events: But, unhappily, for him, if not for us, it soon expired after producing effects directly contrary in their nature, to those intended. The next effort, in order to carry those favorite points, was to call a meeting, which was accordingly done. On the 6th the people generally assembled at the place appointed, and seemed so averse to the measures proposed, that Capt Jones privately went down to the Tender & caused her to move up so near the Town that her Guns would reach the Houses, & put springs upon her Cables,—The people, however, not knowing what was done, and considering themselves nearly as prisoners of war, in the hands of the common enemy (which is our only plea for suffering Capt Jones to carry any Lumber to Boston, since your Honors conceived it improper) passed a Vote, that Capt Jones might proceed in his Business as usual without molestation, that they would purchase the provisions he brought into the place and pay him according to Contract.

After obtaining this Vote, Capt. Jones immediately ordered his Vessells to the Wharf & distributed his provisions among those only, who voted in favour of his carrying Lumber to Boston. This gave such offence to the aggrieved party, that they determined to take Capt Jones, if possible, & put a final stop to his supplying the Kings troops with any thing: Accordingly, they secretly invited the people of Mispecka & Pleasant River to join them; accordingly a number of them came & having joined our people, in the woods near the settlement; on the 11th They all agreed to take Capt Jones & Stephen Jones Esqr, in the place of Worship, which they attempted, but Capt Jones made his escape into the woods, and does not yet appear. Stephen Jones Esqr only was taken, & remains, as yet, under guard. The Capt & Lieutenant of the Tender, were also in the Meeting House, & fled to their vessel, hoisted their flag, & sent a Message on shore to this effect: "That he had express orders to protect Capt Jones; that he was determined to do his duty whilst he had life; & that, if the people presumed to stop Capt Jones's vessels, he would burn the Town." Upon this, a party of our men went directly to stripping the sloop that lay at the Wharf, and another party went off to take possession of the other sloop which lay below & brought her up nigh a Wharf, and anchored her in the stream. The tender did not fire, but weighed her anchors as privately as possible, & in the dusk of the evening fell down & came to, within Musket shott of the sloop, which obliged our people to slip their Cable, & run the sloop aground. In the mean time, a considerable number of our people went down in boats and canoes, lined the shore directly opposite to the Tender, and having demanded her to surrender to America, received for answer, "fire and be damn'd": they immediately fired in upon her, which she returned, and a smart engagement ensued. The Tender, at last, slipped her Cable and fell down to a small sloop, commanded by Capt. —— Toby, and lashed herself to her for the remainder of the night. In the morning of the 12th, They took Capt Toby out of his vessel, for a pilot, & made all the sail they could get off, as the wind & tide favoured; but having carried away her main boom, and meeting with a sloop from the Bay of Fundy, they came to, robbed the sloop of her boom & gaff, took almost all her provision, together with Mr Robert Avery of Norwich, in Connecticut, and proceeded on her voyage. Our people, seeing her go off in the morning, determined to follow her. About forty men, armed with guns, swords, axes & pick forks, went in Capt Jones's sloop, under the command of Capt Jeremiah O'Brian: about Twenty, armed in the same manner, & under the command of Capt Benjamin Foster, went in a small Schooner. During the Chase, our people built them breast works of pine boards, and any thing they could find in the Vessels, that would screen them from the enemy's fire. The Tender, upon the first appearance of our people, cut her boats from the stern, & made all the sail she could—but being a very dull sailor, they soon came up with her, and a most obstinate engagement ensued, both sides being determined to conquer or die: but the Tender was obliged to yield, her Captain was wounded in the breast with two balls, of which wounds he died the next morning: poor Mr Avery was killed, and one of the marines, and five wounded. Only one of our men was killed, and six were wounded, one of which in since dead of his wounds.

The Battle was fought at the entrance of our harbour, & lasted for over the space of one hour. We have in our possession, four double fortifyed three pounders, & fourteen swivels, and a number of small arms, which we took with the Tender, besides a very small quantity of ammunition &c. Thus we have given your honors, as particular an account of this affair as possible. We now apply to you for advice, and for a supply of Ammunition & provisions (the latter of which we have petitioned your honours for already) which if we could be fully supply'd with we doubt not but with the blessing of Heaven we should be prepared to defend our selves.—We propose to convey the prisoners to Pownalborough Goal, as soon as possible, there to await your orders.—We are, with deference, your Honors—most Obedient Humble Servants —

By order of the Comm.

Capt. Moore put a pistol to Samuel Tobey's chest and said he would be killed unless he used his guns to defend the cutter. Tobey, of Sandwich, refused then Robert Avery was threatened in like manner but he complied. When Moore and Avery were hit in the first volley the crew panicked and retreated below decks. Captain Moore was taken to the home of Stephen Jones where he died the next day, June 13.

On June 11, Nathaniel Godfrey, the pilot aboard the *Margaretta* recorded his own account of the events:

June 11th

Laying in Mechias River, about ¼ of a Mile below the Falls, to protect two Sloops belonging to Mr. Jones Mercht. one laying at the Falls, the other ½ a Mile below us, Mr. Moore and the other Officer being aShore at the Meeting House, hearing a Bustle looked out of the Window & saw a Number of People Armed making towards the House, they immediately jumped out, & made their escape in a Boat sent from the Schooner, before their pursuers (who were very numerous) came up with them. A Party immediately went to the Sloop which lay'd at the Falls & plundered her, then assembled to the Number of One hundred within hail of the Schooner, & demanded her to strike to the Sons of Liberty; Mr. Moore enquired what they wanted, was answered Mr. Jones, whom they said was onboard the Schooner. At ½ past 8 o'Clock in the Evening Mr. Moore thought proper to weigh Anchor and drop down towards the Sloop which lay'd below him; which they discovering made themselves Masters of her, & ran her ashore. Mr. Moore then anchored within Fifteen Yards, with an Intent to retake her, & get her off; he was hailed on Shore by the Rebels, once more ordering him to strike to the Sons of Liberty, threatening him with Death if he resisted, upon Mr. Moore's replying he was not ready yet, they fired a Volley of small Arms, which was returned from the Schooner with Swivels and Small Arms. The Firing continued about an hour and a half, Mr. Moore then cut the Cable, drop't down Half a Mile lower, & anchored near a Sloop laden with Boards. In the Night they endeavored to Board us with a Number of Boats & Canoes, but were beat off by a brisk fire from the Swivels & obliged to quit their Boats, four of which in the Morning were left upon the Flats full of holes; we had but one Man Wounded. We hauled the Sloop alongside, took in some Planks, & made a Barricadoe fore & Aft to defend ourselves from the Small Arms. The Captain of the Sloop being well acquainted with the River, carried us down at Daybreak, during the Passage we were continually fired at from the Shore, having a smart Breeze, in jibing, carried away our Booms and Gaff: we saw a Sloop at Anchor about a League off, Mr. Moore came to an Anchor, sent his Boat aboard her, & brought her alongside, took her Boom and Gaff & fixed them in the Schooner. A sloop & Schooner appeared, we immediately weighed Anchor & stood out for the Sea, they coming up with us very fast, we began to fire our Stern Swivels, & small Arms as soon as within reach. When within hail, they again desired us to strike to the Sons of Liberty, promising to treat us well, but if we made any resistance they would put us to Death. Mr. Moore seeing there was no possibility of getting clear, luffed the Vessel too and gave them a Broadside with Swivels & Small Arms in the best manner he was able, and likewise threw some Hand Grenadoes into them; they immediately laid us Onboard, the

Sloop on the Starboard Quarter, the Schooner on the Larboard Bow. At that Instant Mr. Moore received two Balls, one in his right Breast, the other in his Belly. The other Officer was slightly wounded in the Side, one Marine killed, two more Wounded & two Seamen. The Rebels took Possession of the Schooner, & carried her up to Mechias, in great triumph, with their Colours flying. They carried Mr. Moore down into his Cabbin, & asked him why he did not strike when they hailed him, he look'd up and told them "he preferred Death before yielding to such a sett of Villains"—The Rebels had two Killed and four wounded, one of which expired soon after. Mr. Moore was carried to Mr. Jones's house, where he expired the day following in the afternoon. The 18th the Rebels marched those Men belonging to the Schooner (who were not Wounded) to the Congress. Mr. Moore telling them before his death, that I was a pressed Man, I obtained my Liberty, & went Passenger in a Brig to Halifax, for which I paid four Dollars.

Nathl Godfrey

After the battle, Jeremiah was given the honor of hauling down the White Ensign and Capt. Moore's sword was given to young Joseph. James Cole, James Coolbroth, and one named McNeal, all of Machias, were lost in the battle.

Besides James Moore, British marine William Bassett was lost and eight prisoners from the *Margueritta* were sent on to Watertown: sailors Thomas Skinner, John Burrows, Peter Larcher, Thomas Crispo, Joseph Temple, William Bishop, and two marines, William Nurse and John Pardoa. On July 14 they were conducted to the Worcester County jail.

James Moore, of Yorkshire, is usually referred to as a midshipman but according to British records he had passed his examinations for lieutenant in 1772 and was on the *Preston* payroll as a master's mate while awaiting his commission. Additionally, Royal Navy protocol at that time precluded a midshipman from commanding a vessel.

The townspeople immediately petitioned the Provincial Congress of Massachusetts to seize the income from the estate of Ichabod Jones "being an enemy to his Country." He apparently had fled the scene and left his affairs and money in charge of Stephen Jones. They also asked for relief, saying in part:

...and use the money to defray the costs of fitting out the privateers.... We would inform your Honours that in taking the first Tender, one of the men that was Killed has Left a poor Helpless widow & Six Small Children intirely Destitute of the Necessarys of Life; and a number of wounded men who have Lost their whole Summer by being wounded and will Stand in great need of some Relief.

The *Falmouth Packet* was returned to Capt. Flinn on June 13 and by the 22nd was ready to sail but was again detained at the mouth of the river by John Long, William Tupper, William O'Brien, Jabez West, Joseph Wheaton, and three others. Flinn was finally permitted to sail on July 5 for Halifax, Nova Scotia.

The engagement off Machias is considered the first naval battle of the American Revolution. The second occurred three days later in Narragansett Bay when Abraham Whipple (1733–1819) captured the *Diana*, the packet tender for HMS *Rose*. Whipple initially claimed the first naval victory of the war for himself but had not yet heard of the action at Machias.

Tradition has it that guns from the *Margueritta* were put aboard the *Unity* and the sloop's name was changed to *Machias Liberty*.

A few weeks after the battle Admiral Graves sent the schooner *Diligent* and tender *Tapnaquish* to Machias and Jeremiah O'Brien was instrumental in capturing these two vessels as well "without firing a shot."

On July 19 Col. Foster and Jeremiah O'Brien petitioned the Massachusetts General Court for commissions in order to avoid being declared pirates in the event of capture, although it would hardly have mattered to Admiral Graves as the Rebels were considered pirates in any event and England's record of observing the laws of nations was never exemplary in those days. Jeremiah was then made captain of the *Machias Liberty* and the *Diligent*.

Admiral Graves soon began receiving reports of privateers and one stated, in part:

> These pirate Vessels and several others are now cruising about Mechias in the Bay of Fundy, and to the Southward as far as Sheepscut River, with intent to take and destroy all Vessels and People employed in bringing Supplies to the Kings Army and Fleet at Boston.

On July 18 Lt. John Graves, RN, commander of the schooner HMS *St. Lawrence* received an order from Admiral Graves:

> You are hereby required and directed to take Lieut [George] Dawson in his Majesty's Schooner *Hope* under your Command and proceed together in search of these Pyrates or any others you can get Intelligence of, whom you are to do your utmost to take, sink, burn or destroy by all means in your power, wherever you find them, and all persons who shall be actually aiding and assisting them.

In 1780 Jeremiah O'Brien commanded the 24-gun privateer *Hannibal*, which was captured and taken to New York. Jeremiah and his crew were put aboard the notorious prison ship *Jersey* and after about six months he was taken to England and put in Mill Prison at Plymouth. Eighteen months later he escaped, made his way to France, and then arrived home in 1782. He became an officer of militia, receiving the title of Colonel, and in 1811 was appointed by Albert Gallatin as collector of customs. In 1814 Machias was occupied by the British without resistance.

Morris O'Brien died on June 6, 1799, at age 84 and Mary died on August 21, 1805, at age 88. Jeremiah married Elizabeth Fitzpatrick and they apparently had no children but raised his niece Lydia, the orphaned daughter of his younger brother William. Elizabeth died on June 12, 1810. Jeremiah died on September 5, 1818, after a short illness at age 74.

The Namesake Ship

The keel for the *Jeremiah O'Brien* was set down on Way No. 1 in the West Yard on May 6, 1943, and the hull was launched on Saturday, June 19. The average temperature for Portland that June was 64.7, higher than all the other war years, and the temperature on the 19th was 78°, a lovely day for a launching.

The ship was at the fitting out dock for a week and got the Official Number 243622 and call sign KXCH when the paperwork came back. On June 30 the Armed Guard reported aboard. A 3"/50 Mark XXI double purpose gun was installed forward and a 3"/50 Mark XXII was installed aft in place of the usual 5"/38 gun. The ship's eight 20-mm antiaircraft guns were allocated 40,740 rounds of ammunition and the 3" guns got 450 rounds between them. Two .38 cal. revolvers were brought aboard with 120 cartridges. Winter gear, clothing, goggles, overalls, coats, etc., welfare and recreational gear, and cleaning supplies, were stored aboard for 27 sailors and 1 officer. Ensign Charles Lee Foote, D-V(S) USNR, the Armed Guard commander, got a sheepskin officer's coat along with all the gun manuals, signaling equipment, and routine and confidential publications needed. Seven gallons of dark gray paint, formula 5D, was issued to keep the guns protected.

At 2 p.m. on the afternoon of the 30th the War Shipping Administration officially turned the ship over to Grace Line as General Agent for operation. Grace Line had an office at 10 Hanover Square, New York, and 2 Pine St., San Francisco, California, and operated 23 passenger, cargo, and auxiliary vessels of their own. Three of the liners sailed out of San Francisco.

The Sponsor

The lady who sponsored the ship at launching was Ida Lee Starling, the wife of Colonel Edmund William "Big Bill" Starling, chief of the Secret Service's White House detail. The Starlings lived in Washington at the time, much closer to other shipyards, and President Roosevelt wasn't in Maine at the time so how Ida Lee came to sponsor a ship at South Portland is unknown. Neither she nor her husband had any known familial connections to Jeremiah O'Brien. In September 1943 Starling announced he would retire around the first of November so it's possible he was simply taking some summer vacation with his new bride and they went up to Maine.

Edmund William "Big Bill" Starling was born on October 5, 1875, at Hopkinsville, Kentucky, to Colonel Edmund Alexander Starling and Annie Leslie McCarroll Starling. His father had a brick making business behind the family home at 730 N. Main in Hopkinsville and was also a deputy sheriff. In 1879 he decided to run for the office of sheriff but was shot and killed while making a campaign speech. Young Edmund was four. After high school Edmund became a deputy sheriff himself, serving papers in civil matters throughout Christian County on horseback.

In 1898 he went to Lexington with a friend to enlist in Teddy Roosevelt's Rough Riders but on returning to Hopkinsville he was persuaded to join a newly-formed local unit of the National Guard "for the sake of civic pride." He became a first sergeant of the Provost Guard in Columbus, Georgia, and while there a member of his unit was shot. The victim told Starling who did it before he died and Edmund found the perpetrator but then became embroiled in the subsequent trial and during this time his outfit was sent to Cuba so he never served overseas.

In 1901 he became a special agent with the Louisville & Nashville Railroad in East St. Louis then went to Birmingham, Alabama, where he assisted a Secret Service friend with President Roosevelt's visit in 1905. In 1907 he became a stock claim agent with the railroad and in 1910 he accepted a job as Chief Special Agent with the Southern Express Co. chasing train robbers all through Southern swamps and over hills. In 1913 he was offered a position with the Secret Service and on November 14, 1914, he signed up. He was assigned to the White House in December where President Coolidge referred to him as "Colonel Starling," a traditional nickname he had since childhood, like his father before him, and that stuck with him.

Ida Lee Bourne was born on a farm in Lancaster, Kentucky, in 1892. She grew up to be a very attractive brunette and was described as a "central Kentucky beauty." Sometime around 1917 she married James Fred Neighbors, 34, a train master for the Louisville & Nashville Railroad. They lived at 2023 Cherokee Road in Louisville and the next year were lodgers in a large boarding house on Cumberland Ave. in Middlesboro, Kentucky. They separated shortly after as Ida was back on the farm in 1920. Fred remarried in 1924, lived at 2000 Spring Dr. in Louisville, and died in 1929 from a heart attack. He was the chief dispatcher for the L & N at the time.

On December 6, 1922, Ida Lee Neighbors married Harvey White, the city auditor of Louisville, Kentucky. They were married in Washington, D.C., by the Rev. James Shera Montgomery, the chaplain of the House of Representatives, while Harvey was in town on business with the American Legion. They had planned to marry in February 1923 but couldn't wait. They lived at 1439 Willow Place but by 1925 they were living in the Brown Hotel. In 1930 they were living with Ida's sister Allene and her husband, M. Ewing Stults, and their 9-year-old twin daughters Jane and June at 1265 Willow Ave. in Louisville. Stults was the State fire insurance agent and Harvey was selling life insurance. In 1931 Harvey was president of the

American Broadcasting Co. of Kentucky at the same address. Ida Lee apparently didn't have much to do and left shortly after for brighter lights. In 1933 she went back to Washington, D.C., to visit with Edwin P. Morrow, the former governor of Kentucky, who was then serving on the National Railway Mediation Board. She lived at 1150 Connecticut Ave., NW, Apt. 84, as Mrs. Ida Lee White and got a job working as a hostess with a local broadcasting company. Big Bill lived at the Mayflower Hotel at 1127 Connecticut Ave. NW.

Ida Lee was known by her friends as "Lindy Lou" when Big Bill met her. He had never thought much about marriage before, until he met her, and was taken aback when she agreed to his proposal. Their engagement was announced in the society columns on November 2, 1935, and they were married on February 2, 1936, by the Rev. James H. Taylor at the Central Presbyterian Church with President Wilson in attendance. The couple lived at the Mayflower.

In November 1943 Big Bill retired after 25 years in the White House and 10 years as chief of the detail, and they moved to Miami Beach, Florida, but the following July he contracted pneumonia and died on August 4. He was buried at Arlington National Cemetery as was Ida Lee next to him upon her death on October 13, 1946.

Crew Notes for Voyages

The descriptive notes in the crew lists for each voyage that follow include the person's name, age, position, number of years at sea, race or ethnicity, height and weight, next of kin, and any additional descriptive notes and information available from records. This information varies with the amount each purser aboard the ship included on forms or the Immigration Inspector at the port of entry made note of. When available, the person's last ship before joining the *O'Brien* is included along with the ship they signed on after paying off.

Voyage No. 1

Enough of a crew was signed on at South Portland to sail the ship to Boston. They departed South Portland on July 2, 1943, and arrived at Boston the next day where the remainder of the crew, mostly locals, signed on over various dates while a cargo of steel and grain was loaded aboard.

Departed Boston July 21 for Halifax, Nova Scotia, in the 23-ship Convoy BX 64 and arrived July 23.

Departed Halifax on July 25 in the 32-ship Convoy HHX 249 in fog and "somewhat heavy weather" to join a convoy from New York to Liverpool. During this passage the Armed Guard deployed the short-lived Mark 29 anti-torpedo hydrophone gear, which took a difficult 4½ hours. The cumbersome gear had a listening panel, at which someone had to stand watch, a hydrophone to listen, paravanes, and long streamers armed with explosives. When a suspicious sound was detected by the operator the explosive charges were armed and would theoretically explode any torpedo heading for the ship. Ensign Foote reported that the gear left a bright, phosphorescent wake when streaming alongside the ship at night, the device was plagued with breakdowns, slowed the ship's speed by 1.5 knots, and caused them to straggle eight miles behind the convoy.

With all its inconvenience, the device was believed to have destroyed two torpedoes fired at the *Samuel H. Walker* in October 1943. The concussions from the explosions damaged the propeller shaft but the ship was able to make Miami for repairs.

At 10 a.m. the next day they joined the main convoy, which then totaled 73 ships. On August 4, 18 ships left the convoy and were rerouted. The *O'Brien* arrived at Aultbea, Loch Ewe, Scotland, at 12:30 p.m. the next day August 5. Loch Ewe was a staging and routing area for ships and convoys.

Departed Loch Ewe the evening of August 5 with 16 other ships for Methil Docks, Firth of Forth, Scotland, and arrived August 7. Methil was a London & North Eastern Railway port set up for handling esparto grass, lumber, and coal. Esparto, or needle grass, was used extensively in papermaking in Great Britain.

Departed Methil August 7 in a 37-ship convoy for London and arrived August 9 at Victoria Docks late at night.

Departed London August 16 for Methil in a 30-ship, 7.5-knot convoy. At 8 a.m. the next morning loud explosions rocked the ship when minesweepers blew up mines. The convoy arrived on the 18th.

Departed Methil at 8 a.m. on August 19 for Aultbea, Loch Ewe, in a 24-ship convoy. At 8:50 that night the convoy commodore advised all ships that enemy aircraft were in the vicinity and general quarters was sounded. Battle stations were manned for one hour and they arrived uneventfully the next day.

Departed Aultbea in ballast on August 21 in a 19-ship, 9.5 knot convoy to join the Mersey and Clyde Sections of Convoy ON 198 for New York. The next evening at 6:30 the engine room watch reported that the tubes in both boilers were leaking badly. The Convoy Commodore was notified and he instructed the ship to return to Gourock, The Clyde, where they arrived at 9 a.m. the next morning escorted by British destroyer HMS *Hesperus* (H.57).

On August 27, Capt. Southerland and Ens. Foote attended a convoy conference and the next day departed Gourock for New York in Convoy ON 199. Chief Engineer Richardson Montgomery soon reported that the port boiler tubes were leaking, but only slightly, and felt they could keep up with the convoy. By August 31 the ship was in heavy seas and the watch on the forward gun was ordered to the bridge. By 2 p.m. they were in a "moderate gale" and by 7 the ship was having difficulty making headway. On the afternoon of September 1 Chief Montgomery reported that the boilers were using twice the normal amount of water due to leaking and advised that domestic water be rationed.

Just after midnight on the 4th lookouts reported two white flares and by 2 a.m. they were steaming through a heavy oil slick. The day was very foggy and they sounded their convoy position with the steam whistle. The next day hurricane warnings were received and on the 6th the ship was rolling badly in heavy swells. On the 8th Montgomery reported that boiler feed water was very low and he was using permanent ballast water. They arrived at Pier 57 on September 10, none too soon.

During the voyage there was "some slight trouble" with the crew over gas masks. Only 56 masks were on board, not enough for everyone. Ensign Foote noted that Capt. Southerland and 1st Mate Christensen showed great interest in the Mark 29 gear and he also made a recommendation concerning Navy radiomen: "Radiomen attached to ships equipped with Mark–29 gear find little opportunity to do work with radio code, etc. when standing watch at Mk-29 listening panel."

THE CREW

Master

Southerland, Oscar, 51, 5–7/175, Finnish, scar on left index finger. Capt. Southerland was a lieutenant commander in the U.S. naval reserve, had 30 years at sea, and had arrived at

New York on May 12 from Rio de Janeiro after two voyages commanding the 7,572-ton Grace Line motorship *Courageous*. Capt. Southerland was a college graduate who lived in a rented house at 3024 Arunah Ave. in Baltimore with his wife Margarita, 42, and daughters Gloria, 18, and Elaine, 12. He came aboard the *O'Brien* on July 1, 1943, at South Portland, Maine, and stayed on for Voyage No. 2.

Deck Department

Christensen, Charles A., 28, chief mate, 11 years, 5–10/165, tattoo right forearm, Ensign (D-M) USNR. On October 13, 1942, he signed on the brand new Grace Line freighter *Santa Margarita* as second mate and arrived at New York on December 12 from Casablanca. The *O'Brien*'s future skipper, Alfonse de Smedt, was chief mate on the *Margarita*. Christensen signed on the *O'Brien* on July 1, 1943, at South Portland, Maine, and signed on for Voyage No. 2.

Pellegrino, Frank, 27, second mate, 10 years, 6–0/185, Ensign (D-M) USNR. Frank was the junior third mate on the Grace Line passenger vessel *Seminole* when they arrived at New York on May 2, 1943, from Bahia, Trinidad. He signed on the *O'Brien* on July 1, 1943, at South Portland, Maine, and signed on for Voyage No. 2.

Morgan, Oliver Maynard, 35, third mate, 14 years, 6–0/185. In December 1941 Morgan was an able seaman on the new Grace Line freighter *Santa Elisa* and on September 5, 1942, he arrived at New York from Gourock, Scotland, as a passenger on the USAT *Siboney*. He signed on the *O'Brien* on July 1, 1943, at South Portland, Maine, and signed on for Voyage No. 2.

Park, Robert C., 21, radio operator, 1½ years, 5–10/155. Signed on the 1920 Hog Islander *Ann Skakel* on April 8, 1943, at Boston as radio operator and arrived at New York on June 4 from Reykjavik, Iceland. Signed on the *O'Brien* on July 1, 1943, at South Portland, Maine. Paid off and signed on the American Export Lines Liberty ship *Grant Wood* as chief radio operator and arrived at New York on November 1, 1944, from Swansea, Wales.

Ender, Thomas J., 21, junior purser, 8 months, 5–11/170, hammertoe, 5th left. Signed on the Sudden & Christenson Liberty ship *John Jay* on February 18, 1943, at New York as clerk and arrived back there on April 28 from Oran, Algeria. he signed on the *O'Brien* on July 1, 1943, at South Portland, Maine, and signed on for Voyage No. 2.

Gird, John C., 32, bosun, 17 years, 5–11/170, 1 inch scar on cheek. Signed on the *O'Brien* on July 1, 1943, at South Portland, Maine. In April 1942 Gird signed on the 12,591-ton, 1921 Standard Oil tanker *John D. Archbold* at Bayonne, New Jersey. Paid off at end of voyage.

Samaras, Theodore, 53, carpenter, 25 years, Greek, 5–4/145, artificial right eye, wife Mary, 40–07 67th St., Woodside, Long Island, New York. Samaras was the carpenter on the MS *Courageous* under the *O'Brien*'s future skipper, Oscar Southerland, when they arrived at New York on May 12, 1943, from Rio de Janeiro. He signed on the *O'Brien* on July 1, 1943, at South Portland, Maine, and signed on for Voyage No. 2.

Di Lorenzo, Mario Carmen, 19, able seaman, 3 years, 5–6½/180, scar on base of right thumb. He was an ordinary seaman on the Grace Line passenger vessel *Seminole* when they arrived at New York on May 2, 1943, from Bahia, Trinidad. Frank Pellegrino was third mate. Signed on the *O'Brien* on July 1, 1943, at South Portland, Maine. Paid off at end of voyage.

Dias, Manuel Luis, Jr., 31, able seaman, 2 years, 5–10/160, scar on right wrist. Signed on the *O'Brien* on July 1, 1943, at South Portland, Maine. Signed on for Voyage No. 2.

Sullivan, Thomas F., 37, able seaman, 12 years, 5–6/155, 3 inch scars both sides of left wrist. He was an able seaman on the 1915 Pocahontas Steamship coal-fired freighter *Oakley L. Alexander* when they arrived at New York on May 27, 1943, from Port of Spain, Trinidad.

Signed on the *O'Brien* on July 1, 1943, at South Portland, Maine. Paid off and signed on the U.S. Lines 16,532-ton passenger liner *John Ericsson* on January 1, 1944, at Boston as a fire watchman and arrived at New York from Liverpool on March 3, 1944.

Rudnitsky, Sigmund, 22, able seaman, 3 years, 5–4/160. Signed on the *Isaac Sharpless* as a messman on March 19, 1943, at Boston and arrived at New York on May 31 from Hull, England. Signed on the *O'Brien* on July 1, 1943, at South Portland, Maine. Paid off and on October 6 signed on the *Charles A. Dana* at Boston as an AB.

Patrinzi, Vincenzo J., 29, able seaman, 6 years, 5–5/155, signed on July 15 at Boston. Signed on the brand new Coastwise Transportation Liberty ship *Augustine Heard* on February 5, 1943, and arrived at New York on May 1 from Middlesbrough, England. Signed on the *O'Brien* on July 15, 1943, at Boston. Paid off at end of voyage.

Cadogan, Joseph, 55, able seaman, 25 years, 5–10½/190, Irish. Signed on the *O'Brien* on July 19 at Boston. Signed on for Voyage No. 2.

Demanuel, Sebastian, 36, ordinary seaman, 7 years, 5–8½/150. Signed on the *Isaac Sharpless* as an ordinary seaman on March 19, 1943, at Boston and arrived at New York on May 31 from Hull, England. Signed on the *O'Brien* on July 1, 1943, at South Portland, Maine. Signed on for Voyage No. 2.

Corbett, Donald, 32, ordinary seaman, 2 years, 5–7/170, 2 inch scar left wrist. Corbett lived at 697 Broadway in Everett, Massachusetts, and arrived at New York on May 1, 1942, as a passenger on the USS *Munargo* (AP-20) from Gourock, Scotland. Signed on the *O'Brien* on July 1, 1943, at South Portland, Maine. Signed on for Voyage No. 2.

McCormick, Francis S., 27, ordinary seaman, 2 years, 5–8/145. Signed on the *O'Brien* on July 1, 1943, at South Portland, Maine. Signed on for Voyage No. 2.

Schneider, Coleman, 19, deck cadet, 2 months, 5–8½/150. Signed on July 12 at Boston as a cadet midshipman from the Merchant Marine Academy at Kings Point, New York. Signed on for Voyage No. 2.

Engine Department

Montgomery, Richardson G., 40, chief engineer, 23 years, 5–5/170, Irish, brother Robert, 952 St. Marks Ave., Brooklyn, New York. Signed on the *O'Brien* on July 1, 1943, at South Portland, Maine. Signed on for Voyage No. 2.

Shields, William J., 58, first assistant engineer, 25 years, 5–5/162, burned right hand. Signed on the *O'Brien* on July 6 at Boston. Paid off and signed on the *John Catron* at New York.

Morrison, Donald, 52, second assistant engineer, 20 years, 5–6/160, Scotch. Signed on the new Grace Line freighter *Santa Maria* on October 13, 1942, as second engineer and arrived at New York from Casablanca, Morocco, on December 24. Signed on the *O'Brien* on July 1, 1943, at South Portland, Maine. Signed on for Voyage No. 2.

Halpin, Leo G., 26, third assistant engineer, 6 years, 6–0/192. Signed on the *O'Brien* in July 6 at Boston. Paid off at end of voyage.

Gill, Thomas, 24, junior engineer, 2 months, 5–10/164, 3-inch scar under right knee. Signed on the *O'Brien* on July 1, 1943, at South Portland, Maine. Paid off at end of voyage.

Bryce, Herman C., 33, oiler, 12 years, 6–1/165, scar on left elbow. Signed on the Parry Navigation Liberty ship *Helen Hunt Jackson* on December 22, 1942, at San Francisco as third engineer and arrived at New York on June 3, 1943, from Noumea, New Caledonia. Signed on the *O'Brien* on July 1, 1943, at South Portland, Maine. Paid off at end of voyage.

McCarthy, William, 42, oiler, 20 years, 5–6/165. Signed on the *O'Brien* on July 1, 1943, at South Portland, Maine. Paid off at end of voyage.

Card, Lester E., 28, oiler, 3 years, 5–4/145. Signed on the tanker *Ponca City* as an oiler on October 4, 1942, at New York and arrived back there on the 23rd from Curaçao. Signed on the *O'Brien* on July 1, 1943, at South Portland, Maine. Paid off at end of voyage.

Harrington, Timothy F., 40, fireman/watertender, 19 years, 5–7/125. Signed on the Agwilines Liberty ship *Anne Bradstreet* on January 19, 1943, as a F/WT and arrived at New York from Gibraltar on May 8. Signed on the *O'Brien* on July 1, 1943, at South Portland, Maine. Paid off and signed on the *James Manning* and arrived back at New York on February 14, 1944, from Manchester, England.

Hall, Tom C., 18, fireman/watertender, 6 months, 5–11/158, scars on both knees. Signed on the *O'Brien* on July 1, 1943, at South Portland, Maine. Signed on for Voyage No. 2.

Warren, Frederick C., 21, fireman/watertender, 2 years, 5–10/165, both forearms tattooed. Signed on the *Daniel H. Lownsdale* on March 3, 1943, as a F/WT at Port Said, Egypt, and arrived at New York on June 10, 1943. Signed on the *O'Brien* on July 19 at Boston. Paid off and signed on United Fruit's Liberty ship *Champ Clark* on October 1, 1943, at Boston as an oiler. Arrived back at New York on December 5.

Lannan, Richard, 41, wiper, 8 years, 5–7/160, large scar on left side of neck. Signed on the *O'Brien* on July 1, 1943, at South Portland, Maine. Paid off and signed on the 1920 American South African Line freighter *Charles H. Cramp* on September 24 as a wiper and arrived back at New York on December 27 from Trinidad.

Float, John H, 19, wiper, 1 year, 5–9/145. Signed on the 1918 Eastern Gas & Fuel freighter *Glen White* on January 8, 1943, at Boston as a coal passer and arrived at New York on May 19. Signed on the 1918 freighter *Atlantic Trader* on June 3 at Boston as an ordinary seaman and arrived at New York on June 30 from Botwood, Newfoundland. Signed on the *O'Brien* on July 19 at Boston. Paid off and on October 9 signed on the *Abel Parker Upshur* as a wiper. Arrived back at New York on January 5, 1944, from Liverpool.

D'Andrea, James, 22, engine cadet, 2 months, 5–6½/170. Signed on July 8 at Boston as a cadet midshipman from the Merchant Marine Academy at Kings Point, New York. Signed on for Voyage No. 2.

Steward Department

Bernardo, Albert, 39, chief steward, 15 years, Filipino, 5–4/130, signed on July 8 at Boston. Signed on for Voyage No. 2.

Spark Lam, 44, chief cook, 26 years, Chinese national, 5–4/122. Signed on the Grace Line Liberty ship *Thaddeus Kosciuszko* on December 18, 1942, at Baltimore and arrived at New York on May 26, 1943, from Oran, Algeria. Signed on the *O'Brien* on July 8 at Boston. Paid off and signed on the *John N. Maffitt* at New York on February 2, 1944, as chief cook and arrived at New York on March 15 from Liverpool.

Kai Tee, 44, second cook & baker, 25 years, Chinese national, 5–5/122. Signed on the *O'Brien* on July 8 at Boston. Paid off at end of voyage.

Tong Gee Ow, 43, third cook, 16 years, Chinese national, 5–5/164. Signed on the *O'Brien* on July 8 at Boston. Paid off and signed on the *Robert Lansing* on December 7, 1943, at New York as a third cook and arrived back at New York on February 17, 1944, from Hull, England.

Yok Lee Ah, 24, utility, 5 years, Chinese national, 5–4/125. Signed on the Grace Line Liberty ship *Thaddeus Kosciuszko* on December 18, 1942, at Baltimore and arrived at New York on May 26, 1943, from Oran, Algeria. Signed on the *O'Brien* on July 8 at Boston and paid off at end of voyage.

Carista, Vincenzo, 27, messman, 3 years, Italian, 5–7/149. Signed on the Coastwise Transportation Liberty ship *Timothy Dwight* at Boston on April 1, 1943, as a wiper and arrived at New York on May 31. Signed on the *O'Brien* on July 1, 1943, at South Portland, Maine. Signed on for Voyage No. 2.

　　Carista, Nicholas, 18, messman, 4 months, Italian, 5–8/135. Signed on the *O'Brien* on July 1, 1943, at South Portland, Maine. Paid off at end of voyage.

　　Carista, Rosario N., 21, crew messman, 3 years, Italian, 5–11/155. Signed on the *O'Brien* on July 1, 1943, at South Portland, Maine. Paid off and signed on the Matson freighter *Mokihana* as chief cook on December 20, 1943, at Boston and arrived at New York on February 17, 1944.

　　Botelho, Edmund Madruga, 18, utility, 4 months, 5–11/135, 1½ inch scar on left hand. Signed on the *O'Brien* on July 6 at Boston. Paid off at end of voyage.

　　Brown, Joseph, 25, utility, 3 years, 5–7/148, scar on right cheek. Signed on the *O'Brien* on July 7 at Boston. Paid off at end of voyage.

　　Lambert, Louis I., 29, utility, 2 months, 5–5½/132. Signed on the *O'Brien* on July 13 at Boston. Paid off and signed on the Grace Line passenger liner *Santa Rosa* on October 10 at Boston as the engineer petty officer's messman. Arrived at New York on December 11.

Armed Guard (all USNR unless otherwise noted)

　　Foote, Ens. Charles Lee, D-V(S), commanding officer. Dr. Foote was born in Haskell, Texas, on October 12, 1912, obtained a master's degree in Texas, and took his PhD in zoology at Iowa State in 1940. Florence Mary Martindale earned a PhD in physiology at Iowa State, the two connected, and in 1941 Charles accepted an instructor position at Wagner College on Staten Island in New York. Florence did research and they married in August 1941 at Utica, New York. In September 1942 Charles left Wagner and joined the Navy in October. He commanded the 12-man Armed Guard detachment aboard the Gulf Oil tanker *Gulftide* and when the ship arrived at New York on April 11, 1943, from Halifax, Nova Scotia, he reported to the Armed Guard Center in South Brooklyn and was transferred to the *O'Brien*. He stayed on for Voyage No. 2 then was transferred to the Navy research division at Fort Detrick in Frederick, Maryland, where he was the executive officer. He left the Navy as a lieutenant in March 1946 and returned to Wagner the following September. In 1947 the couple moved to Carbondale, Iowa, where they both taught and did research in zoology at Southern Illinois University. Charles and Florence enjoyed sea cruises after the war. Dr. Foote died on November 11, 1963, after an extended illness and Florence died on February 5, 2008, in Carbondale. Southern Illinois still maintains a $750 Charles L. Foote Achievement Award in Zoology.

　　Landrum, Herbert Emmett, Coxswain; Goodsell, James Francis, GM3c; Williams, Morgan Casto, GM3c; Hudson, Lewis Edwin, RM3c; Morick, Harmon Eugene, RM3c; Garbett, Charles Robert, SM3c; Campbell, Howard Leon, S1c; Caron, Robert Nelson, S1c; Chisholm, William James, S1c; Felci, Armando Frank, S1c; Gould, Philip Frederick, S1c; Hodgson, Thomas W., Jr., S1c; Holsapple, Kenneth Lloyd, S1c; Hunt, John Joseph, S1c; Pinkerton, Henry Douglas, S1c; Serra, Georges Jack, S1c; Shaw, Jerome Edgar, S1c, USN; Smedley, Edward Jardine, Jr., S1c; Smith, Raymond, S1c; Stojek, Ludwig Joseph, S1c; Straughan, Alvis Franklin, S1c, USN; Surdi, Gildo Ralph, S1c; Swisher, Clarence, S1c; Sznukowski, Edward Anthony, S1c; Talyai, Charles, S1c; Thomas, James Carwile, S1c; Tyler, Herbert Leslie, S1c.

Voyage No. 2

　　Loaded a cargo of general merchandise, ammunition, and explosives and departed New York on September 22, 1943, in Convoy HX 258. The Mark 29 gear was again deployed, the ship slowed to 4 knots, fell behind, and at 11 a.m. on September 23 an escort vessel signaled the ship to take in the gear and rejoin the convoy. On the 30th Chief Engineer Montgomery reported leaking boilers but said they would be able to maintain their position and they arrived at Liverpool on October 6 without further incident.

On October 17, the day before departing for New York in Convoy ON 207, Captain Southerland and Captain Lester G. Hallett, of the Marine Transport Co. Liberty ship *Bartholomew Gosnold*, which was also equipped with Mark 29 gear, were ordered by the British Naval Control Service Officer, Mersey District, to proceed ahead of the convoy but to deploy their gear only when ordered. The 52-ship convoy was set up by the British as a "bait convoy" to lure U-boats in for an attack where they would be met with extra forces waiting for them. Both east and westbound North Atlantic convoys had air cover all along their routes except between Greenland and the Azores. In order to fill this hole, Capt. Frederic J. Walker, RN, on his sloop (gunboat) HMS *Starling* (U.66) took his 2nd Support Group from Lough Foyle, Ulster, on October 19 and rendezvoused with escort carrier HMS *Tracker* (D.24) in the North Channel. The next day they joined the convoy and put *Tracker* right in the middle of it. The convoy was then steered toward a known German wolf pack. Another group under Cdr. Peter Gretton, RN, was stationed 100 miles to the north keeping station with the convoy. On the 23rd this group sank *U-274* then the entire naval group left Convoy 207 and joined the eastbound Convoy HX 262 on the 26th. The *O'Brien* had no contacts with the enemy and no ships in the convoy were lost or damaged. Three U-boats were destroyed by escort vessels and the *O'Brien* and the *Gosnold* arrived at the Staten Island Army Base on November 3, 1943.

The Crew

Master

Southerland, Oscar.

Deck Department

Christensen, Charles A., chief mate. Signed on for Voyage No. 3.

Pellegrino, Frank, second mate. Signed on for Voyage No. 3.

Morgan, Oliver M., third mate. Signed on for Voyage No. 3.

Milby, Robert A., 21, radio operator, 1 year, 5–10/165. Signed on the American Export Lines *Exmouth* as radio operator on December 4, 1942, at New York and arrived back there on May 2, 1943. Signed on for Voyage No. 3.

Ender, Thomas J., junior purser. Signed on for Voyage No. 3.

Ford, Charles E., 41, bosun, 15 years, 5–10½/170, appendix scar. Signed on the American Export Lines freighter *Explorer* as bosun on December 5, 1942, at New York and arrived at New York on May 15, 1943, from Calcutta. Paid off at end of voyage.

Samaras, Theodore, carpenter. Signed on for Voyage No. 3.

Valentine, Sherman A., 38, able seaman, 15 years, 6–0/158, tattoo right forearm. Signed on the USAT *Siboney* on April 1, 1943, as an able seaman and arrived back at New York on August 8 from Port of Spain, Trinidad. Signed on for Voyage No. 3.

Weingaertner, Walter C., 30, able seaman, 1 year, 6–2/205, tattoo right foot. Signed on for Voyage No. 3.

Dias, Manuel L., Jr., able seaman. Paid off at end of voyage.

Cadogan, Joseph, able seaman. Signed on for Voyage No. 3.

Cook, Alton K., 39, able seaman, 23 years, 5–7/170, tattoos on all fingers. Signed on for Voyage No. 3.

Bron, Daniel, 28, able seaman, 7 years, Dutch national, 5–7/147. Signed on the Wilhelm-sen Co. Norwegian-flag freighter *Touraine* on January 10, 1943, at New York as an able seaman and arrived back at New York on April 17, 1943, from Curaçao, Netherlands West Indies. Signed on for Voyage No. 3.

Corbett, Donald, ordinary seaman. Signed on for Voyage No. 3.

McCormick, Francis, ordinary seaman. Signed on for Voyage No. 3.

Demanuel, Sebastian, ordinary seaman. Signed on for Voyage No. 3.

Schneider, Coleman, deck cadet. Signed on for Voyage No. 3.

Engine

Montgomery, Richardson, chief engineer. Signed on for Voyage No. 3.

Morrison, Donald, first assistant engineer. Signed on for Voyage No. 3.

Whitney, Walter C., 22, second assistant engineer, 4 years, Irish, 6–3/175, scar on upper chest. Signed on the *Ethan Allen* at Boston on September 15, 1942, as fireman/watertender and arrived at New York on April 2, 1943, from Liverpool. Signed on for Voyage No. 3.

Prado, Ralph T., 26, third assistant engineer, 5 years, West Indian, 5–6/145. Signed on the Moore-McCormack motorship *Mormacdale* as assistant chief electrician on July 8, 1942, and arrived at New York on February 2, 1943. Paid off at end of voyage.

McCabe, Edward J., 22, junior engineer, 3 years, 5–10/150. Signed on the United Fruit steamer *Cape Cod* on January 26, 1943, at Newport News, Virginia, as engine cadet and arrived at New York on July 10, 1943, from Port of Spain, Trinidad. Paid off at end of voyage.

Bonem, Clarence C., 21, oiler, 5 months, 5–9/160, tattoo on right arm. Signed on for Voyage No. 3.

Hall, Tom C., oiler. Signed on for Voyage No. 3.

Almindi, Anton, 47, oiler, 24 years, 5–11/175, tattoos on both forearms. Paid off at end of voyage.

Wasko, Michael George, 20, fireman/watertender, 1 year, 5–10/170, burn on left arm above elbow. Signed on the United Fruit Liberty ship *David S. Terry* as fireman/watertender on May 15, 1943, at New York and arrived back there on July 22 from Cardiff, Wales. Signed on for Voyage No. 3.

Joell, Vernon Rudolph, 20, fireman/watertender, 1 year, African-American, 6–2/175. Signed on the U.S. Lines motor freighter *American Press* on May 18, 1943, at New York as a wiper and arrived at New York on July 9. Signed on for Voyage No. 3.

Takacs, Louis, 20, fireman/watertender, 4 months, 5–6/175. Paid off and signed on the *John P. Holland* at Pier 98, Hog Island, Philadelphia, in December.

Victor, George, 31, wiper, 5 months, 5–9/185, incision scar on right arm. Signed on the Carbella Steamship Corp. freighter *Carbella* on May 8, 1943, as a fireman and arrived at New York on August 29 from Recife, Brazil. Paid off at end of voyage.

Twiggs, Martin J., 31, wiper, 10 months, 5–6½/144. Signed on for Voyage No. 3.

D'Andrea, James, engine cadet. Signed on for Voyage No. 3.

Steward Department

Bernardo, Albert, chief steward. Paid off and signed on the Grace Line freighter *Cape Douglas* on January 27, 1944, at New York as storekeeper and arrived at San Francisco on April 26 from Milne Bay, New Guinea.

Wee Sung Ming, 33, chief cook, 15 years, Chinese national, 5–5/115. Signed on the Panamanian-flag freighter *El Mundo* as chief cook in early 1943 and arrived at New York on July 9 from Swansea, Wales. Signed on for Voyage No. 3.

Geo Wee Hie, 52, second cook & baker, 20 years, Chinese national, 5–1/100. Signed on for Voyage No. 3.

Wong Lock, 57, third cook, 27 years, Chinese national, 5–4/110. Paid off after the voyage.

Carista, Vincenzo, messman. Paid off and signed on the *Clara Barton* on January 8, 1944, at Boston as second cook & baker. Arrived at New York on March 1, 1944, from Swansea, South Wales.

Denmark, Dother E., Jr., 27, messman, 2 years, African-American, 5–8/170. Paid off and signed on the *Robert Luckenbach* on December 12, 1943, at New York as a messman and arrived at New York on March 1, 1944, from London.

Preziosi, Salvatore A., 18, messman, first trip, 5–10/170. Paid off and signed on the *Robert Lansing* on December 7, 1943, at New York as a wiper and arrived back at New York on February 17, 1944, from Hull, England.

Smith, Eugene L., 48, utility, 27 years, 5–5/155. Signed on the Coastwise Transportation Liberty ship *Richard Hovey* on June 25, 1943, at New York as a utilityman and arrived back at New York on September 4. Paid off and signed on the 10,195-ton tanker *Fairfax* at New York on February 27, 1944, as a messman and arrived back at New York on May 12, 1944, from Bristol, England, after two voyages.

Sung Hai Yeo, 37, utility, 7 years, Chinese national, 5–4/110. Signed on for Voyage No. 3.

Geber, John, 18, utility, 2 years, 5–3/131, tattoos on both forearms. Signed on the Gulf Oil tanker *Gulfhawk* at New York on July 2, 1943, as a wiper and arrived at New York on August 12 from Greenock, Scotland. Paid off and signed on the *Silas Wier Mitchell* on December 6 at New York as a fireman/watertender and arrived back at New York on February 17, 1944. Geber was on the *Nathaniel Bacon* as a fireman/watertender off Omaha Beach in June 1944 and arrived at New York on August 20, 1944, from Liverpool.

Armed Guard (all USNR unless otherwise noted)

Foote, Ens. Charles Lee, commanding officer.

Landrum, Herbert Emmett, coxswain; Thomas, James Carwile, coxswain; Williams, Morgan Casto, GM3c; Hudson, Lewis Edwin, RM3c; Morick, Harmon Eugene, RM3c; Garbett, Charles Robert, SM 3c; Campbell, Howard Leon, S1c; Caron, Robert Nelson, S1c; Chisholm, William N., S1c; Felci, Armando Frank, S1c; Gould, Philip James, S1c; Hodgson, Thomas W., S1c; Holsapple, Kenneth Lloyd, S1c; Howell, Robert Martin, S1c; Hunt, John Joseph, S1c; Rose, William James, S1c; Serra, Georges Jack, S1c; Shaw, Jerome Edgar, S1c; Smedley, Edward Jardine, S1c; Smith, Raymond, S1c; Straughan, Alvis Franklin, S1c; Surdi, Gildo Ralph, S1c; Swisher, Clarence N., S1c; Talyai, Charles N., S1c; Tyler, Herbert Leslie, S1; Stojek, Ludwig Joseph, S2c.

THE NAVY PASSENGERS

Five Navy enlisted men came aboard on September 22, 1943, when the ship was anchored off Liberty Island in New York Harbor. They left the ship on October 8 at Liverpool, England, and reported aboard the heavy cruiser *Augusta* (CA-31) on Thursday, November 4, 1943, at Greenock, Scotland. Twenty-two days later they headed right back to the United States.

Sickelka, Walter, RM3c, 620–11–02, V-3, USNR, enlisted at Des Moines, Iowa, on December 2, 1941. Changed rating in 1944 to RT2c. Transferred to USNH Portsmouth, Virginia, for treatment on June 16, 1945, and remained ashore.

Williams, Paul, S2c, 811–70–68, V-6, USNR, enlisted at New York City on June 1, 1943. On February 1, 1944, his rating changed to F2c. Summary Court Martial on February 25,

1944. Transferred to USNH Philadelphia for treatment on December 14, 1944, and remained ashore.

Wise, Joseph Vincent, S2c, 245–74–07, V-6, USNR, enlisted at Philadelphia on June 8, 1943. Changed rating to Y3c. Transferred off on September 27, 1945, for separation at Memphis, Tennessee.

Wolfskill, Frederick Donald, S2c, 820–86–97, V-6, USNR, enlisted at Allentown, Pennsylvania, on June 1, 1943. Advanced to S1c in 1944 and transferred off on September 26, 1945, for separation at Bainbridge, Maryland.

Womer, James E., S2c, 635–86–76, V-6, USNR, enlisted at Altoona, Pennsylvania, on June 7, 1943. Made S1c in 1944. Transferred off on November 12, 1945, for separation at the New York receiving station.

Voyage No. 3

Loaded grain, general cargo, and munitions at New York and departed on November 26, 1943, in the 14-ship Convoy HX 268 for the Mersey. At 11:30 that night they nearly collided with another ship that lost steering, veered out of position, and failed to show the breakdown light signal soon enough. On the 29th, 23 more ships from Halifax joined the convoy along with nine escort vessels and one aircraft carrier. Heavy weather set in and the next day the *O'Brien* became separated from the convoy due to weather and ended up ahead of the convoy. Messages were received by flag hoist on December 6 that enemy subs were in the area.

Arrived at Aultbea, Loch Ewe, Scotland, at 9 a.m. on December 10. Departed Aultbea at 8 p.m. with 10 other ships and arrived at Methil at 9 a.m. on December 12. Departed at 4 p.m. the same day in a 17-ship convoy and arrived in the River Humber at 6:30 p.m. and at Immingham Dock, Lincoln, England, at 10 p.m. on December 13 with trucks, tanks, and mail. Immingham was a London & North Eastern Railway port that handled lumber, iron ore, sulphate of ammonia, paper, and coal.

Departed Immingham at 6 a.m. on December 25 loaded with sand ballast and 150 tons of dunnage. The 17-ship convoy arrived at Methil on December 27. Departed on the 29th for Aultbea, Loch Ewe, and arrived on the 31st.

Departed Loch Ewe the same day with 14 other ships and joined Convoy ON 218 for New York off Oversay Island Light on January 1, 1944, in heavy weather. The 50-ship convoy had seven escorts and one aircraft carrier. On January 2 the engineers filled No. 3 deep tank with water ballast to help the ship maintain headway. On the 4th Capt. Southerland was notified their final destination would be Halifax. On the 9th the ship was "pounding heavily" and at 5:45 p.m. steering was lost. It was determined the telemotor had lost oil and the ship would have to heave to for an hour while it was being fixed. That was done but the next afternoon the steering went out again for half an hour. Very heavy seas returned and early on the 11th it was difficult to maintain steerageway. Three ships showed breakdown lights, the convoy was breaking apart, the *O'Brien* regained her position on the 12th, but lagged behind the next day due to heavy seas. On the 14th the ship was ordered to proceed independently to Saint John, New Brunswick. At 8:30 a.m. the next day they left the main convoy with seven other ships and one escort heading for Halifax and at 3:30 that afternoon broke off for Saint John.

At 2 a.m. on the morning of the 16th the radio operator heard an S.O.S. from a ship advising they were sinking after a collision. The *O'Brien* headed toward the reported position and at 9 that morning two ships and one "patrol boat" were sighted.

Captain Robert L. Fairburn's Seas Shipping Co. Liberty ship *George Westinghouse* had collided with a British ship, the 7,900-ton Ocean Steam Ship Co., Ltd.'s steamer *Adrastus*. The *Westinghouse* left Saint John for Halifax in company with the Canadian steamer *Elk Island Park* and escorted by the Canadian-operated fleet minesweeper HMCS *Bayfield* (J08). The ships had been ordered to run blacked out at high speed between designated ocean "stations" but at the discretion of the escort's commander. The *Bayfield's* running lights were on at 9 p.m. when it changed course to 90°T toward Halifax and at about 2 a.m. the next morning the *Bayfield* altered course to 52°T "to avoid a westbound convoy." The *Bayfield* was about one half mile off the Liberty ship's starboard bow and upon seeing this, the *Westinghouse* changed course to 62°T.

The *Westinghouse* had two lookouts on the bow, one on the monkey bridge, and one on each bridge wing and was proceeding at 10½ knots. An Armed Guard sailor was in the forward gun tub and a merchant sailor was on the foredeck in a makeshift wooden shelter built by the carpenter and fitted with porthole glass in front. The sides were covered with canvas that could be pulled back so the lookout could see out on both sides. At about 2:20 the mate on watch observed a "shape which he could not identify" about two points off the starboard bow at an undetermined distance. The bow lookout saw the same thing at the same time and tried to ring the bridge but the phone was not answered. The mate then turned on the ship's navigation lights and went back out on the bridge wing for a second look. Very shortly after he ran back into the wheelhouse, sounded five blasts on the steam whistle, and rang up full astern. The *Adrastus* then struck the *Westinghouse* at about a 38° angle. The *Bayfield* had the *Adrastus* on her radar but never contacted the *Westinghouse*.

The *Adrastus* had been in a westbound convoy until noon of January 15 when she was ordered to proceed independently to Saint John at her full speed of 14½ knots on a zigzag course during the day and blacked out at night. The captain had no knowledge of any ships in the area, had no bow lookout, and was heading 280°T. There was no bow lookout but one was stationed about 156-feet from the bow. The second officer was on the port wing of the bridge and the third officer was on the starboard wing. Just when the second officer went over to talk to the third officer, the phone rang. The second officer answered. It was the stern gunner reporting a white light on the port quarter and a green light on the port bow. The third officer then looked back from starboard and saw the lights on the *Bayfield*. He then ran back across the bridge and saw a large, looming shadow and then saw the running lights of the *Westinghouse* come on. He immediately ordered the helm put over hard to starboard and the engine full astern but it was too late and the ships collided. Lower No. 1 hold began filling with water. The *O'Brien* stood by at the request of Capt. Fairburn until about 2 p.m. while the *Bayfield* rigged a towline to the *Westinghouse*.

The *O'Brien* arrived at Saint John on January 17, 1944, and Capt. Southerland was relieved there on January 19 by Capt. Alfonse A. de Smedt. It was de Smedt's 34th birthday. On January 28 Armed Guard officer Charles Foote was relieved by Lt. Allen R. Memhard, Jr., USNR.

The 6,173-ton, 1921 Grace Line-chartered Shipping Board motorship *Oldham* had left Halifax, Nova Scotia, in Convoy SC 156 on March 29, 1944, for England but on April 3 became disabled when the propeller shaft broke. The tug *Tenacity* was sent out, towing commenced on April 20, and the ship arrived back at Haliax on the 26th. Capt. Southerland took command on June 8, 1944, departed Botwood, Newfoundland, on July 24, and arrived at New York on August 2. He stayed aboard for the next voyage.

The *O'Brien* departed Saint John on February 1 for Halifax unescorted in company with the two small Canadian-flag Imperial Oil Co. tankers *Royalite* and *Sarnolite* as Convoy FH 100A. They arrived on the 3rd covered in thick ice. On February 6 Armed Guard sailors Edwin and Morgan Williams and Howard Campbell were sent ashore for medical care and Joe E. Morris, S1c, was transferred to the *O'Brien* from the *Robert E. Peary*.

The *O'Brien* loaded grain, general merchandise, and munitions and departed Halifax on February 7 joining the 65-ship Convoy HX 278 for Liverpool escorted by six corvettes, 12 destroyers and three aircraft carriers. The *O'Brien* was routed to Oban, Scotland, on February 19 with eight other ships and arrived at Leith on February 23. Leith connects to Edinburgh as one town and handled grain, cattle food, paper, lumber, cement, agricultural products, steel, coal, and steel. Departed for Methil and sailed from Methil on March 6 and arrived at Loch Ewe the next day.

Departed Liverpool on March 9 and joined the 60-ship Convoy ON 227 escorted by eight corvettes, four destroyers, and two aircraft carriers, had the usual submarine warnings, and arrived at the Staten Island Army Base on March 22, 1944.

THE CREW

Master

Alfonse A. de Smedt, 34, 12 years, 6–0/170. Capt. de Smedt was born in Belgium on January 19, 1910, and came to the United States in 1915 with his father Albert, 27, mother Mary, 27, and sisters Gene, 7, and Marie, 1. Albert was a clerk at a shipping company in New York and the family lived at 2149 Southern Blvd. in the Bronx. In 1928 Alphonse was an apprentice steward on the Atlantic Transport Co.'s steamer *Manchuria*. In 1930 the family was at 81 Chestnut St., Rutherford, New Jersey, and Albert was with the International Mercantile Marine. Sons Theodore, 12, and William, 10, had joined the family. By 1939 Alphonse was 3rd mate on the Grace Line ship *Santa Lucia* and in 1941 2nd mate on the *Santa Ana*.

Deck Department

Christensen, Charles A., chief mate. Paid off at end of voyage.

Morgan, Oliver M., second mate. Signed on for Voyage No. 4.

Smith, Russell J., 32, third mate, 15 years, Canadian national, 5–7/135, signed on at Halifax on February 5, 1944. Paid off and signed on the *Winfred L. Smith* on April 25 at Baltimore as second mate and arrived at New York on September 8 from Port Said, Egypt.

Milby, Robert, radio operator. Signed on for Voyage No. 4.

Ender, Thomas, J., purser. Paid off at St. John, New Brunswick, on January 26, 1944, and signed on the old Waterman freighter *Bayou Chico* in April when that ship arrived at New York from Liverpool.

Haas, Albert E., 26, purser, 6 months, German, 5–7/160. Signed on the Grace Line cargo liner *Santa Elena* as assistant purser at New York on July 13, 1943, and arrived back at New York on August 11 from Glasgow, Scotland. He stayed on and arrived at New York from Oran, Algeria, on September 21. On November 6, 1943, the *Santa Elena* was hit by an aerial torpedo north of Algeria, collided with another vessel the next day while under tow, and sank. Crew survivors were brought to Philippeville, Algeria. Haas signed on the *O'Brien* at St. John, New Brunswick, on January 26, 1944, to replace Thomas Ender. Signed on for Voyage No. 4.

Cook, Alton K., 39, bosun. Signed on for Voyage No. 4.

Samaras, Theodore, carpenter. Signed on for Voyage No. 4.

Terry, Trendell L., 21, able seaman, 2 years, Negro, 5–8/150. Signed on the United Fruit Liberty ship *Joseph E. Johnston* at New York as an ordinary seaman on August 22, 1943, and arrived back at New York on October 21 from Liverpool. Signed on for Voyage No. 4.

Weingaertner, Walter C., able seaman. Paid off and signed on the Oliver J. Olson Liberty ship *George Middlemas* at San Francisco on April 13, 1945, as third mate and arrived back at San Francisco on August 22 from Okinawa.

Valentine, Sherman A., able seaman. Signed on for Voyage No. 4.

Corbett, Donald, able seaman. Signed on for Voyage No. 4.

Bron, Daniel, able seaman. Signed on for Voyage No. 4.

Cadogan, Joseph, able seaman. Paid off and signed on Keystone Shipping's brand-new 10,256-ton tanker *Sag Harbor* on October 29, 1944, at Philadelphia as quartermaster-able seaman. They arrived back at New York on November 26 from Swansea, Wales.

Cioffi, Joseph, 24, ordinary seaman, 1 year, Italian, 5–4/135. Paid off at end of voyage.

Demanuel, Sebastian, ordinary seaman. Paid off at end of voyage.

McCormick, Francis, ordinary seaman. Paid off and signed on the Blidberg Rothchild Liberty ship *Harold I. Pratt* as an able seaman on August 25, 1944, at Boston and arrived at New York on January 13, 1945.

Schneider, Coleman, deck cadet. Signed off and went back to school.

Engine Department

Montgomery, Richardson, chief engineer. Signed on for Voyage No. 4.

Morrison, Donald, first assistant engineer. Paid off at end of voyage.

Whitney, Walter C., second assistant engineer. Signed on for Voyage No. 4.

Watson, William, 21, third assistant engineer, 1 year, 5–10/170. Signed on the *Mormacmoon* on May 26, 1943, at Philadelphia as junior engineer and arrived at New York on October 13 from Bandar Shalpur, Iran. Signed on for Voyage No. 4.

Pinheiro, Carlos, 27, junior engineer, 18 years, British subject, 5–7/145. Paid off at end of voyage.

Hall, Tom C., oiler. Paid off at end of voyage.

Wasko, Michael G., oiler. Paid off and signed on the U.S. Navigation Liberty ship *Nathan Towson* as an oiler on January 17, 1944, at New York and arrived back there on May 7 from Belfast, Ireland, via Murmansk. In 1945 he made third assistant engineer.

Bonem, Clarence C., oiler. Paid off at end of voyage.

Ruppert, Henry Earl, 21, fireman/watertender, 1 year, 5–11/170. Signed on the *William Hawkins* at Philadelphia on April 10, 1943, as a F/WT and arrived at New York on September 26 from Suez, Egypt. Paid off and signed on the *P. T. Barnum* on May 3, 1944, at New York as a F/WT and arrived back at New York on June 20 from Cristobal, Canal Zone.

Twiggs, Martin J., fireman/watertender. Signed on for Voyage No. 4.

Joell, Vernon R., fireman/watertender. Signed on for Voyage No. 4.

Tibau, Jose C., 45, wiper, 23 years, Spanish national, 5–9/155. Signed on for Voyage No. 4.

Cuevas, Isaac A., 36, wiper, West Indian, 2 years, 5–7/170. Paid off at end of voyage.

D'Andrea, James, engine cadet. Signed off and went back to school. In January 1945 he signed on the *John W. Garrett* at New York and expected to sail for Halifax of February 20.

Steward Department

Martin, Percy, 64, chief steward, 20 years, British subject, 5–8/135. Arrived at New York on the *George H. Thomas* on October 24, 1943. Paid off and signed on the Grace Line freighter *Santa Barbara* and served as chief steward until war's end.

Sung Ming Wee, chief cook. Paid off after the voyage.

Geo Wee Hie, second cook & baker. Signed on for Voyage No. 4.

Yok Lee Ah, 25, 6 years, third cook, Chinese national, 5–4/130. Paid off and signed on the Lykes Bros. freighter *Sahale* in April at New York then went aboard the Grace Line freighter *Santa Barbara* as second cook & baker and arrived at New York on January 21, 1945.

Qvistgaard, George, 38, messman, 7 years, 5–2/135. Paid off and signed on the big 20,614-ton American Republics Line passenger ship *Argentina* at New York On July 20, 1944, as fourth pantryman and arrived back at New York on August 20 from Gourock, Scotland.

Start, Francis J., 29, messman, 6 months, 5–9/225. Paid off and signed on the *Edward Canby* at Boston on June 12, 1944, as nite cook and arrived at New York from Newport, Wales, on August 7.

Cramer, Noel T., 39, crew messman, 3 years, 5–7/145. Signed on the Parry Navigation Liberty ship *Collis P. Huntington* on July 30, 1943, at New York as chief steward and arrived back at New York on October 15 from Oran, Algeria. Signed on for Voyage No. 4.

Dias, Jose Do Nasimento, 34, utility, 21 years, Portuguese national, 5–8/170. Father, Manuel Do Nascimento Dias of Olhao, Portugal. Signed on the Lykes Bros. Liberty ship *Thomas Paine* at Baltimore on April 10, 1943, as third cook (second trip on the *Paine*) and arrived at New York on October 13 from Fremantle, Australia, via Cristobal, Panama. Signed on for Voyage No. 4.

Sung Hai Yeo, utility. Signed on for Voyage No. 4.

Dong Ah Wee, 37, utility, 9 years, Chinese national, 5–4/130. Signed on for Voyage No. 4.

Armed Guard (all USNR unless otherwise noted)

Memhard, Lt. Allen Ray, Jr., commanding officer. Memhard's father was a lawyer at 39 Broadway in Manhattan. Junior was born on June 23, 1913, graduated from Haverford College in 1935, and joined the Navy on October 2, 1941. He stayed on for Voyage No. 4 and in November 1944 he commanded the 30-man AG unit on the Socony-Vacuum tanker *Champion's Hill*. They left Chester, Pennsylvania, and arrived at New York on December 1 from Aruba. After the war he went into the radio broadcast advertising business. In 1946 he joined N. W. Ayer & Son as the plans-marketing supervisor and in 1947 was the client service supervisor in the Detroit office. In 1950 he was the plans-marketing supervisor in Philadelphia and lived with his wife Judith and sons Charles P. and Richard C. on Crescent Rd. in Riverside, Connecticut. In 1955 he was vice president and head of the Chicago office. In 1960 he was the marketing supervisor at the Leo Burnett Co. in Chicago. He died on April 8, 1981.

Landrum, Herbert E., Coxswain; Thomas, James C., Coxswain; Gould, Philip J., GM3c; Hodgson, Thomas W., Jr., GM3c; Holsapple, Kenneth L., GM3c; Williams, Morgan C., GM3c; Hudson, Lewis E., RM2c; Roberts, Jack William, RM2c; Garbett, Charles R., SM2c; Mason, Robert N., SM3c; Bandy, Daniel G., S1c; Caron, Robert N., S1c; Chisholm, William N., S1c; Felci, Armando Frank, S1c; Howell, Robert Martin, S1c; Hunt, John Joseph, S1c; Mason, Robert Noble, S1c; Mitchell, Buford Veitch, S1c; Morris, Joe Emmett, S1c; Rose, William James, S1c

Serra, George J., S1c; Shaw, Jerome E., S1c; Smedley, Edward J., S1c; Smith, Raymond N., S1c; Stojek, Ludwig J., S1c; Straughan, Alvis F., S1c; Surdi, Gildo R., S1c; Talyai, Charles N., S1c; Tyler, Herbert L., S1c; Williams, Edwin Lewis, S1c

NOTE ON THE COLLISION BETWEEN
THE GEORGE WESTINGHOUSE AND THE ADRASTUS

The United States sued the Ocean Steamship Co. and Ocean Steamship filed a cross libel, each accusing the other of being solely at fault. The district court held that neither party was solely liable and dismissed the suit on the grounds that each vessel was proceeding as directed by military authority and both ships had improper lookouts. Both parties then appealed to the 2nd Circuit Court of Appeals and on August 17, 1951, the court held that because the lookouts were not properly posted on the *Adrastus* and the bow lookout on the *Westinghouse* was "in a most unusual sort of homemade shelter which obviously did obstruct his view to a considerable extent," both parties were held liable for half the damages.

Voyage No. 4

The ship was chartered from the War Shipping Administration by the Army Transport Service while still under the General Agency Agreement with Grace Line.

Departed New York with general military cargo and AFVs on April 12, 1944, for Liverpool in the 81-ship Convoy HXF 287. Routed to Barry Docks, Glamorgan, South Wales, and arrived at the Barry Roads anchorage on the 25th. Barry was a Great Western Railway port that handled coal, lumber, grain, iron, and building materials. In 1913, Barry was the largest coal exporting port in the world.

Departed for Newport, Monmouthshire, Wales, and arrived on April 27. Newport was a Great Western Railway port that handled lumber, steel, iron ore, pig iron, and general merchandise. Sailed for Gourock and arrived on May 21. Departed on June 2 and arrived at Southampton, Hampshire, England, on June 5. The main invasion at Normandy occurred the next day, D-Day, June 6, 1944.

The *O'Brien* left Southampton on June 9 for Pointe de la Percée, Normandy, with troops and equipment in company with several other ships and various escorts consisting of British corvettes and Harbour Defence Motor Launches, U.S. Coast Guard sub chasers, and all the landing forces had air cover. During the passage "several mines were narrowly avoided." Explosions, tracer fire, and numerous flares were observed and the ship arrived off Omaha Beach around 8:30 a.m. on the 10th. The troops embarked to LSTs that came alongside.

At 3:45 a.m. on the 11th the gun crews went to battle stations when enemy planes were seen circling overhead at about 10,000 feet. At around 4 a.m. a JU 88 came down in a dive and dropped four bombs. One splashed about 200 yards off the port bow and three others landed close to another Liberty ship. Twenty-five minutes later, one Focke-Wulf 190 fighter came out from shore toward the ship at about 14,000 feet and then lost altitude. Both 3-inch gun crews fired two rounds each. At 5 a.m., three groups of three Focke-Wulf 190s came out and all guns opened fire on one, expending 12 rounds of 3-inch and 500 rounds of 20-mm. Lt. Memhard did not observe any hits but several others said they saw the plane "go down in smoke several miles out to sea."

The next day, June 12, visibility was poor and no shots were fired at circling aircraft. Lt. Memhard reported:

> In general, it was surprising that more determined and heavier enemy plane attacks were not encountered, particularly so soon after "D" day and since enemy-held territory at this point was only a few miles inland. During the day excellent allied plane coverage was maintained, mainly by Spitfires of several types, Mustangs, Thunderbolts, Lightnings and Typhoons in this area. At night, from dawn to dusk, enemy planes were always about and dropping flares, but practically no damage to allied shipping was observed by the undersigned. "E" [boats] also made frequent attempts to penetrate the destroyer protective ring. On one occasion it appeared that a combination plane and "E" boat attack was being made on the protective ring outside the anchorages.

The ship returned to Southampton on June 14 and left on the second run to Percée on the 17th and returned on the 20th "without incident."

Departed Southampton on June 22 for Belfast, Ireland, in convoy and arrived two days later where they took aboard troops and equipment on July 4. Departed July 6 to Utah Beach in convoy with troops and equipment and then returned to The Solent anchorage off Portsmouth on July 12.

The fourth run was from Southampton on July 15 to Utah Beach with troops and equipment and return to Southampton on July 18 "without incident."

The fifth run was from Southampton on July 21 to Omaha Beach with troops and equipment and return to Southampton on July 26. During the night of the 23rd enemy planes were overhead and heavy 20 and 40-mm firing caused shrapnel to fall on the deck.

After returning to Southampton, a gyrocompass and three repeaters were installed. They had come from Capt. Gustav Andersen's South Atlantic Steamship Co. Liberty ship *John A. Treutlen*, torpedoed on June 29 by *U-984* in the English Channel. The ship was beached near Southampton and declared a total loss. Eight Navy sailors and one merchant seamen were injured and everyone was taken off by *LST-336*. Three other Liberty ships, the *James A. Farrell*, *H. G. Blasdell*, and *Edward M. House* were torpedoed by the same sub on the same afternoon and all were declared total losses.

The sixth run commenced from Southampton on August 2 to Omaha Beach with troops and equipment and returned to an anchorage on the 5th without incident.

The seventh run commenced from Southampton on August 13 to Utah Beach with troops and equipment. The weather turned bad with gale force winds. They returned on the 18th.

The eighth run commenced from Southampton on August 23 with troops and equipment to Utah Beach and returned to Southampton "without incident" on August 26. On the 23rd they observed an explosion near the A. H. Bull & Co. Liberty ship *Louis Kossuth* astern of them at Buoy H4, which they believed to be a mine or torpedo although no torpedo track was observed. Capt. de Smedt prepared to render assistance but the ship signaled they did not need help. The *Kossuth* arrived back at New York from Cardiff on December 28.

The ninth run commenced from Southampton on August 31 to Utah Beach with troops and equipment, returned to an anchorage on September 2 without incident, and moored on the 6th.

The tenth run commenced from Southampton on September 9 to Utah Beach with troops and equipment, returning on the 13th without incident.

At Southampton on September 14, Navy gunner James Potts fell off the gangway about 25 feet to the concrete dock below while he was bringing a sack of mail aboard the ship. His way was partially obstructed by a preventer from a starboard boom on the main mast and it was surmised that while ducking under it he lost his balance and fell. An Army medical unit was right there being loaded on the ship and a doctor splinted a broken arm. Potts was taken to a U.S. Navy hospital and admitted in serious condition.

The eleventh run commenced on September 16 to Utah Beach with troops and equipment then departed for Cherbourg.

Departed Cherbourg on September 24 for Swansea, arriving there on the 26th.

Departed Swansea on the 28th and arrived at Milford Haven the same day. Departed Milford Haven in ballast on September 29 and joined the 72-ship Convoy ON 256 and arrived at New York on October 12 and tied up at Pier 2, North River.

On February 27, 1945, the ship was awarded an Operation and Engagement Star for the Normandy Invasion.

THE CREW

Master

    de Smedt, Alfonse A.

Deck Department

    Pellegrino, Frank, 27, chief mate. Paid off and signed on the Grace Line Liberty ship *John Bidwell* as chief mate. Made two voyages and arrived at New York on September 28, 1945.

    Morgan, Oliver M., second mate. Paid off and on May 21, 1945, signed on the Alcoa freighter *Charles A. Warfield* at New York as chief mate and arrived at San Francisco on September 17 from Eniwetok, Marshall Islands.

    Seymour, Edward, 29, third mate, 3 years, 5–11/160. Paid off at end of voyage.

    Milby, Robert, radio operator. Signed on for Voyage No. 5.

    De Waard, Gerrit, 23, second radio operator, 6 months, 5–11/155. Wife Virginia, 70 Oliver St., Suffern, New York. Signed on for Voyage No. 5.

    Haas, Albert E., purser. Paid off, went to pharmacist's mate school, and made two voyages on the Grace Line Liberty ship *George Abernethy* as purser-pharmacist's mate and arrived at New York from Antwerp, Belgium, on October 31, 1945.

    McGeehan, Thomas R., 19, deck cadet, 6 months, Scotch, 5–6/135. Left school in December 1943 and signed on the Texas Co. tanker *Delaware* as deck cadet. Made two voyages and arrived at New York on March 22, 1944, from Liverpool. Signed on the *O'Brien* and got off after one voyage and went back to school.

    Cook, Alton K., bosun. Paid off and signed on the Grace Line Liberty ship *George C. Childress* on January 10, 1945, at New York as junior third mate. Arrived back at New York on March 12 from Cristobal, Panama.

    Samaras, Theodore, carpenter. Signed on for Voyage No. 5.

    Terry, Trendell L., able seaman. Signed on for Voyage No. 5.

    Bron, Daniel, able seaman. Paid off and signed on the American-West African Line Liberty ship *C. H. M. Jones* at New York. they were expected to sail for Halifax on January 23, 1945.

    Valentine, Sherman A., able seaman. Paid off at end of voyage and continued sailing with Grace Line.

    Corbett, Donald, able seaman. Paid off at end of voyage.

    Klitsgaard, Henry, 20, able seaman, 5 years, Danish national, 5–11/185. Signed on the Agwilines Liberty ship *Pearl Harbor* at Saint John, New Brunswick, on January 22, 1944, as an AB and arrived at New York on March 15 from Newcastle-on-Tyne, England. Paid off and signed on the *Horace H. Harvey* on November 15, 1944, at New York as oiler and arrived back at New York on December 29 from Gibraltar then signed on the *James T. Fields* on January 9, 1945, at New York as an AB and arrived back at New York on March 15 from Liverpool.

    Doyle, Herbert Elgin, 27, able seaman, 1 year, 5–8/168, appendix scar. Signed on the *Alcoa Leader* at Boston on January 12, 1944, as an ordinary seaman and arrived at New York on March 15. Made another voyage and arrived at New York on May 18. Signed on at Southampton, England, on July 29. Paid off and signed on the *James Jackson* as acting AB on November 20, 1944, at New York and arrived back at New York on January 20, 1945.

    Rudesill, James, 40, able seaman, 8 years, 5–2½/155, scar on forehead. Signed on for his second voyage on the Luckenbach freighter *Margaret Brent* as an AB on October 8, 1943, at Philadelphia and arrived at New York on March 23 from Alexandria, Egypt. In an odd twist, a 19-year-old oiler named Ernest Lee Murdock was on the same voyages. He worked his way up to chief engineer and in 40 years would be the volunteer chief engineer on the *Jeremiah O'Brien* in San Francisco. Oblivious to this startling coincidence, Rudesill paid off and signed on the *Crosby S. Noyes* and arrived at New York on April 25, 1945, from Swansea, Wales.

Garcia, Louis S., 19, ordinary seaman, 6 months, 5–2/120. Signed on the *Ephraim Brevard* on December 2, 1943, at Boston as a messman and arrived at New York on February 17, 1944. Paid off the *O'Brien* and signed on the *Fred C. Ainsworth*.

Jones, Osborne P., 36, ordinary seaman, 1 year, African-American, 5–9/165. Signed on March 31 and paid off after the voyage.

Bennes, Emil F., 18, ordinary seaman, 1 year, 5–6/150, signed on March 31. Paid off and signed on the *George Davis* on November 17, 1944, at New York as an ordinary seaman and arrived back at New York on February 6, 1945, from Naples, Italy.

Kusel, Henry, 21, deck cadet, 8 mos., 5–10/165. Kusel arrived at New York from London on March 22, 1944, on the R. A. Nicols Liberty ship *Charles A. Dana* as third Mate under Capt. Viktor Peterson. He signed on the *O'Brien* for Voyage No. 4 the same day. On June 21 he was transferred to the Liberty ship *Pearl Harbor* and on July 18 signed on the United States Lines–operated Army troopship *John Ericsson* at Liverpool as deck cadet under Capt. John Anderson. They arrived at New York on July 27 from Gourock with 346 crew.

Engine Department

Montgomery, Richardson, chief engineer. Signed on for Voyage No. 5.

Lauritsen, Ludvig C., 50, first assistant engineer, 10 years, Scandinavian, 5–8/180. Signed on the *Jose Marti* as second engineer at Baltimore on July 30, 1943, and arrived at New York on February 20 from Belem, Brazil, via Port of Spain, Trinidad. Paid off at end of voyage.

Whitney, Walter C., second assistant engineer. Paid off and signed on the American Mail Line Liberty ship *R. P. Warner* as second engineer. He made two voyages and arrived at Honolulu on August 12, 1945, from Vancouver, B. C.

Watson, William, third assistant engineer. Paid off and signed on the Grace Line Liberty ship *John S. Pillsbury* on January 21, 1945, at New York as second engineer and arrived back at New York on March 29 from Swansea, Wales.

Wentworth, Harris G., 32, junior engineer, 13 years, 5–5/175. Father, Fred Wentworth, Manchester, Maine. Signed on the *John Vining* as deck engineer on February 13, 1943, at New York and arrived back at New York on October 24. Signed on for Voyage No. 5.

Joell, Vernon R., oiler. Signed on for Voyage No. 5.

Erdmann, Francis E., 20, oiler, 1 year, 5–8/175. Signed on the Gulf Oil tanker *Gulfhawk* at New York on February 7, 1944, as a wiper and arrived back at New York on March 23 from Casablanca, Morocco. Paid off and signed on the Agwilines Liberty ship *James Rolph* on June 23, 1945, at Los Angeles as third engineer and arrived at San Francisco on November 6, 1945, from Yokohama, Japan.

Kober, Herman H., 28, oiler, 1 year, German, 5–10/160. Paid off and signed on the *Horace H. Harvey* on November 15, 1944, at New York as oiler and arrived back at New York on December 29 from Gibraltar then made two voyages on the *Sea Porpoise* as oiler and arrived at New York on June 12, 1945, from Le Havre, France.

Twiggs, Martin J., fireman/watertender. Signed on for Voyage No. 5.

Saxvik, Olaf M., 22, fireman/watertender, 1 year, 5–11/165. Paid off and signed on the *John P. Holland* in January 1945 at New York.

Tibau, Jose, fireman/watertender. Signed on for Voyage No. 5.

Miller, Hubert K., 36, wiper, 1 year, 5–8/165. Made his first two voyages at sea from Norfolk on the Tankers Co. tanker *McClellan Creek* as a wiper and arrived at New York from on

February 27 from Aruba. He intended to remain aboard but signed on the *O'Brien*. Paid off and made two voyages on the *Sea Porpoise* as a fireman/watertender and arrived at New York on June 12, 1945, from Le Havre, France.

Ooghe, Ernest A., 22, wiper, 1 year, Flemish, 5–11/165. Paid off and made two voyages on the *Benjamin Rush* out of Philadelphia as a fireman/watertender. Arrived at New York on April 27, 1945, from Plymouth, England.

Steward Department

Kite Lo, 51, chief steward, 10 years, Chinese national, 5–5/150. Signed on the old 1919 Grace Line–operated freighter *Dunboyne* as chief steward on December 17, 1942, at Mobile, Alabama, and arrived at New York on February 5, 1943, from Sanchez, Dominican Republic. Paid off at end of voyage.

Yang Tin Ming, 33, chief cook, 6 years, Chinese national, 5–5/135. Paid off after voyage.

Geo Wee Hie, second cook & baker. Paid off and signed on the Grace Line freighter *Marine Robin* on May 16, 1945, at New York as petty officer pantryman and arrived back at New York on June 2 from Le Havre, France.

Song Foo Hee, 31, third cook, 3 years, Chinese national, 5–5/130. Possibly signed on the Isbrandtsen motorship *Cavalcade* as second cook on November 11, 1944, at New York and arrived back at New York on December 22 from Preston, Cuba. Paid off and possibly signed on the *Thomas Eakins* as utilityman on June 12, 1945, at New York and arrived back at New York on August 12 from Cadiz, Spain.

Cramer, Noel T., messman. Paid off at end of voyage.

Yacynik, John, 19, messman, 1 year, Ukrainian, 5–10, 165. Paid off and signed on the Gulf Oil tanker *Gulfbird* at New York on November 12, 1945, as a messman and arrived back at New York on December 1 from Las Piedras, Venezuela.

Wray, George, 19, crew messman, Canadian national, 1 year, 5–6/160. Paid off after the voyage.

Dias, Jose Do Nasimento, utility. Signed on for Voyage No. 5.

Dong Ah Wee, utility. Paid off and signed on the Grace Line freighter *Marine Robin* on May 16, 1945, at New York as galley utility and arrived back at New York on June 2 from Le Havre, France.

Sung Hai Yeo, utility. Paid off and signed on the United Fruit freighter *Marine Devil* at Pier 19, Staten Island, New York, on February 14, 1945, as galley utility and arrived back at New York on March 21 from Plymouth, England.

Armed Guard (all USNR unless otherwise noted)

Memhard, Lt. Allen R., Jr., commanding officer.

Bandy, Daniel Glendyn, coxswain; Jones, James, GM3c; Potts, James Davis, GM3c; Williams, Morgan Casto, GM3c; Hudson, Lewis E., RM2c; Roberts, Jack William, RM2c; Hardin, Wallace James, SM3c; Mason, Robert Noble, SM3c; Bires, Joseph William, S1c; Christian, Samuel Clifton, S1c; Counts, Luther Wetzel, S1c; Cunningham, Stanley Morrel, S1c; Dennison, Fred, S1c; Gorman, William Robert, S1c; Helbling, Albert Frederick, S1c, USN; Huffstetler, Alvin Leroy, S1c; Lamonica, James, S1c; Murphy, John Thomas, S1c; Pilcher, Robert Roy, S1c; Planeta, John Paul, S1c; Robichaud, Robert Jerome, S1c; Rubin, Melvin David, S1c; Savering, Richard Paul, S1c; Sharpe, Elbert Ray, S1c, USN; Sirrene, John Edwin, S1c; Slaight, Donald Harvey, S1c; Swanson, Clarence Alvin, S1c; Weeks, Donald Oirse, S1c.

The Armed Guard crew was detached at New York on October 18 and a new detachment put aboard the same day.

Lt. Memhard made lieutenant commander in October 1944 and in February 1945 he was attached to Commander Amphibious Group 10 as assistant intelligence officer on the general communications ship *Auburn* (AGC-10) during the Iwo Jima invasion.

THE AUGUSTA

The Navy passengers from Voyage No. 2 arrived on the cruiser at the South Boston Navy Yard on December 1 for repairs and alterations. Work was completed on January 29, 1944, and they soon left for Belfast to prepare for the Normandy Invasion. The *Augusta* was flagship of Rear Adm. Allen G. Kirk, USN, Commander Task Force 122 and Commander Western Naval Task Force. Also on board was Lt. Gen. Omar Bradley and his staff, Maj. Gen. Sir Robert Laycock, and a British general in charge of the British Marine Force. The ship left Plymouth at 2:39 on the afternoon of June 5 in company with cruiser HMS *Bellona* (D.63), *PT-71*, *SC-1321*, and *YMS-231*, *-247*, *-304*, and *-349* and anchored in Fire Support Area #3 off the Omaha Assault Area at 6:17 the next morning, Point du Hoc bearing 228T, distance 8 miles. Between 6:18 and 6:23 they fired 21 rounds of 8-inch main battery ammunition and from 6:35 to 6:43 fired 30 rounds. At 8:05 they anchored in the Omaha Transport Area near the *Ancon* (AP-66), flagship of Commander Assault Force "O" and at 8:12 p.m. moved again and anchored at berth H-31, Oregon Area, inside the screening line.

At 7:17 the next morning they moved closer to the beach and at 11:50 the big minelayer HMS *Apollo* (M.01) flagship of Admiral Sir Bertram H. Ramsay, RN, Chief of all naval operations came alongside with Gen. Dwight D. Eisenhower on board. That afternoon they anchored off the Utah Transport Area and just before 5 p.m. Gen. Laycock and Gen. Head left the ship. They returned to Omaha and anchored. On June 9 they anchored near the *Bayfield* and probably had no idea future Yankee catcher Lawrence Peter "Yogi" Berra was on one of the transport's boat crews. One June 10, the same day the *O'Brien* arrived, Gen. Bradley and his staff departed to establish headquarters ashore. On June 12 they fired 8 rounds of 5-inch anti-aircraft shells and the next day fired 21 rounds and shot down one plane. On June 15 at 2:45 a.m. they fired 60 rounds of AA and at 7:38 fired 18 rounds of main battery ammo at a shore target. The next day expended 5 rounds of AA, the 18th 11 rounds.

On June 19, the *O'Brien's* first birthday, the seas were very rough and *Augusta* lost one sailor overboard, John Duffy, S2c, from New York City. The cruiser remained until June 30 and spent the rest of the war uneventfully in the Mediterranean.

Voyage No. 5

Departed New York on November 1, 1944, sailing independently for Panama with trucks, foodstuffs, machinery, and general merchandise. On the 4th, an Australian destroyer, possibly HMAS *Diamantina* (K.377), asked for their radio call sign and on the 6th a Navy blimp from Cuba requested their call sign and secret identification, which was given by flag hoist. They arrived at Cristobal without on the 9th, discharged their cargo, and departed on November 17 in ballast through the Panama Canal for Antofagasta, Chile, where they arrived on the 25th. The port handled nitrate of soda, bar copper and ore, tin, silver, antimony, borates, hides, and general merchandise. While there, the crew had their first dealings with the inbred corruption of Latin American officials and the widespread theft of anything loose.

Departed on November 28 with copper and lead ingots and plate for Callao, Peru, and arrived there on December 1. The port handled textiles, leather, furniture, chinaware, paints, wheat, coal, dry goods, motor and railway cars, and metals. Departed Callao on December 2 for Balboa, Canal Zone, and arrived on December 8. Sailed for Cristobal, transited the Panama Canal on the 8th, and headed for New Orleans. During a storm on the 11th and 12th the chain locker filled with water and ruined some Navy gear in the bosun's stores. They arrived at New Orleans on the 14th and moored at the Market St. Pier.

THE CREW

Master

Gundersen, Arthur Johannes, 41, 23 years, Scandinavian, 5–7/145. Capt. Gundersen was born in Norway on September 14, 1903, took to the sea, moved to Glasgow, Scotland, and arrived in the United States on April 3, 1929, aboard the steamer *Camero-nia*. He decided to remain in America and work on American vessels. He married his wife Elizabeth, born in Norway on July 22, 1903, on November 1, 1931, in Brooklyn. They lived at 850 50th St. in Brooklyn. When he renounced his allegiance to Haakon VII, King of Norway, and became a citizen on November 9, 1934, they lived at 760 60th St. in Brooklyn. Right before Pearl Harbor, Capt. Gunderson was chief mate aboard the Grace Line steamer *Lara*. On September 23, 1944, he had arrived at New York from Port of Spain, Trinidad, as master of the Grace Line Liberty ship *Frederic Remington*. He stayed on the *O'Brien* for the next voyage. Capt. Gundersen died in Brooklyn on December 9, 1990.

Deck Department

Scott, R. H., chief officer.

Cruickshanks, Reid N., 21, second mate, 21, 5–9/170. Paid off and signed on the Grace Line Liberty ship *John S. Pillsbury* at New York on January 24, 1945, as third mate and arrived back at New York on March 29 from Swansea, Wales.

Ganley, William G., 31, third mate, Irish, 5–11/175, scar on right knee and tattoos on both arms. Wife, Bernice, 39 Charter Oak Pl., Hartford, Connecticut. Signed on the Isthmian freighter *Steel Trader* at New York on March 3, 1944, as an able seaman but was hospitalized at Hull, England on April 14. On April 18 he signed on the Moore-McCormack freighter *Sweepstakes* at Hull as an AB and arrived at New York on May 1, 1944. Signed on for Voyage No. 6.

De Waard, Gerrit, radio operator. Signed on for Voyage No. 6.

Haney, Edwin A., 34, purser/pharmacist's mate, 1 year, 5–6/155, scar on stomach. Mother, Mary, 34 Quentin Rd., Brooklyn, New York. His first two voyages were on the *John C. Kendall* as purser/pharmacist's mate, arriving at New York after the second voyage on August 7, 1944, from London. Signed on for Voyage No. 6.

Thiago, João, 35, bosun, 19 years, Brazilian national, 6–1/235. Arrived at New York on September 23, 1944, as bosun on the *Keguas*. Signed Articles on October 20, 1944. Paid off and signed on the *Charles Tufts* as bosun and arrived at New York on March 13, 1945.

Samaras, Theodore, carpenter. Signed on for Voyage No. 6.

Graham, Arthur, able seaman. Paid off after the voyage.

Terry, Trendell L., able seaman. Paid off and signed on the *James Lykes* at New York.

Salas, Louis E., 24, able seaman, 4 yrs., Spanish, 6–2/180, scar on left hand. Mother, Inez, 132–07 115th Ave., Long Island, New York. Signed on the U.S. Lines freighter *Tintagel* on July 26, 1944, at Philadelphia as an AB and arrived at New York on October 12 from Trinidad. Signed on for Voyage No. 6.

Lopez, Manuel, 39, able seaman, 15 yrs., Spanish national, 5–7/185, wife Maria, Finisterre,

Coruna, Spain. Made three voyages on the Pan American Petroleum Transport Co. tanker *Pan Maine* then signed on the *O'Brien*. Signed on for Voyage No. 6.

Targia, Angelo J., 24, able seaman. Paid off at end of voyage and apparently made only one foreign voyage.

Roper, William S., 23, able seaman, English, 5–7½. Believed to have signed on the *Joseph N. Teal* on July 4, 1944, at Norfolk as an AB and arrived at New York on September 23, 1944. Paid off at the end of the voyage.

Glasgow, Robert W., 18, ordinary seaman, Scotch, 6–0/180. Paid off at end of voyage.

Duffy, Cornelius J., 17, ordinary seaman, 5 mos., 5–10½/155. Paid off and signed on the *Timothy Bloodworth* on January 23, 1945, at the Staten Island Army Base as an ordinary seaman and arrived back at New York on March 1, 1945, from Marseilles, France.

Laroche, Louis Adlere, 18, ordinary seaman, French, 5–9/145, scar under left arm. Paid off and signed on the *Frank P. Reed* in May 1945.

Engine Department

Montgomery, Richardson, chief engineer. Signed on for Voyage No. 6.

Wallace, William, first assistant engineer.

Prado, Ralph T., second assistant engineer. Rejoined the ship after Voyage No. 2. Paid off and signed on the *Louisa M. Alcott* as first assistant engineer. Made two voyages and arrived at New York from Antwerp, Belgium, on September 3, 1945.

Scharpf, Carl A., 24, third assistant engineer, 4 yrs., Scandinavian, 5–7/140. Signed on the Princess Line freighter *Cape San Antonio* at New Orleans on January 7, 1944, as junior third engineer and arrived at San Francisco on March 28 from Milne Bay, New Guinea. Got to New York and signed on the *O'Brien* and paid off after the voyage. Signed on the *John Philip Souza* as second engineer at Baltimore on February 12, 1945, and arrived at New York on April 13 from Port-de-Bouc, France.

Leifken, Joseph J., 18, junior engineer, German, 5–10/155. Josef was 3 years old when he arrived at New York from Esterfeld, Germany, on March 17, 1926, on the liner *Westphalia* with his father Josef, 28, mother Maria, 32, and brother Herbert, 4. The family settled in Rochester. He signed on the Moore-McCormack freighter *Argentina* at Pier 20, Staten Island, in August 1944 and arrived back in New York in October. Paid off at the end of the voyage.

Kemper, Paul Schermerhorn, 45, oiler, 16 yrs., 5–11/170. Mother, Corinne, Rockford, Illinois. Signed on the Grace Line freighter *Santa Teresa* in early 1943 at New York as an oiler and paid off at New York on May 12, 1944, upon arriving from Cardiff, Wales. Signed on for Voyage No. 6.

Joell, Vernon R., oiler. Paid off and signed on the *Joseph H. Chevalier* in June 1945 at the Sullivan Drydock & Repair Co. in Brooklyn, New York.

Wentworth, Harris G., 32, 6 years, oiler, 5–5/175. Signed on for Voyage No. 6.

Twiggs, Martin, fireman/watertender. Paid off at end of voyage.

Tibau, Jose, fireman/watertender. Paid off and signed on the *John N. Maffitt* on February 22, 1945, as a wiper arrived at New York on April 9, 1945, from Antwerp, Belgium.

Halliday, Walter S., 37, fireman/watertender, Scotch/Canadian national, 5–5. A sailor believed to have been admitted into the United States on April 18, 1925, at Detroit to reside in Ashtabula, Ohio, and work the Great Lakes. Apparently made only one foreign voyage. Paid off at end of voyage.

Ondesko, E., wiper. Paid off at end of voyage.

Carnelo, Robarto B., 42, wiper, Peruvian national, 5–3. Mother, Petronila, of Hoache, Peru. Signed Articles on October 23, 1944, and paid off at end of voyage.

Zoetjes, Joannes H., 38, wiper, Dutch national, 5–5/155. Arrived at New York on September 27, 1944, on the Grace Line freighter *Marine Robin*, possibly as chief steward. Signed Articles on October 19, 1944. Paid off and signed on the United Fruit Liberty ship *Jonathan Trumbull* in January 1945 at Brooklyn.

Steward Department

Hegarty, Philip, 40, chief steward, 4 yrs., Irish, 5–6/145, wife Anna, 522 E. 138th St., New York. Made at least two voyages on the Parry Navigation Liberty ship *Robert T. Hill* and arrived at New York from Oran, Algeria, on September 28, 1944, as chief cook. Signed on for Voyage No. 6.

Owens, Tela, 32, chief cook, 5–10/227. Signed on the tanker *Ridgefield* as second cook & baker on September 6, 1944, at New York and arrived back there on October 8 from Liverpool. Paid off and signed on the *James H. Price* as assistant cook on December 27 at Savannah, Georgia, and arrived at New York on March 11, 1945, from Manchester, England.

Low Boon Eng, 34, second cook & baker, Chinese, 4–9/135. Paid off at end of voyage.

Dias, Jose Do Nasimento, third cook. Signed on for Voyage No. 6.

Smith, David C., messman. Paid off at end of voyage.

Magers, D. D., messman. Paid off at end of voyage.

Esposito, Raffaelo J., messman, 32, 16 yrs, 5/8–146. Arrived at New York on October 7, 1944, on the *Louis D. Brandeis* from Algeria as a galley utilityman. Paid off at end of voyage and signed on the *Brandeis* at New York on January 9, 1945, and arrived back there on March 5 from Cardiff, Wales.

Arias, Radamas, Jr., 22, utility, Spanish, 5–8/140, scar on right abdomen. Signed on the Grace Line Liberty ship *Abraham Clark* on October 30, 1943, at New York as a messman and arrived back at New York on November 28 from Newport, England. He signed on for the next voyage but there was a problem of some sort and he never arrived with the ship on March 22, 1944.

Bush, Richard, 21, utulity, 5–8/160. Signed on the *China Mail* as a utilityman and arrived at New York on September 9, 1944. Paid off at end of voyage.

NOTE: When the ship arrived at New Orleans there was no immigration inspection for Voyage No. 5. An officer noted there were 39 people on board at the time of arrival. Two deserters had failed to join the ship, 27 sailors were discharged, 29 signed on for Voyage No. 6 and Capt. Gundersen stated the ship expected to sail on December 29.

Armed Guard (all USNR unless otherwise noted)

Robinson, Ens. Norman Evans, commanding officer. Robinson was born in Melrose, Massachusetts, on February 10, 1915, to Joseph A. and Ada Jane Evans. His father was a carpenter and both parents were from Nova Scotia. Norman enlisted in the Navy at Boston on September 9, 1942, went to Pharmacist's Mate's school, and on November 30, 1943, he was in the commissioning crew of the *Henry R. Kenyon* (DE-683) as a PhM1c. On April 9, 1944, he transferred off and went to 90-day Wonder school at Princeton and was commissioned an Ensign.

Doyle, James Joseph, Coxswain; Crocker, Robert Arthur, GM3c, USN; Morieko, Henry Walter, GM3c; Kuhlman, William Clayton, S1c/signalman striker; Walker, Joseph, S1c/signalman striker; Andrews, John R. S1c; Armour, Wesley R. S1c; Bator, Louis, S1c; Bartels, LeRoy George, S1c; Barnett, Clarence Earle, S1c, USN; Carver, Earl Roy, S1c; Casey, James Daniel, S1c; Conklin, Charles Grant, S1c; Crumley, Orval Franklin, S1c; Curtis, Johnny McDonald, S1c; Davis, John Wesley, S1c; Henzen, Marion LaVerne, S1c; Hassler, Cleveland Joseph, S1c; Kennedy, David Bicking, S1c; Lewis, Charles Edgar, S1c; Martin, Theodore S.,

S1c; Ogonowski, Albert Joseph, S1c; Poskie, George Joseph, S1c; Roy, Kermit Lee, S1c; Salandino, Joseph Peter, S1c; Swan, Robert James, S1c, USN; Williams, Vernon Earl, S1c; Wilson, Robert Lee, S1c.

Voyage No. 6

Articles First Signed on December 16, 1944, at New Orleans. Departed New Orleans on December 29 for and anchored in Galveston Bay, Texas, on New Year's Eve. Arrived at Houston on January 3, 1945. Half the Armed Guard crew was on leave and rejoined the ship in Houston where the ship loaded a cargo of bombs and detonators,

Departed Houston on January 17, 1945, for Galveston where a deck cargo of belly tanks and two LCMs were put aboard. Departed for Cristobal on the 19th and arrived on the 25th. Departed Balboa on the 26th for Manus, Admiralty Islands. Early on Friday, February 16, the ship hit the International Dateline and it instantly became Saturday, February 17. They arrived at Seeadler Harbor, Manus, on February 23.

Departed Manus independently on February 24 with ammunition and airplane belly tanks and arrived at Hollandia, New Guinea, on the 25th to wait for enough ships to form a convoy to the Philippines. Departed on March 3 for Leyte in the 35-ship Convoy LS 2 with two LCMs in tow and their eight crewmen on board. The LCMs apparently slowed the ship causing them to lag and that evening the convoy commodore ordered the LCMs turned loose and sent back to Hollandia. The ship arrived at San Pedro Bay, Tacloban, Leyte, on March 10 and arrived at Mangarin Bay on the 18th.

Departed Mangarin Bay for Subic Bay on March 30 and departed Subic on April 13 in Convoy NLY 118 for Leyte. On the 17th the *O'Brien* and *LST-635* and *718* left Subic Bay and joined the convoy and anchored in San Pedro Bay on the 20th.

All the cargo was discharged and the ship departed Leyte on April 20 in Convoy IG 18 for Hollandia, arriving on the 27th. Departed the same day for Oro Bay and arrived on the 30th.

Departed Oro Bay on May 12 and arrived at Hollandia on the 14th to load cargo. Departed Hollandia for Lingayen Gulf in Convoy GI 27. Several crewmen, including Capt. Gunderson, had contracted malaria and on May 21 the escort USS *Gentry* (DE-349) was contacted for medical advice and help. A highline was rigged and one sailor was transferred off and the *O'Brien* arrived at Subic on May 29.

Departed Subic for Lingayen Gulf on May 30 in Convoy SL 8 and arrived the next day.

On June 8, the ship took on bunkers from the station tanker *Kenwood* (IX-179), the old Texas Oil Co. tanker *Texas*. A minor collision occurred in the heavy swells resulting in some damage to the *O'Brien*. The storm continued and they departed Lingayen on June 9 in Convoy LS 28. The convoy eventually dispersed and the *O'Brien* arrived at Pier 35 in San Francisco on July 6, 1945, after an uneventful trip.

THE CREW

Master

Gundersen, Arthur J. Officially aboard on December 16 at New Orleans. Paid off at end of voyage and on August 2, 1945, took command of the Grace Line–operated ship *Cacique* at New York and arrived back at New York from Barranquilla, Columbia, on September 4, 1945.

Deck Department

Antony, Arthur A., 32, acting chief mate, 5 yrs., 5–8/180. Wife, Evelyn, 1837 Crete St., New Orleans. Signed on the Grace Line freighter *Cacique* on February 28, 1944, at New Orleans as third mate and arrived at New York on April 10, 1944, from Curaçao. Signed on the *O'Brien* at New Orleans on December 22 and paid off at end of voyage.

Ganley, William G., 31, acting second mate. Signed on the *O'Brien* at New Orleans on December 21 and paid off after the voyage.

Crosby, John Lawrence, 20, third mate, 1 yr., 5–8/175. Father, James H., 5331 Laurel St., New Orleans. Signed on the *O'Brien* at New Orleans on December 22. Paid off, went home, and signed on the *Milton H. Smith* at New Orleans in October 1945 as second mate and arrived at New York on May 15, 1946, from Antwerp. Paid off at end of voyage.

De Waard, Gerrit, chief radio operator. Signed on the *O'Brien* at New Orleans on December 16 and paid off at end of voyage.

Callahan, John, 20, second radio operator, 2 yrs., 6–1/175. Father, John, 1804 Washington Ave., New York. Signed Articles on December 20 at New Orleans and declared a deserter on the 29th. Rejoined the ship at Houston. Paid off at end of voyage.

Hubbard, Merrill E., 34, third radio operator, 1 mo., 5–10/140. Wife, Alice, 125 S. 1st St., Princeton, Illinois. Signed on the *O'Brien* at New Orleans on December 20 and paid off at end of voyage.

Haney, Edwin, purser/pharmacist's mate. Signed on the *O'Brien* at New Orleans on December 16 and paid off at end of voyage.

Sterling, William, 28, bosun, 4 years, 5–7/160. Signed on at Houston on January 12 and paid off at end of voyage.

Samaras, Theodore, carpenter. Signed on the *O'Brien* at New Orleans on December 16. Paid off and went back to New York and signed on the *Towanda Victory* in early August.

Lopez, Manuel, able seaman. Signed on the *O'Brien* at New Orleans on December 16 and paid off at end of voyage. Went back to New York and on August 21 signed on the *Mary Lyon* as an AB and arrived at Pearl Harbor on June 13 from Guam.

Salas, Louis E., able seaman. Signed on the *O'Brien* at New Orleans on December 16 and paid off at end of voyage. Signed on the *Zoella Lykes* on July 25, 1945, at San Francisco as an AB and arrived at Seattle, Washington, on November 12 from Tacloban, Leyte, Philippines.

Stallings, Paul Walkins, 20, acting able seaman, 1½ yrs., 5–10/135. Father, Oscar, Box 116, Spiro, Oklahoma. Signed on the *David Wilmot* at New York as an AB and arrived back there on July 12, 1944, after two voyages. On August 8 he signed on Capt. Oscar Southerland's Grace Line motorvessel *Oldham* at Galveston, Texas, and paid off on October 13 at Pier 13, North River, New York. He got to New Orleans and signed on the *O'Brien* on December 17 then paid off and signed on the American Export Lines motorship *Mariner's Splice* as AB for two voyages and arrived at New York on November 9 from Neuvitas, Cuba.

Patterson, Spellman, 21, able seaman, 1½ yrs., 5–10/150. Mother, Ruby, Rt. 2, Pocahontas, Arkansas. Signed on the *David Wilmot* at New York as an AB and arrived back there on July 12, 1944, after two voyages. On August 8 he signed on Capt. Oscar Southerland's Grace Line motorvessel *Oldham* at Galveston, Texas, and paid off on October 13 at Pier 13, North River, New York. He got to New Orleans and signed on the *O'Brien* on December 17 then paid off and signed on the American Export Lines motorship *Mariner's Splice* as AB for two voyages and arrived at New York on November 9 from Neuvitas, Cuba.

Carman, Max F., 23, acting able seaman, 1 yr., 5–11/175. Mother, Laura, Rt. 7, Ottumwa, Iowa. Made two voyages on the Panama-flag Pan-American Petroleum Tramp Co. tanker *Pan*

Mai Ne as an ordinary seaman and arrived at New York on November 15, 1944, from Liverpool. Signed on the *O'Brien* at New Orleans on December 19 and paid off at end of voyage.

Sunday, Vincent, 24, acting able seaman, 3 yrs., Dutch, 5–9/205. Wife, Pauline, Box 325, Sarasota, Florida. Signed on the American Export Lines motorship *New Orleans* on August 25, 1944, at New Orleans as an ordinary seaman and arrived at New York on October 2 from Manati, Cuba. Went home on shore leave, signed on the *O'Brien* on December 18 and paid off in San Francisco.

Douglas, Caral, 20, ordinary seaman, 4 mos., 5–11/155. Mother, Isabel Douglas, 514 Eliza St., New Orleans. Signed on the *O'Brien* at New Orleans on December 20 as Carroll Douglas and paid off at end of voyage.

Kmieciak, Paul John, 21, ordinary seaman, 3 yrs., 5–11/130. Wife, Pauline, 2158-A S. 15th Pl., Milwaukee, Wisconsin. Signed Articles on December 28, 1944, at New Orleans, declared a deserter on the 29th, and rejoined the ship at Houston. Hospitalized at Hollandia on May 16, 1945. On May 26 he signed on the *James A. Bayard* and again was sent to the hospital. He then went back aboard the ship as a passenger and arrived at New Orleans on September 4, 1945, from Manila.

Daly, David R., 18, ordinary seaman, 1 month, 5–8/145. Signed on the *O'Brien* at Houston on January 19, 1945, and paid off after the voyage.

Engine Department

Montgomery, Richardson, chief engineer. Signed on the *O'Brien* at New Orleans on December 16. Paid off after the voyage and signed on the Grace Line Liberty ship *W. R. Grace*.

Tagert, John M., 29, first assistant engineer, 6 yrs., 6–0/220. Wife, Stephanie, 8229 Stroelitz St., New Orleans. Left New York in October 1941 and arrived back at New York on December 18 as senior first assistant engineer on Grace Line's cargo liner *Santa Clara*. Signed on the Pan Atlantic freighter *Pan York* on August 28, 1944, at New Orleans as third engineer and arrived at New Orleans on September 27 from Cartagena, Columbia. Signed on the *O'Brien* at New Orleans on December 20. Paid off after the voyage and signed on the Grace Line freighter *Alden Besse* as chief engineer

Torppa, Ero John, 28, second assistant engineer, 3½ yrs., 5–10/160. Mother, Selma, 507 N. Division St., Hurley, Wisconsin. Left New York in September 1944 on the *Nathaniel Bacon* and signed on the *O'Brien* at New Orleans on December 19. Paid off at end of voyage.

Simpson, Roy E., 23, third assistant engineer, 1 yr., 6–2/160. Father, Claude A. Simpson, 4100 W. Olympic Blvd., Los Angeles. Signed on the *O'Brien* at New Orleans on December 19 and paid off at end of voyage. Signed on the Union Oil tanker *Orson D. Minn* on May 24, 1946, at San Francisco as second engineer and arrived at Port Angeles, Washington, on May 29 from Vancouver, British Columbia.

Wentworth, Harris G., junior engineer. Signed on the *O'Brien* at New Orleans on December 16 and paid off at end of voyage.

Kemper, Paul S., oiler. Paid off and went right back to New York and signed on the States Marine Liberty ship *John H. Murphy* on August 8 as an oiler and arrived back at New York from Rotterdam on September 7. Signed on the *O'Brien* at New Orleans on December 16 and paid off at end of voyage.

Lanier, Clinton, 25, oiler, 6 yrs., 6–1/165. Mother Mrs. K. L. Reynolds, 101 Panama St., San Antonio, Texas. Signed on the *O'Brien* at New Orleans on December 20 and paid off at end of voyage.

Brooks, Melton Green, III, 19, oiler, 6 months, Irish, 5–8/155, ptsosis of left eyelid. Signed on the Cleveland-Cliffs Iron Co.'s Shipping Board laker *Yosemite* at Toledo, Ohio, in 1944 as a coal passer, made two or more voyages, and arrived at Duluth, Minnesota, from Fort William, Ontario, on September 7, 1944. Signed on the *O'Brien* at Houston on January 16, 1945, and paid off at end of voyage.

Anderson, Herbert, 33, fireman/watertender, 1 yr., 6–0/165. Mother, Selma, 109 W. Melendy St., Ludington, Michigan. Signed on the *O'Brien* at New Orleans on December 27 and paid off at end of voyage.

Morris, Wilbert, 42, fireman/watertender, 8 yrs., 5–7/140. Mother, E. Belle Morris, 585 Celtic St., Akron, Ohio. Signed on the *O'Brien* at New Orleans on December 28 and paid off at end of voyage.

Orondez, Louis, 38, fireman/watertender, Honduran national, 12 years, 5–8/175. Signed on at Houston on January 12, 1945, and paid off at end of voyage.

Hemphill, Billie, 16, wiper, 6 mos., 6–0/165. Guardian, Minnie B. Thomas, 2624 5th Ave. S., Birmingham, Alabama. Signed on the *O'Brien* at New Orleans on December 20 and paid off at end of voyage. In 1947 he was a 6-foot, 200-lb., 19-year-old fireman/watertender on the Waterman freighter *Charles Goodyear*.

Wajda, Stanislaus, 31, wiper, 2 months, 5–6/155, signed on at Houston on January 8, 1945, and paid off at end of voyage.

Steward Department

Edwards, Howard, 33, chief steward, 2 yrs., 5–8/140. Wife, Dorothy, 216 Carr St., Fulton, Kentucky. Signed on the *O'Brien* at New Orleans on December 18 and paid off at end of voyage.

Hegarty, Philip, chief cook. Signed on the *O'Brien* at New Orleans on December 16 and paid off at end of voyage and signed on the *Bardstown Victory* at Pier 2, North River, New York in October 1945.

Denny, Edward, 27, second cook & baker, 3 yrs., 5–10/155. Cousin, Miss Bertha Bina, 7009 Union St., Cleveland, Ohio. Signed on the *O'Brien* at New Orleans on December 28 and paid off at end of voyage. Hospitalized at Mindoro, Philippines, on March 24, 1945.

Mestayer, Charles, 18, third cook, 8 yrs., 5–8/135. Father, Stanley B., Loreauville, Louisiana. Signed on the *O'Brien* at New Orleans on December 28 and paid off at end of voyage.

Vasquez, Ivan, 38, messman, Puerto Rican, 3 yrs., 5–9/180. Wife, Rosa at La Osiba, Spanish Honduras, Central America. Signed on the *O'Brien* at New Orleans on December 26 and paid off at end of voyage.

Sumrall, Robert, 17, messman, 3 mos., 6–2/160. Mother, Nessie, 726 St. John St., Bogalusa, Louisiana. Signed on the *O'Brien* at New Orleans on December 27 and paid off at end of voyage.

Vaughn, Don, 19, messman, 4 mos., 5–10/165. Mother, Evelyn Vaughn Whitman, 776 Sarcee Ave., Akron, Ohio. Signed on the *O'Brien* at New Orleans on December 28. Hospitalized at Canal Zone on January 25, off the ship.

Thomas, Emmett, 18, messman, 1 month, 6–1/185. Signed on at the Canal Zone on January 25, 1945, to replace Vaughn.

Dias, Jose Do Nasimento, utility. Signed on the *O'Brien* at New Orleans on December 16. Signed on for Voyage No. 7.

Frazher, Jeff, 17, utility, 6 months, 5–11/150. Signed on at Houston on January 12, 1945, and paid off at end of voyage.

Lause, John, 49, utility, 7 yrs., 5–6/150. Wife, Thelma at Bellefontaine, Mississippi. Signed on the *O'Brien* at New Orleans on December 18 and paid off after the voyage.

Armed Guard (all USNR unless otherwise noted)

Robinson, Ens. Norman E., commanding officer.

Doyle, James, Coxswain; Conklin, Charles, GM3c, hospitalized in the Canal Zone, off the ship; Howell, Ballard L., GM3c, joined at the Canal Zone to replace Conklin; Crocker, Robert, GM3c, USN; Morieko, Henry, GM3c; Andrews, John, SM3c; Kuhlman, William, SM3c; Armour, Wesley, S1c, hospitalized at Olongapo, Philippines. Off the ship; Barnett, Clarence, S1c, USN; Bator, Louis, S1c; Bartels, Leroy George, S1c; Carver, Earl, S1c; Casey, James Daniel, S1c; Crumley, Orval, S1c; Curtis, Johnny, S1c; Davis, John Wesley, S1c, received a telegram at Cristobal on January 25, 1945, saying his mother was in the hospital and he was granted leave; Dickinson, Eryl B., S1c, joined to replace Armour; Hassler, Cleveland, S1c, hospitalized on May 22, 1945, not replaced; Henzen, Marion, S1c; Kennedy, David, S1c; Kermit, Roy, S1c; Martin, Theodore, S1c; Ogonowski, Albert, S1c; Poskie, George, S1c; Salandino, Joseph, S1c; Swan, Robert, S1c, USN; Veatch, Louis Elmer, S1c, joined at Canal Zone to replace Davis; Williams, Vernon, S1c; Wilson, Robert, S1c.

Army Cargo Security Officer

1st Lt. Peter Warner, Jr., USA

Voyage No. 7

With one exception, Jose Dias, an entirely new crew signed Articles at San Francisco on July 11, 1945, for the ship's last wartime voyage. It would appear that that none of the Asian crewmembers wanted to sail in the Pacific and those seamen who were accustomed to shipping out of East Coast ports went back East to get another ship.

Departed San Francisco on the 24th and arrived at San Pedro on the 26th where they took on a cargo of general merchandise and jeeps on deck for Calcutta, India.

Departed San Pedro on August 3, 1945, and on August 15, word was received that Japan had finally surrendered and on August 24 they sighted Guadalcanal about five miles away.

The name evokes memories of every aspect of the war in the Pacific—jungle fighting, aerial combat, and horrendous nighttime naval engagements.

After Japan experienced numerous surprises at Midway, among them the dedication and fierce determination of Torpedo 8, qualities they did not expect in soft, lazy Americans, and then suffered the loss of Guadalcanal, the Japanese high command knew for certain by early 1943 they could not hope to win the war. The cherished dreams of Tōjō's Army—the Nipponese "spirit" and the inherent superiority of the Yamato people prevailing over the weakness of Americans despite their industrial might—was crushed very early in the war. Diplomats like Mamoru Shigemitsu had seen inevitable defeat early on and had tried to resolve the conflict on terms the Army would accept while others like Gen. Yoshijirō Umezu wanted to fight to the death no matter what. By the time the two faced Gen. Douglas MacArthur on the deck of the USS *Missouri* (BB-63) on September 2, 1945, in Tokyo Bay, Shigemitsu had won, although far too late to suit him, and Umezu had lost, unable to defy His Majesty the Emperor.

The *O'Brien* continued on past Guadalcanal and arrived at Port Darwin, Northern Territory, Australia, on September 2. They departed on the 4th for Calcutta and arrived on September 23. Cargo was offloaded and they took aboard general merchandise, aviation fuel, and vehicles.

They departed Calcutta on October 12 and anchored near the port of Shanghai, China. Departed Shanghai on November 16 and arrived at Manila, Philippines, on November 21 where most of the Armed Guard crew was detached from the ship.

Departed Manila on the 26th and arrived at Fremantle, Australia, on December 6 and loaded wool and hides. The Australian passengers were embarked and they departed on December 15. The passage was uneventful and they arrived at a San Francisco anchorage on January 13, 1946, and tied up at Pier 40 on the 17th.

Voyage 7 was the *O'Brien*'s last wartime voyage, after 2 years, 6 months, and 25 days of service since the ship first hit the water on June 19, 1943. The ship was then mothballed at the reserve site in Suisun Bay near Benicia and while a Voyage No. 8 was a distinct possibility, no one in their wildest dreams ever thought it would happen in 1994.

THE CREW

Master

Gerdes, George, 42, master, 20 years at sea, German, 6–1/180. Capt. Gerdes joined the ship at San Pedro on July 27. Hellmuth Gerdes was born on August 17, 1903, in Bremerhaven, Germany, arrived at New York on April 25, 1923, on the steamer *Yorck*, followed the sea, and became a citizen as George Gerdes on October 18, 1928. In 1930 he lived with his wife Kate (Christine), 26, in a rooming house at 304 86th St. in Manhattan. Kate was born in Lehe, Germany, and came to America in 1929. At the end of the voyage, Capt. Gerdes left San Francisco and went back to the East Coast to take command of the Grace Line Liberty ship *Henry Wells* at Baltimore on February 26. He arrived at Wilmington, North Carolina, on May 2 from Tocopilla, Chile.

Deck Department

Moen, Martin C., 49, chief mate, 20 years, Norwegian, 6–0/210. Arrived at San Francisco on May 19, 1945, as chief mate on the Grace Line C-2 freighter *Santa Teresa*. On November 15, Moen became ill and was transferred to the hospital ship *Repose* (AH-16) then lying at Shanghai. He was paid off, base pay $254/mo.

Sgerup, Einar, 35, chief mate, 14 years, Norwegian national, 6–1/160. Signed on at Shanghai on November 15, to replace Moen, base pay $254/mo.

Holmes, David, 24, second mate, 4 years, 6–2/149, from Illinois, base pay $220/mo. Signed on the *Alcoa Patriot* at San Francisco as third mate on September 5, 1944, and arrived at San Francisco on December 3 from Tarawa, Gilbert Islands. Paid off the *O'Brien* and signed on the *St. John's Victory* as second mate on March 29, 1946, at New York and arrived at Honolulu on September 1 from Cebu, Philippines.

Kent, Charles R., 30, third mate, 5 years, 5–7/140, from Minnesota, base pay $202/mo. Signed on the *Agwiprince* at San Francisco on March 9, 1945, as third mate and arrived back there on May 20 from Iwo Jima. Paid off the *O'Brien* and signed on the *Trinity Victory* at San Francisco as third mate on March 5, 1946, and arrived back there on April 2 from Port Alberni, British Columbia.

Petherbridge, Roy E., 20, chief radio operator, 2 years, 5–11/155, from Illinois, base pay $187.50/mo.

Hanyak, Edward L., 19, second radio operator, 1 year, Dutch, 5–10/155, from Pennsylvania, base pay $165/mo. Arrived at San Francisco on July 11, 1945, after two voyages as second radio operator on the Grace Line C-2 freighter *Santa Teresa* from Saipan, Mariana Islands. Paid off the *O'Brien* and went back aboard the *Santa Teresa* as chief radio operator.

Meador, Bruce S., 20, junior assistant purser/pharmacist's mate, 1 year, Scotch, 5–2/200, from Texas, base pay $175/mo. Paid off the *O'Brien* and apparently quit the sea.

Gallagher, Robert, 35, bosun, 10 years, Irish, 5–9/150, base pay $112.50/mo.

Kellner, Carlos Q., 35, tools carpenter, 4 years, Honduran national, 5–9/140, base pay $112.50/mo.

Novick, Frank, 38, able seaman, 5 years, Irish, 5–8/150, from New Jersey, base pay $100/mo. Paid off the *O'Brien* and signed on the *Washington* as quartermaster at New York on July 22 and arrived back there on August 13 from Cobh, Ireland.

Brox, Phillip J., 49, able seaman, 4 years, 5–6/130, from Utah, base pay $100/mo. Signed on the American Export Lines freighter *Cape San Lucas* at Long Beach, California, on August 25, 1944, as an AB and arrived at San Francisco on November 3 from Finschaven, New Guinea. Signed on the *Taos Victory* at Long Beach on February 1, 1945, and arrived at New York on May 31 from Capetown, South Africa. Headed west on leave and signed on the *O'Brien*.

Paddy, Robert J., 20, able seaman, 1 year, Scotch/Hebrew, 5–9/140, from New Jersey, base pay $100/mo. Signed on his first ship, the *Susan V. Luckenbach*, as an ordinary seaman on July 8, 1944, at New York and arrived back at New York from Milford Haven, England, on October 18. Paid off the *O'Brien* and signed on the United Fruit motorship *Long Eye* at New York in July 1946.

Cicic, George, 30, able seaman, 4 years, 5–7/165, from Michigan, base pay $100/mo.

Coats, William C., 19, able seaman, 6 months, 5–9/145, from Texas. Signed on at San Pedro, Calif., July 28, base pay $100/mo.

Anderson, Roy, 19, able seaman, 3 years, 6–0/155, from New York, base pay $100/mo. Apparently missed the ship in Australia as he did not arrive in San Francisco.

Watt, Kennedy, 45, able seaman, 30 years, British subject, 5–8½/140. Signed on at Fremantle, Australia, December 15.

Delgado, Pedro A., 18, ordinary seaman, 1 year, Spanish, 5–5/130, from California, base pay $82.50/mo.

Branson, Layton E., 23, ordinary seaman, 1 year, Irish, 5–11/150, from Utah, base pay $82.50/mo.

Pearson, Oscar Donald, 19, ordinary seaman, 1 year, 5–10/145, from Utah, base pay $82.50/mo. First trip was aboard the *Nancy Lykes* as an ordinary seaman. Signed on at San Francisco on February 5, 1944, and arrived back at San Francisco on April 16. Signed on the *South Africa Victory* on May 4, 1944, at Portland, Oregon, as a wiper and arrived at San Francisco on September 3.

Engine Department

Weyls, Carl B., 54, chief engineer, 20 years, 5–8/145, base pay $384/mo. in 1930 he was an engineer at a foundry in Cleveland, Ohio. The chief retired to Pinellas, Florida, with his wife Beth and died on May 12, 1973.

Swanson, George A., 53, first assistant engineer, 20 years, 6–3/200. Signed on at San Pedro, Calif., July 28, from Illinois, base pay $254/mo. Signed on the *John S. Bassett* as second engineer at Los Angeles on November 21, 1944, and arrived at San Francisco on January 5, 1945, from Honolulu. Possibly stayed on for another voyage.

Kranich, Donald E., 24, second assistant engineer, 4 years, German, 5–10/150, from California, base pay $320/mo. Signed on the *August Belmont* on March 8, 1945, at New York as second engineer and arrived back at New York on June 12 from Murmansk, Russia. Headed west on leave and signed on the *O'Brien*. Paid off and signed on the *Western Reserve Victory* as junior third engineer on February 26, 1946, at San Francisco and arrived back there from Saipan on October 20.

McGinty, Charles Joseph, 35, third assistant engineer, 5 years, Irish, 5–4/130, base pay $202/mo. Paid off and made two voyages on the Grace Line freighter *Whirlwind* as third engineer out of San Francisco and arrived back there on August 16, 1946, from Vancouver, British Columbia.

Pennington, Theodore J., 25, deck engineer, 3 years, 5–9/170, from Missouri, base pay $117.50/mo. Signed on the *Tulane Victory* as fourth engineer at San Francisco on April 28, 1945, and arrived at San Francisco on June 22, 1945, from Tinian, Mariana Islands. Paid off the *O'Brien* and signed on the *Dickinson Victory* at Seattle on March 19, 1946, as junior third engineer and arrived back at Seattle on May 15 from Kobe, Japan.

Schinskey, Thomas L., 26, oiler, 5–8, from Ohio, base pay $110/mo. He was hit by a car while riding a bicycle in Calcutta and taken to an Army hospital. He was paid off $363.14 on October 2 and arrived at New York from Calcutta on December 28, 1945, as a patient aboard the Navy transport *General W. F. Hase* (AP-146).

Santos, Rafael, 24, oiler, 5 years, Puerto Rican, 5–9/150. Reported aboard at Calcutta on September 28 to replace Schinskey. Signed Articles on October 1, base pay $110/mo. Santos had signed Articles in New York on August 4, 1945, as an oiler aboard the Waterman freighter *Topa Topa* and was hospitalized at Calcutta on September 13.

Anderson, Robert H., 25, oiler, 4 years, 5–9/140, from California, base pay $110/mo.

Wolfe, Harold W., 25, oiler, 24, 5–8/140, from Texas, base pay $110/mo.

Taibo, Manuel, 25, fireman/watertender, 3 yrs., Honduran national, 5–7/145. Signed on the *John G. Tod* at San Francisco as a wiper on January 5, 1945, and arrived back there on May 10. Signed on the *O'Brien* at San Pedro on July 28, base pay $110/mo. Paid off the *O'Brien* and signed on the *A. Frank Lever* at San Francisco on March 20, 1946, as an oiler and arrived at Honolulu from Shanghai on November 8. When the ship reached Portland, Oregon, Taibo and another Honduran oiler, Marcelino A. Castro, were detained by the Immigration Inspector for several days, until the 21st.

Hoard, Charles E., 18, fireman/watertender, 1 yr., 5–8/135, from Oklahoma, base pay $110/mo.

Fogle, Howard W., 18, fireman/watertender, 1 year, 5–9/150, from Ohio, base pay $110/mo. Made two voyages on the Black Diamond Liberty ship *Leon S. Merrill* as a fireman/watertender out of Boston and arrived at New York on June 15, 1945, from Plymouth, England. Headed west on leave and signed on the *O'Brien*.

Giacchi, Albert, Jr., 18, wiper, 1 year, Polish, 5–8/145, from New Jersey, base pay $87.50/mo. Signed on the *Jesse Billingsley* at New York on February 23, 1945, as an oiler and arrived back there on April 25 from Antwerp. Headed west and signed on the *O'Brien*. Paid off and signed on the Trinidad Corp. tanker *Fort Mims* as a fireman/watertender on November 12, 1946, at New York and arrived back there on May 8, 1947, from Montreal after two voyages.

Burton, Edward A., 18, wiper, 1 year, 5–8/140, from South Carolina, base pay $87.50/mo.

Steward Department

Lazono, Juanito M., 47, chief steward, 20 years, Filipino, 5–5/145, signed on at San Pedro, Calif., on July 28, base pay $147.50/mo.

Candias, Joseph, 55, chief cook, 20 years, Slovakian, 5–1/139, base pay $132.50/mo.

Flowers, Robert C., 28, second cook & baker, 4 years, Honduran national, 5–5/145, base pay $117/mo.

Dias, Jose Do Nasimento, third cook, base pay $112.50/mo. Paid off the *O'Brien* and headed back East and signed on T. J. Stevenson's *M. I. T. Victory* at New York on March 12 as a galley utilityman. He arrived back at New York from Le Havre, France, on May 11.

La Gates, Aloys F., 17, utility/messman, 1 year, 5–8/135, from Missouri, base pay $87.50/mo. Signed on his first ship, the Robin Line freighter *Robin Doncaster*, on November 11, 1944, at San Francisco, as a wiper and arrived back at San Francisco on April 22, 1945, from Hollandia, New Guinea. Paid off and apparently quit the sea.

Shaw, Morris, 42, utility/messman, 4 years, 5–5/130, from California, base pay $87.50/mo. Paid off the *O'Brien* and signed on the Sprague freighter *Wideawake* on August 1, 1946, at San Francisco as a utilityman and arrived at New York on September 14 from Danzig, Poland.

Tozer, Richard C., Jr., 17, utility/messman, 1 year, 5–9/149, from Illinois, base pay $87.50/mo.

Sizemore, Joseph T., 18, utility/messman, 1 year, German, 5–5/135. Paid off the *O'Brien* and signed on the *Westminster Victory* at New York on March 21 as a messman and arrived back there on April 16 from Le Havre, France.

Mason, Roy O., 17, utility/messman, 1 year, 5–10/145, from Illinois, base pay $87.50/mo. Signed on at San Pedro, California, on August 2. Declared a deserter on December 15 at Perth, Australia, and pay due of $106.20 was turned over to the U.S. Shipping Commissioner. Went aboard the Matson freighter *Morning Light* on March 18, 1946, at Sydney, Australia, for repatriation and arrived at San Francisco on April 15 from Suva, Fiji Islands.

Clarke, Terrance, 28, galleyman, 8 years, Australian national, 6–0/170, base pay $87.50/mo. Signed on at Fremantle, Australia, on December 15 to replace Mason.

Ward, George E., Jr., utility/messman, from Missouri, base pay $87.50/mo. Suddenly became ill on November 15, 1945, just before the ship was due to leave Shanghai and was taken to the hospital ship *Repose* (AH-16) then lying at Shanghai. Paid off $711.32. Signed on the *Robert M. T. Hunter* on July 3, 1945, at Philadelphia as a utilityman and arrived at New York on August 16 from Antwerp.

Porter, Francis D., 17, utility/messman, 1 year, 5–11/185, from Utah, base pay $87.50/mo. Signed on the *Henry Villard* at New York as a galley utilityman on March 30, 1945, and arrived back there from Antwerp, Belgium, on June 1. Headed west on leave and signed on the *O'Brien*. Paid off and signed on the *James Ford Rhodes* at New York on January 31, 1946, as second cook and arrived back there on April 12 from Leghorn, Italy.

Armed Guard (all USNR unless otherwise noted)

McGowan, Ambrose Patrick, lieutenant, commanding officer. Lt. (jg) McGowan commanded the Armed Guard detachment on the *Harold I. Pratt* and arrived at New York on May 18, 1945. McGowan was born to Hugh and Nora McGowan, natives of Ireland, on March 19, 1910. He graduated from college and in 1940 lived with his 67-year-old widowed mother and brother Arthur, 28, at 30 Prospect St., Branford, Connecticut. He was an interviewer at a state employment agency making $1,700 a year. After the war he became an assistant personnel director at a VA hospital and died on March 28, 1986, at New Haven.

Martin, Theodore S., Coxswain, remained on board at Manila; Wilson, Robert Lee, Coxswain; Crocker, Robert, GM3c; Erwin, Bert, GM3c; Morieko, Henry Walter, GM3c; Poskie, George Joseph, GM3c; Andrews, John R., SM3c; Kuhlman, William Clayton, SM3c; Barnett, Clarence Earl, S1c; Carver, Earl Roy, S1c; Casey, James Daniel, S1c; Cook, Ira Jim, S1c; Cunningham, Charles Thomas, S1c; Crumley, Orval Franklin, S1c; Curtis, Johnny McDonald, S1c; Davey, Joseph Sherlock, S1c; Dent, Henry H., Jr., S1c; Dickinson, Eryl, S1c; Flores, Yeon, S1c; Henzen, Marion LaVerne, S1c; Kelly, Thomas Frederick, S1c; Kennedy, David Bicking, S1c; La Fave, Paul Peter, S1c; Luckas, Frankie Lee, S1c; Ogonowski, Albert Joseph, S1c;

Saladino, Joseph Peter, S1c; Swan, Robert James, S1c, remained on board at Manila; Toalson, George A., S1c; Veatch, Louis Elmer, S1c; Walker, Casey Lonzo, S1c; Williams, Vernon Earl, S1c; Bartel, Clifford Francis, S2c.

All of the Armed Guard sailors except Martin and Swan were transferred off in Australia and their quarters aft were used to house war brides coming to the United States.

Quite a few Liberty ships were used to transport soldiers home in the quarters formerly occupied by the Armed Guard sailors. In early September 1945, the *Joseph H. Martin* brought 24 soldiers to Boston, the *Daniel Drake*, 31, and the *Felipp Mazzei* and *John Ireland*, 27 each.

War Bride Passengers

Arthur, Catherine Lillian, 26, born in Glasgow, Scotland, on August 18, 1919, and lived in Perth, Australia. Catherine had her 6-month-old daughter, Maria Florence with her. She married Edward James Arthur, a storekeeper third class on the *Montgomery* (DM-17) at Perth in 1941. He enlisted at St. Louis, Missouri, on October 18, 1939, and reported on board the DM on January 1, 1940. In March 1943 he was transferred to San Francisco for new construction and was assigned to the seaplane tender *Half Moon* (AVP-26) and went to Australia. On January 18, 1944, he was transferred for assignment in the 7th Fleet. They moved to Missouri where Catherine was naturalized. She died in Zephyrhills, Florida, on November 11, 1988.

Benesh, Edith Florence, 27, born and raised in Perth, Australia. Edith had a son Robert Antone, 2. She married Joseph Henry Benesh, a watertender first class on the seaplane tender *Childs* (AVD-1), stationed at Fremantle, Australia, in 1941. He was born on March 13, 1919, and enlisted in the Navy on May 18, 1937, at Omaha, Nebraska, and in 1939 was a fireman on the *Langley* (AV-3). When Pearl Harbor was attacked he was on the minesweeper *Heron* (AVP-2) at Port Clego, Philippines, and was transferred off on December 12, 1943, to the West Coast. He was discharged on July 14, 1952, and they lived in Linn County, Oregon. Edith died in May 1992 and Joseph on October 23, 1998 in Medford.

Czatynski, Doris Lesley, 30, born and raised in Subiaco, Australia. Dorrie L. Nevard married John Czatynski. He enlisted in the Navy on July 29, 1941, in Rhode Island, and was an engineman on submarines based at Fremantle. After he got out in July 1947 they lived in Wilmington, Delaware.

Dexter, Grace, 28, was born and raised in Perth, Australia. Grace Alver married Robert Royal Dexter, a motor machinist's mate first class on submarines based at Fremantle. They lived in Vermont where Robert worked in maintenance at Dartmouth College. He died in 1991.

Guillemette, Dorothy Leslie, 23, born and raised in Christchurch, New Zealand. Dorothy Petrie married sea captain Louis J. "Frenchy" Guillemette, a native of Canada. In 1949 they lived at 50 Rebekah St., Woonsocket, Rhode Island, where Louis was a painter. In 1961 they moved to 2814 10th St., Two Rivers, Minnesota, with daughters Sharon, 13, Susan, 9, and son John 13. It appears that in 1969 Dorothy moved back to Christchurch and on February 17, 1976, they divorced. Louis died on February 8, 1987, at Chula Vista, California.

Konkel, Doreen Liddie, 22, born in North Shields, England, and lived in Perth. Doreen had her son, Elsworth LeRoy, Jr., 8 months, with her. She married Elsworth LeRoy Konkel in Australia. He enlisted in the Navy on October 22, 1941, at Los Angeles, and was in the engine department on the submarine tender *Pelias* (AS-14) stationed at Fremantle. They lived in San Fernando, California, and in the mid–1950s moved to Australia. Elsworth died at Perth in 2005.

Marks, Patricia D., 34, born in Kelmscott, Australia, on August 29, 1911, and lived in Perth. She married Jack Gordon Marks in 1941 in Perth, He was a director with the Bank of

New South Wales and was in the service during the war. After hostilities ended they lived at 19 E. 80th St., Brooklyn. Jack was a law partner with Harry M. Marks at 521 Fifth Ave. They travelled extensively and she was naturalized on June 7, 1948.

Quackenbush, Thora Venetia, 24, born in Greenbrushes, Australia, and lived in Bunbury, Australia, just south of Fremantle. James Victor Quackenbush enlisted in the Navy at Dallas, Texas, on January 4, 1941, and reported on board the light cruiser *Phoenix* (CL-46) on July 23 as a seaman second class and was at Pearl Harbor during the attack. A year later he was a radioman third class and on April 15, 1943, he was transferred off to the Brisbane, Australia, Service Force replacement pool. The resided in Shawnee, Oklahoma.

Yocum, Brenda Kathleen, 20, born in Fremantle, Australia, and lived in Perth. Brenda Miller married Edward Cope Yocum. He enlisted in the Navy on January 18, 1942, at Philadelphia, and on January 26, 1945, reported aboard the submarine *Moray* (SS-300), commissioned that day at Philadelphia as an engineman second class. The sub was stationed at Fremantle. The couple settled in Philadelphia where Brenda kept house.

With no further operational orders forthcoming the crew sailed the ship to the newly-established National Reserve Fleet in Suisun Bay north of San Francisco where the ship was mothballed. The Navy took their guns off the ship, lifeboats and deck equipment were stored in the holds, and all machinery below was doused with Cosmoline. Normal maintenance was done until 1963 then ceased altogether and there the ship sat for 33 years and eight months.

But the Grace Line Liberty ship *Henry Wells* at Baltimore had more work to do and Capt. Gerdes took command on February 26, 1946. The ship arrived at Wilmington, North Carolina, on May 2 from Tocopilla, Chile.

PART VI

Post-War Restoration and
Voyages of the *Jeremiah O'Brien*

The official story of the preservation of the *Jeremiah O'Brien* begins in 1962 when Thomas J. Patterson, Jr., left the U.S. Navy and was hired by the Maritime Administration to help survey all the Liberty ships in the Suisun Bay reserve fleet at Benicia, California, as part of the post-war disposal program. He, along with one other shipmaster and two chief engineers, would go aboard each ship, rank them in order of condition, and specify which ones should be sold for scrap first.

On October 15, 1966, Congress passed the Historic Preservation Act that created a National Register for historic places and established a formal process for adding objects to the list. The Register was administered by the National Park Service and was intended to assist individuals, community groups, and organizations like the National Trust for Historic Preservation. This might have been the impetus for saving a ship and by that time Patterson knew the *O'Brien* was an excellent candidate given its overall condition and original configuration. Steps were then taken to keep the ship off the auction block and in 1970 he became the Maritime Commission's Western Region director.

Patterson said he went back to Washington in 1977 and talked to Capt. Harry Allendorfer, of the National Trust for Historic Preservation, to enquire about getting historic status for ships and applying for aid-in-kind grants. The original intention was to get the ship removed for historic preservation as a non-operating static display museum ship. He enlisted the aid of other Maritime Administration officials and lawyers to work out the details and also received help from other federal officials. Back home, he contacted local people in the San Francisco area to join in the effort and in 1978 a group of interested parties, mainly from the shipping and maritime labor industries, incorporated the non-profit National Liberty Ship Memorial, Inc., to take control of the ship and restore it as a memorial to merchant seamen, the Armed Guard, and the men and women who built the ships. Whether or not Congress got involved and exactly who authorized the transfer is unknown. In any case, the ship was withdrawn from the reserve fleet. The Maritime Commission retained ownership of the vessel, which was typical. When the Navy donates surplus ships for museum displays they never surrender ownership. They remove classified or sensitive equipment and might even remove the propellers so no one gets any funny ideas.

With the official approvals in hand, and with the goal of the NLSM to engage in historic preservation in mind, the Maritime Commission elected to bareboat charter the ship to the

National Park Service as the experts in historic preservation. The Park Service then executed a Cooperative Agency Agreement with NLSM under the Park Service's strict rules for the preservation of historic objects. On July 7, 1978, the ship was declared a National Historic Landmark and placed on the register of the National Trust for Historic Preservation as a historic object. At that time the *O'Brien* was the only National Historic Landmark that moved but since then the San Francisco cable cars have since been added to the list. In August 1978 the ship received a $10,000 matching grant from the National Trust for Historic Preservation to restore the ship's wood furniture and joinery work.

The next problem was getting the ship out of the reserve fleet and into drydock for major exterior cleanup and painting and then find a suitable home where the public could easily visit. Since the original idea was to create a static museum ship that sat at the dock where people could come aboard and look over the ship, like the other vessels at the Hyde Street Pier, the obvious solution was to hire a tugboat and tow it out. But Capt. Ernie Murdock, of the Coast Guard, suggested getting the old boilers and triple expansion engine going again and sail out of the fleet. It was a fantastic idea that had doubters and supporters. No one knew of any steamship that had sat for 33 years and been restored to operating condition. But Murdock also knew the ship had only operated for two and a half years and the odds were very good that the equipment was still in great shape. American President Lines chief engineer Harry Morgan, who became the *O'Brien*'s first post-war chief engineer, agreed and went aboard the ship in June of 1979 with a crew of other volunteers to look things over. It was a dead ship— no lights, no running water, no electricity, no toilets, and no food. John Pottinger, an ex– World War II Liberty ship sailor, was in charge of the reserve fleet by then and provided whatever tools or equipment was needed. They started by hiring a company to steam clean all the Cosmoline off everything and then worked on getting all the machinery going.

One major, indispensible aid they had was the use of a C1-M-AV1 coastal freighter the Army had up at Rio Vista on the Sacramento River. The 388-foot Maritime Commission ship was built in 1944 by Globe Shipbuilding at Superior, Wisconsin, and was operated by the Navy as the *Pembina* (AK-200) in the Southwest Pacific and in occupied Japan. In 1968 it was transferred to the Army Transport Service and named *Resolute*. The ship furnished fuel oil, boiler feed water, and compressed air to run and test machinery, an enormous advantage to the project.

Another big boost came in August 1979 when a matching grant totaling $436,532 was awarded by the Dept. of the Interior, the National Trust for Historic Preservation, and the state of California for general restoration.

On October 4, 1979, the engineers reported they had steam up and the ship was ready to leave. The official record states that at 11:15 a.m. on October 6, 1979, the ship was on "loan" to the Dept. of Interior "for Donation to National Liberty Ship Memorial" and on that day the ship steamed out of the reserve fleet with 503 people aboard to the Bethlehem Steel shipyard in San Francisco. It was a momentous event in American maritime history.

The question of where to dock the ship was next. The spot had to have plenty of parking for volunteers and visitors and be reasonably easy to get to. The National Park Service, being the charter party, owned Fort Mason, the former Army Port of Embarkation in the Marina District of San Francisco. Fort Mason was part of the Golden Gate National Recreation Area, the nation's first urban national park, and Fort Mason had three unused piers. Pier 3 East would be the *O'Brien*'s new home. The sheds on the piers were used for community events and the buildings housed various organizations and businesses. The former firehouse for the base was right at the head of Pier 3 and the building was offered to NLSM for office space, which would have been ideal, but for some reason it never happened. Instead the shore office was upstairs at Pier 1 and an on board office was set up in the after starboard cabin on the boat deck. Fort Mason was a great place for the volunteers but a somewhat out-of-the-way place for visitors to find. The ship could be plainly seen from the Aquatic Park pier but tourists or residents often didn't really know what they were seeing.

The ship left the Bethlehem yard on Saturday, May 21, 1980, for the first Seaman's Memorial Cruise. The ship steamed around San Francisco Bay and then went just outside the Golden Gate Bridge where a memorial service was held for World War II merchant seamen. The ship hove to and wreaths were thrown over the side to remember the young and old who never came home. The ship docked at Fort Mason, passengers disembarked and the volunteers.

Tom Patterson

Thomas J. Patterson, Jr. (1924–2008), was a native of Philadelphia and a 1944 Kings Point Merchant Marine Academy graduate who served in the merchant marine during World War II and in the Navy during the Korean War. When Tom was born his father was a carpenter in Philadelphia and they lived at 6512 Grays Ave. By 1930 dad had become a shipwright foreman and the family, Thomas, Sr., 29, Anna E., 28, Thomas, Jr., 5, Donald W., 6 mos., and Robert A., 1 mo., lived with his mother Anna's parents, William and Katherine Barnes and their son William J., 15, at 6803 N. 21st St. in Philadelphia. By 1935 the family had moved to 6605 Rodney St., Philadelphia, and in 1940 they were at 222 Parker Ave., Upper Darby, Pennsylvania.

In 1943 Tom entered the newly-opened Merchant Marine Academy at Kings Point, New York. An accelerated academic program was in effect to meet the urgent manpower demands, much like the Navy's "90-day Wonder" system. After a short stint in the classroom the cadet midshipmen were sent to sea. In October he signed on the Keystone Tankship Corp.'s 5-year-old, 10,342-ton, tanker *Seakay* under Capt. Alfred K. Jorgensen at Philadelphia.

The ship departed New York on October 17 went to Curaçao and sailed for Milford Haven in Convoy CV 6 then on to Cardiff, Wales, and Liverpool, England. They departed Liverpool on November 18 for New York but were diverted to Aruba due to a submarine alert and they arrived on November 31. They left Aruba on December 2 and arrived back at New York on December 7, 1943, in Convoy CU 9 after an uneventful voyage.

He stayed on for the next voyage under Capt. Jorgensen and left New York on December 15 for the UK in Convoy UC 9. They were detached on January 1, 1944, and sent back to the Delaware Capes. They left the Capes on the 29th and arrived at New York the same day in Convoy CU 13. They left again for the UK on February 18 and were detached again on the 25th due to a submarine alert and ordered to Curaçao. They arrived at New York on March 8, 1944, where Tom got off and went back to school.

Meanwhile, the *Seakay* departed on the 10th for Barry Roads in Convoy CU 17 and on March 18 the ship was torpedoed by *U-311* at 51°10'N/20°20'W. Capt. Jorgensen and the rest of the merchant crew survived. The only casualty was 19-year-old Armed Guard sailor, Laurier Bertrand Gervais, S1c. He was survived by his father Arthur, 59, mom Mary, 55, and sisters Margaret, 27, Yolanda, 20, and Rita, 16. The family lived at 13 Prospect St. in Livermore Falls, Maine.

Tom graduated in December 1944 and in March 1945 he signed on the brand-new 10,296-ton Keystone tanker *Cantigny* as 3rd mate for Voyage No. 1 under Capt. Jorgensen. The ship went to the UK then sailed to the Pacific, calling at Saipan and Ulithi delivering fuels. They went back through the Panama Canal and were at Mobile, Alabama, when the war ended.

Post-war service with Keystone lead to a master's license but he entered the Navy when the Korean War started and served on the troop transport *Union* (AKA-106). After that he was executive officer and, for a very brief time, commander of the radar picket ship *Guardian* (ARG-1), the ex–Liberty ship *James G. Squires*. After leaving the Navy in 1962 he joined the Maritime Administration.

In 1982 Patterson left MARAD to become deputy superintendent of the Merchant Marine Academy with the rank of commodore in the U.S. Maritime Service and in 1985 he retired and returned to California and was awarded the rank of admiral and assumed his position as chairman of the board of the National Liberty Ship Memorial, Inc.

Work on the Ship Commences

In the early 1980s the National Trust for Historic Preservation donated $3,000 for cathodic protection and the restoration of the refrigeration system and the National Maritime Museum Association donated $11,000. This work was completed on May 10, 1983. Memorial Cruises were held annually on National Maritime Day and on May 26–29 the crew made their first port visit, to Sausalito, the former home of Marinship, and participated in the city's fourth annual Maritime Days.

General cleanup, painting, and organizing got underway and gradually departments were formed. An old Norwegian salt named Per Dam was hired at $700 a month to supervise re-rigging of the cargo booms, lifeboats, etc., and to oversee the work on deck as new volunteers came aboard to help out. Per had gone to sea under sail at 14 and served as bosun on Liberty ships during the war.

On September 18, 1984, the American Society of Mechanical Engineers designated the *O'Brien*'s engine a National Historic Engineering Landmark.

The relationship with the Park Service, tentative as it was, initially created considerable hostility on the part of many of the original volunteers aboard the ship, primarily those who were retired merchant seamen and tended to see the ship as just another big, floating, gray thing that could use some improvements. More than a few were heard to say that if any ranger or Park official ever came aboard to tell them what they could or could not do they would leave the ship "so fast it would make your head spin." But the Park Service, for its part, wanted nothing to do with the *O'Brien*. They were having enough trouble keeping their own historic ships at the Hyde Street Pier afloat and didn't want or need any additional responsibilities.

The project presented a golden opportunity for the older volunteers who had been to sea to re-live their youth, get out of the house, fraternize with old salts like themselves and tell stories that one could believe, or not believe, as one chose.

After acquiring the ship, the goal of NLSM became twofold: to clean up the ship, make it presentable to the public, and make it a pleasant place for volunteers to work and socialize. And almost immediately the ship began to serve as an ideal place for those who enjoyed wearing uniforms, particularly Navy-style outfits, and certain modifications made to the ship tended to serve that purpose. Technically, the merchant marine was a uniformed service during the war, as the National Maritime Service, but the unlicensed sailors rarely wore their uniforms and the officers usually wore only their uniform hats at sea—either company hats or Maritime Service hats. Prior to the United States formally entering the war, military officials in England made it very clear that non-belligerents should not wear uniforms of any sort ashore in any part of His Majesty's realm and there was a certain amount of resentment among military and naval officers everywhere over rendering salutes Maritime Service or merchant service officers in general. As a rule, merchant seaman were not welcome at U.S.O. clubs during the war and after the war military veterans groups did not include members of the merchant marine.

Like most Liberty ships, the *O'Brien*'s original flagstaff was a relatively short, vertical pole positioned somewhere on or near the after deckhouse. The *O'Brien*'s flagstaff was welded to the deck just aft of the gun tub on the fantail. On other ships the staff was located somewhere on top of the after deckhouse or even in the gun tub and could be lowered when the gun was in use. For some reason, the original flagstaff was removed in the shipyard and a short gaff with a pulley on it was welded to the mizzen mast and another pole was welded to the hull, angled out from the stern—a typical Navy setup. When a Navy ship is moored, the Union Jack is flown at the jackstaff on the bow and the National Ensign is at the stern pole. When the ship gets underway, the command, "Shift colors, the ship is underway" is given and the Union Jack is put away and the National Ensign is hoisted to the gaff. There is no reason the original setup needed to be changed.

Most of the original interior pea green and gray paint was needle-gunned off steel bulkheads and every steel or wood surface was painted a uniform white. Two rooms on the main deck were left untouched, however. The starboard, forward Navy gunner's room was turned into a little storage and work space referred to as "gunners" and the messmen's cabin located inboard on the port side aft was used for storage.

One of the biggest and most essential modifications was to convert one of the deep tanks into a wastewater and sewage holding tank. The ship was designed to discharge everything over the side, in port or out, but those days were long gone.

The after gun platform has about a two-foot-high steel bulwark welded all the way around the circular part of the platform, which was probably meant to keep gunners and spent powder casings from falling all over the place. A waist-high steel rail was welded on top of this bulwark for increased safety, which was a necessary addition.

The early Liberty ships were armed with whatever weapons could be scrounged up, including .30 caliber machineguns left over from World War I and old 37-mm Army guns, and some of the very early ships left the yard unarmed. But by mid–1943 almost every ship had a 3"/50* mounted in the forward gun tub and a 5"/38 gun mounted on top of the after deckhouse so everyone assumed that a 5"/38 had been on top of the after deckhouse.

Two deck guns were donated to the ship by Vernon M. Richardson, a retired American President Lines chief engineer who founded Merchant Vessel Machinery Replacement, Inc., at Wilmington, California, in 1959. He acquired marine equipment and parts from surplus merchant vessels and sold them to ship operators, refineries, mills, power plants, and mine operators. The guns came from the Navy engine repair ship USS *Palawan* (ARG-10), placed in reserve at Suisun Bay in 1962. The guns were removed and brought over on a 120-foot crane barge donated by the Smith-Rice Co. at Alameda. Mr. Richardson is still in business at 214 Lakme Ave., Wilmington.

While collecting archival documents about the ship it was learned from the Armed Guard officer's reports that the ship never had a 5"/38. For some reason one was not available when the ship was at the outfitting pier so another 3"/50 was put aboard and the ship sent on its way.

Workspace for the volunteers was needed so the No. 5 hold 'tween deck was converted into the carpenter's and machinist's work and storage area with access through the helium bottle locker at the forward end of the after deckhouse portside. The original heavy rubber-gasketed door was retained.

The original carpenter shop is way up in the forepeak behind the chain locker and the bosun's stores and would have been very impractical to use. Access is through a hatch on the main deck and down a vertical ladder. The shop has steel racks for wood storage, including plywood, on the port side. Some of the early Liberty ships built on the West Coast made the access hatch with a diagonal measurement of 47½ inches. Unfortunately, a sheet of plywood is 48" × 96" so the carpenter had to rip a half inch off every sheet of plywood. Carpenters called this oversight "Kaiser's Folly."

The New Skipper

The ship's first volunteer master was Capt. Edward A. MacMichael (1914–1982), of Pennsylvania, an acquaintance of Tom Patterson who had also worked for the Maritime Administration. In July 1936 he was a student at the Pennsylvania Nautical School when he signed on the United States Lines passenger ship *President Harding* for his first trip as a cadet. Six years later he would take part in one of the earliest, harrowing episodes of World War II. In 1940 he was a 25-year-old second mate on the Maritime Commission's 1918 freighter *Tampa*, operated by the American Pioneer Company. The same year he signed on Capt. John M. Hatfield's brand-new United States Lines motor freighter *Sea Witch* as chief mate. The ship left New York in October 1941 on Voyage No. 2 but MacMichael joined the ship at San Pedro, California, on the 28th. They headed for Australia and, as fate would have it, war came in the middle of their voyage. At Australia plans were being made to make an attempt to reinforce the Army Air Corps on Java with about 120 P-40 fighters since the Navy's first aircraft carrier, the *Langley* (CV-1), was available at the time. The *Sea Witch* was in the right place at the right time to help out. The *Langley* took aboard 33 13th and 35th Pursuit Squadron pilots and 32 ready-to-fly planes and the *Sea Witch* took aboard 27 unassembled P-40s in crates.

Before the impending mission, oiler Albert Holmes, 36, paid off on February 5 at Melbourne, ordinary seaman John Haley, 43, and messman Thomas McGrath, 35, paid off on the 20th at Perth and on the day they were due to sail, the 22nd, engine maintenance man Ben Hale, 35, deserted the ship at Fremantle.

On February 22, 1942, they left Fremantle, Australia, to join Convoy MS 5 from Melbourne to Bombay, India. Adm. William A. Glassford, USN, planned for the two ships and light cruiser *Phoenix* (CL-46) to detach from the convoy near Cocos Island and then backtrack to Tjilatjap, the only port left in Java that wasn't yet under Japanese control. The operation was technically under Dutch Adm. Conrad Helfrich's control and based on information he had, he ordered the *Langley* and *Sea Witch* to break off much closer to Tjilatjap, proceed alone, and arrive early on February 28. But there was no airfield near Tjilatjap, there were no mechanics to put the crated planes together, and the Japanese were headed there. When Helfrich learned of this, he contacted Glassford and, with his concurrence, ordered the 31-knot *Langley* to race ahead and get there on the afternoon of the 27th since the carrier had planes that were at least ready to fly. The 14-knot *Sea Witch* would have to make best speed. On shore, Dutch and American destroyer sailors started clearing ground for an airfield but around noon on the 27th the *Langley* was attacked and sunk by Japanese aircraft about 75 miles south of Tjilatjap with the loss of 16 sailors. The *Sea Witch* managed to get in to port unscathed. The planes were unloaded onto lighters and brought ashore, but none ever flew. Capt. Hatfield took aboard 40 soldiers and headed back to Australia through sub-infested waters with reports coming in of Japanese surface ships in the area.

On July 15, 1942, chief steward William Perry, 43, died at Perth. The ship arrived at San Francisco on November 10, 1942, from Brisbane with 42 aboard.

Capt. MacMichael left the ship in mid–1982 for health reasons and died in August.

More Visitors Arrive

At first, the ship was open to visitors only on weekends, an event referred to as "Open Ship Weekend" but this soon changed to daily openings. The gangway admission receipts were modest but kept things going. It was decided to make annual Seamen's Memorial Cruises around the Bay on the third weekend of each May to coincide with National Maritime Day and the idea emerged to run the engine at slow speed, 13-rpms, at the dock on the third weekend of every month so visitors could see the engine run. An engineer would come aboard on Friday night to light off a boiler and the term "Steaming Weekend" was coined by volunteer Bob Burnett for this event. Some volunteers would come aboard Friday night, eat supper at a local restaurant, and on Saturday morning the Steward Dept. would fire up the coal-burning range and serve meals through Sunday lunch. Some volunteers came from a considerable distance away. Steaming Weekends were extremely popular with the volunteers and sometimes a little work even got done.

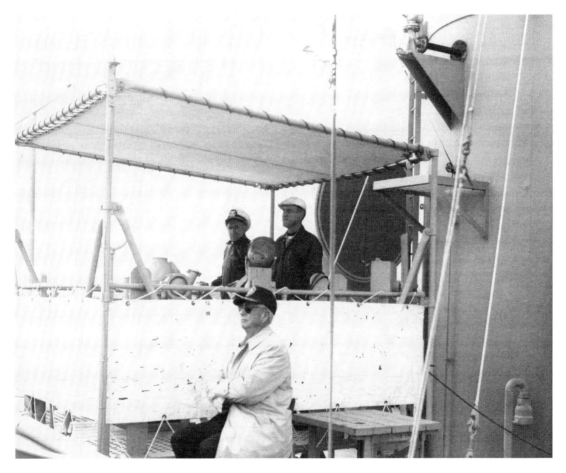

On the monkey bridge on a May Cruise in the 1980s. Bill Krasnoski, the mate in the high pressure hat, was a veteran of the Murmansk Run. When Pearl Harbor was attacked he was bosun on the North Steamship Corp. freighter *Leslie* en route from St. Lucia to Cuba. The ship was sunk on April 12, 1942. In the foreground is Capt. George Jahn, at the time a San Francisco Bay pilot who donated his services for the ship's annual May Cruises. He also served as master of the *O'Brien* on the ship's epic 1994 voyage to Normandy, France. The helmsman is Bob Burnett, an Army veteran, the *O'Brien*'s longtime shipkeeper. Photograph by the author.

At the Port of Sacramento in 1988 from the top of a rice silo. Looking at a map, you would wonder how a big ship could get to Sacramento. First, the elevation of West Sacramento is only 30 feet and sits at the confluence of two large rivers, the Sacramento and the American, and is about 80 miles from the Golden Gate. A 43-mile, 200-foot wide channel connects San Francisco Bay to West Sacramento. The idea goes all the way back to 1899 but wasn't realized until 1963. The Port of West Sacramento handles bagged and bulk rice for export, cement, lumber, and fertilizer. The Sacramento River Delta region is a major rice producer. Photograph by the author.

A system gradually evolved where the Deck Department did their major work on Wednesdays and the Engine Department worked on Thursdays but there were volunteers aboard every day of the week doing something, depending on a person's work, personal, or retirement schedule. The younger volunteers who still worked came on weekends. The normal volunteer workday was 8 a.m. to 3 p.m. and everyone wrote their name and hours worked in a ledger book kept in the crew's mess. Coffee break was at 10 and everyone brought a lunch.

Later on, Capt. Edward C. Lodigiani would come aboard on non–Steaming Weekend Sundays and make a very nice soup and salad lunch for the volunteers who were aboard. Capt. Eddie was born in Springfield, Massachusetts, and in 1940 was a maritime school cadet. He had just turned 23 when he signed on the brand-new Liberty ship *Mayo Brothers* on January 7, 1943, at New Orleans as second mate. They arrived at New York from Algiers on August 13.

The January 29, 1945, edition of *Stars and Stripes* reported that he had been chief mate on an Army transport under Capt. O. C. Jones, of Mobile, Alabama, headed to France with infantrymen when they ran into hurricane weather and 40–60 foot seas. Eddie and four sailors were trying to secure a life raft and were clinging to a steel rail when the rail gave way. Eddie and Gerald Byrne, a 26-year-old Canadian deck mechanic, Fred Henderson, the bosun from Glenwood, California, and two others were washed overboard. By some miracle, Henderson and Eddie were washed back aboard by the same wave that took them off. Byrne managed, by another miracle, to grab a painter and was pulled back aboard but the two other sailors were lost.

Much of the normal work involved routine maintenance and housekeeping, chipping and painting, bringing stores and supplies on board, and moving things around to make room for other things. A large amount of "surveyed" Navy haze gray paint in 5-gallon cans was obtained and used for many years until it ran out.

As time went on, the relationship with the managers of Fort Mason Center began to sour. One of the ways the ship got fuel was through donations of pretty much any liquid that would burn and could be pumped aboard. A backyard mechanic who changed his car's oil at home could leave the used oil at the gate and it would be picked and taken aboard. Likewise, companies that wanted to dispose of unwanted fuels or solvents could bring them down in barrels or even by tanker truck. On one occasion a company had made arrangements well in advance to deliver a large tanker truck of solvent to the ship. Unfortunately, the delivery date coincided with the very popular annual Landscape & Garden Show and the management was very upset about the noise from the pumping. The dock between the shed and the ship was not very wide, about 15 feet, and the show was in the shed on Pier 3 right next to the ship.

Besides the annual cruises in May, there were port visits to Sacramento, Redwood City, and the reserve fleet at Suisun Bay to scrounge equipment. Charter cruises and then Fleet Week cruises made their way into the schedule. The No. 2 'tween deck space was set up as a meeting area and was rented for all sorts of gatherings. Several marriages have taken place on the ship.

Voyage No. 8 and the Return to Portland

Voyage No. 7 ended in January 1946. Voyage No. 8 began in earnest on April 18, 1994, when the *O'Brien* steamed under the Golden Gate Bridge and headed for Portsmouth, England, via the Panama Canal to take part in the 50th anniversary of the Normandy Invasion. According to the D-Day Museum in Portsmouth, a total of 846 merchant vessels took part in the Invasion. The *O'Brien* was the only ship to return but there were several smaller vessels. HMS *Medusa*, the ex-*HDML-1387*, and the ex-*HDML-1410*, converted to the yacht *Fantasia* was there. The *Medusa* has been fully restored to its wartime configuration and appearance by volunteers. *ML 1387* was in the Channel Identification Group at Omaha Beach on D-Day.

A formal proposal for sailing the ship back to France for the 50th anniversary was presented to the NLSM board on December 10, 1987, by Ernie Murdoch, the *O'Brien*'s second chief engineer, after months of informal discussion by numerous volunteers. Those opposing the idea objected to the potential loss of the ship through a catastrophic accident of some sort or through the ordinary perils of the sea. Both were legitimate objections but those who favored the idea prevailed and plans went ahead. As the idea jelled and early reports on the ship's overall condition from naval architects and engineers came back positive, board members made trips to France and England to enquire about available berths and a provisional list of port visits was made up.

One of the primary concerns of the pre-voyage volunteers, perhaps the main concern, was the sailing status of the ship. The *O'Brien* was already a National Historic Landmark and all wondered what effect that would have on the trip. Would the ship be allowed to sail as a 1944 National Historic Landmark, essentially intact and enjoying the same status that vintage automobiles have on public roads? Would the ship sail in the same classification as a yacht and be required to have only the necessary life and safety gear, or would the ship be required to sail "in class" according to 1994 American Bureau of Shipping rules and regulations and Coast Guard safety standards?

CAPTAIN JAHN

Capt. George W. Jahn would be the skipper for the voyage. He had donated his services over the years as a San Francisco Bay pilot when the ship made the annual cruises. He was born on August 25, 1915, in San Francisco. In 1933 he went to sea with Dollar Steamship and by 1935 was a 19-year-old able seaman on the liner *President Wilson* sailing out of San Francisco. In mid–1936 he was sailing with Matson on the big 18,000-ton Oceanic Steamship Co. liner *Mariposa* sailing from San Francisco to Honolulu and Australia. He got his third mate's ticket, signed on Capt. George Sidon's 3,253-ton Matson freighter *Manini*, and by August 1941 he was second mate. On December 16, 1941, the ship left Honolulu and the next day they were torpedoed by *I-175*. The ship sank in a very few minutes leaving 34 survivors in two lifeboats. Able seaman Merritt L. Tompkins was lost aboard the ship and messman Jules H. Simmons died in a lifeboat. One boat with 16 survivors was rescued on the 28th by destroyer *Patterson* (DD-392) and the other boat was found two days later. Survivors recuperated in Honolulu and returned to San Francisco on the Matson liner *Maui* in January 1942.

On August 16, 1943, Capt. George Sidon, 49, took command of the brand-new Matson-operated Liberty ship *William Matson* out of Permanente Metals Yard 2. When they arrived at New York from Calcutta, India, on January 17, 1944, George, now 28, had his master's license and on February 14 he relieved Capt. Sidon at Pier 17 in Brooklyn. They took part in the Normandy Invasion and after another voyage arrived back at New York on December 10, 1944. He continued sailing after the war, ran tugboats, then became a Bay pilot.

As plans moved forward to the point of commitment, the Maritime Administration and Park Service had to sign off on the venture. The Maritime Administration, as owner of the vessel, demanded that the ship meet all current Coast Guard and ABS regulations and consequently, and unfortunately, the ship was transformed from a 1944 freighter to essentially a 1994 "working" commercial vessel.

As the *O'Brien*'s plan began to attract attention, John Boyleston, head of the restored Liberty troopship and former New York City school ship *John W. Brown* in Baltimore, proposed the idea of forming Convoy HX 355—The Last Convoy. The last Halifax-to-England convoy during the war was HX 354. The plan was for the *O'Brien* and the restored Victory ship *Lane Victory* at San Pedro, California, to meet up with the *Brown* off Bermuda and the three old ships would sail to England as a living memorial to the merchant seamen and Armed Guard sailors lost during the terrible days in the Atlantic when the U-boats took so many lives.

The two Liberty ships needed yard work. The *O'Brien* went into the San Francisco Drydock Co., the only commercial yard left in town, while the *Brown* organization chose to use the Bethlehem Steel Co. yard in Maryland, the same yard that built the ship.

San Francisco Drydock was on the ropes financially and by this time the *O'Brien* was seen as the City's ship—the ship that a group of old veterans wanted to sail to Europe for the 50th anniversary of the Normandy Invasion—to relive their youth and remember lost shipmates. No one in town wanted to be the ones to throw a wet blanket on their plan so the company responded and got to work. They figured if the ship got back the bill would be paid and if it didn't make it back, the company would go bankrupt anyway so what was there to lose? Rivets were replaced, heavy, structural crack arresters were welded to the overhead under the main deck, port and starboard, at the forward end of the reefer and dry stores flat and hold No. 3, and a million other jobs were done to please the demanding Coast Guard and American Bureau of Shipping inspectors. One big fear was that the Coast Guard would require the hull strapping that many Liberty ships had added to prevent breaking apart. That one item would have sunk the voyage.

Nevertheless, many unfortunate structural changes were made to the ship while in the shipyard. In the final days, *O'Brien*, maritime industry, and longshore volunteers swarmed over the ship cleaning and bringing stores aboard and the ship was secured for sea. Donations of all kinds came arrived daily but when we left town the organization was deeply in debt.

Back East, things were not going well for the *Brown*. The drydock inspection found that a voluminous number of rivets needed to be replaced. Unfortunately, the Bethlehem shipyard wanted all their money up front. The cost to do the necessary work was out of reach and there was no time for major fund raising. The *Brown* had to bow out.

Out West in San Pedro, the *Lane Victory* was all set to go and on the appointed day they departed for the rendezvous with the *O'Brien* off Southern California. But soon after leaving they found oil in their boiler feed water and put in to Acapulco, Mexico, for repairs. The problem was readily fixed and the crew thought they would be on their way again but the organization's board of directors inexplicably called them back to San Pedro. The *O'Brien* would sail alone.

THE ITINERARY

All of the volunteers who sailed from San Francisco were under Articles and had to participate in abandon ship and lifeboat drills.

The ship departed San Francisco on April 18 and arrived at the Western Approaches to the Panama Canal on the morning of the 30th. Fresh water was taken aboard and garbage taken off at the naval station, and a party was thrown for the crew. Departed at 10 the next morning, transited the Canal with about 125 American passengers, and arrived at Colon around 8:30 and took on fuel oil, water, and stores.

May 2 departed Colon on the Mona Pass-to-Bishop Rock Great Circle Route to England. On May 13 the ship was joined by the training ship *State of Maine*. Arrived off Bishop Rock just after midnight on May 21 and docked at the Portsmouth Naval Base on the 23rd. The other veterans of the Invasion were also at Portsmouth for the planned commemorations on June 6.

June 1 departed Portsmouth for Southampton at 10:45 a.m. and tied up at the same dock the *Titanic* left from at 2 that afternoon. The big liner *Queen Elizabeth II* was also in port.

June 4 departed Southampton for the Solent and anchored out for the big review by the Queen on the royal yacht *Britannia*. The next day President and Mrs. Clinton came aboard from the carrier *George Washington* (CVN-73) and were presented to the crew members who had brought the ship over from San Francisco. This occasion was reported to be the first time the Presidential flag had ever flown on a merchant vessel. Departed around 4 p.m. and headed across the Channel for the coast of France. Anchored off Pointe du Hoc around 2 a.m. on June 6 and left around 1 p.m. for the anchorage off Margate, England, in the Thames Estuary. All of the commemorative events of the day were happening ashore and the *O'Brien* crew was left to ponder the past and perform more or less ordinary work. The volunteer crew of the *HDML-*

A stern view of an old, plain, sea-worn freighter crowded in among 46 sleek, modern warships and beautiful, majestic tall ships at the L'Armada de la Liberté celebration at Rouen, France, in July 1994. The week-long event was attended by more than 6 million people. Photograph by the author.

Home again. Moored at the Maine State Pier on August 11, 1994. Pete Newell's old South Portland Shipyard is directly across the Fore River. Photograph by the author.

At anchor off Kings Point, New York, on August 16, 1994. Photograph by the author.

1387 stood off the invasion beachhead, hoisted a White Ensign, and observed a moment of silence.

June 8 departed Margate at 7:30 a.m., passed the wreck of the *Richard Montgomery*, and arrived at Chatham.

June 15 departed Chatham and arrived at London mooring outboard of the museum cruiser HMS *Belfast* (C.35). There were few visitors in London as anyone wishing to come aboard had to pay the *Belfast* fee first.

June 22 departed London and arrived at Cherbourg, France, the next afternoon.

July 7 departed Cherbourg and arrived at Rouen the next day. The ship participated with 46 other ships in the l'Armada de la Liberté celebration, which was attended by millions from all over Europe and the British Isles. There was a huge fireworks display on the 14th, Bastille Day.

July 17 departed Rouen at 9:30 a.m. and arrived at Le Havre early the next day.

July 22 departed Le Havre for Portland, Maine, and arrived on August 6. Moored at the Maine State Pier directly across the Fore River from the old South Portland Shipbuilding yard.

August 15 departed Portland for New York via the Cape Cod Canal. At 3:30 p.m. passed the northbound *John W. Brown* heading for Halifax, Nova Scotia, both ships exchanging whistle signals. The passing was a momentous event in American maritime history. Transited Long Island Sound and anchored off the Kings Point Merchant Marine Academy the morning of the 16th.

August 17 departed Kings Point with 50 passengers, past New York City, and stopped off Liberty Island where the passengers got off into boats. Proceeded to Baltimore via the Delaware & Chesapeake Canal. On passing Fort McHenry the replica of the garrison flag Francis Scott Key saw was hoisted in the ship's honor, a tremendous salute. Arrived at the Inner Harbor around noon of the 18th.

August 23 departed Baltimore for Jacksonville, Florida, and arrived there on the 26th.

August 27 departed Jacksonville around 4 p.m. for a 3–4-hour trip to the Mayport Naval Station with around 50 passengers. More passengers were embarked to view a boat race the next day.

August 28 departed Mayport at 5 p.m. for Panama and arrived on September 3, went through the Canal the next day, and headed for San Diego. Arrived there on September 15 and docked at the Broadway Pier.

September 19 departed San Diego with passengers and arrived at San Pedro the next day mooring just ahead of the *Lane Victory*. The crew ate dinner on board the *Lane* that evening.

September 21 departed San Pedro early in company with the *Lane Victory*, the official escort of honor. Arrived back at San Francisco on the 23rd and steamed under the Golden Gate Bridge at exactly 8 a.m. from where bushels of flowers reigned down onto the ship. The *Lane Victory* proceeded to Pier 27 while the *O'Brien* continued on toward the San Francisco–Oakland Bay Bridge, escorted by hundreds of small craft, then turned around and tied up astern of the *Lane* at Pier 27.

The ship never went back to Fort Mason. After a stint a Pier 32 the ship moved to Pier 45 astern of the museum submarine *Pampanito* (SS-383) at Fisherman's Wharf.

The trip was five months and five days and 18,000 nautical miles. A total of 107 sailing volunteers from 17 states and two foreign nations made the voyage and out of these, 27 made the entire trip. The ship was crowded with visitors at every port, 10,000 in one day at Portsmouth, England, and the crew was treated to tours and festivities all along the way. An excellent account of the trip can be found in Capt. Walter Jaffee's book *Appointment in Normandy*. Walter was the chief mate on the voyage.

Voyage No. 9

In the summer of 1996 the ship made another foreign voyage, the Pacific Northwest Cruise, visiting Seattle and Longview, Washington; the Esquimalt naval base in British Columbia; Vancouver and Victoria, and Portland and Astoria, Oregon.

On October 6, 1998, the 106th Congress authorized transfer of ownership to the NLSM through the National Defense Authorization Act for Fiscal Year 2000. Capt. Jahn died on January 30, 1999, in San Francisco. The *O'Brien* continues to be a major attraction in San Francisco as an extraordinary part of American history.

Glossary

Able-bodied seaman, able seaman, AB. Rating between Ordinary Seaman and Boatswain. Stood wheel watches and performed general Deck Department duties. Normally six ABs were in a crew and some could be assigned as 8–5 day workers.

Acting capacity. Any temporary position assigned to a person by the Master which the person has not officially attained. In early crews, ABs often served as Acting Boatswains.

A/E. Assistant Engineer.

Armed Guard. Naval detachment assigned to a wartime merchant vessel to operate and maintain the guns, anti-submarine gear, barrage balloons, etc., and assisted with signaling.

Armed Guard Officer. Usually an ensign, lieutenant (junior grade), or lieutenant in the Naval Reserve in charge of the gun crew. Assigned watches as desired. Subordinate only to the Master.

Articles of Agreement, Shipping Articles, Articles. A 12-page, 14 × 17-inch form constituting an agreement between the Master and the crew for the duration of the voyage. The crew signed on in the presence of the Shipping Commissioner of the port, usually one or two days before sailing. The agreement indicated the duration and destination of the voyage, the minimum food rations to be provided, and a promise by the sailor that duties would be conducted in an "orderly, faithful, honest, and sober manner."

Bedroom Steward. A Steward Department utilityman assigned to make the bunks of the Master, Armed Guard commander, and licensed officers in addition to his other duties. Not often seen on Liberty ship crew lists.

Boatswain, bos'n, or bosun. Highest unlicensed Deck Department rating. An 8–5 Petty Officer in the Maritime Service in charge of the anchor, tackle, cordage, and rigging who delegated and supervised all deck work under the direction of the Chief Mate. Next step up was Third Mate.

Cadet. A maritime academy student assigned to a ship for a minimum of six months. Cadets spent four hours a day on ship's work and six hours on their "Sea Projects"—or book work. Most Cadets made two voyages on the first ship they were assigned to because the absolute minimum sea time was six months, without exception. Cadets declared their preference for Deck or Engine while still in school and Engine Cadets further chose a Steam or Diesel course of instruction. The Deck Cadet was assigned to the Chief Mate and the Engine Cadet was under the Chief Engineer's wing.

Carpenter. An 8–5 Petty Officer in the Maritime Service who maintained all shipboard woodwork, built items requested by the Master, officers, or bosun, greased the cargo handling and deck gear, sounded the tanks at regular intervals, assisted with anchoring, and stood gangway, fire, and security watches. Carpenters, usually journeymen, who furnished their own tools were "Tools Carpenters" and those who graduated from a Maritime Service school were furnished a set of tools by the War Shipping Administration. Carpenters on brand-new ships often had a lot of work to do like installing furniture and fittings left undone by the yard workers in their haste to get ships launched, building shelves in storage areas, and even setting up their own shops.

Chief Cook, 1st Cook. In charge of the galley, prepared all meals, and planned the menus with the Chief Steward.

Chief Engineer. Highest rated licensed officer in charge of all engineering functions and spaces on the ship. Reported only to the Master and stood no watches.

Chief Mate, First Mate, or Chief Officer. Second in command, responsible for the stowage of cargo, assigned watches to Deck Department personnel, determined the work on deck to be done and supervised the work through the Boatswain. Normally stood the 4–8 watch.

Chief Steward. Staff officer in charge of the Steward Department who reported only to the Master. Responsible for all consumable stores, bedding, linen, berthing assignments, room furniture, and housekeeping in officers' quarters. Planned menus with the Chief Cook and pitched in at lunch when the 2nd Cook & Baker was normally off duty.

Constructive Total Loss. In marine insurance, the abandonment of a vessel from the owner to the underwriters. In the case of most Liberty ships, War Risk insurance was provided to the operators by the War Shipping Administration so the WSA was essentially self-insured.

Coxswain, Cox., or Coxun. A sailor in charge of a boat and crew.

Crow's Nest. Enclosed cylindrical shelter high on the mainmast for lookouts.

Deck Department. Responsible for the navigation of the vessel, dry cargo, and maintenance of all non-engineering spaces.

Deck Mechanic. An 8–5 Petty Officer in the Maritime Service and member of the Engine Department responsible for maintaining the deck winches and other gear.

Engine Department. Responsible for all propulsion and steering machinery, fuel, pumps and other auxiliary equipment, refrigeration, electrical, plumbing, sanitation, boiler and domestic water supply, cargo and warping winches—most anything that had wires, a pressure gauge, or needed oiling.

F1c. Fireman First class in the Navy, equal to a Fireman/Watertender in the merchant service.

Fireman/Watertender, F/WT. Maintained fire in the firebox and water in the boilers; graduated up from Wiper and was a Qualified Member of the Engine Department, equal to an AB. Normally three in a crew.

First Assistant Engineer. Highest licensed officer under the Chief Engineer. Ran the day to day operation of the engine room and normally stood the 4–8 watch.

Foc'sle. Shortened version of Forecastle, the forward part of a sailing ship where the sailors bunked. The term was transferred to crew cabins on steamships. Sailors took turns cleaning the foc'sle and the cleaner was known as the "foc'sle peggy." By tradition, engineers lived on the port side and deck people lived on the starboard side.

Freighter. A ship that carried palletized, loose, or bulk dry cargo in its holds and liquid cargo in containers.

Galley Utility or Utility. Steward Department worker who cleaned up, washed pots and pans, brought food up from the chill box or freezer, etc., and made coffee, salads, and dressings.

Junior Engineer, Fourth Engineer. Assisted with general engineering duties.

LST. Landing Ship, Tank, a 328-foot ship that ran up on a beach and discharged tanks and other equipment and cargo through large doors in the bow.

Maritime Service, United States. Established in 1938 pursuant to the Merchant Marine Act of 1936 to train sailors. A uniformed service with officer ranks equal to the Coast Guard and uniforms identical to the Navy but with its own cap device.

Master. Short for Shipmaster, highest Deck Department rank equal to the Commanding Officer of a naval vessel. Responsible for the entire operation of the ship and crew and represented and conducted the shipping company's business.

Messman. Seagoing waiter. Three or four in a crew, one or two for the officers' saloon, one for the crew's mess, and one for the Armed Guard mess. The saloon messman normally took care of the Master's quarters. Messman, Galley Utility, and Utility titles were often interchangeable.

Monkey Bridge. Auxiliary steering station located on top of the wheelhouse used in fair weather or when extra vigilance was required, as in convoys during inclement weather. Some were enclosed by the ship's carpenter into a makeshift shelter.

Official Number. Sequential number issued by the Dept. of Commerce to a specific vessel for all time and never re-issued.

Oiler. Oiled all moving parts, graduated up from Fireman/Watertender and was a Qualified Member of the Engine Department, equal to an AB. Normally three in a crew.

Ordinary Seaman, OS. Lowest rating in the Deck Department. Performed routine maintenance, painting, lookout, steering, and household chores. Normally three in a crew.

Petty Officer. In the Maritime Service an unlicensed, non-commissioned officer rating bestowed on persons whose skills warrant the title, such as carpenters, electricians, refrigeration specialists, mechanics, or very experienced seamen who serve as boatswains.

Purser. Staff officer in charge of the Purser's Department who reported to the Master. Completed all the paperwork for the voyage. Liberty ships normally had only one Purser, who was most often a clerk or typist with no experience as a licensed Purser.

Radio Operator. Staff officer in charge of the Radio Department who reported to the Master. Responsible for all radio communications and equipment. Liberty ships normally had only one Radio Operator.

Red Duster. The red ensign flown by British merchant ships.

RM. Radio Man, 3rd, 2nd, or 1st Class in the Navy.

S1c. Seaman First Class in the Navy.

Saloon. The officers' dining and recreation room on a merchant ship, equivalent to the wardroom on a naval vessel.

Second Assistant Engineer. Licensed officer between Third Engineer and First Assistant Engineer. Normally in charge of the boilers and stood the 12–4 watch.

Second Cook & Baker. Did all the flour work and assisted the Chief Cook with breakfast and dinner. A sailor on the 12–4 morning watch normally got the galley range going so it was ready for the baker, who was the first one up.

Second Mate. Licensed officer between Third Mate and Chief Mate who normally did the navigating and stood the 12–4 watch.

Slop Chest. Small store run by the Purser where sailors could purchase clothing, gloves, shoes, uniform items, toiletries, candy, chewing gum, tobacco, etc., whatever the steamship company chose to stock. Merchandise was sold at ten percent over cost and the items purchased were deducted from the seaman's wages at the end of the voyage.

SM. Signalman, 3rd, 2nd, or 1st Class.

Staff Officer. Licensed or unlicensed person on a merchant ship who is entitled to wear the uniform of a licensed Deck or Engine officer, eat in the saloon, and live in a stateroom.

Steward Department. Responsible for feeding the crew, the stowage of dry stores, frozen and perishable foods, linen, cooking utensils and equipment, flatware and china, and housekeeping of the licensed officers' quarters. A Liberty ship was issued 120 coffee mugs and 72 dinner plates.

Tanker. Ship that carried liquid cargo in its holds and additional cargo on deck such as landing craft, PT boats, or airplanes.

Third Assistant Engineer. Licensed officer between Junior Engineer and Second Engineer. Normally in charge of auxiliaries, pumps, generators, compressors, and evaporators and stood the 8–12 watch.

Third Cook. Assisted the Chief Cook with the preparation of vegetables and potatoes, kept galley utensils clean, and assisted the Chief Cook with dinner.

Third Mate. The junior Deck officer who kept the logbook, assisted with navigation, and was responsible for all life-saving gear and equipment. Normally stood the 8–12 watch.

USAT. United States Army Transport.

Watches. On a wartime merchant vessel, six four-hour periods in 24 hours, equivalent to four hours on and eight hours off. Four Deck Department and three Engine Department people were on watch when underway. On deck, a Mate was in the wheelhouse and a sailor at the wheel. At night two sailors were on lookout, one in the crow's nest and one on the bow. Each position rotated every two hours. During the day, the sailors worked two hours on deck and two hours on the wheel. Down below, a watch engineer, fireman/watertender, and oiler worked a four-hour shift. Wipers would be employed if necessary and any sailor could be assigned to day work or watches.

Wiper. Lowest rank in the engine room. Normally worked 8–5 performing general clean-up and housekeeping, painting, and polishing. Assisted with repair work and trained for Fireman/Watertender if so inclined. Normally three were in a crew.

Y3c. Yeoman Third Class in the Navy, the Navy's clerk-typists.

Bibliography

Abbot, Willis J. *The Naval History of the United States*. New York, New York: Dodd, Meade & Co., 1896.

Archibald, Katherine. *Wartime Shipyard*. Berkeley, California: University of California Press, 1947.

Bane, Frank, ed. *The Book of the States, 1943–1944*. Chicago: Council of State Governments, 1944.

Belden, F. Porter. *New York, Past, Present & Future*. New York: Prall, Lewis & Co., 1850.

Berry, Lt. Bob, as told to Lloyd Wendt. *Gunners Get Glory: Lt. Bob Berry's Story of the Navy Armed Guard*. Indianapolis: Bobbs-Merrill Co., 1943.

Bunker, John Gorley. *Liberty Ships, the Ugly Ducklings of World War II*. Annapolis, Maryland: Naval Institute Press, 1972.

Butow, Robert J. C. *Japan's Decision to Surrender*. Stanford, California: Stanford University Press, 1954.

Coman, Edwin T., Jr., and Helen T. Gibbs. *Time, Tide, & Timber, Over a Century of Pope & Talbot*. Portland, Oregon: Pope & Talbot, Inc., 1978.

Commerce Department. *Merchant Vessels of the United States*. Washington, D.C.: Government Printing Office, 1920–1946.

Cornell, Felix, and Hoffman, Allan C., ed. *American Merchant Seaman's Manual*. New York: Cornell Maritime Press, 1942.

Drisko, George W. *Narrative of the Town of Machias, the Old and New, the Early and the Late*. Machias, Maine: Press of the Republican, 1904.

Eddington, Walter J. *Glossary of Shipbuilding and Outfitting Terms*. New York: Cornell Maritime Press, 1943.

Elphick, Peter. *Liberty: The Ship That Won the War*. Annapolis, Maryland: Naval Institute Press, 2001.

Fassett, F. G., Jr., ed. *The Shipbuilding Business in the United States of America*. New York: The Society of Naval Architects, 1948.

Hill, Charles E. *Purser's Manual and Marine Storekeeping*. New York: Cornell Maritime Press, 1941.

Hurd, Sir Archibald, ed. *The Shipping World Year Book*. London: Effingham House, 1939.

Jaffee, Walter W. *The Last Liberty: The Biography of the SS* Jeremiah O'Brien. Palo Alto, California: The Glencannon Press, 1993.

Jones, Herbert G. *Portland Ships Are Good Ships*. Portland, Maine: Machigone Press, 1945.

Kilmarx, Robert A., ed. *America's Maritime Legacy: A History of the U.S. Merchant Marine and Shipbuilding Industry Since Colonial Times*. Boulder, Colorado: Westview Press, 1979.

Lane, Frederic C. *Ships for Victory*. Baltimore, Maryland: The Johns Hopkins Press, 1951.

Lent, Henry B. *Ahoy Shipmate! Steve Ellis Joins the Merchant Marine*. New York: MacMillan, 1945.

Leonard, John William. *History of the City of New York, 1609–1909*. New York: Joseph & Setton, 1910.

McArthur, Lewis. *Oregon Geographic Names*. Portland, Oregon: Oregon Historical Society, 2003.

Messimer, Dwight R. *Pawns of War: The Loss of the USS* Langley *and the USS* Pecos. Annapolis, Maryland: Naval Institute Press, 1983.

Mitchell, C. Bradford. *Every Kind of Shipwork: A History of Todd Shipyards Corporation*. New York: Todd Shipyards Corp., 1981.

Moore, Capt. Arthur R. *A Careless Word... A Needless Sinking*. Kings Point, New York: American Merchant Marine Museum, 1998.

Navy Department. *Naval Documents of the American Revolution, Vol. 1.* Washington, D.C.: Government Printing Office, 1964.

O'Reilly, Tom. *Purser's Progress: The Adventures of a Seagoing Office Boy.* Garden City, New York: Doubleday, Doran & Co., 1944. (Sports reporter Thomas C. Reilly made one voyage on the *Judah P. Benjamin* in 1943, which he calls the *Mulligan Stew* in his wartime-censored book.)

Rohwer, Jürgen. *Axis Submarine Successes 1939–1945.* Annapolis, Maryland: Naval Institute Press, 1985.

Rowland, Lt. Cdr. Buford and Boyd, Lt. William B. *U.S. Navy Bureau of Ordnance in World War II.* Washington, D.C.: Navy Department, Bureau of Ordnance, 1947.

Sawyer, L. A. and Mitchell, W. H. *The Liberty Ships.* London: Lloyds of London Press, Ltd., 1985.

Smith, Eugene W. *Passenger Ships of the World, Past and Present.* Boston: George H. Dean Co., 1963.

Starling, Edmund W., as told to Thomas Sugrue. *Starling of the White House.* New York, New York: Simon & Shuster, 1946.

Talbot-Booth, E. C. *Merchant Ships 1942.* New York, New York: The MacMillan Co., 1942.

U.S. Congress, House Committee on Merchant Marine and Fisheries, *Investigation of Cancellation of Higgins Contract, H. R. No. 2652,* 77th Congress, 2d Session, November 24, 1942.

U.S. Congress, House Committee on Merchant Marine and Fisheries, *Investigation of South Portland Shipbuilding Corporation, H. R. No. 2653,* 77th Congress, 1st Session, November 24, 1942.

U.S. Congress, House Committee on Merchant Marine and Fisheries, *Investigation of the Merchant Shipbuilding Program and Related Matters on the West Coast of the United States, H. R. No. 2031,* 78th Congress, 2d Session, December 7, 1944.

War Shipping Administration. *United States Maritime Service Training Manual.* New York: Cornell Maritime Press, 1943.

Worden, William L. *Cargoes: Matson's First Century in the Pacific.* Honolulu: The University of Hawaii Press, 1981.

Yust, Walter, ed. *1944 Britannica Book of the Year.* Chicago: Encyclopedia Britannica, Inc., 1944.

Index

Ship names are listed exactly as they would have appeared on the vessel itself, so the *Kathleen R. Williams* is in the "K" section. In order to avoid unnecessary duplication, the names of most ships will also serve as the index entry for the person for whom the ship was named. Names beginning with initials or titles, like *A. B. Hammond* or *General Vallejo*, are cross-indexed as Hammond, Andrew B. (N) and Vallejo, Gen. Mariano (N) with an "N" to indicate a namesake ship.

5734